THE DISCIPLEMAKER

What Matters Most to Jesus

Gary Derickson
Earl Radmacher

The Disciplemaker:
What Matters Most to Jesus

Published by Charis Press
Box 1097
5000 Deer Park Drive SE
Salem, OR   97301

Scripture quotations are from the *New King James Version* unless otherwise noted.

ISBN 0-9713870-0-1 (Hardcover)
ISBN 0-9713870-1-X (Softcover)
ISBN 1-56453-052-3 (Hardcover) Schoettle Publishing Co.

BS2615.3   226.5

Cover and Book Design: Lee Fredrickson: IBIS Design

Cover Illustration, "Divine Servant"[r] used by permission of Max Greiner, Jr. For information on Greiner drawings, paintings, sculpture and jewelry, contact: **Max Greiner, Jr. Designs**, P.O. Box 290552, Kerrville, TX 78029

Table Of Contents

FOREWORD

Many who visit the Holy Land have a hope in their heart that they might be able to walk today where Jesus actually walked nearly two thousand years ago. Despite the distance in time and circumstance, modern pilgrims still have this desire. There are several places in Israel where one can feel she or he is *near* to where Jesus had been so long ago. But, amazingly, there are some places in Israel where a person may actually say, "*Here* is where Jesus actually stood. *Here* He walked."

This *sense of place* can be achieved today more than anytime since the actual days of Jesus. This is particularly true in Jerusalem when one sits on the southern steps of the ancient Temple, or when one stands on the pavement at the southwest corner of the Kotel, the famous Temple foundation wall. We have had numerous groups stand on the pavement and sit on the steps. There is something truly lovely to be able to think, Here I am where Jesus actually had been two millennia past!

On one visit a few years ago we had an Israeli archaeologist who did not share our faith in the person and work of Savior Jesus, but who was exasperated with the seeming nonchalance of some members of our group. They were intent on taking pictures, but he felt they seemed emotionally distant from what we were doing. Zvi shouted: "Don't you realize where you are? This is more than a photo-op! You are actually standing where your Jesus stood. Do you really believe in Him? Where are your tears? Where are your shouts? Why no laughter? *Show me you feel something!*"

Great! It took an unbelieving Jewish archaeologist to shake up some members of our group to come to terms with the enormity of their experience!

My wife Beverly and I have just returned from a three-week visit to the country of Israel, two weeks with our group and a week on our own. On our "own" week we visited for the first time the excavation and restoration of biblical Bethsaida (et Tell), the fishing village north of the Sea of Galilee that was home to Andrew, Simon Peter and Philip (see, e.g., John 1:43-45). Believe me, we are adding this site to our itinerary for future groups!

On the day of our visit, the two of us had the entire site to ourselves. We were the only ones there! We ate a snack at a table beside a lovely pond. We walked all over the site, from the base of the tel to the vista overlooking the beautiful Sea of Galilee. We discovered signage that is wonderfully poignant. In addition to signs directing the visitor to the ruins of a large home of a winemaker and a large home of a fisherman, there is a sign pointing out a section of exposed ancient road that was from the time of Jesus. It is only about twenty feet long and perhaps only six feet wide, but there it is. And there we were. Here was a section of roadway inside the city from Jesus' day. It was a road He had walked. Hardly a thing had changed. *And we walked on that little road.* This was a great moment in our lives.

Not everyone can do this. This was an extraordinary experience.

But there are experiences with Jesus that everyone can have, and these may be even more powerful and life changing than walking on an ancient footpath. This may happen when one seeks not a *sense of place* so much as a *sense of meaning*—particularly when meaning is found in Scripture.

One may sit today in a comfortable chair in one's own home, open the Bible, and have a profound, life-changing experience by focusing not on the steps of Jesus but on His words, His teaching, His instruction. And where will one open his or her Bible? Well, one might turn to the Sermon on the Mount, to a series of parables, or to the Olivet Discourse. Each would be immensely rewarding.

Perhaps no passage in the teaching ministry of Jesus that has been written and passed down to us is more significant for Christian growth, for learning as his disciples, than the extended section of the Gospel of John termed the Upper Room Discourse (John 13-17). And as you turn to this great section of the New Testament, you might ask: How may I gain the most from my reading of this passage?

Here is where the present book will serve you. What Dr. Earl Radmacher and Dr. Gary Derickson do in this book is to bring you into the room with Jesus and the disciples. You are an unseen visitor in the upper room. You sit in the shadows and hear with them the deepest teaching of Jesus. You walk along with the disciples as they leave the room and move through the courts of the Temple and then make their way down the Kidron, and you still hear His voice. This is a more powerful experience than you will ever have, even standing on the walkway in Bethsaida. After all, the walkway is just a street of stones, and the experience you might have there is what you might make it out to be. But the teaching of Jesus in this, His most personal expression, may be just what He wants it to be.

Radmacher and Derickson sift through, and interact with, the comments of many who have written on this passage. They analyze the nuances of Jesus' words, point out the direction of His teaching, steer you away from reading ideas into His words that are not really there. Even more importantly, they present a point of view that is quite convincing: Jesus' teaching in this extended section was given to those who already knew Him, but who needed significant growth in the nature of what it means to be His disciples. The salvation truths in these chapters speak concerning sanctification-salvation rather than justification-salvation.

That is, Christian reader, this extended section of the New Testament is tailor-made for you, a person who already has come to faith in Jesus, but who needs continued teaching by Him concerning the life He would have you to live. Radmacher and Derickson bring you into the room. You can nearly hear the breathing of those who heard these words the first time. And then you will hear your own breathing. Here you will enter the roadway of discipleship. This is not just another path. It is even better than a road on which Jesus walked in ancient times in Bethsaida. It is the path you may walk along today, with Him!

Ronald B. Allen, Th.D.
Professor of Bible Exposition
Dallas Theological Seminary

PREFACE

Salvation is one of the great themes of the Bible. For this reason the idea of salvation-history (heilsgeschichte) is considered by many to be the driving force behind the development of the biblical text. Certainly from the time of Abraham, if not from the fall in the garden, God's acts and words within human history have been to elicit a response to His offer of redemption that culminated in the offering of the Son of God on the cross.

Yet there is a more inclusive "center" for theology recognized by other scholars, that of the glory of God. With this in mind, we might understand that God does not only want to redeem us from sin and to declare us innocent of our sin. He wants to create in us the image of Christ. Paul, writing in his letter to the Ephesians, makes plain that all God's work on our behalf is to "the praise of His glory." Salvation, then, is much more than justification. It includes the ongoing work of sanctification, and the culminative work of glorification.

Drs. Gary Derickson and Earl Radmacher have done the Christian community a great service in presenting the fruit of their lengthy and detailed analysis of John 13-17, what is known as the "Upper Room Discourse." As important as justification is, it is only one facet of God's work for and in the Christian believer. It is the lack of understanding of the truths in these chapters that gives rise to the stagnant and immature church today. To be a "pew potato" as a Christian is too often the 20th and 21st century Christian. The challenge of Christ to His disciples immediately before His death provides for the attentive Christian some of the most important ideas for Christian security, comfort, and growth that one finds in the Bible. We find in these chapters Christ's teaching and example of servanthood, the possibility of failure and denial of which each of us is capable, but the comfort and encouragement of God. We discover the secret to Christian maturity in the metaphor of the vineyard and the assurance of God's abiding presence of the Holy Spirit. What is especially exciting and humbling to me is that we may read the actual prayer of Jesus to the Father for each of us—the true Lord's prayer.

Jesus speaks to His believing, though frail, disciples with a message that goes beyond justification, to one of discipleship (sanctification). This post-justification work of God is the concern of Jesus as He teaches His disciples in his final hours before His sacrifice on the cross. These last words take on special significance as Jesus seeks to instruct His disciples who are about to be scattered and even betray Him. In spite of this knowledge Jesus knows that He must provide comfort, direction, and prayer to guide them to be the kind of men who would one day be pillars of the Church, and evangelists to the ends of the Roman Empire.

Derickson and Radmacher provide for the reader a masterful study of these wonderful chapters. They perform many important feats in these few hundred pages. They call the Christian to the neglected area of discipleship. There is much talk of bringing people to Christ (evangelism) but little of the content and process of Christian spiritual growth (discipleship). The authors provide much food for thought in this under-emphasized area.

The authors give an important corrective to interpretative confusion relating to connecting justification with sanctification. This confusion has caused some to reject the clear teaching of Scripture that we are saved by God's unmerited favor, not through any deeds that we may do or not do. The contemporary idea that a believer cannot know if he or she is truly eternally redeemed until the end of life is a theological error perpetrated by both Reformed (perseverance of the saints) and Arminian (one can lose one's justification) scholars and teachers. This is partly due to misunderstanding of the teaching of grace that is expounded by Derickson and Radmacher in this book.

An added theological benefit to this book is putting into balance the purpose stated by John in his epilogue, "that we might believe that Jesus is the Messiah and that believing we might have life in His name." Some have seen the book as mainly evangelistic and some as confirmational. The authors properly explain that both of these aspects are found in the book. John offers theology that brings people to belief in Christ and strengthens the faith of those who already believe.

The book gives to the readers a considerable number of gems, often overlooked or minimally discussed in most works dealing with these chapters. Especially well done is the study of John 15. Dr. Derickson's professional expertise in viticultural studies (M.S. in horticulture at Texas A&M), as well as the scholarly discussion of this chapter, hopefully puts to rest the notion that "cut off" is a correct translation of the Greek term *airo*, to lift up. A plethora of information is provided to understand this often wrongly understood portion of Scripture. Their analysis on Judas and the disciples in the upper room gave to me many insights I had not considered before.

Though the theological and exegetical insight in the book is considerable, it is written in a manner that may easily be understood by the layman and student. For more detailed information, the authors have extensive footnotes that may be consulted. The book has a number of appendixes which give additional information that could not be covered in the main text, and in fact, are themselves worth the cost of the book.

Drs. Derickson and Radmacher have offered to the Christian public, and scholar, a sorely needed study of John 13-17. It should correct much wrongheaded thinking about not only these particular passages of Scripture but certain teaching in the Christian community which confuses justification and sanctification, belief in Christ and being a disciple of Christ.

H. Wayne House, Th.D., J.D.

Distinguished Professor of Biblical Studies

and Christian Apologetics

Faith Seminary, Tacoma, Washington

1991 President of the Evangelical Theological Society

INTRODUCTION

I (Earl) was one of a half-dozen speakers at the annual pastor's conference at Moody Bible Institute several years ago. In the morning series I was the third speaker up, preceded by two of my very favorite motivators. I began by saying, "While Dr. Hendricks was speaking this morning, I got saved ~ **twice!** And then when Dr. Wiersbe spoke, I got saved again. And I am praying that as I speak to you now, you will get saved." You cannot believe the consternation that came over the faces of those fifteen hundred pastors wondering, "What-in-the-world do we have here?"

One of the major problems that we have in America is the failure of the saved to go on being saved. In fact if the saved would get saved, we wouldn't have nearly so much trouble getting the lost saved.[1] (In fact, I'll give you a clue right now about this tremendous discipling discourse of Jesus with the twelve apostles that we are going to study. This is precisely what He is going to make indelible in their minds and hearts.) But come back to the message of that morning at Moody. After the message, one of the VP's of Moody told me that they sold more copies of that tape than of any other message. Furthermore, pastors were coming up to me by the end of the week, slapping me on the back, and saying, "Praise God, brother, I got saved this week."

Basic to an understanding of our magnificent salvation in John's Gospel is a correction of a major theological assumption in our approach to the doctrine of salvation. Most people unwittingly narrow salvation down to justification and all of the marvelous divine transactions that happen at the moment of faith pictured beautifully in favorite passages like John 1:12 and 3:16. But there is so much more in this wonderful doctrine of salvation.

Without minimizing at all what happened to believers at the moment of justification by faith, we must stress that far more of the emphasis of Scripture deals with present tense salvation from the power of sin in a believer's life that we may call sanctification-salvation. And beyond that, even more glorious, is the future manifestation of our salvation which we may call *glorification-salvation*. John contrasts the present and the future of believers with these striking words: "Beloved, now we are the children of God; and it has not yet been revealed what we shall be, but we know that when He is revealed, we shall be like Him, for we shall see Him as He is. And everyone who has this hope in him purifies himself, just as He is pure"(1 John 3:2-3).

A major portion of the message of John's Gospel, therefore, does not have to do with *justification-salvation*, as glorious as that is, but with sanctification-salvation in which regenerated disciples are being impacted by the person and work of Jesus with a view to their transformation into His image by His Spirit (2 Cor 3:18). We learn more about Jesus and His relationship to the Father and Holy Spirit in this Gospel than in any of the others. Here we are given a personal glimpse into His private conversations and inner thoughts. We get to hear Him speak in a whisper as well as to large crowds. We are brought into His presence and helped to understand God better through this unique picture of Jesus provided to us by the beloved disciple.

The Prologue to the Gospel (John 1:1-18) reveals that John intended to accomplish far more than to write a "gospel tract."[2] He reveals in it that he writes to describe the life and ministry of Jesus to men in general, but more importantly, to His disciples in particular. Remember, Jesus chose the twelve in order that they may be with Him and learn from Him (Mark 3:14-15). Since they were already believers in Him, He teaches them far more than how to become believers and be regenerated. That is the starting block for the runner and it is absolutely foundational.

Dead people do not run races but neither do runners get stuck on the starting block. Once they have been given life from the Father of life through faith in the finished work of Jesus Christ, they are ready to get focused on the goal of the race and get into serious training so that they may win. Thus, the master Disciplemaker, Jesus Christ, also teaches them how to trust Him and serve Him so that they can enlarge their capacity to reign with Him in His coming kingdom that is the goal of history. Christ's goal was the crown, not the cross (Heb 12:3). Jesus states this goal succinctly to the church at Laodicea: "To him who overcomes I will grant to sit with Me on My throne as I also overcame and sat down with My Father on His throne" (Rev 3:21). This focus is most often overlooked by students of Christ's training of the disciples.

A large portion of Jesus' instruction which John records must be seen in light of what He said to those who were believing in Him, not just those who would. Thus, a significant portion of Jesus' earthly ministry involved far more than communicating the message of how to be born from above and enter into eternal life. Jesus came to reveal the Father, to explain Him, to exegete Him to us (John 1:18). It is a mistake to take the purpose statement of John 20:31 and, interpreting it in only a justification-salvation sense, make it the sole, or even dominant, purpose of the Gospel as is common among interpreters.[3] Even so, in describing His ministry to men,

John does recount Jesus' focus on issues of regeneration with those who were not yet believing in Him.

John recounted much of what Jesus said in order to communicate what it means to live in fellowship with God. Even Jesus' discussions of eternal life can be better understood when recognized to contain sanctification truths as well as justification truth. (See Appendix 1, "Eternal Life," for a fuller discussion). Jesus often was not explaining *how* to get the life, but *what* it was that they were receiving, the nature and experience of eternal life. Still, we must recognize that much of the first twelve chapters *do* focus on issues of justification as Jesus preached the Gospel of life to a lost world and offered Himself to His own who did not receive Him (John 1:11-13).

But, when His public ministry was complete and He was ready to accomplish His ultimate saving act, He concentrated quality time on communicating with His own who *had* received Him and, performing some of the most important disciplemaking that had happened in His entire ministry. To this end, Jesus gave extensive revelation concerning each member of the Triune God, especially the Father and the Holy Spirit, to His disciples as He comforted and encouraged them with His final words and prayer.

There is no study that we can pursue more profitably than the study of what God is like. To the extent that we know what God is like, to the same extent we can walk our life in Christ. In fact, it may be said, if we never had a wrong thought about what God is like we would never sin.

Jesus was doing more than revealing the Father and the Holy Spirit to His men that evening. He was revealing His own heart. These were perhaps his most significant discipling moments with that core of men who would be the foundation of the church. When they came in for this session, they were hardly ready. They had been bickering among themselves for the last few days as they anticipated the arrival of the Messianic Kingdom (Luke 22:24-30). They had remained blind to the words of Jesus warning of His coming death. Instead, they were full of themselves and lacked the motivational force to weather the coming storm. But they went out from this final session equipped to stand (John 15:3), though the application of this would need time to develop.

In the study which follows, we will examine Jesus' teaching, His last words of encouragement and instruction before His glorification through the cross and resurrection, and learn what He had to say to His closest friends, and to us.[4] Before we get to this marvelous passage of Jesus' last words to His disciples, however, we must first deal with some necessary and extensive data if we are going to understand the text in its context.

CHAPTER ONE

GETTING READY TO UNDERSTAND
CHRIST'S INSTRUCTIONS

Structure of the Passage

The events and conversation known to us today as the Upper Room Discourse should be seen as a single unit of thought. Various scholars attempt to divide this passage into two or three different discourses, sometimes viewing Jesus' washing the disciples' feet as an introductory section preceding the discourse or discourses. Others segregate Jesus' prayer in chapter seventeen from the body of the discourse as well. But, in contrast to these theories, John's intention for the whole section to be read and understood as a single unit is evident from the use of two "book ends" created by the use of "love" (a literary device called an inclusio).

He begins the discourse by revealing Jesus' love for the disciples as the motivating factor in His discussion (13:1) and ends with a record of Jesus' prayer that His love would be expressed in His disciples (17:26).[1] Everything said and done between those two points fits as a single unit of thought and reveals the locus of Jesus' heart that night as He faced Calvary. He loved His own and wanted them to love one another.

Place in the Events of the Passion Week

Many questions have been raised concerning the events in the upper room as reported by John. Was this a Passover meal or was it just some special dinner, eaten with His disciples the evening before the Passover was to be celebrated?[2] Also, if this was the same meal wherein the Lord's Supper was instituted, when was it instituted in relation to the events and words of John's Gospel? Also, did Judas partake of any part of the Lord's Supper? Or, did Jesus institute it only after his departure?

What evidence is there that this was a Passover meal? Matthew 26:17-20 and Mark 14:12-17 identify the day of the meal as the day when the Passover lamb was killed. Luke 22:7-14 specifically identifies this as the Passover meal since it was eaten on the day of Unleavened Bread, the day the Passover was to be sacrificed. Luke 22:13 clearly states that the disciples prepared the Passover and that Jesus then reclined at the table with them. This is followed by the mention of two cups that Jesus passed among the disciples as well as the breaking of bread.

John's opening words, "before the feast of the Passover," does not require that this be the Wednesday before the feast.[3] This phrase could have several possible meanings other than indicating the meal was not a Passover meal. It is more likely a reference to the first phase of the meal that preceded the actual celebration of the Passover that occurred later, during the same meal. Thus, Jesus could have washed the disciples' feet during the supper, but before the Passover ceremonies. Even so, it is worthy to note that verse four indicates that Jesus' action of washing the disciples' feet occurred during supper rather than before it, when it would have been appropriate.

Harold Hoehner's chronology of events is most helpful in understanding how Jesus could eat the Passover and still die as the Passover lamb was being slain the following day. He notes that the Pharisees and Galilean Jews celebrated the Passover a day before the Sadducees of Judea. This came about because the Pharisees and Galileans reckoned their days from sunrise to sunrise while the Sadducees reckoned from sunset to sunset. The Passover was to be celebrated on the 14th day of Nisan of the Jewish religious calendar. The difference in reckoning meant that for the Galileans and Pharisees the 14th lasted from sunrise on Thursday until sunrise on Friday. For the Judeans, their Nisan 14th went from sunset on Thursday until sunset on Friday. In order to accommodate both ways of reckoning, the priests (made up of Sadducees) sacrificed the Galilean/Pharisee Passover lambs from 3:00 to 5:00 p.m., which was considered to be twilight, on Thursday of that year. They then sacrificed the Judean/Sadducee lambs starting at 3:00 p.m. on Friday.[4] So, Jesus, being from Galilee, would naturally celebrate the Passover on Thursday evening and could still die as Israel's Passover lambs were being slaughtered in the temple on Friday.

So, recognizing that Jesus was celebrating the Passover meal with His disciples, we must ask where and how the events recorded by John fit into that evening. In Luke 22:17 and 20, we see that Jesus passes the cup to the disciples twice and that the second cup follows the breaking of the bread. Jesus then prophecies His betrayal immediately after passing the second cup and notes that His betrayer is still at the table with Him (Luke 22:21-22).[5] We can obtain a better understanding of the significance of the cups and where they fit into John's account by first knowing more about the order of events in a Passover meal in the first century.

According to Section 10 of *Mishnah Pesahim*, the Passover meal of the first century included these elements. First, the father or host pronounced two benedictions while preparing the first cup of wine (called the cup of sanctification) that was then passed around to all participants. They next ate a preliminary course of green vegetables, after which the main course of unleavened bread, haroseth (made of crushed fruit and nuts in vinegar), and the Passover lamb was eaten. During this meal the youngest son would ask four questions that would be answered by the father or host. These answers would recount God's deliverance of Israel from Egypt and the meanings of the various elements of the Passover meal.

The meal was followed by the singing of the first one or two Hallel Psalms (Ps 113-118), depending on which school of tradition was followed, and a benediction called the *Ge'ullah'* which remembered God's deliverance of Israel out of Egypt. This was followed by a second cup of wine, called the haggadah cup.[6] The meal was concluded with prayer over a third cup, the cup of blessing, which was followed by singing the remainder of the Hallel Psalms. When the Psalms were finished, a fourth cup was drunk, known as the Hallel cup, or cup of praise.

Based on modern practice, which may be traced back to the first century as well, we know some other elements that may have been included in the Passover meal wherein Jesus instituted the Lord's Supper. Following the first cup and the eating of the green herbs dipped in salt water (the first course above), the middle of three pieces of unleavened bread (called the Matzo) was removed and broken in half, with one half being hidden in a small napkin. After the meal was eaten and before the third cup was drunk, the hidden Matzo was brought out, broken, and distributed in olive size pieces to all participants. This is believed to be the same bread which Jesus broke and said, "This is My body which is given for you," before taking the (third) cup and saying, "This cup which is poured out for you is the new covenant in My blood" (Luke 22:19-20).

With these elements in mind, and recognizing that they were celebrating the Passover meal that evening, we have a picture of the significance of Jesus' words and actions within the other Gospels. We are also able to place the events of John's Gospel within the framework of events record- ed elsewhere. Having done this, it becomes evident and noteworthy that John very clearly does not desire to focus on the "Lord's Supper" aspect of that evening. He purposely avoids the key elements of its institution in order to focus on another significant aspect of that evening's instruction from Jesus that was passed over by the other evangelists. It is in these words and actions of Jesus that John chooses to highlight and recount that we see his focus in this passage is not on issues of justification, but of sanc- tification. It is the instructions of Jesus not contained in the *other* Gospels that John is recounting to the church in his.

Place in the Message of the Gospel

Many interpreters misunderstand Jesus' words because they attempt to fit His discussion into a justification motif within the Gospel that was neither intended by Jesus when He broached this topic that evening or John when he included these scenes and words in his Gospel. This confu- sion caused by interpreters has robbed the church of the depth of meaning and comfort that Jesus intended to communicate to His most intimate fol- lowers as well as the significant words of encouragement they speak to us today (See Appendix 2, "Justification Theology and John's Gospel," for a fuller discussion of this issue).

The Upper Room Discourse is a faithful rendering of a very important portion of a significant evening in the life of Jesus and the lives of His dis- ciples, believing and unbelieving.[7] To attempt to see more in it than either God or John intended is to do Scripture an injustice and results in our missing the blessing intended in its inclusion. Thus, the message is plain- ly given and need not be sought in hidden inferences of the text.

Several points need to be made here. First, the whole section has Jesus' love for the disciples and His desire for them to be influenced and controlled by God's love as its two "book ends." Second, John clearly leaves out the Lord's Supper elements of that evening which we know from the other Gospels. Therefore we are wise to search for the development of Jesus' message from those elements John chooses to include in his account of the evening's activities and conversations. This does not mean that John is denying that the other things happened. No, he assumes them. But, when we look within the movements of this section of John's Gospel we should also recognize that John's choice to exclude the Lord's Supper indicates rather strongly that he did not have issues of justification in view when he recorded this section.

When Jesus met with His men that evening He had several important truths He wanted to communicate to them. The other gospel writers focused on the instruction He gave concerning the significance of His death. John chose to focus on other instruction Jesus gave His men, instruction concerning how they were to live following His resurrection. Thus John wanted to communicate this other important message Jesus had for the eleven that evening, a message the church needs to hear even today.

Since Jesus' instruction focuses on the eleven faithful, believing disciples, it is somewhat illogical to think that He continues focusing on issues concerning their justification (cf. Peter in Luke 22:31). He knows that this is a time when they need encouragement in view of what is about to transpire, encouragement to keep trusting Him and not lose heart. They do not need to hear subtle allusions to the doctrine of justification. They need to be prepared for what is about to happen and the potential of this for them. This is not Basic Training for new converts, but Ranger Training for Christians who are training to reign with Christ (cf. 2 Tim 2:1-15). It is not initial instruction for raw recruits just entering the king's service, but the final preparation of the men who will be in the King's lead combat elements.

This portion of John's Gospel gives us a glimpse into the heart of our Lord in the final hours before His betrayal and crucifixion.[8] It was a time He set aside to spend with those He loved most dearly. He did this in order to give them some final words of encouragement in light of the confusion and pain He knew they would be experiencing very shortly. His concern was for His own, not for unbelievers, as revealed in His final prayer. Thus He said to His Father, "I pray not for the world but for those You have given Me." Even so, His heart reached out not only to the eleven, but to all their spiritual children as well. Though Jesus spoke to the eleven, the latter portion of His final prayer reveals that He had us in mind that evening as well. "I do not pray for these alone, but also for those who will believe in Me through their word" (John 17:20). His words of encouragement include every generation of believers as their ultimate audience.

The scene painted by John in the last supper is an upper room wherein three key events occur as Christ is discipling those who are to be "pillars" in the church (Gal 2:9). First, Jesus models and manifests true humility before His disciples, an act that is prompted by their pride and arrogance (John 13:1-20).[9] Next, we see the response of Judas in betraying Him for selfish motives (13:21-30). Finally, we are allowed to listen in on the last discipling session of Jesus and His disciples. He, in love, prepares them for what is to follow so that their immature faith might endure until His resurrection and then blossom into the world changing faith we see in the book of Acts (13:31—17:26).

We see Jesus' heart attitude in Luke 22:32 as well when, after revealing Satan's desire to sift all the disciples as wheat, He turns to Peter and tells him, "I have prayed for you, that your faith should not fail; and when you have turned again, strengthen your brethren." What did Jesus say to him? "I have prayed that you keep believing," not start believing. His point is that He is praying so that Peter will continue to grow and that he will, in turn, help the others to grow. He will "strengthen" them.[10] In Luke 22 their justification is not the issue. Jesus is not praying that they not become unjustified, but that their faith continues so that they might keep growing! Likewise, in the upper room their justification is not the issue either. Jesus is not telling them how to have justifying faith, but persevering, fruit-bearing faith.

People Being Addressed: Primarily Gentile Believers

One of the first issues that must be clarified is who was the intended audience of the Gospel of John. We should not forget that the Apostles wrote to believers first and foremost. Their epistles as well as gospels were delivered to churches who, in turn, copied and distributed them to other churches.

Luke 1:1-4 is our principal example of how the Gospel's were addressed to believers in order to encourage them in their faith, and not to unbelievers in need of regeneration. Theophilus, a Gentile, was clearly identified by Luke as already being a believer, but as someone in need of further instruction to strengthen his faith. The contents of the other three gospels follows the pattern we see in Luke, namely, that they are written to encourage and instruct believers, and not written for apologetic purposes to unbelievers. This should be recognized as true of the Gospel of John as well. As a result it should not be mistaken for a "gospel tract" as some people tend to do, though it does contain the elements of the gospel repeatedly and is useful in explaining the gospel to an unbeliever. But, its clarity of truth and usefulness in communicating the gospel does not require it be written for that sole purpose.

His Gentile audience can be seen from John's habit of explaining *Jewish terms*, translating Jewish names, and locating Palestinian sites. This indicates that he wrote his Gospel to a predominately Gentile audience who would be unfamiliar with Judea and Judaism. For example, early in the Gospel he moves from the covenant people, Israel, to the broader Gentile audience when he says, "He came to His own and His own did not receive Him. But as many as received Him, to them He gave the right to become children of God, to those who believe in His name" (John 1:11-12). This shift to the Gentile audience is evidenced in translating Rabbi as "Teacher" (1:38), Messiah as "Christ" (1:41), and Cephas as "Peter" (1:42) for readers who would not know the meaning of the Hebrew titles and names. Also, on three occasions he refers to feasts as "the Passover of the Jews" (2:13) or as a feast of the Jews (Passover in 6:4 and Booths in 7:2). On three occasions he identifies and transliterates the Hebrew name of a location, such as the Pool of Bethesda (5:2) with the angelic explanation of the miraculous healings that had occurred there. Both the Sea of Galilee/Tiberias (6:1; 21:1) and the place of Jesus' crucifixion (19:17) are given their Greek and Hebrew/Jewish names. In John 11:18, the relationship of Bethany to Jerusalem is given. Jewish believers would likely have known of the suburb if they had ever visited Jerusalem. But Gentile believers would be less likely to have gone or to know.

John also explains *Jewish customs* to his audience that would have been assumed knowledge even for Hellenized Jews in the latter first century. For example, in John 11:55 he explains the Jewish custom of going to Jerusalem from the outlying regions before the Passover in order to purify themselves. And, in John 19:40, the process of binding Jesus' body in linen wrappings is described as a burial custom of the Jews. This is something that would be practiced by Jews even in Greek cities. His explanation indicates, therefore, he assumes that the readers would not have understood the significance of it otherwise.

Further evidence for an audience of Gentile believers comes from the location of John's latter years of ministry, namely, Ephesus. After Paul's martyrdom John took responsibility for the churches of Asia Minor and ministered there until his own death. This is the context behind Jesus' sending letters to the seven churches of Revelation through him. Again, these letters addressed predominantly Gentile congregations. Thus, it is reasonable that the Gospel should be seen as intended for a similar audience.

Though the evidence of a Gentile audience is strong, it need not mean that John is addressing unbelievers. Gentile believers in Asia Minor would be just as unfamiliar with Judea and Jewish customs as their pagan counterparts. This being said, it does not require that they be unfamiliar with the Old Testament Scriptures. In fact, the prologue of John's Gospel (John

1:1-18) could only be understood by people possessing a developed biblical (Old Testament) as well as theological background. This would be true of Gentile believers in possession of the Greek translation of the Hebrew Bible (called the Septuagint), which was common in the early church. On the other hand, this would not be true of Gentile unbelievers. Thus, the terminology used and explanations given point to an audience of Gentile believers who were familiar with the Scriptures, but not with Judea.

Reason for Writing: To Edify Believers

The many theories on the purpose of John's Gospel reveal the struggle of interpreters to grasp its message. Donald Guthrie provides a long list of purposes proposed by various commentators. They include the following: (1) to encourage faith in a soteriological sense; (2) to supplement the other Gospels (Clement of Alexandria); (3) to supersede the Synoptic Gospels;[11] (4) as a polemic against unbelieving Jews;[12] (5) to combat Gnosticism;[13](6) to present a Hellenized Christianity; (7) to correct a Baptist cult; (8) to pursue an ecclesiastical polemic; (9) to correct the Church's eschatology; (10) or to preserve a tradition suitable for liturgical use.[14]

The difficulty of determining an author's purpose is that we are forced to discern his purpose from the contents of his work, including any statements provided within the text. John 20:31 is a clearly stated purpose within the text of the Gospel of John. However, many commentators see that purpose as exclusively evangelistic. Two problems arise, though. First, this need not be John's *sole* purpose for writing. And second, even if it is his dominant purpose, we must determine what he meant by what he said in his purpose statement.

If John's statement in John 20:31 is made the guide to interpreting the Gospel, that will mean that it is the over-arching purpose which controls the meanings of the various portions of the Gospel. Also, if the purpose statement means that he wanted to engender in his readers justifying faith, then the Gospel is indeed a "gospel tract" and everything should be seen from a justification standpoint with an unbelieving audience in view. But if the message of the Gospel is recognized to be more than the presentation of a plan of salvation, and if that message is recognized as being reflected in the prologue, then a broader purpose must also be seen. In fact, John's meaning in the purpose statement must be evaluated further to see if he meant something more than that he wanted his readers to learn how to be justified.

John's practice is to introduce his message in seminal form in the prologues of each of his major works, John, 1 John, and Revelation. The Gospel's prologue begins with a Christological section that affirms Jesus' deity. The significance of this is worked out in the Gospel's description of the incarnation of the Son of God through His signs and discourses. Also, our experience of Jesus' fullness is introduced in verse sixteen and then defined throughout the Gospel as God's life experienced in our present life and finding its full demonstration in the life to come.

Further, one must ask what "declaring" the Father (John 1:18) has to do with regeneration. In light of John 17:3 and Jesus' statement that knowing God is eternal life, a key purpose of the Gospel must be the revelation of the Father by Jesus which enables men to "know" God in the sense Jesus uses the term in the upper room and in His prayer. This "knowing," which defines what it means to experience life, is different from simple regeneration. This "knowing" is more than cognitive knowledge. It has the sense of *communion* characteristic of 1 John 1 and not of *union*, characteristic of most gospel tracts.

Thus the prologue introduces us to a broader message than regeneration and a broader purpose than just explaining how to be born again. Its audience and the development of key themes reveal that, though John is defining the Gospel and describing Jesus' offer of life, he wants to accomplish far more. This "more" is especially evident in the upper room. The wholistic salvation message of Jesus is evidenced by John 8:30-31 where He immediately leads new believers on to disciple making without any time lapse. This is not the first occasion for this inasmuch as the first use of "abide" in John is immediately given to new believers. Peter really captured this practice when he said in 1 Peter 2:2, "As newborn babes, desire the pure milk of the word, that you may grow thereby, if indeed you have tasted that the Lord is gracious."

A proper recognition of John's readers should help guide our understanding of the purpose of the Gospel and the meaning of his purpose statement in John 20:31. As noted earlier, the weight of evidence points clearly to a readership of Gentile believers. With this in mind, we should then note that John's goal that his readers might have "life in His name" should not be seen in a purely regeneration sense.[15] John is not writing so that his readers might *become* believers, but that they might *experience* through a growing faith in the Jesus of the Bible the eternal life that they received as a result of their initial faith in Him.

The development of the gospel message within the Gospel, though helpful to the unbeliever seeking Christ, is directed to believers to enable them to *understand* their faith and its implications, giving them assurance and enabling them to walk by faith. Thus the Gospel's focus on the deity of Jesus and His revelation of the Father indicates a broader message than one limited to "how to be born again."[16] And, its focus on "eternal life" encompasses much more than issues of regeneration. This is not an "either...or" issue, but a "both...and" issue.

John recorded Jesus' deeds and teachings in order to explain more fully to his readers what it means to receive *and* experience eternal life. Something many believers do not understand is that there is a qualitative difference in various believers' experience of eternal life, not only in this life, but also in eternity. In the process of living and learning in this life today, we are developing the capacity to experience eternal life now as well as in its fullness in the life to come. What we do now impacts what we will experience then.[17]

This can be illustrated from what some take to be purely regeneration-oriented passages within John's Gospel. For example, rather than seeing the story of the woman at the well (John 4) as teaching "how" someone is born again, like most take it, we should see it also teaching what it *means* to be born again. Jesus' words to the woman must be seen in light of what He later says (and in light of John's explanation) in John 7:37-39. There He indicates that the born again person has the potential to experience the abundance of life in this life as a result of the Holy Spirit's presence.

Yes, the woman at the well receives this life by believing Jesus is whom He claims to be. But, it is not the issue of "how to" receive that Jesus focuses on, but rather "what" is received. She will never thirst again. Notice, He does not promise her that her spiritual thirst will be satisfied in heaven, though it obviously will be. Jesus promises her that she need not experience spiritual thirst for the rest of her life on earth. This is so relevant in our world today, when people tend to get stuck on justification-salvation and thus they do not satisfy their spiritual thirst available in sanctification-salvation.

Looking back at chapter three we see that this is true of Nicodemus as well. Though Jesus says, "You must be born again," He does not dwell on the "how to" as much as the "what you get," namely, God's life. This is not to say that the "how to" aspects of regeneration are not addressed in the Gospel. They are almost one hundred times! But Jesus and John also address another dimension. It is not just what you receive that they dwell on, but what you experience as a result of your faith.

The principle for believers that arises in these instances is that you can't believe any more than you know. And, you can't receive any more than you believe. Thus there is an emphasis on the issue of what it is that makes one's life in this life "eternal" and "abundant" (John 10:10) along with how to get it, not only now, but eternally. It is this that John wants his readers to *experience* as a result of their faith.

This progress in faith can be seen further in the emphasis on belief in the Gospel of John wherein there is a progress from the unregenerate to immature believers in John 2, to servants, to friends in John 16.[18] This is what John is after when he says he wants them to "have life in His name" (20:31). He wants to present eternal life in its full experience rather than just discuss how one is to gain it. He wants his readers to have this full life, which comes only as a product of faith placed in Jesus on the basis of an accurate understanding of His person and work.

One cannot experience eternal life apart from knowing the Father (17:3). One cannot know the Father apart from knowing Jesus (14:7). Therefore John describes Jesus as He reveals the Father in order that his readers can know both members of the Godhead. And knowing both members, they can thereby *experience* the eternal life that is available to them on the basis of their sonship, but is dependent on their abiding.

The Gospel's principal purpose, evidenced in the prologue, is to strengthen the readers' faith in (understanding of) Jesus and enable them to understand (experience) their salvation more fully, not simply to get them regenerated. In light of that, when we read the purpose statement of John 20:31, we should listen to him speaking to believers whose faith must be based on knowledge. He is telling them that he has recorded the Gospel so they can accurately understand who Jesus is, the Christ who is Son of God. He is also telling them that the effect of a proper understanding of the Jesus in whom they have placed their faith is that they can *experience* now the kind of life He described in the Gospel, "life in His name," and enter more fully into this "so great salvation" that we dare not neglect (Heb 2:3).

Though the issue of justification is clearly evident in the Gospel narrative, we must beware of assuming that it is the thrust of the Upper Room Discourse, even though that is what most commentators teach. When we move beyond this predominantly justification purpose from this portion of the Gospel, then we are free to see the Upper Room Discourse in its proper light, filling a critical place in the message of the Gospel of John without reducing it to a further description of justification truths.

Literary Arrangement of the Gospel

The Gospel of John is arranged rather simply with five parts. Characteristic of John's writing style, he begins with a *prologue* (1:1-18) in which the major thrust of his message is presented in capsule form. Then, he moves to the main body of his work that, in the case of the Gospel, has three major sections. John begins by describing *Jesus' Ministry to the Nation* (1:19—12:50) in which He reveals the Father and describes both the attainment and experience of eternal life to men and women in every walk of life. For example, in John 1:11, the nation's response to Jesus is described in seminal form. It is then described in detail in the chapters that follow.

This detailing is illustrated through the responses of men such as Nicodemus and the Jewish rulers, as contrasted with the Samaritans in chapter four and the Gentiles who come seeking Jesus in chapter twelve. This is followed by *Jesus' Ministry to His Apostles* (chaps. 13-17) in which He spends His final hours of freedom with the eleven chosen men who are to be the foundation of His spiritual body, the Church. The third section of the main body of the Gospel is *Jesus' Passion and Resurrection* (chaps. 18-21) in which He lays down His life and takes it up again, thereby providing the forgiveness needed for all to receive and experience eternal life. This is followed by a short *Epilogue* (chap. 21) wherein John ties up some "loose ends" and finishes the account of Jesus' post-resurrection ministry.

Message of the Gospel of John

The message of the Gospel, like most books of the Bible, can be summarized into a single synthetic statement. This normally reflects the dominant "theme" within the work. It then details/describes what the author says about this theme. The message of the Gospel of John can be summarized thus: **Jesus, the Christ, the Son of God reveals the Father and grants experience of eternal life to those who are believing in Him.** In the following paragraphs we will discuss the development of this message through the book and explain how the sections and chapters relate to this central message. Following this the place of the Upper Room Discourse in the development of John's message will be discussed more fully.

The subject and focus of the Gospel of John is "Jesus, the Christ, the Son of God." He is the focus of the book from beginning to end and this subject is expressed not only in the purpose statement of John 20:31, but also quite clearly in the prologue. His *deity* is the central emphasis of the book, its subject and dominant theme, not eternal life, Jesus' life, or His person in a broader sense. This does not mean that His incarnation is not dealt with as well. It is. But His deity is what John has chosen for his central focus. For John, understanding the deity of Jesus is of great importance for anyone either to gain or enjoy eternal life (John 10:10).

This emphasis is seen in the prologue where He is described as the Word of God who is God, who reveals God, and who is proclaimed as such by John the Baptist, the forerunner of the Messiah (1:1-18). Throughout His ministry to the nation both His signs and discourses reveal that He is indeed the Christ, the Son of God. His ministry in private to the eleven apostles reveals His revelatory and comforting role as Son of God that will be continued in the person of the Holy Spirit. He is crucified for claiming to be the Son of God and the truth of His claim is finally demonstrated by His resurrection.

The remainder of the message of the Gospel, what John tells us about Jesus, is expressed in the prologue of the Gospel, not the purpose statement of 20:31. The prologue (1:1-18) describes Jesus as the Word who created the world and became flesh in order *to reveal God and give life* to men who believe.[19] He did far more than come to bring life to men (regeneration). He came to communicate, to explain to men, His Father. This is seen in the development of His ministry to the nation, especially in the debates He has with the Jews. This is also seen in His passion and resurrection. Although justification truth is communicated throughout Jesus' public ministry through what He does as well as what He says, it is *not* a focus of His private ministry in the upper room.

In His public ministry Jesus defines what it means to believe in Him through many pictures such as rebirth (3), taking a drink (4,7), eating His flesh and drinking His blood (6), receiving sight (9), and by entering (10). He describes eternal life as a gift that may be received by faith to those willing to believe (3:14-16, 36; 4:13-14, 36; 5:39-40: 6:27, 40-54; 10:27-28; 12:25-26, 50; 17:2-3). It is also something *experienced* in this life, not just the life to come. John 10:10 is the climactic statement of Jesus' purpose in giving eternal life, that it may be *experienced* as an abundant life on earth by those believing in Him.

We need to be reminded again of the breadth of John's concept of "eternal life." For him the term is far more than regeneration truth (initial salvation). Just as salvation in Scripture is much broader than justification, even so eternal life is much broader than the reception of life with initial faith. It is a comprehensive concept involving both this life and the life to come. Jesus came to enable men to enjoy their present salvation, through sanctification, in anticipation of their future salvation, even glorification. Though there are times when the term is used in the sense of future eternal life, it most often includes the experience of God's life in this life as an integral facet of its meaning.

Eternal life is something that Jesus offers to people to experience *now*, as well as later. Thus, His purpose of offering "abundant life" in John 10:10 relates to *experiencing* a quality of life in this life, with more to come in the future. Jesus' declaration in John 11:25, "I am the resurrection and the life," can be seen as purely future. But other places such as with the woman at the well and His offer of living water at the Feast of Booths (7:37-38) clearly promise an experience of a quality of life in this life, especially in light of John's interpretation of Jesus' words in John 7:39. Granted, in each case the experience of eternal life involves the first step of saving faith for entrance into that experience.

But the use of the term "life" or "eternal life" carries with it a broader connotation. "I have come that they may have life, and that they may have it more abundantly" (John 10:10). It is something the individual begins experiencing from the moment of faith and its abundance is to be expressed in this life, as well as after resurrection. Therefore, the idea behind the statement that Jesus "gives eternal life to those who believe in Him" is not solely the justification sense of possessing eternal life, but the sanctification sense of something experienced *now* as well as in the future.

Following is a broad outline based on this understanding of the summarizing message statement for the Gospel. Finally there is an initial outline of the Upper Room Discourse wherein its message is developed more fully.

Broad Outline

I. Prologue: The Word who created the world became flesh in order to reveal God and give life to those who believe in Him. 1:1-18

II. Jesus' Ministry to the Nation: John's testimony and Jesus' signs and public discourses reveal that Jesus is the Christ, the Son of God, and that one may experience an abundant, unending and refreshing, life by believing in Him. 1:19—12:50

III. Jesus' Ministry to His Apostles: Jesus further revealed the Father to His disciples as He comforted and encouraged them in His final words and prayer. 13:1—17:26

IV. Jesus' Passion and Resurrection: Jesus allowed Himself to be arrested, tried, and crucified, dying and rising from the dead, thereby demonstrating that He is the Son of God and producing joy and faith in those who witnessed His resurrection. 18:1—20:31

V. Epilogue: Jesus restored Peter to leadership by the Sea of Tiberias. 21:1-25

UPPER ROOM DISCOURSE

VI. Jesus' Ministry to His Apostles: Jesus further revealed the Father to His disciples as He comforted and encouraged them in His final words and prayer. 13:1—17:26

    A. Jesus modeled humility when He washed His disciples feet and prophesied His betrayal. 13:1-30

        1. Jesus, knowing that His hour to suffer had come, laid aside His garment and washed His disciples' feet. 13:1-11

        2. Jesus explained the true path to blessing (13:17) that the foot washing demonstrated the humility He expects of His followers. 13:12-20

        3. Jesus prophesied His betrayal, revealing Judas as His betrayer by giving him the morsel. 13:21-30

    B. Jesus' provision for the disciples, who faced tribulation following His glorification, was to send a Helper, the Holy Spirit, to comfort and guide them as He convicted the world and gave the disciples peace. 13:31—16:33

        1. Jesus announced His coming glorification and departure. 13:31-33

        2. Jesus commanded the disciples to love one another that would demonstrate that they were His disciples and make them fruitful as they depended on Him. 13:34—15:17

a.   Jesus' new commandment is that they love one another. 13:34

b.   Proof of their discipleship will be their love for one another as they abide in Christ and are enabled by the Holy Spirit to be fruitful. 13:35—15:8

1)   Proof of them being Jesus' disciples will be their love for one another. 13:35

2)   Peter's declaration of his willingness to die for Jesus at the news of His departure resulted in Jesus' warning that he would deny Him three times. 13:36-38

3)   Jesus offered comfort at His departure through the promise of a place in heaven, of the Helper, and of His and the Father making their abode within the believer and giving them peace. 14:1-31

4)   Abiding in Jesus, the true vine, makes a disciple fruitful and leads to answered prayer, while failure to abide makes them useless. 15:1-8

c.   Obedience to Jesus' command to love one another makes disciples His fruitful friends. 15:9-17

3.   The ministry of the Spirit enables His disciples to bear witness of Jesus in a hostile world. 15:18—16:33

a.   Persecution will come upon them because they are identified with Jesus whom the world hates without cause. 15:18-25

b.   The Helper, the Spirit of truth, will enable them to bear witness of Jesus even as He bears witness of Him. 15:26-27

c.   Jesus' provision for overcoming tribulation was the sending of a Helper, the Holy Spirit, who would convict the world and guide believers, revealing Jesus' words to the disciples to whom Jesus would give peace. 16:1-33

1) The persecution they faced included being made outcasts and being killed after Jesus departed. 16:1-6

2) The Helper, the Spirit of truth, will have a ministry of conviction in the world and guidance and disclosure to the disciples. 16:7-16

3) Jesus' response to the disciples' puzzlement over "a little while" was to reveal that they would sorrow soon, but then understand when their joy was made full. 16:17-24

4) Jesus promised that His figurative language would soon be replaced with open explanations and answered prayer as He returned to the Father. 16:25-28

5) When the disciples responded by saying that they believed Jesus came from God, He responded that they would soon be scattered from Him, but that He would give them peace in a world of tribulation. 16:29-33

C. The High Priestly Prayer: Jesus' prayer was for His return to glory, the preservation of His disciples, and unity and love to characterize future believers who would be destined to behold Jesus' glory in heaven. 17:1-26

1. Jesus' prayer for Himself was for the Father to again share His glory with Him since He had completed His work on the earth. 17:1-5

2. Jesus' prayer for His disciples, who believed that He was from the Father, was for the Him to guard them from the evil one, sanctifying them in His word, while they remained in the world. 17:6-19

3. Jesus' prayer for future believers was for them to experience Their unity and love, and to be destined for heaven where they could behold Jesus' glory. 17:20-26

CHAPTER TWO

CHRIST TEACHING BY EXAMPLE
John 13:1-17

We now enter the Upper Room, where Christ's disciples were meeting for the Last Supper they would share together before His crucifixion. Even though they did not know the significance of this evening, Jesus did. He knew all that would transpire, and the depth of need they were about to face, as well as Him. What were the disciples thinking as they came into that room? Luke helps us out at this point. They were thinking about themselves. But Jesus did not waste this opportunity to teach them something about Himself.

An understanding of what preceded this event is helpful in understanding the attitude of the disciples and interpreting Jesus' actions and words in this section. We need to go back a few days before the last supper. An *attitude* of self-centeredness was evident well before their *action* of ignoring the opportunity to serve one another that evening.

The first sign of self-centeredness can be seen more clearly in an event that often escapes our notice. As they traveled toward Jericho, Jesus counsels the rich young ruler to sell all and follow Him (Matt 19:16-22; Mark 10:17-22). He then announces how difficult it is for the rich to enter the kingdom of God (Matt 19:23; Mark 10:23-25). Following this, the group first asks who can be saved, and is told that, "with God all things are possible" (Matt 19:26). Peter then asks a second question, and his words become very informative with regard to the basic attitude of the men the evening of the last supper. He says, "See, we have left all and followed You. Therefore *what shall we have?*" What a brash question! Jesus could have said, "Have you considered what I have left for you?" But no, rather, He chooses another response.

Jesus motivates them with the future kingdom that they are thinking about. He promises them that they will sit on twelve thrones judging the twelve tribes of Israel in the coming reign of Christ and be rewarded greatly for their sacrifices. But then He closes this promise with the final searching comment, "But many *who are* first will be last, and the last first." He next follows this with the parable of the workers in the vineyard who are not rewarded strictly by length of service but heart attitude (Matt 20:1-16; see 1 Cor 4:5). They seem to have missed His point. But rather, we see that even as they continue to travel the road to Jericho and then climb the steep highway to Jerusalem, their minds are on what they can get out of serving Jesus, not on serving one another. Even so, we must commend the disciples for their having the proper goal, the kingdom, even though at times they had wrong attitudes and the wrong time-line (Acts 1:6).

Still, the disciples were listening, because they seem to have understood the promise of twelve thrones and its implication to them that the Messianic Kingdom was about to be inaugurated by Jesus. So, they were anticipating Jesus revealing Himself as the Messiah and bringing in His kingdom, probably during the coming feast. Amid that anticipation the mother of James and John approached Jesus and asked that her sons receive special status in His kingdom, more specifically, the two highest posts in His new government (Matt 20:20-28). The other disciples responded with indignation toward the brothers, implying they were likely in collusion with their mother (who was also Jesus' aunt!).[1] Interestingly, Jesus did not upbraid them for their brashness, but answered forthrightly and responded that greatness in the Kingdom comes through servanthood, not position. Yet, evidently, none of the disciples seemed to be listening.

In Luke 22:24-30 we sense a climax of this wrong attitude in that even during the supper with Jesus the disciples continued to argue among themselves about who would be greatest. We know from Luke that this issue of greatness preceded Jesus' warning of Peter's denial, and so must have preceded the same in the upper room account of John. The events of the foot washing must have occurred between the debate over greatness and Jesus' warning to Peter in Luke 22.

This helps us see the focus of Jesus' action when He arose and washed the disciples' feet. His thoughts and actions were not focused on the cross, but on the problem of pride among his men. What we find is that Jesus had to deal with a destructive attitude in the men who were going to be the foundation stones of the church (Eph 2:20), but who were still quite carnal. He wanted to change their mindset from that of pride and self-centeredness to that of servanthood.

Characteristic of the group was Peter's willingness to die for Jesus, but unwillingness to wash the other's feet. He was after the glorious side of service to Christ, not the humble side. Really, he was being quite selfish in his desires.

In addition to this we must remember that they had just experienced a series of extraordinary events. First, there was Jesus' own commendation of Peter, namely, that his recognition of Him as "the Christ, the Son of the living God" came by revelation from God (Matt 16:16-17). Then there was Jesus' promise that some of them would "not taste death" until they had seen "the Son of Man coming in His kingdom" (Matt 16:28). After this Peter, James, and John had witnessed the vision of Jesus in His heavenly glory on the Mount of Transfiguration and heard His explanation that John the Baptist fulfilled the Elijah prophecy of Malachi (Matt 17:1-13).

Again, as they approached Jerusalem the disciples were anticipating the inauguration of the kingdom and knew that Jesus was the expected Messianic King. Though they had witnessed His transfiguration, the three apostles had not told their companions about it. They also likely did not recognize it as the fulfillment of Jesus' promise that some of them would see the kingdom and so were still anticipating its physical arrival at that time.

Further evidences of the mindset of the disciples are their inability to understand Jesus' warnings of his impending suffering and death (Mark 9:32) and their question concerning who is the greatest in the kingdom (Matt 18:1). These followed quickly on the heels of His promise of the kingdom and His Transfiguration. Their questions and attitudes indicate that they were clearly expecting the kingdom's arrival and so were jockeying for positions in its administration since new kings normally appoint their friends to office.

It is in light of these very selfish attitudes in the group that we see the very unselfish attitude of Jesus contrasted. John takes us into the inner sanctum of their last private moments with Jesus to reveal His tender heart and innermost thoughts in the last hours before His departure. They did not realize the significance of the moment as they entered that room that evening with their Master and Savior, but we should. As we examine these moments Jesus shared with His beloved friends, and through John with us, let us take off our shoes and enter with reverence and awe into the presence of our Savior as we glimpse into His heart and hear His words of love and encouragement once again.

The Humble Act 13:1-11

13:1. Now before the feast of the Passover, when Jesus knew that His hour had come that He should depart out of this world to the Father, having loved His own who were in the world, He loved them to the end.

John begins his account of Jesus' intimate moments with a time marker, a statement of Jesus' self-understanding and omniscience, and a declaration of His deep love for His disciples. Let us begin by focusing on that love Jesus felt and demonstrated that evening.

When John says that Jesus "loved His own . . . to the end," he does not say that Jesus' love and concern for the disciples would end with His death, but that His is an absolute unconditional love. The phrase translated "to the end" carries the sense of "absolutely" or "completely" in this context.[2] It says that Jesus' love for His disciples has no limit. What John is saying by this is that, although the circumstances coming on Jesus would cause most people's attention to be focused either completely or in part on themselves, His love for His disciples is so intense and complete that His focus remains on them in these hours of His own great need. In fact His love is so great that He purposely includes Judas, an unbeliever, among those He serves.[3] We should note that Judas was a disciple, but not a believer. People can be believers without being disciples (cf. John 12:42) or they can be disciples without being believers, as in the case of Judas.

This first verse serves both as an introduction to the whole Upper Room Discourse and as an inclusio with the final verse of the discourse, marking off this section of material in the Gospel so that the readers can recognize the message contained within it.[4] When this verse is recognized as an introduction to what will follow, Jesus' focus on His disciples can be properly understood. These are the men He promised earlier would share His reign with Him, sitting on twelve thrones (Matt 19:28). As He acts, therefore, He may be looking beyond the church to the future glory, when they will join Him as co-regents in His kingdom (Rev 3:21).[5] What He is about to do and say is an expression of His love for this group of men who will one day rule with Him.

Though this is a period of emotional agony for Him, revealed by His ordeal in the Garden of Gethsemane (Matt 26:36-46; Luke 22:39-46), these men remain at the center of His thoughts. With torture and death only hours away, their need in light of what is about to happen to Him is His concern, not Himself. They need instruction that will strengthen their faith and enable them to survive the horrors of the coming hours and days.

They also need instruction that will prepare them to be the kind of men He needs to carry the message of life to a lost world and provide an example for subsequent saints to follow.

Since He loves these men so much, He wants to serve them by meeting their spiritual and emotional needs in this time of His greatest need. Thus Jesus loves them so completely that He takes action to serve and teach them in spite of the fact that they are all full of themselves and not concerned in the least bit about what is about to befall Him. Though they will reign with Him in His kingdom, in their present mission, He does not need kings, but servants. And in our case we need to remember that perhaps we would be better served by attending a "followership" seminar rather than one of the leadership seminar's that are so popular today. That preparation would indeed fit us to reign as kings (2 Tim 2:12; Rev 3:21).

Jesus knows that these beloved men are about to experience traumatic days that, apart from His preparing them, will destroy their immature faith. His words are not an attempt to clarify the gospel to a confused group of men, but preparation for testing, for change, and for His departure. It is His last opportunity to teach them the things that they, who already believe in Him, will need in order to continue His ministry and stand firm in faith.

Jesus' action of footwashing and His words of instruction must be seen in light of their imminent need rather than as a Johannine treatise on justification. This is not to say that justification truths are not expressed or implied by Jesus, as will be seen. But it does mean that such were not the *focus* of His instructions to them, and so should not be ours either. Rather than trying to teach justification truths just before His death and departure, Jesus was giving them a lesson on sanctified living. This lesson began with the most unexpected action on Jesus' part. He donned the appearance of a servant, and served.

13:2-4. And supper being ended, the devil having already put it into the heart of Judas Iscariot, Simon's son, to betray Him, Jesus, knowing that the Father had given all things into His hands, and that He had come from God and was going to God, rose from supper, laid aside His garments, took a towel, and girded Himself.

Before John records the action of Christ, he gives us the source of the action. Jesus knew what to do because He knew what He knew. He knew where He came from. He knew where He was going. He knew what was His mission. He knew all these truths on the basis of the authoritative Word of God. And, that knowledge set Him free to do what He did in taking the role of a servant.[6] We see in this a principle of life that is true of every person. What I know determines how I think. How I think determines what I do.

We see this principle at work in the first five verses of this chapter. In verses one and three we see that Jesus knew what He knew. Then in verses four and five we see that He did what He did on the basis of what He knew. By practicing the principle that our actions are determined by our deepest thoughts Jesus was able to do what He did. Because Jesus knew who He was, He could do what He did. The disciples knew what needed to be done and could have done it, but did not. They could not do what needed to be done because of their mindset. When we come to know who we are, it is amazing what we are able to do. We are reminded of the story in World Magazine by Cal Thomas of a 72-year-old pastor in Mainland China who has spent twenty-one years in prison for his faith. Fifteen of those prison years was for attempting to copy a New Testament. When asked by Cal Thomas how he could "radiate joy in the midst of persecution," he responded, "You must have a mind to suffer. If you have a mind to suffer, you can stand it. But if you don't have a mind to suffer, you can be broken."[7] Humble action does not threaten us if we know who we are. This we will examine in greater detail below.

It is interesting to note that John chose to insert his comment about Satan's influence on Judas in the midst of the introductory description of Jesus' character and attitude.[8] Judas, in contrast to Jesus, does not love. He does not serve. He seeks his own interests rather than the interests of others. In every way he is different from Jesus. A talk on humility in Judas' mind is the *last* thing he needed. He is not interested in a humble servant, but a conquering king. He sits contemplating betrayal even as Jesus is moved by His love to demonstrate and teach humility and service, though He is fully aware of what is about to transpire.

The devil's motivation of Judas contrasts with Jesus' focus on the Father. And where Jesus is submitting Himself to the will of the Father, Judas submits himself to the will of the devil. He represents an expression of pride and rebellion against God that is, in turn, the opposite of humility and obedience about to be modeled by Christ.[9]

Yet, in this attribute of humility the other disciples were not much better than Judas. They certainly lacked humility. Before them was a need that all of them were aware of and any of them could have met. But none chose to meet it. If this had been Jesus' or one of their own homes, there likely would have been a servant boy available to do this very ordinary duty of washing the guests' feet. The disciples obviously were not up to doing such a menial endeavor, or else they would have done it before their teacher. But why were they intimidated by such a task? Why so restrained and insecure?

They really did not know who they were. And they did not know who they were because they really did not know who Christ was. This was made evident by Jesus' question later in 14:9, "Have I been with you so long, and yet you have not known Me, Philip?" And they did not know who He was because they really did not know who God was. Thus, Jesus' following statement, "He who has seen Me has seen the Father." They measured themselves by each other as they jockeyed for positions in the coming kingdom rather than measuring themselves by God.

A. W. Tozer has well stated that every sin we ever commit is because of wrong or inadequate thinking about God. In contrast to them, and Judas, knowing what He knew, Jesus was secure. He knew what He came to do and He knew where He was going when He completed His mission. Thus taking the role of a servant did not threaten Him. He was not intimidated to humble Himself in their eyes. Jesus was going to lead them to that same security. Later, John reminded us all that, "perfect love casts out fear" (1 John 4:18).

Walking through Jerusalem or any village left a person's feet smelling like the animal manure that littered the streets after herdsmen and merchants led their flocks through town to the markets. So, a person's feet were rightly viewed as filthy. As a result, one must "soil" him or her self to wash another's feet. But, since this was a guest chamber provided by a host, the upper room most likely had some rugs covering much of its floor. Customary courtesy called for them to wash their feet before entering the room so that they would not soil and stink up the rugs. Thus washing their feet would simply be an act of common courtesy toward their host, a courtesy they apparently skipped.

For Jesus to wash their feet, then, was to "soil" Himself by taking the position of a Gentile "dog" slave, not a Jewish servant. And, for Him as their teacher and master to do such was a greater violation of societal norms than their failures to wash their own or one another's feet. More than that, where their action was inconsiderate, His was downright shocking!

Should this action by Jesus be interpreted as a picture of His death on the cross for our sins? Beasley-Murray reflects those who focus on the doctrine of justification as the grid through which Jesus' actions and words should be viewed in this Gospel. He says that Jesus' act "was not simply his stripping off his robe and stooping to wash disciples' feet, but his stripping off his glory with the Father and stooping to the humiliation and pain of the cross."[10] There is certainly a great deal of truth in this observation if one wishes to make the footwashing a parabolic picture of Jesus' ministry. It is even legitimate to say that Jesus' act reflects the character of His ministry in that He set aside His glory and position to meet the needs of sinful mankind (Phil 2:5).

But it is illegitimate to say that Jesus is attempting by this action to picture His own self-humiliation. That is not what He is communicating to His men when He stoops to serve them. His purpose is not to teach them about the nature of His sacrifice or ministry. It is neither a picture of the price He had paid in leaving glory, nor of the depth of humility He had exercised in His incarnation. Nor is it a picture of the humiliation He is about to undergo in His crucifixion.[11]

To understand Jesus' actions, we should place them into the context of the events and His instructions to the disciples from the time prior to the Transfiguration until that evening. Then His message to the eleven should lead us to an understanding of the purpose and message behind the action. Viewing it this way, it is better seen as a lesson on humility and service than a picture of sacrifice. Jesus is not warning or informing them again of His coming crucifixion. He has already done that repeatedly before this evening's activities.

He is teaching them humility and mutual servanthood. He is training the eleven to serve. He is modeling for them the outworking of a proper attitude. Notice His statement just a few verses later, "I have given you an example" that they are to practice toward each other (13:15). Jesus is teaching them something about what He expects of them. And so He humbly serves. When they came into the room, they all knew what needed to be done. Any one of them could have done it. But none of them did it. Thus, Jesus, as the master Disciplemaker, teaches them not only by what He says but also by what He does.

We who would teach others need to learn this crucial lesson. Too often, however, we prove to be the legitimate target of the searching statement, "What you do speaks so loudly I can't hear what you say."

13:5. After that, He poured water into a basin and began to wash the disciples' feet, and to wipe them with the towel with which He was girded.

Jesus' actions were not stilted or partial. Having taken the vestige of a servant, He fulfilled the role, washing and drying the disciples' feet. To do this He had to kneel or stoop at their smelly feet and soil His hands on them as He washed off the dust of Jerusalem's manure laden streets. This was not an act of kindness toward victims of disease, like the many lepers He had reached out and cleansed, whose conditions were not self induced. This was an act of humble service to a group of self-absorbed men who had been acting more like spoiled children than the leadership of a future kingdom.

Why was it that none of the disciples had offered to wash the others' feet? Again, Luke 22:24 recounts the conversation that preceded their arrival at the supper. Merrill Tenney rightly notes that each man present with Jesus "would have considered it an admission of inferiority to all the others" to stoop to such a humble task.[12] We know from Luke that it was during the supper that the debate over greatness continued to rage among the men. This debate may have been expressed in terms of where the disciples got to sit around the supper table. During feasts it was customary for people to be seated, at least in part, according to their status as determined by the host or guest of honor, in this case, Jesus. If He had not designated who got to sit where, their debate over greatness could have, in part, been reflected in their jockeying for the places of honor. At any rate, their dispute was sufficiently heated that it did not escape Jesus' notice.

In light of their discussion in the upper room and the maneuvering of James and John on the road to Jerusalem, it is evident that they were in no mood that evening to do anything that might consciously (visibly) denigrate themselves in the eyes of one another, much less Jesus. They were all jockeying for position in the up-coming government of Messiah. And, thinking like the world thinks, their pride and ambition craved prestige, not humiliation. To wash the others' feet that evening might be seen as an admission that the other deserved a better position in the coming kingdom than one's self. None was willing to give the other the opportunity to even think such. In that light, Jesus' act was "a voluntary humiliation that rebuked the pride of the disciples."[13] It is interesting to note that the Rabbinical commentary on Ezekiel 16:9 states, "Human usage is that the slave washes the master; but God is not so."[14]

As noted earlier, a key principle is evident in Jesus as He stoops to humbly serve His undeserving followers. Our actions are simply the product of our deepest thoughts. Jesus' deepest thoughts focused on their good, not His position. He was not striving for position. He had voluntarily relinquished the majestic glory that He had with the Father before the world was.

The same problem Jesus faced with the disciples was evident in the church in Philippi when Paul wrote to them. In fact, Paul may have been reflecting on the events of this evening and the following day as he instructed the church. Early in his epistle (Phil 2:1-4) he commanded the Philippians to pursue unity and to look out for one another's interests "in lowliness of mind" rather than acting from "selfish ambition or conceit." The contrast in attitudes described by Paul matched the contrast in attitudes evident in the upper room.

In turning to Jesus as the example for them to follow, Paul described His motivation and actions in Philippians 2:6-7, "who, being in the form of God, did not consider it robbery to be equal with God, but made Himself of no reputation, taking the form of a bondservant, and coming in the likeness of men." Paul pointed to Jesus' example, not to teach love but to teach humility and servant leadership, the same lesson Jesus was teaching the eleven in the upper room. Paul gave this description of Christ's attitude of humble service to a church struggling with a problem of unity, particularly between two key women in its congregation who were apparently embroiled in a personal conflict that called for the intervention of others to heal the breach in the church (Phil 4:2). When pointing them to Jesus as their example of humble service, he noted Jesus' conscious surrender of His rights and prerogatives as God. He also noted His choice to humble Himself by taking upon Himself the form of a servant and then acting out its implications all the way to death.

How did Jesus humble Himself? In the Greek construction of Philippians 2:7-8 two phrases are parallel, synonymous. Paul's two descriptions of Jesus' action, that He "made Himself of no reputation" and "He humbled Himself" are parallel thoughts describing the same thing. Rather than demanding His rights as God, Jesus, by an act of His own will, revealed His humble attitude by taking the form of a servant and living out its requirements. As F. F. Bruce notes well, in Jesus' act of humiliation the "form of God was not *exchanged for* the form of a servant; it was *revealed in* the form of a servant."[15]

Jesus did not become any less God than He had been before. Rather, He chose to live in obedience to the Father as every human being should, even when that obedience led to death on a cross, a death He did not deserve. Though He had the prerogative as God to be exalted and praised, He willingly subjected Himself, as the representative of all humanity, by humbly obeying, by making "Himself of no reputation," by setting aside His equal rights, and serving. He obeyed and served the Father as every human must. He served men as every human should.

Jesus' action in the upper room was another expression in a practical way of the humility that previously motivated Him to become man and live out the implications of that decision, even to the experience of voluntary death on a cross. In the upper room He was not forgetting who He was or who His men were in relationship to Him. Yet, He still acted the part of a humble servant for the sake of his men. He arose, donned the attire of a servant by taking off His outer robe and wrapping a towel about His waist, and then began to serve. This is quite the contrast to the way to greatness that is taught in the world system around us. Have you heard the statement, "If you don't look out for yourself, nobody else will"? It is quite the opposite in God's pattern for greatness. It is through giving that we receive.

13:6. Then He came to Simon Peter. And Peter said to Him, "Lord, are You washing my feet?"

Peter's response to Jesus is another indication that none of the disciples had washed their feet before the meal.[16] And it is by this that Jesus' intention to teach humble service becomes most evident. He acts in response to their pride and dissension. He chooses such an action to communicate the attitude He demands of them in contrast to the attitudes they have been demonstrating. Jesus wants them to understand the nature of the love He has for them and wants them to live out and so displays that love through humble servitude.

Jesus has likely already washed His own feet when arriving that evening. He has done it precisely because He is concerned about the homeowner and has the humility to display toward him such a common courtesy. He also has the proper humility and self-understanding to do His own washing when no one else is willing to offer the service. Though one of them should have offered to wash His feet, He washes His own rather than asking any of them to serve Him in such a manner, an act they likely have ignored at the time. Thus they continue to focus on themselves, unaware of Jesus' own consideration and compassion amid their maneuverings and bickering.

Jesus' action created a problem for the disciples. Though they were not about to wash each other's feet, they had enough sense to know that it certainly was not Jesus' role to do it.

Jesus' action was horrifying to Peter along with the others. Though he was probably thinking how "politically correct" the others were acting by keeping silent and submitting to Jesus' action, he had to speak. Peter knew Jesus' action violated every rule of social decency. He must have forgotten

Jesus' response to Mary who washed His feet and wiped them with her hair, another socially unacceptable thing. He must also have forgotten how often Jesus did other socially unacceptable things, such as eating with tax collectors and sinners. In this instance, Jesus' action was as socially inappropriate as it would be for someone to ask the President of the United States to clean up a spill in the kitchen at a fund raising dinner. It was not only insulting to the person in a higher position; it was embarrassing for the person of lower social status. This act of Jesus far exceeded anything else He had done in public or private to this point. Peter had to speak up. He could not keep silent and submit.

Peter's refusal in verse six is far more emphatic than English translations can communicate. In Greek, the word order of sentences generally follows the pattern we have in English. But, for writers of Koiné Greek, word order is quite flexible. They can take words out of their usual places in the sentence and move them either to the beginning or end of the sentence in order to draw attention to them, for emphasis. With the role that words play in the sentence (like subject, object, verbs, etc.) being indicated by prefixes and suffixes added to the words, they can be moved like that and the sentence will still make sense to a Greek speaking person. When Peter raises his protest to Jesus, he moves both "you" and "my" from where they would normally be placed in the sentence in order to emphasize his incredulity and alarm at Jesus' action. If we wish to communicate more closely the feeling of Peter, it may be better to paraphrase his response with, "What do YOU think you are doing trying to wash MY feet?!?!"

Lest we think too quickly that Peter was completely out of line, we should remember his high regard for Jesus and Jesus' response to him that is to follow. As A. B. Bruce notes, "This impulse of instinctive aversion was by no means discreditable to Peter, and it was evidently not regarded with disapprobation by his Master."[17] We can see this in Jesus' first response to Peter.

13:7. Jesus answered and said to him, "What I am doing you do not understand now, but you will know after this."

What did Jesus mean when He said, "What I am doing . . . you will know after this"?[18] He was telling Peter He would explain Himself when He was finished with the task of washing everyone's feet. He understood clearly that the disciples could not begin to fathom the significance of His actions or to understand His point. That was precisely why He was doing what He was doing. So, His response to Peter called on him to humbly submit and await instruction. But, Peter was not that kind of follower.

13:8. Peter said to Him, "You shall never wash my feet!" Jesus answered him, "If I do not wash you, you have no part with Me."

Peter's second response was characteristically impetuous, and proud. As A. B. Bruce again aptly notes, "Peter's first word was the expression of sincere reverence; his second is simply the language of unmitigated irreverence and downright disobedience."[19] It smacked of his attitude in Matthew 16 following the feeding of the four thousand when he responded to Jesus' question about who men said He was and declared that Jesus was the Christ, the Son of the living God. After Jesus praised him for his answer and then began to instruct His disciples that His destiny involved suffering and death at the hands of the Jewish leaders, Peter pulled Him aside and began to rebuke Him. Though he had already recognized Jesus as his teacher and social superior, and then had just recognized Him as Messiah and Son of God, he was still sufficiently arrogant to attempt to mold Him to his will rather than visa versa. Now, at the Supper, he again had the brashness to violate their socially defined roles as master/teacher and servant/student and to say "no" to Jesus once again. Though Jesus' actions were embarrassing to Peter socially, he was obligated to submit to his teacher. Though the other disciples had the good sense to submit, Peter could not keep silent.

Jesus' response was equally characteristic and swift. His response was sharp and cut right to the heart of Peter as had been His response at other times. When Peter overstepped his bounds and rebuked Jesus for talking about His coming suffering, death, and resurrection in Matthew 16:21-23, He sharply rebuked him, even addressing him as Satan! And, as He had rebuked Peter previously, so now His words drove a sword into the heart of the issue. Peter must submit, or leave. He could not follow and say no at the same time. Only one way existed for doing things: Christ's way. If Peter wished to remain in the fellowship of that company of men, he had to submit to its Head.[20]

What is the implication of this for us today? Peter's attitude is one that characterizes many believers and churches today. God must do things our way. He must think our thoughts and reflect our values. Often we ask Christian college students if they believe the Bible is the inspired, inerrant, word of God. They say, "Of course!" Then we ask if its command for sexual purity applies to their dating lives. The answer, whether given verbally or in the secrecy of their dorm room, is often, "Of course not! That was for then, not today!"

We not only expect God to act according to our culture and standards, but we have the brashness to demand it of Him. When He acts as Almighty King of the Universe, many of us have the audacity to ask if He is being fair. When something appears in Scripture that gets in the way of modern sensibilities or our culture's view of what Jesus should be like, we reinterpret the Scripture or say that it is no longer culturally relevant to our situation. By doing this many believers today violate Jesus' lordship in their lives. When Peter declared, "never," as A. B. Bruce notes, "he made his own reason and conscience the supreme rule of conduct."[21]

As Jesus' response to Peter was absolute and uncompromising, so is His word to this generation of followers. Either He rules or there is no fellowship. If He were to allow Peter to determine what He could or could not do according to Peter's standards and dictates, then His lordship would be over, not only in Peter's life but also in the life of every believer. Again, A. B. Bruce speaks volumes to us when he notes that the principle of obedience violated by Peter "requires that the will of the Lord, once known, whether we understand its reason or perceive its goodness or not, shall be supreme."[22]

Once God has spoken, we must obey. As John notes in 1 John 1, we either agree with God concerning sin and walk according to His moral purity (in the light), or we deceive ourselves, call God a liar, and remain out of fellowship with Him in our self-deception. It is impossible to have fellowship with a holy God while rejecting His revelation and ignoring the demands of His holiness. It is impossible to walk in fellowship with God while saying "no" to Him when He reveals His will. Jesus told Peter that very thing with His sharp rebuke. He tells us the same as well. It would do us well to listen and respond. Peter was not as slow as many believers today. He responded.

Guess whom we are serving when we say no to Jesus! Don't be afraid to say the truth, even Satan. This indeed is where John would place repentance for a believer as is evidenced in the seven letters to the churches of Revelation 2 and 3.

13:9. Simon Peter said to Him, "Lord, not my feet only, but also my hands and my head!"

Peter's second response was, again, characteristic of him! He demanded more, offering his hands and head. His words might be mistaken by someone as sarcasm, as an attempt to out-do the others in submission. Rather, they should be seen as an over-reaction in response to the threat of expulsion. This makes the best sense, based on Jesus' response to Peter's words. He clearly did not want to be excluded from the fellowship of Jesus and His followers. He had followed Jesus and believed in Him even when the masses walked away (John 6:66-69). He had recognized that Jesus alone was the source of eternal life and that He was sent from God. He did not want anything to disqualify him from continuing in the company of the Messiah. Jesus' rebuke brought immediate submission, even over-zealous submission. By this statement Peter was saying, "I *do* want to have a part with You, more than these others!"

It may be tempting to suspect that Peter was trying to maintain his position of leadership among the followers in the eyes of Jesus. But, it is more likely that he was still just being impetuous and over reacting, as Jesus' next response indicates.

13:10. Jesus said to him, "He who is bathed needs only to wash his feet, but is completely clean; and you are clean, but not all of you."

Jesus' words, first of all, are to Peter and not to the group. This is important to see in order to understand what Jesus is saying here and later in the discourse. Jesus does not address the group until verse twelve, after taking up His garments again and returning to His place at the table. He responds to Peter's honest over-reaction by telling him that his earlier bath was enough. From this, He then hints at a deeper truth, namely that the group is not all "clean" in some different sense.

The term Jesus uses here for "clean" is a broadly used term that includes the idea of ceremonial cleanness and moral purity although it can be used for simple physical cleanness as well.[23] Jesus' use here employs both senses; the spiritual truth pictured in the physical reality. Peter's request implies that he may have been thinking in much the same terms. Jesus' words to Peter are comforting words, "you are clean." Peter has nothing to fear. But Jesus is also thinking of Judas at that point, and so adds that "not all" are clean.

This shows us how much the coming betrayal weighs on His thoughts even as He humbles Himself and washes Judas' feet along with the others. He cannot keep the secret much longer. He has to tell His most trusted friends, but not directly, without interfering with God's eternal plan and Judas' free choices.

What is the significance of Jesus' washing their feet? His reference to cleansing does imply that He is communicating spiritual truths to Peter, at least. But, His instructions to the group as a whole remain focused on the issue of humility, not moral or spiritual cleanness.[24]

Still, Jesus' words to Peter do give His actions another level of meaning. Peter is misunderstanding Jesus' actions at that point and only sees the issue of ceremonial cleanness; thus, his request for his hands and head being washed as well. Jesus then addresses the issue of moral cleanness to Peter, and alludes to Judas' condition when He says that "not all of you" are clean such that only foot washing is needed to make them completely clean. With regard to moral cleanness, Jesus says to Peter, all but one of you have been cleansed and need only a little washing to be properly prepared for the spiritual communion you are imagining, pictured by participation in the Passover meal. So, though the footwashing is not done by Jesus to teach justification truths to the eleven, He does hint at it to Peter, but only to him.[25] And, interestingly, Jesus' allusion to Peter reflects Peter's need for sanctification while alluding to Judas' lack of justification.

Does this raise a problem of multiple meanings? No. Jesus is in the habit of saying things that are intended to have a double thrust or application and thereby force His listeners to think about what He has said. At times, He does not appear to mind being vague. Thus, Jesus repeatedly teaches the multitudes in parables precisely to keep some people from understanding what He is saying and to force others to think long and hard over His words in order to discern their meaning. All of this is part of the single meaning that He has in His mind.

So, what is the significance of Jesus' actions and what He said to Peter as it applies to us? Just as Jesus' washing Judas' feet did not make him a believer in Christ, so participating in the sacraments of the church does not make anyone a believer. Additionally, participating in *any* activity of the church does not make a believer more spiritual either, as washing feet did not change Peter any more than it changed Judas. Note that one may be a disciple without being a believer, as well as being a believer without being a disciple (cf. John 12:42). It is our commitment to and walk with the Lord that counts. God looks at the heart to read our true motives, just as Jesus did with Judas and Peter.

Jesus' statement to Peter concerning his cleanness reveals that the spiritual sense communicated by the foot washing and alluded to by Him reflects the cleansing involved in our sanctification. His last statement, "You are clean, but not all of you," does refer to who is justified and who is not in that group. It is also an evaluation of their hearts. Jesus is indeed saying that Judas is unregenerate. But, His earlier statement, "He who is bathed needs only to wash his feet . . . and you are clean," refers to sanctification.

Yes, Jesus is referring to regenerate persons by His use of "bathed" and "completely clean" in this verse.[26] He uses the term for washing all over (louō) in verse ten when He says to Peter, "He who is bathed...." He then uses a different term for washing (niptō) to say that a bathed person "needs only to wash his feet." The first washing refers to regeneration and the second to the cleansing of sanctification. He thereby affirms Peter's justification as well as his need for cleansing in his sanctification. This sanctifying cleansing will again be alluded to in John 15:3, "You are already clean because of the word that I have spoken to you...."

John reflects on this truth in 1 John 1:9 and teaches that regenerate people need to "wash" themselves of their daily sin by confession. Joseph Dillow aptly concludes from this that, "Christ teaches here that, if a person who has been bathed refuses daily washing, he will have no part with Him. This is what is meant by a carnal Christian." He says further,

> There are two kinds of forgiveness in the New Testament. One pertains to our eternal salvation (justification by faith), the other to our temporal fellowship with the Father. Just as our children may sin within our family, the believer may sin within God's family. Our child is always our child, but until he confesses, our fellowship is not good. In God's family the same principle applies. There is a forgiveness for salvation [i.e., *justification-salvation*] and a forgiveness for restoration [i.e., *sanctification-salvation*].[27]

The Lord referred to the second kind of forgiveness in this verse. Jesus' reference to "no part with Him," since justification is not the issue of the footwashing with Peter, "refers to a severance of fellowship and end of usefulness in Christ's cause."[28] He correctly concludes, "Apparently, true Christians, due to their sin, can 'have no part' with Christ, can be unforgiven, and can be outside His love."[29] This truth recognized, we can then see that Jesus' act of foot washing cannot picture His work on the cross in our justification since it addresses the issue of fellowship, not justification.[30]

To help us understand this idea better, we should look back into the Old Testament. In Exodus 29:4 (also Lev 8:6) the consecration of Aaron and his sons to the priesthood began with Moses bathing them with water.

This was followed by the various sacrifices for their sins and consecration. Then, whenever they approached the tabernacle or offered sacrifices, God required that they wash their hands and feet in the bronze laver (Ex 30:18-21; 40:30-32). Their cleansing for service, though, should not be compared to the cleansing that occurs at regeneration as a part of our justification and the daily cleansing of confessed sin that is a part of our sanctification. The priests were already believers before their initial ceremonial washing.

Hebrews 10:14 relates better to the issue. There the writer of Hebrews says, "For by one offering He has perfected forever those who are being sanctified." This would, again, relate to the complete washing that Jesus said they had already experienced and did not need repeated. Jesus' allusion to their having been fully bathed reminded Peter of the fact that, before coming to the dinner, they would have all bathed themselves at the public bath. Then they would have gone from there to the dinner and only their feet would have been dirty. Peter's request for Jesus to wash more than his feet was inappropriate. Still, Jesus used it to teach him a spiritual truth.

All of this having been said, we must again remember that these words were spoken between Jesus and Peter. And, they related to Peter's request, not the attitudes of the group. Thus, to understand the act as Jesus intended it to be understood by the eleven, we must first and foremost hear His explanation to the eleven, not to Peter. When we do this, we will recognize that He was picturing humility and service, not His coming sacrifice.

13:11. For He knew who would betray Him; therefore He said, "You are not all clean."

John's comment in verse eleven, that Jesus was aware of who would betray Him, reflects again His omniscience and consciousness of Judas' heart even as He was communicating these truths to His true disciples.[31] It is instructive, though, to remember that Jesus knew even as He washed Judas' feet that he was at that time in the process of betraying Him.[32] It was not a decision to be made by Judas, but a conspiracy already set in motion. For Judas, the unregenerate follower of Jesus, these words could mean little. For the others, they were words of comfort.

Jesus' Explanation: Foot Washing Demonstrates the Humility Expected of His Followers, Not Betrayers
13:12-20

Having completed the task of washing His disciples' feet, Jesus redressed and returned to His place of prominence, the chief seat at the feast. He was ready to instruct His men in the significance of His actions. He began their instruction by reminding them of His relationship to them, socially and spiritually.

13:12. So when He had washed their feet, taken His garments, and sat down again, He said to them, "Do you know what I have done to you?"

Jesus began with a question, whose answer He already knew. "Do you understand?" Of course not! Peter's own response had indicated that. Their hearts were clearly not in the right place. But, Jesus' question was not asked for His benefit, but theirs. He was really telling them to listen, and He would explain. Where Jesus had acted on the basis of a clear understanding of Himself and knowledge of God (vv. 1-3), they were clueless. They not only did not really know Jesus in the sense that He was going to acquaint them that evening, but they remained unable to recognize the meaning and importance of His actions apart from plain instruction because of the hardness of their hearts. So, Jesus, having raised the question in their minds, was ready to instruct them.

13:13. "You call me Teacher and Lord, and you say well, for so I am."

Jesus began by reminding his disciples of their relationship to Him. The titles, "teacher" and "lord" were both terms of respect that recognized that Jesus held a social position superior to them. He had been greeted respectfully by one of Judea's leading teachers, Nicodemus, with that title. With this question Jesus metaphorically brought them up short with the obvious in order to lead them to the real point.

Jesus next uses a series of arguments from the greater to the lesser to drive home His point. He first gives the example of the teacher being greater than his students, then of the master over his servant, and finally the sender over the one sent.[33]

13:14-15. "If I then, your Lord and Teacher, have washed your feet, you also ought to wash one another's feet. For I have given you an example, that you should do as I have done to you."

Jesus now drives home the point to His men that if He, the one they clearly regard as their leader, and so social superior, is willing to humble

Himself in order to serve them in a non-leadership capacity, so they should do for one another. D. A. Carson notes well, "One of the ways human pride manifests itself in a stratified society is in refusing to take the lower role. But now that Jesus, their *Lord and Teacher*, has washed his disciples' feet—an unthinkable act!—there is every reason why they *also should wash one another's feet*, and no conceivable reason for refusing to do so."[34] The example Jesus is providing is not that of sacrifice, but of service and humility.[35]

Jesus is teaching here that His disciples have an obligation, a debt of mutual service, when He says that they "ought" to wash each other's feet. When He calls His action an example He draws our attention to the attitude behind the action rather than the action itself. In this instance, the attitude in focus is that of true humility reflected in unrequired service (For a fuller discussion, see Appendix 4, "Footwashing an Ordinance?")[36]. Peter later reveals (1 Pet 5:5) that he learned this lesson from the master Teacher, when he commands us to clothe ourselves with humility toward each other. Paul also commends that same attitude in His description of Jesus in Philippians 2:5-8 (note vv. 3-4). This modeled attitude is the foundation and the basis of all Christians' humble service toward one another. Jesus' whole life has been an embodiment of this attitude. Now He is calling on those who wish to identify with Him to imitate His attitude in practical ways.

13:16. "Most assuredly, I say to you, a servant is not greater than his master; nor is he who is sent greater than he who sent him."

Jesus continues His explanation with a phrase He seems to have enjoyed using. Three other times He has told them "a servant/pupil is not greater than his master." Each time they involve some kind of warning. In both Matthew 10:24 and again in John 15:20, He uses the phrase when explaining that they could expect persecution because of their association with Him. Since He had been persecuted by the authorities, they should expect the same treatment. In Luke 6:40 He says a pupil is not above his teacher and notes that he will become like his teacher while warning them against misleading and judging others (i.e., Be careful what you do because those you influence will become like you, whether you like it or not!).

This last time, though, does not include a warning. Rather, it serves to emphasize the full significance of His act. When we take into account the emphasis of the Greek construction here, Jesus is saying in essence, "If (*since*) I then, your Lord and Teacher (*And you know I am!*), have washed your feet, *then certainly it logically follows as an undeniable corollary to the first truth that* you also ought to wash one another's feet."[37] Carson is insightful in his recognition of the point being made by Jesus. "The point of the aphorism in this context is in any case painfully clear: no emissary has the right to think he is exempt from tasks cheerfully undertaken by the one who sent him, and no slave has the right to judge any menial task beneath him after his master has already performed it."[38] Royce Gruenler also notes well Jesus' message to us today. "Jesus implies that there is no place in God's new society for pride and self-centeredness, for the Son of God is himself a servant. If the Son is first a servant to the Father and then a servant to his disciples, it is imperative that his disciples be servants of the Son and servants of one another."[39]

13:17. "If you know these things, happy are you if you do them."

Jesus follows His explanation with the admonition, explaining experiential salvation that is such a thrust in John's gospel. He uses, here the same word for happy, "blessed," as He did in the Beatitudes of the Sermon on the Mount. And He says that this happiness comes from "doing," not simply knowing. A person who knows and doesn't do is even more culpable than one who doesn't know. To know to do good and not do it is sin. Further, the verb tense of the term He used for doing carries the sense of doing continually (cf. James 1:22-24).[40]

What is the point being made? I do what I believe. And, I can't believe what I don't know. And I can't receive what I don't believe. The key to all of this is what I truly believe in my heart. The wise King Solomon put it this way: "As a man thinks in his heart, so is he." I can really identify with the servant of Christ who said, "Lord, I believe, help my unbelief." Unfortunately, too often we are unbelieving believers. Calvin responded to Jesus' words by saying that "*knowledge* is not entitled to be called true, unless it produce such an effect on believers as to lead them to conform themselves to their Head."[41] As John Calvin has said so eloquently,

man never attains to a true self-knowledge until he have previously contemplated the face of God, and come down after such contemplation to look into himself. For (such is our innate pride) we always seem to ourselves just, and upright, and wise, and holy, until we are convinced, by clear evidence, of our injustice, vileness, folly, and impurity. Convinced, however, we are not, if we look to ourselves only, and not to the Lord also — He being the only standard by the application of which this conviction can be produced. For, since we are all naturally prone to hypocrisy, any empty semblance of righteousness is quite enough to satisfy us instead of righteousness itself. And since nothing appears within us or around us that is not tainted with very great impurity, so long as we keep our mind within the confines of human pollution, anything which is in some small degree less defiled delights us as if it were most pure just as an eye, to which nothing but black had been previously presented, deems an object of a whitish, or even of a brownish hue, to be perfectly white. Nay, the bodily sense may furnish a still stronger illustration of the extent to which we are deluded in estimating the powers of the mind. If, at mid-day, we either look down to the ground, or on the surrounding objects which lie open to our view, we think ourselves endued with a very strong and piercing eyesight; but when we look up to the sun, and gaze at it unveiled, the sight which did excellently well for the earth is instantly so dazzled and confounded by the refulgence, as to oblige us to confess that our acuteness in discerning terrestrial objects is mere dimness when applied to the sun.[42]

This thought, that our actions demonstrate and flow out of our heart motives, continues throughout the remainder of the evening's instruction from Jesus. It is a theme He will develop repeatedly for His men, and us. Thus Jesus will teach this evening that our attitudes toward each other ultimately reveal our relationship with God.

CHAPTER THREE

CHRIST WARNING ABOUT NON-BELIEF
John 13:18-30

A s Jesus was instructing His disciples, there was one who heard every-thing He said, but it did not get past his ears to his heart. Judas still did not believe. Again, as we said earlier, Judas was a disciple, but not a believer. People can be believers without being disciples or they can be disciples without being believers.

Albert Schweitzer was a man who did all kinds of good works, famous for spending his life serving others. He went so far as to use his medical skills as a missionary doctor in Africa. Yet, in his own words he described Jesus as a lunatic. He had the external evidences one might look for when evaluating a person's faith. He did those things we would expect of a disciple of Jesus. But activities apart from faith, even those that characterize a disciple, do not make a person a true follower of Christ, a believer. It is easier to have evidence without believing, than to have believing without evidence.

Judas Iscariot was another man, like Albert Schweitzer, whose actions for a while identified him with those believing in Jesus. But, Jesus knew better, as we see in the following verses.

13:18. "I do not speak concerning all of you. I know whom I have chosen; but that the Scripture may be fulfilled, 'He who eats bread with Me has lifted up his heel against Me.'
Having given them such an admonition, Jesus then tells His men that His words do not apply to all of them. He says, "I know whom I have chosen...," but one of you will attack Me. He quotes Psalm 41:9, wherein

David laments the "defection of a trusted confidant."[1] His quote clearly implies betrayal and attack, not just failure, on the part of one of them. The phrase, "he who eats bread with me," communicates the idea of a very close friend. The term "lifted up" carries the notion of "brute violence, and not of the cunning of the wrestler."[2] Further, "Near-Eastern notions of hospitality and courtesy meant that betrayal by one who is sharing bread is especially heinous."[3] Thus, Jesus is describing Judas' action, not as that of stealth or cunning, but as that of a brutal assault. Jesus is not surprised by the betrayal of Judas, though the others will be. Rather, He is reaching out one last time to Judas and communicating to him just how heinous is his planned deed.

Jesus' words had to impact Judas as he stood among the other men. He had to realize that Jesus knew his heart and plans. He had to feel exposed as his conspiracy was laid bare before him. Even though he may have thought up to this point that his plans had been secret and that Jesus had not known of his meetings with the Jews, he could not think that any longer. Jesus could have said to him something similar to what Elisha said to Gehazi when he asked reward from Naaman (2 Kings 5:26). "Did not My heart go with you as you met with the Jewish leaders and bargained with them?"

Though Judas may have forgotten about Jesus' ability to read the thoughts of men from earlier examples, he must have sensed the same to be happening with him that evening. Yet, he did not change his course. Here, at this point, when Jesus' words exposed him, he was forced to decide what his course of action would be once and for all. We know from what follows what choice Judas made. One is reminded of the words of the song, "There is a line that is crossed by rejecting the Lord when the call of His Spirit is lost." What an example of the depravity of the human heart. How could one be surrounded with greater love and purity than Judas experienced? Yet, he resisted it to the bitter end. How like many today who have abundant opportunity but turn a deaf ear to it (cf. 2 Cor 2:14-17)!

Many theologians relate Jesus' use of "choose" here to the doctrine of election and find it necessary to reconcile what appears to be a departure from the clear teaching of Scripture elsewhere. If Judas were chosen, elect, by Christ, how could he depart from Him and thereby "lose" his salvation (justification)?[4] This is a problem only if justification is the focus of the passage and the point being made by Jesus. But it is not.

We must note, first, that nowhere in this passage is the doctrine of election a part of the purpose of Jesus' instruction to the disciples, at least

not at this point in the evening. It also is not the point of John in recounting the evening's instruction from Jesus. We can see, secondly, that election is not a central issue in any of the Johannine writings. Interestingly,
the place where election is brought in focus in the Gospel, chapter six,
involves Jesus' response to rejection. He explains the response of the unbelieving Jews in terms of election. They are not believing in Him because
they are not elect. Even so, this mention of election is a part of the conversation of Jesus with the Jews and not the focal point of that passage
either. Still, what He says does relate in a secondary manner to the issue
and so must be reconciled with what we know of the doctrine of election
from the rest of Scripture.

One question that must be answered is how Judas could be unregenerate, lost, and still function as an apostle. Remember, he was one of the
twelve apostles sent out by Jesus in pairs to announce the coming of the
kingdom and to perform miracles in Matthew 10 and Luke 9. All indica-
tions from both passages are that he did just as many miracles as anyone
else. There was no reason for any of the apostles or those around him to
suspect his faith was any less than anyone else in the group. He was clearly an apostle exercising apostolic authority. Judas is a clear example of one
who demonstrated external evidence of "faith" without the internal reality (cf. also Matt 7:21-23).

In Matthew 7, when Jesus warned them to beware of false teachers and
to know them by their fruit, He was referring to their teachings, not their
deeds. Why? Because the Pharisees against whom He spoke were doing
innumerable "righteous deeds," even miracles, even casting out demons, but
were not teaching God's truth. This is certainly something for those to pon-
der who teach that we can know a person is or is not a Christian by their
"fruit." If anyone had the external evidences of faith, it was Judas. Not only
did he do the signs and wonders of an apostle but he was trusted to the point
of allowing him to control the finances for the group.

So, how do we resolve this problem? The answer lies in what follows in
both Gospels. After the apostles return, Jesus goes to the Mount of
Transfiguration and then comes down to find them unable to do the same
miracles they had done earlier. The demon-possessed boy is beyond their
power. Why? Because they no longer had faith or were no longer regenerate? No! They no longer had the authority from Christ, the special enablement He had given them earlier. Their miraculous ministry through the
cities and villages of Israel involved a special enablement for a project that
was of a limited duration. The miracles they had performed while going as

His emissaries had not been the product of their faith, but of His power and authority passed to them for that specific ministry. When it was finished, the authority was removed.

At least one of them had performed those miracles apart from faith. Thus, Judas could heal and cast out demons without being regenerate, without believing in Jesus, because his ability to do so was based on Jesus' commission, not his faith. But, in so doing, his fellow apostles accompanying him would naturally mistake that ability for a sign of faith and loyalty to Christ. He would mistake that as an indication of his inclusion in the group by Jesus. Judas would *seem* to belong to the company of faith, though he never exercised faith in Christ. This is reminiscent of Jesus' warning in Matthew 7:21-23. Not everyone who performs miracles in Jesus' name or otherwise identifies himself with Him, even recognizing His deity, will especially be regenerate. They must do that which is God's will for the lost; namely, believe on Christ (John 6:29). Judas knew who Jesus was. Judas performed miracles in His name. But Judas did not receive Jesus as his Messiah/Savior.

Did Judas have a choice when he betrayed Jesus? Or was he hopelessly destined to do this evil deed? Was Judas "chosen" by Christ because he *would* betray and not believe, or because he *had to* betray and not believe? Several parallel passages relate to Judas and must be addressed when discussing his actions and role in God's plan. Matthew 26:15-16 reveals Judas' actions and attitude before his betrayal. He was willing to accept payment for betrayal and actively sought out the authorities and the opportunity to betray Jesus. Matthew 27:3-10 records his actions and attitudes after his betrayal. He was overcome by remorse, returned the money, and then hung himself. Both actions were fulfillments of Zechariah 11:12-13. In Acts 1:16ff, Peter quotes Psalms 69:25 and 109:8 to argue that Judas' actions fulfilled prophecy and disqualified him from being counted as one of the apostles.

Some may argue that Judas was a pawn, helpless, with respect to his role in Christ's crucifixion. Let us never forget, though, that Judas made personal choices throughout the process even as he fulfilled God's purpose.[5] He was not a helpless pawn. He was not a mindless robot. The despicableness of the deed can only be seen in light of personal choices made by him.

Romans 9 is instructive in understanding the relationship of Judas' personal choices and God's sovereign design. He may be compared to Pharaoh, who was raised up by God for the purpose of accomplishing His will. Paul concludes from God's action with Pharaoh that, "He has mercy on whom He desires, and He hardens whom He desires." In Exodus 3:19-20 God states clearly what Pharaoh will do. Then the account of Pharaoh's attitude and actions describes both God hardening his heart (Ex 7:13, 22; 8:19; 9:7, 12, 35; 10:1) and Pharaoh hardening his own heart (Ex 8:15, 32). Thus we see Pharaoh's voluntary and uncoerced will used in conjunction with the outworking of God's plan.

Likewise, Judas' action was the product of his own heart and will even as he fulfilled God's purposes. He was not an unconscious victim. His heart was fully committed to the course of action he took. And he has no one else to blame than himself for what he did that evening. When he stands before Jesus at the Great White Throne Judgment, he will not be able to plead innocence by means of predestination. He will have to admit that he chose to betray and his will was exercised each step of the way until he gave Jesus that fateful kiss.

13:19. "Now I tell you before it comes, that when it comes to pass, you may believe that I am He."

Having revealed His knowledge of Judas' motives and plan, Jesus reveals again His omniscience and sovereignty over the situation. He tells His men that He is telling them what is about to happen with a view to strengthening their faith in Him. They will come to see Him for who He truly is – Almighty God – and to recognize that all that is about to transpire is within the power and domain of His knowledge and control. This becomes very obvious in the encounter with Peter and the soldiers in John 18.

Jesus' use of "I am" in verse nineteen is very significant. He uses the identical expression when approaching their boat as He walked on the water in John 6. He used it again when debating with the Jews at the Feast of Tabernacles in John 8.[6] It is also identical to His seven "I am" statements in the Gospel wherein He describes His divine ministry to mankind. Jesus, having exercised omniscience and claimed foreknowledge, declares again His deity. His whole point to His men, including the one preparing to betray Him, is that He is using these last hours of instruction to prepare them for something that will shake their faith in Him as Messiah and God. Further, He is showing them that none of it will occur apart from His own knowledge and control. When it is over, their faith in Him will be based on His true identity, "I AM."

At this point we need to note another crucial principle that Jesus is using in His process of discipling His men. Earlier we referenced the basic premise of right thinking, namely, our actions are the product of our deepest thoughts. They are the blossom of our thinking. This being true, it is very important to know how to think right. So, a second principle comes to the fore, namely, right thinking starts by thinking right about God. We can never rise any higher in our walk in Christ than our understanding of what God is like. As we noted previously from Calvin's eloquent statement in the very first chapter of his *Institutes*, "it is certain that man never achieves a clear knowledge of himself unless he has first looked upon God's face, and then descends from contemplating Him to scrutinize himself."[7]

In his *Practicing the Presence of God*, Brother Lawrence states, "Counting upon God as being never absent would be holiness complete." As we have stated before, if we never had a wrong thought about God, we would never sin. Our biggest problem is our weak, anemic thinking about God. No one knows this better than Jesus, the master Disciplemaker. Thus, He puts the principle into practice in the training of His men who are destined to be the pillars in the Church that was yet to be established at Pentecost.

13:20. "Most assuredly, I say to you, he who receives whomever I send receives Me; and he who receives Me receives Him who sent Me."

Jesus moves from the fact that they will finally fully recognize Him for who He is, to the significance of that new depth of faith and understanding. In light of who He is, He promises to identify with them as He sends them out as His representatives once again. As He told them the first time He sent them out to represent Him before the nation (Matt 10:40), He again tells them, "He who receives whomever I send receives Me."

Still, they are not representing just Jesus, but God the Father who He has revealed to them. "He who receives Me receives Him who sent Me." This states in a positive way what Jesus proclaimed in a negative way in John 5:19-23. There, He declares that His relationship with the Father is so intimate that His actions originated with the Father and caused those who rejected Him or His works to be guilty of rejecting the Father. Now the disciples will have the same close relationship with the effect that people's responses to them will be equivalent to responding to Jesus personally. Thus this verse repeats earlier themes of reception/rejection introduced in the prologue of the Gospel with the same term being translated "received" there (John 1:11-12), and anticipates the commission of John 20:21.[8] As Carson aptly states, "This verse powerfully ties the disciples to Jesus, and therefore serves as a foil for the failure of Judas Iscariot. The mission of Jesus is here assigned the highest theological significance, the most absolutely binding authority – the authority of God himself. Failure to close with Christ is failure to know God. And because his disciples represent him to the world, their mission, their ministry, takes on precisely the same absolute significance."[9]

Jesus is ready to begin instructing them and preparing them for what is to follow and for their new role in His program. But, first, there is the burden on His heart that must now be revealed to them. And, second, there is the need for Judas, for whom the promise and coming instruction has no meaning, to depart their fellowship forever.

Jesus' Revelation: Judas the Betrayer
13:21-30.

In this section of John's account of the evening, he records Jesus' somewhat veiled exposure of Judas' coming betrayal.[10] We see in His mood and words the depth of pain Jesus felt in knowing that someone He loved was about to betray Him (cf. Rom 5:8). Still, the others remain completely unaware, unable to imagine what Judas is planning. They cannot even fathom that Judas could do such a despicable deed. Yet, they are beginning to sense that this evening portends far more than they had anticipated.

13:21. When Jesus had said these things, He was troubled in spirit, and testified and said, "Most assuredly, I say to you, one of you will betray Me."

The thought of Judas' betrayal hurt Jesus so deeply that He could not keep silent. In this verse, when John uses the verb, "troubled," he is describing Jesus' feelings with the same verb he used in 11:33 and 12:27 to indicate an incredible depth of emotional stirring. What was about to happen, including and especially Judas' betrayal, deeply grieved Jesus. He could not hide His emotions, nor keep completely silent, and so finally revealed His innermost feelings to the group of men. His words, "one of you will betray Me," combined with the emotional anguish that must have suddenly poured forth from Him had to strike a piercing blow into the heart of each man in the room. In an instant the noise level of the room must have dropped into stunned silence.

13:22. Then the disciples looked at one another, perplexed about whom He spoke.

The disciples' response indicates that they were confused and still did not understand fully the implications of Jesus' announcement. We know from Matthew 26:21-25 that the men were both grieved and confused. The faithful eleven must have felt stunned, and even a little frightened. Judas had to know then without a doubt that his plans were discovered and probably felt in serious danger of exposure. Though his blood likely ran cold at Jesus' words, his response to Him indicates the clear and calm mind of a master deceiver. He played the part of a confused disciple to the end as evidenced in his question. Each disciple in turn asked Him, "Surely, it is not me, is it, Lord?" Each question, including that of Judas, was stated as a rhetorical question that, according to its Greek construction, called for a negative answer: "No. It is not." Each question was thus a denial, even by the betrayer.

What we see in their responses is that none of the eleven wanted to betray Him. Nor did they want Him to think that they would betray Him. It also seems that when they were thinking of betrayal, they were thinking more of failing Him at some point than of turning Him over to the authorities and participating in His murder. Since each feared that Jesus might mean him, and none of the others were planning to betray Jesus, then their understanding of "betray" had to be different than "hand over to the authorities." Also, their looking back and forth at each other is another evidence that they did not understand what Jesus was actually saying. They were perplexed and confused rather than suspicious.

Carson provides a good insight into the situation. He notes, "Perhaps the notion of betrayal did not seem very threatening to them, since their Master could calm storms, raise the dead, feed the hungry, heal the sick. What possible disaster could befall him that he could not rectify?"[11] To them, Jesus could not be in any real danger and certainly could not feel in danger. But, the possibility of personal failure, called "betrayal" by Jesus, on their part was far more worrisome, especially when they were vying with one another for a higher position in the coming kingdom.

13:23. Now there was leaning on Jesus' bosom one of His disciples, whom Jesus loved. Simon Peter therefore nodded to him, that he should ask who it was of whom He spoke.
Naturally it was Peter who moved to learn what was on each of their minds. He took into account the other information He had been given by Jesus and acted. It is possible that at this point he remembered the statement of Jesus that not all of them were clean and began to make a connection between the two statements. He did not fully understand its sig-

nificance, yet. But he knew that Jesus had been thinking about the same thing when He had made His "not all are clean" comment to him. Knowing that he was not the one referred to by Jesus, he took measures to attempt to find out to whom Jesus might be referring at that point.

This explains, in part, John's inclusion of Jesus' private words to Peter while washing his feet in the account of that evening. He reported it because it played a key role in the events of the evening, not because it was his purpose to focus on the theological implications of what Jesus said to Peter. Again, Jesus was teaching His men about humility and service, not justification. But, John needed to include His comment to Peter for the account of activities that followed to make full sense.

So, Peter, realizing that Jesus had already alluded to His betrayer, attempted to ascertain his identity. Not being in a position to address Jesus privately, he signaled to another disciple in a better position to ask the question on each of their hearts (See Appendix 5, "Eating at Festive Meals: The Arrangement of the Table.").

Who was the disciple whom Jesus loved? By the process of elimination, the evidence seems to point to John. Inasmuch as the author appears to choose to speak from a third person perspective, we are sure that the "beloved disciple" is not named in the Gospel. Based on this, Andrew, Peter, Philip, Nathaniel, Thomas, and, of course, Judas Iscariot can be eliminated since they are named. We also know from chapter twenty-one that he was among the group who went fishing and that included "the sons of Zebedee and two others." Since James and John were members of Jesus' inner circle along with Peter, they make prime candidates. And, since the writing style of the Gospel is similar to John's epistles when authorial comments are made, and the author consciously excludes mention of himself, it appears best to see John as the beloved disciple.[12]

Of interest also is the fact that both *agapaō* and *phileō* are used to describe Jesus' love for John.[13] Inasmuch as a great deal has been made in sermonizing about the supposed differences between these two terms, caution needs to be taken before giving too much significance to their nuances. Actually, in Greek very little difference exists between the meanings of the two terms. They are synonyms whose difference is more in nuance than in substance. It is popular with Christian writers to make great distinction between the two, with *agapaō* describing a deep love that is reflected in commitment more than emotion and with *phileo* referring more to feelings of friendship. Though such distinctions do hold at times, depending on the context and author's message, the two terms are used rather interchangeably by John and other New Testament writers.

At this point in the Gospel the title of beloved does appear to indicate a special relationship between Jesus and John, though that relationship was not translated into a special leadership position. Peter appears to have always been both the chosen and natural leader of the group and remained such in the church.

13:25-26. Then, leaning back on Jesus' chest, he said to Him, "Lord, who is it?" Jesus answered, "It is he to whom I shall give a piece of bread when I have dipped it." And having dipped the bread, He gave it to Judas Iscariot, the son of Simon.

Peter, being then the natural leader and one to want to be in on every-thing that was happening, signaled to the person in the best position to find out what was going on, he signaled to John. Again, John appears to have been given the third place of honor at the table and so was able to lean back on Jesus' breast and ask Him. Jesus was able to answer him pri-vately, and so chose to do so rather than exposing Judas openly. Thus He answered John plainly as He gave the morsel, the bread of honor, to Judas.

Did John understand the significance of what Jesus had just done? Probably not. Carson suggests that "the momentous nature of Jesus' con-fidence left him temporarily paralyzed—the more so since Jesus himself was clearly taking no remedial action."[14] This sounds good, but is unlike-ly. If he had understood that *treason* was afoot, he would have cried out and kept Judas from escaping the room regardless of Jesus' inaction. John was not the quiet, mousy, type. We must remember that Jesus nicknamed him and James "Boanerges," or "Sons of Thunder," when He chose them as apostles (Mark 3:17).

They were also the apostles who spoke up when the Samaritan village refused to receive Jesus and asked permission to call down fire from heav-en and earned Jesus' rebuke (Luke 9:54-56). John was the apostle, with Peter, who moved quickly to examine Jesus' tomb as soon as word came of His body being missing. John was a man of action. And, if he had under-stood the significance of what Jesus meant by "betray," Judas would not have been able to move toward the door without his shouting a warning.

John does not tell us where Judas was reclining that evening. The normal arrangement of couches around the table basically worked its way from the central place of honor at the joint of the "U" to the lesser positions on each end. If they had three men on each couch, as was customary, there would have been two couches flanking the central couch on one side and one on the other. Probably Jesus would have been able to reach the occupants of all except the farthest couch. It is possible, but unlikely, that Judas had been chosen by Christ to occupy the second place of honor, reclining at His back. Though some have speculated that Peter occupied that place, it would have been difficult for him to signal John with Jesus between them. Also, if Judas were to occupy such a place of honor, he would be able to hear Jesus' whisper. So, we cannot be certain who sat at Jesus' back.

Jesus' action of giving Judas the piece of bread would be quite misleading to the group, including John. His action reflected the custom of the feast wherein the "governor" or central figure of the feast would honor someone else there by taking a piece of bread and giving it to the honored person after either dipping it in wine or sopping up food in it.[15] Ralph Gower notes, "The most honored guest was given a 'token' meal by the host. A piece of bread was dipped into the food and was used as a spoon. The 'bread spoon' and contents were put into the mouth of the favoured guest. This was known as the 'morsel' and was given by Jesus to Judas during the last supper (John 13:26)."[16] The bread Jesus would have used was likely a flat, round, unleavened bread that had a leathery texture and was ideal for scooping food like a large spoon. The bowl Jesus dipped the morsel in (called a "dish" in Mark 14:20) likely contained the *haroseth*. This was a tasty sauce made of crushed dates, raisins and sour wine and was included as a significant element that was always part of the Passover meal.

Jesus' action, while answering the question for John communicated a far different message to the group. His action was the customary way of a host communicating publicly both courtesy and esteem toward a special guest. Jesus would be, in essence, giving Judas a vote of confidence and special status within the group while alerting John to the fact that he was the betrayer. Jesus' act of kindness and respect was not an act appropriate to the kind of betrayal that was actually afoot, at least not from a carnal human perspective. John would certainly not expect Jesus to sit quietly by and allow someone to betray Him to the authorities and precipitate His murder. That was not a "normal" human response.

This also tells us something of the relationship that the other disciples had with Judas. There appears to have been a high level of trust on their parts toward him. Comments about his pilfering the moneybox and evil motives in such places as John 12:6 must be seen in light of later revelation. This is an example that we do not always know people "by their fruits." The fact that he was the group's treasurer, obviously designated such by Jesus, would indicate that he held a position of trust in the group. Jesus' gift of the morsel of food would naturally lead the others to read friendship and trust in Jesus' actions, not anticipation of betrayal.

Though they had heard all of Jesus' previous allusions to His coming death, to this point they had refused to believe that they would see it happen. Rather, they had the more assuring "evidence" of the crowd's response at Jesus' Triumphal Entry just a few days earlier. They had watched the multitudes hanging on each of Jesus' words. They had seen Him defeat His opponents in the temple and streets of Jerusalem. They really did expect Him to bring in the Messianic Kingdom in the next few days or weeks. Thus, being in a state of denial, John and Peter still do not seem to have connected Judas' betrayal with Jesus' predictions of His suffering and death. This might explain their failure to act.

Though the text is silent, there is nothing to indicate that John did not relay the information back to Peter. It would have simply taken a pointing of his finger or a nod of his head in the right direction. Peter's failure to act indicates that he also did not understand the nature of what Jesus meant by "betray."

Going back to the original problem in the group, pride and jockeying for positions in the coming kingdom, it is possible that both men would have felt more relieved than alarmed. In fact, the argument over who would be greatest that preceded this incident may give us some other insight into their attitudes. When they saw Judas identified as the betrayer, they may have been relieved on two grounds. First, they did not think they would have to face the possibility of personal failure (again, not thinking in terms of treachery). Second, one of their competitors for status in the coming kingdom was clearly being eliminated. They may have been thinking, "He'll fail. I won't." In their minds they were not the ones destined to fail Jesus. But one of their competitors would. Ironically, if this were their thinking, their own selfish pride would prove to be a key element, humanly speaking, in the successful betrayal and murder of the One to whom they claimed love and devotion. Our selfishness is always destructive, and usually for others even more so than ourselves. So, as Peter and John enjoy being privy to who will "fail," Jesus speaks His final commanding words to Judas.

Those of us who have served on boards and committees of churches and Christian institutions have had the experience of people who are unwilling to take a stand for that which is right lest there be repercussions against them or their personal goals would be hindered; thus, unworthy or even ungodly things are allowed to continue. We see this with the rulers of Jesus' day who remained quiet for fear of the political power structure (John 12:42). We cannot help but think of the deep disappointment that must have occasioned Paul's sad words to Timothy: "This you know, that all those in Asia have turned away from me, among whom are Phygellus and Hermogenes" (2 Tim 1:15) and again, "At my first defense no one stood with me, but all forsook me" (2 Tim 4:16a).

John's record of the actions of Jesus in the upper room provides a wonderful model later on for the Apostle Paul. No one in that room rose to the occasion to even question Judas and that very night they were all going to flee and forsake Him. But Jesus did not respond with anger or vengeance. Rather He committed Himself to the Father. Later, in like fashion, the Apostle Paul says: "May it not be charged against them. But the Lord stood with me and strengthened me, so that the message might be preached fully through me, and that the Gentiles might hear. Also I was delivered out of the mouth of the lion. And the Lord will deliver me from every evil work and preserve me for His heavenly kingdom. To Him be glory forever and ever. Amen!" May God be pleased to help us focus on the model presented by Jesus (Heb 12:2) and practiced by the Apostle Paul.

13:27. And after the piece of bread, Satan entered him. Then Jesus said to him, "What you do, do quickly."

For Judas, the action of Jesus produced a different effect than the blessing it communicated. First, Satan "entered him." Recall that the devil had previously put the idea of betrayal into the heart of Judas (Luke 22:1-7). Then, Judas departed the company of faith in order to accomplish his evil plan. The morsel was not the means of Satan's entrance into Judas as some suggest but was more likely a final act of love directed toward a man whose heart was set on evil.[17] Jesus loved all of His disciples, including Judas, to the uttermost.

What does it mean that Satan "entered" Judas? Satan's *apparent* entrance onto the scene at this point may seem to some to make Judas the helpless victim rather than the scheming villain. When John said that Satan "entered" Judas, one might take him to have meant that at that point he became satanically possessed, and so controlled. But, we see in

Luke 22 that the same terminology for "entering" was used on a previous occasion. In that instance, Luke describes Satan's action in influencing Judas as "entering" him. It was still Judas who made the choice to meet with the Jewish leaders. We see from this the personal involvement of Satan at crucial times in accomplishing his purpose in opposition to God. There is no indication that Judas was helpless. Rather, he was a willing tool of Satan who suggested the action. Thus his actions were aligned with Satan who was working through him as his agent.

A better answer is that he came fully under satanic dominion or influence.[18] John 13:2 tells us that Satan "put" the plan to betray Jesus "into his heart." We can see from this that Judas was obeying Satan, serving him in the same way we are called to serve and obey God. He was still acting as a free moral agent, not a robot, though he was also a slave to sin. We learn from Paul (Rom 6:6) that every unregenerate person is a "slave of sin." This truth is also expressed in Hebrews 2:14-15, "Inasmuch then as the children have partaken of flesh and blood, He Himself likewise shared in the same, that through death He might destroy him who had the power of death, that is, the devil, and release those who through fear of death were all their lifetime *subject to bondage*" (italics added).

We also know that at regeneration God "has delivered us from the power of darkness and conveyed us into the kingdom of the Son of His love" (Col 1:13). Thus the unregenerate man, as a slave of sin, finds himself existing under the influence of Satan within his domain, and ultimately obeying him rather than God. Even so, with Judas Satan was more personally active in influencing him, than he is with most unregenerate people today. Satan is not omnipresent, but he chooses his battles wisely. At this crucial juncture in history, there was nothing more important for Satan than to destroy Christ, even though this ultimately lead to his own destruction (compare Gen 3:15 and John 16:11).

Does Satan's role in this event relieve Judas of any responsibility? No! Every unbeliever is under the tyranny of Satan. We must remember some key elements of information in order to understand better what is meant by John. First, Judas had made his bargain with the Jewish leaders well before this point in time, before Satan "entered" him. Thus we see the principle of James 1:13-15 in effect, that thoughts precede actions (see also Ps119:11; Prov 23:7). He had already decided to betray Jesus and was simply looking for the opportunity. Second, his action of kissing Jesus in betrayal was something *he* did, not Satan. Jesus addressed him and left responsibility for his actions on him (Luke 22:48). Third, his later remorse reflected an understanding of personal culpability. It was he who had betrayed Jesus. He had not been merely a pawn in a grand battle. He had betrayed innocent blood for selfish, not helpless, reasons.

Judas' departure also was not a loss of regeneration or a departure from faith. He was never a regenerated disciple committed to Jesus as his Messiah.[19] Actually, a disciple is simply a follower. And though Judas *really did* follow Jesus, he did not believe in Him. Jesus' reference to him as a son of perdition argues convincingly that Judas was never a believer, but simply professed faith for the advantage it gave him. Jesus' words in John 6:64 and 17:12, along with John's description of his motives in 12:6 and Peter's conclusion in Acts 1:25, supports this. Still, even with that in mind, Jesus, knowing his heart, offered Judas the piece of bread.[20] This was Jesus' final act of love toward a person who had rejected Him. He was letting Judas know that though He knew his heart, He chose to return a kindness for a wrong planned. He was living out His own command to do good to those who hate you (Luke 6:27-28).[21] Still, Judas had made a decision, and Jesus gave Him permission to enact it.

Judas took action. With Jesus' permission to leave, he got up and proceeded with his evil plan. He went to meet the Jewish leaders and lead them to the place he knew Jesus would be going to next.

13:28-29. Now no one at the table knew for what reason He said this to him. For some of them thought, because Judas had the money box, that Jesus had said to him, "Buy those things we need for the feast," or that he should give something to the poor.

Still, the rest of the disciples remained unaware that Judas' actions were hostile.[22] John was not too stunned to alert the others as some might think. Rather, he was still unclear concerning what Jesus meant. To bestow such an honor on a traitor, though characteristic of Jesus, was beyond the comprehension of the others. They were still thinking like mere men and could not fathom the grace of God exhibited in the person of Jesus before their very eyes. So, knowing Jesus' concern for the poor, it was natural for them to misunderstand what was happening, even John. Judas, on the other hand, did not hesitate to accept the honor as he snatched up the opportunity to act out his evil plot.

John notes that the disciples assumed Judas was being sent on a task by Jesus. His instructions would imply such. He probably ran errands for Jesus whenever purchases were involved since he carried the cash for the group. Since they had just prepared the Passover, probably getting money from the money box earlier that day, they would expect that more supplies would be needed for the days to follow. The Passover, though a separate feast in itself, was followed for the next seven days by the Feast of Unleavened Bread. They would be in need of supplies to carry them through those days. It was also customary during the various feasts to give alms to the poor, a practice that Jesus apparently followed. Thus, Judas' departure to take care of "business" was probably a routine event and so would not arouse attention even at this point in the feast.

Some use this element of the evening to object to the meal being a Passover meal since on such an occasion no one would expect any shops to be open for business. Therefore, they conclude that this meal was the evening before the Passover and the disciples thought he was going to buy things for use on the Passover. But, we must remember that in Judea the Passover did not officially begin until the following morning. And so, one would expect the markets to be quite active that evening as people made their last minute purchases of supplies to carry them through Passover day and its following Sabbath (that year). Carson correctly sees the "feast" for which Judas was to procure supplies referring, not to the Passover feast but to the Feast of Unleavened Bread that followed for seven days after the Passover. He notes,

> The next day, still Friday 15 Nisan, was a high feast day; the following day was a Sabbath. It might seem best to make necessary purchases (e.g. more unleavened bread) immediately. Purchases on that Thursday evening were in all likelihood possible, though inconvenient. The rabbinic authorities were in dispute on the matter (cf. Mishnah Pesahim 4:5). One could buy necessities even on a Sabbath if it fell before Passover, provided it was done by leaving something in trust rather than paying cash (Mishnah Shabbath 23:1). Moreover, it was customary to give alms to the poor on Passover night, the temple gates being left open from midnight on, allowing beggars to congregate there (Jeremias, p. 54). On any night other than Passover it is hard to imagine why the disciples might have thought Jesus was sending Judas out *to give something to the poor*: The next day would have done just as well.[23]

So, Judas' role in the group and the nature of their circumstances were such that his departure and Jesus' instructions could only make sense on a Galilean's Passover evening in Judea.

13:30. Having received the piece of bread, he then went out immediately. And it was night.

John concludes this scene with the terse phrase, "And it was night." This brings the light-darkness imagery, introduced in John 1:5, to its anticlimax. Its first climax came with Jesus' declaration in John 8 that He is the light of the world. A second climax came with the worship of the man born blind in John 9, and will reach new heights a third time with the sunrise of Jesus' resurrection.

The conflict between light and darkness, Christ and Satan, is evident throughout the upper room. Examples of this conflict can be seen in such verses as 13:27, where Jesus confronts His attacker even as Satan enters the scene; 14:30, where Satan, as the ruler of this world is described as coming for Jesus; and then 17:15, where Jesus prays for the apostles' protection from Satan. Further, Jesus has warned His followers just a few days earlier to "Walk while you have the light, lest darkness overtake you, for he who walks in darkness does not know where he is going. While you have the light, believe in the light, that you may become sons of light" (John 12:35-36). Judas has not heeded the warning, and so chooses to depart into eternal darkness. Judas is confronted with the truth of Jesus' person and character in the foot washing, but is not moved to repentance from his evil intentions. More so, with the taking of the morsel and the command of Jesus, not only is Judas' plan set, but his character is revealed to the reader as well. Jesus had said earlier that those who come to Him come to have their deeds (thus character) exposed by the light while those who are evil depart from the light. Thus John comments, "And it was night," as Judas departs.

John did not need to remind his readers that it was night. Jesus and His disciples had been eating for some time and the Paschal meal was always eaten at night. The words are unnecessary apart from their theological and symbolic significance. John exercises his literary genius by telling us in this way that Judas has chosen darkness, night, over Jesus, the light. We know too that "to choose the night, as Judas chose the night, is to choose judgment."[24] "And this is the condemnation, that the light has come into the world, and men loved darkness rather than light, because their deeds were evil" (John 3:19).[25] John Mitchell reminds us: "If we spurn the light, there is nothing left but darkness. Peter could say that the unrighteous are kept in chains of darkness (2 Peter 2:4). Impenetrable darkness is the portion of those out of Christ. Here is Judas who spent three and a half years with this wonderful Savior. And when he left, he not only went out into the darkness at midnight, but he went out into impenetrable darkness. 'Judas by transgression fell.' He made his choice. He went to his own place."26

Oh, how our hearts grieve when we think of a loved one who moves out into eternity without believing on the Lord Jesus Christ! Here is a man who walked with Christ and the other apostles, with all kinds of experiences, and yet did not make the choice. How it must have grieved Jesus' heart to see this one make his decision that would ultimately send him to an eternity in hell.

Yet, with Judas' departure, Jesus now turns to instruct those men whose hearts truly belong to him and whose faith is about to be sorely tested. His message to them in the coming chapters is that He has provided them what they need to face tribulation and be fruitful in the days and years following His glorification. Jesus promises them His peace and is going to send a Helper, the Holy Spirit, to comfort and guide them as He convicts the world. But first, He is going to reveal to them what matters most to Him and the key to their effectiveness.

CHAPTER FOUR

CHRIST REVEALING WHAT MATTERS MOST
John 13:31-35

With these verses, we reach the peak of Christ's concern by way of the mission He gives these men. Having addressed their selfishness and dismissed His betrayer, Jesus focuses His instruction on the Great Commandment that is absolutely crucial to fulfilling the Great Commission. Everything that Christ says after this is an attempt to unfold this central truth. Jesus begins the instruction of those men who truly belong to Him by telling them what matters most to Him. Although He is ready to tell them of His coming glorification that will separate Him from them physically, more than that, He wants them to have the same heart attitude toward one another that He has toward them.

This section begins what is considered by most as the discourse proper, though the words and deeds of Jesus that precede these verses should be seen as integral to the message of John as well as of Jesus to His men that evening. This is also evident from John's commentary on Jesus' actions in John 13:1-5, which really establishes the basis for understanding the rest of what is said and done. "As a man thinks in his heart, so is he." Also, the inclusio of "love" in the first verse of chapter thirteen and last verse of chapter seventeen clearly marks these chapters as a single unit of thought.

Jesus' demonstrated humility and instructions to them had already set the stage for much of what was to be said the rest of the evening. He was preparing their hearts to hear what He had to say even as He washed their feet, along with the feet of one who had not listened and now would not hear. Judas' departure denied him the opportunity to receive the most encouraging words of Jesus' ministry, words we are privileged to hear, words we should receive with reverence.

We must remember that Jerusalem was not a large city, as we think of cities. It is possible to walk completely across the city in thirty minutes, or less, depending on the crowds in the streets. The upper room was most likely in the wealthier part of the city, which would have placed it in the near proximity of either Annas' or Caiaphas' home. It would have taken only a few minutes for Judas to get to either home, if that was where he was to report. It would only take a few more minutes to gain admittance since each of them likely had instructed their guards to be watching for him. Then it would be only a matter of a few more minutes to gather the troops who were on duty at that time, and probably on standby, and head out after Jesus. If he were to find them or some other designated individual at the temple, that would take just a few more minutes. Thus Jesus knew that He had only a short while before their present location would be searched if Judas chose to bring the guard there first. Knowing the relaxed nature of the feast and that it usually was an activity that stretched into the night, it is probable that Judas did, in fact, bring the guard there first.

John considered Jesus' instructions to depart as something worth noting in the same way as Jesus' comment to Peter had been. This serves as another indication that John recounted Jesus' instruction from the foot washing to the prayer accurately (cf. Luke 22). Though he does not report every word Jesus spoke that evening, John's record is not a paraphrase of Jesus' instruction and prayer. Nor is it an example of him putting words into Jesus' mouth in order to develop his own message or theology as some modern theologians would have us believe.

Rather, he is reporting what Jesus said and did that evening in order to faithfully communicate His message to His disciples, John's readers, and to us. Thus, when Jesus said, "Let us arise from here," and John recorded it, it is not a change of subject or a division of discourses. Rather, it is a recounting of Jesus' own instructions as He chose to remove Himself and His men from immediate discovery and possibly "buy" time to finish His instruction and be captured at the place of His own choosing. He knew that Judas knew where He would go next. He also wanted to be there before His captors arrived. He had some final praying to do before He began His final and greatest work on earth. Jesus' instruction continued even as they moved about the city's environs and across the Kidron Valley to the Mount of Olives and the Garden of Gethsemane.

Again, His instruction to arise and to depart does not indicate that two discourses are contained in the one account. Rather, as this was a single period of instruction by Jesus, so John views it as a single unit of thought from his opening words in chapter thirteen to Jesus' final words in chapter seventeen. Further, one should ask, would not Jesus, the master Disciplemaker, in the training of the eleven have carefully planned this final major discipling session as preparation for all that was to follow?

It is instructive to see how His message develops and to note that He has already begun instructing them in humility and love before the meal was finished. Now He returns to His instruction and begins with the central issue, love for each other, the *key* to evangelism. What Jesus is about to say is absolutely crucial for outreach of the Church to the world. No other method, no other passion, no other doctrine is as important for evangelism. In his most famous sermon Francis Schaeffer labeled it "The Mark of a Christian". There is nothing more important to God than relationship.

Jesus' Coming Glorification and Departure
13:31-33

With Judas' departure from their midst, Jesus begins to speak even more plainly to His faithful eleven. He continues His instruction to them with the announcement that He is to be glorified, an enigmatic statement in light of what is about to follow.

13:31-32. Then, when he had gone out, Jesus said, "Now the Son of Man is glorified, and God is glorified in Him. If God is glorified in Him, God will also glorify Him in Himself, and glorify Him immediately."[1]

In less than seventy-two hours Jesus' life on earth will be completed, He will have received His glorified body, and He will be exalted to the right hand of the Father, from which, as Captain of our salvation, He will bring into being the church, the body of Christ.

These verses contain the last occurrence of the title, Son of Man, in John's Gospel. John recorded Jesus' use of the term eleven other times. Tenney notes, "In its general usage it is the title of the incarnate Christ who is the representative of humanity before God and the representative of deity in human life."[2] It is clearly Messianic in tone. Jesus' reference to His coming glorification when He says, "Now the Son of Man is glorified," clearly is the cross and resurrection. In fact, His use of "now" indicates that the departure of Judas to find and lead the Jewish officials to Jesus had begun the glorification process. Jesus is saying by this that His "hour," the time of suffering and death, the completion of His mission on earth, has come.[3] Little did Satan realize that his dastardly deed was putting into motion the final events leading to Christ's ultimate glorification.

With their focus on the imminence of the kingdom, and with Jesus having just announced that one of them is a betrayer, the disciples were still confused concerning what Jesus meant. The title, Son of Man, was in no way associated with suffering in their minds.

Jesus uses "glorify" five times in the first two verses of this section (cf. Phil 2:4-11). Normally the term would mean "exaltation," but here it refers to Jesus' death. So, in what way is the crucifixion glorification? Is Jesus using a euphemism? Or is there greater significance in His choice of descriptive terms?

Jesus appears to use the term with at least two senses in this context. In the first three uses, He is clearly referring to His coming crucifixion. And so "glorify" does not appear to have a "glorious" sense to it.[4] Yet, glorify has its usual sense of exaltation in the last two uses. The dual sense may also be evident in Jesus' prayer (John 17:4-5). Thus Jesus is saying that He will bring glory to the Father through His obedience in death rather than that He experiences glorification in the process.[5] As W. Robert Cook rightly observes, "In Christ's death, burial, resurrection, and return to the Father, the splendor of God's character was manifested in a way it could not have been otherwise."[6]

Jesus is saying that what He is about to endure will bring glory to His Father who will, in turn, respond by exalting, glorifying Him. This is made especially clear through the Greek construction of the sentence. The "if" here carries the idea of "since" and assumes the certainty of what is being proposed. Thus Jesus is saying, "If (since) God is glorified in Him, and we certainly know that He is, then just as certainly God will also glorify Him in Himself, and glorify Him immediately." There is such a certainty in His ability to accomplish in death the payment for the sins of all mankind that it is in reality the road to glory, though not glorious itself (cf. Heb 12:3).

A great deal of theology is contained in these short words of Jesus. First of all, "The unity and equality of Father and Son are evidenced in their mutual glorification by the suffering of the Son."[7] This will be repeated in Jesus' prayer. Shared glory and mutual glorification are characteristic of the Godhead's relationship and a basis for our Trinitarian understanding.[8] God the Father is being glorified in the person of Jesus. It is through Jesus that God will receive glory. Jesus clarifies what He means in His prayer to His Father when He says in 17:4, "I have glorified You on the earth. I have finished the work which You have given Me to do." This looks both at His ministry to that point, and anticipates the completion of His mission on the cross.[9] And, this brings to His mind the next issue the eleven must face. Jesus' glorification involves His departure.

13:33. "Little children, I shall be with you a little while longer. You will seek Me; and as I said to the Jews, 'Where I am going, you cannot come,' so now I say to you."

Having announced His coming glorification, Jesus tells the disciples that He is leaving. Further, He lets them know that they cannot go where He is about to go, reminding them that He had already revealed this truth earlier (John 7:33-34; 8:21). Jesus says this to remind them that what He is saying is not really anything new or shocking. So, He tells them in essence, "I would like to remind you that just like I told the Jews a few days ago, I am leaving. And, no, you cannot come either."

This is the only record we have of Jesus calling His disciples "little children." Yet, whether He used it often or it impacted John as he thought about that evening, it has become a hallmark of John, who addresses his readers similarly in his first epistle (1 John 2:1, 12, 28; 3:7, 18; 4:4; 5:21). Westcott notes that the term translated as "little children" emphasizes the idea of kinsmanship; and the diminutive conveys an expression at once of deep affection and also of solicitude for those who as yet are immature. By using it here the Lord marks the loving spirit of the communication that He makes, and assures those whom He leaves of His tender sympathy with them in their bereavement. At the same time He indicates that they stand in a relation corresponding to that in which He stands to the Father.[10]

There is a marked difference between Jesus' words to the Jews in chapters seven and eight and His disciples here.[11] He tells both groups that they cannot follow Him. The difference is that He promises His men that they *will* follow eventually whereas He tells the Jews that they can never follow. So, where His departure is a permanent separation from one group, it is only a temporary separation for the other. Further, His tone of voice is significantly different. Where with the Jews Jesus is in the midst of controversy with His antagonists, with the disciples it is a tender moment.[12]

Jesus is instructing and encouraging the eleven while they attempt to understand. He is focused on the task of preparing them for what is to come, and they are confused and alarmed over His initial words. But, before being interrupted, Jesus begins His instruction with the issue that has already been exposed as critical to their future service to Him, namely, *their lack of love for one another*.

Love for One Another
Demonstrates Discipleship and Makes Fruitful
13:34—15:17

In light of His coming glorification and separation from them, Jesus commands the disciples to love one another. This *love is the key* to proving their relationship to Him as His disciples and will in turn make them useful and fruitful to Him as His friends. This, the focal point of Jesus' instruction this evening, is marked off by the inclusio of love for one another, found both in this opening verse and again in 15:17.

13:34. "A new commandment I give to you, that you love one another; as I have loved you, that you also love one another."

The new commandment Jesus gives them is to love one another, thereby revealing to the world that they are His disciples. Notice that the recipients of this love are not the world, but the disciples. He does not command them to love the world. Why does He not command them to love the world? Because their love for one another will be Christ's strategy for reaching the world. How fitting that this should be stated to those who were so full of themselves, and their selfish desires for greatness in the kingdom at the expense of each other, that they were not able to respond to the humble task of washing one another's feet. In other words, He is saying, "Peter, I want you to love Andrew. And James, I want you to love John. And not in words only, though those are important and should not be underestimated, but in actions as well."

It seems much easier doesn't it to love people at a distance, especially if they are across the ocean. But the key to effectiveness for Christ is how we love the brothers and sisters right next to us, in our own family, in our own church. What do you suppose would happen in a local church if it took this command as their marching orders for evangelism? Is it possible that we would find it much easier to accomplish the "Great Commission" if we gave priority to the "Great Command"? Undoubtedly, one of the reasons we are sorely hindered in our *outreach* to the world is the disobedience with respect to *inreach* to the brethren.

Three times in John's Gospel Jesus defines what determines whether someone is His disciple or not. In John 8:31 Jesus defines discipleship in terms of "abiding" in His word. Here, it is defined in terms of "loving one another." And in John 15:8, He defines it in terms of bearing "fruit." One should notice also that at both ends of this inclusio (13:34 and 15:17) it is the world, "all" referring to people, that will recognize that they are disciples of Jesus when they love one another. It is not God who is convinced by their love. The world will not hear our doctrine if it is not being demonstrated where they can see it. Paul put this in a powerful maxim: "Speaking the truth in love." A more contemporary expression of it is, negatively stated, "What you do speaks so loudly that I cannot hear what you say."

When Jesus calls His command "new," He does not imply by this that the command to love was not a part of the Mosaic Law. For the command to love is clearly expressed in Leviticus 19:18, "Love your neighbor as yourself," and was recognized earlier by Jesus in Matthew 22:39 as a foundational part of the Mosaic Law, second only to the command to love God. His use of "new" here "implies freshness, or the opposite of 'outworn' rather than simply 'recent' or 'different.'"[13] Though what Jesus is saying is not new *per se*, He is giving it a new depth of meaning as He relates it to positive actions rather than absence of malice, as was characteristic of the Mosaic requirements.[14] He has given love a new standard. In the Old Testament it was "as yourself." Now Jesus says, "As I loved you." This love will be the *key* to the growth and success of the church as was noted by the church father, Tertullian (quoted below).

Jesus' command reveals that He expects us to imitate Him. He does not just say to love one another, but that they are to do it "as I have loved you."[15] John has just told us in the opening words of this discourse that Jesus loves them without limit. Jesus also has just defined love in terms of His humble service by washing their feet. He is about to give the ultimate demonstration of love in giving His life.

We see John's own understanding of Jesus' words in his first epistle. There he defines this same "new" command (1 John 2:7-10) as calling for a love that motivates one not only to die for his or her fellow Christian, but also to meet needs (1 John 3:16-17). He again talks about the demonstrated element of the love Jesus is calling for in 1 John 4:7-11. There He notes that God demonstrated His love by sending Jesus in order to give us life. Thus, the love Jesus calls for is active, practical, and visible, being expressed toward fellow believers in tangible ways.

The first century church seems to have understood and lived out this command. We see it demonstrated in Acts 11:27-30 with the very practical gift for the church in Jerusalem when it faced a famine. The gift is sent from the Gentile churches by the hand of Paul and Barnabas. This love is in evidence in two of Paul's earliest epistles, namely those written to the church of the Thessalonians. Paul is able to describe the church of Thessalonica as being characterized by *love* as well as faith (1 Thes 1:3; 3:6) and that their walks are pleasing to God (1 Thes 4:1). He is able to say to them, "But concerning brotherly love you have no need that I should write to you, for you yourselves are taught by God to love one another; and indeed you do so toward all the brethren who are in all Macedonia" (1 Thes 4:9-10). And, when he writes to them a second time he can say their love "abounds toward each other" (2 Thes 1:3). It is again in evidence in Paul's epistles to the Romans and Corinthians when he talks of the Gentile churches taking up a second collection for the saints in Jerusalem (Rom 15:25-27; 2 Cor 8-9).

Tertullian, a church father who wrote about a century after this Gospel was published reports on the church's practice of receiving gifts that were used to help the destitute, elderly and others suffering for "nothing but their fidelity to the cause of God's Church." He then notes, "But it is mainly the deeds of a love so noble that lead many to put a brand upon us. *See,* they say, *how they love one another*, for they themselves are animated by mutual hatred; how they are ready even to die for one another, for they themselves will sooner put to death. . . . One in mind and soul, we do not hesitate to share our earthly goods with one another."[16] This is certainly reminiscent of the description of love in 1 John and what Jesus means when He commands them, and so us, to love one another.

Jesus begins the core of His instruction with the key to their future effective service toward Him in reaching the lost world with the message of life. They must love one another.

Love for One Another

13:35. "By this all will know that you are My disciples, if you have love for one another."

This love commanded by Jesus is to be such a kind that it convinces the world that we are His disciples. Jesus says that it is by demonstrated love for one another ("by this" looks forward to the content of the "if" clause in the same sentence) that "all will know that you are My disciples."

This same construction is used in John 15:8, the second half of this inclusio, to drive home the same point. Proof of discipleship is in what they (and we) do.

Two key things in this verse are Jesus' statement of the *means* by which their status as His disciples would be proven and the *possibility* of failure. The possibility of failure is seen in His use of the Greek term for "if" which carries the sense, "it may or may not be true."[17] We can fail to love one another. Rearranging the sentence to reflect His emphasis, Jesus is saying, "If you have love for one another, by this *love* all will know that you are My disciples." Implied in this is also the statement, "But if you do not have love for one another, by your failure to love all will *not* know that you are My disciples."

What is Jesus saying? We will not be known as His disciples by our doctrine, as basic as that is; nor by our love for the world, for that can be a gimmick; but by the world's observation of our love for each other in the family of God. It is only by living out mutual love that we prove to the world our relationship to Jesus as His followers. His use of *by this* communicates that the *means* by which the world is convinced of our relationship to Jesus as His disciples is the demonstration of mutual love, love of the same kind as He has for us.

It is also important to note what Jesus does *not* say by this. He does *not* say that failure to love means we are not His disciples. He also does *not* say that mutual love convinces Him or the Father of our status as disciples. Finally, He does *not* say that mutual love makes us disciples.

The audience being convinced is the world of unbelievers. But, does the eleven yet understand? Peter's response indicates that they had other things in mind rather than understanding Jesus' instruction on love.

CHAPTER FIVE

CHRIST COMFORTING WITH TRUTH
John 13:36—14:4

Confrontation with Peter
13:36-38

Having warned His men of His impending departure and of their responsibility to love one another, Jesus was probably about to continue with His message of comfort. But, His instruction was first interrupted by three questions as the disciples tried to grapple with the shocking news. All of them missed the marvelous fact of the *power of mutual love* that He announced. Their response was something like the response of most people who listen to a sermon where the preacher has made a strong appeal and they respond with, "Where are you going for dinner?" or "Who is playing today?"

Notice the three questions and one request of the three disciples in John 13:36, 37; 14:5; and 14:8. They form the basis of the discussion of this portion of Jesus' instruction.[1] Peter asks first, "Lord, where are you going?" And then, "Lord, why can I not follow You now?" He follows these two questions with the promise, "I will lay down my life for Your sake." Thomas next asks, "Lord, we do not know where You are going, and how can we know the way?" Philip then responds to Jesus' answers with a request, "Lord, show us the Father, and it is sufficient for us."

13:36. Simon Peter said to Him, "Lord, where are you going?" Jesus answered him, "Where I am going you cannot follow Me now, but you shall follow Me afterward."

Peter, being the spokesman and leader, is the first to interrupt His master and teacher as he ignores responding to the command. How could loving Andrew help? The idea that loving one another proved anything seems to sweep past the eleven as certainly as it does most of our church-es. How could they love their competitors for positions in the approaching Kingdom's administration? How do you love the person getting the atten-tion and position you desire in your local church?

What would happen if your church really worked at loving one anoth-er as your evangelistic outreach for a year? Would your community become convinced that God was truly at work in your midst? You might be shocked at the impact that loving one another in a love starved world could have. Do not be like the eleven were that night. Be like they became following Pentecost.

Peter, seeming not to hear the command to love, returns Jesus to the beginning of His instruction with his first question. He and the others can hear little else as they grapple with the shocking news of Jesus' departure. He misses the point being made by Jesus and instead persists in learning what Jesus meant by His departure and then declares his willingness to die for Him. Instead of affirming him, Jesus replies to his question and bravado by telling him he will deny Him three times.[2]

It may be too harsh of an assessment of Peter to say that he is only concerned about his own interests at this point. His question is a very real and honest response, even if we see it as selfish. It may not be fair to say that he is totally uninterested in the command to love. It is just that the news of Jesus' departure is of far more immediate concern to him. Until he understands what Jesus means, he will not be capable of hearing anything else. Also, we can be sure that this same question is on the minds of most, if not all, of the other disciples as well. It is just that Peter is quicker to speak than the others.

We need to remember that there is a very real Messianic expectation at work in the minds of the disciples at this time. Jesus has entered Jerusalem on a donkey and been received with great fan fare by the mass-es of people. He has spoken on the Mount of Olives about the end of time and His coming to set up the kingdom. They have been arguing about who will get what position when the upcoming kingdom's government is organ-ized. They, knowing Jesus' power over the natural and supernatural worlds, very clearly expect Him to fulfill *their* Messianic expectations in the immediate future.

To suddenly declare He is leaving, not just the Jews but them, had to be inconceivable! That was the farthest thing from their minds and had to be a shocking blow that cut to the core of their beings. Additionally, they had to know not only of the extent of official opposition to Jesus, but also the extent of the Jews' power to harm them apart from Jesus. With Jesus they could feel a measure of security. He had the protective support of the masses and power over nature. They could not claim the same. Thus, they needed to know what was going on before they were capable of hearing anything else. For Peter, being with Jesus was paramount. If Jesus was relocating, he wanted to be able to stay with Him. Thus, "where" was a very important piece of information needed by him and the others.

Tenney's observation is helpful in understanding the nature of the dialogue between Jesus and the disciples from John 13:36 to 14:4. He says, "The structure of this dialogue offers a contrast between the attempt of Jesus to present some consecutive teaching in preparation of his departure and the nervous unrest of the disciples who were disconcerted by the awareness of impending danger."[3] This is a valuable insight into what is happening during this phase of the evening. Even so, some of Jesus' answers are sufficiently vague to lead to some of their confusion and to spur their inquiry on. Or, it may be that He is not quite ready to speak as plainly as their questions demand (see 16:25-30). There are other things He wants to say before answering the question of "where."

Jesus responds to Peter's question rather enigmatically. "Where I am going you cannot follow Me now, but you shall follow Me afterward." His answer is characteristically both exact and ambiguous at that moment, though its exactness clearly escapes the disciples. It will be much clearer once He has finished His explanations. Tenney again provides good insight into the conversation. He says, "Jesus' answer reflects Peter's underlying meaning, for Jesus' promise, 'You will follow later,' implies that Peter had asked the question so that he might go with him."[4] Yet His answer is still too vague for Peter to comprehend, in a sense meaning two things at once.

Jesus now speaks to them with a series of statements, each appearing to carry a double sense, and so is setting them up for His clearer statements that are coming while answering their immediate questions as well.[5] This reflects His approach to answering questions throughout His ministry. He does not mind being ambiguous. He even seems to delight in saying something that is unclear to the listeners while actually being straight to the point. And, like the Jews who repeatedly missed or misunderstood Jesus' points, the result here is that, as He began to instruct them in preparation for His coming departure, the eleven picked up on the wrong issues.

So, why was Jesus being so vague at this point? He chose to be sufficiently vague to keep them from being overwhelmed by the knowledge of what was about to transpire. In fact, He continued to be vague even when they thought He was speaking openly since none of them seems to have understood He was speaking about crucifixion until it was happening. They *thought* they understood what He meant by departure. But, as we will see below, they never fully comprehended because they were not *willing* to see what He was trying to tell them. Yet, after the fact, His forthright honesty with them was more than apparent to them as they remembered His words and saw them in light of the events between that evening and His ascension.

When Jesus tells Peter that he will follow Him, He uses an ambiguous term for "follow," where a specific term would have been clear. He appears to do this in order to create a double meaning and possibly provoke a momentary misunderstanding that would lead to further discussion and clarification. Jesus seems to have enjoyed the use of *double entendre* when teaching, whether publicly or privately. Here, in answering Peter, Jesus affirms that he "will follow his master to glory but only after the death/resurrection of Jesus makes his own 'following' possible." In the interchange with Peter that follows, Peter's use of "follow" and Jesus' explanation to him repeatedly refers to His going to the Father, His departure from them. But, when Jesus tells them that they will "seek" Him, He seems to have again purposefully set Peter up to misunderstand and ask for further clarification. That clarification comes in later instruction (John 14:4 and 16:5, 17).[6] Thus, Jesus' use of "depart," (*hupagō*) means to "follow" Jesus both to the Father and to martyrdom.

13:37. Peter said to Him, "Lord, why can I not follow You now? I will lay down my life for Your sake."

Though Peter misunderstands His reference to His departure, he does seem to sense, at least in part, that Jesus' life is in some way threatened. This is evident in his response that he is willing to die for Jesus. His response is an honorable commitment, on one hand, and a foolish boast on the other. Such loyalty to death is an appropriate response that any loyal citizen would make to his sovereign. Since Peter expects Jesus to be king soon, such an offer is certainly an appropriate statement of fidelity and commitment to the kingdom and its King. Yet, in the context of the present situation, with the eleven being anything but military men and all selfishly jockeying for positions in the upcoming kingdom, it may be appropriate to see an element of pride or arrogance in his words. At any rate, there is a gross overestimation of his courage and fortitude, which

Jesus does not miss.

13:38. Jesus answered him, "Will you lay down your life for My sake? Most assuredly, I say to you, the rooster shall now crow till you have denied Me three times."

Jesus, on the other hand, understood fully the limitations of Peter and the others. Thus He asks, "Will you lay down your life for My sake?" His question is really a statement. Peter's words are empty, arrogant, and ignorant. As Carson well observes, "Sadly, good intentions in a secure room after good food are far less attractive in a darkened garden with a hostile mob. At this point in his pilgrimage, Peter's intentions and self-assessment vastly outstrip his strength."[7] This is reminiscent of the boasts of the church of Laodicea in Revelation 3:17, and Jesus' response to them. Here, Jesus assures him in no uncertain terms, "Most assuredly, I say to you, the rooster shall not crow till you have denied Me three times." Rather than dying for Jesus, Peter is destined to fail Him that very night (cf. Luke 22:34). Not only does Jesus say that Peter will deny Him, but displays His omniscience and announces when and how many times he will fail. Before the third watch of the night was finished, sometime between midnight and three in the morning,[8] Peter would not only fail to die for Jesus, but would even deny knowing Him.[9]

For Peter, this announcement must be as stinging of a rebuke as Jesus' earlier ones had been. He is silenced by Jesus. Having declared his loyalty to His master, that loyalty has been summarily dismissed as shallow. Actually, Peter is mentally and spiritually denuded by Jesus, right in front of all of his colleagues. If it were possible to self-destruct, then would have been the time to do it. Can you feel his embarrassment and chagrin? We can imagine Peter shrinking back in silence, not to be heard from again until he faces the mob in the Garden of Gethsemane. There, he proves his willingness to die for Jesus as he single-handedly takes on a small army and receives another rebuke for his misguided efforts (John 18:10-11). Can you imagine one man with one sword daring to attack a detachment of elite Roman soldiers as well as a raging mob?[10]

It is only in the dark courtyard, surrounded by enemies, that his nerve fails him and he denies Jesus (cf. Luke 22:31-32). And, lest we criticize Peter too much, we should remember that only he and one other of the disciples followed Jesus after His arrest. The others scattered. It was his courage and devotion to Jesus that placed him in the frightful position of being surrounded on a cold lonely night by hundreds of men and women. How many of us would have done differently? If we were standing there that night, we would have received the same rebuke of Jesus, the same warning of weakness, and have experienced the same failure as Peter. The response of Peter in the weakness of the flesh is not really surprising but what is now to come in the response of Jesus is truly amazing.

As we enter this next chapter in the Gospel, Christ, as the master Counselor, responds to Peter's obvious need—more knowledge of who God is and what He is really like. Remember the principle—our actions are simply the result of our deepest thoughts. We act like we act because we think like we think. The reason Peter and the others were doing and would do unworthy and sinful things was because of wrong thinking. If we never had a wrong thought about God, we would never sin. Every sin we commit is because of wrong thinking and at the heart of wrong thinking is wrong thinking about God.

Jesus knew the source of Peter's problem; thus, this whole chapter is about God. He had to lift Peter's thinking about who God is—Father, Son and Holy Spirit—if He was going to change his actions. For example, Jesus mentions the "Father" more in this chapter (23 times) than anywhere else in the Bible. Furthermore, He introduces the Holy Spirit. The progression is as follows: know, believe, receive. You cannot believe what you don't know and you cannot receive what you don't believe. Christ had made this clear in John 8:31-32.

Words of Comfort

Jesus has given His men a lesson on humble service, announced His coming betrayal, commanded them to love one another, and startled them with the news that He is departing. As they attempt to grapple with the shock of His leaving them, Peter has understood, at least in part, that Jesus faces some danger. Having declared his loyalty and willingness to die for Jesus, only to be told that he will fail Him that very night, Peter and the others are likely in a deep emotional quandary. And rightly so!

If this was a typical situation today, we would probably hear people responding, "How can you possibly think of such a despicable denial?" We would typically expect a serious reprimand from Christ. But to our amazement, there is no further word about Peter's sin! Rather, He directs their attention away from thoughts about themselves to lofty thoughts about the character of the triune God. Christ does the remarkable thing of lifting their thinking from that horrible scene to the provisions that He has contracted with the Father and will further develop Himself in the heavenly mansions. Jesus offers comfort at His departure through the promise of a place in His Father's house, a Helper who will perfectly replace Him in their lives, and that He and the Father will be making their abode within them.

The Amazing Response
14:1-4

Jesus responds to their questions and Peter's bravado with a gentle command for them to calm their hearts and a comforting promise. To calm them, He offers three cures for spiritual heart trouble: faith, His Father's house, and His future coming.

Can you imagine this response from Jesus? After what He has just predicted about Peter's forthcoming denials? He turns and tells them how to comfort themselves in the face of what is about to transpire. When we see what else He said at this point in Luke 22:31-32, we can see why their hearts would be troubled. He warns them that Satan has asked permission to sift them like wheat, and then assures Peter that He has prayed for him. It is then to Peter He turns and commands him to strengthen the others when their ordeal is over. So, in spite of their selfish concerns and bold affirmations of loyalty, Jesus is concerned for their welfare completely. Truly this is unconditional love at its greatest.

Jesus seeks to comfort the disciples by revealing that a part of His reason for departing is His preparation of a place for them in His Father's house. Though this section is a continuation of the conversation of chapter thirteen, it is also an introduction to what follows.[11]

14:1. "Let not your heart be troubled; you believe in God, believe also in Me.

Jesus' first words (cf. Luke 22) following His declaration of Peter's coming despicable denials are, "Let not your heart be troubled." The disciples' response to Jesus' announcement of His departure is evidently one of deep gloom. Fear has gripped their hearts and their faith trembles. His own quick response indicates that He can either sense or see the anxiety on the faces of His men. So He moves to deal with that anxiety quickly with comforting words.

Fear has gripped the hearts of the disciples as to the future. Faith trembles. Jesus knows their need because He Himself had been troubled, though as a perfect man. What a blessing to be comforted by One who has experienced the pain (John 11:33; 12:27; 13:21). Jesus begins, in fact, by asking His men to trust Him as He explains to them what is about to transpire and gives them words of comfort. He tells them what it is they need to know, believe, and receive (cf. John 8:31-32).

Jesus begins giving comfort by instructing His men to calm their hearts, to stop panicking. Though "heart" is singular, Jesus is addressing the group ("your" is plural). His command makes use of a present tense imperative, which in the Greek means that they were at that time letting their hearts be troubled and were to "stop" doing it, *i.e.* not to continue panicking. In other words, Jesus recognizes that the men are allowing His words at this point to alarm them and that they are deeply troubled by what He has already told them. Thus He tells them to calm themselves down.

What was causing their alarm? Jesus had just announced His departure and then told Peter that he was not only *not* going to die for Him, but that he was about to deny Him three times. Further, the disciples knew that there were two kinds of people in Jerusalem: the Romans who hated them because they were disturbers of the peace, and the Jews who saw them as blasphemers. Only Jesus really loved and cared for them. If Peter, who was their natural leader, was doomed to fail, so must they. More importantly, those eleven men understood at this point that Jesus was about to leave them alone to face a hostile situation. They had been with Jesus for the week preceding this night and had clearly seen the antagonism of the nation's spiritual leadership, a leadership that was also politically powerful. They knew of those people who had been excommunicated from their synagogues and the economic and social implications of such rejection.

As long as Jesus was with them, they had little to fear. In the years they had followed Him He had protected and provided for them, sometimes supernaturally. What was to happen with His departure? Luke 22:35-38 contains some additional instruction of Jesus' that follows His announcement of Peter's denial and likely preceded his present comments. There He tells them that the supernatural provision and protection they had experienced when announcing the kingdom earlier (Luke 10) would not be available to them following His departure.

These men had left everything, and risked everything to follow Jesus. Their sudden realization that He was about to leave them had to be emotionally devastating. This is especially true when He seems to be removing all familiar support as well.

Jesus was able to identify with His men in their anguish. The term used by Jesus for "troubled" (*tarassesthō*) here and again in verse twenty-seven is used by John in John 11:33 to describe Jesus' own response to the weeping of Mary and the Jews at Lazarus' tomb, and again in 13:21 to describe His emotions when He announced that one of the disciples would betray Him. Still, He calmed His own heart for their sakes and continued to minister to them as His time of suffering approached. It is noteworthy that Jesus' command was given even as He was living out that same principle. In the face of what He knew was about to happen, He remained at peace and spoke to His men calmly. He expressed His unending love toward them by serving them in this way, even as He had washed their feet earlier. When He would be fully justified in becoming self-absorbed, like they were becoming, He reached out to calm their troubled hearts with calm compassion.

He provides the basis of their response, though, in the remainder of the verse. They are to exercise trust, faith. He provides them with spiritual 20/20 vision. He tells them to "believe in" God and in Him. His command, "believe in" is the strongest expression of faith in the Gospel of John, being introduced in this form in the very beginning (John 1:12) as a description of those who receive the right to become children of God. What a great and powerful word ... *believe* ... a word used by John in this Gospel of belief ninety-nine times. "Only Believe" – Christ could use repent, mourn, confess, etc. But He does not. He gets right to Peter's need, which is to believe.

But "believe" needs a worthy object. And the only worthy object is God. Believing is not unusual. People do it all day long in many different ways. And their actions are simply the result of their beliefs. Emphasizing the importance of the object of belief, A. W. Tozer observes, "I believe there is scarcely an error in doctrine or a failure in applying Christian ethics that cannot be traced finally to imperfect and ignoble thoughts about God."[12]

Why was Peter going to behave so shamefully that night? Because of his wrong thoughts about God. When the eleven need faith to get them through their trauma, Jesus not only commands to believe, but also points them to the proper object of their faith. People become martyrs for wrong objects of faith all the time. Think about the Muslim terrorists who die for their cause, believing their deaths will lead to their heavenly reward. Many communists willingly died for their cause only to have it collapse under the weight of moral, spiritual, and economic corruption.

A difficulty faced when interpreting this verse arises because of the form of the Greek word used twice by Jesus for "believe."[13] When He said, "You believe in God, believe also in Me," the spelling of "believe" allows it to either be in the indicative (stating something that is true, "you believe in Me") or an imperative (a command for them to believe). This permits Jesus' words to be understood in one of four ways. First, and least likely, He may have stated a command followed by a statement of fact: "Believe in God" (command), "you do believe in Me" (fact); *i.e.* "Since you are believing in Me, I want you to also believe in God." Second, He may have stated a fact and followed it with a command: "You believe in God" (fact), "believe also in Me" (command); *i.e.* "I know you believe in God, now I want you to similarly believe in Me." Third, He may have said both phrases as statements of fact: "You believe in God, you also believe in Me," *i.e.* "Your faith in Me is like your faith in God." Finally, He may have intended both as commands: "Believe in God. Believe also in Me."; *i.e.* "Believe in both God and Me."[14]

Further help in understanding this verse is the order of the objects in the Greek construction. "God" and "Me" are moved toward the center of the sentence with "believe" placed at the beginning and end. By doing this Jesus places His emphasis on "believe." Further, the development of the section and what Jesus says following this in no way implies that they do not yet believe in God, but rather that their understanding of Jesus is still deficient. Therefore, the second option (as translated in the NKJV) is the best. Jesus says He recognizes that they believe in God, and then commands them to begin believing in Him as well. This is not to say that they have not "believed in Jesus" up to this point. John has stated clearly that they have. But, they do need to know more about who He is as the object of their faith. Jesus is really reminding them that they need to trust Him at this point in time, not in order to be born again, but in order to calm their hearts.

One might ask, how does this "believing in" relate to salvation? The use of "believe in" in John 1:12 is clearly describing someone who is regenerate. We need to remember that the biblical concept of salvation has a beginning point, but is progressive as well. In fact, salvation may be described as having a past, present, and future tense aspect to it for every Christian. First, there is initial salvation, salvation "past," called regeneration. This occurs when a person initially believes in Jesus and is declared righteous by God, justified, and passes from the domain of Satan into the Kingdom of God, from death to eternal life. The believer is "born again." But, then salvation continues throughout the believer's life.

This second phase can be called salvation "present." The believer continues to be delivered from Satan's dominion and control. This is "being saved" in the present tense, much like Paul described in Philippians 1:9. During this salvation the believer grows in faith and faithfulness as the Holy Spirit sets the believer apart to God and separate from the world. This is also called sanctification.

Finally there is "future" salvation. In this salvation all believers receive their resurrection bodies and enter into eternity with God, enjoying their heavenly rewards in glorified bodies. They share Christ's glory. This is also called our glorification. All three stages of "salvation" are the work of God in us and for us. But, the first two require the exercise of faith on our parts to experience.

At this time in the evening, Jesus is talking to a regenerate group of men (already "saved" in the sense of being born again). He is encouraging them to exercise belief in Him and His Father necessary for deliverance (*i.e.*, salvation) through (not from) the troubles they will be facing in the coming hours.

Having commanded them to believe in Him, He now follows up with the necessary knowledge to exercise such belief. So, Jesus' call for them to believe in Him is immediately followed up with the data that they are going to need to believe. Thus the object of their faith will be sufficiently increased to enable them to meet the demands of the trials they are about to face in the coming hours and days (cf. John 15:3). He asks them to do what Paul the apostle will do in his final days (2 Tim 1:12), to know whom they have believed and to be persuaded that He is able to keep what they have committed to Him. He asks the same of every believer. He does not ask for works, but for belief, belief in Him to keep His word, simply believing what He says about Himself.

Here is counseling at its best. Jesus understands the principles He built into us. He knows that the only way to change the eleven's actions is to change their thinking. "Believe in" is the strongest expression of faith and expresses motion toward. We can see this point of Jesus' by contrasting what He says here with what He says in verse eleven. There He tells the eleven to "believe Me," i.e., My words, what I am saying." Here, Jesus is telling them to relax and have faith in Him, even if they do not yet understand everything that is happening. This is so much like how God deals with us today, calling on us to have faith in Him on the basis of His character and biblical revelation, even as He takes us through trials and circumstances that test our faith. But remember, God never calls on us to exercise blind faith or faith in faith. He provides us the object of our faith, Himself (cf. Isa 1:18; 2 Pet 3:15). They are being asked by Jesus to have faith in Him to tell them the truth and do what is best. If they can have faith in Him, then they can calm their hearts.

Still, this is not an empty invitation to believe. Jesus tells them more about what He will do for them and who He is. Right acting begins with right thinking. And right thinking begins by thinking right about what God is like. Jesus is providing them the right information to use in influencing their thinking.

14:2. "In My Father's house are many dwelling places; if it were not so, I would have told you. I go to prepare a place for you.

Following His command for them to believe in Him, Jesus gives them more to believe. He continues to tell them what he is going to do for *them*, not what they must do for *Him*. He reveals their future destinies and the implications that follow, providing a basis for a calm response to the announcement of His departure. He gives them more to *believe* about Himself and His plans for them—not more to *do* but more to *believe*. And this believing will enable them to receive and to do.

What Jesus gives them to believe is first the revelation that His departure has a positive purpose that is directly beneficial to them. He is going to prepare a place for them within His Father's house. In telling them this He answers why Peter cannot follow, saying that it is necessary for Him to prepare rooms for everyone and promising to take them there in the future. This is somewhat reminiscent of Jesus' words in John 12:26 as He entered Jerusalem. "If anyone serves Me, let him follow Me; and where I am, there My servant will be also." Peter was strongly impacted by this promise from the Lord as is evidenced by his confidence expressed in 1 Peter 1:3-5. "Blessed *be* the God and Father of our Lord Jesus Christ, who according to His abundant mercy has begotten us again to a living hope through the resurrection of Jesus Christ from the dead, to an inheritance incorruptible and undefiled and that does not fade away, reserved in heaven for you, who are kept by the power of God through faith for salvation ready to be revealed in the last time."

Jesus begins His words of encouragement with the announcement that His Father's house contains "many dwelling places" which must be prepared for occupation.[15] What would the disciples have understood by Jesus' words? In John 2:16, when He cleansed the temple, Jesus referred to the temple as "My Father's house." The tabernacle in the wilderness, which the temple replaced as God's dwelling place on earth, drew its design from the heavenly temple (Ex 25:40). Solomon's temple included three stories of rooms that made up the outside walls of the tabernacle (1 Kings 6:1-10). Some of the rooms were used for storage and others were living quarters for the officiating priests. The temple of Jesus' day also had rooms that were used for storage and for priest's apartments. Cook observes that *monai* (plural form of *monē*) "puts emphasis upon the permanence of these dwellings, while the plural number shows that individual provision will be made for all the Father's children. It must not be overlooked, however, that they are all together in one place. Thus the picture is of each child having a suite of rooms in the Father's house."[16] The Apostle John would later give the details about this magnificent city 1500 miles square and 1500 miles high – heaven's high rise (Rev 21:9-21).

But, what did Jesus mean by "prepare"? First, the rooms are already there. John pictures them coming down in Revelation 21:2 and 10, but Jesus is going to prepare them, i.e., make them ready. Jesus has been doing this for almost two thousand years. How long did He take to create the universe? If Christ could take a sunbeam and paint a rose, what will our eternal dwelling place be like? Read Revelation 21:11 and then verses eighteen through twenty. Our future home is a glorious place, carefully and wonderfully prepared for our enjoyment by our Lord who loves us.

After announcing the existence of rooms in the abode of His Father, Jesus reminds them of His own trustworthiness by saying, "if it were not so, I would have told you." This is His way of reminding them that they can believe what He says and that He is not keeping the truth hidden from them. This sets the stage for His repetition of the fact of His departure, but now in a new light. He announces that He is going to prepare a place for them in His Father's house (yes, a fantastic high rise described in Rev 21).[17]

14:3. "And if I go and prepare a place for you, I will come again and receive you to Myself; that where I am, there you may be also.

Jesus follows the declaration of His intention to prepare a place in the Father's house for His men with an explanation of the importance of His going. He says, "if I go and prepare," with the "if" implying that there is the possibility of His not going, though that is His intention. Unlike the Greek "first class" conditional sentences that would carry the sense of "since I go," this one raises the possibility that He might not go. Jesus is saying, "If I go and prepare a place, then I will come get you. But if I do not go, then I won't." The way Jesus says this emphasizes the point that

"His return is as certain as His departure."[18]

But more importantly, Jesus emphasizes the necessity of His departure in this statement. It is for their benefit, not His. If Jesus does not go, then He cannot prepare them a place in His Father's house and cannot come and receive them to Himself in His Father's house. The fulfillment of these promises depends on Jesus' departure. Their opportunity to live in God's presence depends entirely on Jesus' preceding them into His presence. So, Jesus asks His men not only to believe that there are rooms in the Father's house reserved for them (note 1 Pet 1:4), but that His departure includes the preparation of their rooms for their future occupation. Further, they are to believe He will return for them and believe that He will then take them to heaven after the rooms have been prepared. Thus, Jesus is asking them to believe that their separation from Him will only be temporary and that they will follow Him to His present destination in due time.

The idea of Jesus' departure is really not a new concept for the eleven. In John 7:34-36 and 8:21-22 we see that Jesus has already revealed that He is returning to the Father. The disciples at that time, along with the Jews, either do not understand or are not paying attention to the significance of His words. Thus, His announcement now comes as a shock.

When will Jesus come back and receive them to Himself? His promise is somewhat ambiguous in that He uses a present tense form of the verb when He makes this promise. The present tense carries with it a progressive sense. Normally its use indicates something in progress in the present time, though not always. It may also include a more punctiliar idea, in other words, speak of something that happens at a point in time. It can also include the idea of something that happens regularly, known as the gnomic sense.

The present tense verb can have a future sense to it, as is evident in Jesus' use here. In fact, in the conditional construction Jesus uses to say this, the other future tense verbs in the context indicate a future idea rather than some gnomic sense (that it happens routinely). This increases the idea of certainty in the conditional clause just referred to. When used this way it indicates that the future event is considered "so certain that in thought it may be contemplated as already coming to pass."[19] Thus Jesus' use of the present tense to promise a future coming speaks of the certainty of His return.

But, to what does Jesus refer when He says He is returning? Several possible meanings can be given to Jesus' promise. First, He might be thought to be referring to a spiritual coming at every moment of trial. But when did the Lord ever leave in this service? Matthew 28:20 contains His promise to be with us always. A second possibility is that He promises to come at the time of His resurrection.[20] But then what would you do with the rest of the sentence? Third, He might be promising to come for us at death.[21] But Philippians 1:23 and 2 Corinthians 5:8 teach clearly that we go to Him. A fourth possibility is His promise to come in the Spirit. This possibility has some connection with John 14:18, but how would He receive us? The fifth, and best, possibility is that He is promising to come *for* the church (cf. John 14:18, 28; 21:22; Rev 2:5, 16; 3:11; 16:15; 22:7, 12, 20) and so is a reference to the rapture of the church.[22]

14:4. "And where I go you know, and the way you know."

Having revealed the beneficial importance of His departure, Jesus makes another enigmatic statement that He uses to "bait the hook" and draw the disciples into further discussion.[23] He tells His men that they already know both where He is going and the way He is going to take to get there. Looking through the Gospels in retrospect, we can see clearly that Jesus is alluding to His instruction concerning His rejection, death, resurrection, and ascension. Unfortunately, they had not yet understood what He was saying, or had chosen not to believe He meant those things literally. So, He is basically saying, "I have already told you these things and you should know them." But, they did not. Thus we have Thomas' response.

At this point it would be good to review what Jesus had said to the disciples prior to that evening's instruction. Beginning with Peter's confession (Matt 16:16), Jesus had been teaching them of His coming death and ascension to the Father (Matt 16:21-28; Mark 8:31—9:1; Luke 9:22-27).[24] But they had not been listening. In fact, Peter's initial response was to rebuke Him! (Matt 16:22). Soon afterwards, after the three leading apostles saw Jesus' glory on the Mount of Transfiguration, He again explained to them that Elijah had come and that He was to suffer (Matt 17:1-13; Mark 9:2-13; Luke 9:28-36). After healing the demon-possessed boy, Jesus told His disciples, "The Son of Man is about to be betrayed into the hands of men, and they will kill Him, and the third day He will be raised up" (Matt 17:22-23). The disciples became sorrowful at this, but not understanding.

Then, as they approached Jerusalem and certain scribes and Pharisees asked for a sign, Jesus offered the sign of Jonah and said, "For as Jonah was three days and three nights in the belly of the great fish, so will the Son of Man be three days and three nights in the heart of the earth" (Matt 12:40). Next, when Jesus was "warned" by some Pharisees that Herod intended to kill Him, He rejected their warning and then said, "I must journey today, tomorrow, and the *day* following; for it cannot be that a prophet should perish outside of Jerusalem" (Luke 13:33). As He continued to journey toward Jerusalem, after healing ten lepers and being asked by a Pharisee when the kingdom of God would come, He said to His disciples, "The days will come when you will desire to see one of the days of the Son of Man, and you will not see" (Luke 17:22). Further, He warned them that *before* His return to set up the kingdom, "He must suffer many things and be rejected by this generation" (Luke 17:25).

Then, after passing through Jericho, Jesus again told them plainly, "Behold, we are going up to Jerusalem and the Son of Man will be betrayed to the chief priests and to the scribes; and they will condemn Him to death, and deliver Him to the Gentiles to mock and to scourge and to crucify. And the third day He will rise again" (Matt 20:18-19). When James and John sought special status in His coming government, Jesus referred to the "cup" He was to "drink" and then closed His rebuke of their impertinence with the statement, "the Son of Man did not come to be served, but to serve, and to give His life a ransom for many" (Matt 20:28). When Mary anointed Him at Bethany and Judas Iscariot objected, Jesus responded, "Let her alone; she has kept this for the day of My burial. For the poor you have with you always, but Me you do not have always" (John 12:7-8).

Then following His Triumphal Entry into Jerusalem and challenges by the Pharisees, Jesus told the parable of the Vinedressers who kill the owner's son (Matt 21:33-44). The chief priests and Pharisees recognized they were the target of the parable, the evil Vinedressers who would kill the owner's son, Jesus. But the disciples did not seem to pick up on Jesus being the "son" in the parable and it pointing to His coming death. Then later, after some Greeks attempted to meet with Him, Jesus said several things alluding to His coming death, such as, "unless a grain of wheat falls into the ground and dies, it remains alone; but if it dies, it produces much grain," and "if I be lifted up from the earth, will draw all to Myself," and then, "a little while longer the light is with you" (John 12:24, 32, 35).

So, repeatedly Jesus had warned them and alluded to His coming rejection, arrest, and crucifixion. Yet, through it all they had remained oblivious to the implications of what He was saying. They were still just as shocked as if He had said nothing prior to that evening. They were just as confused. Thus, they had more questions.

CHAPTER SIX

CHRIST CONTINUING TO COMFORT WITH TRUTH
John 14:5-11

Though Jesus has answered Peter's question and unfounded promise, revealing to them their future destiny in heaven, the other disciples still appear not to be listening. Jesus has more important things to teach His men. But they are still not ready to hear Him. Rather, they still want to know more about His departure. So, another question and further confusion follows, which Jesus addresses. First, we hear from Thomas.

14:5. Thomas said to Him, "Lord, we do not know where You are going, and how can we know the way?"

Thomas' question begins with a contradiction of Christ. He says, "we cannot know the way to where You are going since we do not know where you are going." The Lord has said, "You do know the way." The *place* is the Father's house. The *way* is the Son. Thomas did know these facts, but the information was still unused and he was unconscious of it. How much we are like this. There is much that we know from the Lord but we fail to believe it and use it. There is a great educational principle of the law of use and disuse. If we don't use it, we lose it. This is why so many people can attend church all their life and never grow in Christ. To Thomas' credit, he was not afraid to admit his ignorance and take it to the light. Jesus also was not hesitant to enlighten him further.

So, Thomas "bit the bait," admitted the disciples' ignorance about where Jesus was going, and asked Him the logical next question. How could they know the way if they could not figure out the destination?

101

They were blind and Thomas was quick to admit it. But, their blindness was not that of hardened hearts like the Jews. They were not rejecting Jesus' person or revelation. Their blindness was that of soft hearts trying to look through the wrong presuppositions. As Mitchell notes, the problem of the disciples was that they "never understood when the Lord Jesus talked of eternity. They didn't see beyond the material kingdom."[1] They were still anticipating the inauguration of the Messianic kingdom and could not fathom how death and departure could fit into *their* eschatological scheme.

Thomas became the group's spokesman at this point. And, lest he be criticized for his seemingly brash or "stupid" question, we need to see him as John depicted him. He was a loyal follower of Jesus who was willing to follow Him into the heart of "enemy territory" following an attempt on His life just days before by the Jewish leaders (John 10:39; 11:1-16). Still, he was not shy about expressing his feelings at that time either. He thought it was suicidal to return, and said so plainly. But, when Jesus went, he followed.

Thomas was not lacking in courage or loyalty. He was just honest about how he felt. Like Nathaniel, he was an Israelite in whom there was no guile. Later, following Jesus' crucifixion and resurrection, he would again be bluntly honest about his feelings and insist that he would not believe Jesus was alive unless he could touch Him and confirm His reality (John 20:24-29). Carson notes, "His question sounds as if he interpreted Jesus' words in the most crassly natural way: he wants an unambiguous destination, for without such a destination how can one meaningfully speak of the route there?"[2] Yet, even in his "crass" question, his open honesty is most evident. Even more important, his response was the response Jesus wanted and so set the stage for further instruction.

A Comforting Explanation
14:6-7

4:6. Jesus said to him, "I am the way, the truth, and the life. No one comes to the Father except through Me.

Jesus answers Thomas by identifying the *destination* as a person, the *Father*. We can be thankful for Thomas' doubt. This answer is a classic statement of the New Testament that we would not have received apart from his question. And, in response to Thomas' response, Jesus clarifies that the way is also a person, *Himself.* When He says, "I am the way," Jesus uses the Greek term for "I" (*egō*) with the verb for "am" (*eimi*) which does not require a subject since "I" is already contained in it. His use of this combination is thereby *very* emphatic. He is saying by this, "I 'and no other' am the way." The answer lies in *who* their attention is focused on, not where. His thumb is verbally bouncing off his chest as He points to Himself and says, "It's I, Thomas!" By focusing on Jesus, they find both the path and destination. F. F. Bruce notes well, "If God has no avenue of communication with mankind apart from his Word (incarnate or otherwise), mankind has no avenue of approach to God apart from that same Word."[3]

Jesus communicates several key concepts in these few words. First, when He says, "I am," He is also saying that He is the object of our faith. Cook notes well that throughout the Gospel of John, Jesus uses this "I am" formula to make "seven claims to deity couched in figurative language" with each claim relating "directly and practically to deep human needs."[4] This is the sixth of those claims and the deep human need involves our eternal destiny, our future dwelling with God. Second, Jesus uses three terms to describe Himself in this claim. He says that He is the "way" to the Father, as well as the "truth," and the "life."

By his use of "and" with the Greek article (translated as "the" in English) before each of the three nouns He indicates that all three descriptions are coordinate ideas and applied equally to Him.[5] He is not saying that He is "the true and living way" or "the way of truth and life." These two ideas would be communicated using a construction that would make them subordinate ideas describing "way," which they are not.[6] Laney describes well the significance of His words. "Jesus is the way to follow; the truth to believe; the life for which we hope."[7] Let us examine these three affirmations further.

The Way. Instead of describing a way, Jesus offers Himself. He does not say "I am a way" – He is not one of several ways. Jesus is being exclusive and making faith in Him an excluding condition for access to God. This is why Christianity presents itself unashamedly as the exclusive way of salvation for mankind. This is reminiscent of John 10:7-9 where He describes Himself as the gate through which His sheep find protection from thieves and robbers. He is the passage to God's eternal presence. "Way" is emphasized through repetition in verses four, five, and six.

He is the only way the lost world can come to the Father as well as the only path a believer has to follow. Those whose minds are set on heaven

have first set their hearts on Christ. But rather than seeing this as simply justification truth, we must remember that Jesus is answering the
question of a *believer* who wants to know how to follow his Messiah into
His kingdom and feels He is deserting him. Jesus tells him, and us, that
our access to the Father, as believers, is through Him. The path we take
in reaching the kingdom and our eternal destiny is through Him. Our
daily fellowship with the Father requires moment-by-moment cleansing
through His blood (1 John 1:7). He is the focus of our hope, our path each
step of the way. Further, Jesus describes with the next two nouns how He
is the exclusive way. He is the way by being the truth and the life.

The Truth. Jesus also calls Himself "the truth," not just a source of
truth. But what does He mean by this?[8] He is the ultimate revelation of
God. He, in fact, brings this issue up in the next verse. They want to know
the way to the Father. Jesus has revealed the Father. He is the embodiment of truth just as they recognize that God the Father is the source of
all truth.[9] If we want to know what is true in this day of competing
philosophies and ideologies, we must look first and foremost to Christ, our
final revelation. Here, again, Jesus' point is most applicable to believers
who want to know how to live for God, though in a secondary manner it
addresses those seeking redemption or regeneration.

He is the one who has communicated clearly to the eleven disciples what
they are to believe and how they are to live. They need not look to anyone
but Him in the coming days and years for the answers to the questions they
will be facing. Their eyes need to remain focused on Him and they need to
believe what He tells them. In the same way, we today must keep our eyes
focused on Jesus, the author and finisher of our faith (Heb 12:2), who has
revealed the person and character of God perfectly. As with the eleven in
that upper room, distraction is a major problem for all of us.[10] But Jesus
does not hesitate to call on them, and so us, to follow Him daily.

The Life. Notice that here Jesus says "I am the life," not, "I present
the life." As revealed earlier in the Gospel, Jesus is life giver. In Him is life
(John 1:4). In John 5:21 Jesus declares to the Jews that He has the authority to give life to whomever He wants and then He follows this with the
claim that He has life in Himself (5:26). This claim is made in light of His
healing the invalid at the Pool of Bethesda and in response to the Jews'
objections to His healing on a Sabbath. In John 10:10 He states His purpose in coming as giving abundant life to His sheep. Then, in 10:17-18
Jesus claims authority over His own life, both to lay it down on behalf of
His sheep and then to take it up again. He takes the title of the

"Resurrection and Life" at Bethany just before raising Lazarus (John 11:25). John understood what Jesus meant because he later calls Him "the true God and eternal life" (1 John 5:20), probably reflecting on Jesus' previous statements and His prayer in John 17:3.

Cook notes that the term for life used by Jesus here, *zoē*, had replaced *bios* as the "higher word" for life by New Testament times, with *bios* taking on the sense of "livelihood" (cf. 1 John 5:17).[11] Thus *zoē* became for the church the "appropriate term to describe the gift of God to man, the gift that is the antithesis of sin and death."[12] Thus when Jesus offers "life" in the Gospel, He offers this higher kind of life. Thus, in John 6, when Jesus offers Himself as the bread of life, the life He offers is *zoē* (cf. 6:17, 33, 35). Again, in John 10 it is this *zoē* that Jesus gives His sheep (cf. John 10:28). This life is the abundant life Jesus promises in 10:10. But, then when He talks about physical life, like in reference to His laying down His own life for the sheep, Jesus uses a different term, *psuchē*. Thus Jesus differentiates between mere physical life and real life. And, He has come to give us more than physical life, but the full experience of life as God intends.

In light of this use of *zoē* by Jesus, we see that the term carries significance as both a justification and sanctification term. Jesus calls Himself the bread of life in John 6. And when the people ask what work they must do to gain bread from Heaven, He points to Himself. They must believe in Him. For anyone wishing to have God's life, eternal life, Jesus is its source. But, there is more involved in this claim. Jesus is telling those who had already believed in Him that He is their sole source of life as well. The experience of eternal life, which is a quality of life more than a quantity (John 10:10), comes to the believer only as a result of walking with the Lord, by faith in and obedience to Jesus. Jesus demonstrates this truth in His own life when He responds to Satan's temptations on the basis of and in obedience to God's Word (Matt 4:1-11).

This truth is evident in 1 John 1:5-10 where walking in the light results from the work of Christ in the life of the believer who is honest about sin and abides in the light through confession of sin with its resultant cleansing by God. In the next chapter Jesus is going to describe this concept further as an "abiding" relationship available to His "friends" who obey Him, who thereby become fruitful. This life can be missed by believers, not through a loss of justification or redemption, but through a loss of fellowship. We have a responsibility to look to Jesus if we wish to experience the life of God expressed in our lives. As Paul says, "beholding as in a mirror" (2 Cor 3:18).

Having made these three exclusive claims concerning Himself, Jesus then states unequivocally that He is indeed the exclusive means for anyone approaching the Father. When He says "except *through Me*" He is saying unequivocally that entrance to heaven is exclusive to Him.[13] When Jesus says, "no one comes," He is including all of humanity. For the unbeliever, that means there is only escape from eternal death through Him, no one or nothing else. For the believer, that means that He is the only means of communion with the Father.

He is more than our sole source of justification. He is also our sole source of sanctification, of access to the Father, our only mediator (1 Tim 2:5). Yes, the Holy Spirit does help our prayer (Rom 8:26-27), but we do not get to the Father through the Spirit. We go through Jesus (Rom 8:34). He is still our only entrance into the Father's presence and our sole path to glory. He is our great High Priest (Heb 7-9). He is the agent of our present sanctification and future glorification. He is everything.

14:7. "If you had known Me, you would have known My Father also; and from now on[14] you know Him and have seen Him."

Remember that Jesus is now filling the resource of knowledge about what He is like to eventually result in changed thinking, and thus changed action, by the disciples.

Having shifted the focus from a path to Himself as the way to the Father, Jesus then describes their ignorance of His Father in terms of their failure to understand Him, Jesus. He does this by first affirming that they had not really "known" Him to that point.[15] This is seen in the significance of His use of "if."[16] The construction of this sentence in the Greek assumes that the first statement is not true. Thus, Jesus' use of "if" here implies that the disciples did not really know Him and so had not known the Father either. Jesus is saying, "If you had known Me, *and you really did not, then* you would have known My Father also (*and you have not*)...." Thus we have Jesus' prayer for the disciples to "know" the Father in John 17:3. Here Jesus is affirming what John stated at the beginning of the Gospel, that He "has declared" the Father in the sense of revealing Him perfectly (John 1:18).

Further, what Jesus did when He made His statement to Thomas was to place "know" at both the beginning and the end of His clauses, thus emphasizing both words in the sentence.[17] He is affirming that they do not yet fully recognize Him for who He is and so cannot really perceive Who He is revealing.[18] In essence He is saying, "If you had acquainted yourselves with Me, you would also have had innate perceptive knowledge of my Father. (cf. John 8:19; 12:44, 45, 49, 50; 10:37-38). He then says from that time forward they both "know" the Father and have "seen" Him. The term for seeing is a concrete, experiential, term referring to physical sight which includes within it the idea of perception as well, rather than an abstract or philosophical term which would have implied a purely spiritual sense.[19]

What has happened that their status can change so suddenly? Jesus said something to them that was revelation to them. What did He say? "Seeing me is the same as seeing the Father." That is why in the prologue of the Gospel (1:18), John tells us, "No one has seen God at any time. The only begotten Son, who is in the bosom of the Father, He has declared (literally: exegeted) Him." What Jesus has given the disciples are words, which when believed, are life to them (John 6:63).

Philip Asks to be Shown the Father

14:8. Philip said to Him, "Lord, show us the Father, and it is sufficient for us."

Philip responds to Jesus' statement with what appears on the surface to be a bold, even arrogant, request. He asks Jesus to show them the Father, affirming at least that he did not think he had seen Him yet. But, if not seen as arrogant, this request could be seen in a positive way. Philip, by faith, responds much like Moses did (Ex 33:18) and asks for the chance to see God's glory.[20] Even more striking is the fact that, in this positive view of his request, Philip's request clearly implies that *he thought Jesus could do it*!

Jesus' response to Philip indicates a third option; he is disagreeing with Jesus. Philip is essentially saying that Jesus is incorrect when He says that they have seen the Father. Gruenler correctly observes, "Philip's request that Jesus show the disciples the Father fails to grasp the truth of Jesus' disclosure, even though Jesus has been manifesting the Father to his disciples for so long a time."[21] Thus Philip's request is more likely an exasperated response and the disciples are still confused.[22]

Seeing Jesus is seeing the Father
14:9-11

Perhaps we need to remind ourselves again as to what Jesus, the master Disciplemaker is doing. Recall what Jesus said in John 13:38? He warned confident Peter that he would deny Him. They are not thinking God's thoughts. They are not even thinking clearly. They have hit bottom emotionally and are grasping for understanding. And now Christ is *lifting* them from where they have fallen with truth about God. Why? Because we will never walk higher in our life in Christ than our knowledge of what God is like. We must remember how basic truth is to action. We cannot act right without believing right. Therefore, Jesus continues to teach His men what to believe so that they can act.

In these verses Jesus teaches significant theology to the disciples, and to us. This is truly "doing theology." What He says is difficult to understand because He is revealing truths concerning the nature of the Godhead that we as mere mortals can never fully comprehend. Yet, we can comprehend some of the truths.

Jesus affirms several things in these few verses. He explains the extent of His revelation of the Father in terms of its expressing their mutual indwelling as reflected in His words and works. To the extent that Jesus speaks His Father's words and performs His Father's deeds, both which He does completely, He is a true expression of His Father (cf. Heb 1:3).[23] If His disciples wish to see what God is like, they need simply to look at Jesus.

One of the truths that Jesus sought to communicate that evening was the reality of His deity (cf. 14:1). The men, to this point, seemed to have understood His Son-to-Father relationship, and recognized that it made Jesus both Messiah and someone to believe in. But they still had not taken the next step in understanding that Jesus was not just "Son of God," but by nature God, also, and worthy of the same worship they accorded God the Father (cf. 18:4-11). Jesus will lead them closer to this understanding later in the discussion. Thomas will finally grasp it when he sees his resurrected Lord (John 20:28). But for now, Jesus must introduce them to the initial ideas, focusing on His revelation of the Father.

14:9. Jesus said to him, "Have I been with you so long, and yet you have not know Me, Philip? He who has seen Me has seen the Father; so how can you say, 'Show us the Father?'

Jesus responds to Philip's request with three accusing questions and a stunning claim. First, His first question reveals that Philip's question exposed the fact that he really does not know Him. He then follows this rebuking question by affirming in no uncertain terms, "He who has seen Me has seen the Father." This expresses John's reflection in the first chapter of the Gospel (1:14) that in Jesus they had beheld "the glory as of the only begotten of the Father." Still, what did Jesus mean when He said these things to Philip and the eleven? Both statements from Jesus require much soul-searching inquiry to understand, then and today.

Jesus' response to Philip is a gentle rebuke. In that rebuke He again uses *ginōskō* to describe the kind of knowledge Philip should have.[24] Philip should have a personal acquaintance with and understanding of Christ based on his three or more years of daily exposure to Him. But, as revealed by Philip's question, in some ways the disciples are as blind as the Jews. Even so, though they are blind in some ways, they have clearly demonstrated that they still know Jesus better than the Jews. For example, in John 6:66-69, after His Bread of Life discourse, when many people stop following Jesus, the disciples affirm their faith in Him and remain at His side. Later, after the disciples have told Jesus who the crowds think He is, Peter affirms that He is the Son of the living God (Matt 16:16).

They *have* grown in their understanding of who Jesus is. So, Jesus' rebuke does not mean that they do not know Him at all, or are completely ignorant of His true identity. Rather, their knowledge is still incomplete. Dillow expresses it well. "What did Jesus mean when He said that Philip did not know Him? Of course Philip did know Jesus in a redemption or regeneration sense. He had believed and followed Christ (John 1:43). But he did not know Him in some other sense." The sense being emphasized by Jesus here is that Philip's question implies that he has failed to grasp "how fully the Son had manifested the Father." In the conversation that follows Jesus will teach that the knowledge He is speaking about "comes only as the disciples obey Him (14:21). In other words, we come to know Him in a deeper sense by means of obedience."[25] So, it is not that they do not know Him at all, but that their knowledge is limited to what they have been able or willing to grasp. As a result they do not know Him very well. I can only receive what I believe. And I can only believe what I know.

Carson and MacArthur seem to fail to see the unconditional love of Jesus in their assessment of the situation when they see Jesus responding with sadness or discouragement in His rebuke of Philip.[26] They forget to see His response to Peter's coming denials in 14:1. Jesus is not discouraged or saddened but offers them comfort. We see this most plainly in Luke 22:32. Jesus is not discouraged, but is praying for Peter and, ultimately, for them so that they will make it through the process and survive Satan's attack (John 17:9). What was the "look" of Christ in Luke 22:61? Was it surprise? No! Compassion. It was not a look of "I told you so," but one of "I know where you are at." Carson and MacArthur are reading into the text what is not there.

In fact, John MacArthur, Jr. takes Jesus' rebuke a step further and says, "Can you imagine how heartbroken Jesus was when after three years of intensive teaching, one disciple turned out to be a traitor, another a swearing denier, and the other ten were men of little faith? How discouraged He must have been! Yet here they were, the night before His death, and they still didn't know who He was. It's sad to realize that after all the repeated displays of Christ's deity, the disciples still didn't get the message."[27] The problem with MacArthur's interpretation of Jesus' response is that he fails to remember that Jesus clearly knows what is about to transpire, not just in the next day or three, but in the years to come (cf. John 13:38; 21:18; and Luke 22:31-34).

Instead of being discouraged or angry, Jesus is always *lifting* these men with truth. He will present this truth figuratively in John 15. He knows not only their failures and lack of understanding, but also the illumination they are soon to experience following His resurrection and the ministry of the Holy Spirit in their lives. He knows also which of them will be martyred on His behalf and the courage, commitment, and faith they will display in the years to follow. The only reference to negative emotions in Jesus in this passage is that of His feelings concerning Judas' betrayal. That did trouble Him, and deeply. Philip's request did not. Thus, Jesus' words should not be seen as an expression of discouragement. Nor should sadness be attributed to Him at this point, especially since John does not do so. Rather, we should see these words as another aspect of His teaching method and, if anything, a rebuke to them for their lack of insight. Jesus is no more surprised by their ignorance than He is by Judas' betrayal or the troop that is at that very moment organizing itself to search Him out and arrest Him.

The next statement of Jesus is loaded with theological impact, both then and today. While Philip asks for a theophany, Jesus affirms plainly that he has been having one for years in the personal presence of Christ! (See John 14:21-24) Jesus is claiming to be the true and complete expression of the Father, such that looking at Jesus is equivalent to seeing God the Father. This is an extremely significant statement, a direct claim to deity. He is saying that every attribute true of the Father is true of Himself, which includes deity. This is the foundational truth to what we now call Trinitarianism. Since Jesus is the full representation of the Father, who is God, and reveals Him so completely that seeing One is equivalent to seeing the Other, He must share in those attributes of the Father which make Him God, and so must be God also.

Why would the disciples not have understood this already? We must remember that they came out of an extremely strong monotheistic background in which they, along with and in the presence of Jesus, daily affirmed the Shema of Deuteronomy 6:4, "Hear, O Israel! The LORD our God, the LORD is one!" They had listened to Jesus pray to the Father, whom He had identified as their God. They had heard Him refer to God as His Father and knew that the two were distinct persons. They clearly understood Jesus to be the Son of God, but had probably not thought in terms of Him being "God" also. They did not yet have a "Trinitarian" theological understanding through which they could assess the data of Jesus' revelation. They had not yet grappled with the concept of three persons sharing the same essence (three distinct persons in one Godhead).

And so, they still were not grasping the significance of His person and presence. It was only now that Jesus was making that connection for them. Remember, the signs recorded by John, after many years of reflection on their significance and on the teachings of Jesus, are done so in order to communicate to the reader His deity. Though the disciples had seen the signs, they still did not have the benefit of the Holy Spirit's coming ministry to help them understand fully their significance. Though the man born blind could fathom the import of Jesus' work in his life (and worshipped Him in response, John 9:38), it was not until after the resurrection that one of the disciples, Thomas in particular, could make the same connection and response (John 20:28).

14:10. "Do you not believe that I am in the Father, and the Father in Me? The words that I speak to you I do not speak on My own authority; but the Father who dwells in Me does the works.

Jesus follows His stunning affirmation that they have seen the Father in Him with a rhetorical question that demands a positive answer. He asks, "Do you not believe that I am in the Father, and the Father in Me?" The Greek construction of the question demands a positive answer, "Yes, I do." Jesus is really saying, "You know very well that I am in the Father and the Father is in Me." This repeats His earlier declaration to the Jews in John 10:38. From this Jesus moves to the significance of that truth, namely, that all He says and does is sourced in the Father.

Jesus affirms by these words the mutual indwelling of two members of the Godhead, Himself and the Father. It is by virtue of this relationship that Jesus can affirm that those who have seen Him have seen the Father. In other words, they have not seen the person of the Father, but His character and nature. By His words and works He has proven His union with the Father. His words prove it in the spiritual realm as they reveal God's character. Mitchell explains it this way. "His words are the claims of One who is God. They are just as supernatural, just as real, just as divine as the words of the Father. All His statements, all His miracles, all His life reveal the Father."[28]

Jesus' deeds prove it in the physical realm and to the human intellect as they reveal His power. Carson's evaluation is insightful. "Jesus' question *Don't you believe...?* presupposes that all disciples *ought* to believe that Jesus is in the Father and the Father in him. This mutual indwelling... is 'a linguistic way of describing... the complete unity between Jesus and the Father'... articulated elsewhere in a statement such as 'I and the Father are one' (10:30). This does not obliterate all distinctions between them: the words and works of Jesus are given to him by the Father..., though the reverse cannot be said. Indeed, it is precisely this degree of unity that ensures Jesus reveals God to us." He concludes from this that the theory presented by some that Jesus is affirming nothing more than the Rabbinical concept that "a man's agent is like to himself" (from Mishnah *Berakoth* 5:5) is highly inadequate. Instead, this is "unique 'sonship' language."[29]

Gruenler explains the relationship as follows. "Father and Son, although two persons, indwell one another so that the Son can say that what he does the Father does. The Son makes himself available to the Father, and the Father defers to work through the Son."[30]

Calvin explained the significance of Jesus' words well and helps us avoid the misunderstanding about whether Jesus is describing a metaphysical union or cooperative relationship. He notes that Jesus' statement, "I am in the Father and the Father in me" does not

> refer to Christ's divine essence, but to the manner of the revelation; for Christ, so far as regards his hidden Divinity, is not better known to us than *the Father*. But he is said to be the lively Image, or Portrait, of God, because in him God has fully revealed himself, so far as God's infinite goodness, wisdom, and power, are clearly manifested in him. . . . this description applies to his power rather than to his essence. *The Father*, therefore, is said *to be in Christ,*

because full Divinity dwells in him, and displays its power; and Christ, on the other hand, is said *to be in the Father*, because by his Divine power he shows that he is one with *the Father*.[31]

Yet, they are not one person. This will be a helpful insight to keep in mind when Jesus begins talking about the unity of believers with one another and with Him and God the Father. Rather than looking for a metaphysical union, we should be looking at relationships.[32]

14:11. "Believe Me that I am in the Father and the Father in Me, or else believe Me for the sake of the works themselves.

Having mildly upbraided Philip, Jesus turns to the group and calls on them to trust His words at this point. But, this is not a command that assumes that they lack faith, as some would understand it. Jesus uses a present active imperative form of "believe" (*pisteuō*) to communicate the sense of "keep on believing." He is introducing them to radical new ideas that they must grasp and asks them to stay with Him. He is also not questioning their faith. He is calling on them to continue in that faith a little further. Cook correctly notes that Jesus' statement of "believe Me" is a use of the verb, to believe, with the idea of the "acceptance of a person's statements as true and is a phase of believing that grows naturally out of trust in the person."[33] This is different from the idea of believing "in" Jesus (a justification sense), as seen in John 6:29-30.

Jesus points to His works as the evidence they need in order to understand what He is saying to them. His works demonstrate His unity with the Father. And, as they express the nature and character of the Father, His works give the men glimpses of the Father in the person and activity of the Son. Still, this appeal to His works is for those who believe in Him. Morris notes, "As elsewhere in this Gospel, faith on the basis of miracles is regarded as better than no faith at all." Yet, "In John the characteristic of the miracles is not that they are wonders, nor that they show mighty power, but that they are 'signs'. For those who have eyes to see they point men to God." They reveal the Father, and the deity of the Son, to those whose spiritual eyes are open to recognize their message. Laney notes Nicodemus' words to Jesus when he met Him (3:2) and then says, "The miracles of Jesus were designed to lead to the truth concerning His Person (cf. 10:38; 20:30-31). They still accomplish that purpose as God through the Holy Spirit touches hearts and draws people to Christ."[34]

CHAPTER SEVEN

CHRIST IDENTIFYING FURTHER POWERFUL RESOURCES
John 14:12-20

Jesus moves from the issues of His being the only way to the Father and the complete revelation of the Father to the significance that those truths had in the lives of His men. Having commanded them to trust His words and recognize His relationship with the Father, Jesus makes to His men another promise that involves another benefit of His departure. He is going to work through them. And, as becomes evident in the verses that follow, He promises to work similarly through all believers.

Greater Works Through Answered Prayer
14:12-14

Jesus shifts His emphasis from the disciples believing Him to anyone believing "in" Him. He makes the transition by continuing the idea of works in the previous two verses, but changing the focus from Himself to His followers. He moves from the fact that He has revealed the Father to them to their responsibility to reveal the Father to the world. He does this by taking the men another step farther by saying that those who believe in Him will do "greater" works than He. In verses twelve through fourteen Jesus applies what He is saying to all who put their trust in Him, not just the apostles.

14:12. "Most assuredly, I say to you, he who believes in Me, the works that I do he will do also; and greater works than these he will do, because I go to My Father.

But what did Jesus mean when He said that we who believe in Him will do "greater works than these"? The three possible meanings of "greater works" include either more extraordinary miracles, effective prayer, or more people saved. In the following paragraphs the three views will be explained and then Jesus' point discussed.

The record of Acts and church history testifies to the invalidity of the idea of more extraordinary miracles. When the Gospel's are compared, we find thirty-six miracles recorded, culminating in Lazarus' resurrection. Only twenty miracles are recorded in Acts. And, though two people are raised from the dead by Peter and Paul, those resurrections are not as stunning as Jesus' restoration of life to a four-day-old corpse which had begun to undergo decay and stank!

The idea of effective prayer does not fully fit with the picture either. After noting that other possible meanings are more conversions or "spiritual works accomplished by the power of the Holy Spirit," Laney offers a different solution on the basis of Jesus' last phrase in the verse, "because I go to My Father." He notes that Jesus then turns the focus of the discussion to prayer in the next two verses and so the "greater things" may then refer to "those things that will be accomplished by prayer in His name," or intercessory prayer and its answer.[1]

The problem with this view is that Jesus is talking about works, works He did and works they will do. He has not been answering prayer *per se*, but revealing the Father to a lost world and calling men to repentance (cf. Matt 4:17; Mark 1:15). This was the ministry and work Jesus had already appointed the eleven to earlier when He sent them out in pairs announcing to the cities and villages of Israel, "The kingdom of heaven is at hand" (Matt 10:7). Though He is going to talk about prayer, and promise them answered prayer, He is promising them something else when He talks about doing greater works than He does.

The best way to understand Jesus' words is to see Him promising that they will have a greater impact on the world in spreading the gospel than He had. Mitchell reflects this third interpretation when he says, "I believe the spiritual miracles of transforming men who are dead in sin and making them eternally alive in Christ is a far greater miracle than the resurrection of Lazarus from the tomb."[2] Thus Jesus is referring to the winning of the lost.

Carson concurs and says that greater works "cannot simply mean *more* works – *i.e.* the church will do more things than Jesus did . . . Nor can *greater works* mean 'more spectacular' or 'more supernatural' works: it is hard to imagine works that are more spectacular or supernatural than the raising of Lazarus from the dead, the multiplication of bread and the turning of water into wine."[3] To understand this statement of Jesus', he notes that Jesus uses similar terminology in John 5:20. There the "greater works" are His resurrection and future judgment of the world. He concludes from this that the greater works means, "many more converts will be gathered into the messianic community . . . than were drawn in during Jesus' ministry."[4]

Gordon Fee also gives arguments in support of an evangelistic sense. He says, "Unfortunately, these verses have been either greatly neglected (How can they be true in light of a church seemingly as often characterized by anemia as by power?) or greatly abused (e.g., by the "faith-formula" televangelists, where "the name of Jesus is the believer's carte blanche with God.")."[5] He looks at the larger context of Jesus' earlier action of foot washing in light of His awareness of who He was, where He had come from, and where He was going. "He will leave, but they will stay to serve as he served. Most of what follows are variations on these twin themes."[6] Thus he concludes that these "greater works" should be "understood quantitatively. These are the works of Jesus, mentioned in verses ten and eleven (including both his deeds and words), that together bring life to those who believe.

Yet now precisely because Jesus is going to the Father, his disciples are to bring the revelation and life of God to an ever-broadening circle. Thus these 'greater works' have in view the 'other sheep' of 10:16, those 'who believe in me through their word' (17:20). That this is John's understanding is made certain by the purpose clause of verse thirteen, 'so that the Father might be glorified in the Son.'"[7]

Mitchell again notes that the context of this promise is Jesus' revelation of the Father. Where people could see the Father in Jesus, today "He is seen by the words and works of His people." He assesses the significance of Jesus' promise well (cf. Matt 5:16). He notes, "Here He is talking about the revelation of the Father in His people. The reason for the greater works is because Christ goes to be with His Father, giving us access into the very presence of God that these greater works may be done."[8] Thus the greater works must be a reference to the quantitative element of the church's ministry. We as a body will accomplish more than He could individually because of the new relationship and empowerment that results from His return to the Father. We see this fulfilled in places such as Acts 3:1-11; 5:1-11; 9:31-35; 9:36-43; and 13:4-13 where multitudes come to faith through the lives and testimony of the apostles.

A final thing to note is Jesus' emphasis on the fact of *His* going to the

Father. Again, He uses the emphatic "I" (*ego*) at a point in the sentence where the present tense verb has the "I" understood to be in it. Jesus says that the greater works will be the works that He "is doing" at that time. Further, He combines this with the connective "and" when He adds greater works to the promise. Thus, Jesus is *not* telling the *way* the greater works are to be done. But Who will be doing them. The results are not due to prayer, pleading, but due to the Lord's promise. It is precisely because *Jesus* has gone to the Father, not because we pray, but because of His presence with the Father, that these greater works will be done.

14:13. "And whatever you ask in My name, that I will do, that the Father may be glorified in the Son.

Concurrent with the promise of doing greater works is the promise of answered prayer, when asked on the basis of Jesus' character. Whether this verse simply continues the thought of verse twelve or adds one more aspect to the promise, it must be read together with verse twelve because of the "and" connecting the two. Westcott sees it as a further development and concludes from it, "The union of Christ, perfect man, with the Father gives the assurance of the greater works; and yet more, Christ, for the glory of the Father, will fulfill the prayer of the disciples" (cf. John 15:8; Matt 5:16).[9]

Jesus promises answered prayer under certain conditions. In this verse and the one that follows, the promise of answered prayer is not without its conditions. In order to understand Jesus' actual promise to us, we will need to examine what He has promised in close detail.

Ask. First, there is an attitude that is to be expressed in the prayer request that is to be heard and answered (cf. James 4:3 where wrong motives block answered prayer). Jesus used a term for asking (*aiteō*) which is normally "used of an inferior asking a superior."[10] This is the action of a supplicant. Our Lord never uses it in the requests He makes of the Father. Instead, He uses *erōtaō* (cf. v. 16). Thus, it is a request, not a demand. It is asked with a clear understanding of who is in charge and what our place is as subject to Him, and not visa versa. Again, this is not a *carte blanche* offer of Jesus, but assumes a proper attitude and understanding of the relationship of the asker to the One asked.

In My name. Second, Jesus conditions prayer's answers on the request being in His name (cf. 14:26; 15:16; 16:23-24). In this light, we need to recall that Jesus had previously taught these same disciples how to address prayer (Matt 5:9-15 and Luke 11:1-4). Now He tells them by what authority they may enter the Father's throne room and approach the Mercy Seat of heaven. How often we hear prayers addressed to Jesus and closed "in Jesus' name." Obviously they miss the point.

Prayer "in Jesus' name" is not a magical formula or a blanket promise. Those who think that simply because they finish their prayer or each specific request with the phrase, "In the name of Jesus," that they will be assured of an answer are self-deceived. They are guilty of using His name as a magical formula, of practicing divination, rather than as the kind of prayer Jesus calls for here. Jesus' meaning is that prayer is to be in accordance with all that His name stands for, consistent with His character. Fee correctly assesses the significance of this condition that has been placed on the promise of answered prayer. "Asking 'in my name' means to be concerned for his concerns, to glorify the Father by making him known and making his life available to those who believe" (cf. 15:8; Matt 5:16).[11] This is an authority no Old Testament saint ever had. We need to understand the significance of the progress of revelation in God's Word. We can certainly appreciate the prayers of Old Testament saints, however we are praying on higher ground.

For My Father's glory. Third, that which is asked, and subsequently answered, must have as its purpose the glory of God. The supreme purpose for all that we do is the glory of God—the manifestation of His excellency.[12] Jesus Christ set the pattern for us (see John 13:31-32, also, 17:4). Earlier He had told these same disciples how to glorify the Father (Matt 5:16) by letting their light shine so people could see their good works. Later, in John 15:8 Jesus again tells them how they can glorify the Father. It is the counterpart to 13:35.[13] So, assurance of its answer can be found in ascertaining whether or not God will be glorified. To do that, it must reflect God's (Christ's) character. We are reminded here of James 4:3, "You ask and do not receive, because you ask amiss, that you may spend *it* on your pleasures."

These are all powerful controls over our prayer life and powerful determiners of whether or not our prayers will be answered. Jesus was promising His men, and us, great power through Him, but with clear limitations. That power was limited to His character and purpose. It was never intended to be subject to our whims and desires.

14:14. "If you ask anything in My name, I will do it.[14]

Jesus restates the promise as a conditional sentence once again, which allows for the possibility of our not asking.[15] He is saying by this, "If (and you may or may not do it) . . . then this will happen if you do, but won't if you don't." Jesus will act on our requests. If we choose not to request His enablement, then He will leave us powerless and unproductive. This idea will be expanded in the vine-branch analogy later in the evening.

Notice, Jesus again repeats "in my name." And, as said earlier, this short phrase contains a wealth of content. It is *the* condition that determines the response of God (Christ or the Father) to every request. Jesus had taught them how to address prayer (Matt 6:9 and Luke 11:2). Some believe that prayer should only be to the Father. This is certainly appropriate because it maintains the principle of submission within the triune Godhead. Yet, we may not want to make this an absolute rule in the light of the words of Jesus in these last two verses.

Benefits of Obedience
14:15-24

Jesus turns from the promise of greater things through answered prayer that reflects His character, to the issue of obedience. Jesus seems to like to use the inclusio as a method of teaching. We see several of them in the upper room. For example, John 13:34 and 15:17 form an inclusio with the commandment to love on another. Then, 13:35 and 15:8 form another one with the topic of being Jesus' disciples. In the previous instruction of 14:1-12, an inclusio may be formed by the phrase "believe in Me." Now, we have another one developing this section by the phrase, "love Me," which occurs in verses fifteen, twenty-one, twenty-three, and twenty-four. This is related to keeping His commandments. *And what is His commandment? We are to love one another* (13:35 and 15:12). Stop and think for a moment. Can you even begin to imagine the potential impact of obedience to this commandment? The way we show our love to Jesus is by loving one another. This proves we are His disciples (15:8; compare NASB) and glorifies the Father. Much is contingent on our obedience, as will be seen below. But first Jesus brings up the issue of motivation.

As we enter into this discussion of the benefits of obedience, we would do well to think of the great words in that classic hymn, "Trust and Obey."

When we walk with the Lord in the light of His Word,

What a glory He sheds on our way!

While we do His good will He abides with us still,

And with all who will trust and obey.

Trust and obey, for there's no other way,

To be happy in Jesus, but to trust and obey.

14:15. "If you love Me, keep My commandments.

For the first time in the Gospel of John, Jesus talks to the apostles about their love for Him. This is very significant in light of all that He has said about His love for them and their love for each other (John 13:34, 35). But, now, as He again moves to the issue of His commandments, the principle one being to love one another (13:34-35), He must address them concerning their personal attitudes and motives.[16] In His desire to *lift* them to greater heights, Jesus has been telling them more about God—His triune person and His works. Jesus knows this truth will have its full effect in their lives (cf. 15:3). And in this portion of their instruction, He directs them to another essential element of their spiritual life, their attitude toward Him.

After raising the question of their love for Him, Jesus then commands them to obey Him as evidence of that love.[17] Jesus' use of "if" in this verse is another conditional sentence and implies that they may or may not love Him.[18] Thus, He is saying in essence, "If you love Me (and you may or may not, then you are obligated to and I expect you to) keep My commandments." John later expands on this principle in 1 John 3:11—5:3. Our love for Christ is a result of His demonstrated love for us and is demonstrated by the practical ways we show love for other Christians.

We need to be careful not to lose the centrality of Jesus' words in John 13:34-35 in this whole evening's discourse. That was their problem when they came to the meeting (Luke 22:24). They did not love anyone but themselves and Jesus is giving them the solution. Their obedience in love for one another will demonstrate their love for Christ and glorify the Father. We need to remember also that He is not talking about believing in Him now, but loving Him. Believing in Him brings regeneration (John 1:12; 3:16; 5:24, etc.) but keeping His commandments demonstrates our love and secures His blessing. This idea will be repeated later to His newly designated "friends" in chapter fifteen where we move to a new level of personal intimacy.

The basic point of this verse, then, is that Jesus says that the one who loves Him can now know what He expects of him, namely, obedience. It seems that we as New Testament believers need to understand the blessing and cursing principle as it relates to God's children. This is spelled out in God's relationship with Israel in Deuteronomy 28-30. There the recipients of the Abrahamic Covenant are given promises and warnings in the Mosaic Covenant that effect their enjoyment of the Abrahamic promises. In particular, their enjoyment of the land of promise depends entirely on their obedience to God's commands. Can you imagine only two men of that generation actually entered the land of promise? And later in Israel's history, the descendents of those who entered the land lost their enjoyment of the land in the Babylonian captivity for their disobedience.

For the New Testament believer, the same is true (cf. Rom 11:22-24; Heb 3:7—4:13). We are given a multitude of promises and blessings from God, including a relationship with Him that permits us access into the very Holy of Holies of heaven through our great High Priest, Jesus. But, behind enjoyment of those blessings and privileges given us freely by God rests a multitude of commandments, expectations. Both in the present and the future our enjoyment of God's blessings is not automatic. It depends on our fellowship with Him. And that fellowship results from a right relationship with Him that is predicated not only on faith, but on obedience as well. And, it is His commandments that we are to obey.

Further, our obedience is not automatic, even when we say we "love" Him. In that light, we can also ask, Is there love when I don't obey? Not really. Interestingly, Jesus does not command us to love Him, but to obey Him. But without love for the Lord and love of the brethren, there will not be obedience; we will not have the necessary motivation to obey. In fact, it is fair to say that when I do not keep His commandments I am not loving Him. That is the way I love Him. Love is a response, not a position. If I am not exercising love, I am not obeying and visa versa. Leon Morris' observation is appropriate at this point. He notes that John's use of the term "love" in the Gospel is not as an abstract emotion, but as "something intensely practical. It involves obedience."[19]

This then sets the stage for the first promise of the Holy Spirit in the upper room. This verse serves as a "hinge" sentence between two portions of Jesus' instruction. By a hinge, we mean that it links the previous section of instruction with what is about to follow. He has taught about His relation to the Father. Now he introduces them to the Spirit and His relation to Him.

The Promise of the Spirit
14:16-20

This is the first of five discussions by Jesus of the ministry of the Holy

Spirit this evening. Here Jesus begins by describing the Spirit as "another Helper" and promises that He will abide in them forever. Next in John 14:26 He promises that the Spirit will teach them and remind them of all that He taught them. The third revelation about the Holy Spirit comes in 15:26-27 where Jesus describes Him as the Spirit of truth who proceeds from the Father and says that His role will be to testify of Jesus. Then in 16:7 Jesus says that He will send the Spirit to them and describes His convicting ministry. Finally, in 16:13-14 He calls Him again the Spirit of truth and promises that He will guide them into all the truth as He glorifies Christ.

Jesus promises the Spirit as someone who will be their "helper." Helper, sometimes transliterated as "Paraclete" (from *paraklētos*), literally means "one called to the side of another" with the secondary notion of counseling, supporting, or aiding. Though it was rarely used as a legal term, "Paraclete" means more than a defense lawyer. In fact, such a use of the term is rare in the extra-biblical literature where it more commonly means "one who appears in another's behalf, mediator, intercessor, helper."[20] As a legal term it referred more to the friend who goes to court with the defendant than to a professional advisor or attorney. The rabbis used the term for an advocate before God, listing things as conversion and good works as a person's "Paraclete." Following New Testament times the term is used by church fathers in more of the legal sense of a helper in court, and only once with a sense of "comforter."[21] Though the use of the term in 1 John 2:1 appears to reflect the more legal aspect of meaning, here in John the focus seems to be more on the "helping" sense of the term.

What is the significance of Jesus' description of the Holy Spirit as our Helper? As Mitchell aptly observes, Jesus' description means that we "have two Advocates—One in heaven pleading my cause at the throne and One in me who pleads my cause and His cause."[22] In 1 John 2:1 we are told of the "Paraclete" work of Christ in heaven on our behalf. Again, in that context He is the righteous friend who has come to our aid, not a defense attorney. Also, Romans 8:26-27 describes the Holy Spirit's helping ministry which enables our effective prayer. This is followed very quickly (Rom 8:31-39) by a description of Jesus' intercessory ministry on our behalf in heaven. Thus we see the continuing ministries of Jesus and the Holy Spirit that Jesus introduced in the upper room.

The following verses grow out of the truths Jesus has just spoken to the eleven as He prepares them for His departure.[23]

14:16. "And I will pray the Father, and He will give you another Helper, that He may abide with you forever,

This verse continues the conditional idea of the previous verse as it introduces the promise of the Holy Spirit as our Helper. This title is given the Holy Spirit only in John's writings (cf. John 14:16; 14:26; 15:26; 16:7; and 1 John 2:1). John's use of the term for Jesus in his epistle is very telling. As he meditated on the significance of Jesus' words in the upper room and wrote his epistle, he chose Jesus' term for the Holy Spirit, identified by Jesus as "another" helper like Himself, to describe Jesus' ministry for us before the Father. He remembered clearly the "alikeness" of the Son and Holy Spirit in their mutual and abiding ministry to believers.

Now Jesus promises the eleven someone like Himself to help them in the coming days. Yet, this promise is conditioned on their love for Him, demonstrated by obedience to His commandments. The condition is love because this sentence continues the apodosis of the previous conditional sentence (the "then" clause). In other words, the condition is "If you love Me." The result is two-fold, involving a command and a promise. The command is for them to keep (obey) His commandments. The promise that follows on that is the giving of the other Helper. This is seen in His use of "and" at the head of this verse that connects the giving of the Helper with their love and obedience.[24] Westcott notes well, "Christ after His departure continues His work for His disciples, and provides for them an abiding Advocate. But the efficacy of His action for them depends upon their fellowship with Him through loving obedience."[25]

The promise made by Jesus is two-fold. He will pray. The Father will give. Jesus' promise to pray (NKJV) to the Father, involves the use of the verb erōtaō rather than aiteō. The term can be used in the sense of prayer, or of someone asking someone for something, a simple request. Jesus' use of this term may indicate that His is a prayer request between equals that anticipates an answer and not a petition from an inferior to a superior.[26] Or it may be an indication of the intimacy of their relationship.[27] His prayer will be efficacious, and the Father will act on their behalf.

Still, Jesus is saying that His request that the Father provide them another Helper in His place whose help is conditioned on whether they obey Him or not. Even so, this is not a veiled threat, but a promise of provision. He knows that if they obey Him, they love Him. He is saying in essence, "You concentrate on obeying Me, and I will take care of the enablement." This shows us where our responsibility lies today. We do not need to worry about whether we can get a second blessing, a fuller bestowal of the Holy

Spirit. We do not need to worry about whether we have enough inner strength to resist sin or serve God. We need only worry about obeying Christ. If we obey Him, He will see our love and provide the strength. This verse is a good reminder to us of both our and God's responsibilities for victorious Christian living.

So, what is Jesus' promise to them and, by application, to us? He promises them another Helper who will help those who are obedient. The term Jesus uses is *allos*, which in some cases means "another of the same kind."[28] What Jesus does not mean by this is that He and the Holy Spirit, the two Paracletes, are the same, identical. At the same time He is also saying that though they are not the same person, they also are not of different natures. Otherwise He would have used *heteros* from which we get our root word "hetero-", as in heterosexual and heterodoxy.

The distinction between the two terms can best be summed up with the idea that *allos* adds whereas *heteros* distinguishes. Also, when He says "another," Jesus is saying that He was the first comforter who had helped them. Fee notes some similarities between Jesus and the Holy Spirit. "As Jesus is 'the truth,' the Paraclete is 'the Spirit of truth'; as the world does not 'see or know' Jesus, so it cannot see or know the Spirit. If Jesus has been with them 'so long' (v. 9), the Spirit 'will be with them forever.'"[29] The difference in ministries between Jesus and the Holy Spirit is that while Jesus was *with* them, the Spirit would be *in* them. Also, the Spirit cannot be crucified since He does not share in flesh and blood and cannot be our representative high priest before God like Jesus (Heb 2:14-18).

Jesus' promise that the Holy Spirit will be with us forever can be combined with Paul's description of the sealing ministry of the Spirit in Ephesians 1:13-14. There He is described as the guarantee that we will receive our inheritance in heaven. We can see from these two key passages that the doctrine of eternal security is implied by this permanent indwelling of the Spirit in believers.

14:17. "even the Spirit of truth, whom the world cannot receive, because it neither sees Him nor knows Him; but you know Him, for He dwells with you and will be in you.

Jesus identifies the other Helper as "the Spirit of truth" who will indwell them. As Jesus has just described Him as "another Helper of the same kind as Me," He now describes this identical Helper with the same characteristic He had assigned to Himself in verse six. As Jesus is *the Truth*, the Holy Spirit is identically the Spirit of truth. The genitive construction translated as "of truth" may be either a descriptive genitive and so mean that He is characterized by truth, or it may be a subjective genitive and communicate the idea that the Spirit communicates truth. Subsequent references to the Holy Spirit by Jesus confirm this second option. In John 14:26 the Spirit teaches. In 15:26-27 He witnesses and testifies. In 16:5 He convicts. And in 16:13 He guides into all truth. This designation, or title, does not mean that the Holy Spirit is just the promise of a presence or inner awareness of truth (an inanimate experience of knowledge) but some*one* to be experienced, "otherwise the promise (in the ensuing verses) of relief from the sense of abandonment is empty."[30] Further, truth is to be a characteristic of His relationship with the disciples. This aspect of Him will be explained in more detail in Jesus' later descriptions of His ministry.

In contrast to them, who will have the Spirit indwelling them forever, the world remains ignorant of Him and is unable to welcome Him. This is reflective of Paul's description of the natural man in 1 Corinthians 2:14-16. The reason for the world's failure to welcome the Spirit is its ignorance of Him. As the world does not recognize Christ, know Him for who He is, it remains in the dark concerning the Spirit as well.

In contrast to the ignorant, rebellious world, Jesus said that the disciples did indeed know the Spirit. The reason they knew Him was because He had been dwelling "with" them and was promised to be "in" them in the future. But what did Jesus mean by this? Is there a significant distinction between the Spirit's ministry before Jesus' ascension and now? Yes. This distinction between the Holy Spirit being "with" and then "in" them indicates a change from the Old Testament economy of selective and temporary indwelling to the New Testament permanent indwelling of all believers.[31] What Jesus is saying is that the Holy Spirit has been at work in their lives. But He is now preparing them for a whole new corporate work of the Spirit that is both individual and corporate.

Before Pentecost there was no corporate indwelling of the Spirit in the community of faith like there is in the body of Christ that began at Pentecost, the birthday of the Church. This change in relationship is a fulfillment of the promise of the New Covenant in Jeremiah 31:31-34 and which is described by Joel (2:28-29) as including the outpouring of God's Spirit on all of His servants.[32] Again, this was fulfilled at Pentecost, as attested by Peter to the nation (Acts 2:16-21). Cook notes well that, "this change in relationship is the key to the believer's *knowing* the Spirit (John 14:17). The reason given . . . as to why Christians may know Him in this indwelling is that 'He abides with you, and will be in you'. . . . The change in prepositions marks a change from nearness to inner presence, and the change in tense from present . . . to future . . . indicates that with the coming of the counselor something that had not hitherto been true was to commence."[33] In the past we have made this an individual relationship whereas the significance of Pentecost relates this promise to the "body" of Christ, the church, as Paul explains in 1 Corinthians 12:12-27. The Holy Spirit's ministry is more corporate than private.

Dwight Hunt, in his thesis on the Paraclete addresses this issue and asks one of the key questions in understanding what Jesus is saying. "How, if He is omnipresent, can the Holy Spirit be given to the disciples or be said to come to them (14:17; cf. 16:7)?"[34] His solution is to recognize these prepositions as "spatial terms, exhibiting the fact that the Spirit 'comes' with *new meaning* to the disciples. . . . Thus, from the point of reference of these men, the Comforter would be seen as 'coming' to them. Their vague notion of the Spirit's work among themselves would be altered at Pentecost to a more precise determination of who He was."[35] He then asks, "What difference can be observed between these two prepositions? The former preposition tells of the relationship that the Spirit had with the disciples (who were still under the Old Testament dispensation) before Pentecost. The latter explains what they can expect after Pentecost. By using para, Jesus was telling them that the Spirit had been "with" them and "in their presence." In the future, however, He would be "within" them (*en*)."[36] Additionally, we should notice that Jesus uses the plural "you" when He makes this promise, again looking more toward the future corporate relationship of the Spirit and the Church at Pentecost created by the baptism in the Spirit which would occur then and henceforth till Jesus returns.

Further, though the first preposition, "with," still carries the sense of association and fellowship, it cannot include the sense of closeness that "in" does with its implication of the blessings that result from indwelling. Thus, "Christians enjoy intimate association with the Holy Spirit; and simultaneously they constitute a dwelling for him."[37] Paul reflects on this when he tells the Corinthian church that they are "the temple of God and the Spirit of God dwells in" them (1 Cor 3:16). Jesus will develop this idea further later in the discussion. Having described the promise of the Holy Spirit and His role as His replacement, Jesus expresses the significance of that revelation in terms of the disciples' immediate need. He explains how it should comfort them in light of His immanent departure.

14:18. "I will not leave you orphans; I will come to you.

Jesus says that the significance of the Holy Spirit's indwelling is that it means, in effect, that though Jesus is going to His Father, He is still not really leaving them. Thus He says, "I will not leave you orphans." Earlier Jesus had referred to the eleven affectionately as "little children" (13:33). Now His use of "orphan" in this verse indicates that He clearly understood the disciples felt that they were about to lose their "natural supporter." Jesus uses "orphan" to describe how they would feel when He died. They had been used to having Him physically present with them and were dependent on His power and presence to protect and guide them just as little children depend on their parents. As they faced a hostile world, His departure made them feel abandoned, powerless, and without direction. So, Jesus now tells them the significance of the Holy Spirit's indwelling. They will have the same companionship, guidance, and protection as they had experienced in His presence.

So, having said, "I am leaving you," Jesus now promises, "I will come to you." But, to what is Christ referring when He says He will come to them? The four possible meanings include: (1) His resurrection appearances; (2) the realization of His presence through the Spirit; (3) His return to take them home; or (4) two or more of these at the same time. The first view certainly fits, having the most immediate fulfillment. Jesus is referring to His return to comfort them following His resurrection. This is evident from what He says in the next few verses and chapters (cf. John 14:19; 16:16, 22).[38]

The second view is supported by the fact that this statement fits with His promise that they would not be without support (i.e., the Paraclete promise is in view). But that does not explain how the coming of the Holy Spirit on Pentecost will turn their present sorrow into joy (16:20), especially in light of the evidence of Scripture. They had *personal* joy long before Pentecost beginning the day of Jesus' resurrection.

The third view does not seem to fit since it relates this statement to His promise to prepare a place for them and then take them to where He is going. The weakness of this is that it would then imply that they would mourn until the rapture of the church or their death. This not only does not fit with what Jesus will say next, but it also does not fit with the data of the post-resurrection appearances of Jesus and the resultant joy and boldness of witness expressed by the disciples. Further it does not fit with the New Testament description of the joyful Christian life.

When Jesus says, "I will come to you," He is intentionally contrasting the experience of the world from that of His disciples in their new relationship with the Holy Spirit. The "world" did not see Him again after the crucifixion, but they did. As was said by Peter in Acts 10:41, Jesus appeared "not to all the people, but to witnesses chosen before by God, to us who ate and drank with Him after He arose from the dead." This also fits best with Jesus' promise in the next verse, "the world will see me no more." Even so, Pentecost is the crucial transition time for their full realization of this promise as evidenced by Acts 1:4-5. After His resurrection Jesus refers to the upcoming promise of the Spirit. Though He was with them again in His resurrection appearances, it was not until the coming of the Holy Spirit at Pentecost that they could say fully that they were not orphaned. Thus, Jesus seems to be referring both to His resurrection appearances – the initial fulfillment of this promise – and to the coming of the Holy Spirit at Pentecost – the complete fulfillment of this promise.

14:19. "A little while longer and the world will see Me no more, but you will see Me. Because I live, you will live also.

The difference between the disciples and the world is explained further by who will see Jesus and who will be excluded from His post resurrection revelation (Acts 10:41). When He says that the world will not see Him, He is clearly referring to His resurrection appearances since in His second coming the world will indeed see Him, as Judge. They will, in fact, all stand in His presence in the Sheep-Goat judgment that precedes the inauguration of His millennial kingdom (Matt 25:31-46). So, this seeing of Jesus must refer to His resurrection appearances, which we know from places like 1 Corinthians 15:5-8 included the saints, but not the unbelieving world. Even so, the disciples clearly did not understand what Jesus meant by this. We see this with the two disciples on the road to Emmaus. They are still puzzled and in need of instruction from Jesus. And, He is still explaining things in Acts 1:4-6. It seems that for the disciples, the lights really do not come on until Pentecost!

This statement is also a clarifying distinction from what Jesus had said to the Jewish leaders earlier. Where He told them that He was leaving and they would not be able to follow Him but would die in their sins, He tells His disciples that they will both see Him again and live! He may be leaving them for a time, but not with the same effect. That leads to another powerful statement of the significance of Jesus' departure and the Spirit's indwelling.

Jesus follows His explanation that they will see Him again with a monumental promise, "Because I live, you will live also." Even so, this promise is not something completely new from Jesus. In John 5:21 He has already said that "the Son gives life to whom He will," and then five verses later says that He has life in Himself (cf. John 11:25). The principle behind this promise, then, is that the life of the Head guarantees the life of the members. This life He promises to His disciples on the basis of His coming resurrection that will be confirmed by His coming to them personally, and then in the person of the Holy Spirit.

14:20. "At that day you will know that I am in My Father, and you in Me, and I in you.

Jesus now tells His men the effect of His coming post-resurrection appearances. They will come to understand the full unity of communion within the Godhead as well as their relationship with God. But when will this occur for them? Jesus' use of "at that day" (en ekeinē tē hēmera) seems to be definite to a specific day. Could this be another reference to His post resurrection appearance or to Pentecost?[39] The context from verse sixteen on is the promise of the Spirit that is obviously Pentecost, not the resurrection. Thus, though with His resurrection appearances some measure of understanding will occur for the eleven, it is not until the full ministry of the Holy Spirit is experienced in their lives that they will fully understand this relationship of mutual abiding.

But what is it that they will understand more fully? Jesus tells them that they will finally come to comprehend the truth of His unity with the Father and theirs with Him and His Father as well. But, what does Jesus mean by each being "in" the other? Also, is it significant that Jesus' use of "you" in this promise is always the plural "you" and not the singular? Hunt properly argues for this being a reference to them as a "collective whole" rather than as individuals. Jesus would abide among the apostles as a group. He would be "with" them more than "in" them.[40] To understand this we need to keep in mind the last words of Jesus (Luke 24, Acts 1). They were still to wait for the coming of the Holy Spirit, the gift from His Father. Again, this is more a reference to the unity of communion rather than to metaphysical union in the sense of mutual indwelling. Though the indwelling of the Holy Spirit is implied in this statement, that is not the focus, as will be seen in Jesus' discussion of His union with the Father through obedience in chapter fifteen. This is a relational idea. Jesus was looking forward to the formation of the Body, the Church. And, in that light, He returns to the question of obedience as it relates to this issue.

CHAPTER EIGHT

CHRIST CALLING FOR OBEDIENCE AND PROMISING HELP
John 14:21-31

God's power is never given indiscriminately. It is never placed at the beck and call of men's egos. Throughout Scripture it is dispensed in the context of obedience as the man or woman empowered by Him followed His instructions. Even Samson, certainly not a model of spirituality and obedience, learned this lesson at the cost of his eyes and his freedom. In the midst of promising His disciples the resources they need to serve Him, Jesus links that help with obedience. Why? Because He has assigned them the greatest task ever given a group of self-centered men. They are to love one another. So, turning to the issue of love once again, He turns their focus to their relationship with Him and God the Father.

Obedience Precedes Fellowship
14:21-24

14:21. "He who has My commandments and keeps them, it is he who loves Me. And he who loves Me will be loved by My Father, and I will love him and manifest Myself to him."
Jesus returns to the issue of His commandment and its relationship to love for Him. Here is the infallible test of love, having and keeping Jesus' commandments. What He says has great significance in the life of the believer, beginning with the disciples and continuing to us today. Keeping Jesus' commandments and loving Him cannot be separated. Jesus says plainly in this verse that keeping His commandments proves our love for

Him. In light of John 13:34-35, the commandment in focus this evening, He is saying that loving one another proves our love for Him. This again, is evidenced by the inclusio of 13:35 and 15:8. This is a corollary, a logical next step, to verse fifteen where Jesus commanded obedience from those who love Him. Here now, He says that keeping His commandment is the indicator and measure of our love.

But He continues the thought further and makes receiving the Father's love contingent on our love for Him, expressed through keeping His commandment, which is to love one another (13:35). We need to realize that this was absolutely crucial to everything—to their mission, to the coming Church, to the kingdom. We can go back to the Disciple's Prayer (Matt 6:9-15) and see how crucial He makes forgiving one another. As a matter of fact, He actually makes our experience of God's forgiveness contingent on our forgiving each other! We tend to lose the import of this today because we are not just eleven, but hundreds of millions. It is love for one another the disciples lack that evening. It is really love for one another Jesus has been talking about. It is, again, love for one another He is looking for when He talks about keeping His commandments. And now, similar to what He said in Matthew 6, He says essentially, "If you want to experience my Father's love, you must love each other." The failure to forgive is a graphic demonstration of the failure to love.

In addition He promises to "manifest" Himself to the disciple who loves, and thus keeps His commandment. This is the greatest apologetic for Christianity. This is what caused Francis Schaeffer to title his message, on John 13:24-25, *The Mark of a Christian*. Notice how all of these men are getting so involved in the accidentals that they are missing the main point. They are not loving one another, but hating each other in their egocentric attitudes and competition for status (cf. 1 John 4:20). But, Jesus envisioned something far different, and so brings them back to the issue of love.

First, Jesus brought their focus back to the issue of how they (and we) were to go about loving Jesus. They were to keep the commandments He had given them.[1] By this Jesus is saying that it is not enough to know His will. The disciple who loves Him will also respond to His will by keeping, obeying, those commandments, the central one being to love the brethren (13:34-35). This having been said, He then describes the benefits an obediently loving disciple will receive as a consequence of that choice.

The experience of the believer who demonstrates his love for Jesus through loving the brethren is that he, in turn, will be loved by God. This shows us that it matters to the Father and Son, in a very personal way, how we respond to one another. And, on the basis of how God works, we see that obedience always brings blessing and disobedience cursing (cf. Deut 28-30). The blessings and cursings offered Israel were not a matter of relationship then and they are not now. Just because they were God's elect nation, blessing was neither automatic nor obligatory on God's part. Just because we are children of God now and have been placed into the body of Christ, the Family of God, blessing is not automatic (cf. Rom 11:11-24).

Experiencing God's love is not automatic, but contingent. As previously noted, we sing the song, "Trust and obey for there is no other way to be happy in Jesus but to trust and obey." But how often do we live it out? Jesus is telling them, and us that, as love for Him is expressed in loving one another, and loving one another in turn causes the Father to love us, loving one another brings blessing in our relationship with God. We can experience God's love by obeying His Son's command to love each other.

But now, some may ask, is this not merited love? Is this not works?[2] The answer to the dilemma is found in Jesus' later instruction, especially in His description of His own relationship with the Father wherein His obedience expresses His love and in turn produces a loving response from the Father.[3] And so the answer is, Yes! But this love is a part of our experience as redeemed saints, part of our sanctification and not our justification. God does not justify by works. The Scriptures are clear on that. But how we live and what we believe and do does indeed effect our sanctification. It has a direct bearing on our *experience* of eternal life's benefits in this life and the life to come.

The Father's love is *experienced* by the obedient believer and, though present to all believers, missed in the *experience* of the disobedient believer. This is the difference between what we often call positional (justification) truths and conditional (sanctification) truths – point versus process. Positionally, we are loved by God because of Jesus' completed work on the cross and the imputation of His righteousness to us. We are justified before God. Conditionally, the daily experience of the believer is affected by his or her confession of sin and obedience to Christ (1 John 1:9). Jesus is discussing *conditional* truths here.

But what did Jesus mean when He said that He would "disclose" Himself to them?[4] This promise by Jesus produced this very question in the mind of at least one of the disciples, and was subsequently explained by Jesus afterwards. So, we will examine this below.

14:22. Judas (not Iscariot) said to Him, "Lord, how is it that You will manifest Yourself to us, and not to the world?"

Judas, the "good guy" one, responded to Jesus' promise of disclosure to His obedient disciples by asking how He was only disclosing Himself to them. Jesus will answer this question more fully in the beautiful allegory of John 15:1-8.[5] Though Jesus' brothers asked a similar question in unbelief (John 7:4), this does not warrant attributing similar unbelief to Judas. Judas was not questioning Jesus' messiahship. There is no indication that his faith or recognition of Jesus as Messiah was in any way shaken by Jesus' statement. Rather, He was trying to fit Jesus' words into his own understanding of the kingdom and of Messiah's reign and thus his own expectations.

Remember, even after the resurrection appearances and forty days of instruction by Jesus, as He was preparing to ascend to heaven in their sight, the disciples were *still* expecting the kingdom to be inaugurated and were *still* asking the same kinds of questions like, "Is it time *now* to restore the kingdom to Israel?" Their faith in Him as Messiah was causing the disciples to attempt to resolve what seemed to them to be contradictory elements in their eschatology and Jesus' instructions. Unlike the Jewish leaders who shared a similar eschatology but rejected Jesus as Messiah when He did not fit their schema, the disciples *were* responding in faith, were *not* rejecting Him as Messiah, but were rather attempting to resolve the apparent contradictions between what they thought was to be expected and what He was saying.

At this point He essentially told them that, where they expected Messiah to make a very public and powerful entrance onto the political scene, He was not going to be manifested as Messiah to the world, but only to them, and not in the way that they think.[6] Any thinking Israelite would immediately pick up on the problem this raised in their anticipation of national deliverance from Roman oppression. And, responding to the new idea, Judas does not ask "why," but "how?" He wants Jesus to explain *how* He is going to manifest Himself to them and not to the world. And, in fact, it is this question that Jesus answers!

14:23. Jesus answered and said to him, "If anyone loves Me, he will keep My word; and My Father will love him, and We will come to him and make Our home with him.

Jesus repeats part of what He has already said, but makes other significant changes. He begins again with the question of loving Him, just as

He had in verse fifteen. But now he changes a few terms from his earlier statement. "You" (the eleven) becomes "anyone" (the church) and "commandments" (*entolē*, exhortations which touch human conduct) are changed to "word" (*logos*, the message as a whole). Further, instead of Him asking the Father who will send the Comforter, He and the Father now make their home with the believer.

By this Jesus promises that He and His Father will abide with anyone who loves Him, evidenced by their keeping His "word."[7] Of interest is Jesus' use of "word" here instead of "commandments."[8] Though this is a more inclusive term and looks at the whole of Jesus' instruction, it still focuses their attention back to what He has been saying that evening. They need to be loving one another and demonstrating that love through servanthood.

Now, how do people understand these words of Jesus'?[9] How does this answer Judas' question? This verse repeats ideas from verses fifteen and twenty-one and links love with keeping His word, which then ties back in with 13:34-35. It takes that link one step farther, though, and talks about its benefit in terms of one's relationship with God, or rather, God's response to the person.

Jesus began His explanation of *how* He would manifest Himself to the disciples and not the world by repeating, in essence, what He had stated earlier, "If anyone loves Me he will keep My word." Remember, in verse fifteen He follows the condition of loving Him with a command to obey. In verse twenty-one He uses obedience as the indicator of one's love for Him. But, here His statement must be seen in relation to what Judas asked and what He is about to say in response. This is best seen as a condition of what follows. This is another (third class) conditional sentence in which the "if" clause allows either thing to be true. If someone loves Jesus, he or she will keep His word. If they do not love, they will not keep. It is as simple as that. But, there is now the additional element of what follows. Those who love Him will also experience what follows. Those who do not, will not. Yes, this is the "why" portion of Jesus' "how" answer. Jesus is saying here "who" will experience this manifestation He is talking about by telling why some will be included and some will be excluded.

These verses are a link between John 13:34-35 and 15:1-8. The command to love one another was given to disciples whose self-centeredness was evidenced in their words (Luke 22) and actions (John 13). Their response to Christ's command (13: 34-35) would determine their fruit or lack of it, and Christ's blessing or lack of it (15:1-8). Jesus is working up to what He is going to say in 15:3, 7, etc. There is progress in these verses. He is working to a conclusion and He will make it vivid with the allegory of the vine and the branches. In verse twenty-one we had loving, obedient children. Here Father and Son take up abode (cf. 15:5). This is more than indwelling. It is a fullness of residence that involves mastery of the house (cf. Eph 3:17).

The blessing of obedience is that God the Father responds to such loving obedience with the benefits of conditional experiences of His love (experienced in our sanctification) that are based on our positional blessings in Christ (possessed in our justification). In fact, as Cook notes, God the Father "loves the believer as He loves the Son"[10] What Jesus is saying in this short statement is that believers can experience and enjoy the same quality of relationship with the Father as He did by simply following His example. This idea is going to be developed further later in the conversation, and so will be discussed in greater detail below. But, having said that the Father will love the believer, Jesus is now ready to move from the "why" to the "how" of Judas' question.

Jesus tells Judas, and the others, that the way in which He will manifest Himself to them and not the unbelieving world, is by He and His Father making their abode *with* them. These are stunning words and had to be a shocking revelation.

Does this mean that all three persons of the Godhead indwell the believer, or only the Holy Spirit?[11] Though many people understand Jesus to be describing the metaphysical union of God and the believer through the Holy Spirit's sealing and filling ministry, He actually does not say that He and the Father will use the believer as their residence, that they will live "in" the believer. Rather, the preposition (*meta*) Jesus uses carries the idea of being "with" someone. It is a reference to the indwelling ministry of the Holy Spirit, though, because of His reference to the Holy Spirit's indwelling the believer in verse seventeen and what He says about the Spirit's ministry in the verses that follow. This promise became a reality for the disciples in Acts 2 on the day of Pentecost when the Holy Spirit filled each of them, thereby empowering them to be Jesus' witnesses. Thus Jesus is referring to the triune God's corporate indwelling of the Church, Christ's body (cf. 1 Cor 12:13 – "in one Spirit were all baptized into one body." See also Eph 4:1-6).

The best answer comes from recognizing that Jesus' use of the preposition "with" does not require that all three persons be present *inside* the believer.

Rather, only the Holy Spirit indwells us as He seals us (Eph 1:13-14). The Father and Son dwell with us in the person of the Spirit, but they themselves are located in heaven.[12] At any rate, this is a statement that necessitates a Trinitarian understanding of the Godhead.[13] Even so, the Spirit's ministry in us is such that the New Testament authors, especially Paul, could speak of every member of the trinity indwelling us. Thus two of Paul's favorite phrases are "Christ in you" and "in Christ" (used over 80 times). He also teaches in Colossians 1 that the Godhead bodily indwells us. And, one of the metaphors of the church is the "temple"—the dwelling place of God. It is the presence of the church that is likely the "restrainer" as the dwelling of the Holy Spirit in 2 Thessalonians 2:7.

Unlike verse two where the abode (same term as this verse) is our future home in heaven and the promise is yet to be fulfilled, at least for those of us who have not departed this life, this verse is fulfilled in our present experience.[14] This promise from Jesus looks forward to the birthday of the church together with all the resulting fireworks at Pentecost. It is now experienced by the church as the body of Christ, baptized by Him into one body, which body is secured and protected by the Holy Spirit until the day of the redemption of the body (Eph 1:13-14) and including every believer (1 Cor 12:13).

The problem Judas was having resulted because he was trying to fit Jesus' promise of *selective* self-manifestation with his understanding of the eschatological promises to Israel which involve the Messiah's *full* revelation and conquest of the world in such places as Daniel, Joel, and Ezekiel. He and the others did not really understand "the promise of the Father" (cf. Acts 1:4-5 and 8). The Church was still a mystery. Jesus, on the other hand, was anticipating the Church, His Bride, who is being developed today. He pointed them to the outworking of the New Covenant promised in Jeremiah 31 and mentioned earlier by Him in the institution of the Lord's Supper as a memorial of His coming death. They still did not understand all of this. He was essentially telling them what He would later say just before His ascension, "Do not get ahead of schedule. There are other things which must happen first!"

It may be possible that this statement on Jesus' part is similar to His promise in Revelation 3:20, which is addressed to the church at Laodicea, not unbelievers. When He says that He is standing outside, knocking, and wants in, He cannot be talking about their need for regeneration, but about having communion with those who are regenerate. Their hearts must be right for Him to fellowship with them. We see this truth developed further in John's first epistle. There he again talks about our fellowship with the Father and the Son that is dependent on our proper attitude toward sin (we confess rather than deny it), our commitment to love the brethren (expressed in actively helping those in need), and sound doctrine (right thinking about Jesus).

Throughout First John the issue is not whether the readers are saints or not, but whether they are living like saints. It is not about how to find out if they have eternal life, but about how to experience that life here and now.[15] Even so, here, the experience of God's abiding presence (conditional truth) is dependent on obedience. Thus, this is not just a reference to the coming of the Spirit at Pentecost, though the fulfillment of this promise began then. It includes the daily experience of the believer in the body of Christ as well. It is a part of the abiding relationship that He will discuss further in the analogy of the vine and the branches.

14:24. "He who does not love Me does not keep My words; and the word which you hear is not Mine but the Father's who sent Me.

Jesus now says negatively what He has said twice positively. Where He had said that love is evidenced by obedience, He now says that lack of love for Him is evidenced by disobedience. One who does not love Him will not obey Him.[16] Of interest is the warning to the church of Ephesus (Rev 2:1-7). Though an orthodox church characterized by service to the Lord and perseverance in the faith, it is criticized by Jesus for leaving its first "love" and is warned of losing its lampstand (God removing His endorsement and blessing from them). Jesus wants obedience for the right reasons, obedience from the heart.

The final statement of Jesus is also significant, especially in light of what He is going to say later about the ministry of the Holy Spirit in imparting His word to the disciples. He is going to tell them that the Spirit does not speak on His (the Spirit's) own initiative. This aspect of His ministry will make Him like Jesus with regard to the Father's words. There is implied in this statement that what Jesus has been saying is not His own words, but those of the Father, that they must be taken seriously, as coming from God. His reference to the Father as the one who sent Him also establishes again the chain of authority and the seriousness of His instruction. To reject what He says is to reject the One who sent Him, namely, the Father.

Two Promises: The Helper and Peace
14:25-31

Promising the Helper, the Holy Spirit, Jesus also promises them peace as He departs in loving obedience to the Father. These verses serve to summarize Jesus' thoughts up to this point. In these we have the second of the five Paraclete promises given by Jesus to the disciples.[17]

14:25. "These things I have spoken to you while being present with you.

Jesus' introduction of this second Paraclete promise is another "hinge" verse (connecting and relating what precedes with what follows). It moves us from Jesus' discussion of obedience being an expression of our love for Him to the ministry of the Holy Spirit through whom the Father and Son indwells the believer. "These things" refers to Jesus' words to them that evening, what He had just said. It sets the stage for the next promise of the Holy Spirit, namely that He will teach them and remind them of what Jesus had taught them. This is also another reminder that He is leaving them soon. In that light, He again speaks words of comfort to His troubled disciples.

14:26. "But the Helper, the Holy Spirit, whom the Father will send in My name, He will teach you all things, and bring to your remembrance all things that I said to you.

Jesus again promises the Holy Spirit as a Helper to them in His absence.[18] Here He says several significant things about the person and ministry of the Spirit. He begins His second description of the Spirit's ministry by saying that the Father would send Him to them in His name.

We see here an example of the sameness of this Helper who has already been identified as "another of the same kind" as Jesus. As Jesus did not come in His own name, but was sent by the Father, so too the Holy Spirit did not come in His own name and was also sent by the Father. And, as Jesus was the Father's representative to the disciples, now the Holy Spirit similarly serves as Jesus' representative.[19]

In His description of the Holy Spirit in this verse and elsewhere in the upper room, Jesus uses a term that argues strongly for the personality, the personhood, of the Holy Spirit. Orthodox Christianity has affirmed that the Holy Spirit is not a force, influence, or some other inanimate element, but a person, the third member of the Godhead. He is as much a person as both God the Father and God the Son. Here, while Greek has masculine, feminine, and neuter pronouns, Jesus refers to the Spirit with a pronoun in the masculine gender. But, its antecedent (the word the pronoun relates to) is not pneuma (translated as "Spirit") but *paraklētos* (translated as "Helper"). But, lest someone attempt to use that as an argument against the personality of the Spirit, *paraklētos* (Helper) is an adjective being used as a noun.

In Greek, adjectives do not have a single gender, but have forms for all three genders and are given the gender appropriate to the word they modify or replace. Thus, if the Holy Spirit was not a person and Jesus wanted to deny the personality of the Spirit, He could have used the neuter form of "helper" rather than the masculine. As a substantive (a word being used in place of a noun), one would expect Jesus to use its neuter form since "spirit" (pneuma) is a neuter word. Also, only a neuter term would be appropriate if it were to express the idea of an impersonal force. Interestingly, Jesus did not change the gender of "spirit," nor did He change the gender of those pronouns that related back to spirit. He used good grammar. Rather, He chose the form of "helper" as a masculine form in order to communicate His personality unquestionably.[20] So, again establishing His personhood, Jesus goes on to describe His ministry.

The Holy Spirit is not only coming to abide in them and help them like Jesus had, but He is also coming to teach them. This raises the question concerning whether this promise is for all believers or only for the disciples? The key to understanding Jesus' promise in this verse is to see "whom" He is addressing when He says this. This is markedly different from what He says in His prayer in chapter seventeen where He prays for His disciples and then for those who would believe through them in later generations. Here, when Jesus says "you," He indicates that the promise is to the eleven. Also, the content of what is promised necessarily involves the eleven. He says that the Spirit would not only teach them, but would remind them of things He had said to *them*.[21]

Necessarily, then, only those who had already been taught by Him could be reminded of what He had said. This is likely the background to the disciples' selection of Joseph and Matthias as candidates to replace Judas in Acts 1:15-26. They needed someone who could speak with apostolic authority, which meant someone who had heard all of Jesus' teachings.[22] In short, we can trust their testimony, contained in the Gospels, precisely because of this promise from Jesus to them that the Holy Spirit would remind them. Their reports of the teachings of Jesus, including those given in this upper room, are reliable and accurate, and not merely musings or paraphrases on what might have been said. John 2:19-22; 12:16; and 20:9 provide us with examples of the Spirit's ministry of reminding them. Having said all this, that the promise is only applicable to those in the upper room with Jesus, there is still "a legitimate secondary application that concerns Christians today. The Holy Spirit comes to live with us and be in us (14:17), too; and he helps us to call to mind, as we need them, the words of Scripture we have first learned."[23]

14:27. "Peace I leave with you, My peace I give to you; not as the world gives do I give to you. Let not your heart be troubled, neither let it be afraid.

Within the context of promising the Helper to them a second time, Jesus next promises them His peace. This is the first of three blessings given to the disciples by Jesus that evening, in fact, offered to all believers who will accept them by faith. Here He offers His peace. Later He gives us His love (John 15:9-10) and His joy (15:11). Unlike the previous verse which we see directed to the apostolic band (though still having application to every believer), this promise is directed to all believers.[24] Its applicability to all believers comes precisely because it is a product of Jesus' presence and faith in Him and not a specific revelatory ministry of the Spirit. We are to respond to the world and to life with these three attitudes. But, first, let us learn about the kind of peace Jesus gives.

This verse is, again, a very significant statement of Jesus that calls for serious consideration by Christians. We must ask ourselves, "Am I experiencing Christ's peace? And what is it anyway?"[25] The world's peace is temporal; it seems best at the beginning but disintegrates as time goes on. Christ's peace is eternal; it grows stronger with time and faith. Whereas Christ's peace was given by Him and expresses a hope, the world's peace is only good enough to use in a greeting. Where Christ's peace is internal and independent of circumstances, the world's peace is completely dependent on circumstances. Where Christ's peace is a positive blessing and the result of a right relationship with God (a Hebrew concept), the world's peace is merely the absence of war or conflict (a Greek concept). Carson notes well, "The *pax Romana* ('Roman peace') was won and maintained by a brutal sword; not a few Jews thought the messianic peace would have to be secured by a still mightier sword. Instead it was secured by an innocent man who suffered and died at the hands of the Romans, of the Jews, and of all of us."[26]

In light of the promise of the Holy Spirit and of His peace, Jesus again commands them to remain calm. His words in the second half of this verse are almost identical to those in verse one. Jesus knew that they were deeply disturbed by each mention of His coming departure. But He could not remain silent about it. He had important things to teach them. Thus, He commands them again to calm themselves and trust Him. In time they will understand.

In time they will have the enablement of the Holy Spirit. In the meantime, they are to keep trusting Him. And following His resurrection, what were Jesus' first words to the disciples? "Peace be with you." And what did He find them doing? They were hiding from the Jews, cowering in fear, filled with anxiety over the danger they now felt as they faced a hostile world without Jesus there to fend for them. Fortunately, those words of Jesus' proved to be more than a mere greeting. They became the characteristic of the persecuted church in the first chapters of Acts as those same men boldly confronted a hostile world in the power of the Holy Spirit. Peter and John's boldness in Acts 4 and Paul's peace in Philippians 4:7 are examples of this promise fulfilled.[27]

14:28. "You have heard how I said to you, 'I am going away and coming back to you.' If you loved Me, you would rejoice because I said, 'I am going to the Father,' for My Father is greater than I.

Having promised them the Helper who will remind them of what He is even then teaching them, and having called on them to calm their hearts, Jesus returns once again to the issue of His departure. He reminds them again of what He has already said. He is going to leave them for a time and then return. Now, though, He turns the tables on them and confronts their selfish anxiety. Instead of being worried about how His departure would affect them, they should have been rejoicing at Jesus' good fortune. Here His use of the Greek "if" construction carries the sense of, "If you loved Me, *and you do not, then* you would rejoice, *and you are not!*"[28] In other words, Jesus basically says that their sorrow is not an evidence of their love for Him, but of their failure to love Him! They are not concerned with what is best for Him, but what they think is best for them. They are being as selfish with regard to Him as they had been earlier that evening in their dealings with one another and their failure to love each other through humble service.[29] None of these were characteristic of the disciples at this point.

So far this evening Jesus has spoken conditionally to the disciples twelve times. This is a good point to pause and bring all these conditional sentences together so that we can catch a glimpse of what Jesus has been saying to the eleven.

Four times He uses the "if" to affirm something which is assumed to be true. First He says, "If (since) I then, *your* Lord and teacher, have washed your feet, you also ought to wash one another's feet" (John 13:14). Serving one another is thereby presented as an expectation and obligation from Christ. Second, He affirms that they already knew what He was teaching them when He says, "If (since) you know these things, blessed are you if you do them" (13:17). Interestingly, the second "if" in this sentence is the optional if, by which Jesus affirms that they may or may not do the things they know. The third time He uses this construction is to affirm God's glorification in the Son. He says, "If (since) God is glorified in Him" (the Son of Man), "God will also glorify Him in Himself, and glorify Him immediately" (13:32). Finally, He affirms their knowing Him when He says, "If (since) you had known Me, you would have known My Father also" (14:7).

Twice Jesus uses "if" to deny something, to declare its falseness. First, He assures the eleven, "In My Father's house are many mansions; if *it were* not *so*, I would have told you" (14:2). With this He actually is saying, "It is so that there are many rooms in My Father's house." The second instance of using this construction is the present verse (14:28) in which He tells the disciples that they really do not love Him.

Finally, Jesus uses the optional "if" construction seven times. Again, this form of the "if" clause leaves open the possibility of it being either true or false, with the resulting second clause being true or false, depending on the truth or falsity of the first. So, to Peter He says, "If I do not wash you, you have no part with Me" (13:8). Participation with Christ is thereby made contingent on his submitting to Jesus' footwashing. Again, in 13:17, the second "if" makes blessing dependent on doing. Then, proof to the world of our being His disciples is made contingent on our love for one another. "By this all will know that you are My disciples, if you have love for one another" (13:35). Jesus' promise to return again and receive us is made contingent on His going and preparing a place for us. "And if I go and prepare a place for you, I will come again and receive you to Myself; that where I am, you may be also" (14:3). Answered prayer is made contingent on asking in Jesus' name. "If you ask anything in My name, I will do *it*" (14:14). Then, twice He expresses the condition of our keeping His commandments being our love. "If you love Me, keep My commandments.

And I will pray the Father, and He will give you another Helper" (14:15-16). "If anyone loves Me, he will keep My word; and My Father will love him, and We will come to him and make Our home with him" (14:23).

In chiding them for their selfishness, Jesus reveals another theologically significant truth to His disciples that has caused great debates to rage within and without the church. His Father is "greater than" Him. But what does He mean by this? Is He less God than the Father? Is His deity diminished in some way? Jesus' affirmation of subordination in this verse must be seen in light of John 10:30, "I and *My* Father are one," and 14:9, "He who has seen Me has seen the Father." Two key New Testament passages help us understand how Jesus can be God, on one hand, and still subordinate to the Father, on the other.[30] First, Philippians 2:5-11 teaches clearly that Jesus was equal with God when He (Jesus) humbled Himself, "made Himself of no reputation," by "taking the form of a bondservant, coming in the likeness of men." Jesus humbled Himself by adding humanity to His deity and choosing to humble Himself. He submitted Himself. The Father did not bring Him into submission.

When Jesus says the Father is "greater than" Himself, it is a relationship Jesus chose and entered into of His own free will. But why would He? Because He added humanity to His deity. And, as a human, as the One taking the form of a bondservant, He accepted the responsibilities entailed in that role. All of humanity owes God submission and worship. Therefore, as a human, Jesus willingly gives to the Father that which is His due from every human being. Second, we see this again in Hebrews 2:16-17, where "in all things He had to be made like *His* brethren" in order to serve as our High Priest, as our representative before the Father.

As God, Jesus could not represent us as our advocate (1 John 2:1). Only in His humanity could He do this. But, the High Priest, no matter how exalted, always serves a subordinate role to God. Jesus *cannot* serve as High Priest without taking a role in which the Father is "greater" than He! But, this does not require inferiority. Jesus has already demonstrated through His washing the disciples' feet that He can assume a servant's role without relinquishing His true identity. As He said to them earlier, "You call Me Teacher and Lord, and you say well, for so I am" (John 13:13). As Teacher and Lord He served them by assuming the dress and posture of a servant. As God Almighty, He serves the Father as the Son by assuming the dress and posture of a servant, a human being. In that way the Father is greater while Jesus never ceases to be God.[31]

14:29. "And now I have told you before it comes to pass, that when it comes to pass, you may believe.

Having chided them for their selfishness, Jesus returns again to His purpose behind all that He is teaching them that evening. Their faith needs to be strengthened and He is preparing them to survive the trauma that is about to beset them.[32] Thus we see again Jesus' ability to not only see the future and see into the hearts of men, but to see into their hearts in the future.

But what did Jesus mean when He said He was telling His disciples these things so that they might "believe"? Recall that this is the word with which He began this chapter. There He had told them, "believe also in Me." Then He began to enlarge their understanding of His person and mission. The key to all of it is "believe." Westcott sees Jesus' use of the term "believe" to include "all the special manifestations of faith."[33] Remember, the disciples did not need to believe for salvation. They were already regenerate. They had already believed in Him as Messiah. Rather, He is talking about their faith in the sense of trusting Him when things did not seem to be going His way. Their faith in Him as Messiah was indeed about to be challenged as He went to the cross, in violation of everything they believed to be true and possible for the Messiah.

Jesus' whole point is not that He is telling them these things to preserve their faith. No, it is going to be shattered. Rather, He is telling them these things so that after they have all come to pass, then their faith will be restored and they will have a more mature, complete, faith. We see this same idea in Luke 22:32, "I have prayed for you that your faith (belief) should not fail." The faith Jesus refers to here is not the faith of someone seeking salvation, but the faith a believer needs to continue living faithfully for the Lord. He is talking about the faith we need to live daily for the Lord and trust Him in every area of our lives as we face trials and tribulations.

Our life in Christ begins by faith in the promises of God and our life in Christ continues by faith in the promises of God. All the way through it is faith alone in Christ alone. Thus we are not sanctified in a different way than we are justified. All the way through it is faith in the promises of God. This chapter of John's Gospel began with the issue of faith in the promises of God, believing, and ends with the disciples being given more things to believe. This is the same teaching that Paul gave in Galatians 3:1-3.

14:30. "I will no longer talk much with you, for the ruler of this world is coming, and he has nothing in Me.

Jesus again reminds His men, time is short. Even as He speaks, Judas has met with the Jewish leaders and a cohort of soldiers is being organized in order to affect His arrest. Jesus identifies the action of Judas with the one motivating him, namely Satan, whom He calls the ruler of this world. Laney notes that the term translated "ruler" is *archōn* and "speaks of one who is a ruler or chief over others, referring to Satan's power over unbelievers and unseen spiritual forces."[34]

We are reminded of Satan's position as ruler of the world when he tempted Jesus. Jesus never questioned his possession of the kingdoms of the earth. And, in fact, Satan will continue to rule the kingdoms of the earth until Jesus returns at the end of the Great Tribulation and establishes His own kingdom. Then He will bind this world's present ruler for a thousand years before administering His final judgment of an eternity in the Lake of Fire. In fact, today in our churches we need to be careful in our teaching and singing not to attribute the present situation to Christ. He is not reigning on earth now (Rev 3:21). Satan is reigning.

This verse reflects one aspect of the double sense of "comprehend" in the first verses of the Gospel (John 1:5) where John says that "the light shines in the darkness, and the darkness did not comprehend it." The term for comprehend (*katalambanō*), can mean either "to understand" in the intellectual sense, or "to overcome" in the sense of to defeat or conquer. The theme's double meaning is developed throughout the Gospel with people either misunderstanding Jesus or trying to destroy Him, or (usually) both. Thus when Jesus says here that the ruler of this world also does not have power over Him, the "mastery/victory" aspect of its meaning is evident in Jesus' words wherein He declares Satan's attempt and failure in His coming crucifixion. Similarly, in John 16:33, Jesus will encourage His followers with the words, "I have overcome the world," using the unambiguous term for victory, *nikaō*.[35]

But Jesus says more than that Satan is making his move to destroy Him. He says that Satan is wasting his time. He says this by noting, in contrast to Judas, Satan "had nothing" in Him. Carson notes that "the words in the original literally rendered are, "He has nothing in me"; though written in Greek, they echo a Hebrew idiom which means, 'He has no claim upon me.' The prince of this world could not possibly have a claim upon Jesus, for Jesus is not of this world. . . . The claim the devil has on all other human beings is their sin, their guilt; but Jesus is guiltless."[36] Further, "The devil could have a hold on Jesus only if there were a justifiable charge against Jesus. Jesus' death would then be his due, and the devil's triumph."[37] F. F. Bruce relates the significance of the phrase as that "there is nothing in Jesus that he can lay hold of so as to gain an advantage over him."[38]

Satan's attempt at conquering Jesus here is like a man attempting to pull the fog from a riverbank with a meat hook. He can flail his hook through the fog all he wants, but it will never take hold of it and move it even an inch. The hook has no ability to exercise authority over the fog. In the same way, Satan, in his coming and in his attack on Jesus, had no point of control. Though Jesus had taken on humanity and the form of a bondservant, He had not participated in Adam's sin like the rest of humanity. He was not of this world, but from God. He was not, and had never been, a citizen of Satan's domain. Satan's authority did not extend to Him. And, even in dying, it was Jesus' authority being expressed, His right to lay down His life and take it again (John 10:17-18), not Satan's. Satan had nothing in Him. Jesus was in control.

14:31. "But that the world may know that I love the Father, and as the Father gave Me commandment, so I do. Arise, let us go from here."

Having stated that Satan had no rights over Him and, by implication, that His death was outside of the control of Satan, Jesus gives the real reason for how the night was going to turn out. This reason is introduced with a strong "but." In contrast to what would appear to be the case, that Satan had gained the upper hand through the agency of Judas and the Jewish leaders, Jesus was about to go through the process of death voluntarily and in obedience to His Father.

We see here the full outworking of the principle of love leading to obedience as it applied to Jesus' relationship with the Father.[39] In so doing, He becomes a model for us (cf. Phil 2:5-11). Carson notes well, "As the love of Jesus' disciples for their Master is attested by their obedience (vv. 15, 21, 23), so also does the Son Himself remain in his Father's love by keeping his commandments (8:29; 15:10). Jesus' love for and obedience toward his Father are supremely displayed in his willingness to sacrifice his own life."[40] Yes, Jesus' obedience is proof of His love of His Father. His love is also seen in this chapter by the fact that He mentions the name of His Father twenty-three times in this chapter alone. "No place in the entire Word of God has as much reference to the Father" as this chapter.[41]

Jesus' final statement in this chapter has been the cause of much debate over whether and how the Upper Room Discourse should be divided. Many see this being used as a literary device by John to end one discourse and begin another. This misses the continuity seen in the following extended metaphor that is the figurative presentation of what was given non-figuratively or plainly in chapter fourteen.[42] Jesus has been doing in straight prose what He will vividly do in poetry in John 15:1-8.

Why would John include this statement here if he did not intend to make a break in the discourse? Because Jesus said this at this time and he is reporting the evening's conversation accurately. This is another example of the eyewitness nature of John's Gospel in that he remembers details which only an eyewitness could report and which, in their reporting, contribute nothing to the flow of thought or "argument" of the text. Therefore, the instruction of Jesus in the next two chapters should be seen as a continuation of what He has already said and not as a separate dialogue (For a fuller discussion of the issue, see Appendix 6, "The Relationship of Jesus' Command to Depart to the Structure of the Discourse."). In fact, as we go through these next two chapters we will again see the same themes cropping up as Jesus repeats key issues which He wants His men to understand before they face the rest of the night and the next three days.

When we ended chapter thirteen, it was disastrous news for Peter. He would deny Jesus. But as we come to the end of chapter fourteen we see that the master Disciplemaker does not mention the sin again that Peter will commit that night. Rather, He has spoken entirely about what the Father, the Son, and the Holy Spirit will do for them. Thus He focuses their attention, not on their present or forthcoming problems, but on the tremendous resources that they have in the Father, Son, and Holy Spirit. What a lesson this is for us who too often tend to rub the face of the sinner in his sin in order to bring him to confession and repentance.

Christ understood very well the principle that right acting begins by right thinking, and right thinking begins by thinking right about what God is like. Having said that now in straightforward prose declarations, the writer now turns to the more graphic picturesque portrayal of the same truth in figurative language. In both cases, however, He is doing the same thing. He is *lifting* them to a higher level of thinking knowing that every wrong action we ever perform is based on wrong thinking about what God is like (cf. Ps 3:3).

CHAPTER NINE

CHRIST ILLUSTRATING PREVIOUSLY TAUGHT TRUTHS
John 15:1-5

Jesus has been *lifting* the eleven disciples up with words of truth and encouragement. He has done this with words of prose—straightforward, plain, literal, declarative propositions. Now, in chapter fifteen He reinforces it with vivid figurative poetic pictures. The instruction contained in this chapter is a continuation of Jesus' instruction as He and the eleven depart from the upper room and move toward the Garden of Gethsemane. We see this in the completion of the inclusio of John 13:34 and 15:17 along with the inner inclusio of 13:35 and 15:8. Again, though some would see these verses beginning a new discourse which moves beyond or further illuminates the issues of the "first," this is a continuation of a single unit of instruction from Jesus to His disciples as He prepares them for the horrors which are about to follow. This is Jesus the master Disciplemaker in action, illustrating and explaining what He has been saying until His pupils have learned enough to continue forward.

When we place these words of instruction into the context of Luke 22, we see that Jesus is indeed continuing to prepare His men before leading them to the place of His arrest. We see this same principle practiced by Paul in Acts 20 when he called to himself the Ephesian elders. He warned them of the danger of false teachers, using the analogy of wolves that would not spare the flock (Acts 20:29). He challenged them to "watch and remember" what he had done among them as he challenged them to defend the their church against false teachers. In the same way, Jonathan Edwards saw the danger of European enlightenment to the faith of his flock and began preaching on the person and work of Christ. His influence was such that he was able to effectively delay its influences in America for another generation.

Jesus continues His instruction with the vivid figurative language (allegory) of the vine and the branches as they walk toward the garden, an analogy that pictures beautifully unique *identification* truths concerning Christ and believers.[1] For in this analogy we see pictured the essence of our relationship with Christ. Where Paul describes Him as the head of the body, the church, here John pictures Him as the whole body (vine). Jesus does not call Himself just the root, but the whole vine, of which each individual branch shares a part in Him. In the same way, Jesus is not just the head of the church, but lives out His life in and through every member of His body, each and every believer.

But, before dwelling further on these beautiful sanctification truths, we must also acknowledge that these verses, the allegory of the vine and the branches, have been the occasion of a great deal of debate concerning their meaning.[2] The information that follows will make vivid the character of God as stated in chapter fourteen. It will help clarify what Jesus meant when He commanded His followers to abide in Him and how His instruction relates to us today.

First, we should note that today few people living in industrialized countries can point to either an agricultural background or a rural past.[3] This has led to a distinct lack of familiarity with all or most aspects of agriculture, including the art and science of viticulture.[4] Since the culture of the Bible was principally agrarian, this modern unfamiliarity may often contribute to a misunderstanding of Scripture by today's students. This can be seen clearly in the differences between the Lordship and Free Grace views of John 15.[5]

When interpreting difficult passages, such issues as grammar, syntax, meanings of key terms and the literary context are of primary importance. But the proper use of historical and cultural data may also productively inform our understanding of key terms and concepts, thereby clarifying what might otherwise be obscure or confusing in a biblical passage (see endnote justifying use of culture beyond Scripture).[6]

In interpreting this passage we need to ask questions such as the following. Who was He talking to in the upper room? What was their spiritual state? What was He preparing them for? Would Jesus spend time discussing justification issues with men who were already believers (justified)? Did Jesus intend to teach that unfruitful followers were not true believers, that they faced divine discipline, or something else? How much should immediate audience, viticultural terminology, and season of the year influence one's understanding of the text?

As this context is His final discourse, Jesus' words are addressed to His believing disciples. Judas has recently departed from their company with the intention of betraying Him, something the others would learn very soon. He is discussing the Father's loyal love, His relationship to them as their source of life and as the One whose ministry to them will be continued through the Holy Spirit following His departure and whose ministry to the world is to be continued through them. The disciples have responded with self-focused anxiety and grief and Jesus is reassuring and comforting them by focusing their attention on the eternal value of what He has in store for them and Him.

In light of His departure and the promised ministry of the Holy Spirit, Jesus introduces this analogy and reveals to them the importance of their continued dependence on Him and what He has told them about the ministry of the Triune God in their lives. They must "abide" (the first occurrence of the word was in John 8:31). Whether He delivers the analogy within the walls of the residence or en route to the garden is uncertain and immaterial. But, the season, since Passover occurred in the early spring, is a critical element to remember in light of Jesus' practice of basing His parables on the world as they could see it right then.

These men are destined to be the pillars of the church, the Body of Christ, to be founded at Pentecost (cf. 1 Cor 12:13). Yet, that evening they have been focused on themselves and need encouragement, lifting up, to direct them where God wants them, to make them fruitful. Peter especially has been stripped bare by the Lord and will be going through the bitterest time of his life that very night (Luke 22:31-34; John 13:36-38). However monstrous their coming sins and failures as the night progresses, he carefully lifts them on to higher ground by showing them the Triune God. Jesus has been doing major cleaning on Peter and the rest of the disciples to deliver them from their pride and arrogance.

Now He will apply the same healing ointment in figurative language showing them the path to fruitfulness. As a result, the central issue of Jesus' analogy involves abiding and fruitfulness in light of His departure and the ministry of the Holy Spirit. Abiding is repeated ten times in the first ten verses. Fruit is mentioned six times. Jesus is clearly teaching that only by abiding in Him, and all that He is, can His followers hope to be fruitful. The result of abiding is that they will bear "much fruit." And this "fruit" has eternal dividends, as will be seen later in the chapter.

This is a call to them to "abide" in Him and what He is like and His teachings through obedience to the command to love one another. If justification and condemnation are issues addressed by the analogy, they can only be seen as secondary, if at all, to the central focus of bearing fruit. But what about the two kinds of branches and the action of the Vinedresser? Everyone agrees that the fruitful branches are regenerate believers. But what of the unfruitful branches? And how about the non-abiding branches? Can the viticultural practices of Jesus' day provide any clues to His use of key terms or on the significance of the burning of non-abiding branches? Yes, as we will see.

15:1. "I am the true vine, and My Father is the vinedresser.

Jesus begins His analogy of the vine and branches by saying that He is the "true vine" and God the Father is the "vinedresser" (or husbandman). He has mentioned the Father twenty-three times already in the immediately preceding context. Now He pictures the loving care of His Father for Him and the disciples through the picture of a vinedresser's concern for his plants.

A vinedresser is more than a mere farmer. His work is not like the typical farmer, who simply plows up a field, plants a crop, harvests it, and waits for next season (We are speaking simplistically here). Grapes are more than an annual crop. They are individuals. A husbandman must know all about grapes, how they grow, what they need, when they need it, and what produces the best health as well as production in the plant. But, to be effective, they not only must know the right things, but they must nurture their plants with loving care.

The vinedresser's grape vines remain with him for decades. He comes to know each one in a personal way, much like a shepherd with his sheep. He knows how the vine is faring from year to year and which ones are more productive or vigorous than others. He knows what they respond to and what special care certain one's need. Every vine has its own personality. And the vinedresser comes to know it over the years. The vinedresser cares for each vine and nurtures it, pruning it the appropriate amount at the appropriate times, fertilizing it, lifting its branches from the ground and propping them or tying them to the trellis, and taking measures to protect them from insects and disease.[7]

So, when Jesus calls His Father the Vinedresser, He is describing Him in terms of His relationship and attitude as well as His actions in the lives of the disciples. We cannot stress enough how important it is to recall the attributes and actions of the Father from the previous context. To call Him a vinedresser is to tell them He cares for them personally and is wise to know exactly what to do to make them fruitful. With such a Vinedresser, the branches can experience complete confidence and security.

When Jesus describes Himself as the vine, He calls Himself the "true" vine. By "true" He means, "genuine." But why does He use this picture of Himself? And, what does He mean by this? He uses the definite article to describe Himself and thereby says I am "the" vine, not "a" vine. This use of the article may indicate that He has a specific image in mind. He is "the" true vine in contrast to something that the disciples might consider the true vine. This emphasis may indicate He is alluding to something in Scripture to which the disciples would be familiar.

Why a "vine" rather than other plants? In the Old Testament the imagery of a grapevine is used to describe Israel. But it does not just designate Israel as a nation. It describes Israel in its relationship to God. For example, in Psalm 80:8 Israel is described as a vine that God brought out of Egypt and planted in the land of promise. In verse fifteen the nation is then compared to a vineyard belonging to God. In this lament psalm, where the Psalmist prays to God to restore the nation, his emphasis is on God's relationship with the nation as the one who cares for it. Isaiah used the same imagery to describe Judah's relationship with God. In Isaiah 5:1-7 the nation is described as the "vineyard of the LORD of hosts" and "the men of Judah" as "His pleasant plant." But in Isaiah, the nation is guilty and unfruitful, facing judgment. In Jeremiah 2:21 God addresses the nation and says that He planted them "a noble vine" but they had turned from Him and become a "degenerate plant of an alien vine." Thus, the Old Testament imagery of Israel as a vine repeatedly focuses on God's care for the nation in light of their failure.

Jesus' use of "true" to describe Himself as the "vine" God cares for can very well be alluding to the nation's failure and to the fact of His *good* relationship with God. Where the nation failed God, Jesus had been the complete embodiment of everything they were supposed to be. This same concept is evident in the first chapters of Matthew. There, Matthew describes Jesus' early life and experiences before beginning His ministry as a parallel to Israel's history. Where Israel came out of Egypt to the Promised Land; so did Jesus. Where they were tempted for forty years in the wilderness, and failed, Jesus was tempted for forty days without failing. There are other parallels as well.

By applying this title to Himself Jesus is "claiming to be the divine source of an abundant spiritual harvest."[8] Hudson Taylor wrote these words as he meditated on the truths of the analogy of the vine and branches, "As I thought of the Vine and the Branches, what light the blessed Spirit poured direct into my soul. . . . I saw not only that Jesus would never leave me, but that I was a member of His body, of His flesh, and of His bones. The Vine, now I see, is not the root merely, but all—root, stem, branches, twigs, leaves, flowers, fruit; and Jesus is not only that: He is soil and sunshine, air and showers, and ten thousand times more than we have ever dreamed, wished for or needed."[9]

When the whole analogy is examined, the focus is not on the nation of Israel and what it should have been. This can be seen by comparing John 15 to the analogy used in Isaiah. Jesus does not focus on Israel/Judah, but on the disciples. He does not focus on the nation's sin and responsibility, but on the disciples bearing fruit. In that same light, the analogy is not focusing on the issue of what is true or false. Jesus is not contrasting true and false believers. Rather He is focusing on the relationship believers have with the Father and the resulting fruitfulness that brings. Thus, the focus of the analogy is on the nature of a vine. It is from this truth that Jesus builds His words of encouragement and cleanses and lifts the disciples unto greater fruitfulness.

Having noted the analogy, we need not attempt to draw too many parallels or contrasts between Israel and Jesus. Rather, we need only recognize that Jesus, as Messiah, does indeed embody everything Israel should be. But, that having been said, the point of the analogy has to do with the nature of a vine, not with the past or present life of the nation. And so, as we listen to the words of Jesus we need to look to first century viticulture in Israel in order to understand His message through this parable. We need to *see* what the disciples were *seeing*. In that light, having introduced the extended metaphor, Jesus begins to discuss the point He wants to make with His disciples.

15:2. "Every branch in Me that does not bear fruit He takes away; and every branch that bears fruit He prunes, that it may bear more fruit.

Jesus describes two kinds of branches in the vine, fruiting and nonfruiting. Along with two kinds of branches are two actions taken by God the Father, the Vinedresser, who is the same, loving Person introduced in the preceding chapter. The problem of interpreting this passage is made apparent by the different and conflicting interpretations given this verse as debate continues concerning the meaning of two key terms. The first term is *airei* and can be translated as either "to lift up" or "to take away."[10] The practice of most translators has been to translate it as "take away" rather than "lift up." For example, the King James uses "taketh away." NKJV, RSV, NASB translate it as "takes away." NIV uses "cuts off." And, NRSV translates it as "removes." In contrast, R. K. Harrison states, "Fallen vines were lifted (Jn. 12:2, *airei*, from *airō*, 'to lift,' *not* from *aireō*, 'to catch, take away,' as in all Eng. versions) into position with meticulous care and allowed to heal."[11] And, since the idea of taking away is sometimes used of judgment in the New Testament, this sense is understood by some as being contained in this verse.

The second term is *kathairei*, and, as you can tell by the similarity in sound, is being used in conjunction with the first word, most likely because of their similarity. The debate is so important that in the following paragraphs we shall detail many of the arguments for the two major positions. Then we shall pause and explain our understanding of how these critical verses should be understood.

Most commentators, accepting the "takes away" translation for the term, see the farmer removing unfruitful branches while cleaning up the fruiting branches in order to make them more fruitful.[12] But it is not an accurate picture they paint. Basically two kinds of pruning occurred in the vineyard, dormant pruning in the late fall and then that accomplished during the growing season. Dormant pruning removed unwanted material from the branches which were to be kept till the following season, including all remaining leaves, as well as unwanted branches and water sprouts. Spring pruning removed succulent sprigs from the fruiting branches, dead and diseased wood, adventitious buds on the trunk of the vine, but *not all* non-fruiting branches. Some non-fruiting branches were kept on the vine. So to what action or actions did Jesus refer in the second verse?[13]

In interpreting the allegory to find the spiritual analogy there are two views. The more common view among students of Scripture, which we will call the justification-salvation view,[14] is that the non-fruiting branches of verse two and removed branches of verse six are nonbelievers within the visible church who appear to be believers but whose lives are spiritually fruitless, superficial Christians.[15] MacArthur embodies this position when he says that "the healthy, fruit-bearing branches . . . represent genuine Christians." He argues further, "We are not saved by works, but works are the only proof that faith is genuine, vibrant, and alive (James 2:17). Fruit is the only possible validation that a branch is abiding in the True Vine."[16] Thus the absence of fruit for him demonstrates the absence of life. And, since abiding is necessary for fruitfulness, failure to abide means failure to believe, to "be saved," to possess life.[17]

The second view, which we are calling the sanctification-salvation view, says that unfruitful branches are initially cared for by God and then eventually disciplined.[18] Chafer is an early proponent of this view and sees abiding within this passage referring to communion with God and not union because the passage's focus is on the believer's walk. Further, he does not see the action on the branches in verse six as an issue of union (justification-salvation), but communion (sanctification-salvation). A believer's failure to abide, and thus bear fruit, leads to discipline from God that may include physical death (James 1:13-15; 5:20; 1 Cor 11:30-32).[19] Dillow concurs with Chafer with the additional aspect that believers not only experience divine discipline in this life but also loss of reward at the judgment seat of Christ.[20]

As can be seen from these two descriptions, their understanding of the meaning of the passage is both different and contradictory to each other. Only one view can be right. The unfruitful branch cannot be both a believer and an unbeliever. The branch that fails to abide cannot be a believer who gets disciplined and a superficial Christian who was never regenerate. The various meanings are not complementary and cannot be harmonized. The question the student of Scripture faces is: Which view has the greatest probability of being correct? And, since both views build their arguments from cultural as well as textual data, it must be evaluated and explained in a way that can answer the issues raised within the text and first century viticultural practices.

The assumption that the Gospel of John has an evangelistic purpose coupled with a lack of understanding of viticulture seems to force most interpreters to look to verse six for an interpretative guide to verse two (See Appendix 8, "The Message of John and Belief in John 20:30-31,"for a full discussion of this issue.).[21] This then lends itself to a position that forces the average interpreter to find "professing" Christians being distinguished from actual. As has just been noted, though, other interpreters have attempted to answer the question from a sanctification perspective and so have differed in their conclusions.

The justification-salvation view sees the Vinedresser taking two actions on the branches in verse two. The fruitless branches are removed while fruitful ones are pruned.[22] Thus the NIV translators, in striving for a dynamic translation render this term "cuts off" which has no relation whatsoever to *airō*. "Cuts off" would have been a possible rendering of *koptō* or *apokoptō*, a word which John knew and used in John 18:10. If He meant that here, He would have used it. He doesn't even use *epairō*. That would have been appropriate if Jesus was referring to someone being taken to heaven as a discipline. As a matter of fact, Jesus prays for the opposite in John 17:15. But, even the term "remove" or "take away" does not have to have the idea of judgment. For example, John uses the compound form of the term (*epairō*) to describe Jesus lifting His eyes heavenward when He prayed His high priestly prayer (John 17:1). But, for those who wish to find judgment in this verse, *airō* is given a negative sense. MacArthur presents a "viticultural" argument to justify this understanding of the verse.

> Vinedressers had two chief means of maximizing the fruit that grew on the vine. One was to cut off the barren limbs. The other was to prune new shoots from the fruit-bearing branches. This all insured that the vine would produce more fruit, not just leafy growth. Verse 2 describes both chores: . . . Barren branches grow more rapidly, and new ones sprout quickly. They must be carefully and regularly pruned. It is the only way to insure maximum quantities of fruit.[23]

This is a nice sounding description, for the non-viticulturalist. But is it what is and was actually practiced? No. Listen to James Boice, a Reformed theologian.

> There are two things that the Father is said to do in His care of the vine. First, He is said to "take away" every branch that does not bear fruit. Generally this has been understood to be a purging away of dead branches in precisely the same sense that branches are said to be "cast forth" and "burned" in verse 6, but I am convinced that most translations have missed the true meaning of the term "take away" in this instance. Undoubtedly, their translation has been made to conform to what they know or believe is coming in verse 6, but the translation is not the best or even the most general meaning of the Greek word *airo* which lies behind it. The word *airo* has four basic meanings, which are, proceeding from the most fundamental to the most figurative: 1) to lift up or pick up, 2) to lift up figuratively, as in lifting up one's eyes or voice, 3) to lift up with

the added thought of lifting up in order to carry away, and 4) to remove. In translating this word by the verb "take away" the majority of translators have obviously chosen the fourth of these meanings, for the reason suggested above. But the verse makes better sense and the sequence of verbs is better if the first and primary meaning of the word is taken. In that case the sentence would read, "Every branch in me that beareth not fruit he lifteth up," that is, to keep it from trailing on the ground.

This translation makes better sense of the passage in every way, and in addition it is much better theology.[24]

This is not only better theology, but would be in agreement with the Psalmist David. When dealing with his enemies he focuses on God and says, "LORD, how they have increased who trouble me! Many are they who rise up against me. Many are they who say of me, "there is no help for him in God." But You, O LORD, are a shield for me, my glory and the One who lifts up my head" (Psalm 3:1-3). We express this vividly in the words of the song, "Love lifted me! Love lifted me! When nothing else could help, love lifted me!"

A major problem this view faces is Jesus' description of both branches being "in Me."[25] This is complicated by the need to determine the significance of Jesus' use of "in Me" in light of Paul's frequent use of the concept ("in Christ") and the meaning he gives it. In the Gospel of John, Jesus uses the phrase sixteen times, six times in the analogy of the vine and the branches.[26] Only once outside of the upper room does Jesus use the phrase to describe a person's union with Him. In John 6:56 He is clearly describing what they must do to become born again. But, even so, this use of "in Me" still reflects the aspect of relationship as well as a believer's position.

The remainder of His uses of the phrase communicate a relational concept more than referring to any "organic" connection (a positional truth such as we find in Paul's use of "in Christ"). For example, in John 10:38; 14:10, 11; 17:21 and 23 it is the Father who is "in" Christ and Christ "in" Him. This certainly has nothing to do with "salvation," but speaks of their communion. Granted, Their organic union is still contained in the phrase. But, organic union is not the point of Jesus' statements. He is talking about their unity of purpose and mind, not essence but function, in these verses. That it does not describe their metaphysical union is evident in that Jesus uses the same phrase in the same way in 14:20 to describe His relationship with the disciples.

In contrast to John, Paul uses "in Christ" ("in Him") with a broad range of meanings, including both the *positional* truth of organic union with Christ and the *conditional* truth of communion with Him.[27] His most common use of the phrase, though, has to do with the positional truth of a believer's being placed into the body of Christ based on the Spirit's baptism (cf. Rom 12:5; 1 Cor 12:13), and thereby being "in Christ." Thus Paul can say things like, "Reckon yourselves to be dead indeed to sin, but alive to God **in Christ** Jesus our Lord" (Rom 6:11). He again says, "Therefore, if anyone is **in Christ**, *he is* a new creation; old things have passed away, behold, all things have become new" (2 Cor 5:17). And, "*In Him* we have redemption through His blood, the forgiveness of sins" (Eph 1:7). It is this sense of "in Me" that Jesus uses here in verse two. Many other places in Paul the phrase "in Christ" or "in Him" is used with the sense of "in the sphere of Christ" or "in His service." These are still basically positional statements because they speak more to the believer's position in Christ than to any communion between the believer and Christ. But, in His analogy of the vine, Jesus begins with a positional statement and then continues His discussion with the relational sense.

Laney attempts to understand Jesus' words by referring to modern viticultural practices and quotes from a circular from the California Agricultural Extension Service entitled "Grape Growing in California." He notes from this circular that "regular pruning is necessary during the vine's growing season." From it he identifies pinching, topping, thinning, and pruning as four actions taken to control growth and improve fruit production.[28] He then sees Jesus' point to be that "as the vinedresser cuts away what would hinder the productivity of the vine, so God the Father, through loving discipline (cleaning, purging, purifying), removes things from the lives of believers that do not contribute to their spiritual fruitfulness."[29]

The problem with his use of this data is two-fold. First, he apparently does not understand the difference between growing season pruning and dormant season pruning. And second, viticulture in California is quite different from Israel and the first century is quite different from the twentieth century. To his credit, he admits that, "the destruction of the Jews at the time of the Arab conquest (A.D. 640) suggests that changes may have occurred in agriculture as the Arab people took over Palestine." This leads him to conclude that the "grammatical and lexical context" is all that is left to the interpreter "to gain a proper understanding of the passage."[30] This last statement has great merit and would be completely true if no way exists of ascertaining the viticultural practices of first century Judea. But there is.

For the sanctification interpretation of the passage the imagery used by Jesus in the vine-branch analogy describes fellowship with God rather than union with Him. Zane Hodges argues well, "With John, the kind of relationship pictured in the vine-branch imagery describes an experience that can be ruptured (John 15:6) with a resultant loss of fellowship and fruitfulness," and so describes "the believer's fellowship with God."[31] And he notes further, "Unlike the salvation relationship, the relationship of a disciple to his Teacher can be lost."[32]

The idea that unfruitful branches cannot be either regenerate or abiding should be rejected. Ask yourself: Does any plant in God's kingdom have fruit instantaneously with life? How does this relate to Jesus' prediction in John 13:38 (note Jesus' words in Luke 12:8-9) that Peter would deny Him? Would the disciples, especially Peter, be considered fruit-bearers that night? Besides the "fruit" of carnality (especially pride), what else were they producing at that time? Dillow responds to such an idea by asking, "If the fruitless branches are only professing Christians, then what bearing did the passage have on the disciples?" He answers this by noting that "the passage gives every indication that it was addressed in its entirety to the disciples to tell them how they could bear fruit in *their* lives. Jesus said to them, 'If you [the disciples, not those to whom they would one day minister] abide in Me, and My words abide in you, ask whatever you wish, an it shall be done for you.'"[33] Cook is in agreement with him when he notes,

Abiding in Christ is to be distinguished from *being* in Christ, although ideally there should be no practical difference between the two. We may observe the distinction by noting John 15:1-11, where the "in Me" branch of verse 2 is seen to be different from the "abide in Me" branch of verse 4. To *be* in Christ is to be born again, to be regenerated, to have had forgiveness of sins through Christ. Thus the disciples are in Christ (v. 2) because they have been cleansed of their sins (v. 3). To *abide* in Christ, however, is to be an obedient follower in fellowship with Christ the Savior and Lord (vv. 4-5, 9-11). An examination of 1 John 3:24 will reveal that obedience is the condition for abiding. Moreover, in John 15:10 our obeying Christ and thus abiding in Him is compared to the Son's obeying the Father and thus abiding in Him; the Son was already *in* the Father by virtue of His sonship, but the Son *abided* in the

Father by obeying Him. We see, then, that just as Christ's abiding in the Father was the maintenance of personal fellowship with the Father, so our abiding in Christ is the maintenance of personal fellowship with Christ.[34]

And, central to this abiding relationship is believing in Christ. In John 6:29 Jesus identified this as the "work" that God required of all who wished to *enjoy* eternal life. "This is the work of God, that you believe in Him whom He sent." In Jesus' thinking abiding, obeying, believing, and loving are all interrelated to one another. Thus the abiding relationship is one characterized by faith which, when developed (cf. 2 Pet 1:5), leads to keeping His commandments, particularly the commandment to love one another.

Dillow correctly interprets *airei* as "lifts up" in this verse. He notes that, in at least eight out of its twenty-four uses in John, this same term is used with the sense of lifting, and not in a judgmental way.[35] He then responds to Laney by noting that Harrison reported how fallen vines in Palestine "were lifted 'with meticulous care' and allowed to heal."[36] Further, in a footnote he remarks that Harrison states that *airei* has *airō* (to lift) as its root rather than *aireō* (to catch, take away).[37] Dillow then points to his own personal observation of viticultural care.[38] He concludes from this that if "lift up" is the meaning, "then a fruitless branch is lifted up to put it into a position of fruit-bearing."

This process was brought home to me (Earl) very vividly on several trips to Israel. When you travel south from Jerusalem past Bethlehem to Hebron, you see mile after mile of grapevines bending down to the ground. In Israel, unlike the United States, the stalks of grapevines are (even today), for the most part, laying on the ground during the nonproductive season—not bearing fruit. But when the time comes for fruit, the vine-dressers begin to lift them off the ground. And today, two thousand years later, you can see the vine-tenders on the West Bank of the Jordan doing it the same way they did it then. They get a rock (about eight to ten inches high), pick up the stalk and put the rock under the top end of the stalk. They go to the next one and do the same thing. Several days later they come back and move that rock back a little further toward the root and do the same to every stalk in the vineyard. Several days later they will repeat the process until they get that stalk positioned properly for fruit-bearing.

In the process the branches have been "taken away" or "lifted" from the ground. This lifting is not judgment, but blessing for the branch. I recall asking a worker in a vineyard near Bethlehem why they lifted the vines. He said that by lifting the vines they allowed the heat from the sun to envelop the branch and thus control the ripening of the fruit. He further explained that if they left the vine on the ground the branches would sink hundreds of little roots directly from the branch into the surface of the soil where there was not sufficient moisture to produce anything except little hard, sour grapes. But if they lifted the branches then they were forced to derive their nutrients from the deep roots of the vine that enabled them to produce the succulent fruit that Israel is known for. As Boice notes,

> It would be a strange vinedresser who immediately cuts off such a branch without even giving it a chance to develop properly. But it would be wise and customary for him to stretch the vine on an arbor or use some other means of raising it to the air and sun. ... to translate the word *airo* by 'lifteth up' gives a proper sequence to the Father's care of the vineyard, indicated by the verb which follows. Thus, He first of all lifts the vines up. Then He prunes away the unproductive elements, carefully cleansing the vine of insects, moss, or parasites which otherwise would hinder the growth of the plant. This last item would have been the ancient equivalent of using insecticides, as is done today.[39]

What a picture this is of how our heavenly Viticulturist tends the branches in Christ! For, in the same way, Jesus' use of this term to describe God's lifting a non-fruiting branch in order to position it for future fruiting need not be translated and interpreted as judgment or removal from the vine, but as lifting it for its good. One cannot help but be reminded of the ever-so-relevant hymn that reminds us of Peter's sinking experience:

> I was sinking deep in sin far from the peaceful shore,
>
> Very deeply stained within sinking to rise no more.
>
> But the Master of the sea heard my despairing cry.
>
> From the waters lifted me, now safe am I.
>
> Love lifted me, love lifted me,
>
> When nothing else could help, love lifted me.

Dillow also argues that this interpretation of the verse does not contradict verse six, but that it rather suggests "that the heavenly Vinedresser first encourages the branches and lifts them in the sense of providing loving care to enable them to bear fruit. If after this encouragement, they do not remain in fellowship with Him and bear fruit, they are then cast out."[40] This casting out is from fellowship, not justification. Cook concurs and notes further that in the Gospel of John *airō* is not used in relation to "the matter of sin" except in John 1:29.[41] Thus it is not a "judgmental" term in this Gospel.[42]

A play-on-words is evident between *airei*, which we understand as "he lifts," and *kathairei*, which the KJV correctly translates as "He purges" or "He cleanses" in contrast to many translations that translate it "He prunes." This meaning is also consistent with Jesus' use of the same word in verse three, namely, "Now you are clean through the word I have spoken to you." *Kathairei* also may mean "he cleanses" and so is linked to John 13:10, "you are clean (*kathairoi*), but not all."[43] Our English word catharsis comes from this Greek term. Though it sounds gross, we understand an enema to be a catharsis of the bowels. In like manner some of us need a catharsis of the brain from time to time. Since Jesus appears to be referring to Judas in chapter thirteen, the justification view says he must be the unfruitful branch that had to be removed, with that removal being judgment, the fire of verse six. *Notice that the "He" of verse two is not the "they" of verse six.*

Much of the difficulty of the passage is removed when exegetes stop attempting to make the sixth verse an exposition of the second. One key element to understanding these verses and their relationship to one another is to note the progression in pronouns as Jesus details this analogy. In verse two Jesus says "He," the Father, takes certain actions with the branches. In verses three through five Jesus uses "you" to describe who is taking an active role as He addresses the eleven men listening to Him at that time. Then in verse six it is "they" who act on the branches, not "He" (the Father) or "you" (the eleven who are the branches). And who are the "they"? In the context the target of the great command of Jesus is the unbelieving world (John 13:35; 15:8). And the "they" of this verse represents the "all" of 13:35. It is the world who evaluates and decides our relation to Christ by our fruit or the lack of it.

Understanding what Jesus intended to say in this passage is made easier by understanding the viticultural practices to which He referred. The weakness of the "taken away in judgment" view of *airei* becomes evident when the term is understood within its viticultural context.

First we should note that *airei* is not an *attested*[44] viticultural term. What we mean by this is that it has not yet been found in any first or second century documents related to viticulture. *Kathairō*, on the other hand, does have at least one viticultural use as given by Baur, and when used in a literal sense *does* carry the idea of cleansing.[45] It has a figurative sense of spiritual cleanness and, building from its viticultural meaning, Jesus uses the term again in verse three. As an attested viticultural term, Jesus' use of it in this analogy must be consistent with its normal use and meaning. His use of parables to teach spiritual truths is based on analogies built from *accurate* portrayals of the natural world. What He describes is what happens. Through analogies with the familiar world the listeners are then able to recognize the spiritual truths being taught.

Since *kathairei* was the legitimate viticultural term describing the process of removing suckers from a fruiting branch, it should be understood that way. And it is by everyone, regardless of how they understand *airei*. Thus, the possibly non-viticultural term's meaning should be understood in conjunction with its clearly attested viticultural counterpart. If it was not a term common to viticulture, Jesus may have chosen *airei* due to its similarity in sound to *kathairei* in order to make a play-on-words (paregmenon, or derivation) and communicate a truth to the disciples.[46] It is more likely that He was in fact using a term used by the farmers of His day to describe their own practice.

Its lack of attestation does not mean that it was not a term common to viticulture, though an argument from silence is not convincing proof either. But, whether *airei* is accepted as a viticultural term or not, its use within the analogy must correspond to a common practice which the disciples would know and understand. Since both *airei* and *kathairei* are used in conjunction with one another, they are better understood as being done simultaneously. Jesus is not putting together two tasks from separate seasons since serious pruning is not done during the spring growth, flowering, and fruit production.[47] Further, on the basis of the relationship of the action to fruiting, Jesus is most likely referring to the stage of seasonal care the vineyards were entering at the time He spoke, namely spring training and trimming.

The approach of most exegetes is to see in Jesus' words a process by which the farmer picks off the adventitious sprigs from the fruiting branches (cleanses them) and cuts off non-fruiting branches (takes them away). Yet with the evidence from Pliny that non-fruiting branches were *preserved* and *nurtured* for use the next season, this translation of *airei* contradicts their practice. As he notes,

> Thus there are two kinds of main branches; the shoot which comes out of the hard timber and promises wood for the next year is called a leafy shoot or else when it is above the scar [caused by tying the branch to the trellis] a fruit-bearing shoot, whereas the other kind of shoot that springs from a year-old branch is always a fruit-bearer. There is also left underneath the cross-bar a shoot called the keeper—this is a young branch, not longer than three buds, which will provide wood next year if the vine's luxurious growth has used itself up—and another shoot next to it, the size of a wart, called the pilferer is also left, in case the keeper-shoot should fail.[48]

It would be better to see Jesus indicating what actually occurred during the Spring, namely, certain non-fruiting branches were "lifted up" (to keep them from touching the ground and setting roots) and tied to the trellises along with the fruiting branches while the side shoots of the fruiting branches were being "cleaned up." The non-fruiting branches were allowed to grow with full vigor and without the removal of any side growth or leaves since the more extensive their growth the greater the diameter of their stem where it connected to the vine and thus the greater ability for the flow of nutrients from the roots to the branches which would produce more fruit the following season. By removing them from the ground and placing them on the trellis the rows of plants would benefit from unhindered aeration that was considered an essential element to proper fruit development.[49] To see *airei* as removal (judgment or discipline) is to contradict the actual practice of the time.

Recognizing the practice described by the two terms, the meaning of "in Me" becomes apparent also. Both kinds of branches may be in Christ and may be abiding since they both existed and were *desired* on *every* vine in Jesus' day. Denying that the unfruitful branch of verse two is attached to the vine violates the reality of the world from which the description arose.

Having discussed in detail the two approaches to this verse, it is best now to interpret it on the basis of the data we have from first century practice and a correct understanding of key terms. What Jesus has said in the first two verses of this beautiful analogy is nothing short of pure encouragement. He has introduced us to a very special "TLC" rule of our Father.

He has told the eleven that God the Father cares for them like a vine-dresser cares for his grapes. Further, they are each a part of Jesus and draw their spiritual life from Him like branches draw life from the vine. Jesus has affirmed that among those who are believers, those who believe in Him and so belong to Him, those who are "in Him," some are ready to bear fruit and some are not.

God the Father is caring for both groups of believers. The ones not ready to bear fruit are being "lifted up" by Him with a view to future fruit-fulness. Thankfully, the Father does not cut off all non-fruiting branches or the vine would never produce fruit. Though they are not fruitful now, they are still important to Him and recipients of His loving concern. The Father is also caring for the ones who are now ready to bear fruit, like the eleven. He is taking those loving actions that will insure their greater fruitfulness. Jesus' point to the eleven in this verse is singular. God the Father cares for all who belong to Jesus regardless of their fruitfulness.

Then what of Jesus' instructions to abide which follow? He will next tell His disciples that they are fruiting branches. They have been "cleansed" (*kathairō*) and so they can anticipate immediate fruitfulness. But that fruitfulness depends on their maintaining a proper relationship with Him. Again, we need to notice Jesus' shift of pronouns from "He" to "you." Here is a good illustration of God's sovereignty and man's responsi-bility at work. I can only believe what I know and I can only receive what I believe. We will soon see too how Christ parcels out relationship for greater fruitage (cf. 15:9ff). He implies by this that there are others believ-ing in Him who are not yet ready to bear fruit, but who need to maintain a proper relationship with Him, abide in Him, in order to eventually bear fruit. This understanding of verses three through five conforms to the cul-tural practices from which the analogy arose.

15:3. "You are already clean because of the word which I have spoken to you.

Having described the Father's concerned care for all believers, Jesus addresses His men in particular. In this verse He tells them that the process of "cleansing" has been completed by His Father through the instruction they have received from Him. The direct implication is that they are therefore "fruiting" branches, and that their "season" of fruitful-ness is upon them.

Jesus' use of *kathairō* seems purposefully to have both a horticultur-al and religious sense, meaning both "to prune" and "to purify."[50] This is similar to the command in Ephesians 5:25-27 for husbands to love their wives like Christ loved the church. In that command the analogy is developed that Jesus "cleansed" the church by washing her with the "word" in order to present her to Himself as "holy and blameless." Similarly, Jesus affirms that He has "purified" the disciples through His instruction. When Jesus says He has cleansed them with the words He has spoken to them, He must be reminding them of all that He has said in chapters thirteen and fourteen, especially the tremendous teachings of chapter fourteen.

"Now you are clean through the word which I have spoken unto you." When I (Earl) think of the cleansing and purifying of our minds through the word of God, a very special event comes to my mind. It was in January of 1989 when my wife and I had just moved temporarily from Portland to Los Gatos, California to start the Bay Area extension of Western Seminary. On the first day in we were busily arranging the office when I received a call from a distressed friend.

"I need to see you," was the plea from Lorelei Dedini. "God didn't bring you down here just to start that seminary. He brought you down here to help me."

As the story unfolded, I learned that she now had a serious recurrence of the breast cancer that had gone into remission five years before. Her doctor told her that she had six months to a year to live. But what was really troubling her was the statement of some of her Christian friends that they had prayed for her and that God was going to heal her.

"How do they know that," she said. "God didn't tell me that."

Well, we looked at the Word and prayed and I said, "Now, I would listen to your doctor and make plans. If God chooses to heal you, well and good. But it appears that you may have a short amount of time to do some strategic things."

Several weeks later the Dedini's took my wife and me to a lovely dinner in Saratoga. Sitting across from me, Lorelei rejoiced, "God is so good."

Strange words from a lovely lady dying at forty-seven? "Tell me about it," I responded.

"Well, some people get taken so suddenly. God has given me time. There are things that we needed to get straightened out." And she went on to spell some of them out. "God is so good," she repeated.

Shortly thereafter, I had occasion to take Lorelei with me to a preaching engagement in Los Altos. The wonderful sixty-voice youth choir was singing a rather jubilant and rocking rendition of "To be absent from the body is to be present with the Lord." Lorelei elbowed me in the side and said, "Get a load of this. They're singing it and I'm doing it." When they finished, I had her step up to the pulpit with me. She was wearing a bonnet on her head because of the devastating work the chemotherapy had done to her lovely head of hair.

She began her testimony of the power of God's word turning to the youth choir, "You have been singing it and I am doing it," and then continued to the whole audience. I shall never forget the scene at the altar after the service. In forty years of ministry I have never had so many people come forward with responses. One stands out. A psychiatrist gave her his card and asked her to make an appointment.

"Oh, thank you, doctor. But I don't need an appointment." She said.

"I know you don't. But I do," he replied.

After getting the seminary classes started, at the end of the semester, my wife and I moved back to Portland. But every time I flew through San Jose I would call Lorelei from the airport. On one visit, we got out her latest X-rays and viewed the growing tumors.

"I don't see how you have room left to breath, Lorelei. It looks to me like you are going to be seeing Jesus soon. And, by the way, when you see Him, tell Him I am coming, too."

"I will," she smiled with a twinkle in her eyes.

The next time I called from the airport, Dominic answered the phone. "Are you coming over?"

"Yes."

"I'll get her ready."

I wondered about the implications of that. When I walked through the front door, they had her bed in the living room. Her beautiful body had wasted to skin and bone. Sores covered it. Tubes were coming out of her nose. But when she heard my voice and saw me, she grabbed my arm and with a strong voice said, "It's the Word. It's the Word. That's what you kept telling me and that's it."

Lorelei wrote her own funeral service that was held before a full crowd at Calvary Church. As a result of the funeral service, a good friend was led to Christ by her husband, Dominic.

This kind of miracle in the lives of believers is replicated over and over again when we dare to take seriously the power of the Word of God. "Now you are clean," Jesus said, "through the Word which I have spoken unto you."

From this and the previous verse we can draw the analogy that God uses His word to purge those things from our lives that keep us, and others, from bearing fruit. Even so, that is not the focal point of what Jesus is saying. Rather, He is saying that the disciples have been prepared for fruitfulness, something which will be defined more fully later, by the action of the Father as He has used Jesus' teaching to "purify" them in the sense of making them fit for service.

The cleansing to which Jesus alludes should not be seen as the believer's cleansing from the penalty of sin that occurs at the time of the new birth (cf. John 13:10). This is not justification truth. Rather, this cleansing is a sanctification truth. This is 1 John 1:9 forgiveness and confession. This, again, is seen in the nature of the purpose of the cleansing. The cleansing to which Jesus refers has prepared them for service, not for heaven. Believing in the Jesus of the Bible gives us heaven—a gift of life— but the process of disciplemaking prepares us for service—the stewardship of that life.

Again, this interpretation fits the context best since service is in view and is, by nature of its being commanded by Christ, something a believer may or may not do. Those who would see this as justification cleansing would hear Jesus saying, "You are all saved (v. 3). And you will demonstrate that salvation by bearing fruit (v. 4)." Rather, we should notice how these words parallel so well what Jesus did to them in 13:4-17. He confronted their sinful attitudes and prepared them for service with a model (i.e., show and tell).

Contrary to seeing this as the cleansing from the penalty of sin that occurs at our justification-salvation, this verse likely has the concept of Old Testament ceremonial cleansing in view. When a priest entered into his period of service in the temple, he began first by going through the process of becoming ceremonially clean before the Lord. This included washings as well as offering certain sacrifices for his sin. When he had completed the cleansing process, he was qualified to serve. This is what Jesus is picturing here more than the idea of God purging specific sins from someone's life.

At the beginning of this discourse the disciples were still egotistical and self-centered, not ready to serve. Jesus had washed their feet and given them an example of humble service to follow. But, regardless of their immature attitudes, the disciples had indeed been set apart to serve God and were now acceptable to Him. So, though the foot washing was not a spiritually cleansing ceremony, Jesus may be alluding to it here as a parallel to the priest's washing as he entered the temple to serve. This may also help us understand the significance of what Jesus is going to say in verse sixteen. As the priests were chosen by God to serve in God's program, so too, the disciples were chosen by Jesus. And, as the priests had first to be made fit to serve by being "cleansed" before entering into service, so too the disciples were "cleansed" by Jesus' instruction, including His washing their feet. But, having prepared them, He continues to instruct them concerning fruitfulness.

15:4-5. "Abide in Me, and I in you. As the branch cannot bear fruit of itself, unless it abides in the vine, neither can you, unless you abide in Me. I am the vine, you are the branches. He who abides in Me, and I in him, bears much fruit; for without Me you can do nothing.

To be fruitful Christians, we must abide in Jesus. This is Jesus' plain teaching in these two verses. As we move from the comforting words of the Father's care in the first few verses, we now enter that portion of the analogy of the vine and branches that stresses the responsibility of the individual believer who wishes to be fruitful for the Lord. Here divine sovereignty and human responsibility come together. Again, we see this in the shift in pronouns from "He" to "you." These are things that the individual believer must choose to do. They are not automatic. But they are our responsibility.

To understand these verses we need to see how they relate to the fruiting branch of the second verse and how we abide. And, also, we need to see what He means by bearing fruit.

It is the fruiting branch (i.e., the branch that will bear fruit that growing season though it has not done so yet), cleansed by the Father through Jesus' words, which is ready to bear fruit. Thus, these verses are describing the response required from the fruiting branch of verse two for fruitfulness to occur. Though they are ready to bear fruit, such fruitfulness will not be automatic.

Rather, we see the interplay of God's sovereignty and man's responsibility. Typically believers misuse verses like Philippians 1:6 and 4:13 and 19 by minimizing human responsibility in spiritual growth and service.[51] We sometimes encounter this form of evangelicalism that emphasizes God's sovereignty to the exclusion of human responsibility. Rather, Jesus says here that the eleven (us, too; cf. 17:20-21) have a part to play in the fruiting process. They (we) have a responsibility to "abide." We might say it this way. As God works sovereignly through us, He sovereignly chooses to work only through those of us who are working (abiding)!

As fruiting is not automatic, abiding, again, is not automatic either. Jesus' command for us to abide indicates that it is possible for a believer to choose not to abide, even one who is ready to bear fruit and has been "cleansed." Peter is a classic example of this. He was clean (13:10) and cleansed (15:3) but he was still arrogant (18:12). He still failed to abide in Christ in the crisis of that night. Remember, we are listening in on a conversation between Jesus and His disciples. This command is being given to *them* first and us second. *They*, by definition of the nature of biblical commands, can *choose* not to abide. Otherwise it does not make sense for Jesus to command *them* to do so.

If abiding is a product of being regenerate, is automatic, then Jesus would not have commanded them to abide. Rather, He would have said something to the effect of, "You will now bear fruit as evidence of your regeneration which I will now describe as abiding since the Holy Spirit will be indwelling you." Or, if He was to speak as some evangelicals, He would have said, "You will now bear fruit because I am at work in you to accomplish My purposes whether you intentionally do anything in particular or not." But that is not what Jesus says. He commands them to abide if they are to bear fruit; thus, it had to be possible for them to fail to abide and fail to bear fruit. This is even more evident when we see that Jesus defines abiding in terms of obedience in verse ten.

We should ask ourselves, then, what has to happen to cause us to obey? Believe! You cannot *do* more than you believe! That is the whole point of what Jesus said about believing in 14:1! You are what you do. And you do on the basis of what you believe. We need to be reminded again of the three-fold principle that we elaborated previously – knowing, believing, receiving. We can only believe as much as we know and we can only receive as much as we believe. Once again, the classic gospel hymn says, "Trust and obey, for there is no other way..."

Yet, even though Jesus tells the eleven this now, as a matter of fact all of them failed to abide (keep believing unto fellowship and sanctification) that night, especially Peter (cf. Luke 22). As a matter of fact, all of them failed to understand His additional teachings that kept them from truly loving and rejoicing in Him ("You don't love Me."). That night they did not stop believing that Jesus was Messiah and Son of God, but they were thinking more of themselves than what He was teaching. He is telling them what they need to know, but they aren't hearing it. Later, after His arrest, Peter and John kept following Him after all others fled. But even Peter did not make it through the night. He eventually denied knowing

Him. But things would get better for Peter. We see this in Acts and John 21:15-17.

Though some might attempt to see in the idea in this verse of Jesus' abiding in us a reference to the indwelling ministry of the Holy Spirit, it may be better to see it otherwise.[52] This will be discussed in greater detail later. The "bottom line" is that our motivation for abiding, and the absolute necessity of abiding, is given by Jesus. This is a metaphor He is using to describe a spiritual relationship. Jesus uses many metaphors in His teaching to enable us to relate spiritual truths to our human experiences. Abiding is a metaphor for relationship. It describes a relationship of submission and dependence on our part and a relationship of nurture and enablement on His. And, Jesus has made clear here that without our abiding in Him and His abiding in us there is no fruitfulness for the believer. The reason: We cannot do anything apart from Jesus' enablement and He will only enable those who "abide" in Him and let Him "abide" in them.

Perhaps it is instructive in passing to be reminded that the wood of the grapevine is worthless as wood. In his work *Christ, His Cross, His Church*, the late J. Vernon McGee notes on page nineteen: "You cannot make furniture of it. You would not go to a furniture mart and ask to be shown the latest models in 'grapevine wood.' You would be shown maple, cherry or walnut, but not grapevine wood. The only value that a grapevine has is to produce fruit." The late Donald Grey Barnhouse confirmed this in his article, "Chain of Glory."[53] He said, In Hampton Court near London, there is a grapevine under glass; it is about a thousand years old and has but one root that is at least two feet thick. Some of the branches are two hundred feet long. Because of skillful cutting and pruning, the vine produces several tons of grapes each year. Even though some of the smaller branches are two hundred feet from the main stem, they bear much fruit because they are joined to the vine and allow the life of the vine to flow through them"

Branches that really get their sustenance from the vine have greater potential than most other plants. That is likely why the grape became a symbol for Israel in prophetic literature (as seen earlier). The promise of God in the Mosaic Covenant was fruitfulness in return for obedience. We see this illustrated in the lives of Caleb and Joshua who chose to trust God when the other ten spies rejected Him. They not only out-lived the men, but entered the promised land and received their reward, the lands they had spied out forty years earlier. God planted them in the land of promise as He planted the nation there and made it fruitful.

We see this same principle in Pauline literature when He talks about Jesus being the head and we being members of His body, the church. The body is absolutely dependent upon the head for direction. But the head is dependent on the body for implementation of its directions (cf. Eph 4:15-16). In that picture we see the relationship Jesus has chosen to have with us, and His choice to work out His purposes through us as we abide in Him by believing Him and keeping His commandments, especially to love one another. This is also why John turns from the issue of fellowship with God in 1 John 1 to abiding. He tells us that if we are abiding in Christ we will also walk "just as He walked" (1 John 2:6). This same concept is described by Paul as imitating God. Of note is John's description of this kind of a believer, who abides in the light (reflecting the theme of the first chapter). He identifies the kind of believer this is, namely, the one who loves his (Christian) brother (1 John 2:10).

But, what if a believer chooses not to abide? What is the consequence for the believer? Jesus addresses that issue next.

CHAPTER TEN

CHRIST EXPLAINING THE RESULTS OF RESPONSES
John 15:6-11

Having described the results of abiding in Him, namely, that they will bear fruit, more fruit, and much fruit, Jesus also explains other significant effects of the daily choices they must make. There are other benefits to abiding in Him that include answered prayer. But there are also consequences to the choice a believer might make to stop abiding.

This pattern of consequences for choices has always been God's procedure for disciplining His children. With respect to the covenant people under the Mosaic Law, God gave specific promises for obedience (Deut 28:1-14) even as He gave specific promises for disobedience (Deut 28:15—29:29). We often hear the chorus sung, "Every promise in the book is mine, every chapter, every verse, every line." What people often fail to realize is that there are specific promises of blessing for obedience. But there are also specific promises of cursing for disobedience! (Note also cursing in Gal 1:9)

Jesus, having promised blessing for abiding, now turns to the issue of its other consequences, both in terms of added benefits, but also of subsequent consequences for those who choose otherwise.

15:6. "If anyone does not abide in Me, he is cast out as a branch and is withered; and they gather them and throw them into the fire, and they are burned.

With this verse the third in a series of pronouns occurs, namely, "they." We have moved from "He" (the Father) to "you" (the eleven disciples) to "they," which now needs to be identified.

Having commanded them to abide and affirmed that, even though they have been made ready to bear fruit by the Father and have been cleansed by the word through the Son, they must abide in Him in order to be fruitful, Jesus goes on to describe the danger of making the wrong choice, of failing to abide. He does this through another "if-then" construction.[1] He says, "If anyone does not abide in Me, *and it is possible to abide or not abide, then* he is cast out as a branch . . ." Assumed in this sentence then is the truth that, if anyone *does* abide, then he is not cast out as a branch.

Choices have consequences. Especially in the spiritual realm, there are very real consequences to the choices we make. And Jesus is talking about some of those consequences in this verse. This is like the sowing and reaping choices of Galatians 6:6-10.

Like verse two, verse six has occasioned a great deal of debate.[2] The difficulty for the interpreter is twofold. First is Jesus' reference to the destiny of the non-abiding branches. Second, the identity of the third pronoun in the allegory, namely, "they." Jesus says that there are consequences from choosing not to abide in Him. He describes those consequences with another viticultural analogy as He describes the destiny of branches that are no longer attached to the vine.

But, Jesus' use of "anyone" does not require that the eleven disciples (the "you" of v. 5) be excluded. Rather, in verse five, where the plural "you" is very much in evidence (used twice), Jesus still uses the third person singular to refer to those same eleven disciples (as well as all believers). After saying "you are the branches" Jesus says "*he who* abides in Me and I in *him*" (italics added). His use of "anyone" in verse six then logically follows the "he who" of verse five and does not distinguish nonbelievers from the disciples. Rather, He is pointing to the individual choices they must each make to abide in Him if each of them wishes to be fruitful.

According to the Lordship view, the unfruitful branches that are "removed" in verse two are synonymous with the non-abiding branches in verse six.[3] They believe their removal symbolizes the judgment of eternal damnation experienced by all the unregenerate, whether they appear to be Christians or do not. Ultimately the problem being addressed by all of these men is that they are unable to resolve the Reformed doctrine of the perseverance of the saints with Jesus' words. That doctrine teaches that all true believers will persevere in good works all the way to the end of their lives. Yet, Jesus' words of warning to Peter in Luke 22 indicate that he did not persevere, though he never stopped belonging. For those who insist on a believer's requirement to persevere in good works to the end of their life, the conclusion, because of the doctrine of election, is that failure to do so means that the person was never a believer.[4] Bearing fruit is obviously good works. Thus, failure to bear fruit would be failure to persevere in good works. Therefore, they conclude being cast out must describe the fate of a nonbeliever whose lack of salvation was demonstrated by his lack of perseverance.

But, what if we were to continue the approach in this verse as sanctification truth rather than justification truth? What if we were to accept this warning as addressed to the eleven men Jesus was addressing right then? What would that do? Well, let us see.

Dillow does not see a justification focus in verse six. He rather says that, "the point of the figure of the vine and the branches is not to portray organic connection but enablement and fellowship. This casting out then is not from salvation but from fellowship."[5] Further, he sees the fire of 1 Corinthians 3:15 as the same as this verse.

> The apostle obviously saw an intimate connection between the believer and his work. To apply the fire of judgment to the believer is the same as applying it to his work. Indeed the believer's works are simply a metonymy for the believer himself. . . . The believer who does not remain in fellowship because of disobedience is cast out in judgment and withers spiritually, and faces severe divine discipline in time and loss of reward at the judgment seat of Christ.[6]

One difference between the two analogies, though, is that Jesus is looking at the person (the branch) while Paul is looking at the person's works. The fire of 1 Corinthians tests the quality of a believer's work in building up the body of believers in a local church, such as at Corinth, or in your local church. Where there is a connection between the two analogies is the relationship between bearing fruit and building quality material into the body of Christ. Only by abiding, and thereby bearing fruit, will anyone be able to build gold, silver, or precious stones onto the foundation of the church, which is Christ. And, in line with Paul's illustration, the non-abiding believer is not going to build anything worthy of reward. His works will be burned up before Christ, though "he himself will be saved, yet so as through fire" (1 Cor 3:15). The judgment is not a pleasant one. But, again, Jesus is not talking about the works themselves, but the branches, including the eleven men listening to Him at that time. Thus it becomes important to see that this branch is neither a nonbeliever nor one who loses his eternal salvation.

For the trained horticulturist, especially the viticulturist, this verse does not present a problem. Verses two and six are not looking at the same time of year. Verse two looks at the Spring while verse six looks at the Fall. Sprigs that sprout from buds along the fruiting branch are cleaned (i.e. *kathairei* in v. 2b) from the branches or trunk of the vine in the Spring (when the action of verse two would be occurring). These shoots would be too small and succulent to do anything more than wither away after being pulled off of the branch. They are sprigs that wither, not branches. They would not have enough wood in them to form a pile and make a fire. There also would not be any adventitious "branches" with sufficient time to develop woody stems, but only succulent sprouts. Even a two foot long sprout would wither to practically nothing in the Spring. To build a fire from branches as is described in verse six, mature wood would have to be removed. This happens in the severe pruning at the beginning of the dormant season after all fruit has been harvested, and all branches look alike. Also, it happens to *fruitful* as well as unfruitful branches.

Rather than being a warning of discipline or judgment, verse six is an illustration of uselessness in light of post-harvest, dormancy inducing, pruning. The best illustration of the uselessness resulting from a failure to abide within the vine-and-branch analogy could only come from the post-harvest pruning. Everything purged in early Spring was either growing from a branch (sprigs and suckers), the branch not being removed, or from an undesired location on the trunk. Only at the end of the season would there be "branches" removed, piled up, and burned. In fact, Jesus may have chosen to allude to post harvest cultural practices specifically because He did not want His disciples to mistakenly link fruitfulness or fruitlessness to divine discipline. Rather, He wanted them to see the importance of abiding itself. In the vineyard, anything not attached to the vine is useless and discarded. A part of the discarding process at the end of the productive season is the burning of dry materials. The burning need not describe judgment, but is simply one of the steps in the process being described. It is simply what happens to pruned materials. Their uselessness, not their destruction, is being emphasized.

If one takes the fire to represent the judgment of nonbelievers in hell, as does the Lordship position and most of those holding to justification-salvation being the issue of the passage, it must be based on the branch's failure to abide, not on its failure to bear fruit. Fruitfulness is not mentioned in verse six, only non-abiding. And, Jesus' excluding it from this verse *is* significant. These are branches of the vine that get carried out and burned. The one who wants to say the burned branches cannot represent regenerate Christians must explain how one can be attached to Christ, a branch, and then become detached without ever having been regenerate, on the one hand, or without losing one's salvation on the other hand.

The "Israel within an Israel" answer given by those who see this verse as justification truth is woefully inadequate. It seems that about the only way to interpret this by someone who wants to find this a commentary on justification would be to find some way to show that those branches were never a part of the vine, that they were never truly "in" Him.[7] Then Jesus is not implying a separation from Him but that the branches *never* abided in Him at all. But then, in doing this, we have Jesus issuing a warning that applies only to unbelievers to a group of men who do believe in Him. They do not need regeneration at this time. Their hearts needed strengthening to keep trusting Him in light of what they will experience over the next three days. These are men who Jesus knows will soon be separated from Him and will not continue in faith, but flee and hide in fear. They have just been passing through a period of failure in their arrogance toward each other and are about to enter another period of failure.

It seems better to ask the question: Who are the "they" of verse six? It clearly does not refer to God the Father nor to Jesus the Vine since both are singular in verse two, while "they" is plural in this verse. It does not refer to the apostles, since they are "you" in this context. The only two options left are either angels or people. If angels, then Jesus is referring to the gathering of humanity by the angels either for the Sheep-Goat Judgment (Matt 25:31-46), or for the Great White Throne Judgment (Rev 20:11-15). These same judgments were alluded to in His earlier parables of the kingdom in the parables of the Wheat and the Tares (Matt 13:24-30) and the Parable of the Dragnet (Matt 13:47-50). To find angels, then, one must see Jesus referring back to the Olivet Discourse and earlier instruction. The weakness of this view is the need to reach out of the context to import "angels." But, there is a better referent within the more immediate context of that evening to which Jesus is most likely referring.

To answer this question it may be best to look again at John 13:35. Jesus pointed His men to the *world* as those who would judge them. "By this all will know that you are My disciples, if you have love for one another." Those outside of Christ look at the fruit (love) of believers toward one another and decide whether they are for real. Charles Colson tells of this kind of love being expressed toward him as a new believer and while he was still in prison following Watergate. He says,

> I'll never forget the day one of them – Al Quie – called to say, "Chuck, because of your family problems, I'm going to ask the president if you can go home, while I serve the rest of your prison term." I gasped in disbelief. At the time, Al was the sixth-ranking Republican in the House, one of the most respected public figures in Washington. Yet he was willing to jeopardize it all out of love for me. It was a powerful witness that Jesus was real: that a believer would lay down his life for another.

As a consequence of this love between believers, Colson notes the response of the reporter who learned of this.

> As I retold the story for the cameras, the interviewer broke down and waved her hand, saying, "Stop, stop." Tears mixed with mascara were streaming down her cheeks. She excused herself, repaired her make-up, and – injecting confidence back into her voice – said, "Let's film that sequence once more." But hearing the story again, she could not hold back her tears. Later, she confessed that Al's willingness to sacrifice had touched her deeply, and she vowed to return to the church she had left years earlier.[8]

Remember Tertullian's quote of pagans who saw the love between Christians expressed in actions? Is it possible that Jesus is thus illustrating through this analogy the uselessness of the branches who do not abide (love the brethren)? Their failure to abide (have fruit) indicates to the world ("they") that they (the disciples) do not represent Jesus, God's vine in this allegory; thus, the world's attitude is to see them as unrelated to Christ, the vine. Thus, they are judged as useless or valueless—fit only for discard—as witnesses for Jesus in the same way that vine dressers judge the pruned materials as useless for future grape production.

If uselessness is not Jesus' point, then the only valid interpretation—for anyone holding eternal security—would be spiritual decline and discipline by death for persistently disobedient believers. Westcott struggles with this verse and his conclusion is illustrative of someone who wants to find this describing discipline by death. He says, "How a man can be 'in

Christ,' and yet afterwards separate himself from Him, is a mystery neither greater nor less than that involved in the fall of a creature created innocent. . . . Death breaks the connexion between the unfaithful Christian and Christ."[9] Thus he is forced to see divine discipline as Jesus' point and not a threat of Hell.

The two verses following this illustration help clarify Jesus' point and will be discussed in detail below. But let it suffice to state now that in this verse Jesus is clearly addressing His believing disciples with the possibility of their failure to abide in Him. And, He is not threatening them with Hell! Rather, He is lifting them (encouraging) to a place of productivity (fruitfulness).

We need to see then that verse six is a vivid portrayal of the result that comes from the failure to believe and obey the commandment that Jesus gave the disciples in John 13:34. History is replete with both the positive and negative results determined by obedience or disobedience of Christ's followers. In the early church they caught hold of the dynamism in Christ's promise of 13:35 and had the result of turning "the world upside down"(Acts 17:6). Listen to Luke's recounting of it in Acts 2:44-47:

Now all who believed were together, and had all things common, and sold their possessions and goods, and divided them among all, as anyone had need. So continuing daily with one accord in the temple, and breaking bread from house to house, they ate their food with gladness and simplicity of heart, praising God and *having favor with all the people. And the Lord added to the church daily those who were being saved.* (Italics added)

The last words of the foregoing recounting by Luke are a specific fulfillment of the promise of Jesus in John 13:35 The same obedience and fulfillment is seen in Acts 4:32-37 and Acts 6:1-7 (especially note the results in v. 7). In 1 Thessalonians, one of Paul's earliest letters, we find the same dramatic results:

And you became followers of us and of the Lord, having received the word in much affliction, with the joy of the Holy Spirit, *so that you became examples to all in Macedonia and Achaia who believe.* For from you the word of the Lord has sounded forth, not only in Macedonia and Achaia, but also in every place. *Your faith toward God has gone out so that we do not need to say anything.* (Italics added)

Ten years later Paul gives similar commendation to the same church:

We are bound to thank God always for you, brethren, as it is fitting, because your faith grows exceedingly, and the love of every
one of you all abounds toward each other, so that we ourselves
boast of you among the churches of God for your patience and faith
in all your persecutions and tribulations that you endure, which is
manifest evidence of the righteous judgment of God, that you may
be counted worthy of the kingdom of God, for which you also suffer
. . . (2 Thess. 1:3-5).

Similar testimonies could be cited over and over down through history. In the third century a man named Cyprian wrote a letter to a friend,
telling him of his decision to convert to Christianity:

This seems a cheerful world, Donatus, when I view it from this fair
garden, under the shadow of these vines. But if I climb some great
mountain and look out over the wide lands, you know very well
what I would see. Brigands on the high rocks, pirates on the sea,
in the amphitheaters men murdered to please applauding crowds.
It is a sick world, Donatus, an incredibly sick world. Yet, in the
midst of it, I have found a quiet and holy people. They have discovered a joy which is a thousand times better than any pleasure
of this sinful world. They are despised and persecuted, but they
care not. They have overcome the world. These people, Donatus,
are the Christians, and I am one of them.

Jesus Christ made clear to the disciples that love (i.e., fruit) would be
the key to success; however, that which seemed to be the normal response
for those early believers, even under persecution, is fairly rare among
those who name the name of Christ in our generation in our country.
Demas in 2 Timothy 4:10 seemed to be a rarity among Paul's associates in
his day but it seems to be closer to the norm in our day.

Is it not ironic that we have to look across the ocean to India and the
late Mother Teresa for a sterling example with international reputation
for one who took seriously the command and promise of Jesus Christ. A
news reporter was commissioned to interview Sister Teresa because of her
outstanding, selfless, life of service. After the extensive interview he said,
"I would not do what you are doing for all the money in the world." To

which, she responded, "Neither would I!" Point well taken. The world did not find fault with her. They simply admired her marvelous testimony as a devoted follower of Jesus Christ. No one questioned her focus.

These are the people who are the "all" in John 13:35 and the "they" in 15:6 who are looking for the love (i.e. fruit) among the believers. What they see in our society – even our evangelical society – is far removed from what Tertullian or Cyprian saw in the New Testament Church or Colonial America saw in Jonathan Edwards, the leading intellectual figure in his day when the minister was considered the most admired man in the community. In the most massive in-depth survey yet conducted on what Americans believe in, among the top twenty occupations Americans most admired, the protestant minister was voted nineteenth and he was given the same position in the bottom twenty of "America's sleaziest ways to make a living."[10]

Randall Balmer, an associate professor of religion at Barnard College/Columbia University, covering the Christian Booksellers Convention for Religious News Service, had the following evaluation of evangelicalism over the past two decades:

> The association's annual convention symbolizes a larger accommodation to American culture on the part of Evangelicals generally. When I was growing up within the evangelical subculture between 20 and 30 years ago, the most stinging epithet you could level against another believer was that he or she was 'worldly.' As Evangelicals have emerged from their subculture into the larger culture of recent years, that suspicion of 'worldliness' has dissipated. . . . Whereas materialism and affluence were once regarded as species of sin, Evangelicals in the 1980's sought to claim their share of the good life, and many invoked God to validate that quest. In the end, the undeniable excesses of the Christian Booksellers Association's annual convention tell us less about the business of evangelical publishing and retailing than they do about the accommodation of American evangelicalism to the values of the larger culture. While the rhetoric of separation from the world continues, evangelicals have, in fact, made themselves rather comfortable in that world.

More recently the world's view may be seen in the review by Nanci Hellmich in the May 21, 2001 issue of *USA Today* of the *Prayer of Jabez*:

Breaking Through to the Blessed Life. She asked the question, "Is 'Jabez' for the needy or the greedy?"

We believe that the foregoing examples are vivid demonstrations of the very thing that Christ warned the disciples about in verse six. When the world at large does not see a different value system from their own among those who profess a unique love relation to Jesus Christ, the believers are belittled, disparaged, maligned, and degraded (i.e. cast out as a branch). Their testimony is useless and non-existent as far as "they" are concerned. With respect to the "they," these believers have failed in Christ's command of John 13:34-35. They have failed in Christ's command of Acts 1:8. They have failed in their love for Christ (John 14:15-24).

On the other hand there is a much better possibility, as we shall now see in the following verses that complete the inclusio of 13:35 and 15:8.

15:7. "If you abide in Me, and My words abide in you, you shall ask what you desire, and it shall be done for you.

In contrast to the uselessness of the one who is "cast out," Jesus offers a major benefit to the one abiding in Him, namely, answered prayer. He does this through another conditional sentence. He says here, "If you abide in Me, *and you may or may not*, and My words abide in you, *and they may or may not, then* you shall ask whatever you desire, and it shall be done for you." Thus answered prayer is conditioned on two things: the disciple abiding in Jesus and His words abiding in the disciple. This is another way of saying that the one in complete fellowship with Him can expect answered prayer.

Our response to those who see abiding as an automatic condition of believers, as we saw in the justification-salvation interpretation of verses two and six, is to notice to *whom* Jesus addresses this condition. He says clearly that it is possible for the disciples sitting in His presence that evening to choose not to abide in Him. The Greek grammatical structure requires that it be understood that those men, clearly believers, clearly disciples, be able not to abide in Him and it must be possible for His words not to abide in them. Thus they could miss out on the mutual communion of such a relationship and its subsequent blessings.

But how does this mutual abiding take place? What are the mechanics of it? Abiding in Jesus is defined in terms of obedience to His commandment to love one another (v. 10) and clearly has 13:34 and 15:17, which are the bookends in view, so to speak, of this inclusio. But how do His words "abide" in us?[11] (See Appendix 9, "Abiding," for a full explanation of Jesus' use of this term and all of its various meanings.) Two things must be true for Jesus' words, His commandment to love (cf. 13:34-35), to "abide" in us. First, we must *know* it. But, what Jesus is discussing here goes beyond mere head knowledge or cognitive input. It cries out for application. Thus, the second thing that must also be true is that His words must be influencing us, affecting our attitudes and decisions. Jesus' word abides in us to the extent that it changes our motives and calls for a response in us.

This is what being a Spirit-filled Christian is all about. The Holy Spirit uses God's word to influence us by affecting our will. He does not speak to us audibly, nor does He make us robots when we are "filled" with the Spirit. Rather, when we look at the parallel passages of Ephesians 5:18-20 and Colossians 3:16, we see that being filled with the Spirit is the same as letting Christ's word "richly indwell" us. The Spirit uses the Scriptures that He inspired (2 Pet 1:20-21 and 1 Cor 2:13) to influence us.

How does the Spirit do this? In the same way that wine affects the person who is filled with it. This is the point of the command in Ephesians 5:18 when Paul says, "Do not be drunk with wine." He is saying that we are to allow the Holy Spirit to effect us in the same way that wine does the person who imbibes it. Wine does not take over the person in such a way as to turn him or her into a robot. Rather, it affects a person in the area of attitudes and judgments. The person under its influence may not even realize that he or she is making different kinds of decisions. But everyone around him can tell. Wine is "indwelling" that person in the sense that it is actively altering the mind that he or she exercises as a "free" agent and not a helpless robot. It is thereby influencing without directly controlling.

What Jesus is saying to His disciples that evening and to us today is that only as His word finds response in us are we truly abiding in Him and producing fruit or experiencing answered prayer. As His word influences us, it is alive and active and an integral element in our decision making process and it thereby "abides" in us (Heb 4:12). In so doing the Holy Spirit is using Jesus' word to affect our motives and worldview.

As we come into line with Christ's character through this process, we in turn ask for those things that reflect His desires (see chap. 14) and values. Then we are said to be asking in His name, according to His character, as a result of our fellowship with Him. Doing this, we can expect Him to answer precisely because we are asking for those things He already wants. This whole process is beautifully woven together in the statement of Paul in 2 Corinthians 3:18, "But we all, with unveiled face, beholding as in a mirror the glory of the Lord, are being transformed into the same image from glory to glory, just as by the Spirit of the Lord." We summarized it in the Nelson Study Bible note: "As believers behold the glory of God in the Word of God, the Spirit of God transforms them into the likeness of Jesus Christ. This is a description of the gradual process of sanctification."

The significance of the effect of this abiding on our prayer is expressed well by Westcott. "The petitions of the true disciples are echoes (so to speak) of Christ's words. As He has spoken so they speak. Their prayer is only some fragment of His teaching transformed into a supplication, and so it will necessarily be heard. It is important to notice how the promise of the absolute fulfillment of prayer is connected with the personal fellowship of the believer with Christ, both in the Synoptists, and in St. John."[12] This truth is expressed in Romans 8:26-27, as Paul describes the ministry of the Holy Spirit in the prayer life of the believer. He intercedes on our behalf according to God's good pleasure in ways we cannot comprehend or approach in our finite humanity.

Mitchell also observes that when we abide in Him "His will becomes our will. . . . Being in fellowship with Him, you will know His will. You will know what He wants done, and you will cooperate with God as a partner in revealing His character and His grace."[13] Thus, answered prayer comes as a result of abiding because the abiding believer's motives and thoughts are in line with Jesus' motives and thoughts which are expressed in His words and works and used by the Holy Spirit to effect our inner being as He indwells us and we study Scripture (cf. 1 Cor 2:13). And, the focus of those answered prayers is likely expressed in what follows of Jesus' conversation, we are praying for fruit. And our prayer for fruit will be answered with fruitfulness.[14]

15:8. "By this My Father is glorified, that you bear much fruit; so you will be My disciples.

Coming to verse eight we are struck by the parallelism of the "by this" to the "by this" of John 13:34. These are the bookends of this powerful inclusio. Having described fellowship in terms of mutual abiding, and having promised answered prayer as a result of such abiding, Jesus moves from the question of prayer to the issue of fruit and relates it to the question of discipleship. How does this work? A combination of Romans 12:1-2 with 2 Corinthians 3:18 provides us with the biblical procedure.

In the crucial hinge verse between the doctrinal and practical sections of Romans, Paul points out that the secret to taking off the masque of the world system around us and letting the real divine nature come shining through is seen in the renewing of the mind. Then, appealing to the same key in 2 Corinthians, namely, metamorphosis, he clearly spells out the process by which the mind is renewed. First, a believer looks carefully at the glory of God as revealed in the person of Christ (John 1:14-18). The more I know of what God is like, the more I am able to believe Him. Second, I will then find myself having hope in his promises because "he is faithful that promised" (Heb 10:23). Third, because of the growing hope that the believer has because of the growing faith, he/she is able to exercise a growing love for the people of God.

This faith, hope, love trilogy is beautifully worked out in Hebrews 10:22-25. There we draw near to God on the basis of faith (the upward exercise of faith in the person of God). And, as we draw near we are cleansed of our sin on the basis of Christ's work on the cross, by the blood of Jesus. Then, on the basis of His cleansing we express our faith by a steadfast hope, a confident expectation of the future promised by God (the forward exercise of hope in the promises of God). This motivates us to encourage each other to strive for love and good works (the outward exercise of love for the people of God). The love and good works are not automatic products of our justification, but expressions of our faith which must be brought forth by us, and which we must encourage in other believers as well if we wish to see them manifested at all.

The last phrase of 2 Corinthians 3:18 ties it all together by the Holy Spirit. We see this worked out in a believer's life. First, a Christian abides in Jesus by believing His promise that He will abide in him/her. Then, as the believer responds to Jesus' revealed will to love other believers, the Holy Spirit brings to that person's mind Jesus' desire and enables obedience. As the believer is influenced by the Spirit and seeks to obey Christ's commandment, he or she will begin to pray for those things which will make loving others possible. This in turn will result in "fruit" which glorifies God. The fruit will, in turn, prove that the believer is indeed a disciple of Jesus. This proof will not be to God, but to the world that is watching that life (cf. Matt 5:16).

So, what does Jesus mean by bearing fruit? Also, how does bearing fruit accomplish these two things? Though He never stops and says, "This is what I mean by fruit," Jesus does define it in the process of this conversation. He defines "fruit" in terms of *love* for one another. But, some see this fruit in terms of evangelism and say that fruit is saved souls.[15] Actually, what Jesus is saying and will say later in this chapter: Fruit is the method, and additions are the product. Remember the "by this" of

John 13:35 and 15:8. It is an evangelistic mission to which He is calling the apostles, and us. But the method is fruiting (loving) one another. All fruit has within it the seeds of reproduction.

Jesus says also that bearing this fruit is significant in that it glorifies God when we bear "much" fruit. The idea of glorifying God is that we "magnify or elevate His estimation in the sight of others" (cf. Matt 5:16).[16] Thus, by bearing fruit (loving the brethren) we participate in that part of Jesus' mission which involved revealing the Father. We see this lived out in the first chapters of Acts. The disciples brought glory to God in the midst of a hostile society as they bore witness to Jesus' resurrection and *thousands* were added to their number. They were extremely fruitful! But why were they fruitful? Not because people were being added. They were fruitful because they were loving one another and being empowered by the Holy Spirit to speak boldly to the questioning world.

They were fruitful whether people were being added to the church or not (2 Cor 2:14-15). It was God who was adding people as the church bore the fruit of loving one another (Acts 2:46-47). Further, what do we see them praying for when pressure came from the hostile world? They asked for boldness to keep proclaiming Christ, not safety from adversity or personal comfort. Remember also, in Acts it was not the miracles that caused the church to be viewed with favor by the people. It was their lives as they bore witness to Christ. And what did the world see? The fruit of loving one another. So we see, first, that bearing fruit led to winning the lost to Christ and did indeed elevate God in the eyes of the lost world (See Acts 2:44-47; 4:31-37; see also the testimony of the early church in Thessalonica—1 Thess 1:2-8; and 2 Thess 1:3-5).

Jesus followed His description of how to glorify the Father with the second statement about the significance of fruitfulness. He said bearing fruit caused them to "become" His disciples. Morris identifies the problem raised by Jesus' statement. "One would have thought that those Jesus was addressing were already disciples. It is possible, with ASV, to supply 'so' (the italics show that this word is not in the Greek). The meaning then will be that the bearing of fruit shows that they are disciples. It is also possible that we should not supply 'so'. The meaning then is that the Father is glorified both in the bearing of fruit and in their continuing to be disciples."[17] Actually, those are not two separate things. Rather, it is cause and effect. The NASB translation of the verse is helpful. In it Jesus says that they will "prove to be" His disciples. Prove to whom? To the world (see 13:35). The world will recognize their relationship with God by the fruit of love.[18] Westcott understands Jesus to be saying that "a Christian never 'is,' but always 'is becoming' a Christian. And it is by his fruitfulness that he vindicates his claim to the name."[19] As Mitchell aptly observes, "Discipleship is living in close, blessed, intimate fellowship with the Savior."[20] And bearing fruit reveals that one is doing just that.

It is wise to pause now and summarize what has been said in these first eight verses of chapter fifteen. When Jesus finished His words in the upper room and made His way to the Garden, He re-enforced His teaching with a visual illustration of it. When He gave the analogy of the vine and the branches Jesus based it on the cultural practice of His day, which was to clean up only the fruiting branches and tidy up the rows during the early spring growth following blooming. Severe pruning and removal of branches did not occur until the grapes were harvested and dormancy was being induced in late Fall. His use of the viticultural term, *kathairei* (to cleanse), which described the removal of sprouts from fruiting branches, should inform our understanding of His use of *airei* (to lift up) in the same sentence. Both actions occurring simultaneously, Jesus was looking at the farmer's care for all of the branches belonging to the vine, whether fruiting or not.

Jesus then moved from the question of the Father's care for them to their need to maintain fellowship with Him if they were going to be fruitful in His service. The sovereign Father will continuously be at work for, "even if we are faithless, He remains faithful. He cannot deny Himself" (2 Tim 2:13). "He is faithful who promised" (Heb 10:23). The preceding context demonstrates this faithfulness (John 14 and Luke 22:28-32). However, we cannot *experience the blessings* of His faithfulness unless we are following His leading and doing His will (cf. 13:17; 14:15-24).

Their failure to abide would result in personal uselessness, not condemnation. Jesus indicated this by describing the Fall, post-harvest pruning which is seen in the practice of burning all of the wood which is not attached to the vine. This is not done by the Vine grower in the allegory, but others ("they") who see by their (the believers) uselessness that they no longer are of value to the vine. Thus, even if His teaching in verse six indicated either discipline or judgment of those who do not abide in Him, *this verse cannot be used to inform the meaning of the second verse as some commentators attempt.* They describe separate practices from opposite ends of the season and would have been understood as such by the apostles (early spring cleaning and care of the branches and late fall removal of all extra growth).

Rather then focusing on the negatives of failure to abide, Jesus then clarified His point to them by discussing the benefits of maintaining fellowship with Him. Notice the double use of "let not your heart be troubled" (14:1, 27). He linked answered prayer to abiding and His Father's glory to their fruit-bearing. Both of these issues, developed and defined in verses four and five, were related directly and *conditionally* to the men standing in Jesus' presence. Both verses six and seven were begun with (third class) conditional clauses that indicated that it was possible for the disciples, undeniably identified by "you" in verse seven, to fail to abide. If they could fail to abide in verse seven, they could equally be described by and subject to the "warning" of verse six.

When the fruitfulness which results from abiding proved their relationship to Christ as His disciples in verse eight, and was seen in light of the promises of verses five and seven, their usefulness as His disciples could only be in view in the warning of verse six. This is especially true since the focus of the whole passage is on those outside of Christ who will or will not respond to Christ depending on how the disciples love (fruit) one another. Jesus was telling them so that they might know how they were going to win the lost. He was telling them how they were going to be evangelists, not how they could get regenerated.

In summary, Jesus was saying that your evangelism is not your sermons to the lost, but how you treat the saints (cf. 13:35). We must pause at this point to stress the importance of this principle for our churches today. *We will never really be successful in carrying out the great commission until we truly implement the great commandment.* We long to see a church plan their evangelism program for the year around the great commandment of John 13:34-35. Then, and only then, will we see the results that the first church saw in Acts 2 and 4.

In these verses, then, Jesus' message to His disciples was a positive encouragement, not a negative warning. He told them that, though He was departing, the Father was still caring for them. Jesus was *lifting* them up with His instruction and had completed the process of preparing them to bear fruit so that the lost would see Christ in them. He had prepared them through His instruction to bear fruit, which they would do very soon. To bear the fruit God intended they needed to continue to rely on Jesus and respond to His instruction. If they chose not to "abide" they were of no value to Christ's mission and could not be used by Him. Having said these things, Jesus was then ready to talk once more to them about their fruitfulness in terms of love for one another.[21] He next defines what they must do to abide in Him and bear fruit.

15:9. "As the Father loved Me, I also have loved you; continue in My love.

Having taught His men that abiding is necessary for fruitfulness and that it makes them disciples, Jesus continues to describe His idea of abiding further.[22] He begins by talking about His relationship with His Father as the model of their relationship with Him. Cook aptly notes that if John's description of Jesus as the *monogenēs* Son of God in John 1:18 "spoke of the Son's *unique* relationship with the Father, these words describe His *intimate* relationship with the Father. This in turn becomes the pattern of the intimate relationship that exists between Christ and the believer."[23] By recognizing the kind of relationship He is describing, the mystery of what He means by "abide" will begin to be unraveled for us.

We see the comparison being made by Jesus in that He begins by comparing His love for the disciples with the Father's love for Him. He does this by beginning with a comparative term (*kathōs*), translated "as" in NKJV, and which carries the idea of "just as" or "even as." He follows this by beginning the next phrase (concerning His love for them) with a term (*kagō*) which means "I also." Thus, Jesus is saying clearly that His love for the disciples is felt and expressed in an identical manner as the Father's for Him. He has imitated His heavenly Father in how He has loved them.

Jesus then follows this pronouncement of His love for them with a command for the disciples to "continue" in His love. How they are to continue will be explained in the next sentence. But, first let us examine what He is saying here. Jesus uses an aorist active imperative to command them to "continue." This same term (*menō*) is translated throughout this passage as "abide" and "remain." By His use of this aorist form of command, Jesus is telling them to *start* abiding in His love.[24] They are to start responding to it and letting Jesus' love have an influence in their lives just as He has commanded them to allow His words to do the same. Recall that they were not doing this when they came into the upper room (cf. Luke 22:12 and John 13:1-17) and also His repeated use of "if you loved me." Rather, they were fighting among themselves and worried about themselves more than about each other or than Jesus.

Concerning what Jesus means by "continue," "remain," or "abide," in this verse, Dillow notes that, "John's favorite term for an intimate walk with Christ is 'abide.' This term is his word for something conditional in the believer's relationship with Christ, fellowship within the family."[25] Again, the nature of a command is such that it may or may not be obeyed. Westcott concurs with this idea and says, "The love of Christ is, as it were, the atmosphere in which the disciple lives. It is not something realized at a momentary crisis, but enjoyed continuously. And this enjoyment depends, on the human side, upon the will of man. It can be made the sub- ject of a command."[26] When Jesus commands them to continue in His love He clearly implies by the command that they may not, and that it is by choices they make that they may or may not. Thus, not every believer can be described as continuing in Jesus' love! It is possible, by disobedience, to fail to continue.[27] How do we continue in Jesus' love? He tells us plainly in the very next sentence.

15:10. "If you keep My commandments, you will abide in My love, just as I have kept My Father's commandments and abide in His love.

Having commanded His men to continue in His love, Jesus describes the condition of doing that very thing - obedience to His commands. He does this by saying two key things. First He conditions continuing in His love on their response of obedience. Second, He offers His own obedience to the Father as their model for how it works. Let us look at these two ele- ments in Jesus' explanation for how we go about abiding in His love.

First, we abide by believing the promises for blessing, by settling down in what He has said (cf. John 14:1). We become a disciple the same way we became a son. We became a son by believing the gospel. We become a dis- ciple by continuing to believe the promises for blessing (13:17). The result of believing Him will be keeping His commandments. Jesus uses another conditional sentence to describe the disciple's responsibility. This condi- tion (third class), again, allows the possibility that the follower of Jesus might choose not to obey. Jesus says, "If you keep My commandments, *and you may or may not do so, then* you will abide in My love." Again, implied in this "if" statement with its result are the twin proposals: "He who obeys Me abides in My love. He who disobeys Me does not abide in My love. The choice is yours." Morris says, "Notice that this is done as an explanation of the means of abiding in His love. This is not some mystical experience. It is simple obedience. It is when a man keeps Christ's commandments that he abides in Christ's love. And once again appeal is made to Christ's own example. He kept the Father's commandments and thus abides con- tinually in the Father's love."[28]

Both Jesus and John are very either/or, black and white. We can see this in many of Jesus' absolute statements. We see this also with John in his first epistle. Compare 1 John 2:15b and 3:10. First he says (1 John

2:15b), "If anyone loves the world, the love of the Father is not in him." Then he later says (3:10), "In this the children of God and the children of the devil are manifest: Whoever does not practice righteousness is not of God, nor is he who does not love his brother." These absolute statements make it nearly impossible for anyone to be a believer if they are not seen as intentionally extreme, rather than true absolutes. In 1 John, the author is telling us that not to love is of the devil, whereas to love is of God. What a parallel this is to Jesus' two opposite descriptions of Peter in Matthew 16:17 and 23!

Dillow correctly recognizes that the Christian who refuses to obey Christ "will apparently no longer remain in Christ's love." He also notes, "This is true even though Paul has declared elsewhere that 'nothing shall be able to separate us from the love of God'" in Romans 8:39.[29] Where Paul is describing a positional (justification) truth, Jesus is describing a conditional (sanctification) truth, the *experience* of the believer. Cook clarifies the most important issue in the debate over whether we are looking at justification or sanctification truths, whether we are defining regeneration or describing its outworking in the life of a believer. He says that

> our obeying Christ and thus abiding in Him is compared to the Son's obeying the Father and thus abiding in Him; the Son was already *in* the Father by virtue of His sonship, but the son *abided* in the Father by obeying Him. We see, then, that just as Christ's abiding in the Father was the maintenance of personal fellowship with the Father, so our abiding in Christ is the maintenance of personal fellowship with Christ. Just as Christ's abiding in the Father was the continuous enjoyment of the position that was His, so our abiding in Christ is the continuous enjoyment of the position that is ours.[30]

Dillow says further,

> We remain in Christ's love by obeying commandments (John 15:9-10). If remaining and believing are equated, then believing is obeying commandments, a thought far removed from John's gospel of faith alone. If *meno* means "believe," a works gospel would be taught, and the verse would be reduced to the absurdity "He who believes in Me believes in Me." And further Jesus would then be saying, "If you believe in Me, and I believe in you, you will bear

much fruit." This is hardly a sensible statement! Furthermore, even if one could successfully argue that *meno* in one place could mean "believe," one cannot allow a possible meaning in one place to govern the clear meaning in so many others![31]

At this point it is very basic to understand that *believing is always the modus operandi of God*, whether it is unto justification or unto sanctification. This is certainly made clear by Paul in Galatians 3:1-3. The object of our believing, however, is the key to the result of believing. To believe the gospel is to become a child of God (John 1:12) and to pass from death to life (John 5:24). On the other hand, to believe the promises of God for blessing as God's child includes an understood response of obedience to the conditional element within those promises, namely, that He will bless as we obey and chastise failure to obey.

We find a parallel to this in the unconditional Abrahamic covenant of the Old Testament and the conditional enjoyment of one of its provisions in the Mosaic Covenant, namely occupation of the land of promise being conditioned on obedience. As a matter of fact, this is the whole issue of the argument of Hebrews and Paul's explanation in 1 Corinthians 10:11 that Israel's experience is given as an example to the Christian of his or her experience in sanctification.

Jesus offered Himself as the model of the believer. He kept His Father's commandments and thereby remained in His love. He proved His love for His Father to His disciples through His obedience to the Father. The Father expressed His love for the Son at such times as the Transfiguration. We see this described by Jesus in John 8:29, where He says, "He who sent Me is with Me. The Father has not left Me alone, for I always do those things that please Him." The disciples' *experience* of Jesus' love was going to be the same way. Thus, Jesus was telling them and us: If we wish to *enjoy* our position before God as beloved sons and daughters, we simply need to live obediently like His Son Jesus did.

15:11. "These things I have spoken to you that My joy may remain in you, and that your joy may be full.

Why did Jesus tell His disciples that He wanted them to obey Him, and promised that they would subsequently experience His love as a result? He told them precisely because He wanted them to enjoy the Christian life as they expressed it to the rest of the world (John 13:35). When Jesus says, "that My joy may remain in you," He is communicating the idea of purpose. His purpose for telling them these conditions of fellowship and fruitfulness was in order that they would also experience His joy. We must obey if we wish to share in Jesus' joy.[32]

From this point and into Jesus' prayer, joy becomes a prominent theme.[33] In contrast to the sorrow and anxiety they are feeling, the disciples should be responding with joy. We see here that they will not be able to experience that joy apart from a relationship of belief in and obedience to Christ, expressed by living out His commandments, something they have not been doing very well to this point (Luke 22). Dillow also notes well that, "to have one's joy 'made full' is not to become a Christian but, being a Christian already, to act like it!"[34]

But what is the nature of this joy? What exactly is being experienced? Jesus was a joyful person who delighted in obeying His Father. He *enjoyed* obeying Him. And He wants us to respond in the same way to Him. We are to enjoy the process and fruits of obeying God, especially by expressing love for one another in practical ways.[35] If we consider the opportunities of expressing love on a regular basis as interruptions that are annoying to us, then we are simply short-circuiting the experience of God's love. We simply cannot *experience* God's love if we are not actively loving God's children.

CHAPTER ELEVEN

CHRIST MOTIVATING TO WORLD WIDE OUTREACH
John 15:12-27

Mutual Love and Friendship with Christ
15:12-17

These verses complete the double inclusio that was introduced in John 13:34-35. We see the focus of love in this section by the even broader inclusio of "love" in the first and last verses of the Upper Room Discourse (13:1 and 17:26). Within this broad section John includes two more inclusios to focus our attention on the importance of what Jesus was saying to the eleven and to us. Of these inner inclusios, the broader inclusio of 13:34 and 15:17 is demarked by Jesus' command to love one another. The inner inclusio of 13:35 and 15:8 give us the result, namely, that the fruit of love for one another will convince the world that we are Christ's disciples. Within the inner inclusio are Jesus' affirmation of Himself as the one in whom they are to believe with the promise of answered prayer, provision of the Helper, His peace, and abundant fruitfulness. Now, having completed the inner inclusio, Jesus is ready to refocus on His command to love one another before turning to the issue of their coming trials and His provision for them to overcome (15:17—16:33). These inclusios can be viewed as follows:[1]

> 13:1 **Jesus' love (expressed):** "having loved His own who were in the world, He loved them to the end."

> 13:34 **Command to love:** "A new commandment I give to you, that you love one another"

> 13:35 **Proof of discipleship:** "By this will all know that you are My disciples, if you have love for one another."

15:8   **Proof of discipleship:** "By this is My Father glorified, that you bear much fruit [love]; so you will be My disciples."

15:17   **Command to love:** "These things I command you, that you love one another."

17:26   **Jesus' love (possessed):** "...that the love with which You have loved Me may be in them, and I in them."

In these verses Jesus has just focused their attention on the promise that bearing the fruit of love for one another would prove to the world that they are His disciples. He now completes His middle inclusio by refocusing them on His central concern, that they will love one another. So, having made abiding in His love and experiencing His joy contingent on obedience, Jesus next presents them with the all-encompassing command, to love one another. This repeats the command He gave them after He washed their feet (John 13:34-35) and ties what He is saying now to what He did and said then. He has embodied the principle of loving them with actions rather than thoughts or mere feelings. He has taken the form of a servant at a time when none of them were willing to serve. He has shown that true love gives of oneself to others without regard to personal status. His love for them has been demonstrated. He has expressed His love further by promising them provision and care in the coming days, assuring them that they will not cease to experience His love fully in His absence.

Though we are two chapters away from that earlier statement, we need to remember that Jesus was only moments away from it and that it is still the backdrop to what He is saying now. This command is defined in these six verses with the phrase "that you may love one another" forming this middle *inclusio*.[2] What Jesus is saying in this section is that by loving one another self-sacrificially as He did them, the disciples' obedience produces an experience of friendship with Christ while making them fruitful in His service.[3] *He is telling them how they will reproduce.* Thus, twice He has said to them, "By this" (13:35) and "By this . . ." (15:8). And these words are just as pointed for us today as they were for the disciples then. To miss it is to bring eternal ramifications at the judgment seat of Christ.

15:12. "This is My commandment, that you love one another as I have loved you.

Jesus begins the section by stating His purpose in instructing them.

He wants them to love one another in the same way He has loved them. When Jesus says, "that you love one another" He may either be stating the purpose or the content of the command. The use of *hina* (translated as "that") with the subjunctive mood in Greek normally indicates purpose (cf. 13:35) rather than content.[4] Further, Jesus' use of the present active subjunctive of *agapaō* (the verb form of "love") can be translated "keep on loving" in this context. But what does He mean by loving one another? Again, He has demonstrated it in His servant attitude and serving actions (13:1-17; cf. Phil 2:5-6). He will demonstrate it in His death (John 15:13).

15:13. "Greater love has no man than this, that he lay down his life for his friends.

Jesus next defines love in terms of self-sacrifice.[5] Thus, Jesus is looking at more than the cross (John 13:1-17).[6] In his Epistle which, again, is a reflection or meditation on the upper room, John defines love further for us in 1 John 3:16-18. It is expressed as a self-sacrificial attitude that motivates us to meet the physical needs of fellow Christians. It motivated Jesus to wash the disciples feet. It is practically and tangibly expressed, not emotionally. It is this love that motivated Jesus to leave heaven, to serve unthankful people, and ultimately to die for us (Phil 2:5-7). It is this love that should motivate us to respond to the needs of other believers.[7] It seems that 1 John 3:17 is especially pertinent because of his use of *bios*—one of the three words for life.

15:14. "You are My friends if you do whatever I command you.

Jesus now introduces a new element into the picture. He had earlier used the analogy of servant and master to describe them in John 13:16. Now He moves to change their status and perspective. He offers them friendship. We can see in the Gospel of John a gradual change in relationship between Jesus and His followers. In John 2:23-24, though many are believing in Him, Jesus does not yet entrust Himself to them. Now, in the intimacy of His last hours with this group of faithful men, Jesus describes the depth of change their relationship has experienced, He now views them as His friends.

Jesus uses another (third class) conditional statement to describe the relationship of obedience to their experience of friendship. And, again, by His use of "if," He clearly indicates that it is something that they might or might not choose to do. Still, their choice would have consequences. Dillow observes that much earlier Jesus had taught that only those who did His

Father's will were counted as His "friends" (mother, brother, sister, etc. i.e., those with whom He really has a filial relation, cf. Matt 12:48-50).[8] He then notes that when Jesus spoke here, "There was no question about the disciples' regenerate state, but there was a question about whether or not they would continue to walk in fellowship with their King and be His 'friend.'"[9] He then states the truth of Jesus' words well. "Friendship with Christ is *not* a free gift; it is conditional." [10] The addition of this condition to friendship shows that it requires commitment on our part if it is to be experienced.[11]

The significance of Jesus' statement is not that *He* becomes *our* friend if we obey Him. Though He is describing a conditional relationship, He is not describing a reciprocal one. This friendship is "carefully qualified" and only one directional.[12] We see this because, though Jesus says that they are His friends, He does *not* call Himself theirs. Thus the friendship is still that of an inferior to his superior. Jesus is not making us His equals, nor making Himself our equal. In the Old Testament we see kings show friendship by inviting persons to eat at their table. Thus David honors Jonathan by inviting Mephibosheth to eat regularly at his table (2 Sam 9). He also invites Barzillai the Gileadite to do the same after he helped him against Absalom (2 Sam 19). But, both men continue to bow to him as king and to show deference to him. Though designated friends, they do not cease to be his subjects. Interestingly, nowhere in Scripture is either God the Father or Jesus referred to as anyone's friend. In all the Old Testament only Abraham is called God's friend (2 Chron 20:7 and Isa 41:8), a title even Moses did not receive (Num 12:7-8) even when God supported him against Miriam and Aaron. This is even more significant when we realize that God is said to have talked to him face to face, "like a man speaks to his friend" (Ex 33:11). So, though Jesus may view us as His friends through our obedience, He remains our Lord.

15:15. "No longer do I call you servants, for a servant does not know what his master is doing; but I have called you friends, for all things that I have heard from My Father I have made known to you.

Jesus now defines what their new status as friends entails. Having linked the status of "friend" to those who obey Him, He describes the significance of that change by contrasting it with the status of a slave. The slave is not made privy to the master's thoughts and plans, whereas a friend is let in on his inner thoughts. It is a relationship of love rather than merely service. Thus Jesus is saying that He is willing to commit himself, to reveal His truths, to them as His friends.[13] Again, this is in contrast to His unwillingness to commit Himself to those believing in Him in John 2:24.

If we look back on the relationship Jesus had with them as their Rabbi, it was one of a master to his servants. Disciples of Rabbis served them, took orders from them, obeyed them. Jesus was clearly in charge and they were His assistants. That is what made His washing their feet so shocking just moments before! But now, Jesus says, they need no longer view themselves as merely His students and servants. They are being admitted to a new relationship of confidence. Jesus will let them in on His innermost thoughts.

Thinking back to the examples of Abraham and Moses (since God spoke to him like a friend speaks to a friend), both of these men were made privy to God's inner thoughts. They were allowed not only to know what He was thinking, but also to discuss those thoughts with Him. Jesus says that such is our relationship as obedient friends.[14] Jesus is even at that time revealing His inner thoughts to them.

Jesus says something else of significance in this verse. He announces that His revelation of the Father is now complete.[15] All that the Father had given Him to reveal to them had been revealed. And now they are ready to bear fruit.

15:16. "You have not chosen Me, but I have chosen you and appointed you that you should go and bear fruit, and that your fruit should remain, that whatever you ask the Father in My name He may give you.

Jesus returns to the issue of fruitfulness and answered prayer after establishing their position as His friends that results from obeying His command to love one another. Though He now calls them friends, they still do not have equal status with Him. This is evident when He states that He chose them to be His friends, not they Him.[16] Mitchell describes this relationship well. "You are not commanded to be friends, but you are called to be friends. You are not commanded to bear fruit, but you are chosen to bear fruit. You are only commanded to love one another."[17] If we are obedient to our calling, we will be obedient friends who are fruitful. And, seeing the conditional nature of this friendship and recognizing that it is a sanctification truth, we should see this as something experienced by the obedient believer and not something automatic to every believer. Thus,

Mitchell can legitimately say that, "you and I can revel in our adoption as sons and heirs, and yet know very little about being a friend of God."[18]

When Jesus says He chose them, He is not referring to election as it related to the doctrine of our justification.[19] The justification of believers is not an issue at this point. Though election does come up with regard to Judas in chapter seventeen, Jesus' point here is not to teach election unto salvation. The "election" to which He refers here is the act of His calling them to service, to fruitfulness.[20] Of those believing in Jesus, these men were chosen by Him and given a special status as apostles. They were further chosen to be the first fruitful followers after His resurrection.

Jesus' choice of this group of men had a two-fold objective as expressed by the purpose clause in this verse. They were to "go and bear fruit." These two verbs describe their (and our) ongoing mission and ministry.[21] But, Jesus appointed them to more than just that.

Jesus' desire for them to go and bear fruit also had a purpose, as expressed in a second purpose clause. The obedience Christ called for, which led to going and fruitfulness had the goal of a permanent impact. The fruit they were to bear would "remain." We can say it this way: "fruit" remaining is the result of "fruit" born (cf. John 13:35; 15:8). Why? Because, fruit has in it the seeds of reproduction. The fruit of love for the saints would reproduce itself in the fruit of lives as the lost world saw the difference in the lives of the saved. Thus Jesus prayed for the ones that would be their fruit (17:20). The opposite result is seen in 15:6. In 13:35 Jesus says their love will prove their relationship with Him to the world. In 15:1-5 He tells them that only by abiding in Him can they bear fruit, can they love one another as He loves them. Then, in 15:6 He warns that the world will reject their testimony if they fail to produce the fruit of love that evidences their abiding in Christ.

But the fruit in this verse is more than more love. Where earlier the "fruit" was their loving one another, here fruit may refer to the people impacted by that love, new believers. It makes much more sense to see people as the fruit Jesus is speaking of since going is necessary to this fruitfulness. We see this repeated in Matthew 28:18-20 that in going they were there commanded to *make disciples*. Also throughout the book of Acts it is the going church which preaches the good news of salvation in Christ and whose gospel bears fruit through large numbers of people believing in Jesus and joining the body of Christ.

A second purpose for their going and bearing fruit that Jesus describes is that it will lead to answered prayer.[22] We can expect, based on the context, the prayer to which Jesus refers will naturally be related to the issue of fruitfulness. As we are loving the saints, God will shine our light so the lost will see and respond to the gospel.

Additionally, seeing the relationship between Jesus' appointment and our dependence in prayer, we must also recognize that, as earlier shown in the analogy of the vine and branches, our fruitfulness depends on His faithfulness, not our will or work. We go while He makes us fruitful. The pressure is not on us to bear, but to obey and go.

15:17. "These things I command you, that you love one another.

Jesus now concludes this part of His instruction with the same statement He began it with, the second half of the inclusio, the command to love one another. But to what does "these things" refer?[23] It refers to all that Jesus has commanded them that evening. Jesus has described love in terms of what it does, in terms of its unselfish nature expressed through self-sacrifice and in terms of the fruit it will bear as they go forth loving each other His way. These are all products of abiding in Jesus and reflecting His character, even as it was demonstrated that evening in humble service to them. All of these truths are necessary elements to expressing mutual love, and so He says that such was His purpose in teaching them.[24]

Expect the Same Hostility Jesus Received
15:18-27

Having told them of His choice of them as His fruitful representatives to the lost world, Jesus now teaches them of the effect that His choice will have on their relationship to that world. In this next section He reveals to them that they will experience persecution because of their identification with the One whom the world hates without cause. In contrast to the love they are to express toward one another, they can expect hatred to be expressed toward them by the world. In this section we see the church's relationship to the world is that it is separate (not of the world), persecuted, hated, and outcast from the world's religious systems, exemplified by Judaism in the experience of the disciples.

They can expect hostility from the world.
15:18-20

Right up front we need to acknowledge what some might think is a contradiction to what we have been saying about love of fellow believers and its evangelistic impact. Jesus earlier told His disciples that the world would recognize them as His disciples by their love for one another. Now He tells them that they will be persecuted by that world. The fact that the world recognizes us as His disciples does not mean that it is a positive recognition, as Paul states very clearly in 2 Corinthians 2:14-17. Some will respond positively, and some negatively. But in either case, Paul says, "Thanks be to God who always leads us to triumph in Christ." That is because our testimony to Him will call forth a response from those observing our love for one another. Those who would come to Jesus will respond positively. Those who reject Jesus will reject His followers as well.

Jesus begins this section of instruction with the description of the opposition they will face from the unbelieving world in general. He provides them with two reasons and the responses they will find, both positive and negative.

15:18. "If the world hates you, you know that it hated Me before it hated you.

Jesus again uses a (first class) conditional sentence in which the "if" carries the idea of "since." This kind of sentence assumes the truth of what is said. Thus when He says "If the world hates you," He is actually affirming that the world's hatred is very real. He is saying in essence, "If the world hates you, *and you know that it does, then* you know that it hated Me before it hated you." The normal attitude of the anti-God world system is hatred and hostility.[25] Today we see this same hatred expressed in diatribes against Christians who are "intolerant" toward lifestyles condemned by God such as sexual promiscuity and homosexuality. We see this in the attacks on Christians in various Communist and Muslim countries. Jesus told them that they could know that this attitude is the normal response of the world, both to Him and to them.[26] In fact, they should not be surprised by it.

As Jesus spoke these words the Pharisees were planning to kill Him. Here when Jesus speaks of the world, it is the world system that is in opposition to God. The disciples' relationship to the world is not an insignificant issue with Jesus. He mentions the world directly thirty-six times and indirectly more than fifteen times in the upper room.[27] John reflects on Jesus' instructions and our relationship to the world and commands us in 1 John 2:15-17 not to love the world which is passing away. Again, in 1 John 3:13 he repeats Jesus' revelation about the world's hatred.

15:19. "If you were of the world, the world would love its own. Yet because you are not of the world, but I have chosen you out of the world, therefore the world hates you.

Why does the world hate the disciples, and all Christians? Jesus explains to them that they are no longer identified with the world and so not accepted by it. Five times in this verse He uses "the world" in contrast to them and thereby emphasizes the antagonism they face from the world.[28] He reveals their separation from the world by describing the nature of that separation and the reason for it.

Jesus begins His explanation by stating that the disciples are not a part of the world's "family" or "group of friends." He begins with a statement that by design affirms the *untruth* of the primary assertion (second class conditional sentence). He says by this, "If you were of the world, *and you know that you are NOT, then* the world would love its own, *which would have included you.*" Directly implied by this construction is the point that they are *not* a part of the world's social group. They (and we) are not included in its company, its family. They are not members of its club, of its clan or gang. The disciples and the world are not birds of the same feather.[29]

Jesus continues His instruction by explaining the reason why the world does not view them as being its "own kind." Jesus has chosen them "out of" the world. Twice in this same sentence Jesus uses the Greek preposition, *ek*, which can carry either the sense of origin and belonging or of departure and separation. It is often translated as "of" or "from" and "out of" when reflecting these two distinctions. In His first use, Jesus gives it the sense of origin when He says, "because you are not *of* the world." He is saying by this that one reason they are not accepted into the company of the world is because they no longer belong to its society. They are no more a part of the world than a Samaritan or an idol-worshipping Gentile was a part of temple worshipping Jewish society. For them this is a clearly understandable concept.

In New Testament times in Jewish society one had to be not only a Jew, but also a member of the synagogue, in order to be included in the social structure of a Jewish community. If one were expelled from the synagogue, as the Jews were doing to those who confessed Jesus, he or she was not only excluded from participating in the synagogue services, but also shunned by its members. This meant that he would have trouble getting work, buying or selling goods, obtaining medical help, or any other personal or social need which might be met by a member of the synagogue community (cf. Acts 6:1). This was a serious enough hindrance to life that some people refused to commit themselves when questioned about Jesus (John 9:22) or became secret disciples (John 12:42-43). They attempted to remain a part of the Jewish world.

Jesus said that the hostility normally placed on those excluded from the synagogue or who were not members of Jewish society would characterize the whole world's response to them. We see this today especially in the Middle East where Muslims who convert to Christianity are shunned by their families, who then hold a "funeral" and sometimes follow it by assassinating them. At best, they are simply rejected by every Muslim and must find work, companionship, and a marriage partner from within the Christian community.

The result of their separation from the world system and Jesus' calling them out of the world is that they will never be a part of the world again. This leads to the conclusion of what Jesus is telling them ("therefore"), namely, the world actively "hates" them. The antagonism that Jesus is describing to them will be a constant experience.[30] The hatred they will face will be permanent and constant. This says something to us today. We see growing antagonism even in the United States toward Evangelical Christianity. Some Christian leaders still entertain the idea that we can "fit into" American society and have a positive dialogue and relationship with these hostile elements. The truth of what Jesus said to the disciples then still applies today. If we are His and bearing fruit for Him, if we are called by Him out of the evil world system, then we will always find rejection and slander the normal response of our society. We live in a nation which is part of the God-hating world, not a Christian or semi-Christian nation. The more we reflect Jesus' character to our society, the more it will respond to us the same way the world of His day did to Him.

15:20. "Remember the word that I said to you, 'A servant is not greater than his master.' If they have persecuted Me, they will also persecute you. If they have kept My word, they will keep yours also.

Jesus again reminds them of what He had said earlier (John 13:16) and then relates that principle to His explanation here. Their identification with Christ, who was rejected, will bring rejection from the world. This therefore provides a second reason they will be hated. As the world hated Jesus, it will hate them precisely because it identifies them as His servants.

Jesus describes two responses they can expect and bases both on how people responded to Himself. He again does this through two "if" statements carrying the idea of "since" (first class conditions) and affirming the reality of what is being said. Thus Jesus is saying that those who persecuted Him will in turn persecute them while those who responded to Him positively (kept His word) will respond the same way to them.[31] We see from this that, when our lives truly reflect the character and calling of Jesus, we will experience both rejection and acceptance from people around us. In a similar vein, Paul describes the world's response to us in terms of the aroma associated with the Roman victory parade. We will smell either as the aroma of death or life (2 Cor 2:14-16).

The more we are like Jesus, the less that response will be because of us and the more it will be a reflection of their attitude toward Him. This should be our goal and should never discourage us. But, having said that, there are many Christians who think they are being persecuted for Christ when in reality they are being rejected because they are obnoxious individuals who irritate everyone around them. Let us be sure that our conduct is Christ-like such that any rejection we face will be for the right reason.

At the same time, let us be separate from the world and its values (cf. Rev 3:14-21 and the values of Laodicea). But, remember that "separate" does not mean physical isolation but spiritual integrity (John 17:15; 1 Cor 5:9-11; 2 Cor 6:14-7:1). They, and we, are to be distinct in the midst of the evil world system such that those in the world will indeed be unable to identify with us. And let us not be ashamed of those differences (2 Tim 1:8). In the process, let us not forget the significant promise of Christ to His disciples in Matthew 5:10-12:

> Blessed are those who are persecuted for righteousness' sake,
> For theirs is the kingdom of heaven.
> Blessed are you when they revile and persecute you,
> and say all kinds of evil against you falsely for my sake.
> Rejoice and be exceedingly glad, for great is your reward in heaven.

We need to regularly remind ourselves of the outstanding returns that Christ promised. The remuneration always far exceeds the renunciation (see Matt 19:27-30). We can never outgive God. We are becoming today by what we do with what He gave us what we will be in the life to come. Today is a day of becoming. Then is a day of being what we have become. We are preparing for the kingdom rule with Jesus Christ. There is a direct continuity between what we become in the present life and what we will be in the next (see Rev 3:21).

They can expect hostility from the Jews.
15:21-25

15:21. "But all these things they will do to you for My name's sake, because they do not know Him who sent Me.

Jesus now gives a third reason for their rejection by the world.[32] They will be rejected because of Jesus as a result of the world's ignorance of God. When Jesus says "for My names' sake" He means by this "because of Me." It is their (and our) identification with Jesus that produces the rejection. It is because this identification separates us from the rest of the world that this results.

But, He says also that they not only are not a part of the world and will be rejected because of their identification with Jesus, but their rejection from an antagonistic world results directly from its ignorance of God.[33] This is a reminder of something Jesus had already said to the Jews while teaching in the treasury of the temple in John 8:19. Though they claimed to worship the God of Abraham and Moses, Jesus said they did not even know Him. Rejection of Jesus was a symptom of a prior rejection of God. Today many Jews and Muslims claim to worship the same God as Christians. Some Christian leaders have said the same. But, by their rejection of Jesus, they actually reveal the fact that they do not know or worship God. In fact, though they identify their god with YHWH of the Old Testament, they are only self-deceived. Their antagonism to the gospel and persecution of Christians in fact reveals their ignorance of God.

Having revealed the third reason for their rejection, Jesus spends the next three verses explaining the significance of what He has just said. The unbelieving world is guilty and has no excuse for their sin in light of both Jesus' words and works.

15:22. "If I had not come and spoken to them, they would have no sin, but now they have no excuse for their sin.

Jesus says that the fact that those who rejected Him also heard Him makes them fully culpable for their sin. Though they do not know God, they cannot claim ignorance as an excuse. Deuteronomy 18:18-19 contains God's promise to Israel that He would raise up a prophet who would communicate His word to the people. Further, anyone's failure to listen would result in God requiring it of him or her, holding each accountable. Thus as Westcott observes, God placed "the responsibility of discernment" on the people and so their rejection of Jesus was inexcusable.[34] This is especially true when we recognize that Jesus fully revealed the Father and spoke with greater authority than any prophet before or after Him. Throughout the other three Gospels it is repeatedly emphasized that, "the generation to which Jesus came bore a greater responsibility than any previous generation."[35]

For example, after healing the man born blind and accepting his worship, He declared, "For judgment I have come into this world, that those who do not see may see, and that those who see may be made blind." Then, in response, the Pharisees ask, "Are we blind also?" Their question is a rhetorical question that, by its design, calls for a negative answer.[36] So, in essence they are not asking Jesus if they are blind, but denying any blindness on their parts. They are actually saying, "We are NOT blind!" Jesus' response is then to say, "If you were blind, *and we know you are not, then* you would have no sin; but, now you say, 'We see.' Therefore your sin remains!" Jesus says here not just that their sin remains, but that they have nothing to say in their defense. The term translated as "excuse" carries the sense of "pretense" or "pretext."[37] In other words, though they might want to cover their real motives and seem righteous, their rejection of Jesus' words exposes their true attitudes. Their sin cannot be hidden behind religious terminology and practices, something distinctly true of the religious leaders of Jesus' day (see Matt 15:1-20).

15:23. "He who hates Me hates My Father also.

The Jewish leaders clearly hated Jesus and eventually plotted His murder, the ultimate expression of hatred. That hatred was about to be brought to fullness in His arrest, trials, and crucifixion. But, their action communicated far more than just hatred toward Jesus. It revealed their hatred of God the Father as well. When Jesus says, "He who hates Me hates My Father also", He puts "Me" and "My Father" into emphatic positions in the sentence by placing them before the verbs where they would normally have followed the verbs like it is translated into English. By stating it this way He can be sure His men will understand that there is "no doubt as to the seriousness of the conduct of the men of His day."[38]

Their antagonism toward Him was actually antagonism toward the God they claimed to worship and serve. Jews today do not worship God, nor do Muslims, even though they claim to worship the God of Abraham. To worship God we must worship Jesus. To love God we must love Jesus. Since Christ and the Father are one, those who hate Christ hate the Father.

15:24. "If I had not done among them the works which no one else has done, they would have no sin; but now they have seen and also hated both Me and My Father.

Jesus provides a second cause of guilt for those rejecting Him. Not only did Jesus' words condemn the antagonistic world, but His works did also. The signs Jesus performed, including those recorded by John, demonstrated His deity and are some of what He is alluding to here. But, Jesus may also be referring to more than just His miracles. He may be referring to His whole life.[39] Even so, His primary focus is His miracles. We see Him alluding to this very issue earlier in His ministry as He debated with the unbelieving Jewish leaders. For example, after healing the man at the pool of Bethesda, Jesus responds to the Jew's criticism by pointing to His works as a greater witness to Him than John the Baptist (John 5:36).

After giving the analogy of the Good Shepherd, when the Jews wanted to stone Him for claiming to be the Son of God, Jesus responded that His works proved His identity and, even if they did not wish to believe Him, they should respond in belief because of His works (John 10:37-38). But, as can be seen in the raising of Lazarus, even in the face of such a powerful demonstration of His authority to create life, some eyewitnesses of the miracle still walked away in unbelief and reported the incident to the unbelieving Pharisees (John 11:45-46). And, just a few minutes earlier, talking to His disciples in the upper room, Jesus points to His works as a cause for their own trust in Him (John 14:11). Thus, one thing we can see in all of this is that, though they may not cause faith, miracles do call for a response by the person who witnesses them and makes that person responsible before God for how they respond.

And how has the Jewish leadership responded? With hatred of Jesus and also, therefore, hatred of His Father. Jesus says further that in His works they have seen both Him and God the Father.[40] Their rejection of Him has resulted in a rejection of the Father while making them accountable for their sin in that they were rejecting obvious evidence and could not claim that they had not been given an opportunity to believe or respond. Their commitment to rejection is then seen in Jesus' description of their attitude as enduring. Jesus chose to describe their awareness and response with perfect tense verbs, translated "seen" and "hated." By this He indicates that their response to each work was hatred which was permanent and which was still affecting their attitudes and actions up to that point. This attitude was described by Jesus in Matthew 12:31-32, popularly referred to as the unpardonable sin. After having heard His words and seen His works, they attributed them to the power of Beelzebub. That is, they attributed the credentials of heaven to hell. They were thereby entrenched in their rejection of Jesus, and would respond similarly to the disciples.

15:25. "But this happened that the word might be fulfilled which is written in their law, 'They hated Me without a cause.'

Jesus then turns to the very thing the Jewish leaders had fallen back on in their debates with Him, the Old Testament Scriptures. "Law" normally means Pentateuch, but can also mean all of the Old Testament, which is how Jesus is using it here, since He quotes from either Psalm 35:19 or 69:4 (both messianic Psalms of David). Further, when He says "their law" He is not saying that it is not Scripture, but that it is Scriptures that they recognize as authoritative. This is similar to his reference to "your law" in John 10:34 when He was debating with them there.[41] Thus, with a sense of irony, Jesus points to their own Scriptures as condemning them for their attitude.[42] Worse yet, their actions were a fulfillment of prophetic Scripture concerning the Messiah's rejection.

In summary, Jesus listed three things that made His opponents' rejection of Him inexcusable. They had heard His revelation of truth and rejected it. They had seen His works and rejected them. They had the Scriptures, and were condemned by them. They were without excuse.

The Holy Spirit and witness.
15:26-27

Having described the guilt of the unbelieving Jews, Jesus turns again to His own men who have responded in faith to those things the Jews have rejected. He tells them that in contrast to the world and Jews who stand guilty, the disciples will get further revelation. This is the third of the five descriptions of the Holy Spirit's ministry to the apostles. In the first one (John 14:15-18) Jesus began by describing the Spirit as "another Helper" (the Spirit of truth) and promised that He would abide in the disciples (and so us) forever. Then in 14:26 He promised that the Spirit would teach them and remind them of all that He taught them. Jesus describes Him there a second time as the Helper, the Spirit of truth, and then further as the one who proceeds from the Father and whose role will be to testify of Jesus and thereby enable them to in turn bear witness. Later, in 16:7 Jesus will say that He will send the Spirit to them and describes His convicting ministry.

And, finally, in 16:13-14 He will again call Him the Spirit of truth and promise that He will guide them into all the truth as He glorifies Christ. Remember the heavy encounter with the Pharisees in John 8. Christ tells them there that they are liars and their father, the Devil, is the Father of lies. Then in John 14, He tells the disciples, "I am the way, the truth, and the life." Now He emphasizes that they are going to receive the Spirit of Truth. Further, we should remember that the first act of discipline by God in the church dealt with a lie and the death brought fear upon all the church (Acts 5). The second thing mentioned in the seven things God hates in Proverbs 6:16 is a lying tongue. Yet there is probably nothing more characteristic of our country today than a lying tongue. In the recent publication, *The Day America Told the Truth*, after extensive national surveys they concluded that 91% of Americans lie as a rather regular procedure and 47% of them defend it.[43] Unfortunately, this is not limited to the world. More and more the church has become very much like the world and has begun to reflect its values and morals, in this area as well as many others.

15:26. "But when the Helper comes, whom I shall send to you from the Father, the Spirit of truth who proceeds from the Father, He will testify of Me.

Jesus begins this third description of the ministry of the Holy Spirit in the lives of the disciples with a contrasting connective which we translate "but."[44] Where the Jewish leadership could not experience the benefits of Jesus' ministry because their rejection was in fulfillment of Old Testament revelation, Jesus promises new revelation to His men through the ministry of the Holy Spirit.

Jesus begins by telling them when they will benefit, at the coming of the Helper. They will be told later to wait in Jerusalem for His coming. But, all they need to know at this time is that His coming is yet future. Still, His coming is also certain. Here Jesus does not say, "if the Helper comes," but "when." As a matter of fact, the Holy Spirit had always been eternally present. But He was shortly going to come alongside the Apostles in a new role, as the Spirit of truth.

Jesus then says that it is He who will send the Spirit of truth to them. Morris notes that, "whereas in 14:16 Jesus said that the Father would give the Spirit in response to His prayer, and in 14:26 that the Father would send Him in Christ's name, now Jesus says that He Himself will send Him from the Father." From this he concludes rightly, "The sending of the

Spirit is an activity which concerns them both."[45]

Jesus then describes the mission of the Spirit. He is sent in order to "testify" of Jesus. In other words, He will bear witness of Jesus even as Jesus bore witness of the Father. It is important to note at this point that the witness is to be a dual witness. As we speak the words of truth from the Word of God, the Holy Spirit brings inner conviction to unbelievers concerning Jesus Christ. Jesus further details this theme of the witness of the Holy Spirit in 16:8-11. Cook describes the theological significance of this statement well. "It should be noted that it is characteristic of John's gospel that the third person of the Godhead points to the second, and the second to the first (cf. John 14:9-10). The Spirit never glorifies Himself, and it is an indictment against certain movements in the contemporary church that they have overlooked this principle."[46]

Without the ministry of the Holy Spirit, I would not be able to give the glory to Christ. Yet, it is not the purpose of the Spirit for me to focus on Him. The Apostle Paul caught this balance beautifully in clarifying this to the Corinthian believers: "Therefore, I make known to you that no one speaking by the Spirit of God calls Jesus accursed, and no one can say that Jesus is Lord but by the Holy Spirit" (1 Cor 12:3). The Holy Spirit is in submission to the Son of God, and it is His task to put the focus on Christ—to give Him the glory. We honor the Holy Spirit most by glorifying Christ.

Again, note that the relationship described by Jesus is a dual witness: He and you. Hunt observes well that what Jesus is affirming is "that there exists an inseparable relationship between the Spirit's witness and that of the disciples." He notes the multiple uses of the second person plural pronoun to refer to the eleven, in which four times the Holy Spirit is described as coming to them. From this we see that Jesus' focus "is on the Paraclete coming to them first and then, together they bear witness to the world."[47]

Finally, in describing the Spirit, Jesus uses the masculine gender pronoun rather than the expected neuter pronoun in an emphatic way to refer to Him as a person. This is again true because its referent is the masculine form of "Paraclete." But also Jesus places emphasis on "He" since the verb already contains the idea of "He" in it and the pronoun is redundant. Cook sees the significance of this to indicate that Jesus is clarifying that the coming of the Holy Spirit is "not merely another manifestation of Christ."[48] Thus the modalist heresy that sees God revealing Himself in three forms, rather than being three persons sharing a single essence, is repudiated.

15:27. "And you also will bear witness, because you have been with Me from the beginning."

The impact of the Spirit's coming in light of His mission of testifying of Jesus (see John 16:8-11) is that the disciples will, in turn, bear witness also. Jesus uses the same verb here as He used in the verse above where it is translated "testify." There He spoke of the Spirit's ministry in the future tense. His bearing witness was yet to come.[49] Now He speaks of the disciples' coming ministry. Thus they could expect the Spirit's personal involvement in the process as they testified to Jesus. Laney says that, "believers never witness alone."[50] This is not necessarily true. If my witness is untrue or distorted it will be alone. When I testify to what the Spirit of truth has promised to convict of, He will testify. Thus a biblical witness will never be alone. When I witness, as my mouth utilizes the things that the Spirit of God is going to testify, I can always be sure that there is conviction of God in the hearer. This provides confidence for me as I go to witness.

Why would they be witnesses of Jesus? Because they were eye witnesses of His glory. He says that they will be witnesses because they have been with Him from the beginning of His ministry.[51]

Though these words are directed primarily to the eleven who had indeed been with Jesus throughout His ministry, it does not mean that believers today are exempt from the responsibility to bear witness of Jesus. The gift of the Spirit, whose mission continues to be that of bearing witness of Jesus to a lost world, means that we too have that same ministry. Having told them that they are going to testify of Him to the lost and hostile world, He again reminds them of the reason for His present instruction.

CHAPTER TWELVE

CHRIST PROVIDING THE PRINCIPLES OF WITNESS
John 16:1-15

They Can Expect Persecution and Death
16:1-4

The persecution the disciples faced included being made outcasts and being killed after Jesus' departure, an unusual ordination, to say the least. Jesus takes another opportunity to tell them what to expect before concluding His instruction to them that evening. He does this through a reminder of just how intense the hostility of the world will become.

Verse four appears to be another "hinge" verse in Jesus' instruction that evening. Commentators tend to place it either with what precedes it or what immediately follows. Or they place the first half of the verse with what precedes and the second half with what follows. As a hinge verse it contains elements of both what Jesus has just said and what He is about to discuss. This shows the connection of His thoughts as He moves from topic to topic. It does not require that this be a formal lecture or structured speech. It also does not mean that this is a literary device of John who is summarizing and manipulating an evening's conversation in order to develop his own theological message. Too many commentators comment on John's style of communication rather than seeing Him quoting Jesus and thus reflecting Jesus' way of saying things. Obviously John has been selective in his choice of material, as is demonstrated by Luke 22. But, he is not putting words into Jesus' mouth or having Jesus teach something He did not teach. We attribute these words and also these transitions to Jesus, and ask what it is He was saying to His men then, and thereby to us today. In the next verse, in fact, we see Jesus addressing the eleven and telling them again His reason for discussing these things with them at this time.

16:1. "These things I have spoken to you, that you should not be made to stumble.

Jesus tells them about the world's rejection and guilt, as well as promises the aid of the Holy Spirit, with the purpose of keeping them from "stumbling."[1] He uses a passive form of the verb for stumbling, thus the translation "you should not be *made* to stumble" ("be stumbled"), and so implies that they might be victimized by the circumstances if they were not forewarned.[2] He uses "stumble" one other time in the Gospel (translated "offend" in John 6:61). There it includes the idea of no longer following Him. It may have the same sense here.[3] And so Jesus' point is that apart from His warning their faith would be shattered and they would give up in defeat. Remember (see Luke 22:31), they were still going to be scattered that very night.

But, they would be regathered when they saw that everything Jesus predicted had happened as He said, and thereby were reminded that He was indeed in control of His own destiny and circumstances (cf. John 10:17-18). It was then that they would understand fully. We see the impact of this in the following months when in Acts 3 and 4 they respond to persecution and threats with faith and boldness rather than fear and trembling. When we look at Peter's actions and words in John 18 and Acts 2 and 4 we can see nothing but stark contrasts. Where he cowers before women and slaves on the night of Jesus' arrest, he boldly proclaims Jesus before thousands and stands firm before the Sanhedrin, the most powerful men in the country apart from Pilate.

16:2. "They will put you out of the synagogues; yes, the time is coming that whoever kills you will think that he offers God service.

Jesus takes His disciples one step farther. Where earlier He had talked about the hostile world in general, He has now moved their attention to the religious community, their religious leaders in particular. The religious community will not only hate them, but will expel them and kill them. This is a worse response than that of the world in general. We can expect the world to misunderstand, but not the religious leaders (cf. Ezek 34). This has already been alluded to in the Gospel. In John 9:22 the parents of the man born blind were afraid to speak up for fear of being thrown out of the synagogue. And, John 12:42 testifies that many Jews remained silent about their faith in Jesus because of this threat.

It would become a very real experience for believers in the years to come. F. F. Bruce tells us that, "At the time when the Gospel was written these words had acquired a special relevance from the inclusion in the synagogue prayers of a curse on the Nazarenes, which was intended to ensure that the followers of Jesus could take no part in the service."[4] Being put out of the synagogue was just the beginning of persecution; death was the ultimate.

The phrase used by Jesus that is translated "offers God service" uses religious terminology. The term for "service" is the noun form of the verb Jesus used when He rejected Satan's offer of the kingdoms of the world in exchange for worship. Jesus quoted the command to worship the Lord and *serve* Him only (Matt 4:40). So, too, here this "phrase expresses the rendering of a religious service . . ., and more particularly the rendering of a sacrifice as service. . . . The slaughter of Christians, as guilty of blasphemy (Acts vii. 57 f., vi. 13), would necessarily be regarded by zealots as an act of devotion pleasing to God, and not merely as a good work."[5] We find this attitude reflected in a rabbinical commentary on Numbers 25:13 which says, "Did he then bring an offering, that power to make atonement should be attributed to him? But this you may learn that every one who sheds the blood of the godless is like one who brings an offering."[6] Saul's persecution of the church in Acts 8 and 9 was the outworking of this very thing.

16:3. "And these things they will do to you because they have not known the Father nor Me.

As He said earlier in John 15:21, the attacks of those who will one day martyr them arises from a world which is ignorant of God. Again, His point is that though it will be religious people attacking them and killing them, even religious Jews, their religious motives did not spring from devotion to God, but to their religion. As we have seen through the centuries of human history, persecution from religious communities has been more intense than that which comes merely from the "world."

16:4. "But these things I have told you, that when the time comes, you may remember that I told you of them. And these things I did not say to you at the beginning, because I was with you.

Jesus again looks to the future and gives His reason for instructing them that night once more.[7] He is not only thinking of the events about to unfold. He is looking, from that context, into the future experience of the church. He also does not expect them to remember what He said that evening. They are indeed going to forget and scatter in great dismay. But, a day is quickly coming when they will need to remember that their suffering was indeed anticipated by Christ. Jesus not only tells them that He is anticipating their future need for assurance, but then explains why He had not told them of this sooner.

Jesus explains to His men that He had not discussed the issues of their rejection and suffering because He had been with them up to that point. He had indeed been able to protect them from harm and had carried the brunt of the hostility. He had protected them. But now things were changing. With Jesus' departure, a subject He is about to return to, they will no longer have the same protection they had enjoyed. In Luke 22:35-37 we see this same truth expressed in another way. Jesus reminds them there of His special provision for them when He sent them out in pairs to announce the kingdom throughout the villages of Judea. When He had sent them out they had experienced supernatural protection and provision. He tells them that from that point on they would not have that same special provision, and must plan for that reality. So too here, Jesus is telling His men that His departure means that they are going to face new challenges. And, as Mitchell summarizes Jesus' warning to them and us as well, He tells them that "the world in its hatred for the disciples . . . are the facts of the Christian life."[8]

Having told them to expect suffering after His departure, Jesus is ready to return again to the issue of His departure which He had introduced at very beginning after washing the disciples' feet. But, before we turn to this further instruction, we need to think a little more about suffering for the faith. Suffering is not failure or something out of God's control. Rather, we should all view this as part of our training. It is "Ranger Training" for the kingdom. We see this truth reflected in passages such as James 1:2-4 and Romans 5:3-5. Trials produce certain traits in a believer: patience, perseverance, character, and hope. These are things we all need.

A soldier goes to Ranger School in the army in order to become a member of the Army's elite corps of shock troops who spearhead the attack on the battlefields. To be able to meet the rigors of combat the soldier is put through an intensity of training that pushes him to the very limits of his strength and will. When he comes out of those weeks of intense suffering and stress he is a different person. He is a Ranger. None of the process is pleasant or easy. But all of it is necessary. The same is true for believers. We are God's shock troops in a hostile world. To serve in His army we must have a strength of character which cannot be gained by reading books. It must be learned by living it. Thus persecution and suffering have proven historically to be blessings from God. It has been through this that faith has often grown strongest and more souls have been won to the Lord as men and women have responded with the boldness of the Holy Spirit's enablement to bear witness all the way to death.

As Jesus finishes telling them to expect persecution and returns to the topic of His departure, He tells them that His provision for overcoming tribulation is the Helper, the Holy Spirit, who convicts the world and guides believers while revealing Jesus' words to the disciples. Finally, He promises them peace.

Their Wrong Response
16:5-6

16:5. "But now I go away to Him who sent Me, and none of you asks Me, 'Where are You going?'

Jesus now returns to the subject of His departure with the goal of explaining its value to them. Having warned them of the world's response to them as His representatives, He continues His instruction by changing the subject with the phrase, "but now."[9] Jesus is simply returning to the point He had been making earlier, the fact of His departure, and refocusing their attention on what He has wanted to discuss from the beginning. Jesus' point is that no one is asking Him any questions now when they ought to be. Note the progression: Nobody is asking now. Before you were asking. Now when you ought to be asking you aren't.

Before going further, we must note that this verse may be seen by some to contradict John 13:36. There the disciples, Peter in particular, asks Jesus very plainly about where He is going. Later Thomas (14:5) asks a second question about His departure.[10] So Jesus' comment seems to go against the obvious record of events. Rather, He is saying essentially that now that it is appropriate to be asking questions, they have gone silent. They have understood what Jesus has said about suffering, and are probably alarmed by all of the "bad news." Of course, we should remember that they still do not understand that His departure includes the cross. They are only thinking in terms of His "walking out" on them. Also, Jesus certainly could remember at that point what questions they had asked Him earlier. Thus His point is that they really have not been listening to Him and are not interested in knowing where He is going. He has just told them that they are going to be hated, persecuted, and martyred by the hostile world. So Jesus' point is more that they are not listening rather than that they are not asking.

But, though fully conscious of what He is about to face, Jesus still has their best interests in mind. He reminds them again that His departure from them means a return to the Father who sent Him. He had already told them about this and identified it as a blessing for both Him and them. But, again, they are not concerned with the benefits of His departure. Rather, they are upset.

16:6. "But because I have said these things to you, sorrow has filled your heart.

Once again we see the heart of a true disciplemaker. Notice that Jesus does not ignore their feelings, even when they are inappropriate, but rather acknowledges them. He tells them that they are completely overcome with sorrow. In fact, they are overcome with sorrow to the point that they cannot see beyond their own loss.[11] Jesus recognizes this and again reminds them of a benefit they are failing to see which, if they could stop and think about it, would completely change their perspective to one of joy. Jesus is constantly discipling and we cannot help but think that He continues to do that with us today even though He is not visible to us. These lessons should speak volumes to us as we study His Word and depend on His Spirit to empower it.

The Spirit of Truth and Witness
16:7-15

These verses contain the last two promises of the Holy Spirit. In these Jesus teaches His men that the Helper, the Spirit of truth, will have a ministry of conviction in the world and guidance and disclosure to them. Much has been written concerning the conviction ministry of the Holy Spirit. These are some of the most difficult verses to interpret because Jesus does not provide many details concerning exactly what He meant. Yet, these are also very significant words and worthy of our study.

16:7. "Nevertheless I tell you the truth. It is to your advantage that I go away; for if I do not go away, the Helper will not come to you; but if I depart, I will send Him to you.

Jesus begins this next promise of the Holy Spirit with a reminder of His sincerity and intense desire that they pay attention to what He is saying.

This is the point of His reminding them that He is telling them "the truth." It is not that He fears that they do not believe Him. But He wants them to listen with an accepting ear on the basis of their trust in Him. Since He is trustworthy, they should accept what He is about to say as true.

Characteristically Jesus models servant-leadership ~ putting others first (cf. Phil 2). Thus, He begins by reminding them that *they* are the ones to gain by His departure. He says, "It is to *your* advantage that I go away." If we think about it we can see His point well. Jesus was not gaining anything that He did not already possess by returning to the Father. We will see this truth in His prayer in the next chapter. In fact, we learn from other Scriptures, like Hebrews 7-9, that Jesus simply moved to another realm of service as our High Priest. His work did not end with His ascension. Interestingly, Jesus uses the same term to describe their advantage as Caiaphas used in John 11:50 when he said that it was "expedient" for the nation that one man die for the people rather than the whole nation perish.

Twice Jesus says, "to you," as He explains the benefit they are to receive in His departure. He is stressing the fact that the Spirit is not given to the world as a conviction directly to the world, but to the believer as an agent to convict the world. He is not saying that the Spirit will convict the world directly, but through "you." That is why the antagonism of the world comes toward the believer. It comes because we are the convicting agent and it does not appreciate what we are communicating (cf. 2 Cor 2:14-16).

In describing His departure Jesus uses two different terms. The first word He chose communicates the idea of "go away" and emphasizes the sense of separation.[12] Then He used a second term to say He would "depart" which emphasizes the sense of a "journey."[13] At least one point that we should glean from what Jesus says is that His departure was a part of His plan and something He was determined to do. The disciples are being asked to accept His and the Father's will. We can see it as a part of His divine plan and an expression of His sovereign control. His glorification involves a departure and a journey. He is leaving this earth and returning to heaven where He will receive the worship and adoration of the heavenly host and where He will minister on their (and our) behalf in a way He could never do while on earth.

But then He continues and describes the particular benefit or advantage that He has in mind at that point in time. His departure is a necessary prerequisite to the coming of the Helper, who He has already identified as the Holy Spirit and the Spirit of truth. He affirms, though, that the Helper's coming is contingent on His departure. Jesus does this in what might seem a negative way and says, "If I do not go away, the Helper will not come." Again, the sense of "if" He uses here is that He may or may not go away. It is the "if" of possibilities. Thus He is saying, "If I do not go away, *and for the sake of argument I may or may not go away, then* the Helper will not come." And then by implication, *"But if I do go, then He will certainly come."* Further, Jesus uses a double negative construction for added emphasis. Thus He is saying, "If I do not go, there is *no possible way* that the Holy Spirit will come." His coming, and all the attendant benefits to the disciples, is withheld as long as Jesus remains on earth.

Some may misunderstand the point Jesus makes here. Some may think that the Holy Spirit could not work as long as Jesus was on earth.[14] But that is not the point Jesus is making. The Holy Spirit was always active on earth, especially during Jesus' ministry (cf. Luke 4:14). But as the Spirit led Jesus, so now He was to work in and through Jesus' disciples. And so, He sends Him to them.

Jesus then states the same promises to them in a positive way. "If I depart, I will send Him to you."[15] This is the same kind of "if" as He had just used. Thus, He still raises the possibility of His not departing, but with the implication of its negative results. His staying would not benefit the disciples.[16] This certainly must have been puzzling to them. Without Him they were left alone in a society where no one cared for them. The Romans hated them because they were disturbers of the peace and the Jewish leaders hated them because they saw them as blasphemers. The only One who truly cared for them was Jesus and now He is telling them that it is to their advantage that He leaves. But we may ask how is it to their advantage that the Holy Spirit comes rather than Jesus staying? The answer to this for *them* is also the answer for *us* and Jesus answers this in the next few verses.

The first benefit of the Holy Spirit's coming is His convicting ministry. In these four verses (8-11) Jesus describes the ministry of the Spirit to the world rather than to believers. Even so, in a sense Jesus is also speaking in part about the ministry of the disciples to the world as well. He has already told them that the Spirit will testify of Him and that they too would be witnesses (John 15:26-27). In this section we see one key way in which the Spirit will "co-witness" with the disciples and us.[17] As Hunt observes well, "The only understanding the world will have of the Spirit/Paraclete will be through its observations of the Church. The Advocate "will bear witness" through and with the disciples to the world with the result that it will be convicted of its sins (16:8-11; cf. 13:25)."[18] He will use us as we bear the fruit of loving one another and impact the lost world with the testimony of our being Jesus' disciples. How will He use us? He will use us to convict the world. We will be His agents. We will be the prick in the conscience of that lost person who sees Christ in us and must respond to Him, whether with faith or rebellion.

Let us recap the truths of John 13:34-35; 15:8 and 15:15. We recognize that it is the fruit (love) of the Church, the Body of Christ, which will be Jesus' witnessing agent (cf. Acts 1:8). This occurs when its members have been brought into "body" relationship by the Head of the Body, Jesus Christ, from His exalted position at the right hand of the Father (Acts 2), and placed in the care of the Holy Spirit (cf. 1 Cor 12:12-13).

16:8. "And when He has come, He will convict the world of sin, and of righteousness, and of judgment:

Again, we must first notice that in this description of the Holy Spirit's ministry, He convicts the world, not believers. In this we have a clear contrast between the ministry of Christ as our Paraclete and the ministry of the Holy Spirit as Paraclete. In 1 John 2:1-2 Jesus serves as our Paraclete on the basis of His being the propitiation for our sins. We know from Hebrews 9:11-15 that He serves as both our high priest and perfect sacrifice. And, as John says in 1 John 1:7 and 9, Jesus' blood cleanses us from all sin. Thus, His ministry as Paraclete is on our behalf, representing us before God and satisfying God's wrath. He is our defense and our hope. The Holy Spirit does not do the same for the world. Cook understands the significance of Jesus' description of the Spirit's work to be related to His completed work on the cross.[19] It is on the basis of what Jesus did that the Spirit convicts the world. But what did Jesus mean when He said that the Spirit would "convict" the world?

Convicts. The Greek term translated as "He will convict" (*elenchō*) can mean either to convict, reprove, or rebuke and has a range of uses, two being possible meanings as it is used in this context. First, it may mean the enlightenment and smiting of conscience.[20] This would reflect such passages as John 3:20 and 8:46. It would thus refer to a *convincing* work of the Spirit in the world, to the lost. Second, He could mean that the Holy Spirit acts as Counsel for the Prosecution in His dealings with the world, in contrast to Jesus' defense of believers before the Father in Heaven.[21] This seems the better sense here, especially in light of John's use of Paraclete with regard to Jesus in 1 John 2:2. We must remember, though, that this sense of "convict" is only used of the world, never of believers. By this use of the word, Jesus says that the Holy Spirit is demonstrating something in a clear light beyond the fear of contradiction. The Holy Spirit is making a case for Jesus Christ through the believer against the world. Christ makes a case for me against the devil at the right hand of God.[22]

Jesus describes three areas of the Spirit's convicting ministry by using the preposition *peri* which can be translated as "about," "concerning," "of," "with reference to," "for," or "on account of."[23] He uses this preposition both in this verse and at the beginning of the next three verses. In the NKJV it is translated "of."[24] If it is understood in terms of content, then Jesus is saying that the content of the Spirit's conviction involves the areas of sin, righteousness, and judgment.[25] The best understanding of this preposition is to see Jesus giving reasons for His convicting the world, thus "on account of," or "because." This same verb, "convict," has the prepositional expression ("about, concerning") after it three other times in the New Testament. In Luke 3 John the Baptist confronts King Herod after he has married his brother's wife, Herodias. And in verse nineteen this verb is used with the preposition to say that John reproved or rebuked Herod "concerning" or "with reference to" Herodias. Thus in this use the verb communicates the idea of confrontation and accusation with the preposition providing the reason for that confrontation.

In John 8:46 Jesus challenges His detractors with the question, "Which of you convicts Me of sin?" Here "convict" carries the more judicial sense of proving His guilt with regard to sin in particular. In this case the preposition looks at the content of their accusation, though it would still carry the sense of "because of." In Jude 15 the term is used with the same preposition to describe God's condemnation of the lost world in the last days when He comes to judge. Then He will "convict" the ungodly "concerning" or "of" their ungodly deeds as He executes judgment upon them. In each of these other three passages the idea behind the use of the verb with the preposition is that of confrontation and exposure. So His convicting ministry is more than just convincing people of sin, righteousness, and judgment. It is confronting them and exposing the truth to them in a way that forces a response.

What exactly does Jesus mean by sin, righteousness, and judgment? Morris notes well that all three areas of conviction relate directly to Jesus Christ and should be interpreted Christologically.[26] We will discuss these three key terms as they appear in the verses that follow. These are the three areas that the Holy Spirit, through the believer, will convict the lost about. Therefore, there are three areas that need to be in our witness. If we expect the convicting work of the Spirit to be active through us, we must be saying what He is authenticating. We must say something concerning sin (not sins, but the sin of unbelief), righteousness with respect to Christ, and something concerning the coming judgment of Satan.[27]

One problem faced in the next three verses is to understand the relationship between sin, righteousness, and judgment, and the clauses that follow each. Do these clauses give the cause or reason for the world's conviction? Or do they explain the content of that conviction? The question arises from Jesus use of a word (*hoti*) that can be translated causally ("because") as in the NKJV, or explicatively ("in that"). Because of the pattern of the three statements, it is most likely that all three have the same meaning. In other words, Jesus is purposefully developing a parallel pattern here. What we see in these verses is that the weight of evidence favors the causal sense, principally because verse ten can only make good sense if understood causally.[28] This sense of the term will be followed in the exposition that follows.

16:9. "Of sin, because they do not believe in Me;

The first verdict of guilt that the prosecuting Holy Spirit will bring against the world is that of its sin which results from its rejection of Jesus. Notice that this is not "sins," but "sin." A specific sin, or aspect of sin is in view, not various sins. This sin is the sin of unbelief. There will never be a person in hell for being drunken or immoral, but only for failure to believe in Jesus Christ who pardons all our sins. The Holy Spirit convicts the world of sin specifically because it has chosen not to believe in Jesus. In the Gospel of John sin is described in terms of failure to believe, and so too here.[29] We see this in John 3:18, "He who believes in Him is not condemned; but he who does not believe is condemned already, because he has not believed in the name of the only begotten Son of God." Jesus says to the Jews after healing the man by the Pool of Bethesda that the one who "hears" and "believes" does not "come into judgment, but has passed from death into life" (John 5:24).

After declaring that He is the light of the world at the Feast of Tabernacles, Jesus says to the Jews, "you will die in your sins; for if you do not believe that I am *He*, you will die in your sins" (John 8:24). We see this in Jesus' confrontation with the Pharisees following His healing of the man born blind. When the healed man met Him, Jesus asked him, "Do you believe in the Son of Man?" The healed man asked for Him to be pointed out to him so "that I may believe in Him." When Jesus identified Himself as the Son of Man, the healed man worshipped Him, the ultimate sign of belief in the Gospel of John![30] Then in His confrontation with the Jews which followed, Jesus concluded their denial of personal blindness by saying, "If you were blind, you would have no sin; but now you say, 'We see.' Therefore your sin remains" (John 9:40-41). Their sin resulted from their response of unbelief (failure to respond with worship) to Jesus. The Holy Spirit will convict the world of this truth.

And how will He do it? Through believers. As we bear the fruit of loving one another before a lost world, and as that world sees Jesus in us, the Holy Spirit will remind it of its sin, of its unbelief, of its separation from God. The testimony of many Christians over the years, abiding in Christ in the presence of their unbelieving co-workers, has been the peculiar awareness of those unbelievers of the Christian's presence. As a Christian officer in the United States Army, I (Gary) was amazed at how often other soldiers would apologize to me after using profanity or cursing in my presence. This is especially intriguing when you consider that during my days in the Army vulgarity and swearing were considered rather macho. But, what I found was that, though they were "committed pagans," these sometimes crude and vulgar soldiers were acutely aware of my presence and felt they had caused me offense. I made them uncomfortable, even after telling them I was not offended. I also found that at times others reacted with intense hostility toward me, without provocation on my part. Some found my choice of language (not to use theirs) or conduct (not to practice their lifestyle) down right irritating. Some just hated me because I was a Christian. Almost all reacted in one way or another.

As the people of Jesus' day reacted to Him, whether good or bad, so too will people today react to us as they see Jesus. Those who do not believe in Jesus, who reject the light, will reject those who bear the light in their lives. The more they see Jesus in us, the more the Holy Spirit bears witness to Jesus through us as His co-witnesses, the more people will become aware of their standing before God. He will convict them—make them acutely aware—of their sin. For example, like Gary, I (Earl) remember a specific occasion when I was serving as station chaplain at Dallas Naval Air Station. I had stepped out of my office to carry out a duty and a weekend chaplain of another faith was left in the office with my chaplain's assistant. When I opened the door on my return, I found a room full of recruits listening to a dirty joke told by the weekend chaplain. He hit the punch line just as I opened the door. Everyone scattered and I heard them saying about the other chaplain, "Chaplain____ is a real regular guy." I went over to my desk feeling rejected. My assistant, feeling the rejection for me said, "Chaplain, I think I know how you are feeling, but just let me tell you that when those guys have a problem or get in trouble, you will be the one they come to." Yes, it is our beautiful responsibility to just let the light of Christ shine through.

16:10. "...of righteousness, because I go to My Father and you see Me no more;

The second verdict of guilt the Holy Spirit will bring against the world concerns righteousness. But what does Jesus mean by righteousness here? And whose righteousness is in view? Here the idea of righteousness can be either righteousness in general, the world's false righteousness, or Jesus' righteousness.[31] The world is found guilty of its false righteousness precisely because the Father vindicated Jesus' righteousness. Thus, His return to the Father is the evidence used by the Holy Spirit to demonstrate Jesus' righteousness and the world's evil. It is the evidence used to force the world to react to Jesus with either belief or hatred (cf. 2 Cor 2:14-16).

This is why no gospel presentation is complete without a focus on the resurrection and ascension of Christ. We see the importance of this truth, and its application, in the Book of Acts. As you go through Acts, notice that nearly every gospel sermon in Acts, no matter how abbreviated, contain a reference to Jesus' resurrection. It is the vindication of His righteousness and a critical truth that must be believed for someone to be born again. This is why it is an unpardonable sin not to believe on Christ. That is also why when we are given the opportunity to give a defense of our hope in Christ (1 Peter 3:15), our witness must include an affirmation of Jesus' resurrection and ascension.

In explaining these truths, the Holy Spirit will co-witness with us to them and affirm Jesus' righteousness before them. We have found that in very few instances do people reject Jesus' resurrection and ascension! They accept it! But, in very few instances have they understood its significance either! Jesus was proven righteous! The world was proven wrong! That calls for a response! And, that leads to judgment. It may be worth noting at this point how many of present day "gospel" messages only preach half of the gospel. There is often a great elaboration on the suffering and death of Christ, but nothing on the resurrection. The death without the resurrection is a tragedy, not a triumph. We would do better to catch the balanced emphasis of the gospel messages in Scripture.

16:11. "...of judgment, because the ruler of this world is judged.

The final verdict brought by the Holy Spirit is that of judgment. Judgment here refers to the judgment resulting from Christ's crucifixion. Jesus is saying that His words in John 12:31 have been fulfilled, and Satan has been judged. This judgment will ultimately be completed with his expulsion from heaven (Rev 12:7-9), capture and imprisonment for a thousand years in the bottomless pit (Rev 20:1-6), and then his splashing in the lake of fire where he will be tormented eternally (Rev 20:10).

But how has he been judged now? In part the judgment of the world comes because in their coming treatment of Jesus, which will be followed by His going to the Father and subsequent vindication, they are bringing about the defeat of Satan. The world's rejection is leading to Satan's defeat when Jesus dies for the sins of mankind and frees man from the clutches of Satan's kingdom. Thus, Jesus' coming death condemns Satan to ultimate defeat. This is why Satan did everything in his power to keep Jesus from the cross. The cross spells doom for Satan. But the world also is then convicted in that it has aligned itself with Satan and subsequently shares in his coming judgment.

The Holy Spirit will expose this truth to the world through believers as He co-witnesses with us. As we share the gospel, a part of our message must be a warning of the coming judgment of God to a world careening toward that fateful day. For those who align themselves with Satan, there is a single destiny. They shall share his fate. They shall swim in the blazing cauldron of the lake of fire, forever, with Satan and his other minions. Why is this their fate? Not because Jesus wants to send them there, but because Jesus conquered their king and has assigned him that destiny, along with all who choose to follow him. When we testify to Jesus' condemnation of Satan on the cross, the Holy Spirit announces the world's condemnation for joining with Satan against Christ. Hell is prepared for the Devil and his angels. The only human beings that will ever go there are those who choose it instead of eternal fellowship with Christ in the heavenly city, the New Jerusalem of Revelation 21.

16:12. "I still have many things to say to you, but you cannot bear them now.

Having described the ministry of the Spirit to the world, Jesus pauses in His description of the Holy Spirit's ministry to remind the disciples once again that He is only telling them part of what they need to know. He has much He would like to say to them, but they cannot handle it. Still, He is about to tell them more about the Spirit's ministry to them and through them in the next three verses. To understand Jesus' point we must understand what He meant by their inability to "bear" more.[32]

When Jesus says they cannot "bear" the additional information He would like to share with them, He uses a term (*bastazein*) that can carry the sense of a crushing burden. Though he uses the same term to describe the Jews taking up stones to stone Jesus, John will also use this word to describe Jesus carrying the cross in 19:17. It is used by Peter in Acts 15:10 when he describes the legalists' desire to bring the Gentile believers under the Mosaic Law. He says they are trying to place on them something too heavy to bear. Paul uses it in his command in Galatians 6:2 for us to "bear" one another's burdens. There he uses a term for burden that has the sense of an overwhelming weight.

So, Jesus' point is that He recognizes that He has given them just about as much information as they can handle and still be able to deal with the events to follow. This is a principle we see Jesus follow in John (cf. John 2:23-24; 15:13f). He knows their limits and is not going to overload them. In fact, Jesus says that they cannot bear the other things He has for them "now," at that time, but that they will be able to bear them later. When He says this, He puts "now" at the very end of the sentence for emphasis, where it normally would have occurred elsewhere. His focus remains on their need and ability, even as His instruction concludes and He gets closer to the time and place of His betrayal.

Do Jesus' words in this verse conflict with what He has already said earlier (John 14:26)? No. There He promised them that the Holy Spirit would remind them of what He had *already* taught them. Following will be a promise of *additional* revelation, things He has not been able to teach them yet. In fact, these next verses promise them that Jesus will complete through the ministry of the Holy Spirit His mission of revelation to them (cf. 2 Peter 1:20-21). In these verses Jesus repeats the same phrase three times with it placed at the end of each sentence for emphasis. He says each time, "and He will declare/announce it to you." Interestingly, the woman at the well used the same term to describe her anticipation of the ministry of the Messiah to the Samaritans (John 4:24).

Having recognized that the disciples cannot handle more revelation from Him at that time, Jesus gives His "fifth" Paraclete promise (16:13-15) to the disciples and describes the Spirit's ministry to them in terms of three works.

16:13. "However, when He, the Spirit of truth, has come, He will guide you into all truth; for He will not speak on His own authority, but whatever He hears He will speak; and He will tell you things to come.

First, Jesus promised them that the Holy Spirit would *guide* them into *all truth*.[33] The Holy Spirit's ministry was one of guiding Jesus' disciples into those truths He had not yet disclosed to them. Jesus had given them as much revelation, as much truth, as they could handle at that point in time. But they would need more. As those who would be used of the Spirit (2 Peter 1:20-21) to write the epistles, they would need more revelation. So He promised them here that the Helper, here again called the Spirit of truth (as in chaps. 14 and 15), would complete the task and could be trusted to provide them all of the information, all of the truth, they needed to effectively serve Christ.

This promise was made to the eleven disciples first and foremost; thus, Jesus said, "He will guide *you*." This He did. And, as a result, along with the promise in John 14:26 of His reminding them of Jesus' teachings, we have the assurance that the New Testament writings contain God's truth, both in the Gospels (they were reminded of what He taught them) and in the Epistles and Revelation (new truths).

Jesus also explained *how* this would be accomplished for them. The Spirit would teach them those things Jesus told Him to communicate. In the same way that Jesus did not speak on His own initiative apart from the Father (John 8:26), so too the Holy Spirit would not be ministering to them independently of Jesus. We see in this the functioning of the members of the Godhead and the full unity of the Trinity. And this meant that they could trust the Spirit's revelation to be in full accord with what Jesus had already taught them and to indeed reflect Jesus' will and words. As Jesus was sent by the Father and faithfully spoke His words, so too the Holy Spirit would be a faithful representative of Christ.

But, can Jesus' promise also be applied to us today? It does not apply to us today in the same way as it did to the original eleven. He was with them physically and taught them. He has not been with us physically. But, there is an aspect of this promise that does still apply. Though we do not receive new revelation, we can and should rely on the Holy Spirit to guide us. He does this through God's word as we allow the Scriptures to abide in us and allow the Spirit to influence us through it (Eph 5:18; Col 3:16). This is what Jesus meant by letting His word abide in us. As Cook aptly reminds us, "For the modern believer, this means the truth as found in the

Bible, for God is no longer giving new revelations about Christ, and the Bible is the only source of truth that we know to be completely and verbally inspired by God."[34] And Hunt speaks well when he says, "All these passages (particularly John 16:12-15) *apply* to the believer today from the standpoint that they teach him that he can know that the Spirit will give him understanding of the Bible. The contemporary believer draws upon the written revelation which the Spirit made known to the apostles."[35]

The second aspect of the Spirit's ministry described by Jesus is that of His providing them *additional revelation* beyond what they had already received from Him. "Things to come" refers back to what Jesus said in verse twelve, "I still have *many things* to say to you, but you cannot bear them *now*" (italics ours). Jesus promises that the Holy Spirit will reveal those *many things* to them. We see these many things in the writings of the New Testament authors, both in the epistles and Revelation.[36]

16:14. "He will glorify Me, for He will take of what is Mine and declare it to you.

A third aspect of the Holy Spirit's ministry to the disciples is that He would glorify Jesus by revealing the things of Jesus to them. Again this follows the same pattern as Jesus' ministry of revealing the Father and disclosing those things He had said and shown to Him.[37] In the case of the Spirit, Jesus would be the focus, the subject of His revelation. He would glorify Jesus by revealing the truths concerning His person and works. From this we see that the Spirit's ministry is completely Christocentric. This is a helpful guide in evaluating many of the modern Christian movements that lay a heavy emphasis on the person and work of the Holy Spirit. As Laney aptly notes, "It is significant that the Holy Spirit works to glorify Christ rather than to draw attention to Himself. This truth may provide insight in determining what works are genuinely of the Holy Spirit."[38]

I (Earl) shall never forget the vividness with which God drove this priority home to me. In 1976 I was conducting several series of Spiritual Gift Conferences in Sydney and Melbourne, Australia for a month. During one series in Melbourne, I had occasion, while in route to a downtown church to travel through a park in which I viewed a beautiful statue far to my right. Though the park was rather dimly lit, I saw the beauty of the statue clearly because of the very appropriate lighting of it. After I had passed through, only then it occurred to me that I would never have been able to see the statue if it had not been for the lights shining on it. Yet it never occurred to me to think of the lights because I was focused on the statue. Truly, the lights were doing their job. It was then that I thought, "How like the ministry of the Holy Spirit in relation to Christ. It is not the purpose of the Spirit to draw attention to Himself but to shine the light on Christ."

Any movement or teaching that glorifies the Spirit, or shifts its focus from Christ to the Spirit, clearly is not a product of the Spirit's work. Clearly this is what the Apostle Paul is saying to the super-spiritual pneumatics in Corinth: "Therefore, I make known to you that no one speaking by the Spirit of God calls Jesus accursed, and no one can say that Jesus is Lord but by the Holy Spirit" (1 Cor 12:3).

More than just revealing Jesus, the Holy Spirit continues Jesus' ministry. As Carson notes, this "does not simply mean that the Paraclete passes on what Jesus declares, but that all the revelation bound up in Jesus' person and mission are pressed home on the disciples." Further, "the content of *what is mine* is nothing more and nothing else than what the Father gave him to say and do;"[39] Thus, the Holy Spirit continues Jesus' ministry of revealing the Father by revealing the Son.

16:15. "All things that the Father has are Mine. Therefore I said that He will take of Mine and declare it to you.

Jesus now defines what He means by "mine" and clarifies its meaning in regard to His relationship with the Father. It seems that this explanation was called for since the next logical question a Hebrew believer might ask is: If the Holy Spirit is glorifying You, is that not taking away the glory that God the Father deserves? Jesus responds to this possible objection by stating that *everything* is His as well as the Father's. Through this Jesus once again indicates His equality with the Father.[40]

But this tells us something else also. Though Jesus has subordinated Himself to the Father and spoken His words and performed His deeds, He has not done it as an inferior. Voluntary subordination is not inferiority. At the same time, He is clarifying for the disciples that, though He has sought to glorify the Father (cf. John 17:3-5, "I have glorified You"), His receiving glory does not detract from the Father's glory. When the Spirit glorifies Jesus, He is not taking away anything belonging to the Father because Jesus and the Father jointly possess everything. We see in this a powerful statement of the unity of the Godhead as expressed in the relationship between the Father and the Son. This same idea will appear again in Jesus' prayer in chapter seventeen. And, implied in this is the truth that the Holy Spirit shares the same equality in the Godhead because He is serving Jesus in the same way that Jesus serves the Father though He is joint possessor of everything. Thus we are able to see implied in Jesus' statement the voluntary submission of equals within the Godhead.

Now, having promised them this ministry of the Spirit and described its nature, Jesus returns again to the issue of His departure.

CHAPTER THIRTEEN

CHRIST PROMISING FULL AND ENDURING JOY

John 16:16-33

Sorrow Will Turn to Joy
16:16-24

Jesus' response to the disciples' puzzlement over His promise to depart for "a little while" was to reveal that they would experience great sorrow soon, but then understand when their joy was made full. In one sense Jesus' instruction is coming full circle. He began the evening expressing His love for them and followed that by announcing His betrayal and departure. He is now completing His instruction with a reminder of His departure before serving them again as their representative before God in prayer. But, having told them all they can bear, He reminds them again of what is about to transpire. He is about to leave them and return to His Father (cf. John 13:1).

6:16. "A little while, and you will not see Me; and again a little while, and you will see Me, because I go to the Father.

Jesus warns them again of His coming departure, but assures them that they will see Him again. In verse ten He had already repeated the warning to them that a time was coming when they would not see Him again. Now He focuses on the immediate of the next few days. Thus, "little while" is a reference to His time in the tomb between His death and resurrection. The reason for this short time of separation is "because I go to the Father." This again relates them back to what He has already said, that He is going to the Father and they should be glad. He has just finished talking about the benefits of His return to the Father in terms of the ministry of the Holy Spirit in them and to the world. And so they should understand this repeated declaration of His departure in a more positive light. But, they do not yet seem to be listening very well.

16:17-18. Then some of His disciples said among themselves, "What is this that He says to us, 'A little while, and you will not see Me; and again a little while, and you will see Me'; and, 'because I go to the Father'?" They said therefore, "What is this that He says, 'A little while'? We do not know what He is saying."

The disciples grab onto the idea of "a little while" and are once again confused. It is interesting to note that they do not ask Jesus what He means, but begin to try to figure it out among themselves. John uses the imperfect tense verb form of "said" to describe their asking, indicating that they continued discussing this among themselves, probably while Jesus was attempting to go on with His instruction. They were still struggling with the ideas He had presented to them that evening, especially since they did not have the conceptual categories to understand that the Messiah would suffer and die, leave them, and be replaced by another Comforter. It is evident from this that they were indeed unprepared to handle more than what Jesus had already told them that evening.

16:19. Now Jesus knew that they desired to ask Him, and He said to them, "Are you inquiring among yourselves about what I said, 'A little while and you will not see Me, and again a little while and you will see Me'?

Jesus then confronts them about their lack of understanding, and their hesitancy to question Him. Rather than listening to Him, they are talking among themselves, and so not getting anywhere. Jesus can see this and speaks up immediately. Their talking back and forth among themselves had to be very visible.[1] Anyone who has taught a class knows how obvious it is when students try to converse in secret while the teacher speaks. Though He had chided them a few times already that evening for their lack of understanding that did not mean that He wanted them to be silent. No. He as the master Disciplemaker expected to interact with them and confronted them when they hesitated to come to Him for clarification.

16:20. "Most assuredly, I say to you that you will weep and lament, but the world will rejoice; and you will be sorrowful, but your sorrow will be turned into joy.

Jesus now begins to answer the real question that needs to be answered rather than the obvious one of what a "little while" means. They are about to face a time of emotional trauma that will be eclipsed by a greater joy after that "little while" is over. Jesus warns them that they are about to experience deep emotional trauma, and that even while they are devastated the world that hates Him will be rejoicing. Of interest is His use of a term for weeping which is always connected to death in the Gospel of John. In John 11:31 and 33, it is weeping in response to the death of Lazarus. Then Jesus' words are fulfilled in John 20:11ff by Mary as she wept outside His tomb after finding it empty.

Still, His words of assurance are that their sorrow will be short lived and will quickly be turned to joy. They need to trust Him. Jesus emphasizes this by changing the kind of contrasting conjunction in His sentence. The first "but" (de: "but the world will rejoice") is a mild contrast and can even be translated as "and" at times, as it is later in this verse (de: "and you will be sorrowful"). The second "but" (alla: "but your sorrow will be turned into joy") produces a strong contrast and is likely used by Jesus to alert them to the significance of the change. Yes, they will experience sorrow, BUT that sorrow will not persist! His point is that "The disciples' sorrow over the crucifixion would be surpassed by their rejoicing over the resurrection."[2]

16:21. "A woman, when she is in labor, has sorrow because her hour has come; but as soon as she has given birth to the child, she no longer remembers the anguish, for joy that a human being has been born into the world.

Jesus gives His men the illustration of a woman giving birth to a child to assure them that their sorrow will only be temporary. He says that though a woman experiences "sorrow" as she begins her labor, she quickly forgets it over the joy of giving birth. Laney notes well that her "soon forgetting" is probably hyperbole on Jesus' part.[3] My own experience is that my wife did not "forget" the pain all that quickly, though years later it is difficult for her to picture its intensity. Still, Jesus' point is that the woman focuses on her child and rejoices in its birth to the extent that the pain she has just experienced is no longer the focus of her attention. This, too, will be their experience.

There is a strong tendency among some to take this verse eschatologically. In other words, they see Jesus referring to the fulfillment of the kingdom promises and to His second coming rather than to the immediate situation the disciples will be experiencing. They base this in part on the fact that the birth pang imagery is a common Old Testament way of describing the judgment of God at the consummation of history and inauguration of His kingdom during a time of tribulation in which He judges the world and purifies Israel. The prime example of this imagery would be found in Isaiah 66:7-14 where it is used in conjunction with the last days. This same imagery is used in Isaiah 26:17-18 and Hosea 13:13-15 to describe Judah and Israel's experience of God's judgment by Assyria because of their continued rebellion against Him.

From this they conclude that Jesus must be referring to the Great Tribulation that precedes His second advent because it was understood as picturing the coming of Messiah in Judaism.[4] Rather, the context makes it plain what Jesus is saying and to whom. Though the term He used, which is translated "anguish," literally means "tribulation" or "trouble," this same term will be used again by Him in 16:33 to describe the experience of the disciples following His departure and NOT during the eschaton. It is the "norm" of their experience as they serve their departed Lord.

16:22. "And therefore you now have sorrow; but I will see you again and your heart will rejoice, and your joy no one will take from you.

Jesus again turns to their present condition and acknowledges that they were even then experiencing "sorrow." But He follows it with the promise that they will see Him again and will then stop sorrowing. But, more than that, they will experience a joy that will permanently replace their sorrow.

Jesus is again looking at their experience of the next few days. His use of "therefore" links this verse with the preceding one and indicates that it is an application of the principle He just stated. Thus it is a clear reference to His resurrection appearances. His point is that, though they are now grieved by the news of His departure and will be plunged into even greater sorrow by His death, He knows there is joy coming very soon.[5]

16:23. "And in that day you will ask Me nothing. Most assuredly, I say to you, whatever you ask the Father in My name He will give you.

Having recognized their grief and told them they are going to experience anguish that will be replaced by joy, Jesus describes to them the significance of His promise. Everything will make sense. Simply stated, this is what He means by "in that day you will ask Me nothing." But even as He says this, His thoughts move to the next blessing He wants to discuss—answered prayer. Thus He has another "hinge" here in the first half of this verse that connects the issue of their sorrow and confusion with their privileged position before God in the verses that follow.

Some wish to make a distinction between the two terms for "ask" which Jesus uses in this verse and the verses to follow.[6] But, as we follow Jesus' use of the two terms through this and the following verses, we see that He is using them as synonyms rather than emphasizing a difference in sense between them. This is especially evident in verse twenty-four where the command to ask follows on the heels of Jesus' statement about their not having yet asked in His name. In that verse they must mean the same thing.

Again, to what day does Jesus refer? He is referring to the day of His resurrection when they will see Him once again. Then everything will make sense and they will finally understand what He has been saying to them that evening.[7]

Carson is a good example of someone who, while seeing the point Jesus is making to His disciples, still wants to read additional theology into Jesus' words. He says, "In the historical setting of the farewell discourse, this clause then becomes an incentive to wait just a bit longer, until they enjoy the understanding thus promised to them. In the evangelistic setting in which John writes, this clause becomes an incentive to 'close with' Christ and become a Christian, for only then can one truly settle one's religious qualms and questions, and rest with quietness in the eschatological community of those who know God and are satisfied."[8]

Carson seems to be reading His justification oriented theology into the evening's discussion on the basis that it is being used by John to communicate something other than what Jesus intended to say that evening. But, when examined in the light of its *actual* historical setting, and when Jesus is allowed to be the one speaking in the passage, there is no evangelistic message in His words. And, to infuse them here is to do an injustice to the message of Jesus to them and of John to us. Remember, these are Jesus' words, reported faithfully by John through the enablement of the Holy Spirit who reminded him of all that Jesus said to him.

Jesus concludes His discussion of His departure with assuring words and reminds them that a time is coming soon when they will finally fully understand what He is saying to them right then. Having assured them, He then turns again to their new relationship that will begin in the near future. He turns their attention to the promise of answered prayer.

The remainder of this verse and the next one seem to form another concluding thought and can be treated as a separate unit. This appears to be the case because Jesus normally uses the formula translated "most assuredly" or "truly, truly" as a way of introducing new thoughts as well as calling the listeners' attention to the seriousness of what He is about to say. Westcott states well the point Jesus now makes. "The questioning of ignorance is to be replaced by the definite prayer which claims absolute accomplishment as being in conformity with the will of God."[9]

Jesus' teaching about prayer in this and the following verses is that it is directly to the Father, and in His name. The Father will grant the request in Jesus' name. Mitchell's reminder is appropriate at this point. Prayer in Jesus' name is not "just tacking His name to your prayers." Rather, "it means that we stand before God in all the merit, all the right-eousness, and all the good standing of the Savior Himself."[10] Prayer in Jesus' name reflects Jesus' person and character and is consistent with all that He is.

16:24. "Until now you have asked nothing in My name. Ask and you will receive, that your joy may be full.

Jesus continues His thought by reminding them that they have not yet asked for anything in His name till then. Now they are to start asking and keep asking, with the promise that if they do they will receive. But there is more. Their receiving will lead to a full expression of joy in their lives.

When He commands them to ask, Jesus uses a present tense impera-tive form of the verb for ask which implies that they are to keep asking, to be persistent in their asking. He teaches by this that answered prayer, even for the disciples who were closest to Him, does not come just because we ask *once* in faith. Rather, it comes as we are persistent in prayer before the Father. This reflects His earlier teaching in Matthew 7:7-11 where He commands us to keep asking, seeking, and knocking. It follows the pattern in Luke 18:1-8 where He teaches persistence in prayer through the para-ble of the widow with the unjust judge.

When Jesus says, "that your joy may be full," He uses a purpose clause to say that the Father's reason for answering their prayer is His desire to bring joy to its full expression in their experience. The idea of joy being "full" looks at its completeness. Joy will be manifested fully in their lives. Further, Jesus is identifying a cause-effect relationship between our receiving answers to prayer and the resulting joy that those answers bring. In application to this promise, Laney aptly notes, "Perhaps when joy is lacking it is because believers have failed to pray. Just as earthly fathers desire the well-being and happiness of their children, so God, our heavenly Father, has these desires for us."[11]

Concluding Thoughts
16:25-28

Jesus concludes His instructions and draws together His thoughts in these final words of encouragement. Having promised them joy and answers in the near future, He promises that His figurative language will soon be replaced with open explanations and answered prayer as He returns to the Father.

16:25. "These things I have spoken to you in figurative language; but the time is coming when I will no longer speak to you in figurative language, but I will tell you plainly about the Father.

Jesus begins by telling the disciples that He has been speaking to them using figurative language. When He says "these things," He is referring to their conversation that evening. The Greek term used normally looks backwards at what has been said or written. And, though it could look only at the immediately preceding paragraph, it seems best to see Jesus including things like the vine-branch analogy and the woman in labor in the figurative language. It also indicates that much of the rest of the conversation can be included.

The term Jesus used to describe "figurative language" (*paraoimiai*) is different from the term for parable in the other Gospels. Though it can mean parable, it can also refer to something obscure or enigmatic. He was most likely including more than the imagery of the vine and the woman in labor when He admitted to speaking to them obscurely. As we have seen, much of what He said was true, but unclear, and would only be clear after the events of the following days. Jesus was only clear enough to bring them along. As we saw earlier, He Himself admitted to keeping them uninformed of things since He was still with them. Then, when it became appropriate, He began to inform them further. His point was not that everything He said was figurative, but that He knew that what He was saying was unclear to them. He was admitting to being purposefully ambiguous that evening. This fits well with His earlier promises that everything would eventually make sense.[12]

16:26-27. "In that day you will ask in My name, and I do not say to you that I shall pray the Father for you; for the Father Himself loves you, because you have loved Me, and have believed that I came forth from God.

Jesus repeats the idea of their asking in His name once again. And, we see from the context, what they are asking for is answers. They have been asking Him and getting answers which they cannot understand because He has been purposefully ambiguous. Now that He promises to speak plainly to them, He tells them that the explanations they ask for from the Father will be granted in an understandable way because the Father loves them. Further, this is a promise of direct access to God. They will not need an intermediary. When Jesus says He will not "pray the Father for" them, He does not use a preposition meaning "on your behalf," but meaning "about" or "concerning." Thus Jesus promises that His role will only be that of "laying the case before" the Father "on their behalf."[13] The Father will be responding directly to them rather than through Jesus.

The Father will lovingly respond to the disciples' requests specifically as a result of their love for Jesus and belief in His mission; that He came from the Father. Also, the Father's love is expressed toward them ("the Father Himself *loves*" is in the present tense) because they have already demonstrated their love for Jesus ("you *have loved* Me" is in the perfect tense which indicates something demonstrated in the past and continuing to the present). To understand the significance of this, we need to remember what Jesus has already said. He is not saying anything new at this point. He has already taught that love for Him is expressed through and demonstrated in obedience. He has taught that we abide in Him and experience His love through obedience. He has also taught that believing in Him means believing in the Father who sent Him. So, Jesus is simply summarizing what He has said to this point in the evening.

Interestingly, when He says "love," Jesus uses *phileō* instead of *agapaō* in these verses. By doing this He seems to be emphasizing the idea of friendship and is saying that the Father's feeling of friendship toward them is a response to their friendship with Jesus. This is indicated by the change in relationship Jesus announced in John 15:15 when He moved them from the status of servants to friends (same root word as *phileō*). But rather than seeing too much significance in His use of this term, we must remember that *phileō* and *agapaō* are synonyms and Jesus appears to use them without making a lot of distinction between them in other places.

Still, He has just introduced the eleven to an idea no Jew could normally fathom. They can be friends of God! They can have a relationship with God that is not distant or dependent on intermediaries such as the priests. God will be personally interested in them and feel affection toward them. What a relationship Jesus has just announced! And, even better, all believers have and may experience this relationship. Thus we have the assuring call of Hebrews 4:16, "Let us therefore come boldly to the throne of grace, that we may obtain mercy and find grace to help in time of need."

16:28. "I came forth from the Father and have come into the world. Again, I leave the world and go to the Father."

Jesus now repeats another theme of this evening's discussion (John 13:1). Just as He came from the Father into the world, He is now ready to return to the Father. This verse summarizes His ministry and reflects the theme introduced in the first chapter of the Gospel (1:11, 14) and repeated by Him throughout His ministry (5:24, 37; 6:38, 62; 7:29; 8:42; 9:39). He had come to earth from the Father in Heaven and now was returning to that place from whence He came. As Laney notes well, this verse is a "summary of the life of Christ—His mission ('I came from the Father'), His incarnation ('and entered the world'), His passion ('now I am leaving the world'), and His ascension ('and going back to the Father')."[14]

Jesus again clarifies to them the nature of His departure. He is leaving the world. They should have understood from this then that He was going to heaven. But that need not mean that they understood it to include the cross. And, in fact, rather than seeing the cross as the departure point, we know from subsequent revelation that Jesus' permanent departure did not occur for another forty-two days! So, He was not talking about His death either. Rather, He was looking at the whole process that would be begun with His crucifixion the following day and completed with His ascension. But, we may ask, what did the eleven understand?

Warning of Failure with a Promise of Peace
16:29-33

The disciples are gong to respond by saying that they believe Jesus came from God. He will then respond that they will soon be scattered from Him, but that He will give them peace in a world of tribulation.

This conversation at the end of Jesus' dialogue is quite informative when one thinks back over what has just transpired. Jesus has been trying to prepare them emotionally for His arrest and crucifixion. They have reacted with dismay at the thought of His "deserting" them and missed the significance of what He has been saying. Even His instruction about the Holy Spirit's ministry has not fully sunk in with them. Yet, having just been completely confused over what "a little while" means, they respond to His final summarization of His points with a declaration of confidence in Him.

16:29-30. His disciples said to Him, "See, now You are speaking plainly, and using no figure of speech! Now we are sure that You know all things, and do not need that anyone question You. By this we believe that You came forth from God."

The disciples really affirm three things in their response to Jesus. They say that they think He is no longer being vague. They affirm their faith in Him. And they affirm their conviction that He has come from God. In so doing, they also thereby affirm their faith in God.

It is worthy to note that they do not say that they understand everything Jesus has said! But, especially by their placement of "now" in an emphatic position in the sentence (evidenced in the Greek), the disciples indicate that they think Jesus has finally stopped speaking in enigmas to them. After what had to seem a long series of vague and confusing statements by Jesus, they feel that they have come to grips with His point. They seem to think that, at least in His last explanation, He is no longer being unclear. Again, this does not mean that they thought they fully understood. They only say that they think He is no longer being vague.

On the positive side, they do say more than *just* that they think they finally understand what Jesus is saying. They reaffirm their faith in Him and His word. They begin this by stating their confidence in Jesus' knowledge. He knows "all things" and need not be questioned. In other words, what He says can be trusted even if He is not understood. They recognize that He truly knows God and has revealed Him to them. And, at the same time, they relate their belief that Jesus knows all things to their understanding of His origin.[15] This makes sense of the idea behind "by this."[16] Thus what they do say, in addition to their confidence in Him, is that they understand His origin. They know that Jesus has come from God. They affirm His preexistence. They may even seem to understand in part where He is returning. But do they? Jesus' response indicates that they are still not fully cognizant of what He is telling them.

16:31-32. Jesus answered them, "Do you now believe? Indeed, the hour is coming, yes, has now come, that you will be scattered, each to his own, and will leave Me alone. And yet I am not alone, because the Father is with Me.

Jesus responds to their statement of faith with a question, "Do you now believe?" He then answers it with His prophecy of their desertion of Him in the hour of His greatest need. But what did Jesus mean by His question? And, does His prophecy deny their faith?

Jesus seems to be responding to their confidence with a measure of irony.[17] Since He knows their hearts and knows how they are going to respond, He is also not really surprised by their present response. In fact, we can conclude that this is really the point He expected to be able to take them to that evening. Again, He has already told them that they will not understand until later, and then only after seeing Him again. Thus, His question when combined with His prediction of their desertion indicates that He is indeed telling them something, namely, that their faith is still immature.[18] They think they are ready. They think they understand. They will soon have their faith and understanding tested, and fail, but only temporarily.

Jesus' response to their overconfidence is to announce that the testing of their faith is about to begin in earnest. The "hour" has come. He has used this term to describe His coming suffering and crucifixion (John 2:4; 12:23, 27; 17:1).[19] He now says that time has come. It is a period of time when the world seems to be winning. It will be a time when the disciples will sense defeat and flee rather than stand with their Messiah.

Jesus' reference to the disciples being scattered likely looks back to Zechariah 13:7, the prophecy of the stricken shepherd, that would be fulfilled that night. He used the same term for "scattered" earlier (John 10:12) to describe the wolf scattering sheep. Jesus knows them. He knows the limits of their courage and faith and knows their coming failures. Rather than standing with Him, they will abandon Him in the face of hostile opposition. But Jesus does not leave them with such a dire prophecy. He says something more about this. Though the disciples are about to abandon Him, He will not be alone. His Father will be with Him.

But, how does this relate to Jesus' cry from the cross, "My God, My God, Why have you forsaken Me?"?[20] Many interpreters believe that Jesus' cry indicates that He was forsaken by the Father on the cross.[21] But this brings up a problem of Jesus' omniscience in light of this statement and what He said earlier. If His cry from the cross actually means that He was forsaken and had not anticipated it, then we have something happening to Him that He did not know was going to happen. This also stands in contrast to what He said in John 8:29, that the Father does not leave Him alone specifically because He always obeys Him. And, suffering on the cross was the ultimate act of obedience on the part of Jesus. So, for the Father to abandon Him on the cross would violate His confidence in their relationship both here and in John 8. Further, 2 Corinthians 5:19 states that, "God was in Christ reconciling the world to Himself." Jesus was not alone.

A better understanding of His words on the cross is to see Him quoting the first line of Psalm 22 and, by implication, pointing to its fulfillment before His listeners' very eyes. This explains why, following His death, the multitude that had previously been jeering at Him returned to Jerusalem beating their breasts (Luke 23:48). They heard His cry, remembered the Psalm, and realized what they had done. They had murdered their own Messiah.

But, what about the eleven? Jesus' words now are certainly not words of encouragement! They have to be shocking, disturbing. And, so, Jesus next speaks to their need once again.

16:33. "These things I have spoken to you, that in Me you may have peace. In the world you will have tribulation; but be of good cheer, I have overcome the world."

Jesus concludes His instruction with a final promise of peace and victory, in Him. He begins by reminding them of His purpose for communicating the truths contained in this discourse. He wanted them to have peace. "These things" looks back on all that He has said to them. The purpose of His instruction is to calm their fears and enable them to have peace even in the midst of apparent defeat by the hateful world.

Jesus next draws a contrast between the two spheres in which the disciples will reside. Though they abide in Christ ("in Me") they will also be in the world.[22] For the believer who has chosen Christ, there will be conflict with a hateful world, even as He described in chapter fifteen. But that conflict need not rob them of peace. Rather, focused on Christ who has overcome the world, they can approach it with confidence.

Having pointed to Himself, Jesus then gives them the basis of their peace: His victory. As victor over the world, Jesus is "the guarantor of peace even in the midst of trouble in the world."[23] It is of interest to note that Jesus does not say, "I will overcome." Rather, He declares His victory as already complete with a perfect tense verb. As Laney notes, "Unbelievers view the crucifixion as symbolic of Christ's defeat. Jesus views it as the moment of victory."[24] Jesus' point is that, though suffering and death still await Him, His confidence in conquering sin and death is such that He views His work and victory as complete. We too should have the same perspective. Though Jesus has not returned and set up His kingdom yet, though Satan is not in the lake of fire yet, we should still live with that day in view. We are victors in Christ! He HAS overcome. We, abiding in Him, are overcomers (Rev 3:21).

CHAPTER FOURTEEN

CHRIST PRAYING FOR HIMSELF
John 17:1-5

This chapter of John's Gospel takes us within the veil to hear the Lord talk to the Father. Truly we are on holy ground. Let us listen to our Savior's words with reverence, awe, as well as appreciation for His love and concern for us this evening before He would offer Himself as the propitiating sacrifice for our sins.

Jesus concluded His evening's instruction of the twelve with a short conversation with His Father that reviewed the major heart issues that had led to that evening's instruction. He prayed concerning His return to glory, the preservation of His disciples, and for unity and love to characterize future believers who are destined to behold His glory in heaven. As Marcus Rainsford notes, "What the Saviour had spoken from God to them He now speaks to God of them, and for them; so faithful is Christ that He will never say anything to us that He will not say for us."[1]

Most people think of the model prayer given by Jesus in Matthew 6:9-14 as "the Lord's Prayer." But this prayer is better designated such, and the one in Matthew should forever be known as the *disciple's* model prayer. David Chytraeus (A.D. 1530-1600) is credited with being the one who originally identified this as Jesus' "High Priestly Prayer."[2] And, in line with that thought, the structure of this prayer may be patterned after Aaron's high-priestly duties recorded in Leviticus 16:17. There, on the Day of Atonement, he first made sacrifices for himself, then for his family, and finally for the nation. Here, Jesus first prays concerning Himself, then for the eleven, and finally for all believers.

Though Jesus is not praying as our high priest at this time, for He would not be appointed to His priesthood until after His ascension, this is a foreview of His heavenly ministry on our behalf as our high priest (Heb

6-8). So, rather than seeing this as a high-priestly prayer, we should see this as a conversation between Jesus and His Father and an insight into the inner fellowship of the Godhead, much like His prayer in John 11. He as the Son speaks with His Father about those people He loves, placing them into His Father's care in anticipation of His own removal from the scene for a short period of time. Even so, this prayer still does picture His work as our Advocate before the Father (1 John 2:1). We see the kind of relationship our Advocate has, and so can have confidence that His ministry on our behalf now is as intimate and effective as it was then. And finally, let us notice that this prayer reflects His ministry on behalf of believers rather than the world.

We should notice, too, the difference in Jesus' prayer from our typical ones. First, there is no confession of sin. There is only one petition for Him. And, every other petition and issue raised throughout the prayer focuses on others as it reflects a desire to see God glorified.

This prayer should not be read in isolation from what has just transpired, nor should it be excluded, as some do, from the flow of thought in the evening's discourse as recorded by John. Rather, it is a continuation of the expression of Jesus' concern for His own, now addressed to His Father rather than to the disciples. We can see this in the issues raised in the prayer, issues already discussed in the previous chapters. Further, in light of the fact that Jesus' prayers in the Gospels are mostly noted and just a few recorded, this, the longest prayer of those recorded, is very significant. But, let us not forget that, though few prayers were recorded, listening to Jesus pray is not an unusual occurrence for the disciples.

Jesus' practice of prayerful communion with His Father evoked the desire in them to learn how to pray, and thus their request for Jesus to teach them (Luke 11:1-4). We also see in this Gospel that Jesus spoke aloud to His Father within the hearing of His disciples, knowing they were listening, on at least two other occasions (John 11:41-42; 12:27-28). As in those two instances, He now addresses His Father, but wants His men to hear and learn from Their conversation. Thus it is appropriate to include this prayer with the rest of the evening's discussion.

Some may find it difficult to reconcile this prayer with the one prayed a few minutes later by Jesus in the Garden of Gethsemane. First, we must remember that Jesus was in the habit of constant prayer, and so it would not be unusual or inappropriate for Him to pray repeatedly this night, especially as His hour of suffering drew nearer. Also, the confident tenor of His prayer here is not lost in Gethsemane. Rather, the issues are different. Where here Jesus is reflecting back on the past few minutes, in Gethsemane He is focusing on the immediate future. And, in Gethsemane we hear Him express His commitment to obey, not a lack of confidence.

Another question often raised has to do with *where* Jesus prayed this prayer. We know it had to be after they had left the upper room (John 14:31) and before they crossed the Kidron Valley (18:1). Based on Josephus' account of the priests opening the Temple's gates at midnight (*Antiquities*, 18:29), this prayer may have been prayed in the temple area on the way to the Garden of Gethsemane. A possible hint of their presence in the Temple courts is Jesus' vine-branch analogy, which may have been given with the great Golden Vine in the Temple complex in view. And, since the Garden of Gethsemane is situated across the Kidron valley on the lower slopes of the Mount of Olives and opposite the Eastern Gate, it is very likely that Jesus and His men would pass through the Temple complex in route to Gethsemane. It also makes sense to see Him pausing there to pray one last time in the Temple before beginning His ministry in the Heavenly Temple as our High Priest (Heb 7-9).

As we begin our study of His prayer, it is significant to note the themes in it: salvation—eternal life; preservation—kept; sanctification—sanctify; glorification—behold His glory. We see also in this prayer that Christ had one consuming desire . . . the glory of God (cf. 13:31, 32), even as He prayed for Himself.

Jesus' prayer for Himself was for the Father to again restore His glory to Him since He had completed His work on the earth. This first portion of Jesus' prayer is highly significant theologically. It is one of the strongest statements of Jesus' deity in the Bible. This truth is expressed through the theme of "glory" which dominates these first verses.

An interesting element of this first section of Jesus' prayer is His reference to Himself in the third person rather than first.

17:1. Jesus spoke these words, lifted up His eyes to heaven, and said, "Father, the hour has come. Glorify Your Son, that Your Son also may glorify You,

Jesus prays with His eyes lifted heavenward. Haenchen correctly notes that John only described Jesus as "speaking" to the Father rather than praying.[3] John uses *laleō* here to say that Jesus "spoke" to His Father. This is a much less common term that *legō* (which also means to speak) and puts the emphasis on the very words uttered. Four other times in the prayer Jesus uses *erōtaō* (John 17:9, 15, 20), which relates more to the concept of prayer than *laleō*. Still, it need not be called prayer to be such, since all communication with God is rightly considered prayer. It is likely that John's decision not to call it prayer as he introduces it relates more to his recognition of Jesus' deity than anything else. He may have chosen to say Jesus "spoke" in order to emphasize the Son-to-Father nature of their relationship and of this conversation between Jesus and the Father.

Some may think that Jesus praying with His eyes lifted heavenward indicates a "position of petition."[4] But that need not be the case since we see Jesus do the same thing in John 11:41 before raising Lazarus. And in that case no petition was made. Rather, Jesus simply acknowledged His relationship with the Father purely for the benefit of those witnessing the miracle. And here we see the unique relationship Jesus has with God the Father as He communes with Him and expresses His desires openly as a Son and not a servant. Yes, He does make petitions. But the uplifted eyes are not especially a petitioning stance with Jesus. It is more likely His customary stance when conversing with His Father, a stance familiar to the disciples.[5]

As we begin our examination of Jesus' prayer, we should note that these first verses sound almost like a contract within the Trinity. Jesus has now finished what He agreed to do in condescending to restrict Himself to the limitations of humanity (Phil 2:6-8) and being humiliated in suffering and death for all our sins. Now He holds the Father, so to speak, to His responsibility to restore His former glory.

Jesus begins His prayer by announcing that "the hour" has come. The "hour" has been the term used by Jesus and John to designate the period of suffering and death that He was to endure as Savior of the world. In John 2:4; 7:30; and 8:20 the hour is not yet arrived. Then in John 12:23, 27; 13:1; and here, it has arrived.[6]

Related to that same theme is a parallel thought, that of Jesus' control. Nothing surprises Him or happens to Him that He is not prepared to face. All the way through death and resurrection, Jesus knows what is going on and is determining His destiny (cf. John 10:17-18, "no one takes it [my life] from Me, but I lay it down of myself"). And, with the "hour" having arrived, we do not see panic, but peace, the peace He has promised the eleven. This prayer, in fact, is a model of calm assurance and communion rather than panic or mere resignation to one's doom. Imagine . . . the pivotal hour that was set in the councils of eternity has arrived (cf. Eph 1:11). This brings to mind Christ's words to Israel in Luke 19:42, "If you had known, even you, especially in this your day." What day? The 173,880th day from the day that the decree went forth (see Daniel 9)! What a comfort and stabilizing truth this is for us.

In the face of what He knows is about to transpire, Jesus' eyes are fixed on the Father rather than Himself. We see this as His first petition asks that the Father would glorify Him, not so that He can avoid suffering, but so that He can in turn glorify the Father (cf. John 12:27 "glorify Your name"). But what does Jesus mean by "glorify" in this verse?[7] When Jesus speaks of His glory (as in verse five), He is speaking of the Shekinah glory He possessed through eternity. His glory was veiled in His humanity (cf. Phil 2:5ff) except for brief moments such as at the Transfiguration (Matt 17:1-2). It will again be revealed briefly at His arrest when He knocks down the cohort with a word (John 18:6), and is again manifested in heaven following His ascension.

When He talks about glorifying the Father and being glorified by the Father, He is referring to the manifestation of His character and attributes for the purpose of inducing a response of praise and worship from men and angels. As Rainsford says, "What is glory, but the manifestation of what God is! and Christ is the manifestation of God."[8] This manifestation of God's character is not just for humanity's edification, but billions of angels are watching and learning from what Christ accomplished on the cross (cf. Eph 3:10-11).

The basic sense of Jesus' request is that He would like the "glorifying" process to begin.[9] The purpose clause (introduced by the Greek, *hina*, "that" or "in order that") shows that Jesus' motivation for requesting glorification by the Father was not selfish, for His own glory, but so that He could in turn glorify the Father. This is a beautiful model for us as we seek for our glory that we may glorify the Son and the Father (cf. Rom 8:17-18; 1 Cor 15:40-43; Rev 4 and 5). We are also promised that we shall share in Christ's glory (cf. 17:22-24).

Jesus is not asking for glorification just for glorification's sake. His desire for glory, for the manifestation of His character and greatness before men, is only with a view to its value in bringing glory to the Father. In other words, when Jesus' character is revealed through what is about to transpire, He will effectively reveal the character of the Father such that men will respond, as they have for centuries, with worship and adoration toward the Father. The angels, too, will marvel and worship God for His goodness. We see in this the same pattern that characterized His life. All He did was for the Father's glory. Even now He has not ceased to reveal the Father in all He does, and will continue to do so into eternity. We think of Jesus' admonition to His disciples in the Sermon on the Mount (Matt 5:16), "Let your light so shine before men, that they may see your good works and glorify your Father in heaven." Jesus is living out this command before the eleven, and us. That which He calls us to, He did completely. As He did all to the glory of God, so too should we.

17:2. "as You have given Him authority over all flesh, that He should give eternal life to as many as You have given Him.

Jesus continues this first petition by asking that His glorification be "to the same degree that He has been delegated authority over all mankind. He has been granted full authority (John 5:19-29; 10:18) and requests full glory."[10] That is the sense of "as" in this verse. Think of it! *All authority* has been given to Christ to give eternal life. God has limited this question of life to His Son. Unless you have Him, you cannot have life. We are shut up to Christ.

This idea is developed throughout the Gospel. It is introduced in John 1:4 where we are told, "In Him was life, and the life was the light of men." Then with Nicodemus Jesus prophecies His coming crucifixion and its eternal significance when He says (3:14-15), "And as Moses lifted up the serpent in the wilderness, even so must the Son of Man be lifted up, that whoever believes in Him should not perish but have eternal life." With the Samaritan woman this life is described as living water which forever removes one's spiritual thirst (4:13-14), and later (7:37-39) identified with the Holy Spirit's ministry to the believer. This life is something that the "dead" will receive when they hear the voice of the Son of God because He has life in Himself (5:25-27).

But only those who "come" to Jesus may have this life (John 5:40). For those who believe in Jesus, He gives the promise that the believer will have everlasting life and will be resurrected because Jesus is "the bread of life" which gives eternal life to those who "eat" His flesh and "drink" His blood by believing in Him (6:40-58). Then, after forgiving the woman caught in adultery, Jesus declares Himself to be the light of the world and offers those who believe in Him the "light of life" (8:12), while warning those who reject Him that they will die in their sins (8:21-23). As the Good Shepherd, Jesus says He provides security for His sheep who hear, know, and follow Him and who are "saved" by entering by Him.

This life He offers is a life *experienced*, not just in the future but

beginning now. It is abundant life that results from communion with Him
as our Shepherd who gives His life for His sheep (John 10:1-10). Then,
with the raising of Lazarus from the dead, Jesus declares Himself to be
the Resurrection and the Life, the source and giver of life even for those
who die physically (11:25-26). Now, as He talks with His Father in the
presence of the disciples, Jesus again mentions His authority as life-giver.
As He does this He speaks, not just of the giving of future eternal life but
of the gift of present eternal life for every believer, a life begun now which
grows in its experience throughout this period of mortal life and then
throughout eternity.

Jesus' authority extends to the entire human race, and not just the
elect. As Jesus says, He has been given authority over "all" flesh. This
reflects the prophecy of Daniel 7:13-14 wherein the Son of Man will
receive dominion and an eternal kingdom in which every nation, language
group, and people group will serve Him. A time is still coming when this
promise will be fulfilled. Here, Jesus speaks of its reality. Since, it is promised by God, who is true, it is reality awaiting its completion. Jesus
acknowledges His authority over all of humanity, not just believers. And,
we should remember that one day even those in hell will acknowledge His
lordship (cf. Phil 2:10-11).

Jesus follows this by describing the purpose behind His authority over
mankind, namely, for granting eternal life. And, as Laney notes, "this gift
is not conferred indiscriminately. It is granted only to the elect—those
'given' to Christ by the Father (cf. 6:37)."[11] We can see this strongly emphasized by Jesus in its repetition in verses six, nine, and twenty-four. Just
because He will rule all of humanity does not mean that salvation is universal. Rather, Jesus affirms that only those chosen by God will inherit
eternal life.[12] Cook notes well, "The cause of eternal life is entirely divine.
It may be traced to God's love as demonstrated in the incarnation (John
1:4) and in the cross (John 3:16; 17:1-2)."[13]

But how does someone know if they are one of the elect? By their
response of faith in God's promise to give eternal life to all who receive His
Son (John 1:12). The "proof of the pudding" in John is always one's
response. Those who are elect come to Jesus. Those who are not reject
Him. How can you know if you are elect? Answer this question: Do I
believe in Jesus and am I coming to Him for life? If you say "yes," then you
are elect. If you say, "I don't care. I like my sin and do not want to have
God deal with it," then you probably are not. Throughout John's gospel, it
is your attitude toward Jesus that exposes your status with Him.

But, some may say, I believe in Jesus, yet I still have sins I commit. Maybe I am not really saved. The answer, again, is in God's faithfulness. Our assurance comes from His promise, not from our performance. We have assurance on the basis of what God has promised and on the basis of His faithfulness. He has said that those who believe in the Son have eternal life. We have assurance because we believe He is being honest with us and because we believe in His Son. Our assurance is not based on our works (visible "fruit"), but on His word. Rainsford explains this basis of our assurance: "I cannot read the Book of Life to see if my name be there; but I can read my name in this Book of God, which is the copy of the Book of Life, and I can know assuredly for the comfort of my own soul that my name is written in the Book of Life above. I have come to Christ, I have believed on Christ; this is the description of those whom the Father has given to Him."[14] I meet this description. I know I am elect. I know I am His. I have eternal life.

17:3. "And this is eternal life, that they may know You, the only true God, and Jesus Christ whom You have sent.

After affirming His authority, Jesus then "defines" eternal life as knowing God and Jesus whom He sent. This is one of the greatest verses of the Bible, on a par with John 3:16 in its comprehensiveness and significance. But, it is also fraught with difficulty if understood incorrectly. So, we must ask two questions of this verse. What did Jesus mean by "eternal life"? And, what did He mean by "knowing" God? We will examine this verse by first understanding its elements, and then by putting it back together and seeing His point.

And this is eternal life. Understanding this term demands that we see the difference between the results of receiving Christ (John 3:16) and the results of knowing God. One mistake of many people is to see this as a comprehensive definition of eternal life rather than as one aspect of it. The biblical teaching on eternal life indicates that there is far more to it than only cognitive data about God. In some contexts it means unending life, life in heaven. In others it describes a quality of life, God's kind of life. But how is it defined in John's Gospel? The bottom line is, knowing God. Daniel had it right in Daniel 11:32 (cf. Jer 9:24 and Isa 26:3). There he prophesies that many will be corrupted by the anti-Christ, "but the people who know their God shall be strong."

Why is knowing God such a key to experiencing eternal life? Because right thinking precedes right living. We cannot *experience* eternal life apart from right living.[15] And we cannot think rightly if we do not have a correct view of God. We cannot have that correct view apart from knowing Him. Right thinking begins with right thinking about God. That is why Jesus came to reveal the Father to us. That is why John begins this Gospel with a theological treatise on the person of Christ and describes Him as being in the bosom of the Father and as explaining Him to us (John 1:1-18). And, as we look at Jesus and get to know Him better, so too, we come to know the Father better. As Paul says in 2 Corinthians 3:18, "But we all, with unveiled face, beholding as in a mirror the glory of the Lord, are being transformed into the same image from glory to glory, just as by the Spirit of the Lord."

What is Paul's point? We become like the object of our attention. As we gaze upon Jesus, we become like Him. That is why our children speak and act like us as they get older. It is often funny, sometimes frightening, to hear ourselves coming from the mouths of our children. It is even more exciting, or frightening, to see our children grow up to do the same things as us, sometimes for the better, sometimes for the worse. Why? Because they have spent their lifetime "beholding" us. As they do that, they imitate us, even in the areas they do not like. This is true of our relationship with God. The more we gaze upon Him through what He has revealed to us in His word, the more we will become like Him, and the more we will experience His life, called eternal life by Jesus.

How does the devil attack Christians in this area? By lowering their concept of God. If he can keep us out of God's word and let humanists and the world's philosophers tell us what to think about God, then he will keep us from knowing God. If the devil can keep us from getting to know God as He really is, he will succeed in robbing us of the kind of life God wants to give us. And, by the way, he does this through more than the secular media. He mounts his attacks sometimes through "Christian" literature.

I (Gary) remember teaching a series on Bible study in a church one summer. I was asked to use a prepackaged program provided by a Christian publisher. As I studied the teacher's manual, it addressed the problem of the parables of Jesus. Turning to Mark 4:10-12, Jesus' explanation, the writer of the manual instructed me to teach that Jesus really did not mean to say that He was keeping some from knowing the mystery of the kingdom. Why? Because the author's "Jesus" could not stand for anyone not to understand. And, his "Jesus" was lamenting the unbelievers' failure to understand rather than explaining it. That author was instructing unsuspecting teachers to teach the opposite of what Jesus said. What do we end up with, another Jesus, one not presented in the Scriptures.

This was Paul's fear for the Corinthians, that Satan would deceive them through false apostles teaching false doctrines (cf. 2 Cor 11:3-4). Why? Because their wrong thinking about God had already led to carnality and horribly offensive sins which had brought God's judgment upon that body of believers (1 Cor 3, 5, 11). They were not *experiencing* eternal life precisely because they were thinking the wrong thoughts about God. They were, rather, experiencing God's discipline.

So, how do we get to know God? First, fill our thinking with a scriptural view of what God is like. Do this by reading through the whole Bible regularly. Especially study the person and work of Jesus as portrayed in the Gospels. Then, we must obey the Word. As Paul says in Romans 6:13, "Present yourselves to God as being alive from the dead, and your members *as* instruments of righteousness to God." We must constantly reject wrong attitudes and thoughts by maintaining the grid of Scripture over our minds and hearts. As we do this, we will have victory over Satan and the resources of our God at our disposal. As we know Him and act on that knowledge, we will experience His life in this life. We will *experience* eternal life.

Eternal life is a prominent theme in all of John's literature. Even so, with all the attention he gives the subject, it is possibly one of the most misinterpreted themes he develops. This has resulted because it is normally read through the grid of a justification motif, where with John it is best understood in terms of its meaning in the daily life of the believer, a sanctification motif. For example, Robert Law, a Reformed theologian, says that eternal life stresses "cause, not effect; not phenomenon, but essence; not conscious experience, but that which underlies and produces experience." He describes it as "the medium of our subconscious," "the animating principle" which produces "fruits and evidences."[16]

For those approaching eternal life from a justification-salvation mode, it is something received, which has an effect on a person's life, not a description of that person's experience of life.[17] The problem with this view is that eternal life is both extensive and intensive. Thus, we have John 10:10. You can grow in the experience of it. It is both a possession and a product. The typical person only thinks extensively. More of what we now have. Wrong! It is also intensive. What we have can be *experienced* more fully!

Law argues that the concept of eternal life as positional truth, something possessed which produces fruit, is implicit in that whole strain of thought in our Lord's Synoptic teaching which regards doing as only the outcome of being. . . . It is implicitly contained, moreover, in the whole Pauline doctrine of the new creation and of the mystical indwelling of Christ in the members of His Body. . . . The efficient source of all faith, righteousness, and love is a new life-principle which is nothing else than the Life of God begotten in the centre of the human personality. In this alone the children of God differ from others. It is not because they believe, do righteousness, and love their brother, that they are "begotten of God," but because they are begotten of God that they believe, love, and do righteousness. The Life is behind and within all.[18]

Now, the possession of life is foundational and productive. It will produce fruit in the person's life. But, a difference we have with typical Reformed Theology is that it seems to miss this dynamic growing quality of eternal life. For them, and the vast majority of Christians, it appears to be essentially static as something possessed. But the Bible is clear that there is far more to eternal life than an unending length of existence. There is a quality of life that can only come from God.

A good example of the problem between the various approaches to John's Gospel is the disagreement between Cook and Wendt on the meaning of eternal life in this verse. Cook reflects well the non-Reformed (and non-Lordship) view when he considers the qualitative "content" of eternal life to be described here. He says that, "the *personal* element is strongly emphasized in our Lord's definition of eternal life. Knowledge here is seen to be an appropriation of three persons, not merely an acquaintance with them (cf. 1 John 1:2). Eternal life is a dynamic relationship rather than a static one, but it is based on static (fixed) truth that endures forever."[19] He also notes that Jesus defines eternal life in this prayer "in practical as well as abstract terms. In its functional aspects, life is best understood both by its privileges and effects. A few of these are enlightenment (v. 8), preservation (vv. 11-12), joy (v. 13), sanctification (v. 19), commission (v. 18), unity (v. 22), and fellowship (v. 24)."[20]

Hans Wendt, on the other hand, does not see the verse describing eternal life, but only the means of obtaining it.[21] Hodges rejects this. And, though he sees eternal life as something possessed, he also sees John focusing on the contingent nature of a person's experience. I believe facts but I experience life. For example, you don't feel yourself in the morning to see if you are alive. You experience life. For example, a very effective and fine Bible teacher, Kay Arthur, seems to misunderstand First John and make its theme assurance of relationship rather than experience and assurance of fellowship. It is talking about how we experience life—or death, in our earthly life. The believer's *experience* of eternal life depends on *obedience* that leads to the *experience* of fellowship with the divine embodiment of eternal life, Jesus.[22]

The believer properly in fellowship (in which sin is not producing a barrier) *experiences* the *quality* of life characterized by Jesus' unbroken relationship with the Father as He walked in obedience to Him moment by moment.[23] This is the whole idea behind First John. Dillow notes well, "We must remember that eternal life in the Bible is not a static entity, a mere gift of regeneration that does not continue to grow and blossom. No, it is a dynamic relationship with Christ Himself."[24] Therefore John's use of eternal life reflects more than the mere possession of future life or the presence of a motivating factor within the believer. It reflects a quality of life experienced by the obedient Christian in this life which quality of life can be lost without the forfeiture of one's future experience of life, without losing one's glorification-salvation.

A couple of Pauline uses of eternal life could really be clarified by this understanding. The promise of eternal life in Romans 2:7, directed toward "those who by patient continuance in doing good seek for glory, honor, and immortality" is seen by most to refer to salvation from eternal condemnation in the lake of fire. But, this would seem to imply that works saves. But, if this is seen as an experience of a quality of life now and into eternity, it makes better sense. How we live will affect our future capacity to enjoy life. Also, Romans 6:22-23 is seen to describe the promise of heaven. But, it is addressed to believers who have been commanded to present themselves to God rather than to sin as slaves of righteousness rather than slaves of sin. It is to believers that Paul says, "now having been set free from sin, and having become slaves of God." It is to believers that he says that the end of having your fruit "to holiness" is "everlasting life."

The next verse explains what he means by what he says to believers whose eternal destinies are already determined. To believers he says that, "the wages of sin is death, but the gift of God is eternal life in Christ Jesus our Lord." What Paul is saying is that believers can only experience the gift of eternal life as they are "in Christ Jesus." And, the only way to do that is to present themselves to God and their members as instruments of righteousness to God (Rom 6:19). The result is an *experience* of eternal life, fellowship with the living God and the expression of His life in their lives in this life. Paul cannot be talking about earning eternal life in the sense of entrance into heaven. Then salvation would be by works. Yet, this eternal life to which he refers is something contingent on something we do besides believe. It is contingent on our presenting ourselves and on our choice to reject sin. It is something that is a product of a work. And, since salvation is free, not the result of any work of man (Eph 2:8-9), this eternal life must refer to something we experience now. It refers to our relationship within the family of God.

To understand the term better, we should begin by examining the broad meanings possible in this seemingly simple phrase. "Eternal life" occurs forty-three times in the New Testament, with twenty-three of those in either John's Gospel or epistles. Additionally, "life" is used ninety-two times without "eternal," including forty-four occurrences in Johannine literature. It has both quantitative and qualitative aspects to its meaning which are recognized by all.[25] The quantitative aspect of eternal life focuses on it as something possessed and as life enduring without end. Its qualitative aspect has experience and expression in daily life in view. It is entered into at regeneration and is experienced in the present.[26] Cook notes that, "in Biblical usage the idea of time is generally minimized or excluded."[27] George Stevens describes well its two aspects when he says that eternal life

> is eternal, not merely in the sense of imperishable or endless, but in the higher sense of the true Godlike life, which by reason of its kinship to God is raised above all limits of time and place. It is life as opposed to the moral death of sin. While . . . eternal life is by its very nature continuous, the emphasis of the phrase lies upon the source and nature of the life rather than upon its continuance. Eternal life is life like that of God, who is its source. . . . Whatever be the exact import of the word "eternal," or the philosophy of its meaning, it is a noticeable fact that it is generally described as a present, rather than a future, possession of believers.[28]

In the New Testament, outside of John's literature, the term for "life" without "eternal" attached can carry the sense of natural life.[29] It is also used figuratively. For example, it is used by Peter to refer to hope as "living" (1 Pet 1:3) and by Paul with reference to the believer presenting himself to

God as a sacrifice (Rom 12:1).[30] Thus life alone carries the normal meaning of the word and its normal senses when modifying other words. When life is combined with the adjective, eternal, it describes the believer's experience following regeneration, whether it is being used with its quantitative or qualitative sense.[31] Though either aspect of its meaning may be emphasized at any given time, both senses are often contained in any given use. This makes it difficult at times to distinguish the two senses. This is true with John as well as throughout the New Testament.

Eternal life is not simply another justification term in John's Gospel. Nor is it a single faceted theme with him. His development of the concept in his Gospel should not be viewed so simplistically, but needs to be recognized as a multifaceted concept, all aspects of which he wants to develop. This may be recognized by the shift in emphasis that is evident in the transition from Jesus' public to His private ministry, in His discussions with believers and nonbelievers. Whereas the *possession* of eternal life is mostly in focus in the early chapters of the Gospel, its *experience* becomes the dominant focus in the later chapters. We say mostly in focus, because even in those early chapters Jesus discusses eternal life in terms of what it means to the person receiving it in this life, not as something to be experienced or enjoyed later. Though one may argue that the first eight chapters of John use the phrase more in terms of its relationship to receiving salvation, in John 10:10 Jesus clearly sees it as something to be experienced by his listeners before they entered into eternity.

Jesus' use of the term in His prayer here also shows that He saw it as far more than something merely possessed. First, it is linked with a relational term, knowing God. Second, it is something to be experienced in this life, not only the life to come.

As noted above, John uses eternal life with its full range of meanings and implications.[32] It is enjoyed by entering into "union with the Father and the Son."[33] Even so, with John eternal life normally is used as a qualitative term. For example, 1 John 3:14-15 is a passage that Lordship people misuse, and most others. They see this saying that a murderer is unsaved. But, they miss the point being made by John. When he says eternal life is not "abiding" in them, he is not saying that they do not possess it. The concept of abiding, again, is that of eternal life influencing, having an effect in the life of, the person. This is the same thing as having God's words richly dwelling (abiding) in us that produces the effect of being filled with the Spirit (Eph 5:18-19—note the parallel with Col 3:16). So, John is not saying that someone who hates his Christian brother is "lost." Rather, he is saying that hatred for one's Christian brother proves that he is not *experiencing* eternal life. God's life is not having an impact in his thoughts and actions. And how is such hatred murder? This is explained further in the following paragraphs.

Jesus proved His love for us by dying for us (1 John 3:16). John's point: Jesus *did something*. He then says we ought to "lay down our lives for the brethren" by meeting their physical needs rather than shutting up our hearts to them (3:17). His point again: We show love by *doing something*, by helping Christian brothers in need. We hate and murder by not helping. That is why he then says (3:18), "My little children, let us not love in word or in tongue, but in deed and in truth." The eternal life we possess is only experienced by us as God's love, God's word, God's spirit, God's life influences us and moves us to action.

When we do not present ourselves to Him and let Him lead, we do not experience His life, but experience death even in this life. As Paul says in 1 Cor 3:1-3, we are carnal, not spiritual, acting like mere men rather than expressing the mind of Christ. And mere men are dead in their trespasses and sins while believers have been made alive by God (Eph 2:1-10; also Rom 8—life and death). Therefore we "should no longer walk as the rest of the Gentiles walk, in the futility of their mind, having their understanding darkened, being alienated from the life of God" (Eph 4:17-18). Rather, "He who says he abides in Him ought himself also to walk just as He walked" (1 John 2:6).

Eternal life for John is far more than future unending existence with God. It describes the believer's present experience of life as well.[34] Vanderlip notes well that with John "believers already possess in the present time the salvation of the age to come. The life of the age to come has moved out of the future into the present. The future will simply bring to consummation and completion the eternal life which is already a present possession."[35] He says also that eternal life "speaks of a new quality of existence so radically different from what a man experiences without it that its opposite can be called 'death' (5:24). The addition of the adjective 'eternal' does not change the meaning of 'life' from a qualitative to a quantitative one."[36] It "refers to the 'life of the age to come,' which has already now entered time and become a part of the spiritual experience of the believer."[37] It is "a higher Divine form of life already existing in believers, as the foundation of the life which eternally endures beyond the grave."[38] This is evident especially in John 10:10 where the life Jesus speaks of is to be experientially enjoyed rather than anticipated. Verses that use "life" in its qualitative sense include John 3:15-16; 6:40, 47, 53, 54, 68; 10:28; and here. This experiential aspect of meaning is also evident in passages that focus on eternal life as a "present possession" for believers, such as John 3:36 and 5:24-26.

Though eternal life is a sanctification term with John, it refers to more than just the present experience of divine life. The danger faced by any view which limits its meaning to just a sanctification sense is the temptation to define its meaning based on verses such as John 17:3 and 17 rather than its use throughout the Gospel. The two references in this chapter do not determine the Johannine sense of eternal life any more than do John 3, 4, 6, or 8. Each passage and use contributes to its broad meaning with the sense resident within its immediate context. Of interest is Stephen Smalley's definition of eternal life as "a spiritual *quality* of life" which involves "a sharing of living fellowship with the Father."[39]

This reflects Smalley's recognition that "life," "eternal life," and "salvation" are not narrow terms with John, but broad terms that he uses with a range of senses as his need arises. As a result, the full range of meaning must be recognized and each use evaluated and interpreted based on its immediate context. First John 5 gives a clear example of how even when used in close-proximity, the term must be interpreted on the basis of its use in its immediate context. In 1 John 5:11-13, John describes eternal life as something possessed. Then in 5:20 he uses it in the sense of something experienced. Just as "know" is a qualitative term, so too is "eternal life." Both may be enlarged! And both Jesus and John enlarge them.

In that light, though he sees it as a present possession for believers, John also does not ignore the eschatological sense of eternal life as something yet to be enjoyed in eternity in his theology. He uses it with this quantitative aspect in passages where life is described as unaffected by physical death. This meaning is seen in such verses as John 5:28, 29; 6:27, 39, 40, 51-58; 11:24-26; and 12:25.[40]

Finally, eternal life should not be viewed as a synonym for the kingdom of God (breadth of meaning) or salvation (breadth of meaning) as some attempt to define it. George Vanderlip, though reflecting the more classic reformed/justification emphasis, helps clarify this problem. He first notes that eternal life is equated with "entering the Kingdom of God in John 3." But then he goes further to point out that this equation does not occur anywhere else with John.[41] It only occurs as part of a quoted conversation. Though John quoted Jesus accurately, his failure to continue to develop a kingdom theme elsewhere should alert us to the fact that it is not a significant concept within his Gospel. He is not attempting to define it or to develop anything from it. He is simply being faithful to record accurately, under the inspiration of the Spirit of truth, the conversation of Jesus with Nicodemus.

In conclusion, the Johannine concept of eternal life is that it is a kind of life enjoyed by believers. It parallels justification, sanctification, and glorification. In that sense it is like salvation. It is a relationship with God that is entered into at regeneration, grows by obedience to an accurate knowledge of God, and has ultimate expression in eternity. It is something to be experienced in this life, not just something to be possessed now and experienced later. But, as Jesus reveals here, there is more to it than even that!

That they may know You.[42] Jesus defines eternal life in this verse in terms of its *goal*, not longevity. He is discussing and defining eternal life from its *divine* perspective, not human. He is speaking in terms of how God views it. The goal of eternal life from God's perspective is knowledge of God, not longevity of existence. We see this from the purpose clause Jesus uses here. Though the Greek term *hina* can be translated as "that" and be used to indicate content (like the content of a statement), when used with the subjunctive mood verb (as here) it normally gives purpose.[43] As Westcott correctly notes, "The definition is not of the sphere (*in this*), but of the essence of eternal life." And further, "Eternal life lies not so much in the possession of a completed knowledge as in the striving after a growing knowledge."[44] Interpreters have been so focused on using this verse as a definition of eternal life that they have missed this aspect of what Jesus is saying. So, if the clause is taken just as a statement of content as most interpreters take it, then the verb in the clause must be given its subjunctive sense, namely, that of *possibility*.

To make the contrast clear, we could translate Jesus' words this way: "Eternal life is defined this way, it is characterized by men having the option/possibility of knowing You." If it is taken as a purpose statement, then He would be saying something like this: "Eternal life, by its definition, has the purpose of causing men to be in the process of getting to know You."[44] If "content" is intended by the clause, then the breadth of it is infinite. Who has mastered the knowledge of God? The more of God I know the greater my experience of Him (cf. John 8:31-32).

If you take the appositional use, and understand both terms as having a beginning (possession) and a growth (experience), there is not a problem. In fact, both senses may be intended. Our experience of eternal life will entail getting to know God better and better throughout eternity. And our growing knowledge of God will lead to a greater experience of eternal life. As Laney correctly notes, "Because 'know' is in the present tense, Jesus must be referring to a growing and vital personal relationship with God."[46] Jesus' purpose in coming was to reveal the Father. Eternal life is given by Him to enable men to know the Father, something that will take an eternity to accomplish. Thus a part of Jesus' revelation of the Father involved giving life to men in order to enable them to continue receiving that revelation eternally (cf. The goal of Paul after 40 years as a Christian in Phil 3 was "that I *may know* Him...").

The approach of some to this verse is to see it from a purely justification oriented perspective. Thus John Calvin saw it simply defining how someone gains salvation. He says (italics his), "He now describes the manner of bestowing *life*, namely, when he enlightens the elect in the true knowledge of God; for he does not now speak of the enjoyment of *life* which we hope for, but only of the manner in which men obtain *life*. And that this verse may be fully understood, we ought first to know that we are all in death, till we are enlightened by God, who alone is *life*. Where he has shone, we possess him by faith, and, therefore, we also enter into the possession of *life*; and this is the reason why the *knowledge* of him is truly and justly called saving, or bringing salvation."[47] We respectfully suggest that Calvin missed the idea.

But one must ask, "Why cannot this be a sanctification theme?" Better yet, rather than pursuing Lordship-salvation, how about Lordship-sanctification? People need to understand that the Bible is basically a manual of instruction for those who have come to faith in Christ. It is for the regenerated—and not simply a "soul-winner" manual. I (Earl) have publicly proclaimed many times that the greatest need is not the saving of the lost but the saving of the saved. If the saved would get saved, we would not have nearly as much difficulty in getting the lost saved. The greatest argument for Christ to the lost is what is happening in the saved. Truly, what we need to do is get off of the error of Lordship-salvation, and on to Lordship-sanctification. If believers will catch the truth of Daniel 11:32; Jeremiah 9:24; John 8:31-32; John 17:3; and on and on, the nonbelievers will see the *proof* of Christ mentioned in John 15:8. So, we ask, why cannot it be addressing believers and encouraging them to pursue the purpose of their salvation?[48]

The only true God. This phrase is used to describe God only here and in 1 John 5:20. When Jesus refers to the Father as "the only true God" He uses a term that carries the sense of "real" or "genuine." As Cook observes,

"The God of Scripture, about whom John writes, is neither false nor counterfeit nor the figment of some man's or society's imagination."[49] The purpose of Jesus' revelation was to show mankind what God is like in truth, in reality. And, here He affirms that there is indeed only One, not many gods, who has the legitimate right to be recognized as God and worshipped. Jesus is affirming also that His revelation of the Father has communicated that truth.

And Jesus Christ whom You have sent. More than forty times our Lord speaks of the fact that He was sent. He had a mission to accomplish. We, also, have a mission to accomplish and, when we are through, God will take us home. No power on earth or in hell can take the Christian away until his job is done. Compare Jesus and Paul. Jesus says next, "I have finished the work which you have given me to do." Paul writes to Timothy, "the time of my departure is at hand, I have finished the race" (2 Tim 4:6-7). When they say this, they both know that their task is done and their departure is sure. They both looked forward to their homecoming to the Father.

Just as eternal life involves a growing knowledge of and a relationship with the Father, so too it does with Jesus as well. Remember John 14:21-24. As stated above, what Jesus is saying here is that eternal life comes through relationship with God that comes through the Son.[50] Having said this, Jesus continues to discuss why men may know God, namely, because He has accomplished the task He was sent to do.

17:4. "I have glorified You on the earth. I have finished the work which You have given Me to do.

Jesus now states that He has finished the task that He was sent to earth to accomplish by the Father. As stated earlier, this almost seems like a contract to which each member of the Trinity has a responsibility. He actually says the same thing two ways in the Gospel, using two words that come from the same root word, and so twice affirms that He has accomplished His task of glorifying the Father. His final word on the cross, "It is finished" (*tetelestai*), came from the same root as "I have finished" (*teleiōsas*) in this verse. Even more interesting is the other time Jesus used this word. In John 4:34, after talking with the woman at the well, Jesus told His disciples that His food was to do the will of the One who sent Him and to "finish" His work!

When Jesus refers to His work as finished, He uses the perfect tense form of the verb, which normally carries the idea of completion with it. Yet, He has not yet gone to the cross and completed the work of our redemption. Thus, though Jesus is looking back at His ministry on earth up to that point, He is also including the cross and resurrection, viewing them as accomplished as well. As Carson notes, the interpretation problem posed by Jesus' words is to decide if He is referring to "everything he has done *up to this point*, or proleptically includes his obedience unto death, the death that lies immediately ahead." He observes rightly, "Either interpretation can be made to 'fit' the passage." He then argues that the words "and now" in the following verse do not introduce the glorification of Jesus, but are drawing a contrast "between the glory that Jesus by his work has brought to the Father on earth, and the glory he asks the Father to give him . . . in heaven." He concludes from this that it makes best sense for this verse to include "*all* the work by which Jesus brings glory to his Father, and that includes his own death, resurrection and exaltation." Thus he sees Jesus speaking "prolepticly" and including His victory over Satan on the cross as a part of His completed work of glorifying the Father.[51]

Mitchell notes the significance of Jesus' statement for us today. "His work was twofold. He came to give mankind the revelation of the heart and character of God, and He came to bring men back into relationship with the Father. This now has become our twofold job."[52] We must be about the business of being God's obedient servants who manifest Him to mankind and thereby continue to bring Him glory. And remember, Jesus told the disciples how that would happen back in John 13:35. We bring God glory by loving one another. In doing this we are bearing fruit before the lost world that then testifies that we are Christ's disciples. And, when they see Jesus in us they will subsequently respond to Him. They will either come to the light and place their faith in Him, or they will reject and hate us even as they reject and hate Him. And, in both responses by the world will God be glorified. But, He will not be glorified if the world does not see the fruit of our loving one another and instead discards us as Christ's disciples.

17:5. "And now, O Father, glorify Me together with Yourself, with the glory which I had with You before the world was.

Jesus next asks to share God's glory. And, in asking this, He describes it as glory previously shared in eternity past.

In this context, the meaning of glory is somewhat different from that of the first two verses. There glory focused on the revelation of God's character. Here glory refers to the expression of God's majestic splendor and honor, expressed by such things as His Shekinah glory. This same glory was allowed to shine forth from Jesus for a few moments at the Transfiguration and at the arrest (John 18:6).[53] It is visible again in Revelation 1 as Jesus appears to John on the Isle of Patmos. Then we see it again as Jesus, the Lamb, stands beside the throne of God in the midst of the cherubim (who guard God's glory) and receives worship from the myriads of angels and men. What Jesus says here is that as He returns to the Father, He wants to receive again that same splendor and honor which He shared with the Father in the past.

In light of passages such as Isaiah 42:8 and 28:11 where God declares that He will not share His glory with anyone else, these words of Jesus' speak volumes about His place in the Godhead. The theological significance of Jesus' words is that He claims here to share "a mutual right to glorification with the Father" and thereby implies "his equality of glory with the Father."[54] Thus, He clearly assumes His own deity in His prayer to His Father. This is made further evident in His use of a preposition, translated here as "with" (*with* Yourself) which in this construction incorporates the idea of being "beside, near, or with" someone.[55] Thus Jesus views Himself as separate in His person from the Father, but looks forward to standing beside Him and sharing glory alongside Him. Jesus is not talking about being glorified (or honored) by Him. He is not talking about bringing glory to Him. He is talking about standing at His side and sharing the same majestic splendor and praise as His Father is receiving.

Jesus' request was answered. We see the answer to this prayer in Ephesians 1:20-21 and Philippians 2:9-11.[56] Following His crucifixion, resurrection, and ascension, He returned to His rightful place in Heaven, took His seat on His Father's throne, and was exalted above every name in the universe. In fact, it was the Father who acted to restore His glory and gave Him the name above every name and demanded that every knee bow to Him. We also see this fulfilled in Revelation 5:6-14 as Jesus stands beside the Father's throne and receives worship by the myriads of angels, the elders, and the four creatures (identified as Cherubim elsewhere) who guard God's glory. They sing out, "Worthy is the Lamb who was slain to receive power and riches and wisdom, and strength and honor and glory and blessing!" Again they praise Him with, "Blessing and honor and glory and power to Him who sits on the throne, and to the Lamb, forever and ever!"

Finally, Jesus' statement that He shared this glory with the Father "before the world was" teaches clearly His preexistence and eternality.

Jesus' own words prove to be powerful arguments for His deity. John the Baptist declared this truth at the beginning of Jesus' ministry (John 1:30). Jesus repeats it at the end.

Now, having discussed His eternal covenant with His Father, Jesus is ready to turn to the needs of the eleven. And so, He prays for them.

CHAPTER FIFTEEN

CHRIST PRAYING FOR THE APOSTLES

John 17:6-19

In this next portion of His prayer, Jesus turns His attention to the needs of the disciples as He prepares to depart their company and return to the Father. In this prayer He focuses on their relationship with the hostile world, and so prays for the Father to keep them safe. Jesus' prayer for His disciples is for the Father to guard them from Satan and to sanctify them in His word while they remain in the world.

This portion of Jesus' prayer can be divided into two aspects. He spends the first half of this section (vv. 6-11a) by focusing on the reason for His requests for the disciples.[1] Then He spends the remainder of His prayer asking for things that will enable their faith to survive in the hostile world in His absence. Several of the themes He has addressed that evening appear in these two portions of this section of His prayer, and so we see that His heart is still focused on the needs of His men.[2]

The Basis of His Prayer
17:6-11a

17:6. "I have manifested Your name to the men whom You gave Me out of the world. They were Yours, You gave them to Me, and they have kept Your word.

It seems that the first thing to be considered here is the strong emphasis on the fact that believers are the GIFT of the Father to the Son. Jesus is now elaborating in verses six, nine, twelve, and twenty-four what was introduced in verse two. What a fabulous thought this is! We were first God the Father's. Then we were His gift to the Son. We are God's gift to Christ and Christ is God's gift to us. The Father's gift to us is perfect, eternal, and marvelous. "They were Yours." This is the emphasis of this verse.

Jesus begins by talking about His stewardship of the Father's gift to Him. If it was important for Christ to exercise faithful stewardship of God's gift to Him, what does that say to us about our stewardship of the Father's gift to us—Christ! How did the Son exercise His authority (John 17:2) over God's gift to Him? He began by manifesting the Father's *name*. Note the instruction of Christ to the disciples in Matthew 6:9-11 as He taught them to pray. We are to say, "Our Father, Hallowed by Your *name*" (italics added). Remember the words of God through Malachi, "My *name* shall be great among the Gentiles." (1:11, italics added). This is a repeated Old Testament theme, and a clear concern of God (cf. Isa 59:19; 66:19; Ps 113:3).

So, in this vein, Jesus begins this portion of His prayer by affirming, "I have manifested Your name to the men whom You gave Me out of the world." In saying He had "manifested" the Father's name, He is again referring to His revelation of the Father that brought Him glory as in verse four. When Jesus says He manifested the Father's name, He is referring to His person and character, not just a name.[3] He has glorified the Father by embodying and expressing His character such that He was able to say earlier in the evening that seeing Him was equivalent to seeing the Father. The Father was revealed in the person of the Son as well as His words. He revealed Him by *life* and by *lips* (John 14:9-11). Christ gave His disciples the same mission (cf. Matt 5:16). This is also the same use of "name" as when Jesus spoke of prayer in His name. Just as answer to prayer is dependent on those prayers reflecting the character and purposes of Jesus, so too Jesus perfectly and completely revealed the Father's character, purposes, and person to the disciples. [4]

Some see Jesus referring specifically to the conversation of that evening and His revelation of the Father to the eleven in the upper room.[5] This idea is strengthened by His reference to those given Him out of the world, whom He has identified earlier that evening as the eleven (John 15:19). But it is better to see Jesus referring to the whole of His ministry to the eleven and not just to that evening. Jesus specifically states this in His answer to Philip (14:8-11).[6]

Jesus also speaks of the Father giving Him the eleven. Though what

He says here applies directly to the eleven, we see that it is also true of all believers based on His use of similar terminology in verse twenty-four. Four times in this chapter (vv. 2, 9, 12, and 24) Jesus describes the disciples as the Father's gift to Him, as well as three other times previously (John 6:37, 39; 10:29). Where previously Jesus was talking with those who were rejecting Him, He now states the truth in the positive context of men who have responded to Him in faith precisely because they *have* been given to Him by God. What Jesus says here and earlier is that God owns those who will believe in Him and gives them to Him (6:37, 39).

Men and women coming to Jesus demonstrate that they belong to the Father. In John 6:44 Jesus affirms that no one can come to Him "unless the Father who sent Me draws him." The term for "draw" can mean literally to drag someone against his will. But in its figurative sense it expresses the idea of pulling on the person's inner life, of attracting them.[7] Thus Jesus affirms that those whom the Father possesses and in turn gives to Him, He does so by drawing them to Jesus so that they respond by coming to Him. He also affirms in that context that men's failure to respond in faith evidences that the Father has not given them to Jesus and thus they are not enabled to receive eternal life (John 6:63-65). How is God's gift of people to Jesus evidenced? By their response of obedience. As Jesus says here, "they have kept" the Father's word.

But what does Jesus mean by "keeping" the Father's word? Confusion might arise if this is made equivalent to obeying Jesus in John 15, the necessary element in an abiding relationship of communion. Rather, Jesus is talking here about responding to the Father as Jesus revealed Him. The word used by Jesus for "keep" has a range of meanings, including "to keep watch over, guard someone or something," "to keep, hold, reserve, preserve someone or something," "to not lose," "to protect," and "to observe, fulfill, pay attention to."[8] It is this last sense of "keeping" which Jesus uses here as is made clear in the following verses. The disciples have responded to Jesus' revelation of the Father through His teachings by believing what He has told them. They have responded with faith to the revelation, to His "word" (cf. 15:3).[9]

Some might interpret this "keep" as "obey." For them this would affirm the Reformed doctrine that true believers will persevere in good works to the end of their lives if they are truly regenerate.[10] But, here Jesus' use of "kept" is as a perfect tense verb and emphasizes a completed work which has continuing effects.[11] Thus, when He says that the disciples have kept the Father's word, He is not looking to the future, but only at the past.

Isn't it interesting to note what Jesus does *not* say to the Father about the disciples? He says *nothing* about the failures of Peter, Thomas, and all of them. But He does say they have kept His word! He does *not* bring up the frailty of His children. He brings up their faith. In other words, Jesus is saying that their response to His revelation to that point has proven that the Father gave them to Him.

In this way they are different from the world, characterized by the unbelieving Jews, in that they have responded in faith to His revelation rather than rejecting Him. Also, He is saying nothing about their future. And, in light of His telling them already that they will fall away (cf. Luke 22:31-34) and be scattered, it is obvious that they will not "persevere" in faith. The focal point of this evening's instruction has been their weak faith that Jesus is bolstering in anticipation of its temporary failure in the next few days. His instruction has been designed to get them through the trauma with a view to reviving and strengthening their weak faith in the future. Thus, even this evening, the revelation Jesus is giving them is not designed to redeem them, but to prepare them for fellowship with God in the years to come. So, Jesus continues to discuss with His Father the content of what they believe.

17:7. "Now they have known that all things which You have given Me are from You.

Jesus affirms that the disciples have come to understand His relationship with the Father. They recognize—*they have known*—that all Jesus has said and done is from the Father. What a beautiful confirmation of the integrity of Christ's Kenosis (Phil 2:7)! And what a pattern of submission He models for us! If he who is very God demonstrates such submission, it becomes us to openly own the Father as the source of all we have. We have nothing but are totally the recipients of God's grace. In contrast to those who seek their own (Phil 2:21), we are to recognize that we are not our own (1 Cor 6:19).

Jesus again uses a perfect tense verb to affirm that their knowledge is complete. They are not still learning that all He has is from the Father, but have fully recognized it.[12] Thus their faith in Jesus is ultimately faith in the Father as well. Even so, Jesus' use of "now" may indicate that this mature level of understanding had only been fully achieved that very evening. And He may even be referring back to their confession in John 16:30.[13] He can see His task of revealing the Father is complete by their response to what He has taught them.

17:8. "For I have given to them the words which You gave Me; and they have received them, and have known surely that I came forth from You; and they have believed that You sent Me.

Notice again the integrity of our Lord's accountability. What a pity that so many followers of Christ feel that they must add to the words of the Father rather than simply faithfully proclaim what He has revealed (cf. Deut 29:29; Rev 21:18-19, Jude 3; Heb 1:1-2). Oh that preachers would be able to say this and not add so much corruption and confusion to the Scripture.

This verse gives Jesus' reason for His confidence that the eleven know that all things are from the Father. It is because of what they believe, the content of their faith.[14] He says they have received His revelation and are convinced that He both came forth from and was indeed sent by the Father. They have believed that which the Jewish leaders refused to acknowledge.

It is important to notice that what Jesus points to is not deeds, but beliefs. He identifies faith in terms of its content, what it assents to, not in terms of what it does. Jesus does not say they are living obediently. Rather, He says they recognize as true and acknowledge the right things. We must not forget that Christ is not writing a theology here, but He is discipling His men who are going to be the pillars of the Church. We need to learn from His model. We need to remember, too, that we can only *receive* as much as we *believe*. And we can only *believe* as much as we *know*.[15] We must remember, too, that here, when Jesus describes His disciples in terms of their faith, it is *what* they believe that He focuses on, not how that belief is expressed (i.e., the "fruit" of obedience). Even so, our actions are the fruit of our deepest thoughts! If we want to change a person's deeds, we need to change their thinking. Though faith may produce good works (James 2 teaches this), faith is an attitude, a conviction, not a deed, and thus not a work. And remember, it is faith that saves, not our works (Eph 2:8-9).

What is it that the disciples have believed, put their trust in? They have believed what Jesus told them, His words. Here Jesus uses a different term for "words" (*rhēma*) than what He had used for "word" (*logos*) in the previous verse. Some commentators make a sharp distinction between the two verses.[16] But Jesus may have simply been using two synonyms for variation. Whether or not we see any distinction between the terms, Jesus says clearly that the disciples have taken Him at His word. That is His point. They believed what He said and accepted His words as the Father's words.

And what have the disciples acknowledged as true? Again, Jesus says that they "have known," indicating that it is something they have already affirmed, that Jesus came from the Father.[17] "Surely" translates the adverb (*alēthōs*) that explains further the nature of their knowledge. Theirs is certain knowledge. They have been convinced of its truth. They are convinced of Jesus' origin.

Jesus defines further the content of their faith. They have not only realized His origin, but also His relationship with the Father. They believed Him when He said that the Father had sent Him and that He was representing the Father. Again, this is something that they have believed already.[18]

17:9. "I pray for them. I do not pray for the world but for those whom You have given Me, for they are Yours.

Jesus' response to their faith is to pray for them (cf. Luke 22:32). He clarifies this by noting that He does not pray for the world, but only for these men whom the Father has given to Him.

This is a good point to stop and note that nowhere in this prayer does Jesus pray directly for the lost world. Actually there is not a place in Scripture where Christ or any of the apostles ever pray for the salvation of a specific lost person. This is quite a contrast to typical evangelical praying. I (Earl) shall never forget an experience in my first pastorate. A woman in the church with five children came to all of the services faithfully—even to the midweek prayer and Bible study. At request time, she always asked us to pray that her husband (Archie) would be saved. This went on for a number of weeks. Then one Wednesday we waited for the regular request. But to our surprise, she said, "Archie got saved this week, so you won't have to pray for Archie anymore." At that point we all mentally scratched Archie from our prayer list. And isn't that the way it happens so often? At the point that Christ and the apostles put him on the list, we take him off.

In Scripture prayer begins when the person exercises faith (cf. Col 1:5, 9). We tend to stop at that time in the life of a new believer when Scripture teaches that we should start. It is interesting to think about what we expect Christ to do! He has finished His work of redemption. Rather than asking Him to do more, it is now up to us to tell the lost about that redemption which is made available to them.[19] Why? Because He is praying for His own and for those belonging to the Father. This is evident when He gives His reason for praying for them, "for they are Yours."[20]

This does not mean that God does not love the world. John 3:16 clearly teaches otherwise. Jesus died for them. But this does show us once again that Jesus is focusing on the needs of His own at this point and not of the world in general. Cook reminds us that "the truth that Jesus Christ is our high priest . . . relates primarily to Christ's word as intercessor and advocate. It is related to believers rather than to the world . . . and includes not only the apostles but all believers of this age."[21] At this point Jesus had not yet been appointed as our high priest (Heb 7-10); that was yet to come following His ascension. But He was praying for those He received from the Father as His disciples. These are the ones He designated as "apostles" because He was sending them out in His name to represent Him to a lost world.

It is truly awesome to realize that the moment we receive our Savior, at that very moment we become the objects of the prayers of the Son of God. We often ask others to pray for us. They often forget. Or they ask amiss. But Christ is always praying for us and always in the perfect will of God (Rom 8:34; Heb 7:25; 9:24). At His death He completed His work for the world. Now He has rested from that work. But He continues incessantly in praying for us. The Holy Spirit reproves the world, and prays for us. If God the Son and God the Holy Spirit pray for us, would it not be good for us to earnestly seek the lost?

Carson seems to overstate the reason for Jesus excluding the world from His intercession. He says, "To pray for the world, . . . in active rebellion against God, would be blasphemous; there is no hope for the world."[22] Jesus *does* pray for some of those who make up the world in active rebellion against God. He prays for those who will come to faith through the ministry of the eleven (beginning in v. 20). Many of those who will come to Him could easily be characterized as actively rebelling against God at the time of Jesus' prayer. Why? Because they are members of the nation and its leadership that is about to crucify Jesus.

Paul is a prime example of someone in active rebellion who at this point in Jesus' prayer is still a member of "the world" and in rebellion against God. So, it is better to see that Jesus is simply saying that He is focusing on those who have already been given to Him by the Father. And, He has not forgotten the others who are yet to be given to Him in the centuries to follow. But, having identified the eleven as belonging to the Father, and thus of deep concern to Himself, Jesus continues to discuss the significance of His and their mutual relationships with the Father ("They were yours"—v. 6.; "They are yours"—v. 9).

17:10. "And all Mine are Yours, and Yours are Mine, and I am glorified in them.

Jesus says two significant things in this verse. First, He expresses the unity of the Godhead in their mutual possession of everything, and the eleven apostles in particular. Second, He says that He is glorified in them.

When Jesus describes His relationship with the Father here, He does so in terms of their mutual sharing of everything. This is expressed through the neuter pronoun, "all" or "everything."[23] This "all" includes the disciples, who are identified as "them" at the end of the verse. As F. F. Bruce notes, "In the reciprocal love which unites the Father and the Son, the Father withholds nothing from the Son."[24] At the same time, everything belonging to the Son also is the Father's. And, everything here includes the whole of creation. There is nothing They do not jointly possess.

Though it is not Jesus' intention to discuss their equality in this verse, it is assumed in the kind of relationship He describes. Thus His claim of "reciprocal ownership" with the Father is a "Christological claim of extraordinary reach."[25] For them to share in this way must indicate an equality that no lesser being could claim.

And even more significant is the statement that Jesus is glorified in those men who they mutually possess. Just as Jesus has shared glory with the Father, now He shares being glorified by men with the Father. But what does He mean by "glorify" here?[26] Jesus anticipates His character and attributes being revealed to the world through the lives of these men in the same way He revealed the Father to the world through His own words and deeds (cf. Matt 5:16). That revelation will result in His being esteemed by men who will respond in faith to the claims of the apostles as they represent Him in the world. Christ has modeled it for them in the upper room when they were seeking their own welfare rather than that of each other. In this light, He now turns again to the final basis for His praying for His men, His departure.

17:11a. "And now I am no longer in the world, but these are in the world, and I come to You.

Jesus finishes giving His reasons for praying for the eleven. He says again, now to His Father, that He is leaving the eleven to return to the

Father and that the eleven must remain in the world without Him. Carson sees Jesus focusing on the cross, with Him here describing His "passion in terms of going to the Father."[27] But perhaps it is better to see Jesus looking beyond the cross since the experience of the disciples in view has to do with their relationship to the world. This is reflected in Hebrews 12:2-3. Jesus was focused on the crown, not the cross. He "endured the cross, despising the shame" but He did it "because of the joy that was set before Him."

The cross was on the way to the crown. The cross was not His focal point. So, rather than seeing Jesus talking in terms of His passion, we should recognize this as a reference to His ascension and exaltation to the place of Messianic authority at the right hand of the Father (cf. Rev 3:21). Just as He has told the disciples that He will no longer remain with them and will send them another Comforter, so now here He repeats that theme to His Father. In light of His coming departure from the disciples and return to His Father where He will share His glory, Jesus expresses to His Father those things He wishes to see accomplished in and for His men. Jesus now turns from the basis of His concern for the eleven to the particular issues that He wishes to address to His Father.[28]

His Prayer for the Eleven
17:11b-19

17:11b. "Holy Father, keep through Your name those whom You have given Me, that they may be one as We are.

Jesus begins by praying for the preservation or protection of the eleven. This is His first request for them.[29] Two things need to be observed about this prayer. First, Jesus prays that the eleven be "kept." The term He uses can mean to "guard" or "keep watch over" someone or something. It can also mean, "to not lose" something. Finally, it can involve the idea of keeping someone or something unharmed or undisturbed, as it does in this verse. Second, Jesus asks that the eleven be kept "through" the Father's name. The preposition He uses can mean either "in," in the sense of location or sphere (the locative case), or "through" ("by means of") in the sense of agency (instrumental case). If it were the first sense, then Jesus is praying that the Father will keep them loyal to Him as a necessary element to their unity.[30] The second use of "in," to indicate agency, focuses on God's character as the basis of their protection.

This reflects the Old Testament concept of God's name expressing His character and power. For example Psalm 20:1 uses the name of God in this sense. And Psalm 54:1 clearly links the name of God with His power through *synonymous parallelism* (cf. *Nelson Study Bible*, p. 876). In Proverbs 18:10 His name is described as a strong tower where the righteous find safety. In each of these cases God's name represents His person and character. When Jesus says "keep through your name" He is asking the Father to exercise His sovereign power on their behalf in accordance with His character and commitment to them.

But what is it that Jesus is asking that the Father protect them from? From what kind of danger? With the protective meaning of "keep" influencing our understanding, we might mistakenly decide that Jesus is asking the Father to be personally involved in protecting the eleven from physical harm. We could then see this request answered in such places as the escape of the disciples when Jesus was arrested (Matt 26:56; Mark 14:50-51), and the deliverance of Peter in Acts 12. This interpretation is strengthened by John's note in John 18:9 that Jesus' request for the disciples to be released by those who came to arrest Him fulfilled His statement in 17:12 that He lost none of them.

But, since that which they are to be protected from is not directly expressed in this verse, and the issue of unity immediately follows in the same sentence, it is probably more likely that Jesus is referring to the Father protecting the disciples from disunity. It may relate more to the issue of protection in the disciples' prayer in Matthew 6:13, "And do not lead us into temptation, but deliver us from the evil one." The context of the following verses, especially 17:15, "keep them from the evil one," also supports this idea of protection. Also, Jesus' words in Luke 22:32, "Satan has desired to have you," fits with this sense as well. Thus Jesus is most likely praying for the Father's involvement in protecting them from Satan's schemes to weaken them through division.[31]

Jesus has taught them earlier that proof of their being His disciples will be their love for one another. When they came into the upper room, they were jockeying for power (cf. Luke 22). Now He prays that the Father will bring about that reality by protecting them from that person (Satan) who could threaten their unity. Remember, it was as Judas broke fellowship and moved to perform the ultimate act of hatred, not love, that Satan entered him. Why did he perish? Because he was not protected. A third possibility is that all these aspects of protection are included in what Jesus means. They are to be protected from physical harm as well as from destructive disunity.

At this point we need to distinguish between union, uniformity, and unity. You can tie two cats together by their tails and throw them over a clothesline and you have union but not unity. Jesus uses the present subjunctive, which can be translated as "that they may go on being one," to describe this unity. They already had essential unity, but they needed to let it come forth in experiential unity.

Three levels of unity exist within the body of Christ. First, there is essential unity. We *are* one in Christ. Second, there is existential unity (John 17). We need to go on *being* what we are. Finally, there will be eschatological unity. One day our existential unity will equal our essential unity. We will experience what we are completely and unhindered by sin.

What is the nature of the unity Jesus describes? When Jesus says, "that they may be one as We are," He prays for a unity among the disciples that reflects the unity experienced within the Godhead. But the unity within the Godhead cannot be perfectly duplicated by humans since a part of Their unity includes sharing the same essence. Yet, They are also a unity in areas that can be duplicated by humans and was to be duplicated by the disciples. Just as the members of the Godhead "enjoy a perfect unity of love, of purpose, of holiness, of truth," so too the disciples should reflect a similar oneness of love, purpose, holiness, and truth.[32]

Just as there is perfect communion between the members of the Godhead, so too the disciples were to experience perfect communion. Westcott aptly describes the relationship for which Jesus prays. "As the divine Unity consists with a variety of Persons, so too the final unity of men does not exclude but perfectly harmonizes the separate being of each in the whole."[33] This is the unity Paul described as the many membered body of Christ living in dependence and mutual appreciation and care for each other in 1 Corinthians 12 (especially vv. 25-26) and Romans 12.

17:12. "While I was with them in the world, I kept them in Your name. Those whom You gave Me I have kept; and none of them is lost except the son of perdition, that the Scripture might be fulfilled.

Having asked the Father to "keep" the disciples through His name, Jesus tells Him that He had done the same during His tenure on earth. He does this by using the same Greek phrase He has used earlier of the Father to say He "kept them" in the Father's name.

Of interest is how the NKJV translates this preposition as "in" (the locative sense) rather than as "through" (the instrumental sense) as previously.

Assuming Jesus intended to express a parallel thought with what He was just asking the Father to do (i.e., "I want You to continue My ministry to them."), we should see both uses of the preposition to be parallel. Thus Jesus affirms that He protected the men from Satan's attack *through* the Father's authority and power (His "name") rather than through His own. This again reflects Jesus' commitment to a ministry in dependence on the Father rather than as an independent agent. He has been a perfect model for His disciples. He did nothing on His own initiative, but only what He saw the Father doing (John 5). And He wants to see the Father continue protecting them as He has done through His Son.

Jesus now uses two terms for "keep" when describing His ministry to the disciples. The first, the same term for "keep" as in the previous verse, "expresses the careful regard and observance" involved in protecting someone or something. The second "kept" (*phulassein*) "describes the protection of something held as it were within a line of defense from external assaults."[34] But, again, these two words are synonyms. And Jesus' use of the second term may indicate the sense He intended for the first. Thus He is talking about protecting them from attack rather than just keeping them committed to the Father.

Jesus protected the unity of the disciples from Satan's attack with only one exception, Judas. But what is the significance of this exception? Does this mean that He failed in His attempt to protect Judas? Does this mean that Judas was "saved" and then lost his salvation? Jesus' use of "except" does not require the idea that Judas was numbered among those "kept," but may simply refer to the phrase, "none of them is lost."[35] In other words, Judas was not protected by Jesus, and so he perished.

Dillow correctly notes that Judas is "the exception" to the group, not a part of it. He points to John 18:9 as evidence. There, Judas was numbered with the cohort who came to arrest Jesus and not the eleven whose release Jesus obtained. Further, there is a contrast between the eleven and Judas. In verse eleven Jesus prays, "Keep them in Your name." Then, in verse twelve He says, "I kept them in Your name." Here we see God, both Father and Son, active in the process of keeping the believers safe from the attacks and influences of the world, in the sense of falling from the faith. He says further, "and none of them is lost except the son of perdition." This use of "lost" cannot refer to physical death. Judas has not yet exterminated himself, but has left the company of faith and walked away from the truth. It cannot refer to a loss of regeneration since that would violate Jesus' own words elsewhere that of those the Father gives Him, He loses none (John 10:25-30). Thus it cannot refer to a loss of union with God. It cannot mean a loss of communion with God in the way that believers can be out of fellowship.

Jesus' designation of him as "son of perdition" must imply that he never belonged to God. He also clearly refers to Judas as lost and not believing in Him even from the beginning (John 6:64, 70). Since in verse fifteen Jesus prays, "Keep them from the evil one," this reference to Judas may look back at 13:27 when Satan entered into Judas' heart and he departed from the company of disciples in order to betray Jesus. Thus, Dillow correctly interprets this preservation in terms of their destiny and says, "The loss from which they are being kept is 'destruction,' or hell."[36] This is also evident from John's explanation of Jesus' statement in John 6:64 that there were some among His disciples who did not believe in Him, "For Jesus knew from the beginning who they were who did not believe, and who would betray Him."[37]

Thus Judas was an unbeliever in the midst of the disciples whose departure proved his character and destiny. He did not lose his salvation. He never had it. He was of the same character as the false teachers in 1 John 2:19 whose departure from the fellowship of the apostles proved they were never of the faith.

This is a good place to pause and note the fallacy of judging one's reality in Christ by his/her external fruit. It is obvious that Judas had more than average "fruit" (outward evidence) or the disciples would not have chosen him to be the trusted treasurer of the group. He obviously displayed "fruit" when he went out as a member of one of the pairs Jesus sent throughout the villages to announce the coming kingdom (Matt 10, Luke 9, 10). He is of the same nature as the false prophets in Matthew 7:21-23. They have lots of "fruit," even of a miraculous nature, but not of God. We need to remember that God has not called us to be fruit inspectors of each other, but to encourage one another to look to Jesus and be changed. As Calvin is reputed to have said, "one look at Jesus is worth a thousand looks at myself when it comes to fruit." Those who look to their fruit to assure themselves, or to others fruit to be convinced of their salvation, are looking amiss. It is what we believe that counts. If I want assurance, I must examine my beliefs, not my deeds. Granted, deeds follow beliefs. What I do grows out of what I believe. But, being a cracked vessel of clay, my deeds often do not match up to what I know to be right, to be God's will. Yet, my failure does not determine my destiny, nor prove it to me or anyone else, only God's decision as He has responded to my trust in Him. My assurance comes from His faithfulness to His promise to accept all who call upon Him. In Judas' case, he never had that faith. He acted the part of a believer, but owed his allegiance elsewhere.

So, what does "the son of perdition" mean?[38] This designation must be understood in light of Hebrew thinking. When a person is described as "a son of" someone, they are being identified with that person or thing's character. For example, Jesus says that those who are peacemakers will be called "sons of God" (Matt 5:9). He means by this that peacemakers reflect the character of God. Thus, for Him to call Judas a son of perdition would indicate that he reflects the character of "perdition," or destruction. Thus, Judas' parentage is found in Satan, not God. Judas' destiny is destruction, not blessing (see also John 8:44).

Finally, was Judas destined to be lost against his will?[39] Some might conclude that Judas was just a pawn in God's plan and was helpless to do anything else. Others see Judas acting as a free agent. It is better to see the combination of human and divine elements. Judas was chosen to be numbered among the apostles, though he was not a believer in Christ. Though he had been exposed to Jesus for years, he had never believed in Him, but chose to betray Him. This should remind us clearly that environment does not determine our faith or character. Judas was in the most perfect of environments, and yet chose not to believe in Jesus. Still, as was noted in our discussion of chapter thirteen, until he took the sop and departed their company, he could have "chosen" to do otherwise.

The text is clear that Judas was making those choices. He had gone to the authorities earlier and bargained with them to betray Jesus for a price. Also, it was not Satan's work, making Judas a puppet, which led to his betrayal of Jesus. Judas had made the bargain *before* Satan "entered" him. We should remember also, we are all born slaves of Satan. It is only at the cross that we are freed from his tyranny. Yet, even as Judas exercised his free choice, this was all part of God's foreordained purpose and plan. Nothing happened with Judas apart from God's planning and permission. Yet, on judgment day Judas will have to admit that *he* did exactly what *he* wanted to do when *he* betrayed Jesus. God permitted it because his action was prophesied and was part of His plan. God did not force him against his will to do it. There will not be one soul who spends eternity in the lake of fire who will claim to have been coerced against his will. Everyone there will have ended up there because of choices made by him or her. They will have no excuse, just as Judas had none.

17:13. "But now I come to You, and these things I speak in the world, that they may have My joy fulfilled in themselves.

Jesus turns from the defection of Judas to focus again on the issue at hand, His return to the Father and the needs of the eleven. In light of His departure and return to the Father, He is concerned for His disciples and reminds the Father that He has been teaching them with a purpose, that they may have His joy (cf. John 15:11; 16:24; 1 John 1:4).

The meaning of "these things" is somewhat ambiguous. It may either refer to Jesus' prayer or to the whole evening's conversation.[40] All through the evening's discipleship session, progress is being made (cf. John 13:7, 17; 15:3, 14-15; etc.). Since Jesus has been reviewing the same issues with His Father that He had discussed with the eleven, it seems best to see the whole evening's conversation. Thus Jesus is saying, "My evening's discussion with the disciples has had the goal of filling them with My joy."

Jesus' reference to speaking in the world is another way of alluding to the fact that He will soon be in heaven and speaking with the Father "face to face" rather than as Son to Father in prayer on earth. But, He is also saying that He has used His time with the eleven to prepare them for His departure and with a very distinct purpose. We need to remember that this whole discourse is of tremendous modeling value to us. Jesus is taking the eleven men from where they are as self-centered, competitive disciples to servants to friends who love each other and display the joy of the Lord.

Jesus wants them to experience His joy.[41] In fact, it is this desire for them to have His joy that may have motivated Him to pray this prayer aloud and in their presence.[42] Even so, we see all of that evening's instructions being given with that ultimate purpose. Jesus is preparing them and comforting them with the anticipation that, as He had said earlier (John 16:22), once all the upcoming events have transpired and they understand this evening's instructions clearly, no one will be able to take their joy away from them. Just as He promised them joy, He now reminds His Father of His desire that they have that which He has promised.

17:14. "I have given them Your word; and the world has hated them because they are not of the world, just as I am not of the world.

What an example to us of the power of the Word of God clearly communicated. Jesus had confidence in the Word. His confidence is such that

He mentions it here in conjunction with their relationship to the world. In doing this Jesus continues to remind His Father of His completed work in the lives of the disciples. As He said earlier to the eleven (cf. John 15:3), "You are already clean (purged, not pruned) because of the word which I have spoken to you." Now He tells His Father, "I have given them Your word."

Jesus again uses *logos* to describe His ministry to the eleven. In this case He has His whole teaching ministry in view and sees it as being culminated and completed that evening. Implied in His giving them the Father's word is their receiving it. The consequence of that reception is, as has He told them earlier (John 17:6), identification with God and not the world system. Thus they have been given to Jesus "out of the world" (17:6) though they are still "in the world" (17:11) while being "not of the world" (17:14). Jesus is next going to pray some more for them, but not that they be take out of the world (17:15), but that they be "sent . . . into the world" (17:18).

This pattern of being in the world but not of the world is a very important teaching for us. Jesus describes believers as "sheep in the midst of wolves" (Matt 10:16). God, through Paul, calls on believers to be "children of God without fault in the midst of a crooked and perverse generation" (Phil 2:14-16). It is the product of the work of God's word in our lives that produces this separation and difference between believers and the lost world. But it is not a separation that involved isolation.

We are not to be isolated from the world (monastic), nor saturated with the world that is so current in much of American evangelicalism's sacrifice of biblical truth for cultural relevancy. But Jesus is talking about penetration of the world (cf. 2 Cor 6:11—7:3). And, such penetration will produce a response from the world. Thus the next point Jesus makes to the Father is that the world has responded to them with hatred because they are not a part of its system. Their identification with Christ, who is not a part of the world, has cost them identification with and love from the world. This truth then leads to Jesus' next request on behalf of the disciples.

17:15. "I do not pray that You take them out of the world, but that You keep them from the evil one.

Jesus prays for the disciples' protection from Satan while specifying that they remain in the world. The three possible meanings of the final phrase can be either "from evil" in a general sense, "from the evil one," a reference to Satan, or from the evil world system.[43] The problem is that the word is an adjective being used as a noun in a prepositional phrase.

Greek adjectives either can have masculine, feminine, or neuter forms. When used as a masculine noun with the article placed before it, it can be translated "the evil one," a term for Satan.[44] But, unfortunately, both the masculine and neuter spelling are identical for the Greek case used here.[45] So, this spelling in Greek means that it could be either a reference to someone in particular (Satan), or the neuter abstract noun, "evil," which does not imply a personal agent such as Satan.

The first possible meaning would involve protection from "evil" in some general, non-distinct sense. An interpretation in line with this abstract sense is reflected by Dillow who says "Jesus prays that we will be kept from hell."[46] But, the context of Jesus' prayer and His use of the article require that more than just some undefined evil be meant. He is talking about something or someone in particular.

The second possible meaning involves protection from Satan.[47] This can be argued for on the basis that the context has Satan in view. In this view the term for "evil" is masculine and looks back on Satan who has been mentioned in John 12:31; 14:30; and 16:11.[48] Further, John uses the same terms in his epistle to refer to Satan. In 1 John 2:13-14 he is the "wicked one" who the young men overcame. In 3:12 Cain is the spiritual child of the "wicked one," identified as the devil in verse ten. Then in 5:18-19 this same phrase is masculine and refers to Satan as "the wicked one." So, here it could be translated "from the evil one" rather than neuter with the sense of "from evil." But, in response to these arguments, we must note that the emphasis in this prayer is the "world" (mentioned 14 times), and not Satan.

We believe the best view is to see Jesus referring to the evil world system. Mitchell notes, "Nineteen times in this passage our Savior speaks of the world as a system, a kingdom of darkness controlled and dominated by Satan. And when you and I become Christians, we are taken out of the world system. . . . God's message for the man of this world is salvation, and for the believer it is separation."[49] Jesus has just said that they are not "of the world" just as He is not of it in the previous verse. Later He is going to pray about sending them into the world, though they are not of it (v. 18). The argument that this interpretation must be rejected because of Jesus' use of the definite article can be answered with a couple of questions.[50] We must first ask, "What about the preposition?" It is the Greek word, *ek*, which carries the sense of "out of" or "from." It indicates separation or departure from. If we take note of the preposition and see the article as an article of previous reference pointing out "the world system" which, of course, is energized by Satan, then "the evil" need not refer to Satan, but the world system.

What then does this mean for the believer? We are no longer slaves of Satan or his world system (cf. Rom 6:16-22; Heb 2:14-15). But, we are also in danger of its influence and attack. We can be overcome by its evil, and fall into sin. While in the world we will face troubles. Jesus promised the eleven that they would be hated because of Him. We can expect the same treatment. And, in fact, millions of our Christian brothers and sisters are facing harsh treatment, including martyrdom, daily around the world. But, we know that Jesus prayed for us then, and prays for us now. Moses, Jonah, and Elijah are all examples of men who asked God to take them from the world and the troubles they were experiencing. Yet they were all three denied their requests. They were left in the world, but delivered from the evil world system by God. Carson's words make a good conclusion to this part of Jesus' prayer. "The followers of Jesus are permitted neither the luxury of compromise with a 'world'. . . that is intrinsically evil and under the devil's power, nor the safety of disengagement. But if the Christian pilgrimage is inherently perilous, the safety that only God himself can provide is assured, as certainly as the prayers of God's own dear Son will be answered."[51]

17:16. "...they are not of the world, just as I am not of the world.

Why are they hated and in need of the Father's protection? Because they are not a part of the world system just like Jesus had said earlier to them in chapter fifteen. By being identified with Jesus who is from heaven, not the world, untouched by the world's evil, in whom Satan has no hold, we too cease being a part of this evil world system. This is a truth we need to meditate on until it controls our view of life, of this world. We need to see the world system as God sees it. One fun thing I (Gary) like to do in my classes is to announce that our government and our system of government are evil. After the students get over the initial shock. I tell them that I am neither a "Repulsivan" nor a "Demoncrat." I am a Divine Monarchist. I look forward to, and pray for, the coming of the Messianic Kingdom. In the arrival of my King, this government, including most, if not all, of its surviving officials (elected and appointed), will be executed and replaced with a new government, a monarchy administered by the saints who have returned to rule with Christ. This is, of course, based on my belief that all governments during the Tribulation will serve the Antichrist and will be removed in the Sheep-Goat judgment described by Jesus in Matthew

25:31-46. Why will our government fall and be replaced? Because it is no less a part of Satan's world system than is any of the remaining communist governments in the world, or Muslim, atheist, or totalitarian. Therefore I should not place my hope in my government, it will not last and does not serve my Savior. I should not place my hope in banks, or the stock market, or property, or anything else in this world. My hope and values are to be located in the person of Christ with whom I am identified.

This truth was of such importance to Jesus that He repeated the thoughts of verse fourteen and set the stage for the next petition. These next three verses focus on the eleven's sanctification.

17:17. "Sanctify them by Your truth. Your word is truth.

Having stated that the disciples are no longer a part of the world system, Jesus requests that the Father set them apart to Himself. To sanctify someone or something means to set it apart from common or ordinary use and dedicate it for some special purpose. In the spiritual realm sanctification means consecration to God's service and thereby also involves separation from evil. Thus Christ will describe Himself as sanctified two verses from now. He is wholly devoted to God and fully separated from evil. And, now He prays that the eleven will experience the same sanctification.

From the context of what Jesus has said already, the "truth," which He next identifies with God's word, is the revelation He has given to them from the Father as well as the additional revelation He will provide them in the years to come, as promised earlier that evening. Though their (and subsequently our) sanctification is a work of the Spirit, it is through God's truth, His Word contained in the Scriptures, that the Spirit works in and through to set us apart and make us useful to God. The sanctification referred to in this passage is looking at a work accomplished by God. In verses seventeen and nineteen the disciples ("they) are recipients of sanctification from God. Notice that in verse nineteen Jesus' sanctification is accomplished by Himself.

Carson notes "in John's Gospel, such 'sanctification' is always for mission."[52] This is true once again here, as can be seen by Jesus comparing their sanctification to His in verse nineteen. This sanctification involves the Word of God, God's truth. Our experience of eternal life, in terms of our sanctification, does not involve a static relationship with God. Even so, it is experienced on the basis of unchanging eternal truths. And as Westcott notes, for the believer, God's truth "is not only a power within him by which he is moved; it is an atmosphere in which he lives."[53] It is the basis of everything a dedicated believer thinks and does.

Jesus again uses the preposition which could be translated either with the locative sense of "in," "in the sphere of," or with the instrumental sense of "by means of." Thus Jesus may be asking the Father to set them apart to Himself within the sphere of His truth, identified as His word. Or, Jesus could be asking Him to set them apart for His service by means of the truth contained in His word. This would be another example of Jesus' use of a word that is intended to communicate more than one truth at the same time.[54] And, either sense would work well in the context.

It seems though, in light of the Holy Spirit's sanctifying work in the life of the believer as taught by Paul in Ephesians 5:18 and Colossians 3:16, Jesus more likely intends the latter sense. He is asking the Father to use His word as the means and measure by which the disciples will be set apart to His service. Mitchell notes well, "Sanctification has a practical side, a daily sanctification, that has to do with our godly walk as Christians in the world. . . . A holy life in a world that hates God is God's program for His people. Obedience to His Word is a sign of discipleship (8:31)."[55] Further, "Sanctification in this sense is not imputed. Justification is imputed to the believer. Righteousness is also imputed. But sanctification isn't imputed; it is more of an impartation, an inwrought work by the Spirit of God because we are in Christ."[56]

Rainsford asks, "Now, *why* is 'the truth' the instrument?" He answers that question by saying, "It is through the truth the love of God is revealed and shed abroad in our hearts; love is a sanctifying principle, 'We love him, because he first loved us'; love is a constraining principle, 'the love of Christ constrains us.'" And further, "The truth is the instrument by which the Holy Ghost is ministered to the soul."[57]

17:18. "As You have sent Me into the world, I also have sent them into the world.

Jesus next compares His commissioning of the eleven with His own coming from the Father. When He says, "*As* You sent Me," He uses a comparative adverb which means that He was sending the eleven "in the same way as the Father had sent the Son."[58] In John 15:26-27 Jesus told them of their commissioning. In John 20:21 we see this fulfilled as He said, "As My Father has sent Me, I also send you." Thus He is looking forward to His commissioning of the apostles, either just after His resurrection or at His ascension (Matt 28:18-20; Acts 1:4-8).

What is the significance of this for us today? We are ambassadors of

Christ. This is truly awesome! Wherever we go, we are representing the One through whom all things have been made (cf. Col 1:15-18). As His representative to a lost world, we are continuing to represent Him and the Father to that world. As F. F. Bruce notes, even though the disciples are no longer a part of the world, even as Jesus was not, they remain in the world because "they are positively sent into it as their Master's agents and messengers. If Jesus does not pray explicitly for the world at this time (v. 9), yet his prayer for the disciples involves hope for the world." Yes! We, as God's representatives, are the hope of a lost world. Let us be the kind of representative for God that we accurately represent Him to the world!

17:19. "And for their sakes I sanctify Myself, that they also may be sanctified by the truth.

Jesus now states the reason for Him setting Himself apart to God's service. It was for the disciples' sakes, in order to accomplish their sanctification. Christ was constantly modeling truth for the disciples. He had lived out before them the role He now gave to them. Think of it. What resources we have in the lives of the apostles and the generations of saints to follow them. Christ did not have a model to follow. He was charting the way. And He charted it perfectly!

When Jesus says, "I sanctify Myself," He uses a present tense verb. On the basis of this most interpreters see Him referring to His crucifixion rather than His life.[59] Jesus is saying essentially, "I am now setting Myself apart to the task remaining before Me so that they can also be set apart to You by means of the truth of Your word."[60] It would seem better to see this use of the present tense verb as a gnomic present and to see Jesus looking at all of His life and attitudes, which will indeed continue through the crucifixion, as the model of the disciples' lives and attitudes (something He has been talking about all evening) rather than His death.[61] Hebrews 12:2-3 tells us that Christ was not focused on the cross but the crown even as He approached the cross. This evening His focus was the crown for the eleven. His ministry with the disciples was preparing them to reign with Him in the coming kingdom, not instructing them about His death. Notice the focus of all of the overcomer passages in Revelation 2 and 3, consummating in 3:21. He who overcomes will be rewarded and will reign with Christ.

If Jesus were focusing on His death, then it would only seem logical to see Jesus thinking in terms of their martyrdoms. But He is not. Rather than seeing Jesus focusing on the cross as He discusses His motivation for ministry to the eleven through the years, we see Him motivating them to service. Jesus committed Himself to His Father's service, to revealing His Father perfectly. To accomplish this He set Himself apart from the world and faced its hostility. He was able to accomplish His task because of His self-sanctification. He had told the disciples that they were to do the same thing.

In the process of ministering to the eleven, He had imparted God's truth, His revelation, to them. Now He asks the Father to use that truth, that revelation, so faithfully delivered by the Son, to set them apart from the world so that they can fulfill the commission that Jesus is giving them to continue His ministry in the world.

How could Jesus sanctify Himself since He is already perfectly holy? "While living in this world Jesus 'set himself apart' to the Father's will and purpose."[62] He did so by devoting Himself to the Father. This is illustrated in the wilderness temptations (Matt 4:1-11). In each of the three instances where Satan tempted Jesus, He responded with loyalty to the Father on the basis of the truth of His Word, and refused to be identified with Satan and his world system. On the basis of God's word Jesus set Himself apart from the very beginning of His ministry. When He cleansed the temple following His Triumphal Entry into Jerusalem, He did so on the basis of God's revealed will for the temple (Matt 21:13). When He stood before the Sanhedrin at His trial and was commanded by the High Priest to tell them if He was the Son of God, He answered them on the basis of Daniel 7:13-14 and the promise of the Son of Man receiving dominion from the Ancient of Days.[63]

In each case He could have taken a different route and avoided the hostility of the world. But, because He had dedicated Himself to the Father and was subject to His word, His word became the separator between Jesus and the world as He responded on the basis of its truth and trustworthiness. We should do the same. This is why every believer has an obligation before God to read His word, to study it, to memorize it, and to obey it. We cannot sanctify ourselves to God by going to church on Sunday and by being spoon-fed tidbits of predigested Scripture by our pastors and expect to walk effectively with God. We must let His word dwell in us by knowing it, thinking about it, and letting it influence our thoughts and actions. There is no other way to be a sanctified saint. Sorry. I know that it is a lot of work. But, have no fear! The rewards for your efforts are eternal!

Now, having prayed for the eleven in particular, Jesus next addresses the Father concerning His care for all of His sheep (John 10:16).

CHAPTER SIXTEEN

CHRIST PRAYING FOR US
John 17:20-26

Jesus' prayer for future believers, including us, was for them to experience the same unity and love that He and the Father experience, and behold His glory. This section of His prayer applies directly to the church today. And, interestingly, the two issues addressed by Him reflect our two greatest needs, unity and hope of seeing Jesus' glory. But, before Jesus talks about beholding His glory, He speaks of *their* glory. We are developing our capacity for glory now. Our glory will be the measure we will have to glorify Him when we share His rule.

17:20. "I do not pray for these alone, but also for those who will believe in Me through their word;

Jesus turns His attention to His spiritual body, the church, by identifying His concern for those who would be reached by the disciples as they fulfilled His mission to the world. It looks, not just at that generation of saints, but at all future saints. Jesus begins now to express His concerns for all the candidates for kingdom positions, for all those who may one day reign with Him.

While "believe" in this verse is a present tense verb it is better translated as future tense as in the NKJV. Westcott interprets Jesus' use of the present tense to indicate that in His view the "Church of the future is regarded as actually in existence" at that point in time.[1] Though there is an element of truth in what he says (there were others believing in Jesus besides the eleven), it must be noted that a present tense verb can be used with a future sense, and the church did not come into existence before the day of Pentecost. The church is composed of Spirit baptized and sealed believers according to 1 Corinthians 12:12-13 and Ephesians 1:13-14.

Thus, it is better to see Jesus looking at future converts through the apostles' ministry. Thus He is using a present tense verb prolepticly, with a future sense. This is made even more evident in that those believing in Jesus will do so "through *their word*," and not through His.

In other words, Jesus is looking at the ministry of the eleven as His representatives, a ministry they have not yet begun.[2] Thus, His prayer is now focused on the needs of the saints yet future to them that day, the needs of the church of the first century through today. Laney correctly sounds a warning to our generation of saints. "It is significant that Jesus anticipated that people would believe in Him (divine sovereignty and election) and that they would do so through the disciples' witness (personal evangelism). The sovereign and elective purposes of God, therefore, never make believers less responsible for personal outreach."[3] This is especially true in light of Jesus' teaching to the eleven in John 15:25-26 and 16:8-11. They had a responsibility to be co-witnesses with the Spirit. We do, too!

17:21. "that they all may be one, as You, Father, are in Me, and I in You; that they also may be one in Us, that the world may believe that You have sent Me.

The first thing Jesus asks the Father for future believers (including us) is unity. This is a growing unity, evidenced in His use of the present tense again, "that they may go on being one." In this request He is continuing the thought of oneness introduced in His prayer for the eleven in verse eleven. Even more so, He is communicating to His Father, and to us, just how important unity is to Him. When thinking of us He did not pray for boldness of witness or purity of life, but for unity among us (cf. 13:34-35, love one another). Unity, mutual love, and effective witness are not separated. *Love begets unity that produces effective witness.*

What exactly is Jesus asking for? And has His prayer been answered?[4] Jesus defines unity, in part at least, by what He says next. The unity for which He prays is patterned after the unity enjoyed by the Godhead. Jesus says that the kind of unity He desires is *just like* that enjoyed between Himself and His Father. This is the sense of "as."[5] So what is the result (cf. 1 Cor 12:25-27)? The result is the same as what Paul exhorted in Romans 12:1-2 with "transformed" (*metamorphaomai*). That is, let the real you come out. Take off the masque and let the glory come through.

Gruenler describes well the kind of unity to which Jesus refers, namely that of relationship. "The Father and the Son are seen to be conversing within the divine Household, Father, Son, and Holy Spirit interweaving their distinctive patterns of personhood within an essential unity, and displaying a characteristic attitude of love and interpersonal communion as servants of one another, always glorifying and deferring to one another."[6] He says further, "The principle of servanthood which Jesus enunciates to his followers . . . is the principle which he implies derives from the interpersonal fidelity and hospitality of each of the three persons of the Triune Family to one another. . . . There is no claim to independent individuality (which would be tritheism) but an assertion of essential identification in loving communion. . . . Servanthood and generosity are the key to life in the divine Community."[7]

This kind of unity is based on Jesus' command in John 13:34-35. It only comes when we love one another through humble service that thinks of their needs above our own. This is the opposite of the attitude of the disciples when they came into the upper room. They did not love one another and so were divided, each vying for dominance over the other. Gruenler continues to describe this unity and its basis well. "The theme of reciprocal equality and sovereignty of Father and Son is interlaced with a typically selfless generosity on the part of the Son toward the Father and the world. Jesus is both Son and servant who embodies in his person the high and the low of the divine Community, both sovereign glory an servant hospitality."[8]

We should reflect the same attitudes and relationships pictured in the Godhead. As Gruenler again notes, "As the divine Community is comprised of a plurality of persons in essential unity, so the effect of preaching and belief in Jesus is the unity of believers in the Family circle."[9] His application of this truth is instructive also. He concludes, "Individuality is real, as are Father, Son, and Holy Spirit; yet true individuality is not separateness or egocentricity but faithful inter-relatedness in oneness."[10]

This is the basis of the Pauline concept of the body of Christ in 1 Corinthians 12. We are one body with many members. But, no member is more or less important than the other. We all need each other. When one member of the body suffers, we all suffer. When one rejoices, we all rejoice. We pass around our honor to compensate for those who lack. We are all attached to the Head, Christ. We do not neglect or ignore any member. In doing this, we express unity within the body, a unity reflective of the Godhead. So, the unity for which Jesus prays is the unity experienced by the members of the Godhead with each other. We are to pattern our relationships with fellow believers after Theirs. In this way we truly reveal the Father and the Son to a lost world, as Jesus will note below. But He does not pray for this unity just for unity's sake. He next gives the two purposes for our expressing a unity like Theirs.

First, unity among believers unites us in fellowship with God the Father and God the Son. Carson sees this as an allusion to the vine metaphor and the idea of the branches being in union with the vine in order to be fruitful. From this he sees the believers becoming "the locus of the Father's life and work *in them* (cf. John 14:12; 15:7)."[11] But this is still looking at Jesus' words from a purely justification perspective. The unity Jesus is talking about here has to do with communion, which is the essence of the vine allegory. This is the relationship of walking with God described by John in 1 John 1. Jesus is praying for the expression of God's life in the lives of believers in this life, not for some metaphysical union with the Father. Again, this is a conditional truth (what the believer is to experience in this life on the basis of his or her obedience) and not a positional truth (what is true because of Jesus' accomplished work on the cross). Jesus prays that the Father will accomplish unity within the church so that the church can experience close communion as God's children now.

But this unity is also to have another effect. It will impact the unbelieving world and convince it that the Father did indeed send the Son. And as a corollary, we should recognize that disunity would have the opposite effect on the world. This is what Jesus means when He says their bearing much fruit will "prove" (see NASB) they are His disciples to the world. How do they do that? By loving one another (John 13:35). And, as unity is the natural expression of the kind of love Jesus calls for, we see that even in this prayer He keeps going back to the basic command.[12]

Ecumenicists use this verse to promote such things as the World Council of Churches and other cooperative programs. They argue that our denominational distinctives and separateness violate Jesus' principle of love and unity. But we believe there is a flaw in their argument in that Jesus is not talking about union, but unity. Morris provides a good caution to the interpretation of this verse. "It is well that we work to bring the sundered denominations together. But it is better to look for a grander unity than that, and it is this grander unity for which Christ prays."[13]

Jesus is not talking about organizational union. He is also not talking about theological compromise. As Carson notes, this unity "is not achieved by hunting enthusiastically for the lowest common theological denominator, but by common adherence to the apostolic gospel, by love that is joyfully self-sacrificing, by undaunted commitment to the shared goals of the mission with which Jesus' followers have been charged, by self-conscious dependence on God himself for life and fruitfulness."[14] In fact, with the World Council of Churches, the groups included in its fold have nothing in common with our faith in Christ. The result is that the organization can only be characterized as anti-Christian.

For true believers, our unity is based on our union with Christ. And, our unity is to be a testimony to the world of the validity of our union with Christ. I (Gary) think of my experience as a Baptist living in Egypt. My family attended the only Baptist church in Cairo. At that time the country had only four non-Muslim religious groups. They were the Baptists, Pentecostals, Presbyterians, and Eastern Orthodox (Coptic). When the Baptists and Pentecostals or Presbyterians got together behind closed doors, they would discuss their theological differences and enjoy a good "debate." But when they stepped out of that room into the Muslim world, they walked arm in arm and presented a united front to a hostile world. This is the unity Jesus desires in the church everywhere.

In that light, let us ask how many church business meetings display unity? Some churches do not seem to think that they have had a successful business meeting unless there has been at least one yelling match or fistfight! Does that express the unity Jesus is praying for? Certainly not! Others will not pass a motion without unanimous consent. Does that express the unity Jesus is praying for? Not really. The unity He prays for goes deeper than mere votes and involves the hearts and souls of men and women who view themselves as sharing in Christ, and so in each other.

17:22. "And the glory which You gave Me I have given them, that they may be one just as We are one:

Related to our experience of unity is the privilege of sharing in Jesus' glory. Thus He says to His Father, "And the glory which You gave Me I have given *them*." Here "them" means future believers, i.e., us! But, what does He mean by "the glory"? Glory is manifestation. The manifestation of the saints is yet to come. Paul's "humble service" is not "glory" but it will result in glory (2 Tim 4:6-8; Rev 2:26-28; 3:21; and 20:4-6). Remember, one aspect of glory has to do with revealing Jesus' splendor and majesty. The other aspect of glory has to do with revealing God's character.[15] The purpose of Jesus sharing His glory (Rev 2:26-28) with us is that it will lead to our unity that should be a reflection of the oneness between the Father and Son. This oneness is defined in the verse that follows.

17:23. "I in them, and You in Me; that they may be made perfect in one, and that the world may know that You have sent Me, and have loved them as You have loved Me.

The unity Jesus prays for includes the mutual abiding relationship He had with His Father being expressed now in Their relationship with believers, thus "I in them, and You in Me." The tendency of some might be to see this as a description of the metaphysical union between God and believers expressed through the Pauline concept of "in Christ." That is a positional truth, something accomplished by God at our justification-salvation, and not something Jesus would need to pray for us to experience.

Dillow cautions us against seeing this as mere justification truth. He notes, "Again it is not a saving relationship which is portrayed by 'in Me' but a life of communion. It is a oneness of purpose and not of organic union which is taught. Jesus expresses its purpose when He says, "that the world may believe" (17:21) and "that the world may know" (17:23). These follow up on 13:35 (they will know by your love) and 15:8 (bear fruit and prove you are disciples). He wants them to have an experience of unity because that *observable unity will prove to the world that they are His disciples,* models of Christian love (17:23). If being 'in Him' referred only to an organic connection, it would prove nothing. But if it refers to an experiential unity of purpose and fellowship, this would have great testimonial impact. It is a unity they do not yet have but must be 'brought to.' For John, to be 'in Me' is simply to have 'complete unity' with Him, not organic connection or commonality of essence."[16] The key to this is *abiding* in 15:1-8, as it is in 1 John. Abiding is nothing more than obedience that grows out of settled believing. Our biggest need is to believe. Remember what Jesus said in 14:1.

The central point of the evening's instruction has now been fully expressed by Jesus. In John 13:34 Christ commands them to love one another. Then in the next verse He gives the command's result. In John 15:8 Christ gives the result again, but with figurative language. Now, in 17:21 and 23 He prays about it. The Lord keeps on track all the way through. Let's not miss the point of His instruction. Let us pursue His desire in our churches.

Why are we to be one as God is one? There are two reasons given by Jesus. First, He wants our oneness to be "perfect" (cf. 1 John 2:5). The Greek concept of "perfect" does not especially mean "perfection," flawless. Rather, it carries the sense of maturity and completeness. That is what Jesus means when He prays that we "may be made perfect in one." He wants our relationships to reflect a level of spiritual maturity and completeness that is recognizable in the world (again, as in 13:35). We see this same idea in Matthew 5:16, "Let your light so shine before men, that they may see your good works and glorify your Father in heaven." The second reason He wants us to express this kind of unity has to do with the world's response. As we are His witnesses in the world, and the world sees us expressing the loving, serving, unity of the Godhead, it will come to know that God the Father did indeed send Jesus and that He loves us in the same way He loves Him.[17]

But what is the significance for us as believers? As we experience this communion of unity with one another and with God, we will also experience God's love in the same way Jesus did while on earth. Therefore we will be privileged to experience a deep and abiding fellowship with God in this life. We will experience eternal life, a quality of life, God's kind of life, in the here and now. Our enjoyment of eternal life in this life will impact the lost world around us and convince them of the reality of our God and the truth of His ultimate act of love in sending Jesus. We cannot be effective witnesses for God apart from this.

17:24. "Father, I desire that they also whom you have given Me may be with Me where I am, that they may behold My glory which You have given Me; for You loved Me before the foundation of the world.

Jesus now turns to our future destiny. Earlier in the evening He had promised the eleven that one day they would dwell with Him in the Father's house. We know from Revelation 21:9-27 that this is a huge house indeed! You could call it God's High Rise (1500 miles high). Now He includes all believers in that promise. He does this by making two requests concerning our future glorification. Jesus' first request is that those who the Father gives Him may be with Him.[18] And it is again for believers, present and future, that He prays. Further, His motive for such a prayer is given next.

Jesus' purpose for wanting the saints to be with Him is so that we may behold the glory the Father bestows on Him.[19] This is a reference to the Shekinah glory, to the glory of Messiah, dominion restored (Dan 7:13). We should notice that there are three glories mentioned in Jesus' prayer. First, there is Christ's eternal glory in verse five. Then there is the added glory because of His finished work in verse twenty-two. We share in this glory (Phil 4:14; Eph 3:13-21). Finally, there is the future moral glory of verse twenty-four which is related to the glory of Revelation 21:23. It is the riches of grace for sinners mentioned in Ephesians 1, the riches of mercy in Ephesians 2, and the riches of glory for the saints in Ephesians 3.

Why did God the Father share His glory with God the Son? Jesus gives this reason next. He loved Him before the foundation of the world. He loved Him from all eternity past. What is exciting for us today is to realize, as Mitchell points out to us, "This divine and perfect and eternal love that the Father has for the Son, and the Son for the Father, is the same love He has for you and me." But that is not all, but "this is the kind of love He wants to see displayed through you and me."[20]

This verse contains the first and only "I will" Jesus uses for Himself. He wants something, namely, that the ones who were given to Him should be with Him to behold His glory. When we look at Revelation 4 and 5 and the glory of God's throne room, and we realize that one day we will be there witnessing His glory and praising Him. . . imagine it! Christ wants us with Him! He wants us to see all of this glory and partake in it!

Looking back over Jesus' prayer for us we see that His thoughts move from justification to sanctification to glorification: our total salvation. He has thought of it all. But, His prayer is not complete. Jesus now turns from supplication for us to a concluding communion with the Father as He again talks about Himself and His heart with the Father.

17:25-26. "O righteous Father! The world has not known You, but I have known You; and these have known that You have sent Me. And I have declared it, that the love with which You have loved Me may be in them, and I in them."

Since these last two verses do not contain any petitions and are introduced with another address to the Father, this may be a separate part of the prayer, its conclusion. Just as earlier in this prayer we have the only place where Jesus calls God the Father holy, this is the only place where He is recorded as saying "righteous Father." Here it is an expression of love and devotion as He finishes this prayer and expresses His heart's desire. We can assume that He used both of these terms on many other occasions as He communed with His Father. And, as the disciples listened in on this intimate discussion, they once again heard Him address His Father with love and respect.

Now Jesus talks about His relationship with the Father and summarizes his prayer. He begins by noting that the lost world has remained ignorant of the Father. Of interest is His use of *ginōskō*, translated as "know" and "declare" five times in these last two verses. He uses the same term throughout, and may possibly be using this term for "know" particularly in order to express its experiential aspect of meaning. *Ginōskō* may at times focus on the experiential aspect of knowledge, in contrast to *oida*, which implies intuitive (non-experiential) knowledge.

This experiential aspect would be the product of a relationship. Thus Jesus is saying that the world does not have an experience-based knowledge of the Father, but He does. This is true precisely because the world has rejected Jesus' revelation of the Father. This is seen in His contrast of the world with the disciples. Where it does not know the Father, the disciples ("these") have come to know precisely that the Father sent Him. They have become convinced of the very thing that our unity will demonstrate to the world, that the Father sent Jesus into the world. But why do they know this? Because, as Jesus next states, He had declared the Father's name, and all it signifies in terms of His character, power, and glory, to the disciples. But then Jesus says something more about His revelation of the Father to the disciples. He says He will continue to declare the Father's name to them.

Jesus next gives the purposes for His revelation of the Father continuing in the lives of the disciples. First, He wants them to express the Father's love. And second, He wants it to be "in" them. When He says that He wants the Father's love to be "in them" He is not saying just that He wants them to experience the Father's love, but that He wants them to be characterized by it. Thus verse twenty-six is the conclusion of the command He gave His disciples, and us, in 13:34-35. As Carson describes it, "The crucial point is that this text does not simply make these followers the objects of God's love (as in v. 23), but promises that they will be so transformed, as God is continually made known to them, that God's own love for his Son will become their love. The love with which they learn to love is nothing less than the love amongst the persons of the Godhead."[21] This is reflected in 1 John 4:12 where our love for one another demonstrates that God dwells in us and that His love has been perfected, brought to a mature and complete expression, in us. This is Jesus' desire for us.

Jesus' last desire was His own presence in believers. Again, this does not especially look at a positional truth but a conditional truth. Jesus asked of His Father that He would be having an impact in the lives of the saints. When He talks of being in us and we in Him, He is talking about the abiding relationship of the vine and branches. He is talking about the *experience* of eternal life as we have communion with Him. Again, this includes the Spirit's ministry in our lives as He influences us through God's revealed will in Scripture and as He changes our motives that in turn change the kinds of decisions we make. Thus, Jesus' prayer was very practical. And every believer should respond with, "Amen!"

APPENDIX 1

ETERNAL LIFE

Eternal life is a prominent theme in all of John's literature. Even so, with all the attention he gives the subject, it is possibly one of the most misinterpreted themes he develops. This has resulted because it is read through the grid of a justification motif, where with John it is best understood in terms of its meaning in the daily life of the believer, a sanctification motif. For example, Law says that eternal life stresses "cause, not effect; not phenomenon, but essence; not conscious experience, but that which underlies and produces experience." He describes it as "the medium of our subconscious," "the animating principle" which produces "fruits and evidences."[1] Further, it is

> nothing else than the Divine Nature itself, regarded, not as abstract being, but dynamically, as the ground and source of all its own manifold activities—as the animating principle in virtue of which the Divine Righteousness and the Divine Love are not mere abstractions, but eternally active forces. And, finally, the Life of God is a principle of self-communication and self-reproduction. . . . To men, Eternal Life is communicated as the result of a Divine act, by which, in the terminology of St. John, they are "begotten of God" and become the "children of God" (τέκνα του θεου). The actual impartation of the actual Life of God is the core of Johannine soteriology.[2]

It is something received, which has an effect on a person's life, not a description of that person's experience of life. Vanderlip argues that "life" and "salvation" are parallel to each other in the Gospel of John and so should be regarded as "equivalents" in Johannine thinking. He points to John 3:16-17 and 10:9-10 as evidences of this equivalence.[3] Lee also sees eternal life and salvation as synonymous, with John using eternal life because it matched better his "positive conception."[4] Law argues that the concept of eternal life as positional truth, something possessed which produces fruit,

> is implicit in that whole strain of thought in our Lord's Synoptic teaching which regards doing as only the outcome of being. . . . It is implicitly contained, moreover, in the whole Pauline doctrine of the new creation and of the mystical indwelling of Christ in the members of His Body. . . . The efficient source of all faith, righteousness, and love is a new life-principle which is nothing else than the Life of God begotten in the centre of the human person-

ality. In this alone the children of God differ from others. It is not because they believe, do righteousness, and love their brother, that they are "begotten of God," but because they are begotten of God that they believe, love, and do righteousness. The Life is behind and within all.[5]

A good example of the problem between the various approaches to John's Gospel is the disagreement between Cook and Wendt on the meaning of eternal life in John 17:3. Cook reflects the non-Lordship/Reformed view well when he considers the qualitative "content" of eternal life to be described in John 17:3.

Eternal life is that we may continually know (γινώσκομεν) the Father (the only genuine [ἀληθινός] God) and Jesus Christ, whom He sent. That is, the *personal* element is strongly emphasized in our Lord's definition of eternal life. Knowledge here is seen to be an appropriation of three persons, not merely an acquaintance with them (cf. 1 John 1:2). Eternal life is a dynamic relationship rather than a static one, but it is based on static (fixed) truth that endures forever (John 17:17).[6]

Wendt disagrees and does not see the verse describing eternal life, but only the means of obtaining it.[7] Hodges rejects this. And, though he sees eternal life as something possessed, he also sees John focusing on the contingent nature of a person's experience. The believer's experience of eternal life depends on obedience that leads to the experience of fellowship with the divine embodiment of eternal life, Jesus.[8] The believer properly in fellowship (in which sin is not producing a barrier) experiences the quality of life characterized by Jesus' unbroken relationship with the Father as He walked in obedience to Him moment by moment.[9]

Therefore John's use of eternal life reflects more than the mere possession of future life or the presence of a motivating factor within the believer. It reflects a quality of life experienced by the obedient Christian in this life that can be lost without the forfeiture of one's future experience of life, without losing one's salvation. To understand the term better, we should begin by examining the broad meanings possible in this seemingly simple phrase.

Range of Meaning

"Eternal life" (*zōē aiōnios*), occurs forty-three times in the New Testament, with twenty-three of those in either John's Gospel or epistles. Additionally, "life" (*zōē*) is used ninety-two times without "eternal" (*aiōnios*), including forty-four occurrences in Johannine literature. It has both quantitative and qualitative aspects to its meaning which are recognized by all.[10] The quantitative aspect of eternal life focuses on it as something possessed and as life enduring without end. Its qualitative aspect has experience and expression in daily life in view. It is entered into at regeneration and is experienced in the present.[11] Cook notes that, "in Biblical usage the idea of time is generally minimized or excluded."[12] Stevens describes well its two aspects when he says that eternal life

> is eternal, not merely in the sense of imperishable or endless, but in the higher sense of the true Godlike life, which by reason of its kinship to God is raised above all limits of time and place. It is life as opposed to the moral death of sin. While . . . eternal life is by its very nature continuous, the emphasis of the phrase lies upon the source and nature of the life rather than upon its continuance. Eternal life is life like that of God, who is its source. . . . Whatever be the exact import of the word "eternal," or the philosophy of its meaning, it is a noticeable fact that it is generally described as a present, rather than a future, possession of believers.[13]

Use of Eternal Life Outside of John's Literature

In the New Testament *zōē* and *zēn* can carry the sense of natural life.[14] It is also used figuratively. For example, it is used by Peter to refer to hope as "living" (1 Peter 1:3) and by Paul with reference to the believer presenting himself to God as a sacrifice (Rom 12:1).[15] Thus life alone carries the normal meaning of the word and its normal senses when modifying other words.

When life (*zōē*) is combined with the adjective, eternal (*aiōnios*), it describes the believer's experience following regeneration, whether it is being used with its quantitative or qualitative sense.[16] Though either aspect of its meaning may be emphasized at any given time, both senses are often contained in any given use. This makes it difficult at times to distinguish the two senses. This is true with John as well as throughout the New Testament.

Johannine Use

Eternal life is not simply another justification term in John's Gospel. Nor is it a single faceted theme with him. His development of the concept in his Gospel should not be viewed so simplistically, but needs to be recognized as a multifaceted concept, all aspects of which he wants to develop. This may be recognized by the shift in emphasis that is evident in the transition from Jesus' public to His private ministry, in His discussions with believers and nonbelievers. Where the *possession* of eternal life is mostly in focus in the early chapters of the Gospel, its *experience* becomes the dominant focus in the later chapters. I say mostly in focus, because even in those early chapters Jesus discusses eternal life in terms of what it means to the person receiving it in this life, not as something to be experienced or enjoyed later.

Though one may argue that the first eight chapters of John use the phrase more in terms of its relationship to receiving salvation, in John 10:10 Jesus clearly sees it as something to be experienced by his listeners before they entered into eternity. His use of the term in John 17:3 also shows that He saw it as far more than something merely possessed. First, it is linked with a relational term, knowing God. Second, it is something to be experienced in this life, not the life to come.

As noted above, John uses eternal life with its full range of meanings and implications.[17] It is enjoyed by entering into "union with the Father and the Son."[18] Even so, with John eternal life normally is used as a qualitative term. "It speaks of a new quality of existence so radically different from what a man experiences without it that its opposite can be called 'death' (5:24). The addition of the adjective 'eternal' does not change the meaning of 'life' from a qualitative to a quantitative one."[19] It "refers to the 'life of the age to come,' which has already now entered time and become a part of the spiritual experience of the believer."[20] It is "a higher Divine form of life already existing in believers, as the foundation of the life which eternally endures beyond the grave."[21]

Eternal life for John is far more than future unending existence with God. It describes the believer's present experience of life as well.[22] Vanderlip notes well that with John "believers already possess in the present time the salvation of the age to come. The life of the age to come has moved out of the future into the present. The future will simply bring to consummation and completion the eternal life which is already a present possession."[23] This is evident especially in John 10:10 where the life Jesus speaks of is to be experientially enjoyed rather than anticipated. Verses that use *zōē* in its qualitative sense include John 3:15-16; 6:40, 47, 53, 54, 68; 10:28; and 17:2-3. This experiential aspect of meaning is also evident in passages that focus on eternal life as a "present possession" for believers, such as John 3:36 and 5:24-26.[24]

Though eternal life is a sanctification term with John, it refers to more than just the present experience of divine life. The danger faced by any view which limits its meaning to just a sanctification sense is the temptation to define its meaning based on verses such as John 17:3 and 17 rather than its use throughout the Gospel. John 17:3 and 17 do not determine the Johannine sense of eternal life any more than do John 3, 4, 6, or 8. Each passage and use contributes to its broad meaning with the sense resident within its immediate context.

Smalley's definition of eternal life as "a spiritual *quality* of life" which involves "a sharing of living fellowship with the Father" is interesting. But, having said that, he also calls it a Johannine synonym for salvation.[25] This reflects his recognition that "life" and "eternal life" are not narrow terms with John, but broad terms that he uses with a range of senses as his need arises. As a result, the full range of meaning must be recognized and each use evaluated and interpreted based on its immediate context. First John 5 gives a clear example of how, even when used in close proximity, the term must be interpreted on the basis of its use in its immediate context. In 1 John 5:11-13, John describes eternal life as something possessed. Then in 5:20 he uses it in the sense of something experienced.

Though he sees it as a present possession for believers, John does not ignore the eschatological sense of eternal life as something yet to be enjoyed in eternity in his theology.[26] He uses it with this quantitative aspect in passages where life is described as unaffected by physical death. This meaning is seen in such verses as John 5:28, 29; 6:27, 39, 40, 51-58; 11:24-26; and 12:25. Wendt also sees this sense in John 4:14; 14:2; and 17:24.[27] Cook sees 6:52-54 reflecting the qualitative sense rather than its quantitative.[28] But even though Jesus refers here to having life "in yourselves" (v. 53), he is speaking in terms of its possession, eternal aspect.

One must not forget that the unending element of eternal life is in effect during the mortal phase of life as well as the immortal phase. Therefore referring to eternal life as a characteristic of a mortal man need not require the term be given a qualitative sense in that sentence.

Finally, eternal life should not be viewed as a synonym for the kingdom of God or salvation as some attempt to define it. Vanderlip, though reflecting the more classic reformed/justification emphasis, helps clarify this problem. He first notes that eternal life is equated with "entering the Kingdom of God in John 3." But then he goes further to point out that this equation does not occur anywhere else with John.[29] It only occurs as part of a quoted conversation. Though John quoted Jesus accurately, his failure to continue to develop a kingdom theme elsewhere should alert us to the fact that it is not a significant concept with John.

In conclusion, the Johannine concept of eternal life is that it is a kind of life enjoyed by believers. It is a relationship with God that is entered into at regeneration, predicated on obedience, and extends into eternity. It is something to be experienced in this life, not just something to be possessed now and experienced later.

APPENDIX 2

JUSTIFICATION THEOLOGY
AND JOHN'S GOSPEL

Though John's Gospel clearly communicates the gospel, its description is comprehensive and wholistic. It describes all aspects of salvation, including the unbeliever's need for justification and the believer's need for sanctification. It describes both aspects of salvation. But, because the Reformed tradition has focused on the issues of justification, the tendency of many scholars from that tradition is to read the gospel through a justification "grid" of reference.

F. F. Bruce and Carson are examples of scholars who we feel read too much justification theology into John's Gospel.[30] For example, they recognize correctly that the literary pattern of the Gospel is to present a "sign" which is followed by a discourse in which the sign's meaning is brought out. But they incorrectly see a reversal of the order with the Upper Room Discourse preceding its "sign," the cross. That is not to say that Jesus did not give instruction that evening covering justification issues. For example, He did institute the Lord's Supper as recounted in other Gospels and by Paul. But that does not require that He be doing the same thing in John. This reflects their justification focus when interpreting the discourse.

Carson argues that the "primary purpose of the Gospel of John was the evangelization of diaspora Jews—a thoroughly eclectic group—and of Gentile proselytes to Jewish faith." He notes the problem raised by these chapters to his theory since they appear to be "written for believers, not to win unbelievers." But then he goes on to argue that these chapters have "unbelievers primarily in view."[31] His arguments are listed and then responded to as follows.

First, the primary focus of the discourse "is not the nature of discipleship, but the nature of Jesus' mission and what takes place after his impending departure."[32] This first argument seems to ignore the contents of Jesus' instructions. Jesus dwells more on what it means to be His disciple than He does on His mission, especially His coming death. He does discuss His coming departure, but not as the principle focus of instruction. It is the occasion of instruction. But, the focus is the disciples' attitudes and conduct in view of His departure and future return for them. It is discipleship.

His second argument is, "To the extent that discipleship is in view at all, there is considerable emphasis on *remaining* in Jesus' word, on continuing in obedience to Jesus' teachings" which he sees as an aspect of "proper *evangelistic* endeavour."[33] In his seeming desire to keep the Gospel as a gospel tract, while admitting that there are clear discipleship issues developed in the discourse, he must relate them to evangelism. Yes, the evangelistic endeavor is a focus of Jesus in this section. The goal of the discourse is evangelization (cf. John 13:35), but the method is discipleship. It is what they are to be doing along with remaining in Jesus' word. In fact, evangelization of the lost is a natural outgrowth of such abiding. But, it is still issues of discipleship, of their relationship to Jesus and His ministry to them, that is the focus of the discourse, not how to be regenerated or what people must believe in order to put their trust in Christ.

A third argument is that "the best evangelistic literature is eager to make clear not only *how* to become a Christian, but also *what it is like* to live as a Christian. Themes detailing fruitfulness in the believer's life, the continued witness and explanations and comfort provided by the Holy Spirit, the prospect of final vindication—these can as easily be seen as incentives to becoming a Christian as edification or exposition for Christians."[34] Yes, this is true, but not a denial that the section was intended as edification for Christians. In fact, this argument lends itself to the view that the weight of evidence in the passage favors an edification purpose far more clearly than an evangelistic purpose.

His fourth argument states that

> a passage such as 15:26-27 not only preserves proper location in the salvation-historical development, but it also accomplishes two more things: it authorizes the kind of evangelism that the Gospel as a whole seeks to accomplish . . . and, in the larger context of 15:17 — 16:4, it openly demands that prospective Christians themselves get involved in witness and evangelism, detailing the cost of failure in this regard. There are only two groups of people: witnessing disciples of Jesus who are willing to suffer for their faith, and 'the world', evil and condemned. . . . The choices are polarized, blunt, demanding – and entirely appropriate to forceful evangelistic literature.[35]

Much of what he says is true about Jesus' words. Jesus does talk to Christians about evangelism. He does warn about persecution. But, Jesus is *not* talking to unbelievers that evening, but to disciples about what He expects of them. Further, we cannot agree with Carson about the polarization of two groups in Jesus' instructions. Jesus is not contrasting witnessing disciples and the world. He is telling disciples how they will see "all" recognize Christ (John 13:35; 15:8). Jesus is describing both the positive and negative aspects of discipleship. He is warning His disciples that the world will hate them. Jesus' instructions are not being used by John to convince unbelievers to turn to Jesus. They are given to encourage believers in their faith and to motivate them to action.

Laney develops his outline of the Gospel and of this section on the basis that it has an evangelistic purpose, expressed in John 20:30-31. He entitles it, "The Strengthening of Belief." He summarizes it by saying, "In this section Christ seeks to strengthen and confirm the belief of His followers in preparation for His crucifixion. Here Jesus teaches His disciples major truths (about service, love, prayer, heaven, abiding, persecution, the Holy Spirit, joy, victory, unity) that will enable them to be more effective in their ministries in those areas after His departure."[36] Yet, this must be seen in light of his view that faith/belief is presented by John as a process which can fall short of saving faith which results in salvation.[37] This concept influences how he understands certain statements of Jesus in this discourse and whether they address believers or include the possibility of professing believers who are not really regenerate. Thus, he must see the possibility that the eleven are still not saved and Jesus is attempting to strengthen their faith to that end. The problem is, in his introduction to the section, he focuses on the issues Jesus addresses with the men, and salvation is conspicuously absent![38]

Carson further identifies a "Passover theme" being developed in the Gospel of John that is behind John's reference to the Passover meal in the first verse. He concludes from this that John was inviting his readers to "see in the footwashing an anticipation of Jesus' own climactic Passover act as the Lamb of God who takes away the sin of the world." He identifies John 2:13, 23; 6:4; 11:55; 12:1; 18:28, 39; and 19:14 as verses developing John's Passover theme.[39]

The problem with his view is that John used the Jewish religious calendar, the feasts in particular, more as chronological markers in the Gospel than as thematic markers. Each of the verses cited by Carson serve as time markers in the Gospel just as John uses other feasts in other passages, such as the unnamed feast in 5:1, the Feast of Booths in 7:2, and the Feast of Dedication (Hanukkah) in 10:22. Thus, John's mention of the Passover feast as a chronological marker need not mean he is developing a Passover theme *per se*. If such a theme were being developed, it must be seen in the discourses or other authorial comments. The closest thing to a Passover theme might be John the Baptist's designation of Jesus as the "Lamb of God who takes away the sins of the world."

Carson's evangelism-justification understanding of the Gospel of John has resulted in an over emphasis in this section on the coming crucifixion of Jesus as its backdrop. This emphasis is evident when he says further that, "the Farewell Discourse must not be treated simplistically, as nothing more than Christian comfort designed to console defeated saints. Rather, it is first and foremost an exposition of the significance of Jesus' "going away" to his Father via the cross. It is elemental theology; *and only as such does it offer encouragement and consolation.*"[40]

To see Jesus' Farewell Discourse as Christian comfort, if that is what

Jesus intended His words to communicate and if John faithfully reported them, is not "simplistic." Carson's focus on the "going away" aspect and his attempt to make it "elemental theology" is really a reflection of his failure to move out a justification focused model of interpretation which attempts to make the Gospel of John a "gospel tract" and to find the doctrine of justification throughout its chapters. If the role of the passage within the development of the message of the Gospel as it relates to Jesus' revelation of the Father is seen, and His focus of love and concern for His own is recognized, then the comforting aspect of Jesus' message is not only most evident, but also highly significant.

The question we should be asking is: What did Jesus want to communicate to the eleven on that night, and through them to us today? Would that not also be what John would want to communicate when he chose to include that material in his Gospel? This answer assumes John's faithfulness to Christ's teaching as well as the historical reliability of his report. He was not manipulating Jesus' actions and words to communicate some personal theology or develop some theme that is separate from Jesus' intentions for that evening. Rather, he was faithfully communicating Jesus' message to the disciples because it had application to his audience then and has application to us today.

One of the weaknesses of modern scholarship is a tendency to see the authors of the Gospels manipulating history and putting words into Jesus' mouth in order to develop "their" theologies. The Jesus Seminar is an extreme example of this, as a group of scholars gathered to decide what Jesus really said or did not say. Granted, the authors of the Gospels were selective in the material they chose to record and Jesus' sayings they chose to report. And, granted, through this selectivity their messages are developed and their "theologies" communicated. Also, it can be assumed that John is as selective as the others when he chooses the material included in his Gospel. But, this does not mean that any of them are saying anything different from what Jesus intended to communicate through that same event and conversation.

So, in this account we should not see John giving Jesus' words meanings apart from those *He* intended to communicate to His men that evening. And, with that in view, the circumstances of that evening and the words of Jesus take on even greater significance when understood correctly.

APPENDIX 3

KNOWING GOD

Knowing God must be studied and understood as a concept since there is no specific word used for this, but rather a series of descriptions. Therefore, this study will be more than just a discussion of the similarities and differences in nuance between *ginōskō* and *oida*, though their relationships and uses by John will be discussed.

Use of Knowing God Outside of John's Literature

The non-Johannine literature does not appear to draw clear distinctions between the meanings of *ginōskō* and *oida* when describing a believer or an unbeliever's knowledge of God, whether experiential or innate.[41] Paul uses the terms six times with regard to knowing God, but does not indicate by his use of the terms that he made any special distinction between the nuances of their meaning. For example, he uses both *ginōskō* and *oida* to describe both believers and unbelievers' knowledge of God. He uses *ginōskō* in Romans 1:21 with reference to the knowledge unbelieving men have of God, though such knowledge does not lead to obedience.[42] The same term in 1 Corinthians 1:21 is used to describe unbelievers' lack of knowledge. In Galatians 4:8 Paul uses *oida* to describe his readers' lack of knowledge of God prior to their conversion, and then *ginōskō* in 4:9 to describe their having "come to know" God in the sense of entering salvation. If the nuance in meanings were significant with Paul, one would expect that he would have used *ginōskō* both times. Finally, 1 Thessalonians 4:5 and Titus 1:16 are examples where Paul uses *oida* to describe the Gentiles and false professors' lack of knowledge of God.

Non-Pauline literature follows the same basic pattern of using the terms as synonyms rather than with distinct meanings. In Hebrews 8:11 both terms are used synonymously and in 10:30 *oida* is used of believers. In Matthew 11:27 Jesus used *epiginōskei* to declare that true knowledge of either Himself or God the Father was limited to those to whom the revelation was given, even among those who "knew" Him in the flesh.

Johannine Use

The Upper Room Discourse and 1 John are the places where the issue of knowing God is most completely developed, though the theme appears earlier in the Gospel. John's use of *ginōskō* or *oida* does not indicate that he consistently distinguished any special nuance of meaning between the two terms. Dillow tries to make a distinction between them, with *ginōskō* containing within it the concept of "an intimate experiential knowledge" while *oida* only indicates a "mental process based on information." When interpreting the Parable of the Foolish Virgins (Matt 25), he describes the foolish virgins as "saved" while "excluded only from the joy of the wedding feast and from co-heirship with Christ."[43] The broader context of the Olivet Discourse makes this interpretation suspect, especially since the final parables end with those being rejected experiencing *eternal* punishment rather than just exclusion from the kingdom (Matt 24:51; 25:30, 46). In contrast to Dillow, Bob George understands John's use of the terms to be "almost interchangeable."[44] But, having said that, he still makes some distinction in that he takes John's use of *ginōskō* to be more than describing academic knowledge or mystical vision. He sees it linked to *pisteuō* and *agapaō*, both which he describes as "fruits" of the Johannine sense of knowledge.[45] John's use of these two terms with regard to knowledge of God will now be examined.

Within 1 John

In eight verses where knowing God is discussed in 1 John, he uses *ginōskō* in each instance but one.[46] In 2:3-4 he affirms that knowledge of God can only be demonstrated through obedience. Here John uses *ginōskomen* in a third class conditional sentence to affirm that only through the keeping (*tērōmen*) of God's commandments can we be sure that "we have come to know Him" (*egnōkamen*). He follows this by affirming that claiming to "have come to know" (*egnōka*) Him apart from obedience makes a person a liar in whom the truth is not exerting an influence (is not "in" him), not in a justification sense as some take the phrase, but in a sanctification sense. Thus John is affirming in these verses that one's confidence that he has "knowledge" of God, not proof of his salvation, grows out of obedience. In 2:13-14 John uses *ginōskō* when affirming his readers' knowledge of God. In 3:6 the practice of sin indicates that one has neither seen nor "known" (*egnōken*) God. In 4:6 only those who "know" (*ho ginōskōn*) God can hear (respond to) the Apostles. Finally, in 4:7-8 love demonstrates a person's "knowledge" (*ginōskei*) of God. What John means by knowledge of God will be discussed below.

John Stott makes a distinction between the meaning of the two terms, with *ginōskō* meaning "we come to know" or "we perceive" and *oida* "generally" meaning "'we know as a fact', not by perception but as something self-evident."[47] Westcott also identifies a difference in meaning, taking *ginōskō* as "knowledge of God gained by experience" in contrast to *oida* which is "the knowledge which is immediate and absolute."[48] Raymond Brown notes that both Westcott and Stott justify their understandings of the two words' distinct meanings with "elaborate explanations for the instances when either verb is used in a way that seems to violate the meaning proposed for it." He concludes rather that, "John may tend to use one verb in one way and another verb in another way, but it is really a question of emphasis and not of sharp distinction."[49] Law, though theologically in line with the Lordship/justification emphasis, differs from Stott and Westcott. "While γινώσκειν always suggests, more or less distinctly, the perception through which knowledge is acquired, εἰδέναι, on the other hand, expresses the fact of knowledge absolutely. It frequently happens, however, that the same experience may be stated from either point of view; and thus it is not possible, in actual usage, to draw any rigid line of distinction between the two."[50]

Gospel of John, Outside the Upper Room Discourse

Within the Gospel *ginōskō* is used forty-five times (nineteen times in the upper room) and *oida* is used seventy-two times (eleven in the upper room).[51] John's pattern within the other chapters of the Gospel does not indicate that he made a consistent distinction between the two terms. For example he uses either or both terms to describe knowledge of things and events. On that basis one may conclude that George's observations hold true and neither term should be given any special theological significance in and of itself. For example, John uses *ginōskō* in John 1:10 to express that knowledge of God that the world lacks. One sees this easily as experiential knowledge. But later in 8:55, while He uses *ginōskō* to describe His opponents' ignorance of God, which we would expect, He chooses *oida* to describe the knowledge of God He possesses, which we would not expect.

Rather than interpreting each passage on the basis of which word was used, the meaning of each term arises from its use within the context of its passage. This is especially significant when examining the concept of knowing God as Jesus developed it in the upper room. Having said all of this, four key passages outside of the Upper Room Discourse are significant in understanding Jesus' (and John's) teachings on what it means to know God. These will now be discussed.

The first significant statement comes in the Prologue of the Gospel (1:10). There John says, "He was in the world, and the world was made by Him, and the world did not know (*egnō*) Him." In light of the reference to "His own" in the following verse, the "world" here refers to the unbelieving world living in darkness and distinct from the elect nation of Israel, "His own." This use of "know" need not require the idea of experiential knowledge, but could include innate knowledge as well.[52] The world was completely ignorant of Him, whereas "His own" could not claim such innocent ignorance. This naturally leads to the statement of verse twelve that, though His own would not receive Him, anyone who was willing, including those in the world, was given the privilege of becoming God's children. Thus, this use of know involves justification truth and is a reference to "saving knowledge" rather than relationship.

In John 7:28-29, while attending the Feast of Tabernacles and while debate was raging concerning His identity, Jesus says to the people "You both know (*oidate*) Me, and you know (*oidate*) where I am from; and I have not come of Myself, but He who sent Me is true, whom you do not know (*oidate*). But I know (*oida*) Him, for I am from Him, and He has sent Me." Jesus used *oida* throughout this discussion. He used it, though, to communicate several aspects of knowledge.

He said that the people did indeed know Him and where He was from. There were those in the crowd who knew His hometown and had known Him personally. Further, they had known of His ministry since the baptism of John and would have heard of John's testimony about Him as evidenced by people's comments. In other words, they knew He was the Messiah from God. This knowledge can be seen as both intuitive and experiential knowledge. Their problem was not in a failure to know about Him, but in not knowing God. Jesus' repeated use of *oida* seems to be in order to communicate to them that their ignorance of God was the reason they were unable to understand what they knew of Him.

Immediately following this declaration Jesus tells the unbelieving Jews that a time was coming when they would seek Him and would not find Him because they could not follow Him where He was going (7:34). Their failure to understand, and the leadership's rejection of Him, left them separated from God in darkness, ignorance, and thus unable to know Him.

Thus, in the context of the discourse, justification is in focus once again. This fits with the development of the message of the Gospel and the theme of knowing God in that those who should have known and responded to Jesus (as noted in the Prologue) fail to because of their spiritual blindness and ignorance. This will be illustrated in greater detail in the healing of the man born blind and the response the Jews give there in contrast to his response of worship. But before the incident with the man born blind, there is another discussion between Jesus and the unbelieving Jews in chapter eight.

In chapter eight, still during the Feast of Tabernacles and following the incident with the woman caught in adultery, the issue of Jesus' identity is raised again in light of His claim to be the light of the world (8:12). Having said that "the Father" bears witness of Him, Jesus' opponents ask him where His "father" is, as if to challenge Him and say, "Bring on your other witness." Jesus' answer is "You know (*oidate*) neither Me nor My Father. If you had known (*ēdeite*) Me, you would have known (*ēdeite*) My Father also" (8:19).

Their failure to recognize Him was symptomatic of the greater problem of a failure to know God the Father. Their ignorance was again a consequence of their non-regenerate status and their rejection of Jesus' revelation of the Father. Having said this, Jesus again predicted His departure and their inability to "follow" Him where He was going (8:21-24).

That Jesus intended this to be understood in a justification sense is made evident by His declaration that they would die in their sins. When

some of the people do believe in Him, Jesus addresses those who believe
(8:30-32) until others in the crowd begin to question (reject) what He is
saying. As the debate heightens and His detractors clearly reject Him,
Jesus brings up the issue of their failure to know God by showing that
their inability to believe in Him is symptomatic of their not knowing God.
Thus, He says to them, "Yet you have not known (*egnōkate*) Him, but I
know (*oida*) Him. And if I say, 'I do not know (*oida*) Him,' I shall be a liar
like you; but I do know (*oida*) Him and keep His word" (8:55). Of interest
here is Jesus' use of *ginōskō* where I would expect Him to use *oida* and
visa versa. Even so, the point made is that their inability to recognize Him
and respond to His revelation of the Father grows out of their separation
from God in ignorance.

So, to this point in the Gospel accounts, the idea of knowing God has
been discussed within the context of conflict with unbelieving Jews who
are rejecting His revelation of the Father and, as His own whom should
have received Him (1:11), responding in unbelief which resulted in spiritual ignorance and blindness. Later in chapter ten, again in the context of
debate, but also while revealing His relationship to those who do believe
in Him, Jesus uses *ginōskō* to describe His knowledge of the Father. He
says there, "As the Father knows (*ginōskei*) Me, even so I know (*ginōskō*)
the Father; and I lay down My life for the sheep" (10:15). Here, in a non-
justification related use of the idea of knowing God, Jesus seems to choose
the term with the experiential nuance in mind.

Within the Upper Room Discourse

Following the departure of Judas, Jesus is talking to men who have
clearly believed in Him and so are considered regenerate. They are distinct from the people with whom Jesus debated in earlier chapters. They
have responded to His revelation and believed in Him such that they have
chosen to follow Him. In this conversation with His own who did receive
Him, *ginōskō* occurs twenty-two times and *oida* thirteen times. In most of
these cases the terms refer to knowledge of immediate things within the
context of the evening's events and have no significant theological significance. Further, their use indicates the general pattern of synonymity,
reflecting more John's desire for variety than a distinction in meaning.
Still, within the six verses addressing knowledge of God, *ginōskō* is used
ten times while *oida* is used only once. The world's lack of knowledge of
God is described three times using *ginōskō* along with the one occurrence
of *oida* (John 14:17; 15:21; 16:3; 17:25). The disciples' knowledge of Christ,
the Father, and the Holy Spirit is described with *ginōskō* (John 14:7, 17;
17:3), as is Christ's knowledge of the Father (John 17:25).[53]

If a pattern is to be found Jesus' use of the terms seems to have
used *ginōskō* more often when speaking with believers and *oida* more
often with unbelievers. If He had not used *oida* that one time here in the

upper room, there may have been opportunity to argue that the difference in their nuance of meaning is significant. This does not work though since synonymity of meaning within Johannine use of the two terms can be seen clearly in the parallel verses of John 15:21 and 16:3 where the unbelieving world's persecution of the disciples reflects a lack of knowledge of God.[54] This, along with the pattern of John 8:55, indicates that no significance should be found in either term alone, but within the concept itself through which Jesus says very significant things about a believer's relationship with God.[55] Having said this, the significance of each use still resides principally in its immediate context. The greater use of *ginōskō* over *oida* in the upper room as it relates to the disciples' relationship with God, I believe, is significant and does indicate that the nuance of meaning is intended to be emphasized by Jesus, at least in part.

Outside of the upper room, Jesus taught that rejection of Him and His word indicated a lack of relationship with God, expressed as a lack of knowledge. In the upper room He teaches that His disciples have moved from not knowing God to a knowledge of Him that includes "seeing" Him, and thus implies an experiential knowledge and relationship (John 14:7).[56] They also can now be said to know the Holy Spirit on the basis of His indwelling presence, again reflecting a knowledge growing out of experience and relationship (John 14:17).[57]

Eternal life is described as knowledge of God and Christ rather than a possession of them or of something else (17:3).[58] It too is relational. Thus, in the upper room Jesus describes knowledge of God as the experiential knowledge a believer has of God in the sense of a growing personal relationship as a consequence of experiencing personal communion. This is seen also in the development of the conversation in the upper room, especially when Jesus tells His men that their relationship with Him has been changed from the kind of relationship a slave would have to that of a friend (15:15). Hodges addresses the sanctification aspect of knowing God well when he says that "fellowship with an individual is the essential medium for acquiring an intimate knowledge of that individual. . . . The same is true also at the level of our relationship to God. While it can be said that in one sense all true Christians know God (John 17:3), it is possible to conceive of a sense in which a true Christian may *not* know God."[59] He understands John 17:3 to affirm that all Christians know God. But then he argues further that "sometimes even genuine believers can be said not to know God or Christ (John 14:7-9). Furthermore, Jesus promised His disciples a special self-disclosure that was predicated on their obeying His commands (John 14:21-23). It is clear that such an experience involves the knowledge of God. Finally, fellowship naturally leads to knowing the One with whom that fellowship takes place."[60] He says also concerning John 14:7,

The format of the conditional sentence in Greek indicates . . . that up to this moment the disciples had—in a special sense—not really known Jesus or His Father. . . . Despite the fact that Philip, along with the other disciples, had believed in Jesus (John 1:40-51; 2:11) and had eternal life, the Person of their Savior remained something of an enigma to them. They had not yet perceived how fully He reflected His Father (14:10) and, in this sense, they did not *know* Him![61]

Dillow concurs that Philip knew Jesus "in a saving sense" since he had believed in Him and followed Him, but "did not know Him in some other sense."[62] He sees Philip as evidence that there may be varying degrees of knowledge among believers. This kind of knowledge of God is not especially characteristic of all believers, but only of those in communion with Him through obedience as evidenced in the command to abide and its link to obedience in John 15:10.[63] He also notes that Jesus' use of know in the upper room "does not refer to the entrance into eternal life at justification but to the continuing experience which Christ called fellowship."[64] He says further, "Knowing Him experientially is not all or nothing. There are degrees. Our fellowship with Christ is not something that happens at a point of time; it is a process which continues over a lifetime and varies in intensity proportional to our obedience."[65] Therefore it is not innate knowledge, but personal knowledge.

Thus obedience may be viewed as the cause or basis of the fellowship that produces knowledge of God in the believer while love of the brethren is the fruit of that knowledge. Knowledge of God can be a contingent and graduated experience for the believer to the extent that a true believer could be described as not knowing God in a personal way even after he has clearly become one of His children. This is not the way it should be, but sadly, it is probably true more often than not because most believers are not obedient.

APPENDIX 4

FOOTWASHING AN ORDINANCE?

Did Jesus institute foot washing as an ordinance of the church along with the Lord's Supper that evening? Allen Edgington views footwashing as an ordinance of the church, established by Jesus at the Last Supper. He provides three arguments for his position. His first argument is that Jesus performed a "physical act that is ceremonial in nature."[66] He defends this by saying that "the graphic detail and the teaching directed to Peter further demonstrate that this was not a lesson in hospitality nor merely an act of humility."[67] Also, "Jesus was not simply carrying out a usual procedure. The significance was greater than the physical act."[68] This greater significance results from two facts: that it was done by Jesus after they had been there a considerable amount of time; and that it was done at the table rather than at the entrance to the house.[69]

Though these observations are true, they do not require an ordinance be instituted. Rather than instituting a new ceremony in the midst of an old one, the lesson was delayed because the discussion of greatness came after the meal was begun and the lesson was a response to that discussion. Further, it needed the delay in order to demonstrate the point being made about servanthood and to highlight their bad attitudes. Thus, seeing the context of controversy and recognizing Jesus' purpose to teach humility as expressed by His own explanation of the meaning of His actions, we do not need to give the physical act more significance than did Jesus.

His second argument is that the act was a "symbolic representation of a spiritual reality."[70] He notes, "Since Peter certainly understood the humility involved in Jesus' action, we may assume that more than humility was in view" in his question to Jesus.[71] Further, "Since Peter was already a believer, to 'have part with Jesus' must have meant to participate in daily spiritual fellowship and intimate communion with him (cf. 2 Cor 6:15). . . . The 'washing' of which Jesus spoke was the reality of which the footwashing was the symbol."[72] "Without introduction, Jesus moves to the spiritual level when he declares that they are all clean except Judas, who is unregenerate. On the physical level, the bath makes one clean. On the spiritual level regeneration makes one clean."[73] He applies this to us by saying, "On the spiritual level, believers are defiled daily by sin as they 'walk' in this sinful world—another 'bath' is not necessary, though they need the daily cleansing which comes from recognizing sin and confessing it. This is what is meant by 'having part with him,' viz., participating daily in intimate fellowship with him."[74] As observed by Laney, it is a mistake to import this spiritual level of meaning into the act when Jesus clearly defined its meaning in His explanation to the men in verses twelve through sixteen.

His third and final argument is that Jesus commanded its perpetuation. He sees this command resident in Jesus' lordship that is stressed in the context of the command wherein He uses the word "ought." He posits further that "the example of the teacher should be imitated by his disciples," and "the comparative καθώς 'just as' does not weaken the sense of the literal example, somehow suggesting that it is impossible to really duplicate Jesus' actions," . . . "obedience was to be evidence of spiritual blessedness," and "Jesus promises that the man who not only knows 'these things' but also does them is blessed."[75]

What Jesus commanded was that they perpetuate His humble service. Laney notes that Jesus chose a term for "example" (v. 15) that avoids the sense taken by Edgington. Rather than saying His act was a type (tupos), referring to "an exact replica," He said it was a "token" or "pattern" (hupodeigma). This term was "often used of something that should spur others to imitate the example." Further, "Jesus was not asking the disciples to replicate His specific actions, i.e., 'wash feet.' Rather, He was calling them to follow His humble pattern of serving others exemplified in the foot washing."[76]

Laney's argument that footwashing is not mentioned in Acts is weak. Neither is the Lord's Supper.[77] But it is significant that Paul, where he clearly saw the Lord's Supper as an ordinance (1 Cor 11), only mentions footwashing as a means of identifying widows who humbly serve others (1 Tim 5:10). His mention of footwashing, then, reflects the same elements of humility and service which Jesus emphasized in His explanation of His purpose for doing it and its meaning to the men that evening in the upper room.

Cook notes four arguments against footwashing as an ordinance. "(1) Jesus' statement in verse 7, 'What I do you do not realize now' . . . would seem strange and meaningless if Jesus had been referring to a mere formality, because the disciples were very much acquainted with the common practice of foot washing. (2) The fact that in verse 15 He used the word ὑπόδειγμα (an example) rather than something like παραγγελία (order, as in Acts 5:28), ἐπιταγή (command, as in 2 Cor. 8:8), παράδοσις (tradition, as in 1 Cor. 11:2), or some other word signifying a command seems to militate against the ritual concept, too. (3) The complementary teaching of John 13:10 is clearly not any more than illustrative of spiritual truth. If foot washing here is to be taken non-figuratively, then the bath must be, also. (4) Finally, in verse 15, where the actual exhortation is found, there is a simile set forth rather than a one-for-one correspondence. The use of the adverb of manner καθώς rather than the relative pronoun ὅ is to be noted. Jesus said to do as He did, not what He did."[78]

Appendix 5

EATING AT FESTIVE MEALS:
THE ARRANGEMENT OF THE TABLE

In early times before the Israelites occupied Canaan, they ate their meals sitting on the ground, something still characteristic of the modern day Bedouin.[79] But, by the era of Judah's kings, they were sitting on chairs around tables (1 Sam 20:24-25).[80] During New Testament times the wealthy ate at tables while the poor often crouched or sat around a common board to eat.[81] This practice can be seen in places like Luke 16:21, the story of Lazarus and the Rich man, where crumbs are mentioned falling from a table, indicating the wealth of the man. Also, the Gentile woman who appealed to Jesus to deliver her daughter from demon possession referred to the crumbs of the children's food falling from the master's table to be eaten by his dogs (Matt 15:27). The term used in the Gospels is *trapeza* and refers to some kind of table having four legs.[82] It was used not only of dining tables, but of the Table of Show-bread and of moneychangers' tables as well.

Reclining at the table had become a symbol of wealth and privilege. The Jewish custom of the first century required that the Passover meal be eaten from such a reclined position in a festive manner rather than the hurried way the Israelites were to eat at the first Passover (Exod 12:11). And so the *Mishnah, Pesha* 10:1, when discussing the Passover liturgy stated that "even the poorest Israelite . . . reclines at his table."[83] This appears to have been intended to symbolize the full inclusion of the poor "in the community on the occasion of the festival meal."[84] So, it had become common, even expected, for everyone to recline and eat such festive meals as the Passover. Interestingly, all references to Jesus eating include the description of Him reclining at table rather than sitting.[85]

At banquets and festive occasions, the tables of the wealthy were arranged one of two ways. Some banquets were eaten with a head table that was on an elevated platform overlooking the other guests, with everyone sitting in chairs at the tables to eat. The most honored guest would sit at the host's right hand with the next most honored guest at his left. The other tables were arranged perpendicular to the head table on the lower level. Others, especially on festive occasions, were eaten around a *triclinium*. In this approach an arrangement of three tables was used, forming three sides of a square and having couches arranged around its outside. The middle area was left open so that food could be served to all the guests from within the inside of the "U" shaped table. The couches were placed close to each other and arranged so that the guests could recline on their left arms, with their heads toward the table and feet away, and eat with their right hands.[86] Each couch was able to hold two or three persons.[87] Either the host, the guest of honor, or the most "important person" lay in the center of the couch located at the center of the table, where the two arms joined. Everyone reclined with heads toward the table and feet pointed away from it at an angle. They raised themselves up on their left elbow and ate with their right hand that was free to reach over the table.

For those reclining on the central couch, the place of greatest honor after that of the host or guest of honor was to his left. The person thus honored lay behind him on the couch. This enabled him to speak directly and privately with the guest of honor without having to twist or turn. The second place of honor involved laying in front of the host or guest of honor that placed the person so honored on his right hand. The person taking that place would be able to lay his head on the breast of the host or guest of honor.[88] Based on the description of Peter signaling the disciple "whom Jesus loved" who then "leaned back on Jesus' breast," we can conclude that the apostle John had been given this third place of honor on His couch and that the Last Supper was eaten around a *triclinium*.

Would these furnishings have been in a borrowed upper room? When Jesus instructed the two disciples to prepare the Passover for the group, He told them to follow a man with a water pitcher and enter the house after him. They were to say to the home owner, "The Teacher says . . .", and he would show them "a large upper room, furnished, prepared," where they were to make things ready for the group (Mark 14:13-15).

Appendix 6

THE RELATION OF JESUS' COMMAND TO DEPART TO THE STRUCTURE OF THE DISCOURSE

As is noted by Segovia there is widespread agreement on the importance of this section of John's Gospel (13:31—14:31) but not on its structure.[89] It also should be noted that he takes a Redaction Critical approach to the text and so has only limited helpful insights from which we may benefit. Also not a lot of agreement exists concerning its meaning. He identifies four major views on the discourse's interpretation:

(1) The discourse represents and is meant to be a rather faithful recollection of Jesus' last discourse to his disciples in the supper room. (2) The discourse seeks to show how the promise of the other world is directly and intrinsically connected with present eschatological existence. (3) The discourse seeks to explain and interpret Jesus' departure from the community. (4) The discourse is an exercise in polemics, constituting in effect an attack on other (Christian) positions.[90]

Though many commentators do not include Jesus' prayer in chapter seventeen as a part of the discourse, Segovia sees the discourse encompassing all of 13:31—17:26. He argues for this on the basis that the "concluding statements of 14:30-31c, the command of 14:31d to arise and depart, and the obvious connection of these verses with the beginning of the passion narrative (18:1-12) appear to divide this farewell into at least two seemingly independent and separate discourses."[91]

This is a logical dividing point, since it involves an apparent scene change, which is a common rhetorical device in narrative literature. But that does not necessarily mean that it divides the Discourse as a literary unit or that it meant that Jesus was changing His subject that evening. Rather, it only faithfully recounts the conversation of that evening and accounts for their movement from the upper room to the garden where the narrative is to continue with Jesus' betrayal by Judas. This is an accurate recollection by John that communicates the urgency of the time and reflects Jesus' understanding of Judas' intentions. Further, John's use of the inclusio of "love" which encompass the material from the first verse of chapter thirteen to the last of chapter seventeen mitigates against leaving out the first part of the chapter from the discourse. Further, the use of two other inclusios (13:34 with 15:17 and 13:35 with 15:8) that incorporate material on both sides of the statement also mitigates against any, but the first, view listed by Segovia.

Segovia believes that "the discourse represents and reflects an anti-Jewish polemic in which the theme of belief is primary and encompasses those of Jesus' departure and return."[92] He comes to this conclusion by relating the discourse to the discourses in chapters five, seven, and eight where similar themes of departure are used in Jesus' conflict with the Jews.[93] He notes Becker's work and identifies the *inclusio* of "Let not your hearts be troubled!" in verses one and twenty-seven of chapter fourteen as "outlining the middle and major section" of the "first" discourse. Another of Becker's arguments that he accepts builds from the departure and return theme he sees reflected in 14:2-3. He notes that, "these two themes are said to provide the basic concerns not only of the proposed middle section but of the entire discourse as well. In addition the two themes are also said to be developed sequentially within the middle section and thus provide the key to its basic structure."[94]

This is an accurate observation, but only in part, in that it is impossible to miss the departure-return theme that traces itself through Jesus' instruction. This was indeed one of the key things He was trying to communicate to His men that evening. His death and departure was not the end and not a reason for dismay. He would take care of them.

Segovia breaks the "first" discourse/section down into: 13:31-38; 14:1-27 (1-3, 4-14, 15-27); 14:28-31.[95] He concludes a polemical character for this section on the basis of his understood *Sitz im Leben* of "a prolonged and bitter confrontation between a Christian community and a parent synagogue(s) from which most of the former's present members have been forced to separate because of their belief in Jesus."[96] Segovia describes his position this way:

> I see the discourse as calling for belief in Jesus on the part of the disciples and specifically for a belief that includes an acceptance of his departure or death as the goal and culmination of his mission. At the same time, I also see the discourse as promising, e.g., Jesus' return to those, and only those, who believe in him. Furthermore, I see this call to belief and its accompanying promise as having an essentially polemical character: they differentiate completely and explicitly the disciples from the unbelieving Jews.[97]

We do not see where "unbelieving Jews" are ever a focus of this section beyond Jesus' promise of persecution. But rather than seeing even that comment as a polemic, it must be seen where it belongs, in a message of comfort and encouragement to persevere in faith amid difficulties which were about to beset them. The pitfall of Segovia's position is that it reads into the text authorial motives based on speculation and supposed problems that may or may not have existed at the time John wrote the Gospel. Further, it ignores the literary design and development of the section itself and of the Gospel as a literary unit of thought. It sees the Gospel being written to combat a problem rather than proclaim a truth. It fails to see the confrontations between Jesus and the "Jews" within the Gospel as developing more important themes than attacks against Jewish or Christian opponents years after the events that are recounted.

The very general way in which John refers to Jesus' opponents throughout the Gospel (especially in contrast to the clearer identifications given by the other evangelists) indicates that he really is *not* focusing on a group of opponents at all, but rather developing other literary and theological motifs, such as the dark-light and rejection-acceptance motifs within his message. Recounting those conflicts was necessary to communicate Jesus' person and message more clearly. They were not included to attack some group who was bothering the church during the time of the Gospel's writing. The Gospel focuses on Jesus' person and purpose, not some later church problem. It was written to tell us about Jesus and explain how to live for Him, not in order to attack someone else.

Jesus' life, His revelation of the Father, and the truths about experiencing eternal life are the focal issues of the Gospel, not merely the medium that John chose in order to grind his theological ax. Recognizing this, and by focusing on Jesus and His message, we should find the textual and literary clues we need to understand this section of the Gospel. We will see this below as we interpret Jesus' instructions to them and to us.

Carson has better things to say about issues concerning the structure and meaning of the farewell discourse. The first issue he addresses is its actual beginning point. He notes that the most common beginning points are either Judas' departure in 13:30 or Jesus' admonition in 14:1. He favors 13:30 on the grounds that "it does see the departure of Judas as much more of a turning point in the plot, and it enhances the link" between the last verse of chapter thirteen and the first verses of chapter fourteen.[98]

Carson notes secondly that Jesus' instruction in 14:31 seems to create a "break" in the material of the discourse and discusses the four major views on its significance. In short they are: (1) that chapters thirteen and fourteen occurred in the upper room while fifteen through seventeen were on the way to the garden; (2) that 14:31 was displaced by some editor and should be at the end of the discourse; (3) that 13:31—14:31 are the actual discourse and fifteen through sixteen are John's "own meditations" on it; and (4) that the two sections of the discourse reflect two versions of the same discourse brought together by the editor of the Gospel.

Westcott reflects a view similar to the third view above. He divides the discourse by Jesus' instruction to depart. He argues,

These two groups of revelation, while they have much in common, are distinguished both by their external form and by a pervading difference of scope. The first group consists in a great degree of answers to individual apostles. . . . In the second group the case is far different. After the little company had left the room a solemn awe seems to have fallen upon the eleven. . . . This outward difference between the two groups corresponds with an inward difference. In the first group the thought of separation, and of union in separation, predominates. In the second group the main thought is of the results of realized union, and of conflict carried on to victory. This progress in the development of the central idea of the discourses influences the treatment of the subjects which are common to the two sections. . . . These last discourses in St. John bear the same relation to the fourth Gospel as the last eschatological discourses to the Synoptic Gospels. . . . The two lines of thought which they represent are complementary, and answer to the circumstances by which they were called out. Speaking in full view of the city and the temple the Lord naturally dwelt on the revolutions which should come in the organization of nations and the outward consummation of His kingdom. Speaking in the Upper Room and on the way to Gethsemane to the eleven, now separated from the betrayer, He dwelt rather on the spiritual revolution which was to be accomplished. In the last case the situation no less than the teaching was unique.[99]

In response to the fourth view he identified, Carson, who seems to accept some form of redaction occurring in the composition of the Gospel, provides a warning to anyone who would listen to theories involving these speculative solutions. He says,

The multiplication of sources and redactors ought to be treated with particular suspicion: most writers will frankly acknowledge that their roughest drafts are their *first*, and that successive polishing, by the original author or someone else, reduces the number of apparent aporias and enhances the smoothness. . . . The interpreter's first job is to make sense of the text as it stands. Not only the witness theme but also numerous bits of incidental evidence suggest that much of the Gospel depends on eyewitness memory. . . . If we take these bits at their face value, 14:31b appears, on initial reading, to be a momentous instance of personal recollection: little of theological value turns on the words 'Come now; let us leave'; their inclusion can be justified only on the grounds of an incompetent editor or *simply on the grounds that personal memory of the events recalled them that way*.[100]

He also gives insightful suggestions for what could have happened. He notes that it is not uncommon to suggest it is time to go and then be delayed from leaving by continued conversation. He then notes, "The troubling question is why the Evangelist should have bothered to report 4:31b at all. Apart from appeal to the power of memory, it might be argued that the decision to record a delay in departure is the Evangelist's attempt to depict yet again Jesus' profound love for his disciples (cf. 13:1), his concern to drill into them certain stabilizing truths that would see them through the crisis ahead (cf. 14:29), his desire to place before them, through his final prayer (Jn. 17), the cosmic sweep of the tragedy and triumph about to befall." He concedes, though, "Alternatively, one could imagine Jesus and his disciples actually leaving at this point, and continuing their conversation in the narrow streets of the old city."[101]

The first view listed by Carson is the best and fits the literary design of John better than the others. The only real change in the development of the Discourse is location. If you take out Jesus' instruction, the flow of thought and development of Jesus' message continues smoothly. Yes, the second section is deeper, as observed by Westcott. But, that is natural since Jesus is moving from the basic ideas to deeper spiritual truths as His men are ready to understand and receive them.

APPENDIX 7

VITICULTURAL PRACTICES IN
FIRST CENTURY JUDEA

Grapes are believed to have originated in the Armenian hills and around the Caspian Sea, *Vitis vinifera* being the first species domesticated and cultivated.[102] Based on Genesis 9 and the grape's center of origin, both Jewish and Christian tradition has considered Noah as the father of viticulture.[103] The importance of grapes within Jewish culture is evidenced by Josephus' mention of them as a "king of fruits" grown within the land of Judah and by their inclusion in the artwork of Herod's temple.[104]

Viticulture was an integral aspect of first century Judah's culture. When Jesus presented the analogy of the vine and the branches to His disciples He was speaking from a familiar context. Because its practice was so widespread it is likely that all of them, including the fishermen, would have seen grapes cultivated either in their villages or on the hillsides around their homes. Below is a description of some of those practices, especially the ones related to understanding Jesus' analogy of the vine and the branches.

Site selection and preparation. Vineyards in Judah were located on nearly any terrain from the hilltops to their steep slopes and the level valleys.[105] The two principle requirements in sight selection were that it had to provide plenty of sunlight and have a year around supply of water. The vast majority of vineyards were situated on the rocky hillsides where most agricultural enterprises were conducted.[106]

Planting and cultivation. The vineyard was started with cuttings from desired varieties. These would be provided from the branches removed in the post-harvest pruning, likely from a nearby vineyard.[107]

An advantage of having a vineyard was that, in contrast to field crops whose tilling and planting time was generally short and intense, maintenance of vineyards could be done at a more leisurely pace with the labor spread over several months rather than days.[108] Blooming occurred in late spring to early summer. From mid-July to mid-August when most people were involved with threshing and winnowing the grain harvest, the elderly and children cared for the vineyards.[109] Plowing and hoeing was conducted during the months of February and March.[110] This tillage of the soil contributed toward weed control and insured proper aeration and maximum absorption of spring rains.[111]

Training of plants. In early Israel the branches of cultivated grapes were either allowed to trail along the ground or were trained to grow over a pole.[112] Shewell-Cooper asserts that training the branches low and parallel to the ground "was the method of viticulture carried out by the Babylonians, who were very far advanced in their agriculture" over the Canaanites and Israelites.[113] The evidence, though, indicates that this particular practice was introduced to Palestine long before Judah's captivity, and probably before the conquest of Canaan. Its mention by Pliny indicates that it was still being practiced in first century Palestine as well.[114] When the stems were trained along the ground the grape clusters were propped up to keep them from contacting and being ruined by the soil.[115] Trellising of vines appears to have been introduced primarily by the Romans as one of their advancements in viticulture and was used extensively in Palestine. It was used as a means of allowing airflow through the branches in order to dry the dew more quickly.[116] Pliny described five approaches to training grape vines "with the branches spreading about on the ground, or with the vine standing up of its own accord, or else with a stay but without a cross-bar, or propped with a single cross-bar, or trellised with four bars in a rectangle." [117] Thus when Jesus related His analogy the disciples would likely have been familiar with both trailing and trellising approaches. Further, though the use of rocks to prop up branches was probably still used in the Negev, the practice in the Galilean and Judean hills most likely reflected the Roman improvements since Pliny took note of that approach being used in Palestine of his day.

Harvest. Harvest time varied throughout the land of Judah depending on local climate. In the Jordan valley some grapes ripened in June while on the coastal plain they came into season in the middle of August. In the mountainous country ripening was delayed until September.[118] The harvest of grapes lasted only a short period since, once grapes have matured, "there is considerable pressure to gather them before they fall from the vines, become dehydrated, or fall prey to insect or animal pests."[119] With the harvest came the making of wine.

Pruning. Pruning of the vineyards occurred at two principal times during the year. Immediately following the harvest the grapes were pruned severely and all leaves were stripped from the plants to induce dormancy.[120] Spring trimming of vines was practiced before blooming as well as after.[121]

The *Oxyrhynchus Papyri*, dated around A.D. 280, contain a contract for labor in a vineyard. It, along with Pliny, represents the nearest viticultural documents to the first century. In this contract the procedure for vineyard management began with "pruning, transport of leaves and throwing them outside the mud-walls."[122] This corresponds to the post-harvest pruning. Following this the workers were committed to "planting as many vine-stems as are necessary, digging, hoeing round the vines and surrounding them with trenches."[123] The planting of stems refers to asexual reproduction of grapes through cuttings and would be done during dormancy using material taken from the plants in the pruning mentioned first. This, being the second stage of labor contracted, argues for the "pruning" to be post-harvest and early dormant season, the severe pruning. The contract continues, ". . . we being responsible for the remaining operations after those mentioned above, consisting of breaking up the ground, picking off shoots, keeping the vines well tended, disposition of them, removal of shoots, needful thinnings of foliage."[124] This describes their responsibilities during the growing season. Direct actions on the vines include "picking off shoots, removal of shoots," and "needful thinnings of foliage," none fitting the description of the removal of a branch. The work is of minor impact on the plant and designed to encourage fruit development while discouraging extensive vegetative growth.

For best results the growth rate of a vine must be maintained within a middle zone. If it has too few growing points it grows too fast and becomes vegetative, producing fewer flowers and so smaller grape clusters. If allowed to have too many growing points, it grows too extensively and its energy is wasted on growth. The clusters do not produce large or juicy grapes. The severe pruning in the early dormant season involves the reduction of the plants to their appropriate number of growing points, the buds. The spring removal of shoots reflects the process of insuring that the plant is not allowed to grow too slowly by spreading its energy among the large number of suckers and water sprouts which appear on the main trunk as well as the fruiting branches.

Duckat is an example of the modern misunderstanding of viticultural practices. Based on Isaiah 18:5 he asserts, "After the plants budded and the blossoms turned into ripening grapes, the vine dressers cut off the barren branches."[125] Pliny refutes him and notes:

> Thus there are two kinds of main branches; the shoot which comes out of the hard timber and promises wood for the next year is called a leafy shoot or else when it is above the scar [caused by tying the branch to the trellis] a fruit-bearing shoot, whereas the other kind of shoot that springs from a year-old branch is always a fruit-bearer. There is also left underneath the cross-bar a shoot called the keeper—this is a young branch, not longer than three buds, which will provide wood next year if the vine's luxurious growth has used itself up—and another shoot next to it, the size of a wart, called the pilferer is also left, in case the keeper-shoot should fail.[126]

Of significance is the number of non-fruiting branches left on the vines. He further notes that after the harvest, when the most severe pruning occurs, it is the fruiting branches that are pruned away and are considered useless.[127] This procedure has not changed since the first century.

Branches are selected for various purposes and accordingly pruned during dormancy. The fruiting branches for the following season are allowed to keep between eight and twenty buds, depending on the cultivar.[128] This serves to regulate the branch's growth rate in the spring at a level that encourages maximum flowering and fruit-set. The non-fruiting branches are pruned more severely in order to encourage vegetative growth with a view to a thick branch which can be used for fruiting the following year. Other adventitious growths, like water sprouts which arise from the roots at the base of the vine, are removed.

APPENDIX 8

THE MESSAGE OF JOHN AND BELIEF IN JOHN 20:30-31

As noted in the introduction to this book, a critical element in interpreting the Gospel of John is an accurate understanding of its purpose as it affects it message. Most commentators turn to John 20:30-31 to determine the purpose of the Gospel. This is because John at least *seems* to be stating his purpose. "And truly Jesus did many other signs in the presence of His disciples, which are not written in this book, but these are written that you may believe that Jesus is the Christ, the Son of God, and that believing you may have life in His name." Based on their understanding of John's statement, those commentators see its purpose as evangelistic. John wrote to engender faith in his readers so that they would come to believe in Jesus and receive eternal life. As a result, Jesus' teachings throughout the Gospel, including in the upper room, are seen in terms of justification truths rather than sanctification. John is said to have selected his material in order to bring people to faith. What he says should be understood in terms of its contribution to justification issues rather than sanctification.

On the surface, when read in isolation, these verses could easily mean just that. Yet, the message cannot be reduced to an explanation of how to be born again. There is far more being accomplished. And so, we are forced to ask, "What if John meant far more than just how to be justified?"

First, we must see why there is far more to the message of the Gospel. Then we can ask what that "more" would be. Beginning in the first chapter, in the Prologue (1:1-18) to the Gospel, certain themes are introduced which do not relate to regeneration or justification issues. The principle theme that evidences this is that of Jesus as the revealer of the Father. After affirming in 1:18 that the Son "has declared" (explained, exegeted) the Father, John spends a great deal of time recounting Jesus' dialogues and deeds which reveal the character and person of God the Father. This idea is again a central focus of Jesus' in the upper room. Eternal life is even defined in terms of knowing the Father (17:3). And, throughout the Gospel, far more is being said about eternal life than that it is something to possess or something future. It is also described as something experienced by the believer in the present (John 10:10). In fact, the descriptions that Jesus gives throughout the Gospel of the experience of eternal life involve present life abundance, not future. This is the only possible meaning of the water of life in John 4:13-14, which is further defined as the indwelling Holy Spirit in John 7:37-38. The abundant life Jesus offers as the Good Shepherd involves the security of His protection in this life (John 10:7-10).

That does not mean that the future life is discounted by Him or by John. It is also addressed in places such as John 6:40 and 10:27-30. But, often Jesus' focus is on explaining how a person could experience God's life, beginning in this life. Eternal life is defined as more than something possessed. It is experienced. Therefore, the eternal life John is talking about in this purpose statement means more than "salvation" in the sense of regeneration or future existence. It is the life of God experienced in the life of the believer. It is as much sanctification truth as justification truth. It is eternal life in its entirety.

As a result of this, John's use of "believe" has more than a justification sense to it as well. It is something believers must do in order to have fellowship with God and experience eternal life. Even believing in Jesus' name is something Christians have to do in order to fellowship with Him and be used by Him. That is why Jesus is still asking the eleven in the upper room if *they* believe Him! Belief is the beginning point of abiding in Christ for every believer. You cannot abide apart from believing. You cannot experience eternal life in this life apart from the first step of believing in Jesus, even as a believer.

APPENDIX 9

ABIDING

Range of Meaning

The term *menō* generally translated "to abide" or "to remain," has a broad range of meaning throughout the New Testament, both literal and figurative. As a transitive verb, it may mean to "wait for, await," or it can also be used with the sense of "to expect someone."[129] As an intransitive verb it means, "to remain in a place, to tarry, to remain, to stay still," and can be used of either persons or things.[130] It also may have the literal sense of living, dwelling, or lodging. Figuratively it can mean someone "does not leave the realm or sphere in which he finds himself" and can be translated as "remain," "continue," or "abide."[131] It can also mean, "to stand against opposition, to hold out, to stand fast," and "to remain, to last, to remain in legal force."[132]

Use Outside of John's Literature

Menō occurs 105 times in the New Testament, with forty-eight of those occurrences in the non-Johannine literature. It is used with the literal sense of waiting for someone in Acts 20:5 and 23. The literal sense of tarrying, or remaining in place occurs ten times in narrative literature (Synoptic Gospels and Acts) and three times with Paul.[133] Nine times (all in narrative literature) it means, "to live" somewhere.[134]

Though it reflects some figurative use in narrative literature, this aspect of meaning is principally found in the epistles. Paul uses it seven times with the sense of remaining "in the realm or sphere in which one finds himself."[135] Seventeen times it carries the figurative sense of remaining in legal force, lasting, or enduring.[136] Its use in Hebrews reflects the sense of continuing, living (eternally), or lasting forever, whether it refers to a person such as Melchizedek, or things such as heaven, the believer's possessions in heaven, love, or God's Word.[137] Finally, Peter uses it to describe God's word as eternal.[138] It also describes "the immutability of God and the things of God."[139] Of note is the absence in Paul of the use of "abide" to communicate his concept of a believer being "in Christ." Further, he does not use it to describe walking in the Spirit.

Johannine Use Outside the Upper Room Discourse

John uses *menō* thirty-four times in the Gospel of John, twenty in 1 John, and three more in 2 John and Revelation.[140] His use of the term in his first and second epistles always reflects one of its figurative senses.[141] For example, in 1 John 2:10 and 3:14 he uses it to express the concept of remaining in the realm or sphere in which one finds oneself.[142] In 2 John

9 this same sense carries with it the idea of obeying or living according to that realm in which one finds himself. It also refers to remaining in legal force, lasting, enduring, or continuing to live in 1 John 2:14, 24, 27; 3:9, 15, and 17.[143] In 1 John 2:17 "remaining" refers to experiencing eternal life, not possessing it.[144] It also means to remain in fellowship (communion) with someone, such as believers in 1 John 2:19.[145] In 2 John 2 the term refers to God's truth having an influence in our lives. In 1 John 4:12-16, it is used by John to refer to the mutual indwelling of God within the believer and the believer in God, the Pauline concept of being "in Christ."[146] Love for others is an evidence of "God's indwelling presence" in the believer.[147]

In the Gospel, John uses *menō* with its literal sense to describe Jesus remaining, tarrying, or living somewhere, and of His body remaining on the cross.[148] He quotes John the Baptist when he uses it with this same literal sense to describe the Holy Spirit's "remaining" on Jesus.[149] Jesus also uses it with the sense of living somewhere.[150]

The term is used, mostly by Jesus, in the Gospel of John with a wide range of figurative senses. Some are difficult to distinguish whether they are to be understood literally in the sense of living somewhere, or figuratively with the sense of remaining "in the sphere."[151] Jesus uses *menō* to express the idea of a person or thing continuing "in the state in which he or it is found."[152] Related to the previous use is the idea of remaining in legal force, lasting, or remaining.[153] Baur notes that a favorite phrase of John, who is quoting Jesus in all his examples, is the use of abiding in something "to denote an inward, enduring personal communion."[154] Jesus also used this term to describe something, such as God's word, influencing a person.[155]

Johannine Use Inside the Upper Room Discourse

In the upper room, Jesus uses the term fourteen times. He refers to the Father "abiding" in Him (14:10) and the Spirit abiding in believers (14:17). Once He uses it with its literal sense of living with them (14:25). Believers are to "abide" in Him, His words, and His love (15:4-10). Jesus conditioned answered prayer on both "abiding" in Him and letting His words "abide" in them (15:7). They were also to follow Jesus' example of obedience in order to abide in His love like He abides in His Father's (15:10). Lastly, Jesus used the term to describe the believer's fruit as something which continues, remains (15:16). Jesus' use of third class conditional sentences in 15:6, 7, and 10 to describe the believer's option of abiding or not abiding is very significant in understanding His use of the term.[156] It is clearly optional for the believer and therefore must be relational rather than metaphysical. This is evident also from His abiding in His Father's love through the relationship of obedience. When used figuratively, the term denotes the dynamics of relationship, interaction, and influence rather than the more static justification aspect of position in Christ or possession of life.

Interpretive Issue

The Lordship approach to Johannine literature argues that the principle meaning given "abiding" by John conveys the sense of union rather than communion. Abiding in Christ is equivalent to being "in" (*einai en*) and conveys a "stronger form" of the Pauline concept of "in Christ."[157] For them it reflects the condition of union associated with the possession of salvation resulting from the "divine indwelling" rather than the expression of relationship.[158] For example, George Findlay says abiding "is more than communion, it is *union*. This Divine κοινωνία is not the intercourse of two separate personalities external to each other, but of the finite knowledge and love with the infinite, that is at once immanent to it and transcendent, the fellowship of the seeing eye with the light that fills the universe, of the spark of kindled being with the eternal Source, . . . which is pervaded and enfolded by the loving will of God."[159]

Further, abiding "is existence in God perpetuated; it is union made restful and secure."[160] It is evidenced by obedience, love, and by holy living.[161] The relational aspect of meaning is resident in the term, though this is not viewed as its primary sense.[162] The Lordship's "union" rather than communion definition arises out of a focus on justification in their interpretation of Jesus' teachings in the Gospel of John. For example, Strombeck says concerning John 15, "'Abide in Me and I in you', does not mean that those who have been cleansed by a similar command on His part must keep themselves in Him." Rather Jesus keeps them and they must simply "remain in continuous union with Him."[163]

Especially in the upper room, *menō* should not be understood as a justification term, but rather as a word Jesus chose to describe living by faith in communion with God, the Pauline sense of walking in the Spirit or being filled with the Spirit. Charles Ryrie defines abiding on the basis of 1 John 3:24 as "habitual fellowship maintained by keeping his commandments."[164] Everett Harrison notes, "Abiding is not to be confused with position. Christ stated the fact of spiritual position before He inculcated the necessity of abiding (John 14:20; 15:4). Abiding is an activity. It means communion with the person of Christ and submission to the will of Christ."[165] Dillow sees it as John's "word for something conditional in the believer's relationship with Christ, fellowship within the family."[166] It means, "to continue in close relationship to" Christ.[167]

Understood from the perspective that Jesus used the term to describe the relationship between Himself and His believing apostles, most of its uses can be interpreted from the perspective of sanctification without placing any stress on the text.[168] The command to abide is a command to maintain fellowship, communion, with God. The Pauline concept of "in Christ" is not a part of the meaning of the term although in John 15 his concept is evident in the "in Me" of verse two.[169] The imagery used by Jesus in the vine-branch analogy describes fellowship with God rather than union.[170] Hodges argues well, "With John, the kind of relationship pictured in the vine-branch imagery describes an experience that can be ruptured (John 15:6) with a resultant loss of fellowship and fruitfulness," and so describes "the believer's fellowship with God."[171] King sees abiding defined as obeying in John 15:10.[172] Cook defends the position well.

> *Abiding* in Christ is to be distinguished from *being* in Christ, although ideally there should be no practical difference between the two. We may observe the distinction by noting John 15:1-11, where the "in Me" branch of verse 2 is seen to be different from the "abide in Me" branch of verse 4. To *be* in Christ is to be born again, to be regenerated, to have had forgiveness of sins through Christ. Thus the disciples are in Christ (v. 2) because they have been cleansed of their sins (v. 3). To *abide* in Christ, however, is to be an obedient follower in fellowship with Christ the Savior and Lord (vv. 4-5, 9-11). An examination of 1 John 3:24 will reveal that obedience is the condition for abiding. Moreover, in John 15:10 our obeying Christ and thus abiding in Him is compared to the Son's obeying the Father and thus abiding in Him; the Son was already *in* the Father by virtue of His sonship, but the Son *abided* in the Father by obeying Him. We see, then, that just as Christ's abiding in the Father was the maintenance of personal fellowship with the Father, so our abiding in Christ is the maintenance of personal fellowship with Christ. . . . Furthermore, a study of John 15:4-11 will show that abiding is the condition for fruit-bearing (vv. 4-5), that abiding brings the confidence of answered prayer (v. 7), and that abiding is commanded of Christians (v. 9).[173]

Dillow concurs, pointing to John 15:10 as evidence of the "conditional nature of the abiding relationship with Christ" and to 1 John 3:24 as revealing that "the abiding relationship is conditioned on obedience."[174]

Finally, since Paul does not use the term to describe the Christian's relationship with God and John does not use "in Christ" (though "in Me" does occur with John) the commonality of meaning is difficult to prove. Further, since the term is used in a theologically significant manner by Jesus in the Upper Room Discourse and then by John in his epistle, those significant uses should be allowed to "set the limits on the meaning communicated" by the term in its passages.[175]

BIBLIOGRAPHY

Books and Commentaries

Abbott, Edwin A. *Johannine Grammar.* London: Adam & Charles Black, 1906.

Bartlett, John R. "The First and Second Books of the Maccabees." *The Cambridge Bible Commentary.* Cambridge: Cambridge University Press, 1973.

Beasley-Murray, George R. *Word Biblical Themes: John.* Dallas: Word Publishing, 1989.

Bernard J. H. *A Critical and Exegetical Commentary on the Gospel According to St. John.* Volume 2. The International Critical Commentary. Edinburgh: T. & T. Clark, 1928.

Boice James M. *The Gospel of John.* 5 Volumes. Grand Rapids: Zondervan Publishing House, 1978.

Brown, Raymond E. *The Epistles of John.* The Anchor Bible. New York: Doubleday, 1982.

Bruce, A. B. *The Training of the Twelve.* Edinburg: T. & T. Clark, 1908.

Bruce, F. F. *The Gospel of John.* Grand Rapids: William B. Eerdmans Publishing Company, 1983.

Bruns, J. Edgar. *The Art and Thought of John.* New York: Herder and Herder, 1969.

Bullinger, E. W. *Figures of Speech Used in the Bible.* Grand Rapids: Baker Book House, 1968.

Bultmann, Rudolf. *The Gospel of John.* Translated by G. R. Beasley-Murray. Philadelphia: Westminster, 1976.

Calvin, John. *Commentary on the Gospel According to John.* Vol. 2. Translated by William Pringle. Grand Rapids: Wm. B. Eerdmans Publishing Company, 1949.

_____. *Institutes of the Christian Religion.* Vol. 1. Grand Rapids: Wm. B. Eerdmans Publishing Co., 1970.

Carson, D. A. *The Farewell Discourse and Final Prayer of Jesus.* Grand Rapids: Baker Book House, 1980.

Cheney, Johnston M. *The Life of Christ in Stereo.* Portland, Oregon: Western Baptist Seminary Press, 1969.

Cook, W. Robert. *The Theology of John.* Chicago: Moody Press, 1979.

Dana H. E., and Julius R. Mantey. *A Manual Grammar of the Greek New Testament.* New York: Macmillan Publishing Co., Inc., 1955.

Dillow, Joseph. *The Reign of the Servant Kings.* Hayesville: Schoettle Publishing Co., 1993.

Dodd, C. H. *New Testament Studies.* Manchester: Manchester University Press, 1953.

Duckat, Walter. *Beggar to King: All the Occupations of Biblical Times.* Garden City: Doubleday & Company, Inc., 1968.

Findlay, George G. *Fellowship in the Life Eternal.* Grand Rapids: Wm. B. Eerdmans Publishing Company, 1955.

Freeman, James M. *Manners and Customs of the Bible.* Plainfield: Logos International, 1972 reprint, New York: Nelson and Phillips, n.d.

George, Bob. *Classic Christianity.* Eugene, Or.: Harvest House, 1989.

Gower, Ralph. *The New Manners and Customs of Bible Times.* Chicago: Moody Press, 1987.

Gruenler, Royce G. *The Trinity in the Gospel of John.* Grand Rapids: Baker Book House, 1986.

Guthrie, Donald. *New Testament Introduction: The Gospels and Acts.* Chicago: InterVarsity Press, 1965.

Haenchen, Ernst. *John: a commentary on the Gospel of John.* Philadelphia: Fortress Press, 1984.

Harel, Menashe. *Dwellers of the Mountain.* Originally published by Tel Aviv University, Department of Geography. Translated by Bathsheba Taub. Jerusalem: Carta, 1977.

Hengstenberg, E. W. *Commentary on the Gospel of St. John.* Vol 2. Translated from the German. Minneapolis: Klock & Klock Christian Publishers, Inc. 1980 reprint of the original 1865 publication by T & T Clark.

Hodges, Zane C. *The Epistles of John: Walking in the Light of God's Love.* Irving, Tx.: Grace Evangelical Society, 1999.

Hoehner, Harold W. *Chronological Aspects of the Life of Christ.* Grand Rapids: Academie Books, 1977.

Hopkins, David C. *The Highlands of Canaan.* Decatur: The Almond Press, 1985.

Huegel, F. J. *Bone of His Bone.* Grand Rapids: Zondervan Publishing House, 1966.

Janick, Jules. *Horticultural Science.* Second Edition. San Francisco: W. H. Freeman and Company, 1972.

Johnson, Elliot E. *Expository Hermeneutics: An Introduction.* Grand Rapids: Zondervan Publishing House, 1990.

Kent, Jr., Homer A. *Light in the Darkness: Studies in the Gospel of John.* Grand Rapids: Baker Book House, 1974.

King, Guy H. *The Fellowship.* London: Marshall, Morgan & Scott, 1954.

Laney, J. Carl. *John.* Moody Press Commentary. Chicago: Moody Press, 1992.

Lawrence (Brother). *Practice of the Presence of God.* Translated by E.M. Blaiklock. Nashville: Thomas Nelson, 1981.

Law, Robert. *The Tests of Life: A Study of the First Epistle of St. John.* Edinburgh: T. & T. Clark, 1909. Reprint, Grand Rapids: Baker Book House, 1969.

MacArthur, Jr., John. *Comfort for Troubled Hearts.* Chicago: Moody Press, 1986.

Miller, Madeleine S., and J. Lane Miller. *Harper's Encyclopedia of Bible Life.* Revised edition of the work by Boyce M. Bennett, Jr. and David H. Scott. San Francisco: Harper & Row, Publishers, 1978.

Mitchell, Curtis. *Let's Live!* Old Tappan: Fleming H. Revell Company, 1975.

Mitchell, John G. *An Everlasting Love.* Portland: Multnomah Press, 1982.

Moldenke, Harold M., and Alma L. Moldenke. *Plants of the Bible.* Waltham: Chronica Botanica Company, 1952.

Morris, Leon. *The Gospel According to John*. New International Commentary on the New Testament. Grand Rapids: Wm. B. Eerdmans Publishing Company, 1971.

Neusner, Jacob. *The Mishnah: A New Translation*. New Haven: Yale University Press, 1988.

Patterson, James and Peter Kim. *The Day America Told the Truth: What People Really Believe About Everything That Really Matters*. New York: Prentice Hall, 1991.

Pentecost, J. Dwight. *The Joy of Fellowship*. Grand Rapids: Zondervan Publishing House, 1977.

Pink, A. W. *Exposition of the Gospel of John*. 3 volumes. Ohio: Cleveland Bible Truth Depot, 1929.

Radmacher, Earl D. *Celebrating the Word*. Portland: Multnomah Press, 1987.

_____. *Salvation*. Nashville: Word Publishers, 2000.

Rainsford, Marcus. *Our Lord Prays for His Own*. Chicago: Moody Press, 1958.

Roberts, J. W. *The Letters of John*. The Living Word Commentary. Austin: R. B. Sweet, 1968.

Rosscup, James E. *Abiding in Christ*. Grand Rapids: Zondervan Publishing House, 1973.

Ryken, Leland. *How to Read the Bible as Literature*. Grand Rapids: Zondervan Publishing House, 1984.

Ryle, J. C. *Ryle's Expositor Thoughts on the Gospels*. John 10:10 to End. Grand Rapids: Zondervan Publishing House, n.d.

Ryrie, Charles C. "1 John" in *The Wycliffe Bible Commentary*. Edited by Charles F. Pfeiffer and Everett F. Harrison. Chicago: Moody Press, 1962.

Schnackenburg, Rudolf. *The Gospel According to St. John*. New York: Herder and Herder, 1968. Volume 3. New York: Crossroad Publishing Company, 1982.

Shewell-Cooper, W. E. *Plants, Flowers, and Herbs of the Bible*. New Canaan: Keats Publishing, Inc., 1977.

Smalley, Stephen S. *1, 2, 3 John*. Word Biblical Commentary. Volume 51. Waco: Word Books, Publishers, 1984.

Stevens, George B. *The Theology of the New Testament*. New York: Scribner, 1947, c1927.

Stott, John R. W. *The Letters of John*. Grand Rapids: Wm. B. Eerdmans Publishing Company, 1964, 1988.

Strombeck, J. F. *Shall Never Perish*. Philadelphia: American Bible Conference Association, 1936.

Taylor, Vincent. *Forgiveness and Reconciliation: a study in New Testament theology*. New York: St. Martin's Press, 1956.

Tenney, Merrill C. "John." *The Expositor's Bible Commentary*. Volume 9. Grand Rapids: Regency Reference Library, 1981.

The Cambridge Bible Commentary. Cambridge: Cambridge University Press, 1973.

Townsend, Anne J. *Prayer Without Pretending*. London: Scripture Union, 1973.

Tozer, A. W. *The Knowledge of the Holy*. New York: Harper and Brothers, 1961.

Trench, Richard C. *Synonyms of the New Testament*. Grand Rapids: Wm. B. Eerdmans Publishing Company, 1960 reprint of the ninth (1880) edition.

Vanderlip, George. *Christianity According to John*. Philadelphia: Westminster Press, 1975.

Wallace, Daniel B. *Greek Grammar Beyond the Basics*. Grand Rapids: Zondervan Publishing House, 1996.

Wendt, Hans H. *The Teaching of Jesus*. Translated by John Wilson. Edinburgh: T. & T. Clark, 1892.

Westcott, B. F. *The Gospel According to St. John*. Grand Rapids: Wm. B. Eerdmans Publishing Company, 1981 reprint.

Wigoder, Geoffrey, Shalom M. Paul, and Benedict T. Viviano. *Almanac of the Bible*. New York: Prentice Hall, 1991.

Wood, Nathan. *The Trinity in the Universe*. Grand Rapids: Kregel Publishers, 1978.

Periodicals

Baker, Alvin L. "Eternal Security Rightly Understood." *Fundamentalist Journal.* 3: 8 (September 1984): 18-20.

Barnhouse, Donald Grey. "Chain of Glory." *Eternity.* 9:17.

Bartlett, David L. "John 13:21-30." *Interpretation.* 43: 4 (October 1989): 393-397.

Chafer, Lewis S. "The Eternal Security of the Believer." *Bibliotheca Sacra.* 106 (October-December 1949): 392-419.

Colson, Charles. "Wanted: Christians Who Love." *Christianity Today* (October 2, 1995): 112.

Dillow, Joseph. "Abiding is Remaining in Fellowship: Another Look at John 15:1-6." *Bibliotheca Sacra.* 147: 585 (January-March 1990): 44-53.

Dodd, C. H. "Eternal Life." *Christianity and Crisis.* 10, April 1950, 33-34.

Edgington, Allen. "Footwashing as an Ordinance." *Grace Theological Journal.* 6:2 (1985): 425-434.

Epp, Theodore H. "Seven Aspects of Abiding in the Vine." Good News Broadcaster. 36: 7 (July-August 1978): 47-48.

Farner, Donald. "The Lord's Super Until He Comes." *Grace Theological Journal.* 6: 2 (1985): 391-401.

Fee, Gordon D. "John 14:8-17." *Interpretation.* 43: 2 (April 1989): 170-174.

Harrison, Everett F. "A Key to the Understanding of First John." *Bibliotheca Sacra.* 3 (1954): 39-46.

Hart, John F. "Does Philippians 1:6 Guarantee Progressive Sanctification?" *Journal of the Grace Evangelical Society.* 9:16 (Spring 1996): 37-58.

Hawkin, David J. "The Johannine Concept of Truth and its Implications for a Technological Society," *The Evangelical Quarterly*, 59:1 (January, 1987): 3-13.

Hodges, Zane C. "Untrustworthy Believers—John 2:23-25." *Bibliotheca Sacra.* 135: 538 (April-June 1978): 139-41.

Laney, J. Carl. "Abiding is Believing: The Analogy of the Vine in John 15:1-6." *Bibliotheca Sacra.* 146: 581 (January-March 1989): 55-66.

Moloney, Francis J. "The Structure and Message of John 15.1-16.3."
    Australian Biblical Review. 35 (1987): 35-49.

Peterson, Robert A. "The Perseverance of the Saints: A Theological Exegesis
    of Four Key New Testament Passages." *Presbyterion*. 17: 2 (1991):
    95-112.

Richard, E. "Expressions of Double Meaning and Their Function in the
    Gospel of John." *New Testament Studies*. 31: 1 (January 1985), 96-
    112.

Robertson, J. A. T. "The Relation of the Prologue to the Gospel of St. John."
    New Testament Studies. 9 (1962-1963): 120-129.

Segovia, Fernando F. "The Structure, *Tendenz*, and *Zitz im Leben* of John
    13:31-14:31." *Journal of Biblical Literature*. 104: 3 (1985): 471-493.

Segovia, Fernando F. "The Theology and Provenance of John 15:1-17."
    Journal of Biblical Literature. 101: 1 (March 1982): 115-128.

Smith, Charles R. "The Unfruitful Branches in John 15." *Grace Journal*. 9: 2
    (Spring 1968): 3-22.

Thomas, Cal. "Lions vs. Pastor Lamb." *World Magazine*. (July 26/August 2,
    1997), 19.

Tukowski, Lucian. "Peasant Agriculture in the Judaean Hills." *Palestine
    Exploration Quarterly*. 101: 1 (January-June 1969): 27.*

Wind, A. "Destination and Purpose of the Gospel of John." *Novum
    Testamentum*. 14: 1 (January 1972): 26-69.

Dictionaries, Encyclopedias, and Unpublished Materials

Albright, Jimmy L. "Wine in the Biblical world: Its economic, social and reli-
    gious implications for New Testament interpretation." Ph.D. disser-
    tation, Southwestern Baptist Seminary, 1981.

Baur, Walter. *A Greek-English Lexicon of the New Testament and Other
    Early Christian Literature*. Translated by William F. Arndt and Wilbur
    Gingrich, 2nd edition of the 5th revised edition. Chicago: University of
    Chicago Press, 1979.

Dictionary of the Bible. Edited by John D. Davis. Grand Rapids: Baker Book
    House, 1954, c1924.

Encyclopedia Judaica. Jerusalem: Encyclopaedia Judaica, 1972.

Hunt, Dwight. "Jesus' Teaching Concerning the Paraclete in the Upper Room Discourse." Th.M. Thesis, Western Conservative Baptist Seminary, April 1981.

The International Standard Bible Encyclopedia. 4 volumes. Revised edition. Grand Rapids: William B. Eerdmans Publishing Company, 1986.

The New Schaff-Herzog Encyclopedia of Religious Knowledge. New York and London, Funk and Wagnalls, 1908-12.

The Oxyrhynchus Papyri. Part 14. Edited by Bernard P. Grenfell and Arthur S. Hunt. London: Egypt Exploration Society, 1920.

Theological Dictionary of the New Testament. Edited by Gerhard Kittel. Translated and edited by Geoffrey W. Bromiley. Grand Rapids: William B. Eerdmans Publishing Co., 1964-74.

Endnotes

Introduction

1 For further elaboration of this, see Radmacher's book, *Salvation* (Waco: Word Publishers, 2000).

2 This term, "gospel tract," is being used in its technical sense and not with any negative implications. This is a term used by scholars to describe a kind of literature, even in the first century, intended to be used in communicating the gospel of salvation to the unregenerate.

3 In John 20:31, John uses the present subjunctive of believe. The present subjunctive normally has the sense of continuing something already in process. Thus, John is writing so that his readers will continue to believe, not so that they can become believers. John is telling his readers that he wants to keep their faith alive and vibrant rather than that he is trying to lead them to faith.

Ζωή, God's life, is eternal life. How can you have something more? Eternal life is both extensive and intensive. When a person is born from above they have eternal life from that moment extensively. But the experience of that eternal life can be greater or lesser. We receive eternal life extensively, and can grow in that eternal life intensively.

4 Carson (D. A. Carson, *The Gospel According to John* (Grand Rapids: Wm. B. Eerdmans Publishing Company, 1991), 480) notes that some modern writers attempt to see in this section of John a "farewell discourse" or "farewell testament" similar to a genre of literature known in both the Hellenistic and Jewish worlds. For example *The Testaments of the Twelve Patriarchs*, written sometime around the first century, claims to be the final words of the sons of Jacob to their sons. Supposed biblical examples of such discourses include Jacob's prophetic farewell to his sons in Genesis 49, Deuteronomy as Moses' last testament to Israel, Joshua's farewell to the tribes (Joshua 24), and David's final words to Solomon and the nation in 1 Chronicles 28-29. Thus Jesus is seen doing the same thing here. Carson points out clearly, though, the key difference between this discourse and the other farewells. Jesus expects to return, none of the others did. If one is to find a "farewell" from Jesus, it is to be found at His final departure at the ends of the Gospels and beginning of Acts, not in the Upper Room. But even in those farewells there remains the promise of His return, a promise which remains true today and calls for our patient endurance in faith as we await its fulfillment.

Chapter One

1 Francis J. Moloney, "The Structure and Message of John 15.1-16.3,"

Australian Biblical Review, 35 (1987): 45. One of the characteristics of this section of the Gospel is John's use of inclusios as rhetorical devices. These will be noted as the discourse is discussed in detail.

2 Some biblical scholars do not see this evening's activities as a Passover meal. For example, Rudolf Bultmann (*The Gospel of John,* translated by G. R. Beasley-Murray [Philadelphia: Westminster, 1976], 464-65) argues from the introductory phrase that it occurred the evening before the Passover and that this was an ordinary meal. One problem with it being an ordinary meal is the reference to their reclining to eat, which was a custom reserved for festivals and special meals. Another problem is that too many other New Testament texts clearly identify it as the Passover meal. Donald Farner, ("The Lord's Supper until He Comes," *Grace Theological Journal,* 6: 2 [1985]: 391-93) is one who agrees with Bultmann when he argues that Jesus was not eating the Passover meal with the disciples. But his basis for agreement is his belief that Jesus was crucified on Wednesday instead of Friday.

3 Carson (*The Gospel According to John,* 460) argues that if those words were taken as a part of the opening words to the section, then they would indicate that the meal could not be the Passover. But, if they are seen as introductory to the footwashing and not the discourse that follows, then the meal could still be the Passover.

4 Harold W. Hoehner, *Chronological Aspects of the Life of Christ* (Grand Rapids: Academie Books, 1977), 88-90.

5 B. F. Westcott (*The Gospel According to St. John* [Grand Rapids: Wm. B. Eerdmans Publishing Company, 1981 reprint], 188) incorrectly argues that the second cup was a later addition to the text of Luke taken from 1 Corinthians 11:25, but that the prophecy of betrayal still necessarily followed the breaking of the bread. Further, he notes that Luke agrees with Paul that the bread was broken and distributed during the meal, and the cup was distributed following the meal. According to Westcott, then, Judas was present when Jesus broke and distributed the bread, but absent when he gave the cup. He concludes that, "the distribution of the Bread must be placed before v. 30 in St. John's narrative, and the distribution of the Cup after." Specifically, the breaking of the bread occurred before verse two and the giving of the Cup after verse thirty-two.

6 In modern practice, the main meal is begun after this cup rather than before.

7 It is improperly understood if it is interpreted as an attempt to respond to various sectarian groups or other second century conflicts in the church.

8 John G. Mitchell (*An Everlasting Love* [Portland: Multnomah Press, 1982], 248) correctly sees this section of the Gospel revealing Jesus' love and

"concern for His own."

9 We should note that this scene likely is the source of Paul's description of Jesus' humility in Philippians 2:5-11 which he identifies as the ultimate model for Christians to follow in order to express love in unity within the Church.

10 The very fact of what Peter ultimately taught in 2 Peter 1:5-9 is a great example of the answer to Jesus' prayer for him! After listing a series of spiritual traits to "add" one on top of the other, he tells us that "if these things are yours and abound, *you will be* neither barren nor unfruitful in the knowledge of our Lord Jesus Christ." He is strengthening his brethren, then and today.

11 The fact that the Gospel includes much new material strengthens this view, though its weakness is that the Gospel by itself gives a very incomplete description of Jesus' ministry.

12 This view is based on the hostile way John refers to the Jewish leaders. Its weakness is that mostly the nation's leadership is hostile and not the Jews in general.

13 This view is based largely on a late first century writing. John seems to emphasize some Gnostic ideas such as "the ideal value of the life of Christ, on the Gnostic antithesis between the lower and higher worlds, and on the importance of the act of 'knowing' in the religious life." The problem with this view is that John does not use the standard Gnostic terminology of *gnosis* (γνῶσις), "knowledge," *sophia* (σοφία), "wisdom," and *pistis* (πίστις), "faith."

14 Donald Guthrie, *New Testament Introduction: The Gospels and Acts* (Chicago: InterVarsity Press, 1965), 246-57.

15 J. Carl Laney (*John,* Moody Press Commentary [Chicago: Moody Press, 1992], 19) argues for an evangelistic purpose of the Gospel on the basis of the supposed purpose expressed in John 20:31, saying, "He designed the gospel to present the orthodox doctrine of the Person and work of Christ, inspiring faith and life in Him." He sees the miracles recorded in John to be "intended to elicit belief in the reader" on the basis of 20:31 and looks to the present subjective verb, "you may believe," to indicate "the entire process of coming to faith and continuing to believe." He then defines believe as more than "intellectual assent to a proposition about Christ. Rather, the biblical concept of 'belief' involves a personal response and commitment to Christ's Person" (20). He notes that the Gospel contains evidence of a progression of belief in various people. He gives the examples of the nobleman of Capernaum (John 4) and the disciples as evidence of progression. This leads him to an uncomfortable position. Laney correctly sees a progress of faith in the Gospel but wrongly infers from this that in "the process of belief there is a stage that falls short of consummated faith resulting in salvation." He argues from the believers of John

2:23 who Jesus did not "believe" in (trust) because He "discerned that their faith was superficial." He provides also the evidence of those in the Feast of Tabernacles (7:31) who were believing in Jesus, also identified by John in 8:31, who Jesus then said were seeking to kill Him in 8:40, followed by Jesus' accusation of the Jews' unbelief in 8:45-46. John 12:11 and 37 also contain this "belief of unbelief," as he calls it (20-21). He sees the problem being that the "superficial" belief resulted from their being "inclined to 'believe' something about Jesus but were unwilling to yield their allegiance to Him, trusting Him as their personal Sin-bearer" (22). Laney sees the theme of the Gospel as "belief" because the term occurs 98 [99] times and is supposedly reflected in the statement of 20:30-31(22-23). This then becomes his interpretive guide and leads to a justification emphasis.

In order to understand the thrust of what John is saying in 20:31, we should translate it in a way that reflects the emphases of key verbs and verbals in the sentence. Emphasizing the senses of the verbs, it may be translated, "I have written in order that you *might keep believing* that Jesus is the Christ, the Son of God, and in order that *while continuing to believe*, you *may continue to experience* life in his name" (italics added).

16 Following John 3, the focus shifts from the need to gain eternal life to how eternal life would be expressed in the life of the one who has received it.

17 For a thorough discussion of this truth, we commend to you Joseph Dillow's book, *The Reign of the Servant Kings,* Hayesville: Schoettle Publishing Co., 1993.

18 Zane C. Hodges ("Untrustworthy Believers—John 2:23-25," *Bibliotheca Sacra* 135: 538 [April-June 1978]: 139-41) notes well that John's use of the phrase "believe in His name" (ἐπίστευσαν εἰς τό ὄνομα αὐτοῦ) is introduced in John 1:12-13 as justifying faith and then is used in 2:23 to describe new believers to whom Jesus could not entrust Himself.

19 In our days we have come to trivialize the word "believe." For many people it means a "blind leap" into the unknown rather than being based on fact or knowledge. For them, the effectiveness of one's belief is dependent on oneself, rather than faith's object. For Jesus, and thus John as well, belief is far different from the popular conception. They do not trivialize its meaning, but deepen it. The way to deepen it is to enlarge the object. John sees its importance for the Christian to be so great that he made the content of his readers' beliefs a focal purpose of his Gospel message (John 20:31). The term "believe" occurs ninety-nine times in the Gospel of John. Therefore it is legitimate to call this the one Gospel of Belief.

Believe (πιστεύω) is the verb form of the Greek noun most often translated "faith." To believe means to exercise faith, trust, confidence in or reliance on something, someone, or someone's word. It is more than intellectual assent.

It is a personal response involving the intellect, emotions, and will. It is a response based on information and not a "blind leap" based on intuition. For example, when Jesus tells Peter he needs to keep believing, He is telling him to act on the basis of what he knows to be true. Again, look at John 20:30-31 and you see the direct correlation between what John wanted his readers to know, and thereby respond to with belief. What we know determines what we do because our knowledge effects our belief and our belief determines our response to what we know.

The object of belief is key. Though what one believes is critical, it is still not as important as who one believes in. For example, Hebrews 11:6 teaches us that people must believe in God's existence and goodness in order to please Him. When we believe God, we respond to His revelation of Jesus' deity and resurrection with confidence that it is true. Belief is a response to knowledge. Jesus and God the Father are repeatedly pointed to as the proper objects of our faith. Thus Jesus told His disciples to believe in Him, to believe what He was saying to them (John 14:1, 11). It is on the basis of Their trustworthiness that our faith has validity. Apart from Them being true and trustworthy, we would be guilty of mere presumption.

Ephesians 2:8-9 teaches us that believing in Christ for salvation is what is required and not a "work" that someone does in order to gain salvation. Rather, it is a response to Christ's promise of deliverance from sin through His work on the cross for all who rely on Him (Rom 10:8-13). Rather than being a work, it is accepting a gift. Thus Jesus pictures believing in Him as taking a drink of water (John 4:10-14) and eating the freely offered bread of life (John 6:32-37). Mark 9:14-29 shows that believing need not be perfect or absolute before God will respond to our prayer. It need only be enough to cause us to cry out to Him for help because its effectiveness depends on its object, God.

In the Gospel of John, one aspect of belief is developed which is significant to its message and is key to our own walk with God. For John, belief is a progressive sanctification idea rather than just a justification truth. Just as faith is absolutely necessary in our justification (Eph 2:8-9), it is also an absolutely necessary element in our sanctification (cf. Gal 3:1-3), our experience of eternal life in this life. If we do not abide, we will not *experience* the abundant life (John 8:31; 15:1-8; 1 John 2:1-3). But having said that, more needs to be said about faith as an element in our sanctification. Where it would be safe to say that any measure of faith leads to our justification before God, there is a difference with regard to our sanctification. The reason for this is that very little need be known to call upon God for deliverance from sin. Hebrews 11:6 tells us that we need only know that God exists and rewards those who come to Him.

Romans 10:8-13 affirms that we must confess Jesus' deity, believe in His resurrection, and call upon Him and we will be saved (justified). Yet, far more is involved in our sanctification. Jesus' instruction of the eleven, His revelation of the Father and promise of the Holy Spirit, was designed, not for their justification, but for their sanctification. They needed to "know" God in order to fellowship with Him and experience "eternal life" in this life. It is this aspect of belief that is focused on in the Gospel, the disciples' growing knowledge of God that would enable them to serve Him and thereby be abundantly fruitful following Jesus' departure. Thus we see the disciples repeatedly described as "believing" in Jesus, beginning with Nathaniel's confession in 1:49, continuing with their response to His first sign in 2:11, until Thomas finally fully understands and falls down in worship in 20:28.

Sanctifying faith is faith which grows in its understanding of who Jesus (and thus God the Father) is and what He expects of us. For the Christian, abiding in God's Word is revealed by obedience to His commands (John 8:31; 15:1-8; 1 John 2:3-11), and love of fellow Christians expressed by personal involvement in helping them (John 15:12; James 2:14-23; 1 John 3:16-18). It is faith that leads to worship and obedience. It leads to works that bear fruit. This faith, focused on in John, is distinctly different from justifying faith.

Chapter Two

1 In the culture of the Middle East, then as well as today, nepotism is considered a virtue and one takes care of "family" first. Matt 12:46-47 reflects this same mentality. Notice Jesus' counter-cultural response in verses forty-eight to fifty.

2 The phrase, εἰς τέλος, if taken temporally, would mean that Jesus kept loving them until He died. Here it is better to see it as an adverbial phrase describing the nature of Jesus' love with which He was loving His men.

3 Royce G. Gruenler (*The Trinity in the Gospel of John* [Grand Rapids: Baker Book House, 1986], 89) believes that John's reference to Jesus' love for "his own" must be understood as a reference to "the redeemed family of believers." We do not see this, since Judas is present and experiences Jesus' loving act with the others. Further, there is nothing in the text that indicates that Jesus ever stopped loving Judas, though he was not really one of Jesus' true "own."

4 This is especially evident because John's use of "love" in this verse and Jesus' final words, praying that God's love would be in the disciples (17:26), forming an inclusio that marks off the Upper Room Discourse from the narrative that precedes and follows it.

5 Hebrews 12:2 describes Jesus' heart at this time, "who for the joy that was set before Him endured the cross, despising the shame, and has sat down at the right hand of the throne of God."

6 As Mitchell (*An Everlasting Love*, 249) reminds us, John notes Jesus' exercise of sovereignty and omniscience even as He chooses to act in humility.

Though Jesus was consciously aware of His own power and position, He did not hesitate to serve the men He had called to follow Him as He prepared them for the "final catastrophe" they were about to face. Merrill C. Tenney ("John," in *The Expositor's Bible Commentary,* Vol. 9 [Grand Rapids: Regency Reference Library, 1981], 136) notes that John's use of the perfect active participle, εἰδὼς, indicates that this knowledge preceded His loving action and served as a motivation for what He did for them. Westcott (*The Gospel According to St. John,* 190) notes well that the "knowledge that He was possessed of this divine authority was the ground of His act of service." George R. Beasley-Murray (*Word Biblical Themes: John* [Dallas: Word Publishing, 1989], 88) describes these first verses of the upper room as containing "an extraordinary contrast between the exalted dignity of Jesus and the depth of humility to which he stooped."

7 Cal Thomas, "Lions vs. Pastor Lamb," *World Magazine* (July 26/August 2, 1997), 19.

8 In verse two a textual problem exists concerning whether the aorist participle, γενομένου, should be preferred over the present participle, γινομένου. The manuscript evidence favors the aorist over the present participle. Significant in this discussion is the fact that the aorist participle does not especially mean that the meal was finished as the NKJV translates it. The synoptic gospels indicate clearly that the meal continued beyond Jesus' announcement of His coming betrayal. For example, after Jesus announces He is going to be betrayed, Matthew says clearly that Jesus instituted the Lord's Supper "while they were eating" (Matt 26:26). Mark 14:17-25 follows the same pattern of events, though Luke's account seems to have Judas present during its institution. Thus, the aorist participle need not mean that the meal was finished, but only that it had been in progress (an ingressive aorist).

9 As this section of the Gospel begins the climax of the theme of light versus darkness, we see the forces of darkness moving to extinguish the Light of Life. Judas is about to depart and betray Jesus, who will in turn be killed by the nation's leaders. Yet Jesus sees this as a battle between Himself and the prince of this world, Satan, a battle Jesus wins. Tenney ("John," in *The Expositor's Bible Commentary,* 136) observes well that in this mention of Satan there is an implication that there is more than a "mere political or theological squabble" in progress between Jesus and the Pharisees. The source of all the conflict that had occurred between light and darkness, Jesus and the Jewish leaders, throughout the public ministry of Jesus is clearly identified in the archenemy of God himself, Satan.

10 Beasley-Murray, *Word Biblical Themes: John,* 90.

11 Ernst Haenchen's (*John: a Commentary on the Gospel of John*

[Philadelphia: Fortress Press, 1984], 106) description of the significance of the foot washing is also characteristic of those who approach the passage from the perspective of a justification-focused theology. He says, "The footwashing which he is about to perform—for the time being only in private of course—is the anticipation of the cross and expresses the meaning of the cross graphically as a deed of Jesus." He argues for this interpretation of Jesus' act on the basis that, "the Evangelist could not represent the death scene itself as an act of love." So, he uses footwashing as a euphemism for crucifixion. This is only necessary if one must find the cross in every part of the Gospel. One must also forget that it is John who recounts Jesus' loving provision for His mother while on the cross (John 19:26-27). Jesus' love and unselfish concern for others was evident, even on the cross. John did not need a euphemistic way of portraying His death as an act of love.

Gruenler (*The Trinity in the Gospel of John,* 90) at first seems to understand the nature of Jesus' actions when he says, "He is about to demonstrate in the humble act of footwashing what divine love is like and what the disciples' relationship to one another should reflect." He says further, "Jesus is inviting his disciples to acknowledge that humility and servanthood are essential characteristics of divine love and must characterize the new society." But he also reveals the characteristic Reformed understanding of Jesus' actions when he says, "the footwashing prophetically anticipates the washing of the cross" (91). His instruction that follows the actions should reflect the focus of those actions, and His instruction was not about the cross, but about servanthood and love. This does not mean that Jesus' going to the cross was not an act of love and humility for which such an action *could* be an illustration. Actually, His condescension to leave heaven's glory and become incarnate was an act of great humiliation. Even so, here Jesus was teaching them something more immediate by His actions and John wants us to see and learn what they saw and learned.

[12] Tenney, "John," in *The Expositor's Bible Commentary,* 136.

[13] Ibid. (Italics his)

[14] *Shemos Rabbah* 25:6.

[15] F. F. Bruce, *The Gospel of John* (Grand Rapids: William B. Eerdmans Publishing Company, 1983), 280.

[16] Westcott (*The Gospel According to St. John,* 191) correctly notes that there is no indication that Jesus began washing the disciples' feet with Judas as some have thought. He feels it is more likely that He began with Peter, which would make his refusal "more intelligible than it would be if others had already accepted it." But, the text indicates that Peter is not the first, since in verse five Jesus has begun washing and "then" comes to Peter in verse six. Peter is sufficiently free-spirited that he would have raised a protest even if

he had been the last one to be washed. It is more likely that Jesus began at one end of the group and worked His way around to the other end. Peter is probably in one of the more central places, being numbered as one of Jesus' three closest companions, and so would have been approached more nearly at the mid-point of Jesus' task.

17 A. B. Bruce, *The Training of the Twelve* (Edinburgh: T. & T. Clark, 1908), 344.

18 F. F. Bruce (*The Gospel of John,* 281) and Carson (*The Gospel According to John,* 463) understand Jesus' words, "after this" in verse seven, to be a reference to the understanding they would have following His resurrection. Thus, his actions were intended to teach the significance of His sacrifice. They were justification truth in parabolic form. Westcott (*The Gospel According to St. John,* 191) makes a strong distinction in the senses of οἶδα and γνώσῃ and interprets Jesus' words to signify that they could not understand His actions until after He was "glorified." He considers it significant that Jesus used different words for "know" in His response. Jesus was saying, in essence, "absolute and complete" knowledge of what He was doing could not be grasped by them at that time in contrast to "the knowledge which is gained by slow experience." He sees "afterwards" (literally "after these things") referring to all of the Passion events rather than just the Upper Room Discourse. Mitchell (*An Everlasting Love,* 251) does not see it as a justification truth, but finds in Jesus' words a reference to the coming indwelling ministry of the Holy Spirit. In other words, they would understand Jesus' actions after Pentecost. All of these interpretations, though possible, do not fit the context well. It is better to recognize that Jesus is telling Peter, "I'll explain myself in a couple of minutes," especially in light of the instruction on humility that follows. His words, "after these things," refer to the task He is performing and the instruction that will follow.

19 A. B. Bruce, *The Training of the Twelve,* 345.

20 Carson (*The Gospel According to John,* 463-64) appears to see more theology in Jesus' response. He argues, "If there were nothing more at stake then [sic] the naked act of footwashing, Jesus' response would seem petty, unbearably rigid. It would sound like fake humility, 'I command you to let me be humble and let me wash your feet – or you're fired!'" He sees Jesus' intention to symbolize the cross as His motivation for speaking such harsh words. His conclusion from this is that Jesus was teaching by His act that "unless the Lamb of God has taken away a person's sin, has washed that person, he or she can have no part with him." This is indeed true, from the teaching of other Scripture, but not Jesus' teaching point here, unless one wants to say that Peter is not yet regenerate. Clearly, having a part with Jesus is not an issue of justification, but sanctification.

Laney (*John*, 240-41) sees the issue of Peter's response involving the person of Christ. He says, "Peter's refusal of His service was in essence a rejection of Christ's Person." Thus his refusal meant he could not be Jesus' disciple. The problem with this is that Peter's refusal more logically arises from an understanding of Jesus' person, and the resulting superior social status which that entailed. No, he is not rejecting Jesus. He is trying again to mold Jesus to his will and ways. This mistaken attitude may be what led to Jesus' question, "Do you know who I am?" as well as His prayer that Peter's faith would not fail.

[21] A. B. Bruce, *The Training of the Twelve*, 347.

[22] Ibid.

[23] Καθαρίζω is related to the noun, καθαρός, which can signify physical, moral, or ceremonial (religious) cleanness (F. Hauck, TDNT, 3:414). First, it describes physical cleanness. For example, in Matthew 23:25-26 Jesus uses it to accuse the Pharisees of washing clean the outside of a cup while leaving the inside dirty, a metaphor for their hypocrisy. Similarly, the linen cloth used to wrap Jesus' body was described as "clean" (Matt 27:59). It is used in Revelation 19:8 to describe the clothing of the church, the bride of Christ. Second, it describes moral cleanness. Jesus used the term with this sense in the Sermon on the Mount (Matt 5:8), explaining its moral sense in His discussion of the Law in which He looked at heart attitudes rather than external actions as the test of moral purity. Paul used it to describe himself as morally clean in Acts 18:6. The third use is the most common in the Gospels, that of ceremonial cleanness. In this use it refers to that which qualifies a person to participate in the community's religious and social life. For example in Matthew 8:1-4, when Jesus "cleansed" a leper by healing him, He made him ceremonially clean and able to participate in the community and its worship once again. Jesus declared all foods ceremonially "clean" in Mark 7:19. Thus, Jesus had available to Him all three senses of the word when He used it in the upper room. We look, then, to the context to determine the sense He intended for His men.

[24] Tenney ("John," in *The Expositor's Bible Commentary*, 136) misunderstands Jesus' actions when he evaluates them solely on the basis of His response to Peter when he objected to His washing his feet rather than in the broader context of the remainder of His instruction. Basically he focuses on the secondary lesson and ignores the primary one when he finds instruction in issues of justification and sanctification rather than humility. He says, "The external washing was intended to be a picture of spiritual cleansing from evil." This is true, at least in part, since it can be implied from Jesus' words to Peter. Peter, and later John, could rightly understand Jesus' actions and words in that way. Jesus' response to Peter indicates that spiritual cleansing

may be an underlying truth. But, Jesus' instruction to the group in verses twelve through seventeen reflects the primary purpose of His actions, which was *not* to teach a lesson on spiritual cleansing. Westcott (*The Gospel According to St. John,* 191) is correct when he says that "it appears to be foreign to the context to introduce any direct reference to the washing in Christ's blood." Laney (*John,* 242) gives the clearest warning against the temptation to ignore Jesus' own explanation and import theology into the text.

> A foundational principle of hermeneutics is, "Do not add to the interpretation when an explanation is given in the text." Another helpful guide is, "Always prefer the clear meaning over an obscure interpretation." Applying these principles to John 13:4-11 one discovers in Jesus' own explanation (13:12-120) that the foot washing teaches a simple but profound lesson concerning the humble service each believer ought to pursue. What is emphasized here is the attitude of service that is to be manifested in daily Christian living.

Thus this is not a picture of Jesus' death, but of service. Carson's (*The Gospel According to John,* 465) analysis of the movement of the conversation between Jesus and Peter also reflects the view that this is a treatise on justification.

> In vv. 6-8 the footwashing symbolizes the cleansing that is the result of Christ's impending cross-work. But Peter's unrestrained (and thoughtless) exuberance (v. 9) opens up the opportunity to turn the footwashing to another point: the initial and fundamental cleansing that Christ provides is a once-for-all act. Individuals who have been cleansed by Christ's atoning work will doubtless need to have subsequent sins washed away, but the fundamental cleansing can never be repeated. It rather misses the point to charge that this view makes the footwashing a mere 'topping up', a symbol not of the fundamental cross-work of Christ and its effects but of progressive Christian experience. *In this verse* that may be so – but the point is that this verse has launched into a new application of the footwashing. The first application used the footwashing to symbolize Christ's atoning, cleansing death; this second application makes the points just elucidated; the third and final application teaches lessons in humility (vv. 12-17). (Italics his)

This is a clear case of reading too much other New Testament teaching into this passage. Though what he is saying is true, and taught elsewhere in Scripture, it is wrong to import those meanings into the text when the flow of the narrative indicates otherwise. Thus Carson's first application is completely absent from the context. The second application is only an implication communicated between Jesus and Peter. Only the third application is the focus of Jesus in the act of foot washing. Though He goes on to discuss Judas's betrayal, it is not the teaching point of His actions either.

25 Though Carson is focused on a justification motif in the Discourse, he still recognizes the message of John. Even so, he is unable to depart from what he sees as the justification focal point of Jesus' act.

> Even when the footwashing is said to point, in various ways, to spiritual cleansing based on Christ's death, both the footwashing and that atoning death are the supreme displays of Jesus' love for his own (v. 1b). The footwashing was shocking to Jesus' disciples, but not half as shocking as the notion of a Messiah who would die the hideous and shameful death of crucifixion, the death of the damned. But the two events – the footwashing and the crucifixion – are truly of a piece: the revered and exalted Messiah assumes the role of the despised servant for the good of others. That plus the notion of cleansing, explains why the footwashing can point so effectively to the cross. But service for others cannot be restricted to this unique act. If the footwashing and the cross are prompted by Jesus' daunting love (v. 1), the fellowship of the cleansed that he is creating is to be characterized by the same love (vv. 34-35), and therefore by the same self-abnegation for the sake of serving others. And that means that the footwashing is almost *bound* to have exemplary significance, just as Christ's death, however unique, has exemplary force. (Carson, *The Gospel According to John*, 467)

The problem with seeing this as a picture of the coming crucifixion is Jesus' own words in 13:34 where He commands the disciples to love one another "as I *have* loved you" That could hardly refer to His death which had not yet taken place. He is pointing them to something He has already done, namely, serving them by washing their feet. This was an act of love, not a symbol of death.

F. F. Bruce (*The Gospel of John*, 282) reflects the same tendency. When discussing verses ten and eleven, he notes a textual problem with "except for his feet." He notes that "the decision whether to retain or to omit the phrase 'except for his feet' tends to be made not so much on the bare textual evidence (which is inconclusive one way or the other) but on one's understanding of the whole passage." For him the phrase suggests that the feet need to be repeatedly washed.

> But what would the spiritual significance be? One popular interpretation throughout the centuries has been a sacramental one: the once-for-all bathing is the initiatory washing of baptism (the inward and spiritual grace, of course, as well as the outward and visible sign), which is unrepeatable; the repeated washing of the feet is another

sacrament—penance, according to some expositors; the Lord's Supper, according to others. . . . Others prefer a non-sacramental understanding of the once-for-all bathing as the initial cancellation of sin and cleansing from guilt that is received in regeneration, while the repeated washing of the feet corresponds to the regular removal of incidental defilement of conscience by confession to God and the guarding of one's way according to his word (cf. Ps 119:9). (282)

He seems to concur with the second interpretation, but then incorrectly concludes, "The foot-washing is thus seen as a parabolic action pointing to the sacrifice of the cross" (283). Again, though there is a lot of truth in his words, Jesus' purpose was not to paint a picture of the cross. He was indeed communicating His concept of love displayed through humble service for others (cf. Phil 2:3-7). We should not allow the loving self-sacrifice of the cross to overshadow the significance of what Jesus is saying to His men at this time. Both messages are of critical importance. The footwashing need not be a parable of the cross, but can stand as a powerful lesson in its own right, as Jesus intended it.

Beasely-Murray (*Word Biblical Themes: John*, 89) is still speaking from a justification perspective when he writes, "Jesus was telling Peter that what he was now doing had the meaning of a *complete* cleansing that is gained by a bath. His washing of the feet of the disciples, accordingly, is a sign of the greater cleansing that Jesus is about to achieve by his sacrificial self-giving." These comments are appreciated, but do not reflect either Jesus' message to Peter nor to us. The cross is not the source of cleansing to which Jesus refers at this point. If anything, John 15:3, where He relates their spiritual cleanness to receiving His instruction, should guide us in understanding the nature of cleanness here. What has made them clean is their choice to follow and believe in Him and His words, not His coming death. Jesus said they are "clean" then, at the supper, not that they will be cleansed soon, at the cross. His words are not anticipating the coming cleansing of His atoning sacrifice. He is referring to their state at that time, before the cross, again, as evidenced in John 13:34.

26 H. E. Dana and Julius R. Mantey, *A Manual Grammar of the Greek New Testament*, (New York: Macmillan Publishing Co., Inc., 1955), 179. The two Greek terms for washing in 13:10 are λελουμένος, from λούω, which involves washing the whole body; and νίψασθαι, from νίπτω, which means to wash a part of the body. The first washing is a perfect tense verb and indicates a completed action whose results continue to the present. Thus it focuses the attention on a resultant state of being, they are clean because they had already bathed. The second term for washing is an aorist tense infinitive that simply looks at an act of washing the feet. But, as an infinitive, the verbal idea contained in it does not focus on the "tense" aspect of its meaning. So, it is not

looking at the washing as being in the past, but only as happening.

27 Dillow, *The Reign of the Servant Kings*, 326.

28 Ibid., 401. (Italics added). Although we agree wholeheartedly with the point that Dillow is making, we think that he has some unguarded and imprecise statements that can lead to erroneous thinking. For one thing, there are not two kinds of forgiveness in Scripture but six according to Wendell Miller is his work *Forgiveness: the Power and the Puzzles*. Again we think that "end of usefulness" is too strong of a statement. Although it may end up there sometimes (cf.1 Cor 9:27; 11:30; 1 John 5:16), that is not the normal situation, for which we thank God. Peter was not at the end of his usefulness when he blasphemously sinned by cursing and swearing that he did not know Christ. A better word would be "disruption" of usefulness. And this really needs to be stressed. It is a black and white issue. We cannot be experiencing fellowship with God and condoning unconfessed sin in our lives at one and the same time.

Μέρος has as its basic and most commonly used sense the concrete idea of a "part, in contrast to the whole" (BAGD, μέρος, 505). Figuratively it can be used of participating or sharing in something. For example, it has this sense in Matthew 24:51 (Luke 12:46) where the evil servant is punished and appointed his *portion* with the hypocrites." In Revelation 20:6 those having a *part* in the first resurrection are called blessed. In Revelation 21:8 the evil "shall have their *part* in the lake which burns with fire and brimstone, which is the second death." In Revelation 22:19 the warning is given that anyone who takes away from the words of the Revelation, "God shall take away his *part* from the Book of Life, from the holy city, and the things which are written in this book." Thus, the idea is that of participation or inclusion in something. Thus, when Jesus uses the term with Peter, He is warning him of expulsion from the group, from being included by Jesus in His purposes and plans. He will be denied fellowship.

29 Dillow, *The Reign of the Servant Kings*, 534.

30 Westcott (*The Gospel According to St. John*, 191) interprets Jesus' words from more of a sanctification perspective. He says, "The reply of the Lord introduces a new idea. From the thought of the act of service as such, we are led to the thought of the symbolic meaning of the special act as a process of cleansing. . . . The 'washing' in itself does not mark an essential change, but is referred to the total change already wrought." He says further, "He who is bathed needs . . . only to remove the stains contracted in the walk of life; just as the guest, after the bath, needs only to have the dust washed from his feet when he reaches the house of his host" (191-92). He gives it a more corporate meaning rather than personal and says,

The apostles as a body were clean. The presence of one traitor, the stain-spot to be removed, did not alter the character of the company any more than the partial soiling of the feet alters the essential cleanness of the man.

Taken in this connection the passage throws light on the doctrine of the holiness of the visible Church. And this the more because it seems impossible not to see in the word *bathed*, as contrasted with *washed*, a foreshadowing of the idea of Christian Baptism. . . . There is however no evidence to shew that the apostles themselves were baptized unless with John's baptism. The 'bathing' in their case consisted in direct intercourse and union with Christ. For them this one special act of service was but an accessory to the continuous love of that companionship. (192)

[31] Tenney ("John," in *The Expositor's Bible Commentary,* 138) says that the term for "know" (οἶδα) used by John in this verse "is generally used in John to denote certain knowledge of a fact rather than experiential acquaintance with a situation or person (cf. 14:4)." Thus when John used οἶδα here to describe Jesus' knowledge he was describing His omniscience and self-consciousness of His purpose and circumstances. Though he is correct in his interpretation of what John was communicating, that does not arise from the term itself. As F. F. Bruce (*The Gospel of John,* 282) notes, "John likes to vary his use of synonyms, as when he uses *oida* and *ginosko* for knowing, or *phileo* and *agapao* for loving." See additional comments on "know" in Appendix 3, "Knowing God." In John the two terms appear often to be used alternately as synonyms, usually without special emphasis upon any nuance of their meaning. Thus it is better to look at the context to determine any emphasis John intends rather than at which of the two terms are chosen.

[32] Thus John used the present participle, παραδιδόντα, to describe Judas as one who was in the process of betraying Jesus at the time Jesus said not all were clean.

[33] Although the term used by Jesus for "he who is sent" comes from the same root word as apostle, His use of the term involves its normal sense rather than as a special designation for the apostles like He used in the other gospels.

[34] Carson, *The Gospel According to John,* 467-68.

[35] F. F. Bruce (*The Gospel of* John, 28-31) imbues a justification emphasis into the upper room at this early point by seeing two meanings within the act of Christ. He says

the Lord gave the disciples two explanations of his washing of their feet . . . The former . . . is theological in character: the foot-washing symbolizes Jesus' humbling himself to endure the death of the cross and the cleansing efficacy of his death for the believer. The latter, unfolded in verses 12-17, is practical in character: Jesus has washed their feet in order that from his example they may learn to perform similar service one for another. ... The second explanation is very much in line with Luke's account of the conversation that took place between the Lord and the disciples at the last supper (Luke 22:24-27).

Though, as seen earlier, a hint of theology may be discerned in Jesus' comment, "Not all of you are clean," this does not mean that His act was intended to teach a theology of the Cross. Interestingly enough, Bruce is unable to depart from his justification model even when the evidence of the Gospel of Luke reinforces the issue of humble service as the focal point of Jesus' instruction. His mind was not on their justification. His mind was on the problem of pride among His men whose limited faith was about to be tested and who would no longer have Him physically present to keep them in line. Jesus was focused on His final words of encouragement and last instructions before His departure. He did not need to get them justified. He needed to teach them to serve one another.

[36] Tenney, "John," in *The Expositor's Bible Commentary,* 137.

[37] This is a first class conditional statement that assumes the truth of the protasis, the "if" clause.

[38] Carson, *The Gospel According to John*, 468.

[39] Gruenler, *The Trinity in the Gospel of John,* 91.

[40] The present subjunctive, ποιῆτε, carries the idea of "keep doing." The third class conditional sentence indicates that it is possible for them *not* to keep doing it.

[41] John Calvin, *Commentary on the Gospel According to John,* translated by William Pringle (Grand Rapids: Wm. B. Eerdmans Publishing Company, 1949), 2:62.

[42] Calvin, *Institutes of the Christian Religion* (Grand Rapids: Wm. B. Eerdmans Publishing Co., 1970), 1:55-56.

Chapter Three

[1] Tenney, "John," in The Expositor's Bible Commentary, 138.

[2] Westcott, The Gospel According to St. John, 193.

[3] Carson, The Gospel According to John, 470.

[4] Westcott (*The Gospel According to St. John,* 193) attempts to reconcile the doctrine of election with the departure of Judas by concluding, in part, that he could not be regenerate. He does this by relating Judas' election to something other than salvation. Judas was elected to the apostolate, not to

eternal life. Carson (*The Gospel According to John*, 470) recognizes that John 6:70 indicates clearly that Judas was counted by Jesus as one of the chosen twelve, both earlier and that evening. He then says, "The reason why he now takes the pains to show that inclusion of Judas was not an oversight or a sign of weakness on his part is so that their faith might be strengthened for the critical hour." Thus election is not always to salvation. "The reason Jesus chose one who would betray him was to fulfill Scripture." Calvin (*Commentary on the Gospel According to John,* 2:63) saw Jesus' reference to His choice of the disciples as a direct teaching on election. He describes election in the life of a believer as affecting their lives, with their works proving their possession of life.

And not only does he ascribe to election their perseverance, but likewise the commencement of their piety. Whence does it arise that one man, rather than another, devotes himself to the word of God? It is, because he was elected. Again, whence does it arise that this man makes progress, and continues to lead a good and holy life, but because the purpose of God is unchangeable, to complete the work that was begun by his hand? In short, this is the source of the distinction between the children of God and unbelievers, that the former are drawn to salvation by the Spirit of adoption, while the latter are hurried to destruction by their flesh, which is under no restraint.

But then he addresses the problem raised by Judas, who is clearly called elect, but who does not persevere in good works to the end. To resolve the problem he identifies a second kind of election. Calvin says,

In another passage he includes Judas in the number of the *elect.* . . . But in that passage the mode of expression, though different, is not opposite; for there the word denotes a temporal *election,* by which God appoints us to any particular work; in the same manner as Saul, who was *elected* to be a king, and yet was a reprobate. . . . And, indeed, the reprobate are sometimes endued by God with the gifts of the Spirit, to execute the office with which he invests them. Thus, in Saul, we perceive, for a time, the splendour of royal virtues, and thus Judas also was distinguished by eminent gifts, and such as were adapted to an apostle of Christ. But this is widely different from the sanctification of the Holy Spirit, which the Lord bestows on none but his own children; for he renews them in understanding and heart, that they may be holy and unblameable in his sight" (*Commentary on the Gospel According to John,* 2:64).

As can be seen with all three of the afore mentioned writers, when issues like the doctrine of election are brought into focus and made teaching points of the passage, problems arise. It would appear that Judas lost his salvation by a conscious choice to reject Christ, by apostasy. Their answer is that he was not elected to salvation, but only to be counted among Christ's followers. Their mistake is that they always relate the term "choose" or "elect" to salvation regardless of its context.

5 F. F. Bruce (*The Gospel of John,* 287), though not holding to eternal security, argues well that the various prophecies he fulfilled do "not mean that Judas in particular was driven to his act of treachery by a decree of fate against which it would have been fruitless to struggle."

6 See John 8:24, 28, and 58.

7 Calvin, Institutes of the Christian Religion, 1:55-56.

8 F. F. Bruce (*The Gospel of John,* 288) sees the two terms for "send," namely *pempo* and *apostello*, in John as "completely interchangeable, with no distinctive nuances" and points to John 17:18 and 20:21 as examples of this.

9 Carson, The Gospel According to John, 471.

10 David L. Bartlett ("John 13:21-30." *Interpretation.* 43: 4 [October 1989]: 393) sees this section providing "the transition between the footwashing and the farewell discourses. More broadly, it provides the transition between the time when the disciples minister with Jesus and the time when one of the disciples betrays Jesus to his death. More broadly yet, the passage recapitulates and foreshadows the great themes of John's Gospel." There is a measure of truth to this. But, though John is a literary master, it appears that Bartlett may be reading far more into the passage than John intended. Yes, it is a transitional section, in a sense. But, one must remember it is also chronologically part of the sequence of events that marked that night.

11 Carson, The Gospel According to John, 472.

12 Westcott (*The Gospel According to St. John,* 194) does not see the designation by the author of the disciple "whom Jesus loved" as a significant title or indication of special status in the group, but that it merely "marks an acknowledgment of love and not an exclusive enjoyment of love."

13 *Agapaō* (ἀγαπάω) is used in John 13:23; 19:26-27 (at the cross with Jesus' mother); and 21:1, 20-25 (by the Sea of Galilee and in the closing comments of the Gospel). *Phileō* (φιλέω) is used once, in John 20:2 (at the empty tomb).

14 Carson, The Gospel According to John, 474.

15 Mitchell, An Everlasting Love, 258.

16 Ralph Gower, *The New Manners and Customs of Bible Times* (Chicago, Moody Press, 1987), 247-48.

[17] Carson, The Gospel According to John, 474.

[18] Tenney ("John," in *The Expositor's Bible Commentary,* 140), for example, says that Judas' "yielding to selfish impulse opened the way to satanic control." He had ceased to be one of Christ's and had become identified with Satan's kingdom. His actions, though his own, were inspired by Satan. Carson (*The Gospel According to John,* 475) sees this as signifying "thorough possession" by Satan

[19] Mitchell (*An Everlasting Love,* 257) argues well that "Judas was never a real disciple of Jesus Christ" and points to Matthew 26 for proof.

[20] F. F. Bruce (*The Gospel of John,* 290) believes that Jesus' action "may have been a final appeal to him to abandon his treacherous plan and play the part of a true disciple." He bases this on the belief that "Satan could not have entered into him had he not granted him admission."

[21] Westcott (*The Gospel According to St. John,* 195) rightly notes that, "at that moment the conflict was decided." Mitchell (*An Everlasting Love,* 258) sees Psalm 41:9 being fulfilled at this point.

[22] Westcott (*The Gospel According to St. John,* 195) also notes well that even John did not understand Jesus' instruction to Judas after seeing Him give the bread.

[23] Carson, The Gospel According to John, 475.

[24] Bartlett, "John 13:21-30," 394.

[25] Bartlett (Ibid., 396) notes further, "Jesus' authority over evil and over Judas is shown by his foreknowledge of what Judas will do. . . . Judas chooses the darkness. Yet what Judas chooses, he waits upon Christ's compelling word to do. . . . darkness encroaches only where light permits."

[26] Mitchell, An Everlasting Love, 259.

Chapter Four

[1] Carson (*The Gospel According to John,* 483), though holding to a justification basis for his interpretation, recognizes that in this verse Jesus embarks "on one of the dominant themes of the discourse: his concern to prepare his disciples for his departure."

[2] Tenney, "John," in *The Expositor's Bible Commentary,* 141.

[3] W. Robert Cook (*The Theology of John* [Chicago: Moody Press, 1979], 75) sees the term being used to designate more than the passion events, but rather it was "the completion of the purpose of the incarnation in toto that was in view."

⁴ Thus Tenney concludes ("John," in *The Expositor's Bible Commentary*, 141), "The Cross would become the supreme glory of God because the Son would completely obey the will of the Father."

⁵ Carson (*The Gospel According to John*, 482) sees these two senses coming together in these words of Jesus. He says, "Now, bringing to a climax a theme developed throughout this Gospel, the Evangelist makes it clear that the supreme moment of divine self-disclosure, the greatest moment of displayed glory, was in the shame of the cross. That is the primary reason why the title *Son of Man* is employed here. . . . Outside the New Testament, the title is associated with glory . . . within the Synoptics, the title is as frequently associated with suffering. In John, the two are dramatically brought together..

⁶ Cook, *The Theology of John*, 75.

⁷ Gruenler, *The Trinity in the Gospel of John*, 93.

⁸ Gruenler notes that these verses "form a chiasm in which the first and last declarations (*a* and *a'*) describe the glorification of the Son, and the two middle statements (*b* and *b'*) the glorification of the Father." From this chiastic description of the relationship of Jesus to His Father, Gruenler sees both "the individuality and unity of Father and Son" being affirmed by Jesus (ibid., 94). In line with these observations is the significance of the choice of words made by Jesus. Westcott (*The Gospel According to St. John*, 197) sees the prepositional phrase translated "in Him" in both verses as a description of the Godhead's "unity of being" (essence) rather than "unity of position" (relationship) that would have used a different phrase ("with You" as in John 17:5). "In Him" is a translation of ἐν αὐτῷ in these verses while "with You" in John 17:5 translates παρὰ σοί. Thus Westcott is making a distinction on the basis of the significance of the prepositions. The preposition ἐν can have either a locative or instrumental sense (Dana and Mantey, *A Manual Grammar of the Greek New Testament*, 86-91). So the preposition translated as "in" can also be translated as "by" and can carry the sense of "by means of" whereas Westcott is giving it a more locative meaning. Thus, God's glorification is coming by means of Jesus, or through what Jesus does. In this case, He is being glorified by means of what Jesus is about to suffer through obediently. As Paul says, God was in Christ reconciling the world unto Himself.

⁹ Concerning the problem of the two tenses of the verb "to glorify," Carson says (*The Gospel According to John*, 486-87), "The aorists, which many grammarians judge must refer to something in the past (if they are in the indicative mood, as here), prompt not a few commentators to think that John is confusing the situation in the church of his day with the ostensible setting, the night Jesus was betrayed. The two instances of the future are then understood either to be setting the record straight, *i.e.* reverting to the perspective

of the ostensible setting; or to reflect a rather botched attempt at mingling futurist eschatology (reflected in the future tense) with inaugurated eschatology (preserved in *at once*). However, it can easily be shown that verbs in the Aorist tense, even when in the indicative mood, can be past-referring, present-referring, and even future-referring, as well as omnitemporal and atemporal (*cf.* Porter, 75-76, 233). A consistent aspect-theory of the Greek verb finds little difficulty, however, by arguing that these Aorists are 'proleptic' (*i.e.* future-referring!), viewing the decisive death/exaltation as virtually accomplished, since the decisive steps have already been taken and the redemptive purposes of God are secure."

10 Westcott, *The Gospel According to St. John,* 197.

11 Though Jesus brought up the Jews at this point, John's inclusion of His mention of them at this point has no polemical overtones, per Fernando F. Segovia ("The Structure, *Tendenz*, and *Zitz im Leben* of John 13:31-14:31," *Journal of Biblical Literature*, 104: 3 [1985]).

12 Segovia's conclusion (ibid., 479) that "the situation of the disciples after Jesus' departure is explicitly likened to that of the Jews in general: these same consequences apply to both groups," is incorrect. Segovia has made too much of a connection between Jesus' warnings of departure to the Jews and His words to the disciples. He does remind the men of what He said previously, but that does not mean that we should view them as three "farewells in the Gospel" as does Segovia (He has identified John 7:32-36 and 8:21-24 as the other two farewells.). Since Segovia perceives a polemical argument in John he concludes that John included these words in order to introduce "a deliberate contrast between the disciples and the Jews with regard to the coming situation" (480). But, this is not the case since the one difference is far too significant, namely, Jesus does *not* tell the disciples that they will *not* be able to find Him. Rather, He indirectly promises the opposite for the immediate future, a promise of the resurrection appearances, and for the farther future when He will take them to be with Him.

Carson expresses an excellent understanding of the literary and historical development of the remainder of this chapter and its relationship to the rest of the discourse. He notes (*The Gospel According to John*, 483-84),

> Having announced his departure, and having insisted that his disciples cannot now come with him (v. 33), Jesus begins to lay out what he expects of them while he is away. Unfortunately, they still cannot get over the unambiguous insistence that Jesus' departure is imminent, and so Peter interrupts and presses the point (36-38). This in turn prompts Jesus to embark on an extended and comforting explanation regarding his departure, before returning to more detailed descriptions of what is expected of them, and what is promised to them, during the time he is

absent from them. In other words, when these chapters are read with literary sensitivity and a modicum of historical realism (instead of treating them as a manual of systematic theology that must have all the points in an abstract and idealized order), passages which have been cursorily dismissed as late additions or awkward displacements make rather good sense where they stand.

Though we are not concerned over the supposed "late additions" or other editorial issues discussed by those scholars who question the authenticity and eyewitness nature of this gospel, we do see this as a significant aspect of John's message. We see Jesus attempting to instruct and encourage while the men attempt to understand.

13 Tenney, "John," in *The Expositor's Bible Commentary,* 142. Calvin (*Commentary on the Gospel According to John,* 2:75) sees Jesus calling the commandment "new" because "laws are more carefully observed at the commencement, but they gradually slip out of the remembrance of men, till at length they become obsolete." He feels that Jesus has called it new because He wants it to be kept with the same enthusiasm as if it were just recently given (76). This is speculative interpretation by Calvin. Westcott (*The Gospel According to St. John,* 197) offers a better understanding of what Jesus meant. He says, "In this case the 'newness' of the commandment . . . must be sought in the newness of the motive and of the scope, inasmuch as the example of the self-sacrifice of Christ, begun in the Incarnation and consummated at His death, revealed to men new obligations of new powers."

14 F. F. Bruce, *The Gospel of John,* 294.

15 Westcott (*The Gospel According to St. John,* 198) considers the clause "as I have loved you" to be ambiguous and says that it "may express either the character or the ground of the love of Christians."

16 Tertullian, *Apology,* 39.7.

17 This is a Third Class conditional clause that does not assume the truth or untruth of the protasis, but does link the truthfulness of the apodosis to it. Thus, if the "if" clause is true, then what follows is true also. If the "if" clause proves false, then what follows does not happen.

Chapter Five

1 Some writers have attempted to see in the four questions of the disciples a Johannine version of the four questions asked during the Passover meal. F. F. Bruce (*The Gospel of John,* 295) notes correctly that "it would be far-fetched to compare the interpositions of the questions of the four disciples to the questions traditionally asked on Passover Eve by four sons – the wise, the foolish,

the simple, and the one who does not know how to ask."

2 Westcott (*The Gospel According to St. John,* 199) interprets Peter's question to indicate that, "his thoughts were fixed upon the material and not upon the spiritual departure and following." He says further, "The reply of the Lord checks and yet encourages the apostle. . . . In checking the disciple the Lord simply points out the impossibility of an immediate following, and does not insist on a contrast of character which makes the impossibility."

3 Tenney, "John," in *The Expositor's Bible Commentary,* 142.

4 Ibid.

5 E. Richard ("Expressions of Double Meaning and Their Function in the Gospel of John.," *New Testament Studies,* 31: 1 [January 1985], 96-112), identifies what he considers an example of such in this section of the Upper Room Discourse in the dialogue between Jesus and the disciples.

6 Ibid., 101.

7 Carson, *The Gospel According to John,* 486.

8 "Cockcrow" refers to the hours between midnight and three in the morning. It got its name from the fact that roosters in Palestine commonly crow during those hours of the night. It was the third of four guard watches, ending as the first light of dawn came around three in the morning.

9 Johnston M. Cheney (*The Life of Christ in Stereo* [Portland, Oregon: Western Baptist Seminary Press, 1969], 218-20) proposes that Jesus warned Peter that he would deny Him six times rather than three. He argues that the evidence of the text indicates an initial warning that he would deny Jesus three times before the cock crowed once, and then a later warning that he would deny Him three more times before it crowed a second time. The first warning follows Jesus' announcement of His departure, institution of the Lord's Supper, giving of the New Commandment (John 13:34-35) and Peter's question about where He is going (176).

The second warning comes after the discussion is completed in the upper room, Jesus has prayed His High Priestly prayer, and they are on their way to the Garden of Gethsemane. This is based on Jesus' statement that the cock would crow "twice" in Mark's gospel. Cheney further proposes that there are more than three accusers identified in the four gospels. Differences in the wording of the two warnings can also be detected in the various Gospel accounts. Cheney's argument is that by recognizing there were two warnings and six denials, all apparent contradictions in the text are removed and "these differing warnings describe precisely what took place with respect to Peter" (185).

Before defending this view, its weaknesses should be addressed. First,

Mark's reference to the cock crowing "twice" need not *require* a second warning. This detail of information could easily be skipped over by the other evangelists as unnecessary to the account while Peter, the recipient of the warning and teacher of Mark, would have remembered it intensely. Their silence is not a convincing argument alone. Further, this silence by the other evangelists could be seen as similar to the mention of two demoniacs by Matthew (Matt 8:28-34), and the mention of only one by Mark (5:1-20) and Luke (8:26-39). It is also similar to the two unnamed blind men healed by Jesus as He left Jericho in Matthew (20:29-33), with only a single individual identified by Luke (18:35-43), who is identified as a person named Bartimaeus by Mark (10:46-52). In these instances we recognize that there were two individuals who received Jesus' ministry in both instances and that the mentioning of only one by an evangelist does not constitute error, but simply reflects their literary focus. In the same way, viewed in isolation from other evidences, both of Cheney's two separate warnings could be harmonized into a single warning with Peter continuing to affirm his loyalty while Jesus repeats twice that he will deny Him three times.

A second argument against six denials is the restoration of Peter in John 21. In this instance Jesus asks Peter if he loves Him three times, presumably because of his three denials. On the surface this would seem a good argument against six denials. But, again, it is essentially an argument from silence. It may be that Jesus asks Peter three times because that is the number of perfection. It may also be that John only reported three of Peter's denials because they matched better literarily with the three restorations. At any rate, John's record does not require there be only three denials, but simply reports only three.

Cheney's position is strengthened when the identity of the servants who confronted Peter is examined in detail. He argues that there are more than three required by the terminology describing them among the four evangelists. So, this evidence needs further evaluation. All four evangelists identify the first accuser as a servant girl. They each use the term παιδίσκη to describe her. Matthew identifies her simply as "a servant girl" (μία παιδίσκη), Mark as "one of the servant girls of the high priest (μία τῶν παιδισκῶν τοῦ ἀρχιερέως), Luke as "a certain servant girl" (αὐτὸν παιδίσκη), and John as "the servant girl who kept the door" (ἡ παιδίσκη ἡ θυρωρός).

Cheney views the references to the second and third accusers as evidence of more than three denials. He says, "There is 'another woman' (Matt. 26:71), a second query by the high priest's maid (Mark 14:69), 'another man' (Luke 22:58), 'another man' (Luke 22:59), and finally 'a kinsman of the one whose ear Peter had cut off' (John 18:26)" (219). In this listing, Cheney identifies the second accuser of Matthew and Mark, the second and third of Luke, and the third of John. The first issue to be answered is this: Who is the second accuser? And then the third accuser needs to be identified.

The second accuser is not the same person in all four Gospel accounts. In Matthew (26:71) the second accuser is simply identified a "another" using the feminine form, ἄλλη. This would indicate another servant girl. Mark (14:69), having identified the first accuser as "one of the maid servants of the chief priest," identifies the second accuser as "the maid servant" (ἡ παιδίσκη), and so concurs essentially with Matthew. Luke (22:58) identifies the second accuser as "another" (ἕτερος), using the masculine form of the word that indicates a different person from the first accuser who is to be understood as a male. This is even more evident when we consider Peter's response in which he begins his denial with the vocative form of "man" (ἄνθρωπε). In contrast, when he responded to the first accuser in Luke (22:57), he addressed her as "woman" (γύναι). In John (18:25) this accuser is anonymous, being simply identified with "he/she said" (third person singular aorist verb). Thus, without Luke's description we might assume the second accuser was simply another servant girl.

The third accuser in all four accounts appears to be someone from a group of servants. Matthew (26:73) and Mark (14:70) simply identify a group accusing Peter. Luke identifies "another" (μῖας ἄλλος τις) with a feminine form of the numeral one, the masculine form for "another" (ἄλλος), and the term for "someone" (τις) which is both masculine and feminine in form. But, for a second time in Luke, Peter answers with the vocative form of "man" in his denial, indicating that the questioner was masculine. John (18:26) identifies the third accuser as a relative of the one whose ear was cut off, and uses the masculine form of the numeral one when he says, "one of the servants of the high priest."

Without Luke's details we might assume just three denials. With Luke's details Cheney's argument is strengthened and the need for six denials becomes apparent. The only way to effectively avoid six denials would be to see Luke inverting the order of people questioning Peter. Then Luke's third accuser would be everyone else's second accuser. This does not seem likely, especially in light of Peter's identifying his questioners' sexes each time.

Therefore, it seems best to harmonize the data and recognize that Peter did indeed deny Jesus six times, three times before the first cock crowing and three times again before the second. How does this effect the question of the historical accuracy of the accounts and the inerrancy of Scripture. Two of Cheney's comments are worth quoting concerning this. He notes that the different datum contained in the reports of the evangelists "demonstrates both the absence of collusion on the part of the human authors and the divine guidance of the One Who knows all the facts to make the four accounts fit as one." When two sets of three denials are seen, all the data fit well without conflict. He notes further, "What the writers did relate, under the Spirit's inspiration, fulfilled their individual purposes and preserved the absolute integrity of the accounts" (220). None of the writers was obligated to report all six denials. In each of their cases, three denials were sufficient to communicate the message of Peter's failure. They never claimed to give every detail of every event. That is not the purpose of any of the Gospels. Rather, each selected the information necessary to communicate their truths. In each case, three denials sufficed to accomplish that goal. Yet, in the process they remembered or learned of different portions of the evening's discussion and events that they chose to incorporate into their accounts. We can know with certainty that everything reported indeed happened. Many more things were said and done, even in the last evening before Jesus' arrest, than have been reported to us.

10 As F. F. Bruce (*The Gospel of John*, 340) notes, the Greek words used to describe the group who came to arrest Jesus include the term σπεῖρα, the technical term equivalent to the Latin word for "cohort," which was used only of Roman soldiers and not of the temple police. From this information he notes, "The fact that Roman troops were there as well as temple police implies that the Jewish authorities had already approached the military command, probably indicating that they expected armed resistance to be offered. That it was the Jewish authorities and not the Romans who took the initiative is shown by the fact that, after the arrest, the Jewish authorities were allowed to take Jesus into their custody."

11 Segovia ("The Structure, *Tendenz*, and *Zitz im Leben* of John 13:31-14:31," 482) correctly notes, "These two imperatives—and specially the second one—govern the entire main body of the discourse: this is a message of comfort and, above all, a demand for full belief."

12 A. W. Tozer, *The Knowledge of the Holy* (New York: Harper and Brothers, 1961), 10.

13 Leon Morris (*The Gospel According to John*, NICNT [Grand Rapids: Wm. B. Eerdmans Publishing Company, 1971], 638) responds to the ambiguity and difficulty of interpreting this sentence by observing, "Perhaps we have here another example of John's habit of using expressions which can be understood in more ways than one, with a view to calling to mind what each means." First, we need to remember that these are the words of Jesus as John recalls them under inspiration of the Holy Spirit and in fulfillment of Jesus' promise in 14:26 that the Spirit would bring to their remembrance all that He said to them. The use of ambiguous statements that call for clarification is a favorite teaching technique of Jesus, as we will see as we continue through this discourse. Thus, ambiguity was intended by Jesus that evening as He taught His men, not just by John later as he recorded his message.

14 Carson (*The Gospel According to John*, 488) notes that the old Latin manuscripts took the two "believes" as imperatives. Westcott (*The Gospel According to St. John*, 200) goes with the double imperative as well. He argues that the changed order of the object "marks the development of the idea" and

that this belief "is 'in Christ' and not in any propositions about Christ."

15 The KJV mistakenly has "many mansions" rather than many rooms. The Greek term, μονή, is more neutral and carries only the connotation of a place to live. NKJV correctly uses "dwelling places."

16 Cook, *The Theology of John*, 229.

17 Carson (*The Farewell Discourse and Final Prayer of Jesus,* 24) describes Jesus' return to His Father's house as a "redemptive journey" which is the means of preparing the place for His disciples. Thus when Jesus says He goes to prepare a place for them, He is saying that the way is via the cross (26). He also says (*The Gospel According to John*, 488) that "in the context of Johannine theology, it is the going itself, via the cross and resurrection, that prepares the place for Jesus' disciples." Though this may be true, the redemptive aspect is not in view when Jesus is saying these things. This is consistent with a justification focused soteriological interpretation of Jesus' words, but is not Jesus' intention at all. The cross is not even implied before verse four. At this point, Jesus is focusing on the fact of His departure, not the means. Further, He is talking to His men who have not been through His crucifixion and resurrection yet and so would not be inclined to understand the terms as symbolic of Jesus' coming work on the cross. Yes, the Holy Spirit will teach them many things in the future, but Jesus is talking to them in the present. And His words must have meaning and bring comfort to them at that point in time. We need to resist our tendency to read future events into the experience of the disciples. This is the same problem as those who read the cross into 13:34, "as I have loved you." How had He loved them? By washing their feet! That is, by doing for them what they could have done and did not.

18 Laney, *John*, 254.

19 Dana and Mantey, *A Manual Grammar of the Greek New Testament*, 185.

20 Beasley-Murray, *Word Biblical Themes: John*, 92.

21 E. W. Hengstenberg, *Commentary on the Gospel of St. John*, Vol. 2, Translated from the German (Minneapolis: Klock & Klock Christian Publishers, Inc.; 1980 reprint of the original 1865 publication by T & T Clark), 189-91.

22 Cook, *The Theology of John*, 159. Amillennialists see this as a reference to His second advent, but not for the establishment of His Messianic kingdom, but as a prelude to the Great White Throne judgment and entrance into the eternal state. For example, William Hendricksen (*Exposition of the Gospel According to John*, New Testament Commentary [Grand Rapids: Baker Book House, 1953], 266) sees this as a reference to Jesus' "second advent." Though

premillennial, Morris (*The Gospel According to John*, 639) also sees this as a "reference to the second advent." Carson (*The Gospel According to John*, 488) notes that "the language used of Jesus' 'coming back' and 'being with' his disciples refers at various places in these chapters to different things: sometimes to Jesus' return to his disciples after his resurrection, sometimes to Jesus' 'coming' to them by the Spirit after he has been exalted to the glory of the Father, and sometimes to his 'coming' at the end of the age." Noting that the language of the verse is ambiguous, he still concurs with Cook and says, "The details of the text argue that these two verses refer to the second advent of Jesus, when he comes to take his followers to be with him forever." Westcott (*The Gospel According to St. John,* 201), on the other hand, sees Jesus intending a multitude of meanings in that one promise. He says, "But though the words refer to the last 'coming' of Christ, the promise must not be limited to that one 'coming' which is the consummation of 'comings.' Nor again must it be confined to the 'coming' to the Church on the day of Pentecost, or to the 'coming' to the individual either at conversion or at death, though these 'comings' are included in the thought. Christ is in fact from the moment of His Resurrection ever coming to the world and to the Church, and to men as the Risen Lord. . . . This thought is expressed by the use of the present *I come* as distinguished from the future *I will come*, as of one isolated future act. The 'coming' is regarded in its continual present, or, perhaps it may be said, eternal reality. . . . Side by side with this constant coming, realized through the action of the Holy Spirit in the life of the Church (v. 26), is placed the personal, historical, reception of each believer (*I will take you to myself*) fulfilled through death" (italics his).

[23] Laney, *John*, 255. Though some of the early manuscripts of the New Testament do not contain the final phrase, "and the way you know," the majority do, and it makes better sense in light of the immediate context (what follows). Richard ("Expressions of Double Meaning and Their Function in the Gospel of John," 98) sees this as another example of the use of double meaning involving "ambiguity leading to misunderstanding" which in turn leads to further clarification and teaching by Jesus.

[24] The chronology of these statements by Jesus is based on Cheney's chronology in *The Life of Christ in Stereo*, now available in *Jesus Christ: The Greatest Life Ever Lived*, Compiled and translated by Johnston M. Cheney and Stanley Ellisen (Eugene, OR Paradise Publishing Inc., 1999).

Chapter Six

[1] Mitchell, *An Everlasting Love*, 268-69.

[2] Carson, *The Gospel According to John*, 490.

3 F. F. Bruce, *The Gospel of John,* 298.

4 Cook, *The Theology of John*, 56.

5 F. F. Bruce, *The Gospel of John,* 299.

6 Interestingly, though he recognizes this principle, Carson (*The Gospel According to John*, 491) still sees the context of Thomas' question making "truth" and "life" supportive ideas. Thus, "Jesus is the way to God, precisely because he is the truth of God . . . and the life of God."

7 Laney, *John*, 256.

8 The various scholars differ on its meaning. For Calvin (*Commentary on the Gospel According to John,* 2:85) this is another justification truth and Jesus' use of truth "means here the perfection of faith, as *the way* means its beginning and first elements." Laney (*John*, 256) also says, "God's redemptive truth has its ultimate realization in and through the Person of Christ (1:17). . . . This truth is not something to be contemplated, but a divine reality to be embraced and lived." For Morris (*The Gospel According to John*, 641) this term also has "saving significance" and points not only to "Jesus' utter dependability, but also to the saving truth of the gospel."

9 David J. Hawkin ("The Johannine Concept of Truth and its Implications for a Technological Society," *The Evangelical Quarterly*, 59:1 [January, 1987]: 10) understands Jesus to be affirming that He is the truth in the Hebrew moral sense rather than the Greek philosophical sense. Here "truth is not 'the reality of the divine', nor is it the goal. Its sense is perhaps best given by reference to the *Acts of Thomas*, where Christ is 'the richness of truth', he who 'mounts the way to truth', 'the teacher of truth'. This guides the exegesis of Jn. 14:6—Jesus is ἡ ἀλήθεια as 'perfect revealer', as 'plenitude' of revealed truth. Thus ἀλήθεια in the Fourth Gospel is not 'an object of intellectual research, but the essential principle of the moral life, of sanctity; for it is the thought of God on man perceived and heard in faith.'"

10 In Hebrews 12:2 we are commanded to look "unto Jesus, the author and finisher of *our* faith" while laying aside the weights of sin and running the race of our lives with endurance. The term for "look," ἀφοράω, carries the sense of "looking away from everything and everyone else" to Jesus (cf. 2 Cor 3:18). It communicates the sense of looking intently and *trustingly* at someone or something (BAGD, "ἀφοράω"). It speaks of our need to be "focused" on Jesus and Him alone. In this verse, Jesus, as the truth, is to be a similar focus for us.

11 There are three major terms for "life" in Greek, ζωή, ψυχή, and βίος. Though ζωή can mean life in the physical sense (Rom 8:38; 1 Cor 3:22; Phil 1:20), it is most often used of the life belonging to God and is experienced by

believers. It is something experienced. On the other hand ψυχή designates physical life and the human soul as the seat of the inner person and of the feelings rather than an experience of life. Βίος was used to describe life in terms of its functions and duration, its conduct, and came to be used also to designate one's possessions. Thus, the three terms, though they may each be translated "life," designate three distinct aspects of meaning (BAGD).

12 Cook, *The Theology of John*, 92.

13 His use of δι' ἐμοῦ involves the idea of agency. He is the agent through whom one comes to God.

14 In the original manuscripts the two words translated in the NKJV (and the other major translations) as "from now on" could also be the spelling for a single word "assuredly." This is because in the original Greek manuscripts the writers did not leave spaces between words and so, if split apart (ἀπ' ἄρτι), they could spell two words which we translate as "from now on." If left together (ἀπαρτι), they would spell the word, "assuredly." The context of what Jesus is saying fits better with the sense of "from now on" rather than "assuredly." He is telling them that, though up to that point they have remained at least partially ignorant of who He is, they shall now have a fuller understanding following His instruction and the things He is about to undergo (cf. 15:3, 5). Note also Jesus' lesson to Peter and the others in John 18:11 (cf. Matt 26:52-53).

15 See Appendix 3, "Knowing God," for a discussion of the significance and use of οἶδα and γινώσκω in the upper room. Ἐπιγινώσκω, a synonym of γινώσκω, is not used by Jesus in the upper room, nor by John in his Gospel.

16 This is a second-class conditional sentence. In 14:2 Jesus had used a third class conditional construction which allowed the "if" clause (protasis) to be either true or false, with the "then" clause (apodosis) being either true or false on the basis of the truth or falsehood of the protasis. In the second-class conditional sentence, the protasis is assumed to be false, as is the apodosis.

17 Unlike English, where word order is rather fixed, Greek sentence construction allows for moving key words around in order to emphasize or to draw attention to them. Thus in this verse, Jesus says, εἰ ἐγνώκατέ με, καὶ τὸν πατέρα μου γνώσεσθε· καὶ ἀπ' ἄρτι γινώσκετε αὐτὸν καὶ ἑωράκατε αὐτόν.

18 Laney (*John*, 256) places significance on Jesus' use of γινώσκω for "know" rather than οἶδα here. He sees Jesus saying that the disciples "knew Jesus, but not in the fullest sense of His messianic Person and work." This is true, but probably not the reason Jesus chose the one term over the other. Rather, He appears to be focusing their attention on the experiential aspect of knowledge. This is evident in what He says following His negative affirmation, that they did not know either Him or the Father.

19 The term Jesus uses here is ἑωράκατε, from ὁράω, meaning, "to see, catch sight of, notice," with the sense of perception (BAGD, 577). But, His use here involves more than mere physical seeing. For that sense Jesus would have used βλέπω. Though both terms can be used for either physical sight or perception, βλέπω has the dominant sense of physical sight and ὁράω is used more to express the idea of perception and understanding (BAGD, 143; Michaelis, TDNT, s.v. "ὁράω," 5:340-44).

20 Laney, *John*, 257.

21 Gruenler, *The Trinity in the Gospel of John*, 97.

22 John MacArthur, Jr. (*Comfort for Troubled Hearts* [Chicago: Moody Press, 1986], 29) describes Philip as "a faithless disciple who wants sight to substitute for faith. He wanted Jesus to back up what He was saying with full visible proof. . . . His belief that Jesus was God and his security were dependent on sight." Rather, let us not mistake difficulty at understanding Jesus and the honesty to question Him as a lack of faith. These men are clearly attempting to comprehend what Jesus is saying to them. And, as is evident in their candid comments, they feel free to interact and ask questions which they believe will lead them to the point Jesus is making. Jesus uses ambiguous statements and confusion as an essential part of His teaching technique, a technique the disciples were likely to be used to by this time. And so it is likely that they were consciously "biting the bait" in their attempt to dialogue with Jesus and to arrive at an understanding of what He was saying. Thus Philip's request would be neither arrogant nor unbelieving but, rather, honest. Later Jesus Himself explains that He has only progressively made Himself and His plans known to them. cf. John 15:15. Thus, it is not a matter of faith but knowledge.

23 In Hebrews 1:3 Jesus is described as the "brightness of His glory" and the "express image of His person." The idea is similar to the concept that the ray of sun is of same character as the sun.

24 Γινώσκω, though a synonym of οἶδα, carries the added sense of experiential knowledge rather than intuitive knowledge (as of just facts). To know someone or something in this sense is to have experience with them. It is not knowledge gained from a book, but from life, from personal exposure. See Appendix 3, "Knowing God," for a further discussion of the two terms.

25 Dillow, *The Reign of the Servant Kings*, 164.

26 Carson, *The Gospel According to John*, 494.

27 MacArthur, Jr., *Comfort for Troubled Hearts*, 30.

28 Mitchell, *An Everlasting Love*, 271.

29 Carson, *The Gospel According to John*, 494.

[30] Gruenler, *The Trinity in the Gospel of John,* 98.

[31] Calvin, *Commentary on the Gospel According to John,* 2:87, (italics his).

[32] In assessing Jesus' instructions at this point, MacArthur (*Comfort for Troubled Hearts,* 31) pursues the "faith" issue again and says, "Philip asked for visual evidence, and Jesus told him to have faith." He criticizes the disciples with this analysis. "After three years with Jesus, Philip—and perhaps the other disciples—didn't have sufficient faith to settle their troubled hearts just by believing. They had to have a visible sign." Though at times Jesus condemned the Jews for asking for signs, John states in John 20:30-31 that Jesus did the signs so that people would believe. Again, the problem with the disciples is not a lack of faith, but of understanding. They clearly believe in Jesus. That is evident by their presence in that particular room on that particular night in spite of the departures of other disciples and in spite of harassment from the Jewish leadership. They do not doubt that Jesus is their long awaited Messiah. They are just unable to decipher the meaning and significance of His departure at this time when they truly expect the kingdom to be inaugurated. These men have faith, even though it may be immature or limited. They believe in Jesus and they believe whatever He teaches them is true. Their problem is in understanding, not believing. This is the same approach that MacArthur uses on Matt 13:4. Yet Jesus says it was a matter of understanding in 13:19!

[33] Cook, *The Theology of John,* 99.

[34] Laney, *John,* 258.

Chapter Seven

[1] Laney, *John,* 258-59.

[2] Mitchell, *An Everlasting Love,* 274.

[3] Carson, *The Gospel According to John,* 495.

[4] Ibid., 496.

[5] Gordon D. Fee, "John 14:8-17," *Interpretation,.* 43: 2 (April 1989): 172.

[6] Ibid., 172-73.

[7] Ibid., 173.

[8] Mitchell, *An Everlasting Love,* 274.

[9] Westcott, *The Gospel According to St. John,* 204.

[10] Laney, *John,* 261.

[11] Fee, "John 14:8-17," 173. Carson (*The Farewell Discourse and Final*

Prayer of Jesus, 109) understands this promise to mean that "prayer in Jesus' name is: (1) prayer in accord with all that name stands for; (2) prayer that seeks God's glory (cf. 15:8); and (3) prayer which is consciously uttered under Christ's lordship, much as baptism in Jesus' name signifies in part coming under Christ's lordship."

12 Glory, δόξα, is a well-worn word, often misunderstood. It can be used for "brightness, splendor, radiance," in the sense of visible "glory," or, as we would say, something being "glorious" (1 Cor 15:40-41). It may also be used in the sense of "fame, renown, honor" (1 Cor 15:43). The plural form of the word is used to depict offices and honors as well as the beings (sometimes angelic) who hold those offices and have that honor (2 Pet 2:10 and Jude 8). (BAGD, s.v. "δόξα") Jesus uses it with both senses of radiance and fame. The verbal form of the word, δοξάζω, can carry both the sense of praising, honoring, magnifying, or of clothing in splendor.

13 There is an inclusio from 13:35 to 15:17 and also from 13:35 to 15:18 that serves to focus our attention on these issues.

14 A textual problem occurs which could effect one's interpretation of this verse. In some manuscripts "Me" is included after "ask" and so Jesus says, "If you ask *Me* anything in My name, I will do it." Thus Morris (*The Gospel According to John,* 647), after accepting the inclusion of "me" concludes, "Prayer may be addressed to the Son as well as to the Father." But, the majority of manuscripts, including all of the Byzantine, do not include "me." And, looking at the verse within its context, it is better to go with the NKJV and not to include it. Thus, we are asking God the Father in the name of Jesus the Son.

15 This is another third class conditional sentence. In these sentences the "if" clause may or may not be true and the "then" clause is then true or false depending on the "if" clause.

16 Jesus use of τὰς ἐμάς is emphatic. What He is saying is, "I mean *My* commandments."

17 A textual problem found between various early manuscripts containing this verse has to do with whether "keep" is in the future indicative (τηρήσετε) or aorist imperative (τηρήσατε). As can be seen, there is but a single letter difference between the two words. If it is in the future indicative, then Jesus is saying, "If you love me (and you may or may not), then you *will* keep My commandments." In other words, keeping His commandments will be evidence that they (we) love Him. If it is in the aorist imperative, then Jesus is saying, "If you love me (and you may or may not), then *start keeping* My commandments." In other words, our love for Him obligates us to keep His commandment.

Carson (*The Gospel According to John*, 498) is an example of someone who considers the future indicative rather than the aorist imperative to be the correct reading of the verse. Westcott (*The Gospel According to St. John,* 205) sees the true reading to be "you will keep" and says, "The imperative reading gives a false turn to the thought. Love carries with it practical devotion, and this calls out the intercession of the Lord; or, in other words, love for Christ finds practical expression in love for the brethren, which is His commandment." Thus he sees love being such a compelling force that a command would not be necessary. Laney (*John*, 260), too, reflects this understanding and says: "The one who truly loves (*agapaō*) Christ will demonstrate it by obedience" (keeping His commandment). Also, "The authenticity of our love for Christ is measured by our obedience to His will" (261). This interpretation seems to anticipate Jesus' words in verse 21 where Jesus does say that obedience demonstrates love.

Though the UBS sides with the future indicative form, the majority of manuscript evidence, including an essentially unified Byzantine text as well as ample representation from the Alexandrian texts, indicates that the aorist imperative is the best rendering, as is reflected in the New King James. If love compelled keeping His command, then the future indicative would have been appropriate and Jesus would have been saying that our keeping of His command would prove our love. The future indicative would create a cause-effect relationship between love and obedience. Interestingly, He does say that in verse 21, but not here. It is probable that the change in the text occurred because some Alexandrian scribe was trying to make the two verses "agree." In contrast, the aorist imperative creates a reason-response relationship between love and obedience. Love is the reason we obey, our motive.

[18] Third class conditional sentence. "If 'A' is true (and it may or may not be true) . . . then 'B' would be true too."

[19] Morris, *The Gospel According to John*, 655.

[20] BAGD, 618.

[21] J. Behm, "παράκλητος," in *Theological Dictionary of the New Testament* (Grand Rapids: William B. Eerdmans Publ. Co., 1967), 5:803-14.

[22] Mitchell, *An Everlasting Love*, 276.

[23] Specifically, verse ten through fourteen clearly cannot take place unless Jesus first goes away and sends "one corresponding to Him in His stead. In general, therefore, the whole context involves the conditions that could be expected to prevail after Jesus' crucifixion, resurrection, and ascension" (Dwight Hunt, "Jesus' Teaching Concerning the Paraclete in the Upper Room Discourse," Th.M. Thesis, Western Conservative Baptist Seminary, April 1981, 34-35).

24 As Dwight Hunt ("Jesus' Teaching Concerning the Paraclete in the Upper Room Discourse," 35) notes, "The crasis conjunction (κἀγώ), conjoining verses fifteen and sixteen, suggests a close relationship between the individual's keeping of the commandments and the Lord's requesting the Father for Him to send the Counselor. The first condition, it seems, for this life of grace in the age of the Spirit will be obedience to the directives of the Lord Jesus Christ."

25 Westcott, *The Gospel According to St. John,* 205.

26 BAGD, 311-12. Richard C. Trench (*Synonyms of the New Testament* [Grand Rapids: Wm. B. Eerdmans Publishing Company, 1960 reprint of the ninth (1880) edition], 145) notes that in the New Testament "our Lord never uses αἰτεῖν or αἰτεῖσθαι of Himself, in respect of that which He seeks on behalf of his disciples from God; for his is not the *petition* of the creature to the Creator, but the *request* of the Son to the Father. The consciousness of his equal dignity, of his potent and prevailing intercession, speaks out in this, that often as He asks, or declares that He will ask, anything of the Father, it is always ἐρωτῶ, ἐρωτήσω, an asking, that is, as upon equal terms (John xiv. 16; xvi. 26; xvii. 9, 15, 20), never αἰτέω or αἰτήσω." He notes further, "It will follow that the ἐρωτᾶν, being thus proper for Christ, inasmuch as it has authority in it, is not proper for us; and in no single instance is it used in the N.T. to express the prayer of man to God, of the creature to the Creator." The only possible exception is 1 John 5:16.

27 Gustav Stählin (TDNT, s.v. "αἰτέω", 1:192-93) says, "Jesus uses αἰτέω only of the prayer of others, not of His own (cf. Jn. 16:26), which is always for Him an ἐρωτᾶν (Jn. 14:16 etc.) or δεῖσθαι (Lk. 22:32), though Martha thinks nothing of applying the term αἰτεῖν to Him too (Jn. 11:22). Perhaps in explanation we might suggest that the basic meaning of αἰτέω is to want something, in the first instance for oneself. When Jesus prays, however, there is no question of His wanting things for Himself, but only for others. Again, αἰτέω might easily suggest a far from humble demanding, whereas Jesus never demands (Schlatter). Again, αἰτέω seems to presuppose a lesser degree of intimacy than ἐρωτάω; hence αἰτέω is used of the requests of the disciples to God, but ἐρωτάω of the requests of the disciples to Jesus, and of those of Jesus to God." This position is strengthened by John's use of ἐρωτάω in 1 John 5:16 for the believer asking God for the life of another believer sinning a sin "not unto death." There he seems to make it a fairly clear synonym of αἰτέω.

28 It is popular among Christian teachers to say that the first term means "another of the same kind" while the second signifies "another of a different kind." But, actually, ἄλλος and ἕτερος are synonyms and little distinction exists between their meanings (cf. Matt 16:14; 1 Cor 12:8-10; Heb 11:35-36). As F. Büchsel (TDNT, s.v. "ἄλλος," 1:264) notes, "If even in ancient Greek it is very difficult to make a clear distinction between ὁ ἕτερος (the other where

there are two) and ἄλλος (another where there are many), since the latter shades into the former and the former into the latter, in the κοινή and the NT this kind of distinction becomes quite impossible." Indeed, there are ample New Testament examples where ἄλλος is used in the sense of "another of a different kind" as well (cf. 1 Cor 15:39-41; 2 Cor 11:4) Still, use in any given context helps us to see the sense given the term there. For example, in Galatians 1:6-7 the distinction is made between the two terms. And so, as Hunt ("Jesus' Teaching Concerning the Paraclete in the Upper Room Discourse," 36) notes, "Though the differences between the adjectives ἕτερος and ἄλλος seem more apparent than real at times, the use of the latter here in 14:16 has a definite purpose. Jesus' followers must know that the paraclete will not be someone with whom they are unfamiliar." Carson (*The Gospel According to John*, 500) argues that Jesus' use of ἄλλος here does not especially mean "another of the same type" because of His use of the term in John 5:31-32 to refer to John the Baptist as another witness along with Himself. Yet, by looking at the context of Jesus' discourse in John 5 it is evident that John is another witness of the caliber of Jesus. Jesus' use of another is indeed similar to His use in the upper room and does not support Carson's view.

[29] Fee, "John 14:8-17," 174.

[30] Carson, *The Gospel According to John*, 500.

[31] Hunt ("Jesus' Teaching Concerning the Paraclete in the Upper Room Discourse," 48-49) argues for a permanent individual indwelling of the Holy Spirit in all Old Testament saints as well as New. He sees Jesus' promise here being "spatial terminology" which relates to their corporate experience rather than individual. The weakness of his view of individual indwelling in the Old Testament is seen in the New Covenant promises and the non-corporate nature of revelation given by the Holy Spirit (He reminded individuals and inspired individuals to write Scripture, not the community of faith).

[32] The weakness of Hunt's ("Jesus' Teaching Concerning the Paraclete in the Upper Room Discourse," 61-62) view referred to previously is expressed he says, "If the Holy Spirit brought about regeneration upon all believers in the New Testament as well as the Old, the fact of His individual indwelling in the Old Testament must also follow. . . . Regeneration happens at the moment when spiritual life is imparted. Indwelling begins at regeneration and continues on beyond that point. . . . Both Romans 8:9 and 1 Corinthians 6:19, 20 teach individual indwelling of each person at the moment of salvation." Both Romans and Corinthians are post-Pentecost and under the New Covenant of Jeremiah 31. God's ability to "keep" people is not a product of the indwelling Holy Spirit, but of His faithfulness to justify them eternally on the basis of their believing Him at some point, as with Abraham. The Holy Spirit's role in the believer as a guarantee of our inheritance (Eph 1:13-14) looks, again, at

God's faithfulness rather than describing a means of producing eternal security. Hunt is guilty of reading the special status of the body of Christ, the Church, into the Old Testament.

Perhaps Hunt goes too far in saying that the Old Testament saints were indwelt by the Holy Spirit in the same way the New Testament Saints are indwelt. The point at issue is the fact that there was no corporate indwelling in the Old Testament as Christ is preparing them for at this point. The actual occurrence will be the very essence of Pentecost. The point is not simply indwelling so much as corporate.

33 Cook, *The Theology of John*, 123-24.

34 Hunt, "Jesus' Teaching Concerning the Paraclete in the Upper Room Discourse," 42.

35 Ibid., 43. Westcott (*The Gospel According to St. John*, 205) recognizes a similar relationship between the prepositions and notes that in this discussion of the ministry of the Holy Spirit, Jesus uses three different ones to "describe the relation of the Holy Spirit to believers. He is 'with (μετά) them.' He 'abideth by (παρά) them.' He is 'in (ἐν) them.' The first marks the relation of fellowship . . . The second that of a personal presence . . . The third that of individual indwelling . . ."

36 Hunt, "Jesus' Teaching Concerning the Paraclete in the Upper Room Discourse," 47-48.

37 Carson, *The Farewell Discourse and Final Prayer of Jesus*, 55.

38 Morris (*The Gospel According to John*, 651) notes that though His first promised return in verse three likely looks at His second coming (which would be the third view on this verse), here "Jesus takes up the thought of a return to the disciples which will meet their immediate need. . . . It is true, as many commentators point out, that He comes in the coming of the Holy Spirit. But here Jesus is surely referring to the post-resurrection appearances."

39 F. F. Bruce (*The Gospel of John*, 330) understands "that day" to refer to "the day when Jesus will have returned to the Father and sent the Spirit to be with and in his disciples," thus to Pentecost. Laney (*John*, 263) and Morris (*The Gospel According to John*, 652) see it as a reference to Jesus' resurrection appearances.

40 Hunt, "Jesus' Teaching Concerning the Paraclete in the Upper Room Discourse," 47.

Chapter Eight

1 The term (ἔχω) used here and translated "has" in the NKJV has a wide

range of meanings. It can mean to have or hold, in the sense of possessing. It can mean to keep, receive or get, to consider or think. It can also mean to be able, to be married to someone, to wear, or to be situated somewhere in relation to somewhere else. These are just some of the meanings, with other variants depending on the context in which it is used. Carson (*The Gospel According to John*, 503) believes that in this passage the term carries the Greek concept of "to grasp with the mind." Morris (*The Gospel According to John*, 653) describes the significance of what Jesus says by noting that to "have" commandments "appears to be to make the commandments one's own, to take them into one's inner being. Jesus speaks not only of 'having' the commandments but of 'keeping' them, *i.e.* to observe them in daily life is more than to have a firm intellectual grasp of their content."

² Morris (*The Gospel According to John*, 653) attempts to avoid the problem of merited love and says, "It might be possible to understand from this that the Father's love is thus merited. But this is not the thought of the passage. . . . This does not mean that He hands out rewards on the basis of merit. It means rather that love calls to love." Westcott (*The Gospel According to St. John,* 207) also attempts to deal with this problem and notes, "the passive form (*shall be loved by*) seems to bring out the idea of the conscious experience of love by the object of it. The believer loves and feels in himself the action of the Father through Christ."

³ Carson (*The Gospel According to John*, 503) rightly observes, "The idea . . . is that the ongoing relationship between Jesus and his disciples is characterized by obedience on their part, and thus is logically conditioned by it. They love and obey Jesus, and he loves them, in exactly the same way that he loves and obeys his Father, and the Father loves him. . . . The groundwork is being laid for the 'oneness' between Jesus and his disciples that mirrors the oneness between Jesus and his heavenly Father."

⁴Westcott (*The Gospel According to St. John,* 207) notes, "The exact force of the word (ἐμφανίζω) is that of presentation in a clear, conspicuous form. . . . It conveys therefore more than the idea of the disclosing of a hidden presence (ἀποκαλύπτω) or the manifesting of an undiscovered one (φανερόω)."

⁵ Carson (*The Farewell Discourse and Final Prayer of Jesus,* 57) correctly notes, "The problem Judas faces is that he cannot imagine how the Messiah, popularly conceived, could show himself to devotees but not to the world; nor why he should want to." He then incorrectly concludes from this that "the real question in the mind of Judas, therefore, concerns the nature and validity of Jesus' messiahship, not the distinction between his coming to his disciples after the resurrection and his coming to the disciples by the Spirit." It is dangerous to guess about what isn't given to us in the text.

⁶ Laney (*John*, 263-64) correctly observes that Judas "was concerned over

the prospect of Christ's disclosure being private rather than public. Like his Jewish countrymen, he expected the Messiah to appear in glory before the whole world, judge the Gentiles, and restore the kingdom to the Jews." But, he wrongly concludes from this that Judas' question implies that he was wandering "why this previously announced plan had changed."

7 The problem of these verses is that they may be viewed in one of three ways. Either they are justification truths, sanctification truths, or are intended as neither. As justification truths, the abiding presence of the Father and Son must mean possessing salvation, with loving Jesus and keeping His word being equivalent to believing in Him. This is another way of saying that those who believe in Him will be saved. Jesus is describing saving faith in terms of what it does, its fruit, and salvation in terms of its benefits. As sanctification truths, Jesus would be addressing only believers, with "anyone" referring to any believer. The believer's love and obedience would be just that, something a believer may or may not do. It would not be assumed to be automatic for believers, thus being commanded by Jesus earlier. Every command to believers in the New Testament necessarily *assumes* that there are believers who are not doing/obeying it and that believers are capable of not doing it and remaining believers. Those things not commanded, like being baptized in the Holy Spirit, are automatic and not contingent on obedience. If *they* do not happen, it means the person is not a believer, not that they are disobedient. Jesus and the Father making their abode with someone describes a blessing which only believers experience. If Jesus is speaking strictly in terms of sanctification truth at this point, He would be describing something contingent for believers and not automatic. He would not be describing positional truths, but conditional truths. On the other hand, it is more likely that Jesus is not discussing either justification or sanctification truths at this point. Rather, He is answering the question raised by Judas, how He will disclose Himself to them and not the world.

8 Carson (*The Gospel According to John*, 498) sees Jesus' choice of the term "word" as significant and concludes that "the plural forms ('commands', *entolai*) likely focus on the individual components of Jesus' requirements, while the singular 'teaching' (*logos*; . . .) focuses on the Christ-revelation as a comprehensive whole." As a result, Carson, et al once again miss what Christ's command is. None of them go back to 13:34-35, the key to the whole passage. This idea is weakened when we realize that He uses the plural form of logos in the next sentence synonymously with commandments earlier. It is more likely that Jesus is using the term here as a synonym for commandments as well and the use of the singular simply arises from it being a more comprehensive term than commandments and includes all of the body of His teaching rather than specific instructions. We should note His words in 15:3, "the word which I have spoken to you," i.e., 13:34-35. In other words faithfulness

to do that command was going to produce fantastic results. The "bottom line" is still obedience to what Jesus has said.

⁹ Carson (*The Farewell Discourse and Final Prayer of Jesus,* 60) represents the justification approach to understanding Jesus' words. He says, "It appears, too, as if loving Jesus, obeying Jesus, and having faith in Jesus constitute elements of an indivisible whole. It is impossible truly to love him without trusting him and obeying him. It is impossible truly to obey him without loving him and trusting him. It is impossible truly to trust him without loving and obeying him. But the one who truly loves, obeys, and trusts Jesus Christ is the one who receives the Spirit of truth and the blessings he brings."

Much of what he says is true, but not his conclusion. For example, Cook (*The Theology of John,* 93, footnote 42) provides a similar description of the relationship between saving faith and obedience in the Gospel of John. He first points us to John 3:36 where obedience is juxtaposed with faith/believing. From this he concludes, "If the antithesis of believing is disobedience, then it follows that faith involves obedience to something. That 'something' is the testimony of God to His Son as found in the gospel (John 5:24; cf. 14:23-24; 15:10, 14; 1 John 3:23). Also, it should be noticed that belief in the Son brings 'eternal life,' but disobedience to the Son even obscures one's vision of 'life' in its ordinary dimension."

With regard to this passage, Carson is correct when he says, "the passage does not concern itself with explaining how a member of the world becomes a disciple of Jesus Christ," though he then makes loving, obeying, and trusting Christ necessary steps in one's salvation, or at least assurance of salvation. In other words, it seems that for Carson, one must *do* something in order to be saved. But, having observed that Jesus is contrasting the community of saints with the lost world, beginning in verse fifteen, he wrongly concludes that the purpose of this passage is to force

> Christians to examine themselves to see if their life is characterized by love for Christ, obedience to Christ, and faith in Christ, and by a deepening awareness of the fathomless depths of God's love; or by worldliness as the fourth Gospel presents it. There is no middle ground, however strenuously we may seek to carve one out. The stark duality confronts us with an unsparing demand for wholehearted commitment. If it declines to comment on such anomalies as the temporary backslider or the believer who remains on a liquid diet long after he should have graduated to solid foods (e.g., Heb. 5:11-14), at least it portrays unambiguously that one is either a child of God or a child of the devil, a follower of Jesus or a follower of the world, a person who enjoys the presence of the Spirit of truth or a person who cannot accept him. All the rest is qualified explanation or lame excuse (61).

As can be seen in this long quote, Carson moves quickly to a justification motif and sees John's motive in including it in the discourse as providing a test of whether one is saved or not. If you fail the test, question your salvation! He also dismisses 1 Corinthians 2:14—3:4 where Paul clearly distinguishes three kinds of people in this world: the natural man (unbeliever), the spiritual believer, and the believer who acts like a natural man ("carnal" believer). Simply because Jesus does not name this third category does not mean it does not exist. Also, if John is being true to Jesus' words, Jesus' purpose for including this must be found. His reason for saying it this way at this time to this group of men is very significant in helping us understand what He meant by what He said.

Though there *is* a contrast between the world and Jesus' disciples in this passage, it is *not* a contrasting description of who is saved and who is not. Jesus is not responding to Judas with a test of whether he is saved or not. Rather, it contrasts the relationship, or lack thereof, that the two groups have with God in terms of their knowledge of Him and communion with Him. Yes, and this is precisely what he will picture for them in the vine and the branches. He is telling Judas both *who* will experience the special manifestation and *why*. Where the world is excluded from experiencing Jesus' coming manifestation of Himself, those who believe in Him, described in terms of love and obedience to His word, His disciples, can expect to experience it fully. Laney (*John*, 264) correctly says, "Essentially Jesus is saying that love issuing in obedience is the necessary prerequisite for His self-disclosure to His disciples. Those who are characterized by loving obedience will be loved by the Father and will enjoy a special fellowship with the Father and Son." This is seen in the details of His promise that follows.

Carson seems to misunderstand both Judas and Jesus in this passage (57). His misunderstanding is expressed in this assessment of the conversation. He says first that Judas' question "calls into question the validity of Jesus' messiahship" and that by this response "Jesus implicitly calls into question the validity of his follower's discipleship." Neither thing is happening. Judas, as noted earlier, is trying to put the pieces of a confusing puzzle together and attempting to understand Jesus. Jesus is taking him and the others to a new understanding of His ministry as Messiah and their place in the program of God (cf. 15:15 "all things that I heard from My Father I have made known to you."). He has not gotten them there yet and is willing to be ambiguous as He puts out pieces of the puzzle for them to muse over. He then uses Judas' question to continue His purpose of instruction and moves beyond it even while answering it.

[10] Cook, *The Theology of John*, 45.

[11] Carson (*The Gospel According to John*, 504) says, "Those who think that the Father and the Son are present in the believer *only through* the Holy Spirit

see the indwelling in this verse as indistinguishable from the gift of the Spirit. Others join with Augustine in thinking that this text coupled with vv. 25-26 argues for the indwelling of the Triune God in the believer (*In Johan. Tract.* lxxvi. 4)."

12 Though God is omnipresent, that does not mean that He is in everything (Panentheism). Omnipresence may be better understood to mean that everything is present to God simultaneously rather than visa versa. Thus Jesus can still be omnipresent while having a human body that can only be in one place at a time.

13 Thus, Westcott (*The Gospel According to St. John,* 208) aptly affirms that Jesus' use of "we" when He says, "We will come to him and make Our abode with him," "implies necessarily the claim to true divinity on the part of Christ."

14 Cook, *The Theology of John*, 230, footnote 34. Even so, Carson (*The Gospel According to John*, 504) sees this as eschatologically significant and says, "However conceived, this is an anticipation, an inauguration, of the final, consummating experience of God after the parousia, when the words of the Apocalypse will be fulfilled: 'Now the dwelling of God is with men, and he will live with them...'" Maybe so, but for the believer today, it is a very practical promise of God's presence in our lives as we walk this earth and await the coming of our Lord."

15 Granted, there are some "tests of life," but these are always directed at the false teachers who were never a part of the apostolic faith (1 John 2:19) and provided as a means of identifying them, not of testing the readers' salvation. In fact, each "test" is followed by assurances from John that his readers are indeed regenerate. For example, the test of 2:3-11 is followed by the assurance of 2:12-14. The warning and test of 2:18-23 is followed by the assurance verses twenty-four through twenty-seven.

16 Laney (*John*, 264) understands the use of the present participle with the negative to mean "the one who keeps on not loving me." This could be a reference to a persistent lifestyle of rejecting Christ and might answer the fear of someone who might feel that a single act of disobedience could cost them their salvation (the Arminian) or indicate they were never saved (the Calvinist). We can conclude that this is a pattern of choice expressed over time.

17 Some scholars who divide the evening's discussion into two discourses, such as Beasley-Murray (*Word Biblical Themes: John*, 93), see these verses forming an "epilogue to the first discourse." There are not two discourses, but a single conversation from Jesus, though this section does crystallize much of what He has said to this point.

18 Hunt ("Jesus' Teaching Concerning the Paraclete in the Upper Room

Discourse," 80) notes that this title for the Spirit (Holy) "occurs only here in John's Gospel. The emphasis here is on the adjective ἅγιον that stresses the divine function of making holy. He is set apart just as Jesus had been before them." This may be reading more into the title than should be there. Rather, as an adjective it describes the character of the Spirit, namely, that He is holy.

[19] Carson (*The Farewell Discourse and Final Prayer of Jesus,* 70) notes that the Spirit's coming in Jesus' name could have two possible senses. Jesus is either saying that the Father would send the Spirit "as a result of Jesus' prayer" on their behalf, as in verse sixteen, or that He would send Him with Jesus' authority in order to act in His place. Laney (*John,* 264) understands Jesus to be saying that He would be sent at Jesus' request. Westcott (*The Gospel According to St. John,* 208-9) differs from Laney and says, "The purpose of Christ's mission was to reveal God as His Father, and through this to make known His relation to men, and to humanity, and to the world. The purpose of the Mission of the Holy Spirit is to reveal Christ, to make clear to the consciousness of the Church the full significance of the Incarnation. Christ's 'name,' all, that is, which can be defined as to His nature and His work, is the sphere in which the Spirit acts; . . . The sense of the promise is completely destroyed if 'in my name' is interpreted as meaning nothing more than 'as my representative' or 'at my intercession.'" It is very possible that Jesus intended both senses in this, especially in light of the things He says about the role and ministry of the Spirit.

[20] Cook, *The Theology of John,* 62-63. Westcott (*The Gospel According to St. John,* 209) concurs with the significance of Jesus' use of the term and notes that Jesus thereby "brings out the personality of the Advocate."

[21] Jesus may have given this promise in a form called synonymous parallelism, a common Semitic approach seen often in Hebrew poetry and wisdom literature. If that is the case, the two ministries are one and the same, a reminding ministry.

[22] Carson (*The Farewell Discourse and Final Prayer of Jesus,* 71) notes the broad significance of what Jesus said is that "one primary function of the Counselor is to teach." From this he draws four implications of Jesus' statement here about the Holy Spirit. First, Jesus' promise here is "meant to alleviate the apostles' fear." Second, "the Holy Spirit will explain things they did not understand at the time they were first uttered" (72). Third, "the Holy Spirit would teach those first disciples the significance not only of Jesus' words, but of the events themselves" (73). And finally, "there is an implicit but unavoidable suggestion that the community of believers will be around for some time. . . . The promise, in short, was for further revelation for an ongoing community; and in this sense the promise anticipated the New Testament canon" (73-74).

Calvin's (*Commentary on the Gospel According to John,* 2:101) interpretation of Jesus' promise basically agrees with Carson except at this last point. He sees Jesus' description of the Spirit's ministry to be that of reminding, but not of providing new revelation *per se*. Still, it is the Holy Spirit who bore along the writing apostles and other authors of inspired Scripture according to 2 Peter 1:21. Gruenler (*The Trinity in the Gospel of John,* 104) notes well, "Jesus is here laying the hermeneutical foundation for a credible exegesis of the gospel material." Carson agrees (*The Gospel According to John*, 505), and expresses well the significance of Jesus' words. "John's purpose in including this theme and this verse is not to explain how readers at the end of the first century may be taught by the Spirit, but to explain to readers at the end of the first century how the first witnesses, the first disciples, came to an accurate and full understanding of the truth of Jesus Christ. The Spirit's ministry in this respect was not to bring qualitatively new revelation, but to complete, to fill out, the revelation brought by Jesus himself." Rudolf Schnackenburg (*The Gospel According to St. John,* [New York: Herder and Herder, 1968, vol. 3. New York: Crossroad Publishing Company, 1982], 83) understands the ministry of the Spirit differently. He says that He continues Jesus' revelation, "not by providing new teachings, but only by taking what Jesus himself 'taught' to a deeper level."

23 Carson, *The Farewell Discourse and Final Prayer of Jesus,* 74.

24 Though any passage of Scripture has but one interpretation, and many passages are directed to specific persons or groups (and so not directed to us today), 2 Timothy 3:16-17 indicates that many applications may be made, based on the truth of an accurate interpretation. The proper practice is to find the principle of the passage or the character trait of God revealed in the passage, and to apply that principle or deduce applications based on God's character. In doing this we may find dozens of applications from a single interpretation based on how that interpretation and its principle of life impacts on various circumstances.

25 Carson (*The Farewell Discourse and Final Prayer of Jesus,* 75-76) sees three dimensions to God's peace. The "first dimension of peace is vertical—peace with God" and the "second dimension of peace in the Scriptures is horizontal: it is peace with men. . . . The third dimension of peace is personal; and that is the peace primarily in view in John 14. This peace is a personal serenity which is not based on an ability to avoid troubles, but on a faith which transcends them." I. John Hesselink ("John 14:23-29." *Interpretation.* 43: 2 [April 1989]: 177) says, "the gift of peace which is offered is the opposite of the troubled and fearful hearts of the disciples. Peace here clearly means the absence of fear and anxiety." Laney (*John,* 265) notes that the word Jesus used for "peace" (εἰρήνη) was used in greetings (John 20:19, 20; Gal 1:3) and as a farewell (Eph 6:23). It was also "used to describe harmonious relation-

ships between men (Mark 9:50; Rom 14:19) and between nations (Rev 6:4)." He says further, "The word 'peace' is also used in the New Testament to describe the spiritual well-being of true believers (Rom 5:1; Eph 2:14; Col 1:20). The message of salvation is essentially a message of peace between God and mankind." Still, though the same word might be used, there is a marked difference between Christ's peace and the world's peace.

26 Carson, *The Gospel According to John*, 506.

27 Some commentators see an eschatological element to Jesus' promise in this passage. Hesselink ("John 14:23-29," 175) is an example of this position and says that "...peace, like salvation, justification, and sanctification, has an eschatological dimension. Here we experience Christ's peace imperfectly; the fullness awaits the life in glory. Yet what Christ promises his disciples here is an assurance, a tranquility, an inner strength which they will enjoy from the resurrection onwards, first in his postresurrection appearances and then more fully after Pentecost." He sees this on the basis of Jesus' use of "a little while longer" in verse nineteen and "at that day" in verse twenty.

28 This is a third class conditional sentence in which the protasis (the "if" clause) is assumed to be false for the sake of argument, and so the apodosis (the "then" clause) is also false.

29 F. F. Bruce (*The Gospel of John*, 306) observes that the phrase "if you loved me" implies "that love involves some insight into the heart and mind of the person loved and some sympathy with him in hope and purpose."

30 One needs to understand whether the work of Christ is being considered or the being of Christ. The former is referred to as the economic trinity, i.e., the Trinity of function or *work*; and the latter is referred to as the ontological trinity, i.e., the Trinity of *being*. Thus speaking of the work of the Trinity, Christ says, "My Father is greater than I." But speaking of the being of the Trinity, He says, "I and My Father are one."

31 Laney (*John*, 266) correctly observes, "Jesus is clearly presented in John as the divine Son of God (20:30-31). Yet in relationship to His incarnation and messianic office, the Father is in a position of authority over Christ. Although coequal with the Father in the Godhead, in His incarnation Jesus became the submissive, obedient, subordinate Son (dv. 13:16; 1 Cor. 11:3; Phil. 2:6-8). Equality and hierarchy are not mutually exclusive concepts." Carson (*The Gospel According to John*, 507) identifies the theological issue that has on occasion arisen from this verse. "My Father is greater than I" he notes "is often cited, out of context, by modern Arians who renew the controversy from the early centuries that is connected with the name of Arius." He identifies the problem we face in understanding this issue as well as presenting a cogent argument in favor of the orthodox faith.

The problem is how to put together that strand of Johannine (and New Testament) witness that places Jesus on a level with God (1:1, 18; 5:16-18; 10:30; 20:28), with that strand that emphatically insists upon Jesus' obedience to his Father and on his dependence upon his Father (4:34; 5:19-30; 8:29; 12:48-49), not to mention John's description of the origin and purpose of the Son's mediation in creation, revelation and redemption as being in the Father's will (1:3-4, 14, 18; 3:17; 5:21-27). It cannot be right to depreciate the truth of one strand by appeal to the other. Arians deploy the latter strand to deny the former: Jesus is less than fully God. Gnostics deploy the former to deprecate the latter: Jesus may in some sense be divine, but he is not fully human. In each passage the immediate context resolves most of the difficulties . . . The *greater than* category cannot legitimately be presumed to refer to ontology, apart from the controls imposed by the context.

Carson (*The Farewell Discourse and Final Prayer of Jesus,* 80-81) notes also, "for Jesus to say that the Father is greater than he is does not prove that the Father enjoys superiority at the ontological level, nor that Jesus is something of an inferior deity. . . . In its context, the statement that the Father is greater than the Son functions as the *reason why*, if the disciples really loved Jesus, they would have been glad of his departure. The argument appears to be something like this: if they loved Jesus, they would want what was best for him. Return to the Father would mean return to the glory he shared with the Father before the incarnation."

[32] Carson (*The Gospel According to John,* 508) understands Jesus' point well. He says, "If Jesus tells his disciples these things now, it is not to shame them but to ensure faith when the events of which he speaks actually occur. Jesus said the same thing with reference to the treason of Judas Iscariot (13:19)."

[33] Westcott, *The Gospel According to St. John,* 210.

[34] Laney, *John,* 266.

[35] Richard, "Expressions of Double Meaning and Their Function in the Gospel of John," 104.

[36] Carson, *The Farewell Discourse and Final Prayer of Jesus,* 83.

[37] Ibid., *The Gospel According to John,* 509.

[38] F. F. Bruce, *The Gospel of John,* 306.

[39] As Laney (*John,* 266) notes "that" is best translated as a purpose clause meaning "in order that" and thereby "indicates that Christ's obedience is

intended to show the world His love for God."

⁴⁰ Carson, *The Gospel According to John*, 509.

⁴¹ Radmacher, "The Word As Truth: Its Authority," in *Celebrating the Word* (Portland: Multnomah Press, 1987), 20.

⁴² Laney (*John*, 267) and Morris (*The Gospel According to John*, 661-62) are examples of this approach. In contrast, though Westcott (*The Gospel According to St. John*, 211) sees them leaving the room at that time, he believes that Jesus continued His discussion as they walked through the streets of Jerusalem.

Chapter Nine

¹ Allegory and allegorization are different. An allegory, like *Pilgrim's Progress* or C. S. Lewis' *Chronicles of Narnia*, purposefully give certain elements of the story symbolic meanings which guide the interpreter to a clear understanding of the author's intended meaning. Leland Ryken (*How to Read the Bible as Literature* [Grand Rapids: Zondervan Publishing House, 1984], 202) notes that the parables of Jesus "are realistic stories, simple in construction and didactic ('aiming to teach') in purpose, that convey religious truth and in which the details often have a significance beyond their literal narrative meaning." Thus, though elements of a parable may signify something else, calling them allegories does not mean that they are to be interpreted allegorically. Allegorization is a method of interpretation in which a meaning other than the literal meaning is sought. In allegorization a "spiritual" sense is understood to underlie the author's intended meaning that we know of as its literal sense. In the allegorical approach every element has some special sense that is in no way connected to the literal meaning of the passage. There is no real correspondence or logical relationship between the element of the story and the meaning the allegorist gives it. To call the parable of the vine and the branches an allegory is to say that Jesus intended certain elements of the story to be understood figuratively, such as the Father being represented by the Vinedresser, Jesus by the vine, and the disciples by the branches.

² At least three interpretations of the passage exist, namely, that the unfruitful branches of verse two and burned branches of verse six represent Christians who lose their salvation, that they represent superficial Christians who never had salvation, or that they represent unfruitful Christians who are cared for by God and then eventually disciplined with death (Charles R. Smith, "The Unfruitful Branches in John 15," *Grace Journal*, 9: 2 [Spring 1968]: 3, 7). The second and third views, both Calvinist, are represented by men such as Laney and MacArthur who reflect the Lordship (justification) view, and Chafer,

Cook, Dillow, and Hodges who reflect the Fellowship (sanctification) view.

[3] I (Earl) shall never forget the event that brought Dr. Derickson and me together to write this book. Among the several hundred papers that were being presented at the Evangelical Theological Society's meetings in Chicago in 1994 was one by Gary Derickson entitled "Viticulture's Contribution to the Interpretation of John 15:1-6." I was really attracted to his presentation because I had come to the same conclusions on John 15:2 as a result of visiting the vast vineyards of Israel in 1973 after the Yom Kippur War.

[4] The section discussing verses one through eight derive in great part from my (Gary) article published in *Bibliotheca Sacra*, 153 (January-March 1996): 34-52, entitled, "Viticulture's Contribution to the Interpretation of John 15:1-6."

[5] Laney, "Abiding is Believing: The Analogy of the Vine in John 15:1-6," *Bibliotheca Sacra,* 146: 581 (January-March 1989): 55-66; and Dillow, "Abiding is Remaining in Fellowship: Another Look at John 15:1-6," *Bibliotheca Sacra,* 147: 585 (January-March 1990): 44-53. Their arguments are generally built from lexical and textual clues, though Laney does refer to present cultural practices. Still, neither refers to any first century data that might enlighten meanings within the text to support their understanding of key terms.

[6] The passage could be interpreted accurately enough with the information provided in the text apart from external historical and cultural data. But, once it is misinterpreted by being taken from its context and external meanings are added, then correcting the misinterpretation may be aided by corrective information from the same external sources being used by those misinterpreting the passage.

[7] In modern times our vineyards have grown in size and the individual notice has probably been lost in most cases. But in ancient times the vineyards were smaller and so each vine could be known by the vinedresser. Even now, vinedressers know their vineyards well and can describe their characteristics in terms of areas and varieties of grapes being grown.

[8] Cook, *The Theology of John*, 57.

[9] In F. J. Huegel, *Bone of His Bone* (Grand Rapids: Zondervan Publishing House, 1966), 105.

[10] When you lift something up you take it "away" from its location. Thus, the term reflects the range of meanings involved in that action.

[11] R. K. Harrison, s.v. "Vine," in *The International Standard Bible Encyclopedia* (4 vols. revised ed. Grand Rapids: William B. Eerdmans Publishing Company, 1986) 4:986. Actually, the problem of this use of the term

is that both αἴρω and αἱρέω are spelled the same way as third person singular present tense verbs since αἱρέω contracts to αἴρει. Thus it is impossible apart from context to determine which of the two root words are being used.

12 In contrast there have been many who have seen this positively rather than negatively. They will be named and their views given below.

13 Some of the confusion caused by modern interpreters can be clarified with an adequate understanding of the viticultural practices of the first century. See note at Appendix 7, "Viticultural Practices in First Century Palestine."

14 Salvation has three aspects to it in a believer's life that are reflected in the three tenses. Justification is salvation *past*, something accomplished once by God when He delivered us from the condemnation and *penalty* of sin, which begins our possession of eternal life. Sanctification salvation is *present*, what God is doing in our lives today as He delivers us from the *power* of sin. It involves our present enjoyment of eternal life. Glorification salvation is *future*, what we will enjoy after God has delivered us from the *presence* of sin.

15 Laney, "Abiding is Believing: The Analogy of the Vine in John 15:1-6," 55; Robert A. Peterson, "The Perseverance of the Saints: A Theological Exegesis of Four Key New Testament Passages," *Presbyterion,* 17: 2 (1991): 108; James E. Rosscup, *Abiding in Christ* (Grand Rapids: Zondervan Publishing House, 1973), 42. Laney (*John,* 270) says that Jesus in this context "is referring to disciples, broadly defined as interested listeners. Some disciples bear fruit, and others, like the 'disciples' who turned away from Jesus' hard teaching (6:60, 66), bear none." Gruenler (*The Trinity in the Gospel of John,* 106) follows this same approach and says, "Abiding in him brings life and fruitfulness to the believer; not abiding in him means death and destruction for the unbeliever."

16 MacArthur, *The Gospel According to Jesus,* 168.

17 Robert Law, *The Tests of Life: A Study of the First Epistle of St. John.* (Edinburgh: T. & T. Clark, 1909. Reprint, Grand Rapids: Baker Book House, 1969), 220; Rosscup, *Abiding in Christ,* 42; J. C. Ryle, *Ryle's Expositor Thoughts on the Gospels,* John 10:10 to End (Grand Rapids: Zondervan Publishing House, n.d.), 328; Smith, "The Unfruitful Branches in John 15," 13-14.

18 Proponents of this view include James M. Boice, Lewis S. Chafer, W. Robert Cook, Joseph Dillow, Zane Hodges, John G. Mitchell, A. W. Pink, and Charles C. Ryrie to name a few. As we have stated, salvation is a very broad term that includes physical and spiritual deliverance. For the believer it has past, present, and future aspects. In the past we were justified, and thereby delivered from the power, dominion, guilt, and condemnation of sin. We were

made alive to God without cost by the regenerating work of the Holy Spirit in us after God the Father declared us righteous by imputing our sin to Christ and His righteousness to us.

In the present we are also experiencing salvation. We are being delivered from the power of sin here and now. At the same time God is at work in our lives, conforming us to the image of Christ through a process we call "sancti-fication," the believer is at work obeying the commands of Jesus that bring His love and manifestation in our lives (John 14:15-24). Sanctification is the phase of salvation a believer experiences in this life as God prepares him for the life to come. In sanctification the believer experiences all the benefits of his justification and "works" (Eph 2:10) to bring his life (experience) into con-formity with his position in Christ. The Holy Spirit is at work conforming us to Christ as He prepares us to spend eternity with God in heaven.

The final phase of salvation is our coming glorification, when God's work in us will finally be completed and we will be like Christ. We will then be delivered from the second death and enjoy our eternal life that includes both *relationship* with and *rewards* from God forever. Thus it is legitimate for a believer to say, "I have been saved, am being saved, and will be saved." When we discuss various aspects of our salvation, we often need to use other terms than "saved" or "salvation" to describe what aspect of the multifaceted expe-rience to which we refer. Thus in this book we have identified the *justification-salvation view* and the *sanctification-salvation view* in order to make clear what aspect of our salvation the two views focus on in their discussion of this passage. For further explanation see Radmacher, *Salvation* (Nashville: Word Publishers, 2000).

[19] Chafer, "The Eternal Security of the Believer," *Bibliotheca Sacra* 106 (October-December 1949): 402-3.

[20] Dillow, "Abiding is Remaining in Fellowship: Another Look at John 15:1-6," 51-2.

[21] For example, Smith ("The Unfruitful Branches in John 15," 9), after saying that the basic sense of the word is "removal," argues, "Since the con-text must determine what kind of removal is in view, it is certainly not the best method of exegesis to interpret the word in a manner that is contradic-tory to the context. . . . In the context, verse 6 describes the taking away in no uncertain terms as a taking away to judgment."

[22] Hendricksen, *Exposition of the Gospel According to John*, 294-95; Homer A. Kent, Jr., *Light in the Darkness: Studies in the Gospel of John* (Grand Rapids: Baker Book House, 1974), 181-82; MacArthur, *The Gospel According to Jesus*, 166; J. H. Bernard *A Critical and Exegetical Commentary on the Gospel According to St. John*, Vol. 2. The International Critical Commentary (Edinburgh: T. & T. Clark, 1928), 479; Peterson, "The

Perseverance of the Saints: A Theological Exegesis of Four Key New Testament Passages," 108. Representative of the justification-salvation view, Laney ("Abiding is Believing: The Analogy of the Vine in John 15:1-6," 57) identifies "two divine actions" being taken on the branches of verse two. Those that are fruitful are "pruned" (καθαίρω) while the fruitless ones are "removed" (αἴρω). He sees the unfruitful branches of verse two as the cast-out branches of verse six. Judas would be an example of the kind of people who initially identify with Jesus and then fall away and are the ones who, though they appeared to belong to the faith, were in fact pruned out and destined to destruction. He defends his interpretation of αἴρει as "remove" rather than "lift up" on the basis that thirteen of its twenty-three uses in John's Gospel should be translated with the sense of "take away" or "remove" while only eight times does it mean "to take up" or "to lift up" (58). Thus the majority of uses points to a judgmental sense. But, one may ask, when interpreting a word with a range of meanings, does the "majority" rule? No. Context and use determines meaning more than number of uses. Further, in the nearer context of John 17 this same term does not mean, "to remove out of."

23 MacArthur, *The Gospel According to Jesus*, 168.

24 James M. Boice, *The Gospel of John* (Grand Rapids: Zondervan Publishing House, 1978), 4:227-28.

25 Smith reflects the justification salvation approach to the passage and rejects the sanctification interpretation of "in Me" in verse two. He argues ("The Unfruitful Branches in John 15," 10),

> Those who hold that the unfruitful branches represent Christians base their interpretation largely upon this phrase and allow it to determine their view of the rest of the passage. Most commentators, however, have felt that the rest of the passage is so clear that this one phrase should be carefully weighed in the light of the whole context. . . . The familiar technical usage of the phrase "in Christ," as it is found in Paul's prison epistles, was not until many years later. At the time when Jesus spoke these words no one was "in Christ" in this technical sense because the baptism of the Holy Spirit did not begin until Pentecost. When these words were spoken, to be "in Christ" was not different from being "in the kingdom." Jesus' parables about the kingdom being composed of wheat and tares, good and bad, fruitful and unfruitful, are very familiar.

Laney ("Abiding is Believing: The Analogy of the Vine in John 15:1-6," 63), though also taking a justification approach to this passage, invalidates Smith's argument by noting that the phrase clearly refers to salvation (justification) elsewhere in the Gospel of John. Even so, he (63-64) attempts to refute the argument that "in Me" in verse two indicates that the unfruitful branches are believers by making it an adverbial phrase modifying the verb "bearing" rather than as an adjectival phrase modifying "branch." The difference in translations is such that, instead of saying, "Every branch in Me not bearing fruit" (adjectival, "in Me" modifies "branch"), Jesus would be saying, "Every branch not bearing fruit in Me" (adverbial, "in Me" modifies "bearing"). Thus for Laney bearing fruit occurs "in the sphere" of Christ and emphasizes the "process of fruit-bearing" rather than the "place."

Dillow notes Smith's argument that "in Me" is only a general reference to people being in the Kingdom rather than to the Pauline concept of being in Christ since both the present Kingdom and future millennial Kingdom contain a mixture of true and false believers (Smith, "The Unfruitful Branches in John 15," 10). He responds ("Abiding is Remaining in Fellowship: Another Look at John 15:1-6," 45) by pointing out that professing Christians are not in Christ. He says that "it is unlikely that 'in Me' can refer to an 'Israel within Israel' (i.e., the truly saved within the professing company) in view of the consistent usage of 'in Me' in John's writings to refer to a true saving relationship." He asserts that the phrase "in Me" always refers to fellowship with Christ in its sixteen uses in the Gospel (The phrase, "in Me," occurs in John 6:56; 8:38; 14:10 (twice), 11, 20, 30; 15:2, 4 (twice), 5, 6, 7; 16:33; 17:21 and 23.). Dillow concludes, "It is inconsistent then to say the phrase in 15:2 refers to a person who merely professes to be saved but is not." Further, "The preposition ἐν is used 'to designate a close personal relation.' It refers to a sphere within which some action occurs. So to abide 'in' Christ means to remain in close relationship to Him" (cf. John 13:8, Jesus' use of μέρος). Jesus' use of the phrase refers to "a life of fellowship, a unity of purpose, rather than organic connection" which is distinct from the Pauline concept of "in Christ" (46). He argues well from the use of the term to describe the relationship of Christ and the Father and His non-relationship with Satan (John 14:30) that it does not speak of "organic connection or commonality of essence, but of commonality of purpose and commitment." Its use in John 17:21 indicates a unity of purpose rather than organic connection. "If this 'in Me' relationship referred to organic connection, Jesus would not have prayed for an organic connection between Him and believers because it already existed" (47). He concludes from this, "To be "in Me" is to be in fellowship with Christ, living obediently. Therefore it is possible for a Christian not to be "in Me" in the Johannine sense. This seems evident from the command to "abide in Christ." Believers are to remain in fellowship with the Lord. If all Christians already remain "in Me," then why command them to remain in that relationship? It must be possible for them not to remain" (47-48). Westcott (*The Gospel According to St. John*, 217), though not a proponent of the sanctification view, concurs in part when he notes, "Even the unfruitful branches are true branches. They also are *"in Christ*," though they draw their life from Him only to bear leaves.

[26] John 6:56, "He who eats My flesh and drinks My blood abides **in Me**,

and I in him." 10:38, "...believe that the Father is **in Me**, and I in Him." 14:10, "Do you not believe that I am in the Father, and the Father **in Me**? The words that I speak to you I do not speak on My own *authority;* but the Father who dwells **in Me** does the works. 14:11, "Believe Me that I am in the Father and the Father **in Me**, or else believe Me for the sake of the works themselves. 14:20, "At that day you will know that I *am* in My Father, and you **in Me**, and I in you. 14:30, "I will no longer talk much with you, for the ruler of this world is coming, and he has nothing **in Me**. 15:2, "Every branch **in Me** that does not bear fruit He takes away; and every branch that bears fruit He prunes, that it may bear more fruit." 15:4, "Abide **in Me**, and I in you. As the branch cannot bear fruit of itself, unless it abides in the vine, neither can you, unless you abide **in Me**." 15:5, "I am the vine, you are the branches. He who abides **in Me**, and I in him, bears much fruit; for without Me you can do nothing." 15:6, "If anyone does not abide **in Me**, he is cast out as a branch and is withered; and they gather them and throw them into the fire, and they are burned." 15:7, "If you abide **in Me**, and My words abide in you, you will ask what you desire, and it shall be done for you." 16:33, "These things I have spoken to you, that **in Me** you may have peace. In the world you will have tribulation; but be of good cheer, I have overcome the world." 17:21, "that they all may be one, as You, Father, *are* **in Me**, and I in You; that they also may be one in Us, that the world may believe that You sent Me. 17:23, "I in them, and You **in Me**; that they may be made perfect in one, and that the world may know that You have sent Me, and have loved them as You have loved Me.

27 He uses "in Christ" (ἐν Χριστῷ) in Rom 3:24; 6:11, 23; 8:1, 2, 39; 9:1; 12:5; 15:17; 16:3, 7, 9, 10; 1 Cor 1:2, 4, 30; 3:1; 4:10, 15, 17; 15:18, 19, 31; 16:24; 2 Cor 2:17; 3:14; 5:17, 19; 12:2, 19; Gal 1:22; 2:4, 17; 3:14, 26, 28; Eph 1:1, 3; 2:6, 7, 10, 13; 3:11; 4:32; Phil 1:1, 13, 26; 2:1, 5; 3:3, 14; 4:7, 19, 21; Col 1:2, 4, 28; 1 Thes 2:14; 4:16; 5:18; 1 Tim 1:14; 2:7; 2 Tim 1:1, 9, 13; 2:1, 10; 3:12, 15; Phm 8, and 23. He uses "in Him" (ἐν αὐτῷ) in 2 Cor 1:19, 20; 5:21; 13:4; Eph 1:4, 9, 11; 2:15; Phil 3:9; Col 1:17, 19; 2:6, 7, 9, 10; and 2 Thes 1:12.

28 Laney ("Abiding is Believing: The Analogy of the Vine in John 15:1-6," 57) identifies H. E. Jacob, "Grape Growing in California," Circular #116 (California Agricultural Extension Service, The College of Agriculture, University of California at Berkeley, April 1940) as his source.

29 Ibid.

30 Ibid., 60.

31 Hodges, "1 John," in *The Bible Knowledge Commentary, New Testament* (Wheaton: Victor Books, 1983), 888-89. Others who take the "lifts up" view include James M. Boice in *The Gospel of John*, 5 vols. (Grand Rapids: Zondervan Publishing House, 1978) 4:228; A. W. Pink, *Exposition of the Gospel of John*, 3 vols. (Ohio: Cleveland Bible Truth Depot, 1929), 3:337; and John

Mitchell, *An Everlasting Love*, 286-87. George Vanderlip (*Christianity According to John* [Philadelphia: Westminster Press, 1975], 31) notes that in the Gospel of John "life" occurs thirty-two times from chapters one through twelve and then only three times from chapters thirteen to twenty because Jesus was then with His disciples who had "come to possess life and therefore the subject matter of the book advances to other themes."

[32] Hodges, *The Epistles of John: Walking in the Light of God's Love* (Irving, Tx.: Grace Evangelical Society, 1999), 81.

[33] Dillow, "Abiding is Remaining in Fellowship: Another Look at John 15:1-6," 51-52.

[34] Cook, *The Theology of John*, 133-34 (italics his).

[35] Dillow, "Abiding is Remaining in Fellowship: Another Look at John 15:1-6," 50. He lists John 5:8-12; 8:59; 10:18, 24 as examples.

[36] Ibid., 50-51. See footnote 10 for Harrison's discussion on αἴρω.

[37] Ibid., 51, footnote # 17.

[38] Ibid., 51.

[39] Boice, *The Gospel of John*, 228.

[40] Ibid.

[41] Cook, *The Theology of John*, 71.

[42] *Airō* has a range of possible meanings in the Greek. Jeremias notes that its basic meaning is "to lift up," and that it can also have the sense of "to take up and carry" or "to carry off." In the Testament of Solomon 23:3 it is used with the sense of "to lift from the ground" (J. Jeremias, TDNT, 1:185-86). The use of *airō* in the Gospel of John reflects all of these various senses of the term. Following are the occurrences of airw: John 1:29, The next day John saw Jesus coming toward him, and said, "Behold! The Lamb of God who **takes away** the sin of the world!" John 2:16, And He said to those who sold doves, "**Take** these things **away**! Do not make My Father's house a house of merchandise!" John 5:8-12, Jesus said to him, "Rise, **take up** your bed and walk." And immediately the man was made well, **took up** his bed, and walked. And that day was the Sabbath. The Jews therefore said to him who was cured, "It is the Sabbath; it is not lawful for you **to carry** *your* bed." He answered them, "He who made me well said to me, '**Take up** your bed and walk.'" Then they asked him, "Who is the Man who said to you, '**Take up** your bed and walk'?" John 8:59, Then they **took up** stones to throw at Him; John 10:18, "No one **takes** it from Me, but I lay it down of Myself." John 10:24, Then the Jews surrounded Him and said to Him, "How long do You **keep** us **in doubt**?" John 11:39, Jesus said, "**Take away** the stone." John 11:41, Then they **took away**

the stone *from the place* where the dead man was lying. And Jesus **lifted up** *His* eyes and said, . . . John 11:48 "If we let Him alone like this, everyone will believe in Him, and the Romans will come and **take away** both our place and nation." John 16:22, "Therefore you now have sorrow; but I will see you again and your heart will rejoice, and your joy no one will **take** from you." John 17:15, "I do not pray that You should **take** them out of the world, but that You should keep them from the evil one." John 19:15, But they cried out, "**Away with** *Him,* **away with** *Him*! Crucify Him!" John 19:31, the Jews asked Pilate that their legs might be broken, and *that* **they might be taken away**." John 19:38, Joseph of Arimathea, being a disciple of Jesus, but secretly, for fear of the Jews, asked Pilate that he **might take away** the body of Jesus; and Pilate gave *him* permission. So he came and **took** the body of Jesus. John 20:1, Now on the first *day* of the week Mary Magdalene went to the tomb early, while it was still dark, and saw *that* the stone **had been taken away** from the tomb. John 20:2, Then she ran and came to Simon Peter, and to the other disciple, whom Jesus loved, and said to them, "They **have taken away** the Lord out of the tomb." John 20:13, She said to them, "Because they **have taken away** my Lord, and I do not know where they have laid Him." John 20:15, "Sir, if You have carried Him away, tell me where You have laid Him, and I **will take** Him **away**." 1 John 3:5, And you know that He was manifested **to take away** our sins, and in Him there is no sin.

43 F. F. Bruce, *The Gospel of John*, 308.

44 It is interesting, however, that Jeremias (TDNT, 1:185) uses "to lift from the ground" as his first reference.

45 BAGD, 386.

46 E. W. Bullinger, *Figures of Speech Used in the Bible* (Grand Rapids: Baker Book House, 1968), 304. He describes this figure as a repetition of words "derived from the same root," and "are similar in origin and sound, but not similar in sense."

47 Once fruit gets on the vine, the greatest problem is bugs and disease. And a diseased branch *may* be pruned, but not because it is not producing fruit. It would be pruned *in spite of* its bearing fruit!

48 Pliny, *Natural History,* 17.35.

49 Pliny, *Natural History,* 17.35.

50 Richard, "Expressions of Double Meaning and Their Function in the Gospel of John.," 102.

51 John F. Hart ("Does Philippians 1:6 Guarantee Progressive Sanctification?" *Journal of the Grace Evangelical Society,* 9:16 [Spring 1996]: 37-58) notes the misuse of this verse as a promise of progressive sanctification

which is to be culminated in our glorification, when in reality it points to the Philippians' personal involvement in Paul's ministry through giving. Rather than being a promise of God's faithfulness in their sanctification, it promises God's involvement in making their participation in Paul's ministry effective.

52 Cook, *The Theology of John*, 123.

53 Donald Grey Barnhouse, "Chain of Glory," *Eternity*, 9:17.

Chapter Ten

1 This is another third class conditional sentence which assumes for the sake of argument that the "if" clause may or may not be true and that the "then" clause then is true if the first clause is true and false if the first clause is false.

2 The justification salvation interpretation identifies the burned branches in verse six as unbelievers who are destroyed in Hell (Peterson, "The Perseverance of the Saints: A Theological Exegesis of Four Key New Testament Passages," 108). MacArthur (*The Gospel According to Jesus*, 171) is typical when he says "the imagery of burning suggests that these fruitless branches are doomed to hell." Laney ("Abiding is Believing: The Analogy of the Vine in John 15:1-6," 62) points to John 6:37 and Jesus' promise not to cast out any who come to Him as proof that the branches being cast out cannot be believers. But, the Greek terms for "cast out" in 6:37 and this verse are not identical. In 6:37 ἐκβάλω ἔξω is used while here ἐβλήθη ἔξω is used. The use of different terms, though somewhat synonymous, limits the similarity. Laney says further, "Belief is the connection that unites the vine and branches. Without belief there is no abiding. The absence of abiding indicates deficient (transitory or superficial) belief. . . . There is no fruit without faith, and there is no faith without fruit. . . . While Reformation theology affirms that faith alone saves, it affirms with equal conviction that the faith that saves is not *alone*" (65-66).

Laney rejects the idea that burning refers to discipline on believers on the basis that the removal of the branches is "a prelude to judgment, not of blessed fellowship with Christ in heaven" (61). Smith ("The Unfruitful Branches in John 15," 17) concurs and says, "But if these branches be taken as Christians, what can the removal signify? The taking to heaven of sinning believers, as suggested by Chafer, does not remove them from Christ or from profession in Christ. If Jesus wanted to teach the truth that sinning believers may be removed to heaven it does not seem likely that He would have chosen this figure. What happens to dead and removed branches is not good." Peterson and Smith note that when Jesus refers to unfruitful, removed, and burned branches He uses the third person. But He refers to the disciples in the second person. Peterson ("The Perseverance of the Saints: A Theological

Exegesis of Four Key New Testament Passages," 109) concludes from this that Jesus "carefully distinguishes his disciples from the unfruitful branches which are headed for God's judgment."

3 Laney ("Abiding is Believing: The Analogy of the Vine in John 15:1-6," 60, 65) points to the "natural flow" of the context that Jesus is referring to the same people. MacArthur (*The Gospel According to Jesus*, 166) looks to the context and key players, including Judas, to argue for false believers being represented by "barren branches" which are judged. He later posits, "Every gardener understands this principle. Fruitless branches are detrimental to the vine. They take sap away from the fruit-bearing branches. Wasted sap means less fruit. Even after careful pruning these branches will remain barren. There is no way to make them bear fruit" (170). He also points to Romans 9:6 and 11:17-24 to argue, "A person can be in the family tree but not be a true Israelite. Likewise, one can be a branch on the True Vine without really abiding in Christ." He relates the "cutting off" to 1 John 2:19 and the departure of the antichrists from the apostolic fellowship (171). In a similar vein, Ryle (*Ryle's Expositor Thoughts on the Gospels*, 335) argues against unfruitful believers and says, "One principle is that no one can be a branch in Christ, and a living member of His body, who does not bear fruit. Vital union with Christ not evidenced by life is an impossibility, and a blasphemous idea. The other principle is that no living branch of the true vine, no believer in Christ, will ever finally perish. They that perish may have looked like believers, but they were not believers in reality."

4 This is different from the doctrine of eternal security. That teaches that all believers remained regenerate, saved, for eternity apart from any effort on their part because God saves them completely.

5 Dillow, "Abiding is Remaining in Fellowship: Another Look at John 15:1-6," 53.

6 Ibid.

7 The alternate view to this verse, if it is to be seen as addressing eternal judgment, is to take the Arminian position that believers can lose their salvation (justification). Then Jesus would be saying to His disciples that if they do not remain in the faith they will be cast into hell, lose their salvation. Again, these would not be words designed to calm their fears, but to create new ones, especially in light of the failure they are about to experience.

8 Charles Colson, "Wanted: Christians Who Love," *Christianity Today* (October 2, 1995), 112.

9 Westcott, *The Gospel According to St. John,* 217.

10 These are the results in the book *The Day America Told the Truth: What People Really Believe About Everything That Really Matters*, authored by

James Patterson and Peter Kim and published by Prentice Hall Press in 1991.

[11] Much ado is made by some of the significance of Jesus' use of ῥήματά for "words" here instead of λόγος, "word." For example, Carson (*The Gospel According to John*, 517) says, "Jesus' *words* (*rhēmata*) are all the individual utterances that together constitute Jesus' 'word' (v. 3; *logos*)." F. F. Bruce (*The Gospel of John*, 309-10) notes first, "There is no practical difference between Jesus' personal indwelling in his disciples and his words' remaining in them." Then he continues, "The 'words' (plural) here are *rhēmata*; the 'word' (singular) of verse 3 is *logos*. The *logos* is his teaching in its entirety; the *rhēmata* are the individual utterances which make it up. . . . In John 14:13 f. the promise of answered prayer is made to the one who believes in Jesus; the same promise is made here to the one who remains in him and in whose heart his words have a permanent residence." Westcott (*The Gospel According to St. John*, 218) makes the same kind of observation. "The *words* (ῥήματα), the definite sayings, here specified, go to make up "the word" (ὁ λόγος, v. 3)." But, the question must be asked, "So what?" The bottom line is that Jesus is calling for abiding.

[12] Westcott, *The Gospel According to St. John*, 218.

[13] Mitchell, *An Everlasting Love*, 291.

[14] My wife, Ruth, and I (Earl) have greatly appreciated the book by Anne J. Townsend, *Prayer Without Pretending* (London: Scripture Union, 1973), in the careful way that she handles this very important subject.

[15] Various options have been proposed for what He meant, both here and in verse sixteen. The most common options are the fruit of the Spirit, such as in Galatians 5:22-23 and the salvation of the lost (i.e., new believers/disciples). Less common options include the possibility that Jesus is looking back at Isaiah 5 and the issues of righteousness and justice, or that He is referring to the fruit of our lips, i.e., praise to God, as in Hebrews 13. Neither of these last two options appears to have any immediate textual support.

The first option, that Jesus is referring to the fruit of the Spirit, is held by many Bible interpreters. F. F. Bruce (*The Gospel of John*, 310) is an example. "Receiving an answer to the prayer of faith appears to be one form of spiritual fruit-bearing. . . . The 'fruit' of which this parable speaks is, in effect, likeness to Jesus (the same may be said of the nine-fold 'fruit of the Spirit' in Gal. 5:22 f.). Those who manifest such likeness show conclusively that they are truly disciples of his. . . . the faith that leads to union with Christ is the faith that manifests itself in true discipleship, a discipleship of obedience, love and joy." The problem with this view is that its proponents are importing the idea of the fruit of the Spirit from Paul back to Christ, or John. They are ignoring 13:34-35. Secondly, Jesus' description of this fruit as something that "remains" in verse sixteen indicates strongly that He is not discussing attitudes. Also, His focus on His choice of them as it relates to this fruit does not seem to fit the idea of attitudes, though they certainly had not had good attitudes that evening. Finally, when He says "much" fruit, would He be saying by this "many different character traits and attitudes" or "full manifestations of character traits"? The idea of "much" indicates something more measurable than attitudes. Rather, we must note the "they" of verse six and the "all" of 13:35. Loving one another, expressed in actions is an attitude that has had its goal reached, has resulted in an action. It is something that can be seen.

The second major view of what Jesus means by "fruit" is people. Carson, Gruenler and Laney are representative of those who see salvation of the lost as the fruit to which Jesus refers. Carson and Gruenler sees it thus because they see conversion of the lost as the "mission" of the church to the world (Carson, *The Gospel According to John*, 523; Gruenler, *The Trinity in the Gospel of John*, 111). Laney makes the connection because of the analogy of the vine. For them salvation of the lost fits the context better, especially in light of Jesus' prayer in chapter seventeen. Jesus has called them to be "fishers of men," and this is another way of repeating the same idea. He has earlier talked about them doing "greater works" than He. If we view those works in the area of evangelism, then this fits the picture as well. This also fits better with what Jesus will say in verse sixteen. There two key terms, "go" and "remain," indicate an evangelistic mission more than attitudes or character traits. The problem with this second view is that it does not keep its focus in the immediate context. Further, the answer is not found in an "either-or" solution, but both. The fruit of loving one another was the method, additions to the Church was the product.

[16] Laney, *John*, 275. Carson (*The Gospel According to John*, 518) notes "the fruit that issues out of their obedient faith-union with Christ lies at the heart of how Jesus brings glory to his Father."

[17] Morris, *The Gospel According to John*, 672.

[18] Laney (*John*, 276) notes that there is a textual problem among many of the Greek manuscripts where "be" or "become" has been spelled two different ways and so could have two different meanings. One spelling (γένησεσθε) gives it a future tense idea and "suggests that the disciples will become more of what they already are, thus glorifying the Father." The other spelling (γένησθε) makes it a present tense verb of possibility (subjunctive mood) and so "makes fruit-bearing and becoming disciples grammatical coordinates that together glorify the Father." Having identified the two possibilities he then notes that regardless of which spelling someone chooses, "being a disciple means to bear fruit and thus glorify the Father."

[19] Westcott, *The Gospel According to St. John*, 219.

[20] Mitchell, *An Everlasting Love*, 291.

[21] This completes the inclusio of 13:35 to 15:8, proving to the world that they are His disciples.

[22] Carson (*The Gospel According to John*, 510) notes that there are many "intricate" links between verses one through eight and nine through sixteen. He says, "Both sections speak of 'remaining', the first of remaining in the vine/Jesus, the second of remaining in Jesus' love (vv. 4-7, 9-10). Both hold up fruitfulness as the disciple's goal [the ultimate goal actually is evangelism] (vv. 5, 16); both tie such fruitfulness to prayer (vv. 7-8, 16). And both sections are built around a change in salvation-historical perspective, *i.e.* both depend on a self-conscious change from the old covenant to the new: under the image of the vine, Israel gives way to Jesus (*cf.* notes on v. 1), and under the impact of fresh revelation, 'servants' give way to 'friends' (v. 15)." Thus he sees verses nine through sixteen serving as "commentary on the metaphor, a recapitulation of some of the same themes without directly appealing to the metaphor" (511). This is very helpful, especially since this section does not allow for a justification grid of interpretation, but better fits a sanctification perspective.

[23] Cook, *The Theology of John*, 45 (italics his).

[24] Laney (*John*, 276) interprets this as a "constative aorist" and thereby sees Jesus referring to "the action of abiding in its entirety, from beginning to end... The imperative enjoins the disciples to remain mindful of and responsive to Christ's love."

[25] Dillow, *The Reign of the Servant Kings*, 174.

[26] Westcott, *The Gospel According to St. John*, 219.

[27] Carson is an excellent example of someone who understands Jesus' words on the basis of an emphasis on justification truth rather than sanctification truth. In order to square what Jesus says in this chapter with the Reformed doctrine of the perseverance of the saints, the issue of one's salvation must come to the fore. He begins well in his assessment of these verses following the vine-branch analogy. For example he notes (*The Gospel According to John*, 520), "The relationship between the Father and the Son is frequently set forth in chs. 13-17 as the paradigm for the relationship between Jesus and his disciples. The immediate link with the preceding verses is the 'remain' language. Remaining in the vine (v. 4) has already been tied to obedience to Jesus' words (v. 7); now the same point is made a different way." These are good observations. He continues further (*The Farewell Discourse and Final Prayer of Jesus,* 95) and correctly observes that "Jesus does not suggest that our obedience somehow earns his love, . . . Were this the case, the divine love would not be prior; and we know that it is (3:16; cf. 1 John 4:10f.)." He also observes, correctly, "In the context of John 15, Jesus is talking about

his *love for his disciples*, not how they became his disciples. Being a disciple, being an intimate of Jesus, entails certain responsibilities. For a start, it requires obedience: only obedience ensures that the disciple will remain in Jesus' love." This, too, fits well with a sanctification understanding of Jesus' instruction. But then he continues by saying (*The Farewell Discourse and Final Prayer of Jesus,* 96), "Similarly, in the extended vine metaphor of the preceding verses, no branch can bear fruit unless it remains in the vine; and the branch that does not bear fruit is lopped off and burned. Where there is growth and fruit-bearing by virtue of connection with the vine, there, too, is life; where there is neither growth nor fruit-bearing, there is no life. In terms of discipleship, Jesus explains the metaphor by saying, 'This is to my Father's glory, that you bear much fruit, *showing yourselves to be my disciples*' (15:8)." He seems to take demonstrating our commitment to Jesus as disciples to mean proving that we are saved by our fruit.

The basic thrust of the justification/Lordship view is that fruit proves spiritual life and the absence of fruit means no spiritual life, no salvation. Again, this grows out of the theological position that those who are truly saved will persevere in doing good works all the way to the end of their lives because God is doing it in them and God does not do anything imperfectly or incompletely. One's failure to persevere in good works must necessarily indicate that God is not working in them, that they are not saved, because God cannot fail to accomplish His will which includes them doing good works. Thus, Carson seems led to conclude (*The Farewell Discourse and Final Prayer of Jesus,* 96) that, "the text is not telling us that fruit-bearing makes a person a disciple, but that fruit-bearing is the necessary and visible sign that one is in truth a disciple." You do not become a disciple of Jesus by obedience, but prove you are saved by your obedience. For Carson, "disciple" is synonymous with "saint." Every believer is a disciple. Every disciple is a believer. He argues for this by resort to an unrelated metaphor used by Paul, poor hermeneutics. "The vine metaphor becomes akin to Paul's metaphor of the olive tree in Romans 11, with Jewish branches being broken off and Gentile branches being grafted in. But John 15 does not speak of 'grafting' at all. The context does not raise the Jew/Gentile distinction, but speaks of branches *in Christ* that are cut off. Christians (whether Jew or Gentile) are in view" (97). His own recognition of the differences between the two passages is telling. They are not related and cannot be used to interpret each other.

John 15 indeed does not talk about grafting, because salvation is not an issue. Still, he must deal with the problem of the passage, and attempts to fit it into his theological grid. He does this by questioning the accuracy of our understanding of the gospel. He says,

> A genuine resolution of this problem will begin with the recognition that our theology of conversion is probably inadequate. We are

inclined to think that once a person has made a decision, he is saved, and that is that. There is some biblical evidence to support this view: a person who has faith in Jesus Christ has indeed come to experience the new birth (John 3), and the simple instruction to the Philippian jailer should not be freighted down with endless qualifications (Acts 16). Nevertheless, there is much biblical evidence to suggest that a person's spiritual condition should be addressed more phenomenolog-ically than ontologically: that is, more according to his behavior and responses than according to what is going on in his very being. True conversion in the Scripture presupposes some genuine change in what a man truly is; but this does not stop the biblical writers from dealing with what a man says and does. Only God can assess the heart; you and I are left to assess words and deeds (97).

Other than his last statement about God assessing the heart, Carson has just preached assurance of salvation by works. We can know we are saved by what we do! In fact, if we do not do good works, we are not saved even if we think we have made a decision for Jesus. He confirms, in fact, that works are the only legitimate proof that a person is saved when he says that "genuine conversion is not measured by the hasty decision but by the long-range fruit-fulness" (98). He uses the departure of false teachers from the apostolic circle in 1 John 2:1-9 as proof of his point and says "John unambiguously insists that their very apostasy proves they were never true believers." This is true. But John is very clear in that passage that they were indeed *never* true believ-ers. Notice Carson's view. "True faith holds fast till the end." But even more telling, "A person may believe, in the sense that he has come to thorough assent; he may pass all tests a discerning church may offer, and be baptized; he may become a disciple, a follower of Jesus in the sense that he adheres (as far as anyone can see) to Jesus' teachings; he may give his testimony and taste something of new stirrings for holiness because of the company he is keeping. To all who are limited by the phenomenological, that person is a Christian, a brother. He is a branch; he is a seed that is sprouting and growing. But if at that point he rejects the truth, remains fruitless, or wilts before opposition, the biblical writers I have cited concur in this: he could not possibly have been a true believer in the first place" (98-99).

There is *some* truth in what he says. But, there is no biblical statement that a person is saved because they *made a decision to believe*—only that they believed. It *is* possible for someone to fake faith and deceive the church. It is possible for someone to say the right words while not understanding and fail-ing to actually believe in Jesus. No one doubts that. But, to deny that a true believer may falter at times in his faith, may fail to obey the commands of Christ and live in disobedience, is to deny the realities of Peter's experience (cf. Luke 22) when he denied Jesus or the realities of the problems the

Corinthians faced with sin in their midst.

Finally, we can agree with Carson when he says, "as Jesus remains in his Father's love by means of obedience, so the believer must remain in Jesus' love by means of obedience. That is what it means to remain in the vine; that is what intimacy with Jesus entails. Failure at this point calls in question the validity of our commitment to Jesus Christ" (99). We can agree with his first point. And yes, failure should call into question the validity of our *commitment* to Jesus, not of our regeneration.

[28] Morris, *The Gospel According to John*, 673.

[29] Dillow, *The Reign of the Servant Kings*, 534.

[30] Cook, *The Theology of John*, 134.

[31] Dillow, *The Reign of the Servant Kings*, 407.

[32] Carson (*The Gospel According to John*, 521) correctly evaluates Jesus' statement in light of the context of the evening's events and discussions. He says, "The Son does not give his disciples his joy as a discrete package; he shares his joy insofar as they share his obedience, the obedience that willingly faces death to self-interest."

[33] Laney, *John*, 277.

[34] Dillow, *The Reign of the Servant Kings*, 163.

[35] Morris (*The Gospel According to John*, 673) describes Jesus' point this way. "He had the joy of living the completely fruitful life and He wants the joy that He already has to be in them too as they live fruitfully."

Chapter Eleven

[1] These inclusios do not form a chiastic structure, though they may appear to on the surface. This is evident because of the material John includes in his report of the evening's conversation, such as the disciples' questions and Jesus' responses, some of which appear to disrupt the flow of Jesus' instruction.

[2] Remember, an inclusio is a literary device that marks off a section of material by putting "book ends" at the beginning and end. This literary device alerts the reader to look at everything between the two similar, or identical in this case, statements as a single unit of thought.

[3] Moloney ("The Structure and Message of John 15.1-16.3," 45-46) sees a chiastic structure in verses twelve through seventeen: mutual love in verses twelve to thirteen (A), commandment in verse fourteen (B), title in verse fifteen (C), election in verse sixteen "a" (D), function in verse sixteen "b" (C1),

commandment in verse seventeen "as" (B1), and mutual love in verse seventeen "b" (A1). He interprets this to mean, "The commandment of Jesus that his disciples must love one another is based upon his prior loving and entirely unsolicited choice of them (v. 16a). What they are called to be: friends and not servants (v. 15) and the tasks that they are to perform: to bear abundant fruit and to ask successfully for the gifts of the Father (v. 16b) is to be understood only in terms of the prior love of Jesus for his own. It is this love which must shine forth in the mutual love of his disciples, prepared to lay down their lives in love for one another (vv. 12-14 and v. 17)." Further, "at the very centre of the central passage stands an all important message: all that touches the essence of being a disciple of Jesus—union with him, mutual love and sharing his experience of persecution and death—has its source in the disciple's being chosen by Jesus."

[4] Westcott, *The Gospel According to St. John,* 220. The verb form, ἀγαπᾶτε, may be either a present subjunctive or a present imperative. In either case it gives the ἵνα the same purpose sense rather than content.

[5] Westcott (ibid.) notes well, *"This* points backward to *I have loved you;* and *that one lay down* does not seem to be a simple explanation of *this,* but rather a declaration of the spirit and purpose of love."

[6] Morris, *The Gospel According to John,* 674. Laney (*John,* 277) notes that Jesus used a similar phrase in John 10:11 when describing the Good Shepherd, clearly a reference to His coming death, and so sees Him referring to the cross. But, this seems inaccurate to us in the light of John 13:12.

[7] Gruenler (*The Trinity in the Gospel of John,* 110) describes it well, and reflects John's own understanding as was noted, "True friendship is ultimately defined by disposability, the willingness to give everything, including one's life, for the sake of the friend." Carson seems more balanced at this point. He says (*The Gospel According to John,* 521), "At one level, this axiom lays out the standard of love Jesus' disciples are to show to one another; at another, it refers to Jesus' death on behalf of his friends - even if the disciples could not have understood this point when they first heard the words."

[8] Dillow, *The Reign of the Servant Kings,* 105.

[9] Ibid., 194.

[10] Ibid., 325-326.

[11] Laney, *John,* 277-78.

[12] Carson, *The Farewell Discourse and Final Prayer of Jesus,* 105.

[13] F. F. Bruce (*The Gospel of John,* 311) does not see such a change of status occurring. He says, "We should not infer from 'no longer' that Jesus had

formerly called his disciples 'slaves' (*douloi*), or treated them as such. The point is rather that now, in the upper room, he is admitting them to the inner motives of his ministry and impending sacrifice."

14 Gruenler (*The Trinity in the Gospel of John,* 111) notes well that what Jesus says is really a paradox in our way of thinking since "the privilege of being called friends is a result of first being servants. Once the servant has made himself disposable to the Son, he is taken into the confidence of the Family and is accounted a friend."

15 Westcott, *The Gospel According to St. John,* 221. Jesus' use of the aorist tense (ἤκουσα and ἐγνώρισα) communicates the idea that He is referring to His past teaching and that their knowledge of the Father is now complete.

16 Haenchen, *John 2,* 132; Laney, *John,* 278.

17 Mitchell, *An Everlasting Love,* 294.

18 Ibid.

19 For example, Laney (*John,* 178) sees Jesus' use of "chose" as "a strong argument for the doctrine of election."

20 Westcott (*The Gospel According to St. John,* 221) notes that when He speaks of His choosing them, Jesus could either be referring to discipleship in general, or to apostleship in particular in this verse and favors the latter. He feels that Jesus' use of "appointed" indicates more "the assignment of a special post, which here carries with it further duties." Carson (*The Gospel According to John,* 523) agrees and notes, "The verb commonly occurs, with a personal object, in contexts where people are being 'set apart' for particular ministry." This is made more plausible by Jesus' nine-fold repetition of the pronoun "you" (*humas, humeis*) that he sees bringing "out the distinctive responsibility of the apostles" (Westcott, *The Gospel According to St. John,* 221).

21 Laney (*John,* 278) observes that Jesus uses present tense (subjunctive) verbs with the purpose clause to communicate the sense of continuous action. They were to "keep going" and "keep bearing fruit."

22 Laney (*John,* 279) again notes Jesus' use of ἵνα ("that," or "in order that") "indicates that answered prayer grows out of obedience and fruit-bearing." F. F. Bruce (*The Gospel of John,* 312) relates this back to the vine analogy and says that "the promise of answered prayer is made to the disciple who remains united to Jesus as the fruit-bearing branch is united to the vine. United to Jesus, that disciple can plead his prevailing name with confidence in the Father's presence. Jesus lives in his disciples' lives and prays with their hearts and through their lips." Westcott says (*The Gospel According to St.*

John, 222), "In the former passage prayer was regarded as the echo of Christ's own words. Here it is regarded as flowing from the new connexion (*ask the Father*) realized in the revelation of the Son (*in my name*). . . . In the former place stress is laid upon the action of Christ; in this upon the privilege of the believer."

23 Morris (*The Gospel According to John,* 677) sees it looking at all of Jesus' commandments in the upper room, thus looking both backwards and forwards. This leads him to place this verse with the next section rather than seeing it related to the previous paragraph. He observes correctly though (678) that it indicates that all of Jesus' "commandments contained in the discourse are for a single purpose, that the disciples may engage in mutual love."

24 This has the same purpose clause as in verse twelve.

25 Westcott (*The Gospel According to St. John,* 222) sees in this hatred the idea "of a persistent, abiding feeling, and not of any isolated manifestation of feeling." F. F. Bruce (*The Gospel of John,* 313) directs us to the writings of Tacitus (*Annals,* 15.44.5) to see that "the earliest extant reference to Christians in pagan literature charges them with 'hatred of the human race'."

26 The term Jesus used for "you know" (γινώσκετε) can be either in the indicative or imperative. The NIV translates it as an imperative with the sense of "keep in mind." The NKJV translates it as an indicative. Though either translation does not affect the thrust of what Jesus is saying, we feel the indicative is best. Jesus is not commanding them to know something, but telling them what they do know.

27 In John 14:17, 19, 27, 30, 31; 15:18, 19 (five times); 16:8, 11, 20, 28 (twice), 33 (twice); 17:5, 6, 9, 11 (twice), 13, 14 (three times), 15, 16 (twice), 18 (twice), 21, 23, 24, and 25, the term κόσμος is used directly. The world is further alluded to as "they" or "them" in John 15:6, 20 (twice), 21 (twice), 22 (three times), 24 (three times); 16:2, 3, and 9. He also refers to "all flesh" in 17:2.

28 Westcott, *The Gospel According to St. John,* 223.

29 Laney (*John,* 279-80) notes well that "the basic premise here is that the world has a friendly affection (*phileō*) for its own kind, but it hates (*miseō*) those who have turned their back on spiritual darkness to walk in the light. . . . The world loves its own—those who belong to its system, commend its values, and follow its ways. . . . The world hates believers because of the essential difference in nature between the unbelieving world and the followers of Jesus."

30 Morris (*The Gospel According to John,* 679) notes that by His use of the present tense verb for "hate" Jesus "indicates a continuing attitude" of hatred would be directed toward them.

[31] Laney (*John*, 280) summarizes His point this way, "The disciples could expect to have fellowship with Christ in His sufferings and to share as well in His success." F. F. Bruce (*The Gospel of John,* 313) provides us with one of the best examples from the New Testament, namely, Saul, the persecutor of the church. He says, "The close association between his persecution and theirs finds expression in the voice from heaven which Saul of Tarsus heard on the Damascus road: 'Why do you persecute me?'"

[32] Moloney ("The Structure and Message of John 15.1-16.3," 35-37) identifies a possible inclusio from 15:21—16:3, marked by the phrase "These things they will do to you." He sees another between 16:4 and 33, marked by the phrase, "These things I have told/spoken to you." His argument is that "there is a shift in content between 16.3 and 4. Throughout 15.1-16.3 the themes of abiding, love and hatred have been developed. The rest of chapter 16 centers upon the themes of speaking, memory and sorrow which leads to joy." Further, "There is a deliberately contrived inclusion formed by the command to love one another" in 15:12 and 17. "The whole of this central section will stress the theme of mutual love, but it will focus upon the theme stated in v. 16a: 'You did not choose me, but I chose you.'" He then argues, "The final section must, therefore, run from 15.18-16.3. Although the *literary* links between the opening and the closing statements of the unit are not so clear, there is a very powerful link at the level of theme: they both deal with the hatred of the world" [italics his]. The major units as he sees them are: 15:1-11 "dedicated to the theme of the need and the results of remaining or not remaining in Jesus", 15:12-17 "dedicated to Jesus' command that the disciples must love one another", and 15:18-16:3 "dedicated to the theme of the causes and results of the hatred which those who abide in Jesus will generate." Further, "In general terms, one can claim that around the central argument of love there is the positive theme of abiding in Jesus, and its exact opposite, the negative theme of the hatred which such abiding will create." His admission that his theory lacks literary linkage that make the inclusion more apparent is telling. This may be a case where one does not exist even though the words are identical. The inclusion of 15:12-17 is fairly easy to detect and defend. These further ones are more difficult. Still, his observations are helpful and the content of what Jesus says does seem to indicate it is better to divide sections at 16:4 than at the end of chapter fifteen. Also, it is better to see Jesus moving through various themes rather than using these themes to create inclusions. In fact, Jesus is going to use the phrase "these things I have told you" several times in the process of this final portion of His instruction (15:11; 16:1, 4, 25, 33). He is clearly summarizing His teaching and giving them reasons for why He has spoken to them about these issues at that time. But they do not form inclusions.

[33] Laney (*John*, 280) correctly observes, "Rejection of the Son is the same

as rejection of the Father (15:23), and it logically follows that those who reject both will reject Christ's disciples."

34 Westcott, *The Gospel According to St. John,* 223.

35 F. F. Bruce, *The Gospel of John,* 314.

36 It is begun with the negative particle μὴ that calls for a negative response from the listener.

37 Carson, *The Gospel According to John,* 527. He lists Mark 12:40; Acts 27:30; Philippians 1:18; and 1 Thessalonians 2:5 as examples. In Mark 12:40 the term describes the motives of the Pharisees who devour widows homes and then pray long prayers in public and is translated by "for appearance's sake." In Acts 27:30 the sailors were letting down the boat in order to escape on the "pretense" of laying down an anchor. And in 1 Thessalonians 2:5 Paul denies coming to them with a "pretext" for greed. The idea in all of these uses involves conscious deception in which the person is attempting to appear differently than they actually are.

38 Morris, *The Gospel According to John,* 681.

39 Ibid.

40 Ibid., 681-82.

41 And, as F. F. Bruce notes well (*The Gospel of John,* 314), "The fact that Jesus quotes this 'law' as authoritative indicates that it was not exclusively *their* law; the Evangelist, like his Master, accepted it as the word of God."

42 Carson, *The Gospel According to John,* 527.

43 James Patterson and Peter Kim, *The Day America Told the Truth: What People Really Believe About Everything That Really Matters* (New York: Prentice Hall, 1991).

44 He uses δὲ rather than ἀλλὰ in this sentence that still provides a contrast, while connecting what He is saying logically to what has preceded.

45 Morris, *The Gospel According to John,* 683. Laney (*John,* 282) concurs. "In as much as John 14:26 reveals that the Father will send the Spirit in Christ's name, it must be concluded that the Spirit is sent by both. The further statement that the Holy Spirit 'goes out from the Father' was the basis for the decision of the Synod of Toledo (A.D. 589) to add the clause 'and the Son' to the words of the Constantinople Creed (A.D. 381) regarding the 'procession' of the Spirit."
This issue of the procession of the Spirit led to what is known as the *filioque* debate that led, in part, to the split between the Roman and Eastern churches. In this debate the Roman church, and subsequently Protestants,

contend that the Spirit proceeds from both the Father and the Son while the Eastern Orthodox Church sees Him proceeding only from the Father. Carson (*The Gospel According to John*, 529) responds to this debate by saying, "It would be easy to dismiss the debate as much ado about nothing, since it is almost certain that the words 'who goes out from the Father', set in synonymous parallelism with 'whom I will send to you from the Father', refer not to some ontological 'procession' but to the mission of the Spirit." F. F. Bruce (*The Gospel of John*, 316) concurs when he says, "The statement that the Spirit 'proceeds from the Father' has probably no metaphysical significance; it is another way of saying that the Spirit is sent by the Father." Westcott's observation is helpful in understanding Jesus' point and the fact that He was not addressing the ontological issue. He notes that the preposition (παρά) Jesus chose to use "in both clauses expresses properly position ("from the side of"), and not source (ἐξ, "out of")" (224). He notes further that the word translated "proceeds" can either "describe proceeding from a source, or proceeding on a mission. In the former sense the preposition *out of* (ἐκ, *e*) would naturally be required to define the source . . . on the other hand the preposition *from* (*from the side of*, παρά, *a*) is that which is habitually used with the verb *to come forth* of the mission of the Son . . . The use of the latter preposition (παρά) in this place seems therefore to shew decisively that the reference here is to the temporal mission of the Holy Spirit, and not to the eternal Procession" (224-25).

In other words, Jesus does not intend to address the issue argued over in the church. He is simply describing the ministry of the Spirit without getting into the issues of the essential nature of the Godhead. Still, this statement does provide another proof of Christ's deity in that we see Him doing what the Father does and exercising the same authority as the Father (Cook, *The Theology of John*, 54).

46 Cook, *The Theology of John*, 36 (footnote).

47 Hunt, "Jesus' Teaching Concerning the Paraclete in the Upper Room Discourse," 94. He says further, "The question remains, why did Jesus make these statements concerning the co-witness of the Spirit in this passage? The immediately preceding and following passages provide the answer: persecution. They would need to know that not only was the Paraclete within their midst (14:16, 17), teaching and reminding them (14:26), but that He also would provide power for their witness even in the midst of incredible pressure to compromise due to persecution" (96).

48 Cook, *The Theology of John*, 64.

49 Here the spelling of the word can be either the present tense or the imperative (it is spelled the same for both). Thus He is either saying "and you also *will* bear witness" (NKJV) or "and you also *must* bear witness." Carson (*The Gospel According to John*, 529) identifies the two options and then con-

cludes that the change in form "prompts the reader to think that the imperative is meant." One must ask, though, what change in form? The form is the
same in both places. We may have a case here of confusing tense and mode. F.
F. Bruce concurs with him (*The Gospel of John,* 315). "Since the disciples' witness is mentioned in the present tense, whereas the Spirit's witness is foretold
in the future tense, the present *martyreite* may be imperative (as it has been
rendered above) rather than indicative ('you bear witness')." Westcott (*The
Gospel According to St. John,* 225) disagrees and points to 3 John 12 for evidence that favors the indicative rather than imperative. He says that 3 John
12 was molded after this verse. Therefore "the present tense is used of the witness of the disciples, inasmuch as their witness was already begun in some
sense, in contrast with that of the Spirit, which was consequent upon Christ's
exaltation." Carson (*The Farewell Discourse and Final Prayer of Jesus,* 127)
says further, "the coming Counselor, the promised Spirit of truth, will testify
to the world concerning Jesus; *and the disciples will join in that witness.* That
is the reason why they are being left behind."

[50] Laney, *John,* 283.

[51] F. F. Bruce, *The Gospel of John,* 316.

Chapter Twelve

[1] His use of "these things" (ταῦτα) with the perfect tense "I have spoken"
(λελάληκα) looks back to what He has just said rather than forward to what He
is about to say.

[2] F. F. Bruce (*The Gospel of John,* 317) interprets this to mean that, "they
might feel resentfully that they should have been forewarned and conclude
that he had let them down."

[3] Hunt, "Jesus' Teaching Concerning the Paraclete in the Upper Room
Discourse," 97.

[4] F. F. Bruce, *The Gospel of John,* 317. In footnote six on page 221, he
explains, "The Hebrew text of this rewording was discovered among the frag-
ments from the Cairo *genizah*; cf. S. Schechter, 'Geniza Specimens: Liturgy',
JQR 10 (1898-99): 657. It is attested also in an early fifteenth-century
Bodleian MS. But, having been devised to deal with a temporary situation,
the rewording was allowed to lapse when the situation passed. See further K.
L. Carroll, 'The Fourth Gospel and the Exclusion of Christians from the
Synagogue', BJRL 40 (1957-58): 19-32 and (for a different point of view) R.
Kemelman, '*Birkat Ha-Minim* and the Lack of Evidence for an anti-Christian
Jewish Prayer in Late Antiquity', in *Jewish and Christian Self-Definition,* ed.
E. P. Sanders, II (London, 1981), 226-244. See also W. Horbury, 'The
Benediction of the *Minim* and Early Jewish-Christian Controversy', JTS n.s.

33 (1982): 19-61."

5 Westcott, *The Gospel According to St. John,* 226. He says further, "The Midrash on Num. xxv. 13 ([*Phinehas*] *made an atonement*) may serve as a commentary. 'Was this said because he offered an offering (*Korban*)? No; but to teach then that every one that sheds the blood of the wicked is as he that offereth an offering' ('Midrash R.' *ad loc.*)."

6 *Numbers Rabba* 21.4. F. F. Bruce (*The Gospel of John,* 317) notes, "There were some militant Zealots who regarded the killing of an apostate as an acceptable sacrifice to God." He also remarks in note three on page 326 that this attitude was not universal among the Zealots.

7 A problem of the text in this verse, and a reason many place it with the following section, is the presence of the strong adversative form of "but" (ἀλλά) which Westcott (*The Gospel According to St. John,* 226) sees breaking the development of Jesus' thoughts and changing the subject.

8 Mitchell, *An Everlasting Love,* 303.

9 His use of δέ is more as a transition than an adversative. Thus though it is translated as a weak adversative ("but"), it really is just being used by Jesus to change the subject. Morris (*The Gospel According to John,* 695) understands that Jesus' point in using this transition is to alert the disciples to the fact that things are now different.

10 Laney (*John,* 287) suggests that Jesus simply meant, "the questioning was not persistent. Or perhaps the disciples' thoughts were on their own loss rather than on what the departure would mean to Him." He explains this on the basis that "it is most natural, when trouble comes, to think of ourselves instead of others." Carson (*The Gospel According to John,* 533) provides a better solution and says, "In the flow of the argument both in 13:36 and in 14:5, it is not clear that either Peter or Thomas was really asking the question formally represented by their words." Rather, they are raising a protest at His suggestion that He is about to leave them and are expressing an "unspoken question" which is "Why are you leaving me?" He notes further that the "disciples have been asking several questions of that sort; they have not *really* asked thoughtful questions about where Jesus is going and what it means for them." As Westcott observes (*The Gospel According to St. John,* 227), the disciples are so focused on their own loss at His departure that they do not think to ask how Jesus is affected by it.

11 Laney (*John,* 287) understands correctly that Jesus' use of a perfect active verb form for fill "indicates that there was room for nothing else" in their hearts.

12 The first two terms are ἀπέλθω from ἀπέρχομαι that means, "to go, go away, leave."

[13] Westcott, *The Gospel According to St. John,* 227. NKJV translates πορευθῶ, from πορεύομαι, as "depart." The term can be translated as "go, proceed, travel, or journey." It can sometimes also carry the idea of "to go away." It may also imply the sense of going to perform a task or going to a goal (F. Hauck and S. Schulz, TDNT, 6:573). In this discourse πορεύομαι alternates with ὑπάγω as synonyms when Jesus speaks of departing to His Father (575-6). Interestingly, πορεύομαι is used in Acts 1:10-11 and 1 Peter 3:22 to describe Jesus' ascension.

[14] As Carson (*The Gospel According to John,* 533) observes, "The thought is not that Jesus and the Holy Spirit cannot, for unarticulated metaphysical reasons, simultaneously minister to God's people, or any other such strange notion." In fact, Jesus and the Holy Spirit had been ministering simultaneously in the lives of the disciples. Jesus has affirmed in 14:17 that the Holy Spirit had been dwelling "with" them already. Carson sees the reason as "eschatological" in nature in that the coming of the Holy Spirit is a characteristic of the "age of the kingdom of God." The logic of this verse is that the age of the Holy Spirit is the age of Messiah. He must be glorified in order to bring the Holy Spirit. Pouring forth the Holy Spirit is just a proof of the Messianic King. But Jesus is not talking about inaugurating the kingdom at this point. Rather, He is talking about enablement for service to Him by the Holy Spirit.

[15] Mitchell notes well (*An Everlasting Love,* 305) that in this promise "we have the Father giving the Spirit in answer to the Lord Jesus' request. The Spirit is sent by the Son in cooperation with the Father. The Father, heeding the request of the Son, sends the Spirit. Notice the remarkable cooperation of the Godhead."

[16] In John 7:39 we have a parenthetical statement by John explaining Jesus' promise of the Spirit and noting that He had not yet been given.

[17] Hunt, "Jesus' Teaching Concerning the Paraclete in the Upper Room Discourse," 103.

[18] Ibid., 38.

[19] Cook, *The Theology of John,* 76.

[20] Laney and Carson are representative of the first interpretation, that of enlightening and smiting the conscience. Laney (*John,* 288) says that this term "implies a rebuke that brings conviction." He notes, though, that in legal contexts it can also refer to cross-examination "for the purpose of convincing or refuting an opponent." Even so, he understands Jesus to be using it in a non-courtroom sense of simply "awakening or proving guilt." Carson (*The Farewell Discourse and Final Prayer of Jesus,* 139) concurs with this concept and says convict "in this context does not mean 'secure a conviction before a

judge,' but rather 'drive home personal conviction in an individual's heart and mind.' The aim of the Spirit's work is not to produce a guilty verdict—that already stands (3:18, 36)—but to bring the defendant to see the perilous condition in which he stands. That may prompt him to enter a plea for mercy; for only mercy will save him." He notes (*The Gospel According to John*, 534) that in classical Greek this term focused on the idea of "putting to shame, treating with contempt, cross-examining, accusing, bringing to the test, proving, refuting," and that it carried the same focus in Koiné Greek as well. He notes also that of its eighteen occurrences in the New Testament, all involve revealing someone's sin and usually include a call to repentance (Matt 18:15; Luke 3:19; John 3:20; 8:46; 1 Cor 14:24; Eph 5:11, 13; 1 Tim 5:20; 2 Tim 4:2; Titus 1:9, 13; 2:15; Heb 12:5; James 2:9; Jude 15, 22; and Rev 3:19). Based on the pattern of its other uses, he interprets this use of the word to mean that the Holy Spirit convicts the world "in the personal sense, *i.e.* not arguing the case for the world's objective guilt before God at the final Great Assize, but shaming the world and convincing it of its own guilt, thus calling it to repentance" (536). Paul uses this same term with this sense in 1 Corinthians 14:23-25 when he talks about unbelievers responding when the secrets of their hearts are exposed by the exercise of prophetic gifts within the Corinthian church rather than uninterpreted tongues.

[21] F. F. Bruce (*The Gospel of John*, 318) represents this second view. He looks at a different aspect of the word's meaning and use in New Testament times and sees a different kind of convicting ministry. He says, "The Spirit is the 'advocate' or helper of those who believe in Jesus, their counsel for the defense. But in relation to unbelievers, to the godless world, he acts as counsel for the prosecution." He says further, "His very presence will be a demonstration to the world which condemned Jesus that he was in the right and they were in the wrong. . . . This is not quite the same as what is often called the Spirit's 'convicting' work in the heart, leading to repentance and faith" (319).

[22] Morris and Westcott blend the two. Morris says (*The Gospel According to John*, 698), "The Spirit convicts the world in two senses. In the first place He 'shows the world to be guilty', *i.e.* He secures a verdict of 'Guilty' against the world. But in the second place we should take the words to mean also that the Spirit brings the world's guilt home to itself. The Spirit convicts the individual sinner's conscience. Otherwise men would never be convicted of their sin." Westcott (*The Gospel According to St. John*, 228-29) sees Jesus using the term in its widest sense rather than a specific focus. He notes that, "he who 'convinces' another places the truth of the case in dispute in a clear light before him, so that it must be seen and acknowledged as truth. He who then rejects the conclusion which this exposition involves, rejects it with his eyes open and at his peril."

²³ These are all possible meanings when it is combined with a genitive noun as in this instance.

²⁴ Jesus uses three clauses involving ὅτι with the subjunctive that normally forms a purpose clause.

²⁵ Laney (*John*, 288-89) says the preposition is "usually translated 'because of,' 'with regard to,' or 'concerning' after verbs of judging or censuring" and he sees this emphasizing the content more than the reason. Westcott (*The Gospel According to St. John,* 229) rejects this first option and says, "The conjunction is not to be taken simply as explanatory ('in so far as'), but as directly causal; 'because this and this and this is beyond question, the innermost secrets of man's spiritual nature can be and are discovered.'" Thus he holds to the second possible meaning, that He will "convict the world of its sin *because* they do not believe." In other words, He is giving the reason He is convicting them rather than the content of His conviction. This second option is best, especially in light of verses ten and eleven. Carson (*The Gospel According to John*, 537) sees the preposition Jesus chose (*peri*) to tell "what" the world is guilty of with each of the explanations ("because") in the next three verses giving a reason for the Spirit's involvement in conviction. He concludes from this, "Just as Jesus forced a division in the world (15:20) by showing that what it does is evil (7:7; 15:22), so the Paraclete continues this work."

²⁶ Morris, *The Gospel According to John*, 699.

²⁷ Laney (*John*, 290) summarizes verses nine through eleven well and says, "There is a logical order presented here to the convicting ministry of the Holy Spirit in relationship to an unbeliever. First, the sinner needs to see his state of sin from God's perspective. Then, he needs to know that the righteousness of Christ demonstrated provides the basis for salvation. Finally, the sinner must be reminded that if he refuses Christ's provision, he faces certain *judgment*. These verses could well provide a pattern for personal witness."

²⁸ Hunt, "Jesus' Teaching Concerning the Paraclete in the Upper Room Discourse," 107-9.

²⁹ Beasley -Murray, *Word Biblical Themes: John*, 96. Haenchen (*John 2*, 143) notes that basically the only sin in the Gospel of John is "to be blind when God shows himself." He bases this in part on Jesus' words in 15:22-24 and says that, "there can only be sin where there is revelation (and man closes himself up to it)." Westcott (*The Gospel According to St. John,* 229) describes sin as "essentially the selfishness which sets itself up apart from, and so against God. It is not defined by any limited rules, but expresses a general spirit. . . . The Spirit therefore, working through the written and spoken word, starts from the fact of unbelief in the Son of Man, and through that lays open what sin is." Morris (*The Gospel According to John*, 698) sees unbelief as a

"classic illustration of their sin." Laney (*John*, 289) concurs and says, "The Holy Spirit secures a verdict of guilty against the world because of the sin of unbelief. Certainly the greatest act of rebellion against God is the rejection of His beloved Son."

[30] We see this evidenced in Thomas' response to Jesus' post-resurrection appearance. When confronted by the risen Christ, he responded with "My Lord and my God!" (John 20:28)

[31] Carson (*The Gospel According to John*, 537-38) notes that this is the only place the term, "righteousness," is used in the Gospel and sees it as the world's righteousness. He points to its parallel with "sin" in the previous verse to indicate that it must have the world's righteousness in view. Thus it is a false righteousness. He says (*The Farewell Discourse and Final Prayer of Jesus,* 141) righteousness "must be taken ironically to refer to what the world holds to be righteousness even if God judges it to be unrighteousness." Laney (*John*, 289-90) says that here righteousness "refers to what is right in terms of God's will," thus God's righteousness. He rejects Carson's view on the basis of Acts 3:14. "Jesus, the Righteous One, embodies the perfect standard of what is right as God has determined it. . . . Christ's return to heaven, to be welcomed by the Father, is the ultimate proof that He is the perfect pattern of righteousness that God accepts. The Holy Spirit will convict unbelievers of their failure to accept the standard of righteousness that God approves—that righteousness exemplified in the Person of Christ, who remains the ultimate standard of righteousness for the world." Westcott (*The Gospel According to St. John*, 229) concurs and says, "In Christ was the one absolute type of righteousness. Just as sin is revealed by the Spirit to be something far different from the breaking of certain specific injunctions, so righteousness is revealed to be something far different from the outward fulfillment of ceremonial or moral observances." Morris (*The Gospel According to John*, 699) takes Jesus to mean that "the Spirit shows men (and no-one else can do this) that their righteousness before God depends not on their own efforts but on Christ's atoning work for them." F. F. Bruce (*The Gospel of John,* 319) relates it to Jesus and says, "His condemnation, promulgated after due process of law, is now shown to have been utterly unrighteous; his return to the Father is the demonstration of his righteousness – and at the same time the vindication of the Father's righteousness."

[32] Laney (*John*, 290) asks and then attempts to answer the logical question that arises from Jesus' statement. "Why were the disciples unable to receive further teaching from Jesus at this time? Two suggestions are worthy of consideration. First, the disciples were limited in their ability to understand the truth because they had not yet received the illuminating ministry of the Holy Spirit. Second, apart from the indwelling ministry of the Spirit,

they were not able to live out the implications of Jesus' teaching." In response to Laney we can ask, What did the Old Testament saints do? Noah, Abraham, Joseph, David, etc.? They had the illuminating ministry of the Holy Spirit back then, as well as the inspiring ministry (2 Pet 1:21).

33 Carson (*The Gospel According to John*, 539) translates Jesus' words to say the Spirit will guide them "in all truth" rather than "into all truth." He then says, "If there is a distinction between '*in* all truth' and '*into* all truth', it is that the latter hints at truth the disciples have not yet in any sense penetrated, while '*in* all truth' suggests an exploration of truth already principally disclosed." He notes that some MSS use "in" (ἐν) rather than "into" (εἰς) all truth. And, though the majority of texts favor the second reading (into), he favors the first reading (in). From this he applies the promise to Christians in general rather than the disciples in particular and says, "The notion of 'guidance'. . . in all truth has nothing to do with privileged information pertaining to one's choice of vocation or mate, but with understanding God as he has revealed himself, and with obeying that revelation" (540). F. F. Bruce (*The Gospel of John,* 320) concurs and says, "It is not that he will guide them 'into' all the truth; they had already been introduced to the way of truth by Jesus, and the Spirit would guide them further along that way." But this explanation is deficient. First, the vast majority of manuscripts favor the idea of "into all truth" rather than "in." Second, the context of what Jesus has just said, namely, that there were things He wished to tell them which they could not handle at that time, requires a different sense. And finally, He is clearly addressing the eleven at this point with regard to His conversation with them that evening and what it is that He wants *them* to know.

34 Cook, *The Theology of John*, 120-21.

35 Hunt, "Jesus' Teaching Concerning the Paraclete in the Upper Room Discourse," 87.

36 Carson (*The Gospel According to John*, 540) on the other hand sees "things to come" to refer to "all that transpires *in consequence* of the pivotal revelation bound up with Jesus' person, ministry, death, resurrection and exaltation." Thus it is not only a reference to doctrine or truth, but to events as well. But he does not see this referring to eschatological revelation. Morris (*The Gospel According to John*, 701) concurs. "More likely 'the things to come' is a way of referring to the whole Christian system, yet future when Jesus spoke, and to be revealed to the disciples by the Spirit, not by natural insight. Not a few scholars discern an eschatological reference. . . . This is not impossible, but it does seem to be reading something into the words. It is better to take the sense as, 'He will show you the whole Christian way'." Westcott (*The Gospel According to St. John,* 231) also sees "things to come" as a reference "mainly to the constitution of the Christian Church, as representing hereafter

the divine order in place of the Jewish economy."

37 Westcott, *The Gospel According to St. John,* 231. As Hunt notes ("Jesus' Teaching Concerning the Paraclete in the Upper Room Discourse," 84), "Here in these verses is an illustration of the different responsibilities within the Trinity. The Spirit glorifies the Son by taking His teachings from Him, and the Son glorifies the Father (cf. John 5:30; 7:16; 14:10) by receiving His teachings from Him. Thus, the Spirit glorifies the Father."

38 Laney, *John,* 291.

39 Carson, *The Gospel According to John,* 541.

40 As Morris notes (*The Gospel According to John,* 701), "There is no division in the Godhead. . . . Just as the Spirit is concerned to set forward the things of Christ so is He concerned to set forward the things of the Father."

Chapter Thirteen

1 Morris (*The Gospel According to John,* 704) is correct when he notes that John's statement that Jesus "knew that they desired to ask Him" does not require supernatural knowledge on His part, though He likely had it.

2 Laney, *John,* 293. Westcott (*The Gospel According to St. John,* 232-33) sees in Jesus' words a reference to the church's attitude until His second coming. But this misses the point of Jesus as He meets the immediate needs of the disciples. Further, it takes away the comfort for them, especially in light of what He says in the next two verses. Thus it is better to see Him referring to the time between His death and first resurrection appearance.

3 Laney, *John,* 293.

4 As Morris (*The Gospel According to John,* 706) notes, "This leads to the well known thought of the birth pangs that would precede the coming of the Messiah." Carson (*The Gospel According to John,* 544) develops this concept further and says, "The model of a woman in childbirth generated a popular metaphor in the Judaism of Jesus' day: 'the birth pains of the Messiah' refers to a period of terrible trouble that must precede the consummation. It is not unlikely that this verse alludes to this eschatological theme, only here the intense suffering is borne by the Messiah himself." He says further, "John is here earthing his realized or inaugurated eschatology. By showing the coherence of Jesus' death/exaltation with the parousia, he not only declares the former to be a properly eschatological event, but makes the entire period between Easter and the consummation the onset of the eschaton." F. F. Bruce (*The Gospel of John,* 322) notes the source of this idea (Babylonian Talmud, tractate *Sanhefrin 98b*) and correctly responds, "It is unlikely that there is any allusion here to the rabbinical teaching about the 'messianic birth-pangs',

the time of distress which will precede and herald the dawn of the new age."

5 Carson (*The Gospel According to John*, 544) takes Jesus' use of "now" as proleptic and sees it reflecting the cross rather than the feelings of the men at that moment. It is better to see Jesus recognizing their feelings at the moment. This is especially true in light of His recognition that they will be scattered and will weep bitterly in just a few hours. Calvin (*Commentary on the Gospel According to John*, 2:151) wrongly understood Jesus' promise that He "*will see* his disciples" as a reference to the Holy Spirit's indwelling. Again, the context indicates that Jesus is looking at only the immediate future and what they are feeling at the moment and will experience in the coming days. Thus Jesus turns their attention to the promise of joy.

6 For example, Laney (*John*, 294) notes the different nuances each word *may* have. "Two different Greek words are translated 'ask' in v. 23. The first word, *erōtaō*, is used here in the sense of asking a question. The second word is *aiteō*, used for making requests or asking favors. It is a word used of a subordinate person seeking something from a superior."

7 Westcott (*The Gospel According to St. John*, 233) still places the time of joy on the day of Pentecost and says "that day" refers to the time period between Pentecost and Jesus' second coming. Laney (*John*, 294) also sees it as a reference to the day of Pentecost. It is better to see Jesus referring to the day of His resurrection. Carson (*The Gospel According to John*, 545), reading this passage eschatologically, says, "This does not mean that Jesus here refers to the end of history and *not* to the period after his resurrection, but that he is referring to the period after his resurrection *as* the end of history." But why must He be talking about the end of history? This interpretation arises from the idea that the imagery of a woman in labor requires an eschatological sense. It also looks for John's theology being communicated years after the event rather than Jesus' message to His men that evening. This is a case of reading too much theology into the passage and missing Jesus' words as a result. Rather than attempting to see the Upper Room Discourse as a Johannine theological treatise, we should see it for what it was intended. It is an accurate rendition of Jesus' final instruction to His men before His arrest.

8 Carson, *The Gospel According to John*, 545-46.

9 Westcott, *The Gospel According to St. John*, 233. Morris (*The Gospel According to John*, 707) notes, too, the significance of what Jesus is now saying. "The disciples had hitherto asked Jesus many questions. Not least was this the case in the upper room . . ., and this makes a reference to questions very appropriate. But they had not prayed to Him. There is no reason for thinking that the words would have made them think at this time of prayer to Jesus. Moreover 'verily, verily' commonly introduces a new thought. It does

not simply repeat the old. The asking in prayer at the end of the verse thus appears to be something different from the asking at the beginning. The alternative view is that the whole verse has to do with prayer. In that case Jesus is saying that prayer will be directed not to Him, but to the Father."

10 Mitchell, *An Everlasting Love*, 316.

11 Laney, *John*, 295.

12 Laney (ibid.) understands Jesus to be promising to "declare the truth of the Father to spiritually enlightened men" during the forty days between His resurrection and ascension. Rather, He is looking even farther into the future and referring to the Holy Spirit's ministry of revelation and explanation. Just as Jesus came to reveal the Father (John 1:18), He would complete the process in the future with clear instruction through the One He was sending to minister to them in His absence.

13 Westcott, *The Gospel According to St. John*, 234.

14 Laney, *John*, 296.

15 Laney's interpretation of the significance of their words may be appropriate. He (ibid.) says their statement, "and do not need that anyone question you," may "refer to the fact that Jesus knew their very thoughts and was able to answer their questions even before they asked." Based on this he concludes, "Christ's full knowledge was convincing evidence of His divine origin."

16 This is communicated through the preposition ἐν with the instrumental case noun that carries the sense of "by means of this."

17 Carson (*The Gospel According to John*, 548) sees Jesus responding with irony and exasperation. But then he observes, "Yet in one sense they had spoken more truly than they knew: Jesus did *not* need to question them to know what was in their minds, and he knew perfectly well that the coming test would find them all wanting."

18 Morris (*The Gospel According to John*, 713) understands Jesus to be pointing out the inadequacy of their faith rather than calling it into question. Westcott concurs (*The Gospel According to St. John*, 236). Laney (*John*, 297) notes well that Jesus' words could be translated either as a question or a statement. He also says, "Jesus may be saying, 'At this time you are trusting me.' And by implication one might add, 'But an hour of crisis is coming when that faith will be tested.' Jesus was not questioning the reality of the disciples' faith. He was perhaps raising doubts as to its power and steadfastness."

19 John uses it with this same sense in 7:30; 8:20; and 13:1.

20 Matt 27:46; Mark 15:34.

[21] For example, Laney (*John*, 297) says, "Becoming sin for the world, Jesus would be forsaken even by the Father, as God through Christ judged mankind's sin."

[22] Carson (*The Gospel According to John*, 550) notes well "this *in me* language is probably an extension of the metaphor of the vine (ch. 15). As F. F. Bruce (*The Gospel of John*, 326) notes, His point is that they should not be taken aback by tribulation, but see it "as a token of their Lord's approval and a harbinger of eternal bliss (cf. Rom. 8:17; Phil. 1:28). With this assurance they may well enjoy inward peace. Laney (*John*, 297) observes that these two spheres are either spiritual and eternal or material and temporal. Further, "Temporal life in this world will be characterized by 'trouble' (*thlipsis*) or 'tribulation.' The word is used in a general sense to speak of the 'pressing affliction' that the disciples must endure as they identify with Christ in an unbelieving world (cf. 15:18-25). . . . Yet although believers face intense pressure from the world, they can enjoy internal peace in Christ."

[23] Cook, *The Theology of John*, 115.

[24] Laney, *John*, 297.

Chapter Fourteen

[1] Marcus Rainsford, *Our Lord Prays for His Own* (Chicago: Moody Press, 1958), 35. Originally, lectures on St. John XVII by M. Rainsford, minister of Belgrade Chapel, London, n.d.

[2] F. F. Bruce, *The Gospel of* John, 328; Carson, *The Gospel According to John*, 552.

[3] Haenchen, *John 2*, 150.

[4] Laney, *John*, 300.

[5] Rainsford (*Our Lord Prays for His Own*, 31) notes, "We often find our Lord *teaching* His disciples to pray, and we read of Him spending even whole nights in prayer; but we never find Him praying *with* His disciples. Indeed, there would seem to be something incongruous in Christ kneeling down *with* His disciples for prayer; there must always have been something peculiar in His petitions." His observation is mostly correct, though we do see Jesus leading the group in prayer, even in the upper room when He gave thanks for the elements of the supper. Still he is correct in that we do not see Jesus ever praying as an equal within the group in a group prayer meeting. When He prays with the disciples, He is praying as their head, and not as an equal.

[6] Note the classic use of the perfect ἐλήλυθεν to designate its having arrived.

[7] Westcott (*The Gospel According to St. John*, 238) understands Jesus' use

of the term to mean that, "the 'glorifying' of the Son is the fuller manifestation of His true nature." It has as its end "the fuller manifestation of the Father." Thus "glorify" really means to reveal or "bring into full display Jesus' divine character and attributes through His impending death and resurrection" (Laney, *John*, 300). Carson (*The Gospel According to John*, 554) fuses the meaning of "glorify" with "glory" when he says that "in this context the primary meaning of 'to glorify' is 'to clothe in splendour', as v. 5 makes clear. The petition asks the Father to reverse the self-emptying entailed in hs [sic] incarnation and to restore him to the splendour that he shared with the Father before the world began. The cross and Jesus' ascension/exaltation are thus inseparable." There is truth in what he is saying; though he errs when he uses verse five to interpret verse one (the same kind of error he made in John 15, using verse six to interpret verse two). The cross and exaltation of Jesus are interrelated, but not in this prayer, as will be seen below.

8 Rainsford, *Our Lord Prays for His Own*, 43.

9 His use of the aorist imperative for the verb "to glorify" carries the sense that the action has not begun yet.

10 Laney, *John*, 301.

11 Ibid.

12 As Haenchen (*John 2*, 150) comments, "The continuation, 'to all whom thou hast given him,' shows that only a selection is intended. The expression, 'all flesh,' only appears here in John. The Evangelist believes that Jesus only gives salvation to the elect;"

13 Cook, *The Theology of John*, 93.

14 Rainsford, *Our Lord Prays for His Own*, 54.

15 Remember, we *receive* eternal life by believing, but we *experience* eternal life by abiding.

16 Law, *The Tests of Life*, 62, 187. He says further, it is "nothing else than the Divine Nature itself, regarded, not as abstract being, but dynamically, as the ground and source of all its own manifold activities—as the animating principle in virtue of which the Divine Righteousness and the Divine Love are not mere abstractions, but eternally active forces. And, finally, the Life of God is a principle of self-communication and self-reproduction. . . . To men, Eternal Life is communicated as the result of a Divine act, by which, in the terminology of St. John, they are "begotten of God" and become the "children of God" (τέκνα τοῦ θεοῦ). The actual impartation of the actual Life of God is the core of Johannine soteriology" (55-56).

17 Vanderlip (*Christianity According to John*, 35-36) argues that "life" and

"salvation" are parallel to each other in the Gospel of John and so should be regarded as "equivalents" in Johannine thinking. He points to John 3:16-17 and 10:9-10 as evidences of this equivalence. Edwin K. Lee (*The Religious Thought of St. John* [London: S.P.C.K., 1950], 191) also sees eternal life and salvation as synonymous, with John using eternal life because it matched better his "positive conception."

[18] Law, *The Tests of Life*, 201-3

[19] Cook, *The Theology of John,* 94 (italics his).

[20] Ibid., 95

[21] Hans H. Wendt, *The Teaching of Jesus,* trans. by John Wilson (Edinburgh: T. & T. Clark, 1892), 1:245.

[22] Hodges, *The Epistles of John*, 76-77.

[23] Hodges, *The Gospel Under Siege,* 64-65.

[24] Dillow, *The Reign of the Servant Kings*, 136.

[25] Cook, *The Theology of John,* 93-95; C. H. Dodd, *New Testament Studies* (Manchester: Manchester University Press, 1953), 168; Law, *The Tests of Life,* 296; *Wycliffe Bible Encyclopedia,* S.v. "Eternal life," by M. C. Tenney, 1:552.

[26] J. Edgar Bruns, *The Art and Thought of John* (New York: Herder and Herder, 1969), 58; Cook, *The Theology of John,* 93; Westcott, *The Epistles of St. John,* 215.

[27] Cook, *The Theology of John*, 91.

[28] George B. Stevens, *The Theology of the New Testament* (New York: Scribner, 1947, c1927), 231-32.

[29] Bultmann, TDNT, 2:861.

[30] Ibid., 862.

[31] Ζωὴ αἰώνιος, occurs three times in the Septuagint, with each use reflecting the quantitative aspect of meaning. In Daniel 12:2 it speaks of the life to come, evidenced by its resulting from resurrection. Even so, here its qualitative sense is implied since two groups are identified in terms of their post resurrection experiences, whether of life or disgrace and contempt. Both are described as "eternal" and experience unending existence. But only one group's existence is enjoyed, those described by "life." In 2 Maccabees 7.9 "eternal" modifies ἀναβίωσιν (being made new) that also describes life following resurrection. The phrase still refers to the experience of future life rather than quality of life experienced in this life, even though the emphasis in this statement includes quality as well as duration ("The First and Second Books of the Maccabees," in *The Cambridge Bible Commentary* (Cambridge:

Cambridge University Press, 1973), commentary by John R. Bartlett. Finally, in 4 Maccabees 15.3 eternal life is used to refer to the immortal expression of life rather than quality of mortal life.

[32] Cook, *The Theology of John,* 93; Vanderlip, *Christianity According to John* 33; Wendt, *The Teaching of Jesus,* 1:244-48.

[33] Lee, *The Religious Thought of St. John,* 192.

[34] Dodd, "Eternal Life," *Christianity and Crisis* 10, April 1950, 34; Law, *The Tests of Life,* 188-89.

[35] Vanderlip, *Christianity According to John,* 37.

[36] Ibid., 33.

[37] Ibid.

[38] Wendt, *The Teaching of Jesus,* 1:249.

[39] Stephen S. Smalley, *1, 2, 3 John* in Word Biblical Commentary, Vol. 51 (Waco: Word Books, Publishers, 1984), 10 (italics his).

[40] Wendt (*The Teaching of Jesus,* 1:249) also sees this sense in John 4:14; 14:2; and 17:24. Cook (*The Theology of John,* 93) sees 6:52-54 reflecting the qualitative sense rather than its quantitative. But even though Jesus refers here to having life "in yourselves" (v. 53), he is speaking in terms of its possession, eternal aspect. One must not forget that the unending element of eternal life is in effect during the mortal phase of life as well as the immortal phase. Therefore referring to eternal life as a characteristic of a mortal man need not require the term be given a qualitative sense in that sentence.

[41] Vanderlip, *Christianity According to John,* 41.

[42] Of note is the absence of the noun for knowledge (γνῶσις) in John.

[43] Daniel B. Wallace (*Greek Grammar Beyond the Basics* [Grand Rapids: Zondervan Publishing House, 1996], 475) uses John 17:3 as his example of apposition, one of the four uses of ἵνα with the subjunctive. He also notes, "Although not frequent, it is almost idiomatic of Johannine literature." Also see John 15:8, 12; 1 John 3:23; 4:21; 5:3; 2 John 6; 3 John 4.

[44] Westcott, *The Gospel According to St. John,* 239.

[45] Cook (*The Theology of John,* 94) defines eternal life as "continually knowing" the Father and Jesus on the basis of his understanding of the meaning of the present indicative γινώσκομεν). Westcott (*The Gospel According to St. John,* 239) notes that the "tense of the verb (γινώσκωσι) marks continuance, progress, and not a perfect and past apprehension gained once for all."

[46] Laney, *John,* 301.

[47] Calvin, *Commentary on the Gospel According to John,* 2:166. Carson *(The Gospel According to John,* 556) follows Calvin's approach. At first he seems to see it differently and states "it is clear that the knowledge of God and of Jesus Christ entails fellowship, trust, personal relationship, faith." But then he follows this observation with the statement: "There is no more powerful evangelistic theme."

[48] Carson *(The Farewell Discourse and Final Prayer of Jesus,* 180) correctly observes, "Eternal life is best seen not as everlasting life but as knowledge of the Everlasting One. To know God transforms a person and introduces him to a life he could not otherwise experience. Knowledge of God is eternal life; to know God is to have eternal life." These are great definitions and true observations. But then he also defines receiving eternal life and seeing God's glory as parallel concepts, as synonymous ideas *(The Gospel According to John,* 556). In each of these definitions he appears to be looking at eternal life in terms of its possession, and not its purpose or progressive experience by the believer. Still, he is not far from the point Jesus makes, though it is a subtle difference (but not merely a difference in semantics). All that he says is true of eternal life and is taught elsewhere in Scripture. But, it seems that here Jesus has been focusing on different aspects, its divine and progressive aspects.

[49] Cook, *The Theology of John,* 43.

[50] Mitchell, *An Everlasting Love,* 326. F. F. Bruce *(The Gospel of John,* 329) describes well the theological significance of what Jesus has said in this short verse. "Eternal life, then, consists in the knowledge of God. Since the knowledge of God is mediated through the revealer whom God has sent, and is indeed embodied in that revealer, the knowledge of the revealer is one with the knowledge of the God who is revealed. Nor is this knowledge a matter simply of intellectual apprehension: it involves a personal relationship." And, as Gruenler *(The Trinity in the Gospel of John,* 123) observes, "For believers to know Jesus Christ is to know God and to experience eternal life."

[51] Carson, *The Gospel According to John,* 557.

[52] Mitchell, *An Everlasting Love,* 328.

[53] Laney *(John,* 302) sees the transfiguration as "a revelation of the future glory He would enjoy in the kingdom (Matt. 17:1-2)." This is true in part. But the transfiguration was also an expression of the glory He already had before He veiled it in His incarnation. Carson *(The Gospel According to John,* 557) concludes from this "the incarnation entailed a forfeiture of glory." Hugh Ross's discussion of extra-dimensionality in his *Beyond the Cosmos* is significant at this point. When Christ became man, He squeezed Himself into our four dimensions. How many dimensions of space and time do you suppose

Jesus had before His incarnation (cf. ἐκένωσεν in Phil 2:7). He "emptied" Himself of perhaps a dozen or more dimensions. But, in light of the transfiguration, we must conclude rather that Jesus only veiled His glory. He did not "forfeit" it.

54 Gruenler, *The Trinity in the Gospel of John,* 124. Also, cf. *The Trinity in the Universe*, by Nathan Wood.

55 When used with the dative (in this case: σεαυτῷ) παρὰ "denotes nearness in space" (BAGD, 610).

56 Eph 1:20-21, "which He worked in Christ when He raised Him from the dead and set Him at His right hand in the heavenly places, far above all principality and power and might and dominion, and every name that is named, not only in this age but also in that which is to come." Phil 2:9-11, "Therefore God also has highly exalted Him and given Him the name which is above every name, that at the name of Jesus every knee should bow, of those in heaven, and of those on earth, and of those under the earth, and that every tongue should confess that Jesus Christ is Lord, to the glory of God the Father."

Chapter Fifteen

1 Carson, *The Gospel According to John*, 557.

2 Rainsford (*Our Lord Prays for His Own*, 101-3) identifies seven "considerations" and seven "petitions" made by Jesus in His prayer. The seven considerations He brings to the Father's attention include: First, He manifested the Father's name to them, "Thus He enshrines them, as it were, in the name of His Father, baptizing them into all that name involves." Second, He pointed out "the Father's own interest in them." Third, He noted "the gift of them." The fourth consideration was "their reception of Himself and His message." The fifth was "in the power of which He presents them to the Father." Then, the sixth was the world's hatred with the seventh being their separation from the world. His seven petitions included: "keep them," sanctify them, unite them, let them be "with Me", glorify them, let Your love be in them, and, "let Me be in them."

3 As Morris (*The Gospel According to John*, 723) correctly notes, "The 'name' stands for the whole person (see 1:12). To manifest the name of God then is to reveal the essential nature of God to men."

4 Rainsford (*Our Lord Prays for His Own,* 108-9) explains the phrase, "manifested Your name," in terms of Old Testament practice. He notes that, "the servants of God were wont to inscribe the names of Jehovah upon the

monumental pillars where the displays of His grace, his salvation, or of His kindly care had been manifested." He provides examples from Genesis 22:14; Exodus 17:15; Ezekiel 48:35; Exodus 15:25; Jeremiah 33:16; and Judges 6:24. Then he says, "But saved sinners are His true monuments, 'the men which thou gavest me out of the world.' And every name of God shall be inscribed upon them. And Jesus Himself shall be the inscriber" on the basis of Rev 3:12. There is indeed great truth in what he says, but this is really not what Jesus had in mind at this point. He Himself is the manifestation He has in mind, not the disciples.

5 F. F. Bruce, *The Gospel of John,* 330.

6 Mitchell (*An Everlasting Love,* 330) differs from most and sees Jesus referring to the name, "Father," with Him focusing on the changed relationship of the disciples with God. The problem with this is that in the upper room He does not focus on their Father-son relationships. Also, Jesus has been calling God His Father throughout His ministry as He did when He taught them to pray (Matt 6:9; 7:9-11). So, it is better to see Him saying that He has completed His mission of revealing the Father to the disciples, a ministry (actually to the world) introduced in the prologue (1:18) which will be culminated on the cross. Mitchell sees an advance over the Old Testament. The OT did not reveal God as Father—the heart of God. He had been revealed by many names but never as Father—the heart of God. In the OT we see the majesty of God— the great and terrible God but now, in Christ, we see the wonders of the heart of God.

7 BAGD, 251 (ἕλκω).

8 BAGD, 814-15 (τηρέω).

9 Carson (*The Gospel According to John,* 559) argues well that "a good case can be made that when in the Fourth Gospel Jesus refers to his *words* (plural) he is talking about the precepts he lays down, almost equivalent to his 'commands' (*entolai,* as in 14:21; 15:10), but when he refers to his *word* (singular) he is talking about his message as a whole, almost equivalent to 'gospel'." If this is the case, then Jesus is not saying that they have kept His commands, but that the eleven have responded in faith to Jesus' revelation of the Father. They have believed Jesus' testimony.

10 This doctrine is one of the "Five Points" of Calvinism, namely, Perseverance of the Saints. It differs from the doctrine of eternal security in that it does not teach that once a person is saved he or she remains saved. Rather, this doctrine teaches that *if* a person is saved, that person will *persevere in good works* to the end as evidence of his or her salvation. If someone fails to persevere it is because they were never regenerate in the first place. This has been discussed in part in the section of the vine and the branches.

11 Or as Laney (*John*, 303) puts it, it gives "emphasis to the point of culmination and the existence of its finished results."

12 As Laney (ibid.) observes, "The disciples recognized that 'everything' (*panta*) given to Christ comes ultimately from the Father. The Father is the source of Christ's mission (12:44; 13:3), His authority (5:27), and His teaching (7:16; 8:28; 12:49)." Thus, per Carson (*The Gospel According to John*, 559), "they had come to the deep conviction that Jesus was God's messenger, that he had been sent by God and that all he taught was God's truth."

13 Mitchell (*An Everlasting Love*, 330) believes Jesus is remembering Peter's words in Matt 16:16 when He says they believed that the Father sent Him.

14 This is evident from His use of ὅτι to indicate reason, "for" or "because."

15 Though Carson (*The Gospel According to John*, 560) has stated earlier that fruit (deeds) proves the presence of spiritual life and that perseverance in good works is a necessary expression of the presence of spiritual life, he correctly observes here, "In this verse there is little distinction between the knowledge and the belief of the disciples."

16 For example, Westcott (*The Gospel According to St. John*, 241) says, "The teaching which was before (v. 6) regarded in its unity, is now regarded in its component elements (τὰ ῥήματα)." Further, "The contrast between 'the word' (λόγος), the complete message, and 'the saying' (ῥῆμα), the detached utterance, is frequently important in St. John, and yet difficult to express without a paraphrase." Yet Laney (*John*, 303) cautions us that, "John, being prone to variation, may intend no significant difference in meaning between the two words." Though John is credited for this variation by Laney, it should be noted that John is quoting Jesus and it is likely that Jesus also used variation in His instruction as reflected by John. The choice of words is not John's doing, but a reflection of John's faithfulness to record Jesus' words accurately. Carson (*The Gospel According to John*, 560) is in similar agreement with Laney and notes that this term for words (ῥήματα) does not refer to Jesus' "teaching as a whole nor his itemized precepts, but his actual 'words' or his 'utterances'."

17 This is the aorist tense of γινώσκω, indicating an action in the (undefined) past.

18 He uses the aorist tense of πιστεύω here as well.

19 Read chapter eight of *Let's Live!* by Curtis Mitchell (Old Tappan: Fleming H. Revell Company, 1975) for an encouraging discussion on prayer.

20 Laney, *John*, 304.

21 Cook, *The Theology of John*, 107-8.

22 Carson, *The Gospel According to John*, 561.

23 He uses τὰ and πάντα, both neuter pronouns which by their use includes more than the disciples, though His later use of αὐτοῖς refers to them in particular.

24 F. F. Bruce, *The Gospel of John,* 331.

25 Carson, *The Gospel According to John*, 561.

26 Westcott (*The Gospel According to St. John,* 242) defines it as making either God or Christ known and acknowledging Him "as being what He is." Laney (*John*, 304) correctly sees this use of glorify by Jesus to be "emphasizing the ongoing impact of the disciples' personal faith and witness."

27 Carson, *The Gospel According to John*, 561.

28 Cook (*The Theology of John*, 109) perhaps sees this as a part of Jesus' high-priestly ministry. But, as noted above, since that ministry could not start prior to His appointment, we should see this as Jesus' prayer of concern for those men as one member of the Godhead speaking with the other.

29 Of interest is the fact that this is the only place Jesus addresses His Father as "*Holy* Father" or even refers to Him as holy.

30 Carson (*The Gospel According to John*, 562) argues that if it is understood to have locative force, the "passage must then be rendered 'keep them in your name', *i.e.* 'keep them in loyalty to you' or 'keep them in full adherence to your character'." He says the context of verses six through eight favors this option. "In short, Jesus prays that God will keep his followers in firm fidelity to the revelation Jesus himself has mediated to them. The purpose of such faithful allegiance, Jesus avers, is *that they may be one as we are one*..

31 Carson (*The Farewell Discourse and Final Prayer of Jesus,* 189) understands Jesus point to be "not that they may progressively achieve unity, but simply that they may be a unity continually." He further notes that the implication of what Jesus says, "seems to be that various dark forces will strive to break up this unity." He notes (*The Gospel According to John*, 562), "They are not kept *as* a unity; rather, their unity is the purpose of their being kept."

32 Carson, *The Farewell Discourse and Final Prayer of Jesus,* 190.

33 Westcott, *The Gospel According to St. John,* 243.

34 Ibid.

35 Ibid.

36 Dillow, *The Reign of the Servant Kings*, 170.

37 Carson (*The Gospel According to John*, 563-4) sees Judas' "exceptional

status" being established by two things. First, Jesus describing him as the son of perdition could refer to either character or destiny. Second, "The reference to the fulfillment of Scripture also assures the reader that the defection of Judas is foreseen by Scripture, and therefore not evidence of a failure on Jesus' part." Alvin L. Baker ("Eternal Security Rightly Understood," *Fundamentalist Journal,* 3: 8 [September 1984]: 19) points to Judas as a nonbeliever, not a believer who lost his sonship based on Jesus' affirmation in verse twelve. "Jesus made it clear that Judas was not an exception to His keeping of true disciples (cf. John 6:46ff.; 6:70; 13:18)." Again, Carson correctly notes, "Jesus' prayer for his disciples, in this context, therefore *excludes* Judas Iscariot, for otherwise one would have to conclude that Jesus failed in the responsibility that had been assigned him" (563).

38 Laney (*John,* 305) says, "The expression 'doomed to destruction' (*apōleia*) is the very antithesis of the concept of salvation and indicates that Judas was an unregenerate man. Morris (*The Gospel According to John,* 728) says this designation "points to character rather than destiny. The expression means that he was characterized by 'lostness', not that he was predestined to be 'lost'."

39 Morris (*The Gospel According to John,* 728) says, "The reference to the fulfilling of Scripture brings out the thought of divine purpose." He adds: "There is a combination of the human and the divine, but in this passage it is the divine side rather than the human which receives stress." F. F. Bruce (*The Gospel of John,* 332) disagrees with this and says, "Despite the predestinarian flavour of the language, Judas was not lost against his will but with his consent." Then he reflects the Arminian understanding that Christians can lose their salvation and says, "Judas, like the other disciples, had been given by the Father to the Son, but even among those so given apostasy is a solemn possibility."

40 Carson (*The Gospel According to John,* 564) notes that if "these things" refers to the prayer, then the "prayer demonstrates the depth of Jesus' communion with his Father, and this constitutes a paradigm for the intimate relationship with the Father that the disciples themselves will come to enjoy. . . . But more probably *these things* refers to the entire farewell discourse."

41 Rainsford (*Our Lord Prays for His Own,* 239) notes that Jesus' use of "My joy" can have three different senses as used by Him. First, Jesus may have intended it with the sense of "The *joy* which is Mine to bestow", the joy which He could give them and us. Second, it could be the joy "of which He is *the object, subject,* and *element.*" It is our response to Him. Then it could also refer to "*His own personal joy.*" He sees Jesus intending all three senses simultaneously.

42 Laney (*John,* 306) notes, "Jesus intended that they be comforted by the

fact that He had committed them to the Father's safe keeping."

[43] Rainsford (*Our Lord Prays for His Own*, 283-87) asks how God has answered Jesus' prayer, "Keep them from evil"? He notes that it is not "from outward tribulations, distresses, persecutions, obloquy, and even violent assaults from the world, the flesh, and the devil" on the basis of 1 Cor 4:9-13 and personal experience. He says, "The experience of the Church of God, and the individual experience of every member of it, also proves that we are not secured from *spiritual conflicts*" and notes Eph 6:11-12. He also says we are "not secured from *temptations* arising from various sources; they are even called in Scripture '*fiery trials*,' not only resulting from the malice of the devil, and the weakness of self, but from contact with the evil which is in the world, the entanglements of the world, evil companionships which we cannot get rid of, evil influences, and evil associations." Then, again, "Nor are we secured from *humiliating failures* in service." Also, "we are not secured from *grievous bodily suffering*, nor from crushing bereavements, loss of health, loss of substance, death itself; and *painful* dying." Again, "we are not secured from *the burden of self*, we are not secured from the conscious coldness, hardness, and deadness of our own corrupt heart and nature." Finally, he notes, "we are not secured from *actual sin!*" He then sees Jesus praying that we be protected from "spiritual hurt" on the basis of Psalm 121:7. "That is the only evil *to us* which can hurt *the soul*; all the other things which we may think evil, and call evil, shall work together for our good." Therefore, "No evil, no hurt, no loss, no spiritual evil, can evermore prevail to injure the soul of any child of God, whether it arise from the evil one, or from the hatred of the world to Christ and to His cause, or from our own poor, wretched, fallen nature, or from the dominion or the consequences of sin."

[44] We translate the Greek article as "the" and words without the article with the indefinite "a."

[45] Τοῦ πονηροῦ is in the ablative case with the preposition ἐκ.

[46] Dillow, *The Reign of the Servant Kings*, 500.

[47] As Westcott (*The Gospel According to St. John*, 244) says, "Just as Christ is Himself the medium or sphere in which the believer lives and moves…, so the prince of the world, the evil one, is the medium or sphere in which they live and move who are given up to him." He says further, "The relation of man to good and evil is a personal relation; and the Lord prays that His disciples may be kept out of the range of the pervading influence of His enemy.

[48] F. F. Bruce, *The Gospel of John*, 333.

[49] Mitchell, *An Everlasting Love*, 335.

[50] Laney, *John*, 306.

51 Carson, *The Gospel According to John*, 565.

52 Ibid., 566.

53 Westcott, *The Gospel According to St. John*, 245.

54 The use of double entendre involves a word having two meanings simultaneously. Though it may seem ambiguous or confusing at first glance, when both meanings are explored and meditated on, the full significance of what is being said comes to the fore.

55 Mitchell, *An Everlasting Love*, 337.

56 Ibid.

57 Rainsford, *Our Lord Prays for His Own*, 307.

58 Laney, *John*, 308.

59 Reformed theology seems to remain focused on the cross almost like Rome, except that it doesn't have the crucifix. And, the eschatology of Rome seems to have kept Catholicism from serving the goal of history.

60 For example, Morris (*The Gospel According to John*, 732) understands Jesus' self sanctification here to mean His coming death and says that His words point "us to Calvary and all that Calvary means." Laney (*John*, 308) reflects this same justification approach to the interpretation of His words and says, "The last half of the verse indicates the intended purpose of Christ's sanctification. He set Himself apart to do God's will and to go to the cross to provide a basis for the disciples' own sanctification. Through His death the way was prepared for the disciples to be 'set apart' to God, both in their salvation and service for their Lord." F. F. Bruce (*The Gospel of John*, 334) basically concurs with them and sees this as "a Johannine counterpart to the Gethsemane prayer." Carson (*The Gospel According to John*, 567) too sees the same sense here and says, "The sweep of the Fourth Gospel demonstrates that the central purpose of the mission of the Son is his death, resurrection and return to glory. . . . At the same time, the second part of the verse, *that they too may be truly sanctified*, suggests that the sanctification of the believers consequent upon Jesus' sanctification of himself must be something akin to what he undergoes. Here it seems best to find a parallel in the notion of the consecration of prophet or priest to particular service."

61 The idea of a "gnomic present" tense verb is that it describes action which happens on a routine basis. An example of a gnomic present would be the statement, "The sun rises in the east." It is something that happens routinely and is described with a present tense verb.

62 Laney, *John*, 308.

[63] He is going to rule this world in righteousness (cf. Isa 11) and bring in everlasting righteousness and when He does, He will turn the kingdom over to God the Father (cf. 1 Cor 15:28).

Chapter Sixteen

[1] Westcott, *The Gospel According to St. John,* 245.

[2] And, as Morris (*The Gospel According to John*, 733) notes, "their word" stands "for the whole of their message. Their message is one which will lead to faith in Christ."

[3] Laney, *John*, 309.

[4] Rainsford (*Our Lord Prays for His Own*, 372) says yes, and on that basis eliminates many possible things for which Jesus could have been praying. He argues first, "Our Lord's prayer must have been answered. He could not pray in vain. And if this be so, then it is a divine fact, a most blessed reality, that all His believing people *are one*, according to His own words." On the basis of this affirmation, he identifies four things the unity cannot be (373). First, He "does not here speak of an absolute, complete, and perfect *uniformity* between believers in His name. If He did, His prayer had not been answered, for no such uniformity exists." Second, He does not speak of a union between the different *sects* and denominations of the professing Christian church." Third, "The Lord does not pray that His people should be more united in His Father's purpose, because this would be *impossible*." And, fourth, "The Lord does not pray that His people may be more united one to another and to Himself *in fact*, no need for this, because they are in fact united."

From the elimination of these options, he then concludes, "First, there is that union which all the Lord's believing people have one with another as members of the same body, as children in the same family, as living stones in the same spiritual temple, the foundation stone of which is the Lord Jesus Christ" (374). "Second, there is union between the body, made up as it is of many members, and the glorious Head Himself" (376). Third, "as the Father is in Him, and He is in the Father, so His people may be one with Him, and with the Father" (378). He notes that Jesus' use of "*as* here is not the *as* of equality—only the Father, the Son, and the Holy Ghost can be united in equality; but it is the *as* of similitude and likeness." Thus there exits a three-fold union: "the union between the Man Christ Jesus, and the Second Person in the Trinity, the Son of God" (379), then, "a love union between the Father and the Son" (380), and finally, "a union of will between the Father and the Son" (381). This is a little *too* expansive on what Jesus intended to communicate. It would be better to see Him saying, "that they may *be* (existential unity) what they already *are* (essential unity).

⁵ Laney (*John*, 309) understands this to mean that just as in the Trinity the three distinct Persons share one divine essence, "in the Body of Christ there are many members, but they share in a unity of the Spirit (1 Cor. 12:13)." Westcott (*The Gospel According to St. John*, 246) attempts to describe this unity. He says, "The true unity of believers, like the Unity of the Persons in the Holy Trinity with which it is compared, is offered as something far more than a mere moral unity of purpose, feeling, affection; it is, in some mysterious mode which we cannot distinctly apprehend, a vital unity . . . In this sense it is the symbol of a higher type of life, in which each constituent being is a conscious element in the being of a vast whole." F. F. Bruce (*The Gospel of John*, 335) sees this as a "unity of love" and Jesus is asking that future believers get to participate "in the unity of love which subsists eternally between the Father and the Son." Beasley-Murray (*Word Biblical Themes: John*, 99), on the other hand, sees this as a justification truth and describes it as "a unity grounded in the being of God and in the redemptive action of God in Christ." He says further, "In the former petition the redeemed become one by participating in the fellowship of the Father and the Son; in the latter, the participation is through their union with the Son, for the Son of God is the one Mediator between God and man. Clearly this is a unity that cannot possibly be achieved by the efforts that people—even Christian people-can make. It is the fruit of God's redemptive work in Christ." Mitchell (*An Everlasting Love*, 341) takes note of the significance of Jesus' use of "as" in this verse and says that, "He is dealing with an internal unity. The union of believers will be the same as the union between the Father and the Son. . . . This is a vital relationship in life between God and the believer." He clarifies further, "It's not union in organization, but an internal unity in love, in life, in purpose, and in desire" (343).

⁶ Gruenler, "John 17:20-26." *Interpretation*. 43: 2 (April 1989): 178.

⁷ Ibid., 179.

⁸ Ibid., 180.

⁹ Ibid., 180-81.

¹⁰ Ibid., 183.

¹¹ Carson, *The Gospel According to John*, 568.

¹² Morris (*The Gospel According to John*, 733-4) provides good insight into this verse as well as what Jesus will say in verse twenty-three. He says, "In both places we have four parts. Here they are as follows: (1) 'thou, Father, art in me,' (2) 'and I in thee,' (3) 'that they may be in us' (4) 'that the world may believe that thou didst send me.' In v. 23 these are the four parts: (1) 'I in them,' (2) 'and thou in me,' (3) 'that they may be perfected into one;' (4) 'that the world may know that thou didst send me'. In each case the effect of this

structure is to add solemnity and emphasis. Jesus prays first that the disciples may be one and then that they may be 'in' the Father and the Son, just as the Father and the Son are 'in' one another. . . . This does not mean that the unity between the Father and the Son is the same as that between believers and God. But it does mean that there is an analogy. The Father is in the Son and does His works (14:10). The Son is in the Father. The two are one (10:30) and yet are distinct. So in measure is it with believers. Without losing their identity they are to be in the Father and the Son. Apart from the Son they can do nothing (15:5). In other words the unity for which He prays is to lead to a fuller experience of the Father and the Son."

13 Morris, *The Gospel According to John*, 728.

14 Carson, *The Gospel According to John*, 568.

15 And so Carson (ibid.) correctly defines glory here as "the manifestation of God's character or person in a revelatory context; Jesus has mediated the glory of God personally to his first followers and through them to those who believe on account of their message." Laney (*John*, 310) follows this same sense and defines glory here in terms of humble service, and misses it entirely. "The path of greatness through humble service is the glory in which both Jesus and believers may share."

16 Dillow, *The Reign of the Servant Kings*, 405.

17 Morris (*The Gospel According to John*, 735) notes that whereas in verse twenty-one "the purpose was that the world might believe that the Father sent the Son. Here it is that the world may know that the Father sent the Son." From this parallel he concludes, "Actually there is little difference, since for John believing gives further knowledge, and knowledge to all intents and purposes means faith." He has it backward. More knowledge of God provides more to believe and the more we believe, the more we receive. And the more we receive, the more the light shines through us. And the clearer the light shines, the more the unbeliever sees Christ and believes.

18 Mitchell (*An Everlasting Love*, 344) notes that this is "the only time in our Lord's ministry upon the earth where He said to His Father, 'I will,'" and then points us to Isaiah 14:13-14 for a contrast with Satan.

19 Laney (*John*, 311) sees this reference to glory to be the same as the previous sense in verse twenty-two, "His glorious reputation as demonstrated by His Person and work." He bases this on his understanding that the last half of the verse provides a definition of glory as "the evidence of the Father's eternal love." But then we must ask, "What kind of glory would the Father give the Son?" Carson (*The Gospel According to John*, 569) is more correct when he identifies this glory as "an unambiguous reference to v. 5, where Jesus prays to be restored to the glory that he had with the Father before the world

began." And, "the glory of Christ that his followers will see is his glory as God, the glory he enjoyed before his mission because of the Father's love for him" (569-70).

20 Mitchell, *An Everlasting Love*, 347.

21 Carson, *The Gospel According to John*, 570.

Appendix

1 Law, *The Tests of Life*, 62, 187.

2 Ibid., 55-56.

3 Vanderlip, *Christianity According to John,* 35-36.

4 Lee, *The Religious Thought of St. John,* 191.

5 Law, *The Tests of Life,* 201-3.

6 Cook, *The Theology of John,* 94 (italics his).

7 Wendt, *The Teaching of Jesus,* 1:245.

8 Hodges, "1 John," 892.

9 Hodges, *The Gospel under Siege,* 64-65.

10 Cook, *The Theology of John,* 93-95; Dodd, *New Testament Studies,* 168; Law, *The Tests of Life,* 296; *Wycliffe Bible Encyclopedia,* S.v. "Eternal life," by M. C. Tenney, 1:552.

11 Bruns, *The Art and Thought of John,* 58; Cook, *The Theology of John,* 93; Westcott, *The Epistles of St. John,* 215.

12 Cook, *The Theology of John,* 91.

13 Stevens, *The Theology of the New Testament,* 231-32.

14 Bultmann, TDNT, 2:861.

15 Ibid., 2:862.

16 Ζωὴ αἰώνιος, occurs three times in the Septuagint, with each use reflecting the quantitative aspect of meaning. In Daniel 12:2 it speaks of the life to come, evidenced by its resulting from resurrection. Even so, here its qualitative sense is implied since two groups are identified in terms of their post resurrection experiences, whether of life or disgrace and contempt. Both are described as "eternal" and experience unending existence. But only one group's existence is enjoyed, those described by "life." In 2 Maccabees 7.9 "eternal" modifies ἀναβίωσιν (being made new) that also describes life following resurrection. The phrase still refers to the experience of future life rather

than quality of life experienced in this life, even though the emphasis in this statement includes quality as well as duration ("The First and Second Books of the Maccabees," in *The Cambridge Bible Commentary* (Cambridge: Cambridge University Press, 1973), Commentary by John R. Bartlett. Finally, in 4 Maccabees 15.3 eternal life is used to refer to the immortal expression of life rather than quality of mortal life.

[17] Cook, *The Theology of John,* 93; Vanderlip, *Christianity According to John,* 33; Wendt, *The Teaching of Jesus,* 1:244-48.

[18] Lee, *The Religious Thought of St. John*, 192.

[19] Vanderlip, *Christianity According to John,* 33.

[20] Ibid.

[21] Wendt, *The Teaching of Jesus,* 1:249.

[22] Dodd, "Eternal Life," 34; Law, *The Tests of Life,* 188-89.

[23] Vanderlip, *Christianity According to John,* 37.

[24] Lee, *The Religious Thought of St. John,* 198; Vanderlip, *Christianity According to John,* 36-37.

[25] Smalley, *1, 2, 3 John,* 10 (italics his).

[26] Vanderlip, *Christianity According to John,* 38.

[27] Wendt, *The Teaching of Jesus,* 1:249.

[28] Cook, *The Theology of John,* 93.

[29] Vanderlip, *Christianity According to John,* 41.

[30] F. F. Bruce, *The Gospel of John*, 291; and Carson, *The Gospel According to John*, 455.

[31] Carson, *The Gospel According to John*, 481.

[32] Ibid.

[33] Ibid.

[34] Ibid.

[35] Ibid., 481-82.

[36] Laney, *John*, 25.

[37] Ibid., 21.

[38] Ibid., 237.

[39] Carson, *The Gospel According to John*, 460-61.

[40] Carson, *The Farewell Discourse and Final Prayer of Jesus,* 19. (Italics

his)

41 The synonym of γινώσκω, ἐπιγινώσκω, does not occur in any Johannine literature.

42 If this verse had used οἶδα, then a Pauline distinction might be argued.

43 Dillow, *The Reign of the Servant Kings*, 395.

44 Bob George, *Classic Christianity* (Eugene, Or.: Harvest House, 1989), 207.

45 Ibid.

46 Within the epistle γινώσκω occurs twenty-three times (2:3, 4, 5, 11, 13 [twice], 14, 18, 29; 3:1, 6, 19, 20, 24; 4:2, 6 [twice], 7, 8, 13, 16; 5:2, 20) and οἶδα fifteen times (2:11, 20, 21, 29; 3:2, 5, 14, 15; 5:13, 15 [twice], 18, 19, 20).

47 John R. W. Stott, *The Letters of John* (Grand Rapids: Wm. B. Eerdmans Publishing Company, 1964, 1988), 94. He applies this distinction in meaning to John's use of both terms in 5:20 and says (197), "This real God Christ has given us understanding to *know* (*ginoskomen* in contrast to *oidamen* at the beginning of the verse). We might paraphrase 'we know as a fact that the Son of God has . . . given us understanding to come to perceive and know in experience him who is real' . . ." (italics his).

48 Westcott, *The Epistles of St. John*, 46.

49 Raymond E. Brown, *The Epistles of John,* in The Anchor Bible (New York: Doubleday, 1982), 250.

50 Law, *The Tests of Life,* 366.

51 γινώσκω : 1:10, 48; 2:24, 25; 3:10; 4:1, 53; 5:6, 42; 7:17, 26, 27, 49, 51; 8:28, 32, 52, 55; 10:14, 15, 27, 38; 11:57; 12:9; **13:7, 12, 28, 35; 14:7, 7, 9, 17, 20, 31; 15:8; 16:3, 19; 17:3, 7, 8, 23, 25, 25,** 19:4; 21:17. οἶδα : 1:26, 31, 33; 2:9, 9; 3:2, 11; 4:10, 22, 25, 32, 42; 5:32; 6:6, 42, 61, 64; 7:15, 27, 28, 28, 29; 8:14, 19, 19, 37, 55, 55; 9:12, 20, 21, 21, 24, 29, 29, 30, 31; 10:4, 5, 22, 24, 42, 49; 12:35, 50; **13:1, 3, 7, 11, 17, 18; 14:4, 5, 15, 21; 16:30;** 18:2, 4, 21; 19:10, 28, 35; 20:2, 9, 13, 14; 21:4, 12, 15, 16, 17, 24.

52 Bringing the Pauline teaching of innate knowledge of God being rejected by the world in Romans 1 into the theology of this section is probably not appropriate, especially if that is used as the basis for making a distinction between meanings of οἶδα and γινώσκω.

53 Some MSS (B, C*, L, Q, Ψ) use ἤδειτε in place of γνώσεσθε (including ℵ , P66, D) or ἐγνωκειτε (A, C3, Θ, φ, vg) for knowing the Father in 14:7. Textual support is strongest for the use of γινώσκω. John 17:25 says, "O righteous Father! The world has not known (ἔγνω) You, but I have known (ἔγνων) You; and these have known (ἔγνωσαν) that You have sent Me."

54 John 15:21, "But all these things they will do to you for My name's sake, because they do not know (οἴδασιν) Him who sent Me." John 16:3, "And these things they will do to you because they have not known (ἔγνωσαν) the Father nor Me."

55 John 8:55, "Yet you have not known (ἐγνώκατε) Him, but I know (οἶδα) Him. And if I say, 'I do not know (οἶδα) Him,' I shall be a liar like you; but I do know Him and keep His word."

56 "If you had known (ἐγνώσκατέ) Me, you would have known (γνώσεσθε) My Father also; and from now on you know (γινώσκετε) Him and have seen Him."

57 "...even the Spirit of truth, whom the world cannot receive, because it neither sees Him nor knows (γινώσκει) Him; but you know (γινώσκετε) Him, for He dwells with you and will be in you."

58 "And this is eternal life, that they may know (γινώσκωσιν) You, the only true God, and Jesus Christ whom You have sent."

59 Hodges, *The Gospel under Siege,* 56 (italics his).

60 Ibid., "1 John," *BKC-NT,* 887-88.

61 Ibid., *The Gospel under Siege,* 56 (italics his).

62 Dillow, *The Reign of the Servant Kings,* 164.

63 Ibid.

64 Ibid.

65 Ibid., 165.

66 Allen Edgington, "Footwashing as an Ordinance." *Grace Theological Journal.* 6:2 (1985): 425-26.

67 Ibid., 427.

68 Ibid.

69 Ibid., 426.

70 Ibid., 427-28.

71 Ibid., 428.

72 Ibid.

73 Ibid., 429.

74 Ibid.

75 Ibid., 430-31.

76 Laney, *John,* 243.

[77] Ibid.

[78] Cook, *The Theology of John*, 110 (italics his).

[79] L. Goppelt, TDNT, s.v. τράπεζα , 8:209.

[80] Gower, *The New Manners and Customs of Bible Times*, 246.

[81] Geoffrey Wigoder, Shalom M. Paul, and Benedict T. Viviano, *Almanac of the Bible* (New York: Prentice Hall, 1991), 178.

[82] Goppelt, TDNT, s.v. τράπεζα, 8:210; Wigoder, Paul, and Viviano, *Almanac of the Bible*, 178.

[83] Translation by Jacob Neusner in *The Mishnah: A New Translation*, New Haven: Yale University Press, 1988.

[84] *The Anchor Bible Dictionary*, 6:303 (s.v. Table, Fellowship).

[85] Though the term for reclining at table could be a figure of speech simply for fellowshipping, it is more likely that the meals reported by the evangelists were all banquets or other special occasions.

[86] Gower, *The New Manners and Customs of Bible Times*, 246; Wigoder, Paul, and Viviano, *Almanac of the Bible*, 178.

[87] Goppelt, TDNT, s.v. τράπεζα, 8:210.

[88] Morris, *The Gospel According to John*, 625-26.

[89] Segovia, "The Structure, *Tendenz*, and *Zitz im Leben* of John 13:31-14:31," 471.

[90] Ibid., 471-72.

[91] Ibid., 471.

[92] Ibid., 474.

[93] Ibid., 475-76.

[94] Ibid., 477-78.

[95] Ibid., 478.

[96] Ibid., 488-90.

[97] Ibid., 478-79.

[98] Carson, *The Gospel According to John*, 477.

[99] Westcott, *The Gospel According to St. John*, 195-96.

[100] Carson, *The Gospel According to John*, 478.

[101] Ibid., 479.

[102] *Dictionary of the Bible*, s.v. "Vine, Vineyard," by E. W. G. Masterman,

959; n.a., *Fauna and Flora of the Bible*, 188.

[103] Harold M. Moldenke and Alma L. Moldenke, *Plants of the Bible* (Waltham: Chronica Botanica Company, 1952), 242-43.

[104] Josephus, *The Jewish War*, 3.10.8; also *Jewish Antiquities*, 15.11.3.

[105] Menashe Harel, *Dwellers of the Mountain*, Orig. pub. by Tel Aviv University, Department of Geography. Trans. by Bathsheba Taub (Jerusalem: Carta, 1977), 18-21. 1 Ki 21:1; Song of Sol 1:14; Hos. 14:7 mention vineyards in the Jordan valley, thus level places.

[106] Jimmy L. Albright ("Wine in the Biblical world: Its economic, social and religious implications for New Testament interpretation" [Ph.D. dissertation, Southwestern Baptist Seminary, 1981], 91) looks to Isaiah 5A:1, Jeremiah 31:5, and Amos 9:13 for planting practices, and concludes that it was done generally on hills because of Psalm 80:10-11.

[107] *The Oxyrhynchus Papyri*, Part 14, "1631. Contract for Labor in a Vineyard," 18; Pliny, *Natural History*, 17.35.

[108] David C. Hopkins, *The Highlands of Canaan* (Decatur: The Almond Press, 1985), 227.

[109] Lucian Tukowski, "Peasant Agriculture in the Judaean Hills," *Palestine Exploration Quarterly*, 101: 1 (January-June 1969): 27.

[110] Ibid.

[111] *The New Schaff-Herzog Encyclopedia of Religious Knowledge*, s.v. "Wine, Hebrew," 382; *Dictionary of the Bible*, s.v. "Vine, Vineyard," 959; Hopkins, *The Highlands of Canaan*, 227.

[112] *Encyclopedia Judaica*, s.v. "Vine," 16: 156; James M. Freeman, *Manners and Customs of the Bible* (Plainfield: Logos International, 1972 reprint, New York: Nelson and Phillips, n.d.), 360-61; W. E. Shewell-Cooper, *Plants, Flowers, and Herbs of the Bible* (New Canaan: Keats Publishing, Inc., 1977), 75; Hopkins, *The Highlands of Canaan*, 228.

[113] Shewell-Cooper, *Plants, Flowers, and Herbs of the Bible*, 75; also Hopkins, *The Highlands of Canaan*, 228. This is reflected in Ezekiel 17:6. Albright, in his dissertation, points to Isaiah 16:8 as an indication of an earlier practice.

[114] Pliny, *Natural History,* 17.35 says, "This is better for wine, as the vine so grown does not overshadow itself and is ripened by constant sunshine, and is more exposed to currents of air and so gets rid of dew more quickly, and also is easier for trimming and for harrowing the soil and all operations; and above all it sheds its blossoms in a more beneficial manner."

[115] Walter Duckat, *Beggar to King: All the Occupations of Biblical Times* (Garden City: Doubleday & Company, Inc., 1968), 264; Madeleine S. Miller

and J. Lane Miller, *Harper's Encyclopedia of Bible Life* (revised edition of the work by Boyce M. Bennett, Jr. and David H. Scott. San Francisco: Harper & Row, Publishers, 1978), 183.

116 Pliny, *Natural History,* 17.35.

117 Ibid.

118 *The New Schaff-Herzog Encyclopedia of Religious Knowledge,* s.v. "Wine, Hebrew," 382.

119 Hopkins, *The Highlands of Canaan,* 229.

120 Ibid., 228.

121 Pliny, *Natural History,* 17.35.

122 *The Oxyrhynchus Papyri,* Part 14, "1631. Contract for Labor in a Vineyard," 18.

123 Ibid.

124 Ibid.

125 Duckat, *Beggar to King: All the Occupations of Biblical Times,* 264.

126 Pliny, *Natural History,* 17.35.

127 Ibid. When discussing propagation practices, he says, "Vines give more numerous kinds of shoots for planting. The first point is that none of these are used for planting except useless growths lopped off for brush-wood, whereas any branch that bore fruit last time is pruned away."

128 Jules Janick, *Horticultural Science* (Second Edition. San Francisco: W. H. Freeman and Company, 1972), 240-48.

129 BAGD, 504; Hauck, TDNT, s.v. "μένω," 4:574-88.

130 Ibid.

131 Ibid., 503.

132 TDNT, s.v. "μένω," 4:574-88. Hauck also says, "Religiously μένειν is a mark of God and of what is commensurate with Him."

133 Matt 26:38; Mark 14:34; Luke 19:5; 24:29; Acts 18:3, 20; 20:15; 21:7, 8; and 27:31, 41. Paul refers to people still living among the readers (1 Cor 15:6), his own expectation of still living among his readers (Phil 1:25), and Erasmus' staying in Corinth rather than following him (2 Tim 4:20).

134 Matt 10:11; Mark 6:10; Luke 1:56; 8:27; 9:4; 10:7; Acts 9:43; 16:15; and 28:16.

135 BAGD, 504. Widows, the single, and married are to remain in whatever marital state they find themselves (1 Cor 7:8, 11, 20, 24, 40). Women are to

"continue" in the faith (1 Tim 2:15) and Timothy is to "continue" in the things he has learned (2 Tim 3:14).

136 Matt 11:23; Acts 5:4; Rom 9:11; 1 Cor 3:14; 13:13; 2 Cor 3:11, 14; 9:9; and 2 Tim 2:13.

137 Heb 7:3, 24; 10:34; 12:27; 13:1, 14. Also see 1 Cor 15:6; Phil 1:25. BAGD, 504.

138 1 Pet 1:23, 25. In 1:25, μένει is a translation of קוּם in Isa 40:8.

139 Rom 9:1; 1 Pet 1:23, 25; 1 Cor 13:13; 2 Cor 3:11. Hauck, TDNT, s.v. "μένω."

140 Μένω in Rev 17:10 reflects the literal sense of living or dwelling.

141 Μένω is found in 1 John 2:6, 10, 14, 17, 19, 24, 27 (twice), 28; 3:6, 9, 14, 15, 17, 24 (twice); 4:12, 13, 15, 16 (three times). Brown (*The Epistles of John*, 195-96) sees three meanings for εἶναι ἐν which are also parallel to μένειν ἐν: (1) "indwelling pertinent to God" as in John 10:38; 14:10, 11, 17, 20, 23; 15:2; 17:21, 23, 26; 1 John 2:5; 4:4; and 5:20; (2) "indwelling of other realities in the Christian" as in John 11:10; 12:35; 15:11; 17:26; 1 John 1:8, 10; 2:4, and 15; and (3) "miscellaneous theological uses" which he did not categorize.

142 Dodd, *The Johannine Epistles*, 83-84; Hodges, "1 John," 896; Guy H. King, *The Fellowship* (London: Marshall, Morgan & Scott, 1954), 38; J. Dwight Pentecost, *The Joy of Fellowship* (Grand Rapids: Zondervan Publishing House, 1977), 89; J. W. Roberts, *The Letters of John*, The Living Word Commentary (Austin: R. B. Sweet, 1968), 44, 48, 91; and Westcott, *The Epistles of St. John*, 56. Also Smalley (*1, 2, 3 John*, 61) takes a more eclectic approach to the epistle and does not see either purpose as dominant.

143 BAGD, 504; Dodd, *The Johannine Epistles*, 61; Stott, *The Letters of John*, 103, 117-18; Brown, *The Epistles of John*, 355-59; Smalley, *1, 2, 3 John*, 124; Hodges, "1 John," 892; Pentecost, *The Joy of Fellowship*, 66.

144 Brown, *The Epistles of John*, 315, 327; Dodd, *The Johannine Epistles*, 43; Hodges, "1 John," 891; Ryrie, "1 John," 1470; Smalley, *1, 2, 3 John*, 88-89; Stott, *The Letters of John*, 106. Roberts (*The Letters of John*, 59) varies by seeing abiding in this verse as describing the believer's "fellowship with God" as a "foretaste or earnest of the life to come."

145 BAGD, 504; King, *The Fellowship*, 54; Roberts, *The Letters of John*, 64; Stott, *The Letters of John*, 110; Westcott, *The Epistles of St. John*, 72.

146 Brown, *The Epistles of John*, 521-22, 524, 526; Dodd, *The Johannine Epistles*, 114; Hodges, "1 John," 899; King, *The Fellowship*, 96; Stott, *The Letters of John*, 166, 168-70. Smalley (*1, 2, 3 John*, 247, 249, 254-55) agrees with this.

147 King, *The Fellowship*, 94; Stott, *The Letters of John*, 167.

148 John 1:38, 39; 2:12; 4:40; 7:9; 10:40; 11:6, 54; 12:34; and 19:31. Edwin A. Abbott, *Johannine Grammar* (London: Adam & Charles Black, 1906), 334.

149 John 1:32, 33.

150 John 8:35; 12:24; 21:22-23.

151 2 John 9. This could also have the sense of allowing the "teaching" to influence one's life.

152 BAGD, 504 identifies John 8:31; 12:24; and 15:9 as examples of this. John 8:31 does not seem to relate. In John 15:9 Jesus commands us to "abide" in His love. Only John 12:24 is a clear example of this use, as well as 12:46.

153 Jesus uses μένω to refer to God's Word abiding in men (John 5:38), Jesus' words (John 15:7), men abiding in God's Word (John 8:31), food which is given by Him and which "endures" to eternal life (John 6:27), the truth (2 John 2), and to the Pharisees' sin "remaining" because they refuse to admit their spiritual blindness (John 9:41). John quotes the Baptist using μένω to refer to God's wrath "abiding" on men (John 3:36). The permanency of the possession is expressed through the use of the ἔχειν τι μένον ἐν ἑαυτῷ according to Baur (BAGD, 504). He also notes Jesus' words in John 14:17, ὅτι παρ' ὑμῖν μένει καὶ ἐν ὑμῖν ἔσται, describes the Spirit of truth remaining with someone. Finally, the wrath of God is described as remaining on someone (μένει ἐπ' αὐτόν).

154 BAGD, 504. His example is that of God's relationship with Jesus in John 14:10. Jesus uses this sense of μένω to describe the disciple's relationship to Himself in such places as John 6:56; 8:31; and 15:4-7.

155 John 5:38.

156 His use of the first class conditional clause (εἰ plus the indicative) when describing the certainty of the world's hatred toward believers in verse eighteen is very significant in demonstrating the possibility of believers not abiding.

157 Hauck, TDNT, s.v. "μένω." Also seeing the term as equivalent to Paul's ἐν Χριστῷ are George (*Classic Christianity,* 204) and Vincent Taylor (*Forgiveness and* Reconciliation [New York: St. Martin's Press, 1956], 122).

158 Brown, *The Epistles of John,* 403, 447; Stott, *The Letters of John,* 146.

159 George G. Findlay, *Fellowship in the Life Eternal* (Grand Rapids: Wm. B. Eerdmans Publishing Company, 1955), 146.

160 Ibid.

161 Brown, *The Epistles of John,* 421; Dodd, *The Johannine Epistles,* 64, 94-95; Stott, *The Letters of John,* 121, 131, 154.

162 Dodd, *The Johannine Epistles,* 32, 46, 58; Law, *The Tests of Life,* 54.

163 J. F. Strombeck, *Shall Never Perish* (Philadelphia: American Bible

Conference Association, 1936), 215.

164 Charles C. Ryrie, "1 John" in *The Wycliffe Bible Commentary,* ed. Charles F. Pfeiffer and Everett F. Harrison (Chicago: Moody Press, 1962), 1468.

165 Everett F. Harrison, "A Key to the Understanding of First John," *Bibliotheca Sacra* 3 (1954): 44.

166 Dillow, *The Reign of the Servant Kings,* 174.

167 Ibid., 406.

168 Cook, *The Theology of John,* 134; Hodges, "1 John," 888.

169 Hodges, "1 John," 888-89.

170 Ibid., 898; Chafer, "The Eternal Security of the Believer," 402-3.

171 Hodges, "1 John," 888-89.

172 King, *The Fellowship,* 71.

173 Cook, *The Theology of John,* 133-34 (italics his).

174 Dillow, *The Reign of the Servant Kings,* 174.

175 Elliot E. Johnson, *Expository Hermeneutics: An Introduction* (Grand Rapids: Zondervan Publishing House, 1990), 24.

General Index

Abbott, Edwin A., 447

Abide, 25, 32, 122-23, 130, 135, 140, 150-52, 156, 160, 166, 170-73, 175-76, 178-81, 184-87, 189-92, 211, 230, 242, 246, 316, 331-35, 349, 396-97, 412, 447

Abided, 160, 179, 193, 335

Abides, 105, 120, 126, 170, 173, 176, 185, 187, 192, 261, 333, 397

Abideth, 381

Abiding, 9, 27, 32, 81, 105, 124, 130, 138, 151, 156, 160-161, 165, 170-73, 175, 177-78, 184-86, 190-93, 198, 202-203, 226, 246, 255, 260, 271, 296-97, 300, 307-308, 331-35, 339, 341, 350, 383, 392-96, 398, 401-402, 405, 410-12, 426, 447-48

Abode, 32, 91, 97, 136-37, 383, 386

Abraham, 9, 200-201, 208-209, 380, 420

Abundant, 27, 29-30, 58, 96, 104-105, 154, 197, 253, 330, 349, 408

Abundantly, 30, 350

Acts of Thomas, 373

Adultery, 252, 313

Advocate, 123-24, 144, 222, 248, 275, 387, 418

Agapaō, 65, 242, 359, 362, 378

Airei, 155, 161, 163-65, 189

Αἱρέω, 161, 393

Αἰωνιος, 302-303, 427, 440

Aireō, 155

Airō, 155, 157, 161, 163, 399

Ἀγαπάω, 362

Agapaō, 65, 199, 311

Albright, Jimmy L., 444-45

Alive, 102, 116, 155, 159, 185, 256, 258, 261, 345, 394

Allegory, 134, 136, 150, 155, 176, 180, 189, 294, 391

Allen, Ronald B., 7

Allos, 125, 380

Almighty God, 61

Almighty King, 48

Alone, 21, 49, 92, 100, 145, 147, 193-94, 214, 222, 244-45, 257, 260, 264, 291, 302-303, 315, 368, 373, 399, 401

Ancient of Days, 290

Angels, 179, 228, 251, 267

Anointed, 100

Antichrist, 286

Antichrists, 401

Anxiety, 91, 142, 151, 195, 388

Apokoptō, 157

Apostasy, 362, 407, 434

Apostle, 59, 66, 69, 95, 97, 177, 213, 232, 320, 359, 361, 367

ABOUT THE AUTHORS

Gary Wayne Derickson was born to Glen and Christiana Derickson in Pasadena, Texas in March of 1953. He grew up in a Christian home and witnessed his parents' growing faith. One day just before his seventh birthday he stood by the dining table listening to his father explain the gospel to a friend. After he left, Gary asked his father to tell him, too, how he could become a Christian. His father gladly explained the gospel to his young son. A couple of weeks later, at a revival meeting in their church, Gary felt God's drawing him during the alter call and received Christ as His Savior. Then, as an eight-year-old, he sensed God's call to service. During a Sunday morning worship service alter call he went forward to tell his pastor of His calling. He also offered to preach for him if ever he needed a substitute. His pastor stopped the service and shared his offer with the congregation. All laughed, thinking it was cute. But Gary was serious.

Gary's life was rather normal through High School, other than his family moved numerous times and spent his six and seventh grade years in Egypt. In High School he involved himself in the Future Farmers of America program and worked in his father's tomato greenhouses. By the time he graduated from High School he had mostly forgotten His calling. He chose to attend Texas A&M University and study Horticulture, with a dream of earning a doctorate in greenhouse tomatoes, growing them, and getting rich. His freshman year he was led by the Lord to become involved with the Campus Crusade for Christ group. As a sophomore he sensed God's leading into the Corps of Cadets where he shared the gospel, led Bible studies, and discipled other men. After completing his R.O.T.C. training and being commissioned a Second Lieutenant, Gary remained at Texas A&M for two more years, both to earn a Masters of Science in Horticulture and to continue discipling three friends.

Gary served four and a half years of active duty in the U.S. Army Transportation Corps at Fort Eustis, Virginia. His assignments included commanding a platoon of five tugboats, serving on Battalion staff, and as a company executive officer. Throughout his career he led Bible studies and served in local churches. Intending to stay for a thirty-year career, he began praying for God's leading—just as an exercise. After a year of prayer he realized that God's calling when he was an eight-year-old was still there. So, he resigned his commission and enrolled at Dallas Theological Seminary.

Gary studied biblical exposition at Dallas Seminary and earned his Masters of Theology degree in 1986. Wanting to study further, he continued doctoral studies under four godly men: Drs. Elliot E. Johnson, Stanley D. Toussaint, J. Dwight Pentecost, and Homer Heater. Writing his dissertation on First John, he earned his Doctorate of Philosophy degree in 1993 and was awarded the Donald K. Campbell Award in Biblical Exposition. He left Dallas to teach at Western Baptist College in Salem, Oregon, where he continues to minister until the present as a Professor of Biblical Studies and Chairman of the Ministries Division.

During his doctoral studies Gary met Rebekah, who was in the Masters of Arts in Biblical Studies program at Dallas Seminary. They were married in 1991. God also has blessed them with a son, Ian. They presently live in Salem, Oregon, attending and participating in the life and ministry of First Baptist Church.

Earl Radmacher was born almost seventy years ago in Portland, Oregon just a couple of miles from Western Seminary where, in the providence of God, he would later serve on the theological faculty for thirty-three years (1962-1995) and in administrative positions as Dean of the Faculty, (1964-1965) President (1965-1990), and Chancellor (1990-1995). In 1995 he was designated President Emeritus and Distinguished Professor of Systematic Theology Emeritus.

His parents, who were immigrants from Romania and Austria, settled in Portland in 1913 where they brought eight children into this world, Earl being the last. The whole family was very active in local churches so every Sunday found Earl spending all day in church—Sunday school, morning worship, potluck lunch at the church, recreation break, youth service, evening service, and after service. Even though he had heard the gospel preached Sunday after Sunday, he did not personally receive Christ as his Savior until he was fourteen years of age. He has often stated that sitting in church Sunday after Sunday doesn't make one a Christian any more than sitting in a garage makes one a car.

At that juncture in his life, Earl came in contact with another Earl—Earl Gile—a faithful Sunday school teacher who lived right across the street from the grade school he had attended, and he opened up his home as an outreach to boys from the school. Mr. Gile's church rented the school gymnasium on Thursday nights and made it available for boys to play basketball if they came to Sunday School on Sundays. That sounded like a good deal, so he went. Shortly after that, the teacher announced a forthcoming boys camp at Twin Rocks Beach, Oregon. He decided to go; and there, at fourteen years of age, he accepted Christ as his Savior.

Although the church preached the gospel faithfully, they didn't go beyond the gospel to build up believers in the faith. He has often said, "As a believer, I didn't need a birth message, but I did need a growth message. That being absent, I tended to flounder, and my growth in Christ was stunted. Thus, the high school years were a disaster as far as the things of Christ and spiritual growth were concerned."

As graduation time neared, he took the normal batch of tests to determine which line of work he should pursue. The tests indicated mathematics or mechanics, so he decided to go the route of mathematics and join it with money by starting a career in a saving and loan institution. He started as a file clerk and worked up to an investment statistician that year.

His plans in the investment business were dramatically interrupted, however, by a visit to Portland of a new evangelist on the scene, Billy Graham, in August of 1950. A friend invited him to go to the meeting and, although he had little spiritual appetite at that time, God seemed to press him toward the affirmative. As the poet Francis Thompson has written: "He tracked me down the corridors of time." As it turned out, Earl not only went that night but every night thereafter for six weeks. The only meeting he missed was the women's meeting (they wouldn't let him in!).

After listening to the powerful preaching of Billy Graham for six weeks, at the conclusion of the last service, he found himself standing to his feet, going forward, grabbing Cliff Barrow's hand, and telling him that God had called him to preach. His next question was, "What do I do now?" Cliff said, "You go to college and prepare" and he recommended his alma mater in South Carolina.

Once again, God had a man prepared to help him take the next step. As the tabernacle cleared out, he saw a man he hadn't seen since grade school. In the beautiful providence of God, this man, Jerry Burleson, was going to the same college in South Carolina that Cliff Barrows had recommended, and he was looking for one more rider. Although it was just two weeks before Fall semester, Jerry assured him that they would accept him on probation though his recommendation. He worked nights for two weeks training another person for his job so that he could leave with the good graces of his employer.

Twelve years and four degrees later (Bob Jones University, B.A., M.R.E.; Dallas Theological Seminary, Th.M., Th.D.), together with broad opportunities of experience in preaching and teaching, overseas missions and military chaplaincy, local church pastor and parachurch ministries, rural and urban outreaches, he ended up not in the pastorate, but in the training of evangelists, pastors, and teachers at Western Seminary. His years there involved traveling over ten million miles and preaching and teaching over twenty thousand hours in over a thousand Bible conferences and thousands of churches.

Among the numerous books and articles that Dr. Radmacher has authored or edited are the following books: *You and Your Thoughts* (1977), *The Nature of the Church* (1978, 1995), *Can We Trust the Bible* (1979), *What to Expect from the Holy Spirit* (1983), *Hermeneutics, Inerrancy, and the Bible* (1984), *The NIV Reconsidered* (1990), *The Nelson Study Bible* (1997), *Nelson's New Illustrated Bible Commentary* (1999), and *Salvation* (2000).

Dr. Radmacher has often stated, "In my wildest dreams fifty years ago, I could never have imagined the exciting plans that God, in His sovereign grace, had for me." His life mission is found in 2 Timothy 2:15, "Study to show yourself approved unto God, a workman who has no need to be ashamed, rightly dividing the word of truth." His personal life verse is 2 Corinthians 3:18, "But we all, with unveiled face, beholding as in a mirror the glory of the Lord, are being transformed into the same image from glory to glory, just as by the Spirit of the Lord."